INTERPERSONAL COMPARISONS OF WELL-BEING

Edited by Jon Elster and John E. Roemer

INTERPERSONAL COMPARISONS OF WELL-BEING

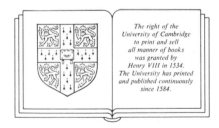

The right of the
University of Cambridge
to print and sell
all manner of books
was granted by
Henry VIII in 1534.
The University has printed
and published continuously
since 1584.

Cambridge University Press

Cambridge

New York   Port Chester   Melbourne   Sydney

Published in collaboration with Maison des Sciences de
l'Homme, Paris

Published by the Press Syndicate of the University of Cambridge
The Pitt Building, Trumpington Street, Cambridge CB2 1RP
40 West 20th Street, New York, NY 10011, USA
10 Stamford Road, Oakleigh, Melbourne 3166, Australia

©Cambridge University Press 1991

First published 1991

Printed in the United States of America

Library of Congress Cataloging-in-Publication Data

Interpersonal comparisons of well-being / edited by Jon Elster and John E.
Roemer.
p. cm. – (Studies in rationality and social change)
"Published in collaboration with Maison des sciences de l'homme,
Paris."
Includes index.
ISBN 0-521-39274-8 (hardcover)
1. Social justice. 2. Social ethics. 3. Utilitarianism.
I. Elster, Jon, 1940–   . II. Roemer, John E. III. Maison des
sciences de l'homme (Paris, France) IV. Series.
HM216.I67 1991
303.3'72 – dc20   90-26400
                                                                          CIP

British Library Cataloguing in Publication Data

Interpersonal comparisons of well-being. – (Studies in
rationality and social change).
1. Ethics
I. Elster, Jon 1940– II. Roemer, John E. III. Series
171

ISBN 0-521-39274-8 hardback

Contents

Contributors

C. d'Aspremont
CORE
Université Catholique de Louvain
Louvain, Belgium

Charles Blackorby and David Donaldson
Department of Economics
University of British Columbia
Vancouver, Canada

John Broome
Department of Economics
University of Bristol
Bristol, England

Jon Elster
Department of Political Science
University of Chicago
Chicago, Illinois

L.A. Gérard-Varet
Ecoles des hautes études en sciences sociales
Marseilles, France

James Griffin
Keeble College
Oxford, England

Peter J. Hammond
Department of Economics
European University Institute
San Domenico di Fiesole (FI), Italy

Aanund Hylland
Department of Economics
University of Oslo
Oslo, Norway

Daniel Kahneman and Carol Varey
Department of Psychology
University of California
Berkeley, California

Ignacio Ortuño-Ortin
Department of Economics
University of Alicante
Alicante, Spain

John E. Roemer
Department of Economics
University of California
Davis, California

Thomas M. Scanlon
Department of Philosophy
Harvard University
Cambridge, Massachusetts

John A. Weymark
Department of Economics
University of British Columbia
Vancouver, Canada

Acknowledgments

The conferences on which this book is based were funded by a grant from the Alfred P. Sloan Foundation. We received assistance as well from the Institute for Governmental Affairs at the University of California at Davis and the Center for Ethics, Rationality and Society at the University of Chicago. We thank all three organizations.

Jon Elster and John E. Roemer

epithelial cells were being shed in living cholera patients, they would
have to appear in the stools [78]. (It is mucus rather than desquamated
cells that give rice-water stools their characteristic appearance [78, 151].)
William Osler (1892) also maintained that epithelial desquamation was
not the cause of the cholera syndrome, but took place as a result of
post-mortem autolysis [322]. This view was later supported by Good-
pasture [164] and Dutta [106] on the basis of the appearance of post-
mortem material affixed within an hour of death.

In more recent years, the desquamation hypothesis was revived when
Burnet caused a sensation in 1947 in the then rather sleepy cholera
world with a report on the desquamation of intestinal epithelium *in
vitro* by cell-free cholera filtrates [41]. Had cholera exotoxin at last been
discovered? Could the boring and fruitless work with cholera endotoxins
now be dropped? Burnet had already made a considerable impact with
his work on influenza virus and, in particular, with his influenza virus
receptor-destroying enzyme (later shown to be neuraminidase) which
was produced not only by the virus but also by *Vibrio cholerae*. He
had now found two more enzymes in cholera culture filtrates—a mucin-
destroying enzyme, that is, a mucinase, and a tissue-disintegrating
enzyme as well:

> the mucinase . . . can rapidly destroy the viscosity and hence the mechanical
> protective and lubricating properties of intestinal mucus—this action can take
> place in isolated gut segments in the living animal and if the enzyme, as
> seems likely, is produced in large amounts in the bowel of a cholera patient,
> it might well play a major part in facilitating desquamation of the intestinal
> epithelium. The third agent [i.e., the tissue-disintegrating enzyme], on which
> very little work has so far been done, by breaking down some presumed
> components of the cement substance between cells would also favour the
> desquamating process.

(The tissue-disintegrating enzyme apparently sank without trace, but
would surely be far more important in breaking up intestinal epithelium,
and so bringing about desquamation, than the more vaunted mucinase,
which would merely liquefy the film of mucin lying on the epithelium.)
All this was up-to-date exciting work and it seemed that the problem
of cholera toxin was about to be solved[23] and dealt with. Some thought

---

23. One of the authors (van H.) remembers his late chief at that time, Lord Florey,
a noted mucinogogue, declaiming with stirring enthusiasm and pride in a fellow Australian
that the cholera problem was now quite simple—the cholera mucinase stripped the
protective layer of mucin from the intestinal epithelium, so cholera should be looked at
as a kind of internal third-degree burn, and no wonder that all that fluid poured into
the gut! (See also [171].)

cholera could be prevented by incorporating mucinase in cholera vaccine, since mucinase was neutralized by its homologous antibody, but this idea was never tried out in practice [216, 261][24] because the desquamation hypothesis soon fell to the ground. We shall see that a few years after these excitements, Gangarosa used the recently invented device, the Crosby capsule, to obtain samples of the intestinal wall of living cholera patients in Thailand, and was able to show that the integrity of the epithelium was preserved during the disease. This finding, together with the demonstration by Gordon that large molecules of polyvinylpyrrol-idone did not leak into the gut in cholera (as they might be expected to if the epithelium were stripped from the wall), finally put an end to the desquamation hypothesis. By that time, something else had been found to take its place—cholera exotoxin.

The Animal Model

If all the work on parenterally administered preparations was such a waste of time and effort, what enteral animal model could have produced more relevant information? Koch, it may be remembered, was unable at the first cholera conference to report successful infection of experimental animals with the cholera vibrio and abandoned artificial reproduction of the disease by the organism as an essential criterion for ascribing the disease to the organism. But by the second cholera conference, he was able to change his mind. Nicati and Rietsch, who had been the first runners in the confusion over cholera toxin with their injections of young and old cholera culture filtrates parenterally into dogs, had successfully infected dogs and guinea pigs by introducing whole cultures directly into the duodenum [306]. Koch soon had similar success when he presented the cholera vibrio enterally to guinea pigs. To achieve this, he had first to neutralize the acidity of the stomach by giving the animals sodium carbonate. A broth culture of the comma bacilli was then injected directly into the stomach, and this was followed immediately by an intraperitoneal injection of opium to reduce intestinal motility. The animals died within one to three days, with their intestines distended with an alkaline, colourless, flocculent fluid representing an almost pure culture of comma bacilli [235]. This could surely be called cholera! These experiments were followed by many others in which

24. If mucinase assists the cholera vibrio to colonize the intestine, or promote its action, it might still be a good idea to incorporate it in any cholera vaccine and so generate antibodies to it. The antimucinase element would then be antibacterial rather than antitoxic. The same may perhaps be said of other cholera enzymes and antigens. Excessive purification of bacterial products for active immunization is to be deplored (see p. 197).

the cholera vibrios were enterally administered with and without opium and other substances to guinea pigs, rabbits and other animals by injection or by a tube into the stomach or the duodenum, or by feeding. While these experiments confirmed the role of the cholera vibrio in the disease, they threw no light on the question of the cholera toxin. In none of these experiments do cell-free preparations from cholera cultures seem to have been introduced into the small intestine. But even if cell-free filtrates of cultures producing what is now known to be cholera exotoxin had been introduced into the small intestine of animals, it is unlikely that any effect would regularly have been observed, because exotoxin is not regularly produced by any culture grown anyhow.

Metchnikoff made an observation in 1894 that many years later (see next section) was to be applied successfully for testing the activity of cholera toxin. He reasoned that the normal intestinal flora of adult rabbits inhibited infection with the cholera vibrio, and showed that suckling rabbits (but not adult rabbits) could be orally infected with cholera vibrios with resultant fluid accumulation in the bowel, diarrhoea, dehydration and death. He did not test the effect of cell-free culture filtrates [279].

An even better animal model was invented in 1915, but, unfortunately, it does not seem to have been noticed, nor its value recognized, and it fell into desuetude at once. Violle had failed at the Institut Pasteur in Alexandria to produce cholera in rabbits by introducing cholera cultures directly into the small intestine after laparotomy. Even when inoculated in very great quantity, the vibrios were eliminated within 24 hours [439, 440]. He and Crendiropoulo then developed a technique of tying off a 10-cm length of the highest part of the small intestine at both ends, to provide "une anse", a loop. Injection of a "toxigène" culture of vibrio into such a ligated loop was generally followed by abundant growth of the vibrios in pure culture with the contents of the loop assuming a rice-water appearance: "in a word, a striking analogy is seen between these lesions and those of a case of human cholera; death follows in about twelve hours". Whether death followed from cholera, with exudation of fluid being provoked only in such a small part of the small intestine, is highly debatable. It was more likely due to the effect of the intestinal obstruction. Voille and Crendiropoulo themselves pointed out that "a control intestinal loop, that is one not inoculated with vibrios, shows no cholera lesions. Nevertheless because of the high ligature, the death of the animal rapidly follows". With a loop several times longer than 10 cm, the growth of the vibrios was much feebler and the lesion less pronounced. With a single ligature of the intestine, inoculation of vibrios above or below the ligature did not produce the typical cholera lesion [441]. Violle and Crendiropoulo never stated why it occurred to them to prepare a short ligated loop in the small intestine—perhaps they wanted to confine their inocula in small volumes since they had had no success with unligated intestine, and little or no success if the ligated loop was too long.

Although the cultures inoculated into their ligated loops were stated by Violle and Crendiropoulo to be "toxigène", it does not seem to have occurred to them to use their model for testing the effect of any preparation of cholera toxin, whatever they may have considered cholera toxin to be. They did not test cell-free cholera filtrates (which might have revealed the existence of exotoxin), or dead cholera bacilli or other endotoxin preparations (which might have disposed of the myth of enteral toxicity of endotoxin). Nothing new was learned, and no more was heard of the model until it was reinvented 40 years later.

The Discovery of Cholera Toxin

Koch, it may be remembered, had started his address to the first cholera conference in 1884 with the statement that little progress had been made in research on cholera during the preceding 10 years because there had been no cholera in the countries where research on other infectious diseases had been advancing, and in India, where there was plenty of cholera there was nobody to do the research. In the first half of the twentieth century, cholera was no longer a serious problem in Europe and the stimulus to do research on it had died down. But in India, cholera never ceased to be a problem, and by the mid-century India had produced its own research workers, with abundant incentive to take action. The benefits of their work came just in time for the seventh cholera pandemic and the renewed interest in cholera in Western countries, mainly the United States of America.

In India, research on the cholera toxin problem advanced simultaneously and independently on two fronts in the 1950s in N. K. Dutta's laboratory in the Haffkine Institute in Bombay and in S. N. De's Department of Pathology of the Nilratan Sircar Medical College in Calcutta, on the other side of India. It was De, undoubtedly, who discovered cholera exotoxin, in 1959.

In 1953, De reinvented *de novo* the ligated intestinal loop of Violle and Crendiropoulo—"reinvented" rather than revived, because at the time De was unaware of Violle and Crendiropoulo's 38-year-old short paper in the proceedings of the French Société de Biologie, which had rapidly sunk into obscurity (De, personal communication, 1978). It came to his notice only 8 years later, when he happened to read an abstract of it in the *Tropical Diseases Bulletin* of 1915.[25] De did not explain, any

25. This is reported in a footnote in De's monograph on Cholera [96].

more than Violle had, what led him to try ligated intestinal loops. He performed laparotomies on a number of rabbits and tied off one segment of about 5 inches in the middle of the small intestine of each rabbit with silk ligatures. He then injected 1 ml of peptone water containing a loopful of a 24-hour culture of the Ogawa strain of *Vibrio cholerae* in the experimental loops and uninoculated peptone in control loops. After 24 hours, the control loops were still collapsed, and the experimental loops distended with a rice-watery fluid rich with a pure culture of the cholera bacilli and containing some albumin. The presence of this albumin led him to conclude that cholera bacilli caused an increase in capillary permeability, and that the protein was rapidly reabsorbed, thus explaining the already well-known (e.g., to Snow) observation that the protein content of cholera stools was low [98]. De was at this stage still under the influence of the endotoxin doctrine. He had previously claimed that intraperitoneal injection of washed cholera vibrio cells caused an intraperitoneal accumulation of protein-rich fluid [101], and he clearly believed that the effects he was observing in his ligated loops were due to the action of endotoxin on intestinal capillaries. Violle never had tested the effect of cell-free cholera culture filtrate in his intestinal loops, and it was six years before De got around to doing the crucial experiment. In 1959, he reported experiments in which two 4-inch ligated loops, separated by 12 inches, were used in each of 14 rabbits. Sterile filtrates of 18-hour cultures of Ogawa and Inaba strains of the cholera vibrio were injected into one loop, inoculated culture medium in the other. The next morning, all 14 control loops were still collapsed and all 14 experimental loops were distended with a fluid containing about the same concentration of sodium and potassium ions as plasma water, and about 25 percent less chloride ions. There was no figure for, or comment on, protein content, but a figure of 0.69 mg nitrogen, were it all derived from protein, could account for no more than 0.4 percent protein, as compared with 1 to 3.8 percent protein observed in the previous experiments with whole live cultures. De made no comment in his paper on the question of cholera toxin, except (with every justification!) to use the title: "Enterotoxicity of bacteria-free culture filtrate of *Vibrio cholerae*" [95]. This short essay deserves to go down as a classic in the history of cholera, and, indeed, as later developments have shown, in the history of cellular physiology and biochemistry.

In the following year, De clearly showed not only that it was a cholera exotoxin that caused fluid accumulation in the small intestine, but that cholera endotoxin did not have such an effect. He used three preparations from cultures of Ogawa and Inaba strains: (1) sterile filtrates of cultures grown on a liquid medium consisting of 5 percent peptone water; (2) sterile cell-free endotoxin-containing extracts of cells obtained by growing cultures on solid agar medium, harvesting the cells in saline, disintegrating the cells ultrasonically, centrifuging down and discarding the cell residues, and filtering the supernatant fluids; (3) as (2), except that the harvested cells were thoroughly washed with saline before ultrasonic disintegration.

Sterile filtrates from liquid cultures, i.e., (1) above, consistently caused an accumulation of fluid in ligated intestinal loops, as before, thus demonstrating the presence of an enterotoxic exotoxin. Sterile ultrasonic lysates of washed bacterial cells, i.e., (3) above, consistently failed to cause an accumulation in ligated loops, thus demonstrating that endotoxin had no enterotoxic action. Ultrasonic lysates of unwashed bacterial cells, (2) above, occasionally swelled ligated loops, because not all the exotoxin had been washed away [100]. These experiments should finally have exorcised the endotoxic irrelevance that had haunted cholera research since Pfeiffer invoked it in 1892. Indeed, they eventually did so, but their point was not recognized immediately. Even De at this stage could not entirely shake off the endotoxin, or parenteral administration of toxin. He showed that the enterotoxin-containing preparations did not cause a significant fall in blood pressure when injected intravenously into cats, whereas endotoxin-containing preparations did cause a marked and persistent fall. From this he concluded that both exotoxin and endotoxin played a part in the pathogenesis of cholera. But the effect of neither exotoxin nor endotoxin, when administered parenterally, is of any relevance to cholera, because neither toxin acts beyond the wall of the gut in the disease. The fall in blood pressure in cholera is due to the decrease in blood volume that results from the exudation of blood ultrafiltrate into the lumen of the gut.

In his next paper, De made another important contribution to the question of cholera toxin. He showed that cholera exotoxin is not produced by every culture of the cholera vibrio. Conditions for toxin production are very exacting—it depends on the strain of the subculture, the nature of the organic components of the medium, the concentration of these components, the salts, pH, aeration of the medium, and the time and temperature of incubation of the culture [99]. Considerations of this kind have long been well understood by exotoxinologists. They underline the fact of life that any strain of the cholera vibrio growth on any medium under any conditions may well not produce cholera exotoxin, and therefore that the chances of cholera researchers in the pre-De era ever actually having had cholera toxin in their hands could have been slim—not that that matters, because the bath water that might have contained the baby was invariably thrown out anyway, and attention concentrated on the irrelevant parent cells.

Soon after De reinvented Violle's ligated loop, Dutta revived the infant rabbit model first used by Metchnikoff in 1894. He confirmed that in infant rabbits feeding or intraintestinal inoculation of cholera vibrios led fairly consistently to the development of watery diarrhoea [107]. In the same year that De published his paper on "Enterotoxicity of a bacteria-free culture filtrate of *Vibrio cholerae*", Dutta published a paper entitled "Role of cholera toxin in experimental cholera" [108]. But what he had in mind was endotoxin, not exotoxin, for the preparation he administered orally to infant rabbits was Gallut's preparation of endotoxin, which was an autolysate of a heavy suspension of washed cholera vibrios killed by the acid resulting from the fermentation of glucose by the organisms [148]. Dutta was logical in using an endotoxic preparation because he intended to test whether endotoxin, which he assumed was the only cholera toxin, would produce cholera-like symptoms when given orally to infant rabbits. The rabbits fed the preparation became sick after 6 hours and suffered diarrhoea—first mild, then more severe—and died after 12 to 24 hours. Dutta was satisfied that he had reproduced cholera in these animals, but it is unlikely that this was due to endotoxin. De, it will be recalled, showed that ultrasonic lysates of cholera vibrios failed to cause distension of ligated intestinal loops if the bacilli were washed before lysis, and were inconsistently toxic if the bacilli were not washed before lysis—i.e., exotoxin-contaminated endotoxin preparations caused fluid accumulation; exotoxin-free endotoxin did not. The Gallut preparations were lysates of very heavy suspensions of vibrios, and if they had not been washed, or not washed well enough, before autolysis, the final doses administered might well have contained enough exotoxin to produce the effects observed.

A few years later, after the appearance of De's classic 1959 paper, Dutta repeated his observations on the effect of orally administered endotoxin preparations in infant rabbits, using extracts of ultrasonically disintegrated rather than autolysed washed vibrios [323]. He referred to De's observations with ultrasonically disintegrated unwashed vibrios and stated that they only occasionally caused distension of ligated intestinal loops. He missed the important point that extracts of properly washed vibrios were never active and ignored the essence of De's paper, namely, that 1 ml of the simple culture filtrate derived from about one ten-thousandth the number of organisms needed for the doses used by Dutta caused fluid accumulation in the small intestine. It does not seem to have occurred to Dutta to test the effect of cholera culture filtrate in his suckling rabbits, although he did in effect do so when he produced cholera by feeding sterile-filtered stools of cholera patients, which can be regarded as a contaminated preparation of a culture filtrate [108].

De's work was not accepted at first, nor its significance realized. For example, Jenkin and Rowley, who had already invested heavily in endotoxins, were unable to repeat De's observations on the effect of cholera culture filtrate and claimed, astonishingly, that his results were due to the combined action of the old favourite, endotoxin, plus the new favourite, mucinase, plus a new-comer to the field, lactic acid [215]. Instead of such a complicated idea, they might have been better advised to consider the far simpler idea that their cholera culture filtrates contained no exotoxin. We have seen that it is all too easy to grow a culture of the cholera vibrio producing no exotoxins. In any case, the lactic acid hypothesis was soon demolished by S. B. Formal and his colleagues [142] at the Walter Reed Army Institute of Research in Washington, D.C.

The ligated intestinal loop was at first understandably regarded with suspicion. It seemed (as it was) unnatural and was liable to yield false positive reactions with non-exotoxic materials if the loops were too short and the material injected too rapidly [100]. For these reasons, and because, on the other hand, he failed to get positive reactions with culture filtrates (which did not necessarily contain toxin!), Formal, who had been interested in the technique, gave it up. This, as we shall see on p. 170, was to have a repercussion. In time, the reservations about De's ligated intestinal loop diminished as it came in for more and more use in the study of other diarrhoeal diseases as well as cholera. False positives seemed to become rarer as experience was gained in handling the small intestine, and it was found to be feasible, and very convenient, to tie off as many as 24 loops in a single rabbit.

Cholera toxin, or cholera exo-enterotoxin, to be specific both about its nature and about its site of action, had at last found its way out of a maze of confusion, soon to fall into the welcoming arms of a scientific community that was ready and able to make the fullest use of it.

III

The Intervention by the U.S.A.

1. The Doldrums

The first half of this century was the period of inactivity in the West between the second and third watersheds suggested at the beginning of Chapter 1. The sixth cholera pandemic ran its course for the first quarter of the century, causing few deaths in Western Europe and none in the Americas, and consequently was of little concern to the West. But cholera had not lost its hold on the East, and there, at any rate, two Westerners were involved in the problem in the first two decades of the century—the Englishman, Sir Leonard Rogers, professor of pathology at the Medical College of Bengal in Calcutta; and the American, Andrew Watson Sellards, working in the Biological Laboratory of the Bureau of Science in Manila in the Philippines.

Like everybody else, Rogers believed that the relief brought to cholera patients by intravenous infusion of saline was a delusion, reviving the patient but reviving the diarrhoea as well. Latta's lesson of persisting with infusion in spite of the diarrhoea simply was not learned, perhaps because he died within a year, in 1833, before he had time to spread his gospel. Rogers stated before the Royal Society of London in 1909 [369] that "although all who have used transfusions testify to the remarkable immediate improvement in the pulse and general condition, yet this is commonly of such brief duration that many think it only serves to needlessly prolong the agony of the patient, so that of recent years it has been only exceptionally resorted to in India". He recalled his own experiences at the Calcutta Medical College when he infused patients with 2 pints of "normal" saline containing 1 drachm sodium chloride per pint (i.e., 0.68 percent, or 117 mEq/l). Immediate effects, "little short of marvellous", would be obtained, but within 2 to 12 hours the rice-water stools would recur. Rogers stated that repeated transfusions "usually" failed to save such patients, but he did report that a colleague had found some reduction in mortality on continued transfusion—possibly better results might have been obtained with saline solutions isotonic with blood, i.e., containing 154 mEq NaCl/l; indeed, he stated later that a 0.95 percent salt solution (163 mEq/l) "appeared to be distinctly more favorable" than the previously used hypotonic solution. But whatever solution he used, the diarrhoea would have recurred and he would still have been discouraged. Rogers then came to the following conclusion about rehydrating cholera patients:

> On thinking over the causes of this comparative failure, the following possible explanations occurred to me. The great loss of fluid through the stomach and bowels produces a concentration of the blood, which might be expected to increase the proportion of salts it contains, and therefore present a greater osmotic resistance to further draining off of fluid through the damaged intestinal mucous membrane. Thus, a conservative process, tending to check the diarrhoea, would come into action, which would be interfered with by the injection into the bloodstream of large quantities of normal salt solution of lower salt content than the now concentrated hypertonic blood serum. The drain through the bowel would therefore be restarted, and the restored fluid and blood pressure rapidly lost again, as is so commonly seen in actual practice. If this view is correct, the indication would be to inject hypertonic salt solutions, so as to supply sufficient fluid to restore the circulation, and at the same time maintain the conservative beneficial hypertonicity of the blood, which would tend to carry more fluid into the circulation, instead of removing it through the damaged bowel wall.

Rogers then proceeded to put his theory into practise by rehydrating cholera patients with a hypertonic salt solution, twice as strong as before, i.e., 2 drachms sodium chloride per pint, or 234 mEq/l, in a single injection of 3 or 4 pints (1.7 or 2.3 l). The results, in a series of 72 cases, were encouraging—the mortality was only 27.5 percent compared with an average of 61.2 percent during the previous 5 years at the Calcutta Medical College. "Another striking feature", remarked Rogers,

> was the far less tendency of the hypertonic solutions to restart the copious rice-water stools, which so commonly renders the use of normal salines of such temporary value. It is not too much to say that at the Medical College Hospital, where cholera patients are usually brought in an advanced stage of collapse, the simple substitution of 2 drachms of salt to the pint instead of one, for transfusion, has so revolutionised the treatment, that, whereas formerly it was considered a matter for surprise if a severe case of cholera recovered, it is now a great disappointment when such a case is lost in the collapse stage.

We have seen that Rogers's idea of transfusion with hypertonic saline was based on his assumption that the concentration of salts in cholera blood was hypertonic, and, because water osmotically follows salt, this would check the flow of water away from the blood to the lumen of the gut as the disease got worse. It was to maintain this "conservative beneficial hypertonicity of the blood" that he advocated the infusion of hypertonic saline. He must, therefore, have been taken aback, though he did not admit it, when his analyses showed him, apparently, that the salt concentration in the blood of some cholera patients was lower than normal. Actually, his data are confusing. He states that the sodium chloride content of the blood of normal Bengalis is 0.80 percent (i.e., 137 mEq/ml, whereas in fact it is much closer to 100 mEq/ml) and finds a mean value of 0.72 percent for 3 out of 4 fatal cases, and of 0.90 percent for 11 non-fatal cases. All these data must be regarded with reserve because they do not take into account the volume contributed to the blood by the protein in it (see p. 17, n12). Rogers is erroneously credited with using hypertonic replacement fluid because he thought cholera blood was hypotonic [445], whereas he had reasoned precisely the opposite, that it must be hypertonic, and must be kept that way. Today we know that cholera blood and stools are isotonic, since the salts pass unhindered with the water from the blood into the gut, and that, therefore, they do not concentrate in the blood like the proteins, whose molecules are too big to pass through the walls of the blood vessels and the cell walls of the intestinal epithelium.

Rogers's idea of restoring the blood volume of cholera patients with infusions of hypertonic saline might have been based on a false premise, and may not have been good physiological practise, but the fact remains that his saline solution did restore blood volume and its hypertonicity did have the then desired effect of preventing the recurrence of diarrhoea. He did succeed in halving the death rate from cholera, which is an achievement that deserves respect. A variant of his hypertonic saline continued to be used in Calcutta and Dacca until 1963 (see p. 123).

About the same time as Rogers was working on cholera in Calcutta, Sellards was studying the disease in Manila [393]. His particular concern was the uraemia that often develops in severe cholera, which he thought, erroneously, was associated with the loss of sodium bicarbonate from the blood into the stool, as had been demonstrated by O'Shaughnessy in 1832 [319], and the consequent fall in blood alkalinity. If a normal subject is given an intravenous injection of 5 g of sodium bicarbonate, his urine will be rendered alkaline, but Sellards found that the urine of cholera patients was often strongly acid, and remained acid even after injection of 90 g of sodium bicarbonate over a 24-hour period. This acidosis, and the uraemia, could be prevented by the infusion first of 2 l of 178 mEq $NaHCO_3$/l before the infusion of normal saline.

Sellards was not the first to use alkaline infusions in the treatment of cholera—O'Shaughnessy had proposed and Latta had used it nearly 80 years previously, and Sellards pointed out that it had long been recommended by various authorities, including the great authority on tropical diseases, Sir Patrick Manson,[1] who suggested infusion of a solution containing sodium chloride and sodium carbonate (the more alkaline Na_2CO_3, distinct from bicarbonate, $NaHCO_3$) [270]. However, the two patients whom Sellards treated with sodium carbonate both died, and he turned to sodium bicarbonate. This recommendation was adopted by Rogers [371]—he had already reduced the cholera death rate from 60 percent to 30 percent, and with sodium bicarbonate he was able to reduce it further to 20 percent.

2. Cairo 1947:
NAMRU-3 and the Beginnings of Effective Rehydration

The revival of the West's interest in cholera started with a bang in September 1947, when there was a rogue outbreak of classical cholera of unknown origin in Egypt which captured the interest of Commander Robert Allan Phillips, MC, USN, who happened to be in Egypt at the time in command of the U.S. Naval Medical Research Unit Number 3 (NAMRU-3) in Cairo. This was the beginning of his lively, distinguished, and sometimes controversial career of research on cholera—and consequent saving of many lives—that was to culminate 20 years later in his receiving the highly regarded Albert Lasker Award for Clinical Research, and many other honours. This first encounter was also the beginning of the involvement in the cholera problem of the United States of America—the Navy, the Army, the Department of State, the Department of Health, Education, and Welfare, and the academic world.

The Origins of the NAMRUs

There are at present only two NAMRUs; once there were five. They are under the Navy's Bureau of Medicine and Surgery (BUMED), and they owe their origins to academics in the Naval Reserve at the beginning of the United States' involvement in the Second World War, and to the naval tradition of research on tropical diseases that stems from the work of Admiral Edward Rhodes Stitt in the early part of the century. He was a noted parasitologist who realized that the Navy should have an interest in tropical diseases since its sailors and marines were liable

---

1. Who also recommended for the cholera patient that "his thirst should be treated by sips of iced water or of soda-water, or champagne, or brandy and water". One hardly supposes he had the common Indian patient in mind.

to be exposed to them in foreign climes. What was to become NAMRU-1 was conceived as long ago as 1920 by Dr. Albert Paul Krueger of the medical faculty of the University of California at Berkeley, who, being convinced that infectious diseases such as influenza were the worst enemies the military faced, suggested the setting-up of small, well-trained, well-equipped infectious disease research units. But it was not until 1934 that he succeeded in convincing Rear Admiral Rossiter of the need for such units. He was commissioned in the Naval Reserve and organized and commanded Naval Research Unit-1 as a reserve unit on the Berkeley campus. In January 1944, its name was changed to NAMRU-1, with its primary interest being research on communicable diseases in areas of specific interest. It was disestablished in 1974. NAMRU-2 was first commissioned in June 1944 at the Rockefeller Institute in New York City under Thomas H. Rivers, having arisen from a BUMED conference on infectious hepatitis and scrub typhus that were occurring in the South and Southwest Pacific. Among the Rockefeller Institute scientists belonging to this unit were D. D. van Slyke, V. P. Dole, P. B. Hamilton, M. McCarthy, Lewis Thomas—and R. A. Phillips and, briefly, J. Smadel, both of whom we will meet again. The rebirth of NAMRU-2 in another place and the origins of NAMRU-3 will be discussed below. NAMRU-4 was established in June 1946 at Dublin, Georgia, under the command of Comdr. John R. Seal (subsequently to become chairman of the Cholera Advisory Committee of the National Institutes of Health, as we shall see). It was originally authorized for rheumatic fever research and was moved to Great Lakes, Illinois, in 1948 and its purpose broadened to conduct research on acute respiratory diseases in military personnel with the object of providing means of prevention and control of these diseases. It was disestablished in 1974. NAMRU-5 started in December 1965 as a field facility of NAMRU-3 at Addis Ababa in Ethiopia, and was organized as NAMRU-5 in June 1974 under Capt. Craig K. Wallace (whom we will also meet again) with the object of conducting research on tropical and infectious diseases prevalent in Ethiopia and neighbouring countries. With the change of government in Ethiopia, it was disestablished in 1978. There are now only two NAMRU's—Number 2 in Manila and Number 3 in Cairo.

NAMRU-3

NAMRU-3 owes its particular origins to the U.S. Typhus Commission which was set up by order of President Roosevelt in December 1942, following the landings of American and British forces in French North Africa the previous month. The object of the commission was to deal with typhus during the war and to anticipate the possibility of post-war typhus epidemics such as had occurred in the wake of the First

World War. Under the sponsorship of the Navy, the Army and the Public Health Service[2], research laboratories were set up in Eastern Europe and in Egypt, the laboratory in Egypt being staffed by American, British and Egyptian scientists and technicians.

R. A. Phillips joined the staff of this laboratory in Egypt in 1944. He had joined the Naval Reserve in 1940 and was working in the Rockefeller Institute in New York when the United States entered the Second World War. He had been sent to the Naval Air Training Station in Pensacola, Florida, to work in the Harvard Fatigue Laboratory, but had been recalled to the Rockefeller Institute in 1944 to join the newly established NAMRU-2, a group which was working on problems of body fluid balance in connection with finding blood substitutes for transfusion of wounded soldiers suffering from blood loss. These studies required a reliable method of determining the specific gravity of blood that could be carried out in the field with a minimum of equipment. Phillips and D. D. van Slyke and others developed such a method,[3] little knowing that it would later play a crucial part for Phillips in determining the degree of dehydration of cholera patients. It was to be a stroke of good fortune for the later treatment of cholera by NAMRU-2 that they should have happened to develop this technique for an entirely different purpose.[4] The technique consists in letting drops of whole blood, or of blood plasma, fall into a series of standard solutions of copper sulphate of graded concentration and therefore of graded specific gravities. According to whether a drop falls or remains stationary or rises in a particular copper sulphate solution, its specific gravity is higher than, or the same as, or lower than that of the solution. In his researches on the dehydration and rehydration of cholera patients, Sir Leonard Rogers [371] had used a similar method, but with solutions of glycerine, in which the drops of blood or plasma dispersed so rapidly as to make accurate observation difficult. Copper sulphate solutions had the advantage that they coated the drops of blood or plasma with a skin of copper proteinate and so stabilized them; moreover, they had almost exactly the same temperature coefficients of expansion as blood or plasma. Thus, it was possible with a single drop—any sized drop, at whatever temperature was ambient—to determine the specific gravity

2. The PHS, later to be part of the not yet extant Department of Health, Education, and Welfare, now the Department of Health and Human Services.

3. Preliminary accounts which were published during the war in Navy [342] and Army [343] medical journals make no reference to cholera; the full account, which was published after the war, mentions cholera [344].

4. Later it was to be discarded by others in favour of a clinical assessment of the patient's condition (see p. 140).

of blood or plasma in a matter of moments; and any particular bottle of copper sulphate solution could be used for up to 100 determinations.

The Typhus Commission established its laboratories in an annex of the Abassia Fever Hospital in Cairo. Some members of the NAMRU-2 group, including Phillips, joined it in 1944; others, Under T. Rivers, fitted out a mobile field laboratory, intending to take it out to New Caledonia in the Pacific in June 1944. By this time, Guam had been recovered from the Japanese and Rivers's team went out there in January 1945 to establish a laboratory for tropical diseases[5], which was disestablished in 1947.

In the Typhus Commission laboratory, Phillips's assignment was to set up a more sophisticated biochemical laboratory than the one already there. He carried out electrolyte and protein balance studies on typhus patients, using his copper sulphate method of determining the blood specific gravities. He wanted to see if by feeding them they could gain weight, and he carried out metabolic evaluation studies on them. (And after the liberation of the concentration camps at Dachau, he went there, too, to examine typhus patients.) The fact that there was no serious typhus outbreak in Egypt during or after the war is thought to have been due in a large part to the work of the Typhus Commission Laboratory.[6] At the end of the war, in 1945, the Typhus Commission withdrew from Cairo. It seemed a pity to abandon its well-organized laboratory and to discontinue the collaborative efforts with the Egyptian scientists. The Americans were pleased that an avenue had been opened, and the Egyptians were pleased that the joint effort had been so worthwhile.

Early in July 1945, Phillips wrote to Capt. T. J. Carter at the Navy Bureau of Medicine and Surgery in Washington suggesting that the Navy take over the Typhus Commission Laboratory "for the further study of the physiological and biochemical aspects of Typhus Fever and other diseases prevalent in the Middle East area, which represent an occupational hazard to the armed services, particularly the Navy". He had in mind carrying on with studies of liver function that had already been made in the laboratory. He pointed out that all three of the officer personnel and three of the enlisted personnel who had been working on the biochemical aspects of typhus fever had been supplied

5. Thus fulfilling the original intention of NAMRU-2, which was to "operate a laboratory in the Pacific to study diseases of military importance".

6. Perhaps the Laboratory also played a part in the winning of the war in North Africa. At any rate, Phillips is quoted (in an article called "These Americans Must Be Gods" in a popular magazine) as having said, "if we hadn't checked the typhus epidemic among Egyptian stevedores unloading war material back in 1942 we might have lost the battle of El Alamein" [221].

by the Navy and were anxious to continue with the work they had been doing. He noted that the Typhus Commission already had approved the Navy's request for the transfer of the laboratory equipment to the Navy. He requested five officers, one of them being himself.[7]

Phillips's suggestion was accepted, and the director of the Typhus Laboratory, Dr. C.J.D. Zarafonetis, turned the laboratory over to the U.S. Navy in September 1945.[8] The renewed collaboration took the form of a new NAMRU—Number 3. It was designated for administrative purposes in January 1946 and, pending a formal agreement with the Egyptian government, an epidemiological unit was established on a temporary basis under the command of Capt. T. J. Carter as an interim measure in order to have a Navy presence in Cairo. At this point, however, Phillips had no notion of joining the regular Navy, and wished to continue his studies on blood and fluid imbalance. He therefore resigned from the Naval Reserve in June 1946 and returned to the United States. He went to the newly founded Alfred I. Dupont Institute in Delaware to join some of his former colleagues from van Slyke's laboratory in the Rockefeller Institute to carry on with the studies they had begun there. But Phillips was soon contacted and asked if he had any interest in joining the regular Navy in order to return to Cairo and take command of NAMRU-3. He joined the regular Navy in December 1946 and awaited orders. These soon came, and in June 1947 he arrived in Cairo to take up his new command and to negotiate the formal policy agreement concluded between the United States and Egyptian governments in June 1948.[9]

Phillips, with his colleagues Lts. M. K. Johnson and R. H. Weaver, had hardly arrived in Cairo when cholera invaded Egypt—on 22 September 1947—for the first time since 1919. It was a rogue outbreak, and the country was ill prepared for it. There had been a minor outbreak in Syria, but in Egypt it started in an important trading centre on the eastern fringe of the Nile delta close to a canal supplying drinking water for the cities and villages along the Suez Canal. In three days it reached Cairo, in five, Ishmailia; in three weeks all of lower Egypt was involved and by October all upper Egypt. By December, it was

7. Correspondence retrieved from NAMRU-3 by J. R. Seal in 1979.

8. Karnow avers that the Typhus Commission "agreed to turn [its laboratories] over to another American organisation—provided one could be found within seven days. Delegated to turn up a new sponsor, Phillips rushed back to Washington and made his pitch for support to every likely agency. Only the Navy was flexible enough to take over. . . " [221].

9. It is a measure of NAMRU-3's standing with the Egyptian government that it has continued in full and uninterrupted operation since that date, despite heavily strained relations between the U.S. and Egypt after the six-day war in 1967.

gone—according to Kamal [220], as a result of strenuous sanitary measures—but not before it had caused 33,000 cases, with 20,000 deaths.

This was Phillips's first encounter with the disease, and there could not have been a better man for such an encounter. With his concern with the balance of body fluids and the composition of blood, he was well qualified, and he must have been greatly interested. He decided that NAMRU-3 should investigate the disease immediately by means of physiological studies on cholera patients admitted to the Abassia Fever Hospital in severe shock. He wanted to determine accurately the loss of water and dissolved salts from the blood of cholera patients with a view to improving the treatment by means of rehydration. By the time he came onto the scene, the death rate from cholera had been reduced by Rogers's hypertonic and Sellards's alkaline infusion from 60 percent to 20 percent. Phillips proposed to make biochemical studies on 40 cholera patients, not forgetting the treatment of these patients. As he commented, "It must be remembered that, although our work was of a research nature, the primary motive was to achieve the adequate treatment of the patients" [458].

Patients were rehydrated first with plain normal saline (i.e., 154 mEq NaCl/l). After the first week, when loss of bicarbonate could be measured, small volumes of 476 mEq $NaHCO_3$/l were administered in proportion to the bicarbonate lost, in this way achieving cures of acidosis. Biochemical studies showed that as far as the salts were concerned, cholera blood did not differ essentially from normal blood, i.e., it was close to isotonic, except that the loss of sodium bicarbonate was more severe than that of other salts [458]. On the basis of the data obtained, they proposed rapid rehydration with slightly hypertonic solution containing 179 mEq Na^+/l, 3.4 mEq K^+/l, 123 mEq Cl^-/l and 60 mEq HCO^-_3/l (see Table 1.2, line 13). The patients' state of dehydration was rapidly determined by measuring the specific gravity of the blood or plasma by means of the copper sulphate method so recently, fortuitously and fortunately, developed by the NAMRU-2 unit at the Rockefeller Institute in New York. From the specific gravity, the volume of fluid needed for rehydration could easily be calculated (see p. 83). Of the 40 severely ill patients so treated, only 3 died, of whom at least 1 was beyond rescue by any means [218]. Thus, within a few months of intensive research, with no advance notice, and with no previous experience of cholera, NAMRU-3 had reduced the death rate in acute cholera to 5 to 7.5 percent.

The NAMRU-3 team concluded that their investigations "seemed to show that the diarrhoea of cholera constitutes the entire pathologic aspect of the disease and that all the derangements of function seen can only be accounted for on this basis". They also concluded that "the Vibrio comma plays no part in the disease once the diarrhoea has been initiated; that the vibrios present are reduced to the status of saprophytes which usually persist in the intestine only so long as the bowel contents remain abnormally alkaline". These were clear-sighted conclusions. Their conclusion about cholera toxin was also clear-sighted, even if they denied its existence. They concluded that there was no cholera toxin because their patients recovered so quickly and so well. Clearly, they were still under the influence of Koch's doctrine of systemic action of toxin, and since they could see no systemic effects they deduced there was no toxin. It did not seem to have occurred to them (as it had to Snow) that the toxin might act locally on the walls of the intestine.

Twenty years later, when Phillips received the Albert Lasker Award for Clinical Research, he revealed that he had intended in Cairo to do accurate balance studies on his cholera patients that could be achieved only if the fluids they received were carefully measured and introduced intravenously. However, he was unable to do this "because my young doctors said it was inhuman to withhold from a cholera patient water given by mouth" [341]. Indeed, in Egypt, "oral fluids were vigorously forced, even in patients who persistently vomited" [218]. Phillips had to wait 11 years before he could carry out his water and salt balance studies in which all fluids and salts were administered intravenously.

NAMRU-2

The cholera outbreak in Egypt came to an end in December 1947. Phillips remained in Cairo, resuming his studies on blood substitutes until early in 1952, when he returned to the United States to join the Navy Bureau of Medicine and Surgery in Washington. It was there that he conceived the idea that was eventually to give rise to the reactivation of NAMRU-2 (which had been disestablished on Guam in 1947) in Taiwan. In Cairo, he had acquired a taste for, and a proficiency in, medical diplomacy, an interest in tropical diseases, and a liking for living in foreign parts. He reasoned that if the Navy had a NAMRU in the Middle East it should also have one in the Far East. This suggestion was taken up and he and a group of experts of various interests, including Joseph Smadel, at that time Director of the Division of Communicable Diseases at the Army Medical Service Graduate School in Washington (now the WRAIR; see p. 92), travelled out to the East to find a suitable place for such a research unit. They visited a number of places, including Guam, Okinawa, Kuala Lumpur, Japan, and Taiwan. They chose Taiwan because there existed strong ties between the Americans and the Chinese at the Peking Medical College and they were made to feel welcome there, but, according to Phillips's wife, Hope, mainly because Taipei was the only place where dry ice was

FIGURE 3.1. Dr. Robert A. Phillips, Medical Corps, U.S. Navy, in his laboratory at the Naval Medical Research Unit, No. 3, Cairo, 1948. (Courtesy of Dr. F. M. Neva.)

available.[10] In May 1955, negotiations between the United States and the Republic of China were completed, authorizing the U.S. Navy to conduct research on tropical diseases in the Western Pacific from headquarters in Taipei in a building that had formerly been the nurses' dormitory for the National Taiwan University Hospital. All expenses that were payable in Taiwan currency (including about 75 percent of operating costs) were to be drawn from U.S.-owned Chinese currencies under U.S. Public Law 480, Eighty-third Congress.[11]

Phillips arrived in Taipei in September 1955 to reactivate the dormant NAMRU-2 in these new surroundings.[12] It took two years to construct the additional buildings needed and to equip the unit, and the formal recommissioning under Phillips's command did not take place until November 1957.[13] The reactivated unit, and its detachments in the Philippines (1961), Vietnam (1966) and Indonesia (1970), carried out a number of investigations in the countries where they were stationed, and during field trips to Pakistan, Thailand, Borneo, Korea and the Ryukyu Islands, on tropical diseases—bacterial, viral, rickettsial, amoebic and zoonotic, and it promoted training of military personnel in a way that could hardly have been available to academic students. But one of its first concerns happened to be cholera. When NAMRU-2 was commissioned in 1957 there was no cholera in Phillips's area of interest, but history was soon to repeat itself. Just as cholera broke out shortly after his arrival in the Middle East, it broke out again in 1958, the year after he had settled down in the Far East.

3. Bangkok 1958: NAMRU-2 and the Rationalization of Rehydration

Except that it induced an intense interest in cholera and its physiology in Phillips, the Cairo outbreak in 1947 did not, from a scientific and

10. The availability of dry ice had also been one of the attractions of Cairo.

11. Public Law 480, 83rd Congress, generally known as PL 480, was passed during President Truman's administration under the "Food for Peace" program for assistance to a number of countries. It provided that payment by these countries for food, and for other projects mutually agreed upon between the United States and the local country, should be made in the currency of the local country and spent in that country.

12. Phillips got things started by advancing the one-dollar rent for the former dormitory from his own pocket, or, rather, from his wife's purse.

13. When the U.S. Embassy in Taipei was destroyed during a civil disturbance in May 1957, Phillips invited the Ambassador, Mr. Carl Rankin, to move the embassy into his facility, which he did, for several months. This was when Phillips strengthened his friendship with a member of the embassy staff, Jack Conroy, who had helped him with negotiations with the Taiwan government, and with whom, within a few more years in another place, he was to have a critical encounter (see p. 95).

medical point of view, leave much of a mark on others. Eleven years after the publication by the NAMRU-3 group of its papers reporting that the fluid loss in cholera was isotonic, and that by replacement of it with alkaline isotonic saline they had reduced the death rate further from about 20 percent to 5 to 7.5 percent among those treated with alkaline hypertonic saline, Pollitzer made no mention of their work in his otherwise comprehensive monograph. Indeed all he has to report about rehydration during that outbreak in Egypt was that, in other hands, hypertonic saline (24.1 percent mortality) proved to be superior to isotonic saline (33.7 percent mortality).

But in 1958, there was an outbreak of cholera (due to the classical *Vibrio cholerae*) in Thailand that attracted a great deal of attention—so much that eventually it was to lead to an explosion in knowledge of cholera and a revolution in its treatment. Of course, outbreaks of cholera occurred around the many mouths of the Ganges every year, and as often as not twice a year, and of greater magnitude, but they never invited the attention of the Western scientific world the way the Bangkok episode did. Thailand had been invaded by cholera about every decade, the previous attack having lasted from 1943 to 1947, typically causing 19,000 cases with 13,000 deaths. In May 1958, it struck again, in Dhonburi on the right bank of the Chao Phraya river opposite Bangkok, to which it soon spread, killing 2,372 people between 23 May 1958 and 7 October 1959 [67]. It was a considerably less lethal attack than those during the previous 50 years, but it attracted considerably more attention.

In March 1958, Captain Phillips and his second-in-command at NAMRU-2, Lt. Comdr. Raymond H. Watten (who succeeded Phillips as commander of NAMRU-2 and was later in command of NAMRU-3 in Cairo), were attending a conference in Tokyo. After they had been there about a week, they read in the American armed forces paper, the *Stars and Stripes*, that there was a major outbreak of smallpox in East Pakistan, and at the same time an unusually heavy flare-up of the always endemic cholera in the capital, Dacca. Phillips was eager to tackle the cholera problem again. This was the first outbreak since his unit had been commissioned in 1957 and he believed it was ready to deal with it. He went forthwith to the American Embassy in Tokyo and through the naval attaché caused a message to be sent to the U.S. International Cooperation Administration in Dacca offering the assistance of his NAMRU-2 in the cholera epidemic. He and Watten then returned to Taipei, where they found a message waiting from Dacca asking for particulars of what NAMRU-2 proposed to do and how many people would be sent. The message came from Dr. Cockburn, chief medical officer of the Dacca Office of the then International Cooperation Administration (ICA), now the Agency for International Development (AID), of the United States Department of State. ICA had already asked Dr. Alexander Langmuir, head of the Epidemiology Division of the Communicable Disease Center[14] in Atlanta, Georgia, to bring out a team to investigate the smallpox. Phillips replied that NAMRU-2 could send a bacteriologist and some clinicians to consult with the East Pakistani government on the cholera epidemic, and a few days later he was invited to bring his team to Dacca. Thus it was that AID entered into its long and fruitful engagement with the cholera problem.

Phillips's team, consisting of himself and Watten, three other scientists and three technicians, flew from Taipei to Dacca in a C-47 provided by the 13th Air Wing of the U.S. Air Force in Taipei. It was an exhausting journey lasting two and a half days, with stops at Hong Kong, Taipei (again), Clark Air Force Base in the Philippines, Saigon and Bangkok, but at least it gave Phillips and Watten plenty of time to discuss the cholera question. Phillips told Watten how he had assessed degrees of dehydration of cholera patients in Cairo by means of the copper sulphate method for measuring plasma specific gravity, and how according to the value he had been able to calculate how much intravenous fluid a patient should receive for proper rehydration. He told him how his studies had not been as successful as he had hoped because his patients had been miserable with thirst, had been given fluid by mouth at the insistence of his young colleagues, and so had vomited, thus making it impossible to carry out accurate studies of the balance of output and intake of fluid and electrolytes. Here, like Phillips's previous interest in fluid balance and its application to cholera studies, was another fortunate coincidence, because Watten, too, had had experience of balance studies. Before coming to Taiwan he had worked with a Navy medical department research team at the U.S. Naval Hospital in Oakland, California, that was concerned with one of the first artificial kidneys on the west coast used for treating patients with renal shut-down due to shock, trauma or poisoning. If such patients could be kept alive long enough by means of the artificial kidney, their own kidney function would return. The research on the development of this technique required very careful studies of the balance of intravenous input of electrolyte and fluid and output by the kidney, and insensible losses through respiration and perspiration, with nothing given by mouth. It had been important not to overload the patients with potassium. To Watten's way of thinking, the kidney patient was in a similar condition, but in

14. The CDC, part of the U.S. Public Health Service (PHS), now with the more ambitious name of Center for Disease Control, but the same initials.

reverse—retaining rather than losing electrolytes—and he suggested doing the same kind of balance studies on cholera patients. Phillips agreed, and asked Watten to draw up a proposal.

When the exhausted NAMRU-2 team arrived in Dacca in April they received a gala reception from Dr. Cockburn and his ICA officers, accompanied by newspaper reporters, photographers and newsreel cameramen. The next day, the newspapers carried stories about the American team that had arrived. Since a team of Russian doctors also arrived at about the same time to assist the Pakistani government, the U.S. State Department was glad to be given an opportunity to counter the Russian move in this way.

In Dacca, the NAMRU team set up a laboratory in the newly erected building of the Ministry of Health near the airport. They had brought some equipment for bacteriological and virological investigations, but no intravenous fluids or clinical equipment. They set up a bacteriological laboratory, went out into the country to get samples of blood and stools from patients and confirmed that the disease organism was the Inaba strain of the classical *Vibrio cholerae*. They also went to the cholera ward of the Mitford Hospital in Dacca, where Watten saw his first case of cholera. The patients were being treated with Rogers' hypertonic saline, but the NAMRU team did not feel that an offer to undertake any studies on rehydration would be acceptable. In the laboratory, the virologist in their group, Dr. Dam Ping Wong, offered to assist in the production of smallpox vaccine, but otherwise there was very little to do. Phillips returned to Taipei after 10 days, leaving Watten in charge, and Watten filled the time reading Pollitzer's reviews on cholera in the *Bulletin of the World Health Organization* that were subsequently revised and brought up to date and published as a monograph in 1959. He was impressed by the historical aspects but disappointed by the clinical and laboratory studies. There was no careful measurement of fluid output and only vague studies on the various electrolytes. There was a jumble of confusing data resulting in a jumble of confusing ideas for therapy. This stirred him into preparing the protocol for a detailed electrolyte and fluid balance study that he and Phillips had discussed on their flight to Dacca. After they had been in Dacca for two weeks, Langmuir and several young men from the Public Health Service's Epidemiological Intelligence Service (EIS) arrived to study and assist with the concurrent outbreak of smallpox. They stayed for several weeks but, according to Watten, were not able to do much, either. Watten was bored by the inactivity and wanted to return to Taipei but was dissuaded by Cockburn of the ICA, who thought the American medical presence should continue in Dacca as long as there was a Russian presence.[15]

But after four weeks, at the end of April, Watten returned to Taipei without Phillips's permission, leaving Comdr. R. E. Kuntz in charge of the remainder of the NAMRU-2 team, which remained in Dacca until June, when it rejoined NAMRU-2, not in Taipei, but in Bangkok, to take part in the important events that were now taking place there.

A few weeks after Watten's return to Taipei, cholera broke out in Thailand. The Thai authorities were not unprepared for it. From early March, they had received reports from the World Health Organization (WHO) Epidemiological Intelligence Office in Singapore that Calcutta was having more cases of cholera than the usual number of 100 to 200 a month, and it was feared that heavy air traffic between Calcutta and Bangkok might bring the disease to Thailand. Accordingly, on 11 April, the Thai Division of Communicable Disease Control requested the Thai Red Cross and the Thai Department of Medical Service to increase production of vaccine and medicine, and a week later ordered increased vigilance by the quarantine officer at Bangkok Airport. On 2 May, it issued a notice on Thailand Radio advising everyone to be vaccinated, and on 6 May provincial health officers were instructed to vaccinate the population and keep a close watch for cholera [399]. On 23 May, it struck.

When word came to Phillips in Taipei of this outbreak, he was ready. He and Watten had discussed and agreed on the protocol for detailed balance studies. He got in touch with—or was contacted by, the record is not quite clear—the American Embassy in Bangkok and offered—or was invited to offer—the services of his NAMRU in dealing with the outbreak. Watten states that Phillips cabled the embassy, but the embassy may have taken the first step. Phillips had a friend working at the SEATO[16] desk in the Bangkok Embassy, J. J. Conroy, who had moved there from the embassy in Taipei, where he had helped Phillips negotiate with the Taiwan government in setting up NAMRU-2. Conroy's memory of the sequence of events is that he telephoned Phillips from Bangkok and asked him if he would be willing, and if they could get Washington's approval, to bring his team to Bangkok. Phillips would have to get

---

15. The Russians returned to Dacca in March 1969 and collaborated with the Pakistani and American scientists (in the PSCRL; see Chapter 4) on the treatment of cholera with cholera bacteriophage, a virus discovered in 1915 that destroys and dissolves bacteria. It had been noted 20 years after the discovery of bacteriophage that the mortality rate fell rapidly after the beginning of the cholera season and this was thought to be due to the multiplication of bacteriophage. However, it was concluded that bacteriophage "has no place in the treatment of cholera" [271].

16. Southeast Asia Treaty Organization; see p. 95.

Naval approval and Conroy would have to get SEATO agreement and U.S. State Department approval.[17] After a series of dispatches, the concurrences were obtained from all quarters within a few days, and Phillips, Watten and a new arrival, Comdr. Francis M. Morgan,[18] and a number of technicians, together with 1,500 pounds of equipment and 20 cases of intravenous fluids, set off from Taipei to Bangkok in the U.S. Air Force's C-47. It took them two or three days to set up a laboratory on the ground floor of the priests' ward of the Chulalongkorn and a patients' ward on the floor above. By the end of the week, they were ready to treat patients in collaboration with two members of the staff of the Chulalongkorn University Medical School, Yachai Na Song-kala and Bunam Vanikiati. Phillips was now able to have done what he was prevented from doing 11 years previously in Cairo. Under Watten's supervision, water and electrolyte balance studies were done on 25 patients, all of whose fluid output—stools,[19] vomitus and insensible loss—was carefully measured and analysed, and all of whom received fluid only intravenously. These careful studies confirmed that the concentration of electrolytes in the plasma of cholera patients is essentially the same as in normal subjects, i.e., isotonic, if corrections are made for the increased concentration of protein in the cholera plasma (see p. 17). In other words, the loss of electrolytes from the blood in cholera is essentially isotonic, but there are important differences: the concentrations in the blood of the two most abundant electrolytes, sodium and chloride, are slightly, essentially insignificantly, higher, but there is a distinct fall in potassium and a loss of 50 percent or more of bicarbonate (as observed in 1831 by O'Shaughnessy and in 1910 by Sellards). These losses are reflected by corresponding increases in their components in the stools. In fact, the electrolyte composition of cholera stools is remarkably constant [455]. The loss in bicarbonate is particularly serious, since it leads to acidosis, as we have seen. The NAMRU-2 team concluded that the aim of rehydration should be to restore the

17. The question of who invited whom can be embroidered. Watten relates that while the NAMRU-2 team was in Bangkok, an Army colonel came from Kuala Lumpur and was enraged to find the Navy there since it was the Army, being closer in Malaysia, that should have been called in. Phillips replied that they had been invited by the Royal Thai Government because the Navy had not waited to be invited, but had invited an invitation. However, the Army did send some of its people to Bangkok the next year (see p. 91).

18. Later they were joined by a civilian biochemist, R. Q. Blackwell.

19. Initially, the patients lay on four-poster beds with slatted bottoms. Holes were cut in the middle of these bottoms and the patients were stretched on two folded-over mattresses laid on the two sides of the hole, with the buttocks over the hole and a stool collection bucket below. Later, the "Watten cholera bed", thought by the Thai nurses to be "the greatest thing since peanut butter", was invented; see p. 83.

blood to its proper volume as fast as possible, then to correct the acidosis, and then to maintain a balance between the output of water and electrolytes in the stools (plus urine, vomit and insensible loss) and input of water and electrolytes by intravenous infusion.

Studies by NAMRU-2 continued on a diminishing number of patients in a number of visits to Bangkok, and with analysis of stools specimens transferred to Taipei in 1959 and 1960. By 1961, cholera had virtually disappeared from Thailand. However, in September of that year, cholera broke out in Manila in the Philippines—"fortunately, for us"—as Phillips put it [341]. This was in fact the beginning of the seventh cholera pandemic, due to the El Tor biotype of the cholera vibrio. NAMRU-2 had previously been invited to study the incidence of *Entamoeba histolytica* infections in the Philippines, and now it was invited to introduce its methods of treatment of cholera, to assist the Philippine Department of Health, and to conduct research in the San Lazaro Hospital in Manila.[20] This led to the establishment of a NAMRU-2 detachment in the Philippines, dealing with several other tropical diseases besides cholera. Cholera research was continued in Manila in successive years to 1964. Cholera also broke out elsewhere, to be pursued by NAMRU-2. This became a pattern:

> Since cholera was not present in Taiwan itself (except for a brief epidemic in 1964), the technique used by NAMRU-2 for the study of the disease was as follows: Upon hearing of an epidemic the Navy proffered the services of NAMRU-2; upon receipt of acceptance a team of three or four scientists and 8 to 12 technicians with all the necessary supplies and equipment was immediately airlifted by Navy or Air Force planes from Taipei to the stricken area. After indoctrinating local physicians and nurses in the Navy method of treating cholera, permission to conduct research was requested and usually granted [341].

In the autumn of 1963, cholera broke out in South Korea and a NAMRU-2 team was sent out to advise the Korean government. In 1964, it appeared in South Vietnam, and within less than 14 hours a NAMRU-2 team arrived in Saigon with 15,000 pounds of equipment and supplies. Since this turned out to be a major outbreak of the disease, studies on it were transferred from Manila to Saigon. Lesser outbreaks were dealt with in a similar way in East Pakistan, Malaysia and Sarawak. In 1964, while the NAMRU-2 team was in Manila, there was an outbreak of

20. In 1979, after the "normalization" of relations between the United States of America and the People's Republic of China, NAMRU-2 was moved from Taiwan (the Republic of China) to the Philippines.

cholera—as it happens, a minor one—in their base, Taiwan. The team decided not to return to Taipei, but to leave the problem in the capable hands of the wife of one of their members (Blackwell) who had remained at the base. She was a physician who had learned the technique of rehydration during the studies in Thailand (her native country). She and two or three Chinese medical officers set up treatment centres in local hospitals to demonstrate rehydration techniques and soon had the disease under control.

The outcome of all this work was a routine for the rehydration of cholera patients that led to the reduction in the death rate from about 20 percent in the pre-Egypt days, through 5 to 7.5 percent in Egypt in 1947, to 0.6 percent.[21] The recommendations for treating patients admitted to cholera wards with a history of copious watery diarrhoea during a cholera epidemic can be summarized as follows:

1. The patient is weighed, then placed on a "Watten cholera bed", i.e., an army canvas cot with a 9-inch hole in the centre through which passes a sleeve attached to a similar hole in a rubber or plastic sheet. The sleeve is placed in a calibrated bucket (or a plain bucket with a dipstick) which receives the stools from the patient lying with the buttocks over the hole.

2. A 3-ml sample of blood is taken through a hypodermic needle inserted in a suitable vein. The needle is left in place and through it an infusion of isotonic saline (9 g NaCl/l, 154 mEq/l) is started, at a rate of 100 ml per minute.

3. In the meantime, the specific gravity of the sample blood, and of its plasma, is rapidly measured by the copper sulphate method in order to determine the volume of fluid needed to restore the patient's blood plasma to normal specific gravity, which is 1.025. For every 0.001 elevation of the plasma specific gravity above the normal value, the patient will need a volume of intravenous fluid equal to 4 ml multiplied by the body weight in kilograms (e.g., a 50-kg adult with a plasma specific gravity of 1.030 would need 1,000 ml of fluid, and a 20-kg child with the same plasma specific gravity of 1.030 would need 400 ml of fluid).

4. The rapid administration of fluid is continued until the calculated volume has been administered and the plasma specific gravity restored

21. NAMRU-2 apparently wished to give this method full publicity, for the identical paper, by Wallace and five others, was published in three, if not four, journals at the same time, namely 447, 448, 449. A footnote in the Chinese journal stated that the paper was also to appear in a better-known journal, viz. the *Bulletin* of the World Health Organization, but there appears to be no trace of it in that journal between 1962 and 1968.

to 1.025.[22] The infusion rate can then be slowed down to about 3 ml per minute. The rehydrated patient, though nearly restored to health, continues, or starts again, to have diarrhoea, and the object now is to match the fluid output as measured in the bucket under the bed with fluid input.

So far, we have been concerned only with the restoration, and then the maintenance, of the blood volume; but other losses from the blood also have to be corrected, the first of which is the alkali. In order to correct acidosis, the NAMRU-2 procedure, in Bangkok, was to administer 1 litre of 2 percent sodium bicarbonate ($NaHCO_3$) after every 8 litres of isotonic saline, but later in the Philippines, the ratio was changed to 1:3 (see lines 14 and 15, Table 1.2). There is somewhat of a mystery about the ratios of saline to bicarbonate in the NAMRU-2 regimen. American workers later in Dacca and Calcutta referred to Phillips's 1:2 regimen, but this does not seem to have been documented anywhere. It may also be necessary to correct for loss of potassium, which may otherwise lead to depression of the heart muscle, neuromuscular disturbance and perhaps kidney damage; on the other hand, infusion of too much potassium may have harmful effects.[23] NAMRU-2 considered that potassium at a concentration of 10 mEq/l would satisfy the needs of cholera patients under a variety of conditions and could be used with impunity as long as diarrhoea continued [457].[24] On the whole, the practise today is to rehydrate cholera patients with a solution containing sodium and potassium anions and chloride and bicarbonate cations very similar in constitution to cholera stools,[25] and, as we shall see, a common single-solution fluid is the "5:4:1" solution generally used in the Cholera Research Laboratory at Dacca consisting of 5 g NaCl, 4 g $NaHCO_3$ and 1 g KCl per litre, shown in line 18, Table 1.2. With children under five years of age, rehydration therapy has to be slightly different because the effects of dehydration are manifested more

22. At this stage, the specific gravity of the whole blood can be measured and the observed value used as normal, and thereafter the more quickly determined whole blood specific gravities can be used instead of the plasma values. But we shall see that clinicians now prefer to estimate the state of hydration of a cholera patient by evaluating the quality of the pulse, the blood pressure, the appearance of the neck veins and the turgor of the skin (see p. 140).

23. Sir Leonard Rogers used to administer potassium chloride, but on a visit to England was told by some physiologists that infusion of potassium was unnecessary and possibly harmful, so he gave it up [370].

24. Potassium solutions are often given by mouth as an adjunct to intravenous infusion. In the East, these might economically take the form of green coconut water, a good source of potassium.

25. Greig was horrified at the suggestion that cholera stools (presumably filtered and sterilized) might make a suitable infusion fluid, but, considered in terms of electrolyte concentrations, it was at least an entirely logical notion [182].

rapidly and rehydration has to be done more carefully, and complications of electrolyte imbalance and acidosis that are seldom seen in adults tend to develop. The rehydration solution is a little different, containing a little more potassium and a little less sodium, from that used with adults [358]. Nowadays, cholera patients are also given the antibiotic tetracycline (see p. 133) because it halves the duration of the diarrhoea and so lessens the volume of rehydration fluid needed and the duration of hospitalization.

Phillips has stated: "Cholera cures itself, like a common cold. The problem is to keep the patient alive by giving him enough fluids fast enough. If he has no other complex diseases, any patient who can get treatment will survive" [337]. The treatment is not only almost perfectly effective, it is also very simple. To quote Phillips again: "This regime would enable even a 12-year-old boy or girl of average alertness to provide adequate treatment in the average patient and to cull out those requiring training medical knowledge" [337].

Although the method of saving cholera victims by intravenous rehydration had been greatly refined and simplified by Phillips and his successors, and the excellence of his efforts was recognized in his receiving the Albert Lasker Clinical Research Award in 1967, the technique has the disadvantage that it is not possible to apply it on a large scale in underdeveloped countries where cholera is most likely to occur. The reason for this is that the infusion solutions have to be sterile, and the water in which they are made has to be distilled to eliminate fever-producing substances. Since a cholera patient may require more than his own weight of infusion fluid, and sometimes two or three times that amount, enormous volumes of fluid would be needed to cope with an epidemic. This does not take account of sterile needles and tubes required, the necessity for having to move large volumes of fluid about and the need for hospitalization. Phillips, of course, realized this, and even in Egypt was considering ways of rehydrating patients by mouth, because if the fluids could be administered by mouth[26] the water used need not be distilled, the solutions need not be sterilized and the patients would not need hospitalization. Oral rehydration was eventually to be made practicable—it will be discussed in Chapter 6.

4. Bangkok 1959: The Army and the First Civilians

NAMRU-2 was the first but not the only American party to take an interest in the outbreak of cholera in Thailand. In the following year, the Army (through the Walter Reed Army Institute of Research, WRAIR),

---

26. The fluids so far considered are ineffective by mouth because the cholera-poisoned gut is unable to absorb them.

the Public Health Service (through the National Heart Institute of the National Institutes of Health) and a university (Jefferson Medical College, Philadelphia) also sent their representatives to Bangkok, and they all carried out excellent studies on the problem. The decennial Bangkok episode was neither extensive nor long-lived, yet it captured the interest of the United States in a way that the annual, or rather biannual, and far more serious, epidemics in East Pakistan and West Bengal had not.

It is not unlikely that geopolitical considerations would have made the U.S. Department of State (through the ICA, which held the strings of the relevant foreign aid purse) look with favour upon an opportunity to render assistance in this matter of cholera to Thailand (rather than India or East Pakistan) at that juncture. The split between North and South Vietnam had occurred in 1954, and by 1958 it was clear that there was going to be trouble in Southeast Asia. The Southeast Asia Treaty Organization had come into being in 1956, and although East Pakistan was part of SEATO, it was a long way from where the interest of the architect of that treaty, Secretary of State John Foster Dulles, was directed at that time, for he was convinced that the North Vietnamese would not let the South Vietnamese alone. Thailand, which was much nearer, was also part of SEATO, and the buildup of Americans in Thailand had already begun in 1955–57. Thailand was West-oriented, it had never been a colony, and it had always been on the winning side. In the Second World War it had accepted the Japanese, but at the end of the war, in 1945, it had joined the United Nations. With such considerations, a request for help from the Thais would have had a high level of impact on the State Department, and simply would not have been ignored.

The Setting

The Bangkok outbreak engaged American interest at a time when there was, on the whole, little domestic interest in tropical disease, for there was no more tropical disease in the United States, the last residue of it, malaria, having been eliminated from the New Orleans area in 1948. The tropical medicine community in the United States essentially died out after the Second World War, as it had in Great Britain after it lost its colonies, and in the United States interest was now focused, not on areas where there were tropical diseases, but on Europe and the Marshall Plan and the North Atlantic Treaty Organization (NATO). Young men were not interested in going in for tropical medicine, and there were no research grants for it because what the country, and Congress, were now concerned with, and where the money and the talent went, were the major domestic causes of death—cancer, heart disease and stroke. Senator Lister Hill, Congressman James Fogarty and

James Shannon, Director of the National Institutes of Health, were engaged in "the Great NIH Take-off", making it attractive to Congress, the Executive and the medical profession of the United States, and, with its budget increasing each year by 15 to 20 percent (in a time of no inflation), building it into an immense and powerful empire of medical research. The National Institutes of Health now occupy a campus of 306 acres in Bethesda, Maryland, near Washington, D.C. They comprise 11 Institutes and the National Library of Medicine, formerly the Library of the Office of the Surgeon General of the Army. They are one of six components, another of which is the Center for Disease Control, formerly the Communicable Disease Center in Atlanta, Georgia, of the Public Health Service (PHS), which were transferred from the Federal Security Agency to the newly formed Department of Health, Education, and Welfare, DHEW,[27] in 1953. The PHS arose from the Marine Hospital Service established in 1798 under President John Adams for the relief of sick and disabled seamen (and the badge of the PHS still carries a fouled anchor). The NIH are descended from the one-room Laboratory of Hygiene established under the Marine Hospital Service in 1887 on Staten Island for research on cholera (let it be noted) and other infectious diseases. It was redesignated the National Institute (singular) of Health in 1930 and pluralized in 1948 (see p. 11).

Domestic Cholera Research

In the years preceding the Bangkok outbreak, research on cholera was proceeding only in a desultory fashion in the United States and elsewhere in the West. Working on a grant from the Army, William Burrows was pursuing the false trail of endotoxins in Chicago. In 1952, he was engaged in a collaborative study with Charles Lankford of the University of Texas in Austin, who had been asked by the Army microbiological laboratory at Fort Detrick (set up during the war to study preventive measures against germ warfare) to study the cholera vibrio, because so little was known about it. The stock of vibrio cultures they had were genetically degraded and therefore they travelled (under the auspices of the World Health Organization) to India to get freshly isolated cultures from cholera patients in the Nilratan Sircar Hospital (of S. N. De's medical college) in Calcutta. When Lankford returned to Texas, he made a decision to carry out an investigation that was going to have a most important influence on the eventual purification of cholera toxin by a pupil of his, Richard A. Finkelstein, whose fundamentally important work we will later discuss. He decided to work on the basic nutritional requirements of the cholera vibrio, in order to make

---

27. Since 1980, the Department of Health and Human Services, DHHS.

a study of its properties such as virulence and toxin (i.e., endotoxin) production, and also with the view to preparing a whole-cell vaccine against the organism. Finkelstein had come to Lankford's department as a graduate student to work for a master's degree on a problem of resistance to streptomycin in salmonella organisms. When he had taken his degree, he wanted to work for a Ph.D. with Lankford on the gonococcus, a subject on which Lankford had made pioneer studies, but Lankford considered this too difficult a subject for a microbiological tyro and put him onto the nutritional requirements of the cholera vibrio instead. Finkelstein tackled this problem unwillingly, but efficiently. He developed an entirely synthetic culture medium for the growth of the cholera vibrio. Later, as we shall see, he put this medium to good use when he supplemented it with a well-known mixture of amino acids prepared from casein (casamino acids). This synthetic-casamino, acid-supplemented medium (syncase) not only supported the growth of the vibrio, but also its toxin production. After a three-year virological interlude, Finkelstein went, in 1958, to work under Sam Formal at the Walter Reed Army Institute of Research, one of the few other institutions in the United States where there was an interest, if rather subdued, in the cholera vibrio. His subsequent career is discussed in Chapters 8 and 10.

At the WRAIR, the only work being done on cholera at the time of the Bangkok outbreak, or, rather, completed shortly before it, was that by Joseph Lowenthal, who had joined the staff under Geoffrey Edsall, director of the Division of Immunology, in 1952. Edsall's interest in cholera arose from his participation in the Commission on Immunization, one of the several commissions of the Army Epidemiological Board[28] which had to deal with those immunizations that did not have, as influenza and enteric diseases had, a commission of its own. The Commission on Immunization had considered cholera, among other infectious diseases, because it was a potential problem for the armed forces, and had a contract with Kenneth Goodner at Jefferson Medical College. Lowenthal worked for four or five years in Edsall's division, at Goodner's suggestion, on the cholera mucinase which was still being thought of as being responsible for the alleged desquamation of the intestinal tract. This theory was soon finally to be demolished in Bangkok.

In Philadelphia, Kenneth Goodner at Jefferson Medical College had been doing research for some years on the cholera vibrio. Goodner advocated the notion that one day cholera would invade the United

28. Later the Armed Forces Epidemiological Board (AFEB).

States again[29] since there were many areas where it could flourish—large cities, rural areas with inadequate sanitation and migrant labour camps. He and his young colleagues Harry Smith and Rolf Freter studied the growth characteristics of the cholera vibrio and its immunology, and were interested in the still fashionable mucinase.

Another American worker who had long been working on the cholera vibrio was Oscar Felsenfeld. In 1944, he was publishing papers on cholera lecithinases from the Chicago Medical School. Later, he joined the Walter Reed Army Institute of Research, and after the war he spent several years as a member of WRAIR working on cholera vibrios in the U.S. Army 406th General Medical Laboratory in Japan. He also was the first head of the Army's Thai Cholera Laboratory in Bangkok.

In Europe, there was even less interest in cholera. Before the war, Arthur Gardner, at the Sir William Dunn School of Pathology of the University of Oxford, had prepared "the charter of present knowledge on the antigenic structure of cholera and cholera-like vibrios" (Pollitzer), and at the Institut Pasteur in Paris, Jean Gallut and Pierre Grabar were working on cholera endotoxin, on a small-molecular toxin that hardly saw the light of day, and on cholera vaccines.

The Inner Circle

The Bangkok outbreak captured the interest of a powerful and influential group of distinguished medical research workers in the general neighbourhood of Washington. It was an "Inner Circle", an old boy network, of people in the upper management of science who were old enough still to be interested in tropical diseases despite the trend away from them. They were closely tied together by bonds of common experience and interest, longstanding friendship and mutual respect, and by the fact that many of them had worked at the Rockefeller Institute (at the same time as Phillips) before the United States entered the Second World War—indeed, they were sometimes referred to as the "Rockefeller Rocket". They were: (1) James Shannon, Director of the National Institutes of Health since 1955, an outspoken man of considerable power and energy and, obviously in his position, influence. (2) Joseph Smadel, Associate Director for Intramural Research of the NIH since 1956. He had previously been Director of the Division of Communicable Diseases at the Walter Reed Army Institute of Research since 1950. He joined the Army (having been rejected by the Navy on physical grounds) in 1942 as chief virologist of the First Medical General

29. A prophecy fulfilled in the late 1970s, when it began to occur on the coast of Texas.

Laboratory in Europe. He led the mission to study the control of typhus in Italy and Egypt, and with Woodward (see below) showed in Malaya that scrub typhus patients could be cured, and at the same time immunized, by treatment with the antibiotic chloramphenicol, which they found also to be highly effective against typhoid. He was an outspoken and ruthless man of considerable drive and force of character (alluded to as "our beloved bastard" in the minutes of the National Foundation for Infantile Paralysis). If such a close-knit group of equals could be said to have had a leader, it was Smadel. He died in 1963. (3) Colin MacLeod, who had played an important part at the Rockefeller Institute, with Oswald Avery and Maclyn McCarthy, in the work that was, after a long lag, to lead eventually to the recognition of DNA as the chemical basis of heredity. At the time we are now concerned with, he was professor of Experimental Medicine at the University of Pennsylvania, and was later to become a member of President Kennedy's and then President Johnson's Science Advisory Committee, and Deputy Director of the White House Office of Science and Technology. MacLeod was an experienced and proficient microbiologist with a particular interest in bacterial toxins. He died in London in 1972, on his way to the Cholera Research Laboratory in Dacca. (4) Theodore E. Woodward, professor of Medicine at the University of Maryland School of Medicine in Baltimore. He was an old and close friend, and fellow campaigner in foreign parts, of Smadel. (5) Woodward's "most irascible, unpredictable and sensitive friend" [465], Kenneth Goodner, who was, as we have already seen, the only member of the Inner Circle who at the time was actually working on the cholera vibrio. He was a bachelor and he and Smadel and Woodward were particularly close friends, and would go duck hunting on Chesapeake Bay, sharing a piece of land on the shore. He died in 1967. Tangential to this Inner Circle were some others: Richard Mason, Director of WRAIR; Geoffrey Edsall, who succeeded Smadel as Director of the Division of Communicable Diseases at WRAIR; and two who were not on the eastern seaboard, Thomas Francis, of the University of Michigan in Ann Arbor, and John Dingle, of Western Reserve University in Cleveland. Most of these people were serving on the Armed Forces Epidemiological Board or one of its commissions, such as the one on immunization.

There are different accounts of how the army and civilian teams came to go or to be invited to go, to Bangkok in 1959, but whatever way it was, it was mediated largely through the Inner Circle. Robert Gordon (now Special Assistant Director of NIH), who went to Bangkok from NIH, avers that in 1958, after NAMRU-2 had dealt with the cholera in Bangkok, Phillips, back in Taipei, anticipating a further outbreak in Bangkok in the following year according to pattern, contacted all the other U.S. federal services, including the PHS, advising them that he was planning ahead for further studies and inviting them to join in the effort. Eugene Gangarosa, who went to Bangkok from WRAIR, believes that it was a WRAIR man who made the suggestion. This was Oscar Felsenfeld, then with the 406th General Medical Laboratory (see p. 92, who had come to Bangkok to study the outbreak. These are, one might say, the NIH and WRAIR versions. There is also the version of the third party who went to Bangkok, the Jefferson version. Probably all three are correct in their ways, but the Jefferson version appears to have had the most weight. Goodner had a good friend, an alumnus of Jefferson Medical College, in Bangkok, Dr. Luang Binbakya Bidyabhed, Under-Secretary of State in the Thailand Ministry of Public Health. Like many Thais, Dr. Bidyabhed had an alternative and more frequently used name, Pyn, presumably derived from the first syllable of his first name Binbakya (Luang is a title—Prince—not a name). While he was doing post-graduate work in roentgenology at Jefferson, he and Goodner had become good friends, and during the summer of 1958 Goodner offered to send a team of bacteriologists to help the Thais investigate the outbreak of cholera. Since the number of cases was decreasing, Pyn thought it inadvisable for the Jefferson team to come out immediately, suggesting rather that they remain on the alert. When the second peak of cholera came in December, Goodner prevailed on Pyn to invite teams from Jefferson Medical College, the National Institutes of Health and the Army to come out to Thailand to investigate the cholera epidemic in its second year, 1959. The team that went out worked together in the Chulalongkorn Medical College in Bangkok, closely with Phillips, Watten and Blackwell of the NAMRU-2 team. It was the first opportunity for the American home contingent to look at this nineteenth-century disease (as far as the Western world was concerned) with the eyes of modern medicine. Except for Phillips's excellent physiological work, 11 years before in Cairo, and now continuing in Bangkok, there was no modern work on the basic science of the disease.

The Army

We will discuss the Army's contribution first because after NAMRU-2 the Army was the first to have a man out in Bangkok, Lt. Col. Oscar Felsenfeld, an experienced cholera bacteriologist, as we have seen. The Army's tradition of medical research in foreign parts is a little older than the Navy's. Its first venture abroad was Lt. Bailey Ashford's investigation of hookworm-mediated anaemia in Puerto Rico in 1899. In 1900, Maj. Walter Reed led the Yellow Fever Commission in Cuba and established that the disease was carried by mosquitoes, and Lt. Charles Craig began his studies of amoebic dysentery in the Philippines.

That year also saw the establishment of the first American (not to say military) medical research laboratory overseas, in the form of the first of three successive U.S. Army Medical Research Boards in the Philippines. In 1930, a medical research laboratory was established in Panama. Immediately after the Second World War, in 1945, the U.S. Army 406th General Medical Laboratory was established in Tokyo as a regional and general support laboratory for the Army medical services.[30] Later, other army medical research laboratories were established in Malaysia, Thailand, Brazil and Kenya. In the United States, the Army has seven medical research laboratories, the one of most concern to us being the Walter Reed Army Institute of Research in Washington, established in 1893 as the Army Medical School,[31] with Walter Reed as the first secretary of the faculty [112]. In 1952, as a result of outbreaks of tropical diseases occurring in the theatre covered by the 406th laboratory, WRAIR sent out a number of experts, including Felsenfeld, whom the 406th supported by means of various supplies, such as housing, airplanes, helicopters, vehicles. In 1953, a cholera project was established under Felsenfeld to collect and study cholera strains from Taiwan, the Philippines, Malaya and India. In 1955, Felsenfeld went to Thailand when the 406th laboratory gave medical support, in collaboration with Thai medical authorities, to a mapping mission of the 29th Engineer Company in a remote area in Thailand on the border with China. He continued his cholera studies (including studies on El Tor strains) in the following years, and in 1959 when the cholera broke out in Bangkok again, he went there with his wife, who was also a bacteriologist. The WRAIR sent five men to join them—Col. F. L. Orth, Maj. W. R. Beisel, Capt. E. Blair, Capt. E. J. Gangarosa and Capt. S. Halstead.[32]

Gangarosa and Beisel had previously worked with Col. W. H. Crosby on his capsule, a device that could be passed through the mouth, oesophagus, and stomach into the small intestine of a living subject, there to obtain a biopsy sample of the epithelial lining that could be

30. It also supported the Navy—Gen. Joe Blumberg, who was deputy director of the 406th at the time, states that it helped Phillips set up his NAMRU-2 laboratories in Taipei.

31. Today, much of the military medical teaching (and research) is done in the magnificent new Uniformed Services University of the Health Sciences in Bethesda, close to the National Naval Medical Center and the National Institutes of Health.

32. Finkelstein had joined WRAIR in 1958, and states that when he arrived there he was told by his chief Abram S. Benenson (of whom more later), Director of the Division of Communicable Diseases, that if he would work on cholera he would be sent to Bangkok. Finkelstein therefore agreed to work on cholera, but was not sent on this mission to Bangkok, possibly because he was a civilian and the others all army officers. However, Finkelstein did eventually go to Bangkok with excellent effect; see p. 172.

used for microscopic and biochemical studies [88]. Smadel had been interested in finding out whether desquamation of the intestinal tract took place in cholera, and in discussing the mucinase hypothesis of Burnet (p. 57), had suggested that the question of desquamation could be clarified only if it were possible to study the intestinal wall during active purgation. It occurred to Gangarosa that the Crosby capsule might be the ideal instrument for this purpose. It was a most fortunate coincidence that Gangarosa should have been associated with Crosby, and thus, like Phillips with his copper sulphate method for determining dehydration, for reasons unconnected with cholera, happen to be equipped with a technique that could immediately and effectively be applied to the cholera problem. Indeed, when in collaboration with Piyaratn and Benyayati of the Chulalongkorn Hospital Medical College, and Sprinz back at WRAIR, they were able to show that the integrity of the intestinal epithelium was unassailed, and there was thus no desquamation [151]. Gangarosa went on to Calcutta and made similar findings, confirming his Bangkok observations.

The NIH

Smadel had always been much interested in cholera, but when the invitation to send investigators to Bangkok came to him at the National Institutes of Health, and he tried to interest those Institutes that were concerned with infectious diseases, he met with little enthusiasm for cholera, owing to the shift of interest to domestic diseases already mentioned. Curiously enough, the only Institute that responded was the National Heart Institute, whose director, James Watt, had previously done research on diarrhoeal diseases among the Indians in the Southwest of the United States. He persuaded one of his staff, Robert Gordon, to take an interest, and Gordon proceeded to Bangkok to join Phillips's team. For the third time, the cholera problem was to find a man fortuitously pre-equipped at the right time with the right technique to investigate it. Gordon had recently been studying the permeability of the intestinal tract to proteins in a variety of diseases. His technique had been to give intravenous injections of radioactive polyvinylpyrrolidone, a molecule about as large as a protein. If this material appeared in the intestinal tract, it would mean that the wall of the tract was desquamated and therefore permeable to proteins. O'Shaughnessy had found 128 years previously that there was no appreciable protein in cholera stools, and the NAMRU-3 team also had not found significant amounts of protein in the stools of their cholera patients in Egypt, but others thought there was protein (e.g., De; p. 61). Gordon tried his techniques on cholera patients in Bangkok. He showed that intravenous polyvinylpyrrolidone did in fact not appear in the intestinal tract of normal subjects or cholera patients. This confirmed that the intestinal wall was intact in cholera and was not desquamated [168]. This study went very nicely hand in hand with Gangarosa's studies with the Crosby capsule that led to the same conclusions. Thus, there was no histological damage to the intestinal wall in cholera—the lesion was biochemical and invisible. The nature of this invisible biochemical lesion was to be revealed during the next decade.

Orth, the leader of the Army mission, made a survey of the distribution of the cholera vibrio in Bangkok and its suburb, Dhonburi [315].

The Academics

The Jefferson Medical College bacteriologists Sweeney, Harry Smith and Rolf Freter, joined Felsenfeld and his wife at the Chulalongkorn Hospital. Goodner himself did not go to Bangkok on this occasion. They carried out studies on the immunological aspects of cholera, taking cultures of the vibrio from stool samples from cholera patients, and also serum samples, and studying their immunological properties, in collaboration with a distinguished Pakistani bacteriologist, Dr. K. A. Monsur, of the Public Health Laboratory in Dacca, who, as we shall see, later was to join the Pakistan-SEATO Cholera Research Laboratory. This work provided a test that was needed for epidemiological and immunological investigations of cholera vaccines [163].

IV

The SEATO Cholera
Research Program and the
Pakistan-SEATO Cholera
Research Laboratory in Dacca

1. The Program

While Phillips was in Bangkok in June 1958, he met his good friend from Taipei, John Conroy, who had previously been in the American Embassy in Taipei and was the officer who had helped him to negotiate the agreement with the Chinese government to establish NAMRU-2 in Taipei. Conroy was now the U.S. State Department's SEATO officer in the American Embassy in Bangkok. SEATO was one of Secretary of State Dulles's regional treaties. It was basically a military alliance of three Asian countries—the Philippines, Thailand and Pakistan—with the United States, the United Kingdom, France, Australia and New Zealand, set up in 1956 on the basis of a collective security pact signed in Manila in September 1954. In 1958, the base of SEATO was broadened so that it was not just a military alliance but involved economic and social factors as well. The treaty now contained an additional article— Article 3—that was quite new to collective defence treaties. This article pledged the participating countries "to assist each other and, by self-help and mutual co-operative effort, to lift the standard of their own people and to bring economic and social progress to their countries" [391]. That encounter between Phillips and Conroy led to a meeting that was going to have a considerable effect on research on the cholera problem. The object of their discussion was an idea of Phillips's to set up a medical research laboratory in Bangkok, modelled on the NAMRU experience, as an appropriate non-military function of SEATO. Conroy was very receptive to this idea and asked Phillips, when he was back in Taipei, to send him a proposal in writing. In September 1958, Phillips submitted a proposal to Conroy for the creation in Bangkok of a SEATO medical research laboratory costing $400,000, of which half was to be spent on a building and half on equipment. The proposal reached Clifford Pease, a member of the U.S. State Department's International Cooperation Administration (ICA), who had just been put in charge of the Far East/Near East area of its Office of Health. He was about to travel to the Far East, and so was able to discuss the proposal with Conroy in Bangkok, and later with Phillips, who happened at the time to be in Manila. By the time he returned to Washington in December 1958, the SEATO desk in the ICA had earmarked $400,000 to meet the request. In their discussions, Phillips and Pease had agreed and recommended that in establishing a medical research laboratory it was essential to make a long-term commitment, and to find operating funds in addition to the $400,000 for buildings and equipment. The ICA at that time was not willing to commit itself in this way, and no more was set aside for a possible SEATO laboratory than the $400,000 already earmarked. Thus, at this stage, there was no clear idea what to do with the money, but at least the camel had got its nose under the edge of the tent.

As it happened, Pease had become concerned with the question of cholera for a quite unconnected reason. ICA had become interested in the arousal of interest in cholera in Bangkok in 1958 by the Inner Circle, and Pease was asked to organize a meeting at the ICA office in Washington of those concerned to discuss plans for further study of the cholera problem in the summer of 1959. The meeting was held in late December 1958, and was attended by Smadel, Edsall, Goodner, Woodward, MacLeod and a number of others. There was an excellent discussion, but it was no more than an informational discussion; no action was called for, and none was proposed. A few days later, however, Pease conceived the idea of interesting the Inner Circle in the Phillips-Conroy suggestion of a SEATO medical research laboratory in SEATO territory. He suggested to Smadel and Edsall that since it did not seem possible to obtain a long-term commitment for a SEATO medical research laboratory it might be possible to use the SEATO-earmarked money for a SEATO cholera research programme. The idea was well received, and Smadel convened, and presided at, a meeting at the National Institutes of Health of an "Ad Hoc Committee for Research on Cholera" on 30 January 1959. Those present were: J. E. Smadel (Associate Director of NIH); Margaret Pittman (Bureau of Biologics, NIH); R. J. Colton (NIH); J. H. Hundley (Special Assistant on International Affairs, NIH); G. Edsall (WRAIR); A. Langmuir (CDC); H. DeLien (Division of International Health (ICA); J. R. Kingston (U.S. Navy); A. Wilson (Du Pont Institutes); W. Burrows (University of Chicago); and K. Goodner (Jefferson Medical College).

Those attending the meeting had been given a background report on a "Preliminary plan for cholera research work to be undertaken by, or under the auspices of, the World Health Organization".[1] This report envisaged three main series of studies in India (not a member of SEATO) under the auspices of the World Health Organization, namely (1) field studies combined with laboratory work on cholera epidemiology, (2) studies on environmental sanitation, and (3) adequately large field trials of cholera vaccines in order to correlate data on the efficacy of vaccines with laboratory assays. Anyone reading the minutes of that meeting would not realize that the fund of $400,000 under discussion had been earmarked for SEATO purposes. It was noted that the U.S. efforts in connection with the smallpox epidemic the previous year had engendered much good will and that an intensive research programme in cholera might create further goodwill, as well as lead to badly needed and potentially useful research efforts. Smadel referred to $400,000 that might be made available by ICA for a programme of research on cholera which would have to be carried out under contracts between NIH and universities.[2] It was agreed that studies on cholera should fall into two categories: (1) those best done in base laboratories with modern facilities, which would largely be concerned with studies on the microbiology of cholera and on vaccines; and (2) those requiring access to patients with cholera, which would largely be concerned with field trials of vaccine and various studies on patients. It was agreed that the best location for vaccine field trials was Calcutta, in collaboration with WHO. Smadel hoped that light would be shed on the means by which cholera spread, on the factors which made individuals resistant or susceptible to the disease, on "the cause of the primary lesion in the intestine which results in the passage into the lumen of the gut of torrents of fluid", and on which vibrio antigens would provide the best immunity against the disease. He touched on the fact that cholera tended to happen in areas distant from highly developed medical research communities, where it was difficult to study or treat the disease, and hoped the collaborative studies in the field and the laboratory would overcome the difficulty. The group's estimate for the cost of carrying out its suggestions for vaccine and antibiotic trials in India and perhaps else-where, for clinical studies and for laboratory studies on vaccines and

1. It is not clear who had prepared the report, nor for whom it was intended. A photocopy appears to have "From Pollitzer thru Burrows" handwritten on it.
2. The research would not be done in government laboratories because the funds would have to be "obligated" within six months of receipt by NIH, but contracts with universities could extend over a number of years.

bacteriology, would, over a period of three to five years, come to a total of about $369,000.

Pease had not been invited to this meeting, presumably because he was a government administrator and not, though medically qualified, a practising scientist. When he was informed over the telephone of the meeting's conclusions, he pointed out that the proposed activities were not the object for which ICA had allocated the $400,000. The allocation had been made under the SEATO umbrella with a political motivation, and therefore it was necessary that it should give rise to something that was not only visible, but visible in the SEATO area. So it was decided to call a second meeting. In the meantime, the U.S. Government had put its proposal to SEATO to initiate a special project on cholera, and the SEATO council, at its fifth meeting, in Wellington, New Zealand, on 8–10 April 1959 had approved the proposal, in which member governments of SEATO were invited to participate [3].

The second meeting of the Ad Hoc Committee on cholera was held in Atlantic City on 14 April 1959. Those attending (in addition to Burrows, Goodner, Kingston, Pittman, Smadel and Hundley, who had attended the first meeting) were Pease, Abram S. Benenson of WRAIR, G. Presson of the NIH's Office of International Research, and F. S. Cheever of the University of Pittsburgh in the chair. Sweeney, Smith and Freter of Goodner's group, who had just returned from cholera studies in Bangkok, also attended. Pease reported the recent approval of the proposed cholera project by the SEATO council: the $400,000 allocated for the purpose would be held in the Asian Economic Development Fund until project agreements had been signed (before 30 June 1959) with the three SEATO countries mainly concerned with cholera, namely, Thailand, Pakistan and the Philippines, committing these countries and the United States specifically to cholera projects. He thought the State Department definitely wanted some sort of laboratory established, preferably, but not necessarily, in Bangkok. India would not be able to co-operate officially in the project, but would not object to individual scientists participating in some fashion, and would probably co-operate with a WHO-sponsored project. The committee agreed to prepare a statement for ICA to use as a basis of discussion for the agreements with the cholera project countries, and to send a U.S. team, including Mason, Goodner and Smadel, to the Philippines, Thailand, Pakistan, India and WHO in Geneva to discuss further developments of the cholera project. They also agreed that a vaccine trial in India (as had been proposed by Pittman) was essential, but that it was to be approached outside the present SEATO programme.

A month after the meeting in Atlantic City, NIH and ICA jointly, with the advice of the Ad Hoc Committee on cholera, drew up a

"Proposal for Cholera Research Program" for fundamental and applied investigations in the field and the laboratory with the object of increasing knowledge of cholera and approaching more effective public health control of the disease. It was proposed that a research laboratory should be established in conjunction with an established institution in Southeast Asia, probably at Bangkok, and that the laboratory should be closely linked with three academic research laboratories in the United States, namely, the University of Chicago (for studies on immune response to cholera vaccine and to the disease); Jefferson Medical College, Philadelphia (for fundamental investigations on the cholera organism); and the University of Pittsburgh (for studies on viral agents that might be associated with, or involved in, susceptibility or resistance of individuals to cholera).

The proposed cholera research laboratory in Southeast Asia would have as its programme three main activities: (1) research on the epidemiology and bacteriology of cholera and other diarrhoeal diseases; (2) the training of selected nationals from SEATO countries both in the cholera research laboratory and in cooperating research laboratories in the United States, and (3) to serve as a base for field studies. The hard core of the staff of the cholera research laboratory would consist of an experienced microbiologist and an epidemiologist, one being the director and the other the assistant director, selected by NIH. The remainder of the staff would be nationals of the host country or other SEATO countries. The laboratory would be guided, and its progress evaluated, by a committee consisting of one member to be nominated by each of the co-operating SEATO countries; one member of each of the co-operating U.S. laboratories; and one member designated by NIH, who would be chairman and the director of the laboratory *ex officio*. Observers from India and WHO would be invited to attend the meetings of this Advisory Committee which would take place each year, usually at the site of the laboratory.

A team of six—four members of the Inner Circle, namely, Smadel (at the head), Goodner, MacLeod and Woodward, and two who were tangential, namely, Dingle and Mason—left for the Far East and South Asia on 1 August [308]. They did not waste any time. After visiting the SEATO countries of the Philippines, Thailand and Pakistan, as well as Japan, Taiwan and India, inspecting sites and discussing scientific, political and organizational possibilities, they had their draft prepared by 10 September 1959.

The visits to Japan, Taiwan and India were obviously not with the view to establishing a laboratory, since these countries did not belong to SEATO, but in order to discuss cholera. The group had had many contacts with Japan, including the Army's 406th Laboratory (from whence

Felsenfeld had gone to Thailand to study cholera), but it did not consider that country, even if it were a member of SEATO, to be a suitable country for a cholera research laboratory because there was hardly any cholera and it was too far away from the United States. The same considerations, more or less, applied to Taiwan, where, in any case, NAMRU-2 was stationed, with its already proven (and soon to be tested again) mobility that enabled it to appear swiftly on the scene of any cholera epidemic. India, particularly West Bengal, had much cholera, as well as outstanding workers in the field, particularly in Calcutta, and was willing to collaborate with any cholera laboratory established in a SEATO country. Cholera could not be eliminated from West Bengal unless it was eliminated also from its neighbouring country, East Pakistan, which belonged to SEATO. As to the three SEATO countries visited, they all had claims to consideration since they all had cholera to some degree and were all strategically situated with regard to those parts of the world where cholera was endemic, or likely to be epidemic. But in 1959, East Pakistan was the only part of SEATO that had endemic cholera.

At the time the team visited the Philippines, there had been no cholera since 1926. Suitable laboratory facilities could be made available for a SEATO laboratory, but it did not seem worthwhile since there was no cholera. There was diarrhoeal disease of other origins in the Philippines and a study of this might be a useful supplement to studies on cholera diarrhoea elsewhere. Had the team visited the Philippines two years later, it might conceivably have come to another conclusion because, as we have seen (p. 82) cholera broke out in the Philippines in 1961, to be adequately dealt with by Phillips's mobile expert team from NAMRU-2 in Taiwan.

Thailand, of course, had just recently been the centre of interest in cholera, and the present expedition was the outgrowth of the cholera epidemic in Bangkok in the previous year (continuing into the present year). Thai medical scientists were interested in the disease, and there were excellent laboratory space and facilities that could be made available at the Army Institute of Pathology, at the Chulalongkorn Hospital, and at the Pasteur Institute. The team considered that Bangkok would continue to be an important location for research on cholera for the next few years, and recommended that it be the site for "one of the SEATO cholera laboratories" until epidemic cholera disappeared from Thailand. As we shall see below, this recommendation was accepted in the limited form it was proposed.

In the end, the advisory team decided on East Pakistan (formerly East Bengal, now Bangladesh), which contains the Ganges, Brahmaputra and Meghna Rivers, whose delta region, like West Bengal in India, is a region of high cholera endemicity and epidemicity. The team found the East Pakistan Government, not surprisingly, greatly concerned about the cholera problem and keen to have research done on it. The medical profession of East Pakistan had had much experience of cholera and looked forward to research that might lead to the disease's control. They were on an excellent footing with local ICA staff and visiting public health workers. As it happened, they also had excellent space to offer for a research laboratory. The price of East Pakistan's main crop, jute, had been high some years earlier and the government had built a large Institute of Public Health in the Mohakhali district of Dacca. The price of jute then fell and they had a fine building on their hands with very little in it in the way of equipment. They therefore were able to offer one of the wings for a cholera research laboratory, which would provide ample space for a research laboratory as well as an infectious disease ward for scientific studies on cholera patients. Moreover, there was housing available for visiting scientists.

Conferences were held at Karachi with the Minister of Health (Lt. Gen. W. A. Burki), the Director General of Health Services (Brig. Gen. M. Sharif), and the Director of the ICA mission (Mr. J. S. Killen), and it was agreed that the Pakistan government would take the initiative in providing support in the form of personnel, space, etc., for cholera research in East Pakistan, and that the ICA mission, Pakistan, would consider equipping a laboratory in Dacca. In their report of 10 September 1959, the Advisory Team "recommended that a base in Bangkok be kept operative during the coming epidemic season for continuation of the clinical and physiological studies that have produced so much important information during the past two years". It further "recommended that a base be established during the coming year in Dacca for clinical, laboratory and field studies of cholera and other acute diarrhoeal diseases in the endemic area of East Pakistan". As cholera and resultant activities in Bangkok decreased, as past experience suggested it would, the Dacca laboratory should become the major base for future operations, and for the training and development of young scientists from SEATO countries. It was recommended that funds allocated by SEATO countries for investigations on cholera should be used for the stimulation and support of research and training that would not be financed by other means. Thus, investigations in the United States should be supported by NIH funds and other granting agencies, and funds for sending young scientists for training in the United States and elsewhere should be supplied by the country of origin. Finally, it was recommended that a scientific conference on cholera be held annually.

An appendix listed the cholera problems to be investigated: (1) Clinical and physiological studies on normal persons and on patients with cholera and other acute diarrhoeal diseases. (It is worth noting, in view of the present intense world-wide interest in all diarrhoeal diseases—see Chapter 9—that the Advisory Committee from the beginning stressed the need to study other diarrhoeal diseases besides cholera.) No mention was made of studies on cholera toxin, nor on the means by which cholera diarrhoea occurred. (2) Epidemiological studies: the duration of the epidemics of cholera and other diarrhoeal diseases in Thailand; the role of human carriers; the influence of supplying water from tube wells on the incidence of cholera in rural areas of East Pakistan. (3) Vaccination: whether the disease conferred immunity, and for how long; the efficacy of current cholera vaccines. (4) Susceptibility to cholera; the role of nutrition, and of the bacterial and protozoal flora of the gut. (5) Basic studies in the United States and elsewhere.[3] (6) Training and conferences: the need to train cholera investigators in the immediate future—workers from Southeast Asian countries needed more laboratory training, while those from other SEATO countries needed more clinical and epidemiological training. In particular, it was essential to send a young Pakistani bacteriologist to the United States as soon as possible for intensive study on the bacteriology and immunology of the cholera vibrio; for three or four young physicians to be apprenticed in the Dacca laboratory and then sent to the United States (and perhaps India) for further training; and to work out a continuing programme for training in the Dacca laboratory.

It will be recalled that the Ad Hoc Committee had agreed that the SEATO $400,000 should be handled through the NIH extramural mechanism, providing prompt disbursement of the funds to institutions wishing to use them for cholera research in their own laboratories, but these ideas were now seen by the Advisory Team to be impractical, and it was suggested that the bulk of the SEATO money should be used for the direct support of field operations. Funds for fundamental laboratory work in cholera in the United States and elsewhere should be obtained through regular NIH research grants, or from other granting agencies.

While the Cholera Advisory Team was on its travels in August 1959, the SEATO Cholera Research Program was formalized by an interagency agreement signed between the ICA and the U.S. Department of Health, Education, and Welfare, asking the NIH to assume responsibility for the development of the SEATO Cholera Research Program and allocating the $400,000 to enable the setting-up of a programme of training and fundamental and applied laboratory and field investigations of cholera

---

3. These do not appear to have been enumerated.

and the establishment of the cholera research laboratory in an Asian SEATO member country.

The visit to Pakistan by the Cholera Advisory Team in August 1959 and the appearance of this report in September were swiftly followed by a further visit to Pakistan in October by James H. Hundley, Special Assistant on International Affairs at NIH (who had acted as Secretary to the Ad Hoc Committee), with the intention of securing agreement with the governments of Pakistan and of East Pakistan and the ICA mission in Pakistan in as many areas as possible in order that planning for the SEATO cholera research laboratory could begin. It was agreed (1) that the laboratory would be established in the building of the Institute of Public Health in Dacca, and equipped and staffed so that research could begin in October 1960; (2) that the laboratory would be equipped, operated and financially supported by the NIH (with the SEATO funds), the ICA and the governments of Pakistan and East Pakistan; (3) that the scientific direction of the research programme would be in the hands of NIH, advised by a Committee of Cholera Research to be established by the Director of NIH, and exercised through the Director of the laboratory, and that the laboratory would be operated as a project under an agreement with the ICA mission in East Pakistan until July 1963, when it and its operation would be turned over to the governments of Pakistan and East Pakistan.[4]

The governments of Pakistan and East Pakistan would provide: (1) the space for the laboratory; (2) local labour and materials for the necessary modifications to the building; (3) local recurring operating costs; (4) a trained bacteriologist, 3 young scientists, 4 technicians, 11 non-technical staff; (5) a 20-bed cholera and dysentery ward; (6) accommodations for staff working overnight; (7) space for an animal house; (8) an undertaking to assume total responsibility for the laboratory when SEATO funds would be exhausted and NIH participation withdrawn in July 1963; (9) co-ordination of its medical care and public health activities in cholera with the programme and plans of the laboratory.

The NIH would undertake: (1) to establish a Committee on Cholera Research to advise the Director of NIH on the operation of the SEATO Cholera Research Program; (2) to disburse the SEATO fund of $400,000; (3) to find for the Dacca laboratory a senior research microbiologist and an epidemiologist, one to be the Scientific Director of the laboratory; (4) to organize an annual conference on cholera; (5) to assist the four

---

4. In fact, the agreements were extended and fundamentally remained unchanged until 1971–1972, after the war by which East Pakistan became the People's Republic of Bangladesh (see Chapter 11).

U.S. laboratories expecting to co-operate in the programme to find funds outside the SEATO fund; (6) to design the laboratory in Dacca and purchase the necessary imported equipment and supplies with SEATO funds.

The ICA would be responsible for: (1) the provision and servicing of two motor vehicles; (2) finding funds in 1961 to complete the scientific equipment and supplies of the laboratory; (3) establishing the laboratory as a project under the administrative direction of the ICA mission, East Pakistan; (4) co-ordinating its public health activities in cholera with the programme and objectives of the laboratory; (5) providing funds for a six-month fellowship to enable the Pakistani scientist appointed research bacteriologist of the Dacca laboratory to study in the United States.

In December 1959, a formal agreement was made between the governments of the United States and Thailand to establish the Thailand-SEATO Cholera Research Laboratory, as recommended by the Cholera Research Advisory Team (p. 100). It was situated in the Royal Thai Army Institute of Pathology in Bangkok with financial support from the Thai government and the United States government through the SEATO Cholera Research Program, WRAIR and the ICA programme in Thailand. The Director-General was the Undersecretary of State for Public Health of Thailand (our friend Pyn) and the Executive Director was Oscar Felsenfeld, assigned by WRAIR but now temporarily responsible to the Director of the NIH. The U.S. workers involved in the programme of the laboratory were those who had already been concerned with the cholera outbreak in Bangkok—members of NAMRU-2, WRAIR and Jefferson Medical College, continuing with the research they had already started. The laboratory existed for a year and in January 1961 was succeeded by the Thailand-SEATO Medical Research Laboratory, a broad-based medical research laboratory interested mainly in problems other than cholera, and operated co-operatively by the government of Thailand and WRAIR. The U.S. component was established as the U.S. Army-SEATO Medical Research Laboratory, Bangkok, with Felsenfeld reassigned to WRAIR.

In October 1960, a formal agreement was signed by the U.S. government and the government of Pakistan creating the Pakistan-SEATO Cholera Research Laboratory in Dacca. The laboratory was to be financed by funds from the governments of Pakistan and the United States, but governments of other SEATO nations who wished to take part were invited to do so. The U.S. government was the main source of funds, which were to come from four main sources: (1) funds made available to NIH by ICA for the laboratory; (2) Pakistan rupees made available from United States–owned Public Law 480 funds under the terms of an NIH research agreement with the laboratory; (3) direct contributions and administrative support from the ICA program in Pakistan; (4) direct contributions from NIH, particularly in payment of salaries of U.S. staff from the National Heart Institute and the Office of International Research. The government of Pakistan made available the physical facilities at the Institute of Public Health, including utilities, the loan of certain personnel, and an annual contribution to the laboratory's operating fund. There were to be lesser contributions from other SEATO countries— thus, the United Kingdom was to make an annual contribution of £10,000 and Australia was to contribute two motor vehicles and the services of an anthropologist to work with the epidemiology section.

The NIH undertook the responsibility for immediate scientific direction of the laboratory under the overall guidance of the Directing Council, and for the appointment of the Director of the Laboratory. The Directing Council was to consist of (1) a representative from each of the nations taking part in the laboratory programme, (2) the Secretary-General of SEATO, and (3) the Director of NIH. In addition to the Directing Council, there was to be a Technical Committee appointed by the Director of NIH to advise the Director of the Laboratory and the Directing Council on technical aspects of the laboratory programme. This Technical Committee was to consist of three research scientists from the United States, the United Kingdom and Pakistan, who would receive advice from a panel of experts made up of scientific workers from different SEATO countries interested in various aspects of the cholera programme.

The Director of NIH was advised by a Cholera Advisory Committee which he had already established on 23 December 1959 to inform him on phases of the operation of the SEATO Cholera Research Program and assist him in its technical direction. This was in effect a formalization of the Ad Hoc Committee on Cholera. Its first members consisted of the advisory team (less Dingle), supplemented by William Burrows of the University of Chicago, F. S. Cheever of the University of Pittsburgh, Capt. James Kingston, U.S.N., and Clifford Pease of ICA. Smadel was the first chairman.

There was no mention of any particular connection of the laboratory with any academic institution in the United States, as had been proposed in the original memorandum that was to serve as a basis of discussion for the advisory team in its dealings with countries that were likely candidates for the laboratory. In fact, the idea was dropped when the Dacca laboratory became the predominant objective.

The laboratory in Dacca was to be organized in sections for clinical research (including a cholera ward), bacteriology, water study, epidemiology, administration and general services, to be housed in an entire wing of the Institute of Public Health, consisting of three floors. The first floor was to be a 20-bed cholera ward with the usual ancillary facilities; the second and third floors were to be devoted to office space, a library and laboratories for clinical, physiological and bacteriological studies. The epidemiology section and the animal facilities were to be separately housed.

The senior members of the staff of the Pakistan-SEATO Cholera Research Laboratory were appointed. The first Director, the late Fred L. Soper, recently retired from the directorship of the Pan American Sanitary Bureau, assumed his duties in February 1961. The Deputy Director and head of the epidemiology section, Joe L. Stockard of the U.S. Public Health Service, was the first on the spot, having reported for duty in Dacca in early September 1960. The head of the bacteriology section, Kazi Abdul Monsur, of the Public Health Laboratory in Dacca, returned to Dacca in December 1960 after having made special studies of the cholera vibrio in Goodner's department at Jefferson Medical College and at NIH.

The Pakistan-SEATO Cholera Research Laboratory became operational shortly after it was inaugurated at a SEATO Conference on Cholera in Dacca on 5 to 8 December 1960 [391]. This conference was attended by 55 participants, many of them distinguished, from 5 countries in the East and 4 in the West. Cholera had again, after 60 years, become a matter of concern to the West as well as the East, partly out of Western concern for the East, partly because improved communications were threatening its spread.[5]

In Chapter 3, we mentioned the geopolitical considerations which are likely to have made the U.S. Department of State favour assistance to Thailand in 1958, but the choice of East Pakistan as the site of a SEATO Cholera Research Laboratory seems so obvious that it is reasonable to ask why the advisory team even considered any other locations. Cholera is endemic in East Pakistan, and occurs only in epidemics roughly every 10 years in Thailand; the big outbreak of cholera in Dacca in 1958 occurred a few months before the epidemic in Bangkok, and attracted the attention of Phillips, and of ICA, before the Bangkok epidemic. Yet it was the Bangkok epidemic that aroused the interest of the Inner Circle and it was Bangkok that the advisory team looked to before Dacca. Why? Was it that cholera in Dacca was not news, but was news in Bangkok, and therefore more compelling? Or was it simply a matter of Pyn's being a friend of Goodner's and the advisory team's

5. The 1867 Kumbh Fair epidemic took two years to reach Europe; the 1892 epidemic took five months with improved sea and land communications to make the same journey. What was going to be the effect of air travel? The answer was to come the very next year, when the seventh cholera pandemic broke out.

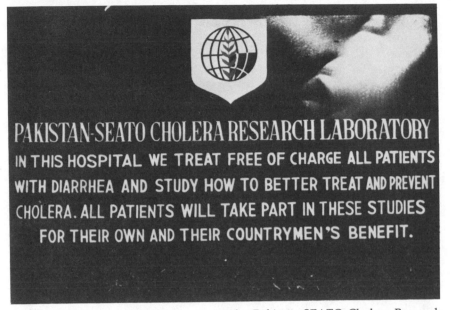

FIGURE 4.1. The sign at the entrance to the Pakistan-SEATO Cholera Research Laboratory emplaced at Inaugural Conference, 1960.

having had a warm and lively welcome from the enthusiastic young King Rama, who gave them a two-hour audience when only half an hour had been intended? Or was it that Bangkok was more "glamorous" than Dacca, which at that time was considered so isolated and unattractive that the Americans who were there were the only ones who would find Calcutta by comparison attractive enough to go there for their rest and recreation leave?

2. Early Years at the Pakistan-SEATO Cholera Research Laboratory

Although the Cholera Advisory Team had acted swiftly in 1959, and it had been agreed that the Pakistan-SEATO Cholera Research Laboratory (PSCRL) to be established in the building of the Institute of Public Health in Dacca would be equipped and staffed in time for research to begin in October 1960, and although the first member of the staff reported for duty in September of that year, and the laboratory was officially opened in December, not much progress was made in the first two years. It would have been surprising if there had not been an initial lag period.

The first member of the staff of the PSCRL to report for duty was Joe L. Stockard, Deputy Director and epidemiologist, and acting Director until the arrival of the first Director, Fred L. Soper. Stockard arrived in Dacca on 2 September 1960, and was joined in December by the head of the bacteriology section, K. A. Monsur, who had spent some time making special studies of the cholera vibrio in Goodner's department at Jefferson Medical College and at NIH. Work on the new laboratory was in progress when Stockard arrived, but activity was erratic because the plans for the three floors of the laboratory had been drawn up by American architects working in offices in NIH. They were used to U.S. materials and workmanship, and drew up blueprints suitable for American contractors, but the contractors in Dacca were not used to working according to American blueprints and went about their work in their own way. Terrazzo floors were still being installed in the upper two storeys of the three-storey wing of the Institute of Public Health that had been assigned to the PSCRL; attempts were being made to install the plumbing; the electricity supply had not yet been installed; the first shipment of equipment had arrived and was being stored; laboratory benches were being made by local carpenters out of local material; and difficulties were experienced in recruiting suitably qualified staff willing to work for salaries that were less than half those they could earn in commercial organizations. In addition to having to cope with all these problems (and settle down in an alien land), Stockard had to make all the arrangements for the Inaugural Conference that was to be held within three months, and this entailed all kinds of unforeseeable difficulties. Thus it was that when Stockard went to Karachi to meet Soper in March 1961, he had a rather discouraging report to give him.

Stockard and Soper were followed in October 1961 by Robert S. Gordon, Jr., of the National Heart Institute at Bethesda. Gordon, as we have seen, had already had some experience of cholera research in Bangkok in 1959. While the laboratory was still being planned, the United Kingdom offered to make a contribution of £10,000 to it, and this, according to Gordon, encouraged Smadel to broaden the laboratory's interests. It had been intended that these should be focused on bacteriological and epidemiological research, but now the clinical chemistry of cholera could also be embraced, and Gordon was asked if he would take charge of such an endeavour. A cholera ward was to be installed on the ground floor of the PSCRL and operated by the government of Pakistan, and laboratory research on samples from the ward patients was to be carried out on the upper two floors. Gordon did not think such a plan would be workable, because he did not believe that he, or any other Western clinical investigator, could undertake the responsibility of handling samples from patients being treated by another group of physicians. A clinical research team should be formed that would have responsibility for the care and experimental treatment of patients as well as laboratory research. This would entail having more than one physician. Smadel agreed to this and so a clinical research unit was set up, and another physician, O. Ross McIntyre, was engaged.[6]

In January 1962, a committee consisting of four of the original exploratory team—Smadel, Goodner, Woodward and MacLeod—afforced by Shannon from NIH and Phillips from NAMRU-2, paid a visit to the laboratory to report on its first year. Progress had been solid, but some senior staff were about to be lost, notably the Director, Soper, and Monsur, who had been appointed Director of the Institute of Public Health, but was being retained as a consultant to the PSCRL. It was important that they should be replaced as soon as possible. The committee expressed the opinion "that the problem of cholera is of such broad significance to world health that any activity short of one which brings the techniques of science to bear directly and importantly on the many problems of the disease is short-sighted and inadequate". The PSCRL had "already established itself as a key factor in the apparatus that will be required to eradicate the disease", and it was important that the laboratory should be given enough financial support to enable it to acquire a high level of staff and appropriate physical facilities. The laboratory staff members recommended to "continue their planning with less regard to the funds which have been available up to the present than to the importance of the task they address themselves to".

The visiting committee members were concerned about the lack of progress with the cholera ward. They considered that the ward was needed for a number of reasons, and recommended that it should be opened early in the spring of 1962, "even though expedients must be devised for food and laundry services".

The opening of the ward did not, in fact, take place in the spring of 1962, but in November of that year. When Gordon had visited the laboratory on the occasion of the Inaugural Conference in December 1960, he had found that the cholera research ward that had been built on the ground floor by local workmen according to plans drawn up by architects in NIH "looked lovely", but was quite unworkable, partly for the lack of laundry and food services mentioned by the visiting

---

6. At the same time, other physicians were engaged for the future: W. B. Greenough for 1962–64, and J. Lindenbaum and M. L. Reiner for 1963–66. Gordon was to return to the NIH in 1964. His intention was that there should be a number of physicians serving for two-year periods in the Public Health Service, overlapping by one year, so that there always would be two in residence, one in his second year, the other in his first; this pattern continued throughout the sixties.

committee. The architects had not been told that the cholera ward was not part of an existing hospital with all the usual amenities, such as laundry and food services, and consequently these were absent. Nor had they been told what kind of a disease cholera was: There was a waiting room for cholera patients where they were supposed to sit on chairs, presumably actively purging, while waiting to be seen.

The first thing Gordon and McIntyre did when they came to Dacca in October 1961 was entirely to replan the cholera ward. They got their own first contacts with cholera, and the beginning of their own feel of the disease, by going to the Mitford Hospital in Dacca, and to the hospitals in Narayanganj and Khulna. By good fortune, they found a Danish architect in Dacca, Jean Deleuran, who was interested in hospital architecture, having spent many years in hospitals himself as a poliomyelitis patient. He agreed to redesign the cholera ward. He went with Gordon to look at cholera patients in the Mitford Hospital, learned about the disease and the way it was treated, then devised relatively easy means by which the cholera ward could be redesigned at modest expense. An outbuilding was attached to serve as a sanitation centre for such procedures as cleaning bedding and bedpans, and weighing and disposing of cholera stools. Thus, by November 1962, the ground floor of the PSCRL was made into a small but completely self-contained hospital of 20 beds.

In 1962, Soper returned to the United States, having done what he came to do, which was to lay down a firm basis for an administrative agreement for the PSCRL. He modelled this agreement on the proposal he had devised when he founded the Institute for Nutrition for Central America and Panama, which ensured an autonomous organization with its own Directing Council and Technical Committee. He was succeeded as Director of the PSCRL by Abram S. Benenson, who came from the Walter Reed Army Institute of Research, where he had succeeded Smadel as Director of the Division of Communicable Disease. In the summer of 1962, Gordon was joined by another physician, W. B. Greenough, III, a graduate of Harvard University who had just completed his medical residency training at the College of Physicians and Surgeons in New York. It was as well that he came, because Gordon's other colleague, McIntyre, had to go home within a month or two, due ironically enough to the first case of so-called "non-cholera" diarrhoea (see Chapter 9) to be seen at the PSCRL.

Perhaps the main reason for having a cholera ward at the PSCRL was that it was necessary for an important mission the laboratory had to fulfil under its charter, namely, the conduct of carefully controlled field trials of the efficacy of cholera vaccines. In such trials, it would be necessary to compare the cholera attack rates of people treated in

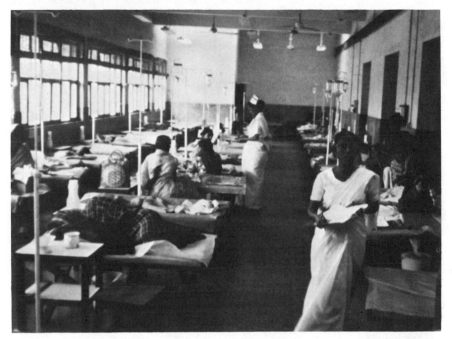

FIGURE 4.2. Ward at Pakistan-SEATO Cholera Research Laboratory. (Courtesy of Dr. Carl Miller.)

advance with cholera vaccine and with placebos. It followed, therefore, that even if the cholera vaccine were completely effective, half the people in the trial would be at risk of cholera and some of them would contract it; then it would be necessary to treat them in a cholera ward.

In addition to the laboratories and the cholera ward in Dacca, it was necessary to set up a field surveillance facility for the vaccine trials and for epidemiological studies. In 1964, Benenson, Robert O. Oseasohn (who succeeded Stockard as epidemiologist in 1963) and M. Fahimuddin (a local consultant, later a full-time member of the staff) visited the countryside, mainly in motor launches, since it is a wet countryside, to find a suitable area for proposed field trials. Several local village headmen wanted their villages to be selected for the economic advantage to be gained; others were afraid and wanted nothing to do with the project.

Finally, due largely to Fahimuddin, a group of 23 villages in Matlab thana, a subdivision of Comilla District about 40 miles southeast of Dacca, was chosen because of continued high prevalence of cholera in the recent past, and because the Gumti River, a tributary of the Meghna

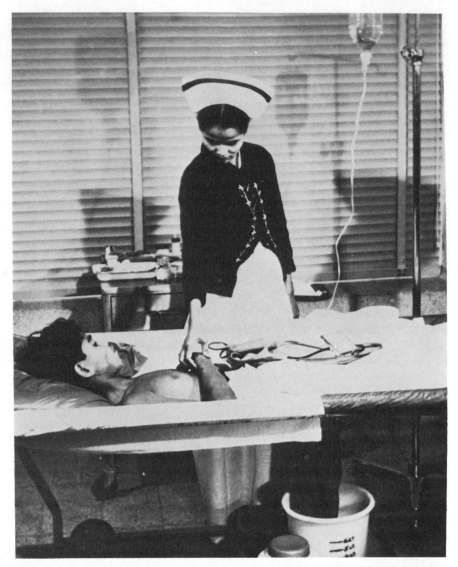

FIGURE 4.3. Cholera patient under treatment at Pakistan-SEATO Cholera Research Laboratory. Note tube delivering stools from the "Watten Cot" to graduated bucket below.

River, allowed easy access by houseboat for case-finding and treatment. The census of 1961 had shown that Matlab thana was one of the most densely populated areas of East Pakistan, the population of the 23 villages being 24,000 (more than 1,500 people per square mile). The census lists were revised by a house-to-house survey, and each inhabitant

FIGURE 4.4. At Pakistan-SEATO Cholera Research Laboratory, Dacca, 1962, left to right, Robert Gordon, Joseph Smadel, Abram Benenson.

was allotted a number, prefaced by a letter identifying his village [316]. Forward medical care was provided at Matlab Bazaar, a centrally located market community on the banks of a creek flowing into the Meghna River opposite the point where it joins the Padma River. Dacca is reached by motor speed boat in 2 to 3 hours (or by country boat with large loads in about 3 days) via the Meghna and its tributary, the Lakhya, to the river port of Narayanganj, and thence 20 miles by road.

Benenson had another reason for the clinical care facility at Matlab Bazaar—it was to be a model for any Bengali physician to copy with the very simple means at his disposal. It started in a small tin hut with a physician and a nurse in constant attendance, and later a barge was provided by the government of East Pakistan, and a tent by the U.S. Navy. Later facilities were moved to a more substantial building, under Mizamur Rahman's direction.

When Gordon and Greenough first started work in the cholera ward, they were the only physicians on the staff, with two new Bengali senior nurses, Mrs. Hadhi Ghose and Mrs. Anisa Saad, who proved to be not only highly competent themselves but capable of effective supervision of local aides and attendants. They were responsible for all the patients until the summer of 1963, when Sister Dorothy Torrance arrived from Great Britain and took charge of the ward. The first laboratory technician,

Mr. Mafiz, was acquired from the Pakistani army. He set up and supervised a clinical laboratory that carried out reliable blood and urine tests, thus relieving the research laboratories of responsibility for tests for patient care. Bazhur Rahman, the pharmacist, also came from the Pakistani army. He was later, during a cholera emergency in January 1964 (see p. 139), to prevent a disaster by running a "factory" for making intravenous replacement fluid. Mr. Razzack was the motor mechanic who took over the maintenance of the laboratory vehicle fleet from the AID garage. Not only could he deal with every kind and nationality of automobile or truck, but, more importantly, he maintained the outboard motors of the fleet of 37 motor boats that patrolled the field surveillance area of the laboratory. The sight and sound of those motor boats during the cholera seasons probably raised more goodwill for the United States than many far more expensive and less effective operations. Gordon and Greenough were joined in January 1963 by three more physicians assigned by the Pakistani government, Mujibur Rahaman (now Deputy Director of the laboratory; see Chapter 9), Rafiqul Islam and Majid Molla, and by March the medical team was integrated and working well, with the Bengali physicians being responsible for primary care and the American physicians acting as consultants and beginning to take up research. Later, they were joined by a fourth Bengali physician, A. K. Jamiul Alam, who walked into the ward one day and asked to be engaged, and since he was well qualified and very much interested in cholera he, too, was engaged. He was to remain in the laboratory until his death in 1978, and during the Civil War in 1971 he and Mujibur Rahaman played a most important part in preserving the laboratory under very difficult circumstances. Among the other Bengali scientists there were the epidemiologist Moslemuddin Khan, the bacteriologists S.S.H. Rizvi (who took over from Monsur) and Imdadul Haq, K.M.S. Aziz (now Scientific Director of the Laboratory; see Chapter 11), a marine biologist by training, who was involved in a number of important laboratory investigations, particularly those concerned with cholera toxin. His brother, K.M.A. Aziz, an anthropologist, played, and still plays, an important part in that capacity in the care and operation of surveillance of the area of the laboratory [6]. Another physician who served the laboratory, not as a staff member but as a member of the first Directing Council, was the distinguished and much loved A.K.M. Abdul Wahed of the Department of Health, Social Welfare and Local Government in Dacca. He was well versed in experience and knowledge of cholera and used to go about the country visiting patients on his bicycle, with bottles of infusion fluid hanging from the handlebars.

The foreign, very largely American, scientific staff employed at the PSCRL during its first ten years is listed in Table 4.1. By agreement between Shannon and Langmuir, the control of epidemiological aspects

Table 4.1
Expatriate scientific staff employed at the Pakistan-SEATO Cholera
Research Laboratory, 1960-1970.

Role	Name	Country	Years
Directors:	Dr. Fred L. Soper	U.S.	1961-1962
	Dr. Abram S. Benenson	U.S.	1962-1965
	Dr. Robert A. Phillips	U.S.	1965-1970
Epidemiologists:	Dr. Joe L. Stockard	U.S.	1960-1963
	Dr. Robert O. Oseasohn	U.S.	1963-1965
	Dr. Robert M. Glasse	Australia	1963-1965
	Mrs.Robert M. Glasse	Australia	1963-1966
	Dr. Wiley H. Mosley	U.S.	1963-*
	Dr. William M. McCormack	U.S.	1965-1968
	Dr. Albert R. Martin	U.S.	1966-1968
	Dr. Kenneth J. Bart	U.S.	1968-1970
	Dr. William E. Woodward	U.S.	1968-1970
	Dr. George Curlin	U.S.	1969-*
	Dr. Alfred Sommer	U.S.	1970-*
Clinical Research:	Dr. Robert S. Gordon	U.S.	1961-1964
	Dr. O. Ross McIntyre	U.S.	1961-1962
	Dr. William B. Greenough	U.S.	1962-1965
	Dr. John Lindenbaum	U.S.	1963-1966
	Dr. M. L. Reiner	U.S.	1963-1965
	Dr. Norbert Hirschhorn	U.S.	1964-1967
	Dr. James O. Taylor	U.S.	1965-1968
	Dr. David B. Sachar	U.S.	1965-1967
	Dr. Joseph L. Kinzie	U.S.	1966-1968
	Dr. W. Kendrick Hare	U.S.	1966-*
	Dr. Ruth Hare	U.S.	1966-*
	Dr. Robert S. Northrup	U.S.	1966-1969
	Dr. Richard A. Cash	U.S.	1967-*
	Dr. David R. Nalin	U.S.	1967-*

* Remained beyond 1970.

of the work of the PSCRL and the appointment of epidemiologists after Oseasohn were placed in 1964 in the hands of another branch of the Public Health Service, namely, the Communicable Disease Center (CDC) in Atlanta, where Alexander Langmuir, a consultant to the Technical Committee of the PSCRL, and a member of the Cholera Advisory Committee, was chief of the Bureau of Epidemiology. Their first appointments, in 1965, were W. H. Mosley as head of epidemiology, assisted by W. McCormack.[7] Mosley was assigned to Dacca until 1971,

7. Langmuir states that when he discussed this matter on a visit to Taipei with the Director-Elect of the PSCRL, R. A. Phillips, he was informed in Phillips' navy way that "no military operation will go without at least three men, one on duty, one off duty and one in reserve" (service in the PHS counts as military duty). However, financial, administrative and housing problems prevented the appointment of a third epidemiologist.

FIGURE 4.5. Attendees at Technical Committee meeting, Pakistan-SEATO Cholera Research Laboratory, January 1966. Front row, left to right, Robert Gordon, Gustave Dammin, William Verwey, Doris Parkinson, Margaret Pittman, General M. S. Hague, William Burrows, Luang Binbakaya Bidyabhed and Charles Williams. Standing, left to right, Abram Benenson, A.K.M. Abdul Wahed, Kenneth Goodner, Robert Black, Alexander Langmuir, John Seal and Robert Phillips.

but McCormack and his successors had two-year assignments. In addition to these two-year assignments by the CDC, there were many short-term assignments of young men from the Epidemiology Intelligence Service to enable them to gain experience in the field. In 1966, a chemistry section was established by Kendrick Hare and Ruth Hare. This enumeration of staff members of the PSCRL is not complete, and it takes no account of the very many visitors who came from all parts of the world to work for short periods of time.

When Gordon and Greenough first started work in the new cholera ward in November 1962, they were the only expatriate physicians on the staff. They had a totally new organization with a new set of nurses whom they had to train to record output and input of fluids, a technician to run the clinical laboratory, some attendants and orderlies, and a medical chart and record-keeping system of their own, but no practical experience in the management of cholera patients. It seemed wisest to begin with patients who were not critically ill, so they started their

FIGURE 4.6. Members of the Directing Council, Pakistan-SEATO Cholera Research Laboratory (PSCRL), 1969. Seated, left to right, Willard Boynton (representing U.S.), S. A. Mallick (Pakistan), David Wraight (SEATO), and John Seal (NIH). Standing, left to right, Robert Phillips (PSCRL), Robert Cruikshank (U.K.), Patrick Talmon (PSCRL), Kendrick Hare (PSCRL), Walter Magruder (NIAID), and Jean Rogier (AID).

new ward as a convalescent ward for patients transferred from the Mitford Hospital who were recovering and seemed out of danger. Their experiences with their first patients are reported in Chapter 6.

Benenson returned to the United States in 1965 and his place as Director of the PSCRL was taken by R. A. Phillips, who retired from the U.S. Navy and his command of NAMRU-2 in Taipei to accept the appointment. It was, of course, an inevitable appointment, and Phillips ran the laboratory and dealt with the committees such as the Directing Council and the Technical Committee in Dacca, and the Cholera Advisory Committee at NIH, in his customary way—with hard-headed and ruthless energy, imagination and style, and, from time to time, a little refreshing and sometimes productive eccentricity. He believed in getting the best possible advice and would invite scientists of many disciplines from many parts of the world, sometimes for reasons that were not clear, to come to the laboratory (always flying first class on PL 480 money) to act as consultants. He was always the laboratory-oriented physiologist

FIGURE 4.7. Dr. Robert A. Phillips and General Jesus Vargus of the Philippines, Secretary-General of the Southeast Asia Treaty Organization, 1969.

first, and in the laboratory his first concern was to find means of dealing with disease. But he had little interest in the large-scale practical application of such laboratory knowledge. We shall see that this in the end brought him into conflict with the young physicians and epidemiologists who were anxious to apply a fundamentally important finding that he himself had made to large-scale treatment of cholera patients in the field. He retired from Dacca at the end of 1970, shortly before the outbreak of civil war between East and West Pakistan that led to East Pakistan's becoming the People's Republic of Bangladesh, and the PSCRL's thus losing its first two initials but continuing, after some initial difficulties, to remain a CRL for several more years before undergoing a further modification of its objectives and its constitution.

V

The Johns Hopkins Center for Medical Research and Training in Calcutta

By the time, in November 1962, the PSCRL in Dacca was ready with its newly completed cholera ward to tackle the cholera problem in earnest, another, quite independent, American group had come onto the scene in Calcutta, not more than 125 miles to the southwest, but separated from Dacca by the tension then existing between India and Pakistan.[1] This was the JHCMRT—Johns Hopkins Center for Medical Research and Training—or, rather, the cholera research program element of it, consisting initially of Charles C. J. Carpenter and R. Bradley Sack. The International Centers for Medical Research and Training (ICMRTs) were American university centres in foreign parts established with the support of the National Institutes of Health in 1961. There were five of them—those of the University of California in Kuala Lumpur; the University of Maryland in Lahore; Tulane University in Cali, Colombia; Louisiana State University in San José, Costa Rica; and Johns Hopkins University in Calcutta. Originally, the JHCMRT in Calcutta, like the others, was known as the ICMRT, but since this was likely to be confused with the Indian Council for Medical Research, the "I" was replaced by "JH" within a few months. In 1968, the "T" was also dropped because the NIH wished to de-emphasize the training aspect of the program.

Carpenter had just finished his house staff training at Johns Hopkins University School of Medicine early in 1962 and had carried out investigations on salt and water transport at the Laboratory of Kidney and Electrolyte Metabolism at NIH (thus gaining experience in techniques he was later to apply to the cholera problem). Being eager to work in

1. To travel from one city to the other at that time, one had to fly 800 miles via the city of Kathmandu in neutral Nepal.

an underdeveloped country (without having any particular problem in mind), and having therefore paid a visit to Calcutta in the summer of 1962, where he saw his first cholera patients, he accepted an appointment as head of the Cholera Research Program of the JHCMRT in Calcutta. He and Sack went to Calcutta in the autumn of 1962 and were joined the following April by three colleagues from Johns Hopkins, P. E. Dans, S. A. Wells and E. Hinman. The clinical studies of the Cholera Research Program were carried out in the Infectious Disease Hospital in co-operation with A. Mondal, the Physician-in-Chief, D. Mahalanabis (who was later to direct the Medical Relief Programme for the Indian government at the time of the mass migration of Bangladesh refugees to West Bengal; see Chapter 9), P. P. Mitra and S. R. Khanra. Laboratory studies were carried out at the Calcutta School of Tropical Medicine in co-operation with R. N. Chaudhuri, the Director; D. Barua,[2] Professor of Bacteriology; and S. N. De, who a few years previously had discovered cholera toxin (Chapter 2).

Thus, the JHCMRT cholera research program was well provided with facilities, and with the close collaboration of Indian colleagues steeped in experience of cholera. It was therefore ready for action as soon as it came into being—it did not have the two-year-long lag period of teething troubles of the PSCRL.

During the interepidemic period from November 1962 to early March 1963, Carpenter and his colleagues made their first observations on cholera patients, and on patients suffering from diarrhoea not due to the cholera vibrio, in the adult male ward of the Infectious Disease Hospital [56]. The patients were being treated with a modification of Sir Leonard Rogers's "hypertonic saline regime" and the death rate was about 30 percent. They observed that hypovolaemic shock, uraemia and acidosis were the most common causes of death and, being aware of Phillips's work, concluded that the death rate could be reduced "by more prompt and exact replacement of saline and alkali". They also observed that there was little difference between patients suffering from true cholera and those with non-cholera diarrhoea (see Chapter 6), except that in the former the diarrhoea was generally more severe. For their subsequent studies in the cholera epidemic period in April and May 1963, to be discussed in Chapter 6, they set up a "metabolic ward" to which they admitted the first two hypotensive, or hypovolaemic (i.e., having low blood pressure due to low blood volume), males who arrived each morning in the Infectious Disease Hospital with a history of acute diarrhoea.

---

2. At present with the Division of Communicable Diseases of the World Health Organization in Geneva.

The JHCMRT Cholera Research Program and the PSCRL differed in several respects. The emphasis of the JHCMRT was mainly clinical, although we shall see in Chapter 6 that some important bacteriological work was carried out. Having a small research ward with selected patients, young adult males, attached to a large hospital, the physicians could make intensive studies. In this respect, the JHCMRT Cholera Research Program bore a closer resemblance to the cholera program of NAMRU-2 in its various locations than to the PSCRL ward. There were, according to Carpenter, a number of reasons why it was easier to carry out clinical research projects. There were more cholera patients from whom they could choose their cases; they had perhaps better laboratory arrangements for monitoring their clinical investigations; and they had a continuing relationship with Johns Hopkins University School of Medicine, which had a firm commitment to clinical investigations abroad. It was possible to bring over as many Johns Hopkins–trained physicians as were necessary to meet the demands of clinical research at any time. There were five of them collaborating with Indian physicians in the first clinical studies in 1962 and 1963. And the Calcutta program provided outstanding training for American academics—no fewer than seven full professors of medicine, including five division heads, received their introduction to clinical investigations under the cholera program.

The PSCRL cholera ward was the adjunct to a bigger operation. As we have seen in Chapter 4, its main purpose was to treat cholera patients who had not been protected by vaccine during vaccine trials, but from the beginning the ward admitted any case of severe diarrhoea that was presented, and, as we shall see in Chapter 6, by 1964 it was the only centre for treating cholera in Dacca. From the beginning, the experience of the ward was, therefore, derived from the treatment of infants, children, pregnant women and old people with complicating debilities. The physicians at PSCRL consciously tried to favour simple methods of treatment that could be used by indigenous physicians; indeed, they were obliged to do so because they had to handle such a varied load, often fluctuating from no cases on one day to over a hundred on others.

The two institutions between them were able to study cholera for a large part of the year, the PSCRL in the winter and the JHCMRT in the summer. This was because of the extraordinary difference that there is, or was,[3] in the seasonality of cholera in Calcutta and Dacca despite their closeness to each other and the indistinguishability of their climates or of any other determinable factors that could conceivably affect the

3. The difference in seasonality applied to the classical cholera vibrio; with now-reigning El Tor vibrio, the cholera seasons are more spread out, with lower peaks.

incidence of cholera. In Dacca, the cholera season starts at the end of October, after the monsoon, reaches its peak during the months of November, December and January, and disappears with the arrival of the hot, dry months of March, April and May. In Calcutta, the cholera season reaches its peak during these hot, dry months of March, April and May and ends with the onset of the monsoon rains in June [152].[4]

Carpenter was succeeded as Director of the JHCMRT Cholera Research Program by others who also made notable contributions to cholera research, as we shall see. In May 1964, Craig Wallace, who had been with Phillips's NAMRU-2 in Taipei and the Philippines, took over from him, to be succeeded in turn by Nathaniel F. Pierce in 1966, who was followed by Sack, who had returned to the United States in 1964 and came back in 1968. Thomas Simpson followed Sack in 1970, and in 1972 the Johns Hopkins Cholera Program moved from Calcutta to the Cholera Research Laboratory in Dacca, where it remained until 1978. By that time, the laboratory in Dacca had become more internationalized, as we shall see in Chapter 11, and it was felt that too strong a Johns Hopkins element was undesirable. The Johns Hopkins program then moved to work on diarrhoeal diseases in the Gorgas Laboratory in Panama, but the old ICMRTs—then ICMRs—came to an end in May 1980, to be replaced by the NIH with the International Centers for Infectious Disease Research (ICIDR).

4. The experienced physician Abdul Wahed maintained that there were two cholera seasons in Dacca—one in October, November and December, and another in March, April and May as in Calcutta [391], but it has since transpired that the March to May season is due to non-cholera diarrhoea (discussed in Chapter 6) [460]. There were also two cholera (or diarrhoea) seasons in Bangkok, in the summer of 1958 and the winter of 1959 [67].

VI

Learning to Deal with Cholera

1. Rehydration and the Problem of Acidosis and Pulmonary Oedema

When, at the end of 1962, the physicians at the PSCRL and the JHCMRT first began to turn their attention to the treatment of cholera patients, they were equally inexperienced in dealing with the disease. At this time, the rate of mortality among treated patients on the Indian subcontinent was about 30 percent, because they were still being rehydrated with Sir Leonard Rogers's hypertonic saline, or, rather, a modification of it, in the Mitford Hospital in Dacca and the Infectious Disease Hospital in Calcutta. This is understandable—Phillips's method of treatment that had been so successful with his patients had not had the time to be properly tried by these hospitals. The physicians knew about the method, but they had not known about it long enough to overcome their understandable reservations about it. NAMRU-3's method of treating acidosis with sodium bicarbonate, if necessary, according to how much had been lost from the blood, had been published in some detail in 1948, but in a journal apparently so obscure [218] that even the all-embracing Pollitzer made no reference to this classic paper in his 1959 monograph. By 1951, the United States Army at least was paying some attention to the recommendations of its sister service, because its official method of treatment entailed infusing 1,500 ml of isotonic saline[1] followed by 500 ml of hypotonic saline containing 18 g of $NaHCO_3$ per litre during the first 2 hours, followed by 1,000 ml of isotonic saline every 3 to 4 hours. An account of this regimen appeared in an official Army publication and was reprinted in Shattuck's textbook on *Diseases of the Tropics* [397], and recorded by Pollitzer, but apparently it was not seen, or made no impression, or was rejected, on the Indian

---

1. With chance prevision containing an unexplained apparent irrelevance, thiamine chloride, that was to be included again, briefly, in the treatment regimen at the PSCRL 12 years later.

subcontinent. Phillips's principle of treatment as amplified by NAMRU-2 in Bangkok was published again in a well-known American journal in 1959 [456], but without any technical detail of the manipulations involved. It was expounded once more by Phillips in 1960 in Dacca at the inauguration of the PSCRL (which was, of course, attended by many local physicians), with an appendix sketchily summarizing the method of treatment, which he stated could be placed in the hands of "even a 12-year-old boy or girl of average alertness", but the proceedings of the meeting were not published until 1962 [337]. As we have seen in Chapter 3, the treatment was spelled out step by step in some detail in early 1962 in Taiwanese and Philippine journals (no doubt out of courtesy to NAMRU-2's hosts) and in a NAMRU-2 official report to the U.S. Navy [447, 448, 449], but in spite of a statement in one of these journals that it would also appear in a journal more likely to be read by Pakistani and Indian public health officials, namely, the *Bulletin of the World Health Organization,* it did not, and even if it had, it could hardly in that short time have had much effect in Dacca and Calcutta before the Americans began to deal with cholera patients there at the end of 1962.

As we have seen in Chapter 4, the American physicians at Dacca, not having had any experience with the treatment of cholera, thought it wise to begin with patients who were not critically ill, and so started their new ward as a convalescent ward for cholera patients transferred from the Mitford Hospital who were recovering and seemed out of danger. The experience with the first 23 convalescent patients was almost free of trouble, and so, although a few patients relapsed temporarily into moderate diarrhoea, it was decided to be more adventurous and transfer a patient from the Mitford Hospital who was still actively purging. This was "around Thanksgiving" (i.e., the third Thursday of November), and that is when the trouble began. They treated the patient by the standard NAMRU-2 technique of first treating hypovolaemia by rehydrating rapidly with saline, then countering possible acidosis by infusing bicarbonate, and the patient developed pulmonary oedema (as a result of a dangerous condition of the heart; see below) and died. They retreated for a while, then transferred another patient (number 36) in the acute phase. Again, pulmonary oedema developed, but the patient did not die. When Benenson and his colleagues had visited the Mitford Hospital the previous July, they had found (as had Phillips and Watten on their visit to Dacca in 1958) the patients being rehydrated with the old hypertonic saline of Sir Leonard Rogers. They were told by the Mitford physicians that they did not use the NAMRU-2 method of rehydration because it led to pulmonary oedema. The Americans had been inclined to believe that the trouble could be due to the Mitford infusion solutions possibly containing fever-producing pyrogens,[2] perhaps on account of contamination, and that they could avoid this difficulty at the PSCRL. But their experience with the two patients who got pulmonary oedema after infusion of pyrogen-free fluid showed that the problem must lie elsewhere. They decided, therefore, that it would be easier to take in fresh patients whom they could treat from the beginning, rather than transferring convalescent patients.

From the last week of December 1962 to the end of April 1963, they treated 77 patients by initially rehydrating them with isotonic saline to correct the most serious condition, i.e., the decline of blood pressure (hypotension) due to decrease in blood volume (hypovolaemia), and then infusing them with a maintenance fluid closely resembling that recommended by Phillips at the SEATO Conference in Dacca in December 1960 (Table 1.2, line 16). This maintenance fluid was PSCRL's newly evolved 5:4:1 solution, containing 5 g NaCl, 4 g NaHCO$_3$ + 1 g KCl per litre (Table 1.2, line 18) [178]. As we shall see below, these patients also received an antibiotic and vitamins. By the spring of 1963, the PSCRL had come to realize that if there was any clinical evidence (moisture at the bottom of the lungs evidenced by pulmonary râles on auscultation of the chest) of incipient pulmonary oedema, the patient should first receive isotonic sodium bicarbonate. In all, only five cases of pulmonary oedema, with three deaths, were encountered at the PSCRL between 1962 and 1964, all in patients who had received inadequate treatment elsewhere before admittance to the PSCRL ward [179].

Carpenter had seen several cases of pulmonary oedema in cholera patients in the Infectious Disease Hospital when he visited Calcutta on his preliminary reconnoitre in the summer of 1962. When he returned to Calcutta towards the end of the year to take up his duties with the JHCMRT, his first step was to make preliminary studies on cholera patients in the Infectious Disease Hospital during the interepidemic period of November 1962 to early March 1963. Patients with weak radial pulse were routinely receiving Rogers's hypertonic saline regimen, or, rather, an unfortunate variant of it that had been made in 1941 and had been "traditional" (to use Carpenter's word) throughout East and West Bengal since then. (The Director of the Calcutta School of Tropical Medicine, R. N. Chaudhuri, who was to be very helpful to JHCMRT, had in 1950 recommended an isotonic regimen, with sodium lactate or bicarbonate if there were signs of acidosis [70], but this does not seem to have been adopted in the Infectious Disease Hospital.) The

---

2. Rogers had had trouble with pyrogens and probably for this reason had reduced the volume of hypertonic fluid administered; see Carpenter et al. [58].

traditional regimen consisted of an infusion of 600 ml hypertonic saline (231 mEq/l), followed by 600 ml isotonic saline (154 mEq/l), 600 ml isotonic saline containing 5 g glucose, and 50 ml of 7.5 percent sodium bicarbonate (line 17, Table 1.2) [56]. The series of infusions were repeated at eight-hour intervals when considered necessary. The hypertonic saline induced a terrible thirst in the patients, who seem not to have had easy access to drinking water, and Carpenter remembers[3]

> the unending cacophony of voices, some faint and whispered, some plaintive and some quite assertive, calling "jal" (pronounced jawl, the Bengali word for water) superimposed on the background of a smaller number of voices calling "pani," the Hindi word for water. . . . Some were nearly wild with thirst, and the resultant thrashing about resulted in dislodging of the intravenous infusion equipment, sometimes with fatal consequences.

During the cholera epidemic in Calcutta in the spring of 1963, this hypertonic regimen was compared by Carpenter with an isotonic one, with free access to drinking water (see below) and, to quote him again,

> The contrast between the extreme discomfort and agitation of the patients treated for only four hours with hypertonic saline, as compared to patients who received isotonic saline with drinking water, was as stark as any I've seen, and made an immediate impact even on those physicians who had been advocating the use of hypertonic saline for many, many years. This simple change altered the whole ambience of the cholera ward, in that the extremely uncomfortable, agitated patients, incessantly pleading for water, were replaced by patients who were comfortable, quiet and cooperative.

We have seen in Chapter 3 that Rogers introduced his hypertonic regimen, on the basis of erroneous reasoning, for the sole purpose of avoiding the recurrence of diarrhoea that took place when cholera patients were rehydrated with isotonic or hypotonic saline. In the climate of opinion then prevailing, recurrence of diarrhoea on rehydration was regarded as failure, and had been regarded so by everyone, including so wise a man as John Snow, since Latta introduced rehydration in 1832. Latta was the only one to realize that rehydration had to be persisted with. Rogers was justifiably satisfied that his regime halved the death rate from cholera, but it is not clear whether he achieved as much success in his desired objective of preventing the recurrence of diarrhoea. All he has to say about this is that "another striking feature was the far less tendency of the hypertonic solution to restart the copious rice-water stools, which so commonly renders the use of normal

3. Carpenter, private communication, 1980.

saline of temporary value", but we are left without knowing how far "far" is. Carpenter found in his comparative study of cholera patients receiving hyper- and isotonic infusions that there was no significant difference in the rate of stooling but the patients received hypertonic saline for four hours only, and then isotonic saline and bicarbonate (see below) [58]. The change to the less hypertonic solution took place in 1941, when it was reported that certain cholera patients receiving the Rogers regimen developed hypoglycaemia [69]. The new solution, which was used for the next 22 years, was not only less hypertonic but, more importantly, less alkaline (22 mEq HCO_3/l compared with 56 mEq/ml, lines 17 and 12, Table 1.2), and it is by no means certain that the patients always received any or all of the 50 ml of bicarbonate prescribed. It was perhaps this lack of sufficient bicarbonate that brought the rate of mortality back to about 30 percent, the figure Rogers obtained before he took Sellards's advice and added sodium bicarbonate to his hypertonic saline. But Carpenter suggests that Rogers's greater success may have been due to his insistence that the patient be under continuous observation, since his condition might deteriorate precipitately, such that corrective measures must be taken immediately; Rogers could provide this continuous care because he never had to deal with more than 500 patients a year in the Calcutta Medical College Hospital, whereas 40 to 50 years later the Calcutta Infectious Disease Hospital had to deal with 4,000 to 5,000 patients a year and was unable to give so much attention to each patient [58].

At first, the Indian physicians, who in fact were aware of the NAMRU-2 regimen, were reluctant to apply it to their own patients because they thought their cholera was of a more severe type, and that although Phillips's conclusions might apply to Thai and Filipino patients they might not apply to Indian patients. Benenson shares this view. He writes (private communication, 1980): "There isn't any question in my mind that the disease [in Dacca] differed from that in the areas where Bob Phillips developed it [his regimen]. The cases that I saw in Saigon were very much milder than those that we had in Dacca. One of my questions [see below] continues to be the difference in the physiological state of the individual in the Subcontinent, in contrast to that of those in Egypt, Bangkok, Saigon, Manila". Similar points were made by Craig Wallace and by Abdul Wahed at a round-table discussion on the management of cholera patients at the second SEATO-Sponsored Cholera Research Symposium in Hawaii in January 1965. In retrospect, Sack, too, is not surprised by the attitude of the Indian physicians, since he found a similar attitude in practically every developing country he later visited as a WHO consultant, not specifically with regard to intravenous rehydration of cholera patients, but with the treatment of other diarrhoeal diseases, and with other medical problems. Everybody, he states, is convinced that his diseases are different from other people's, and that his children are better nourished, or worse nourished, than other children (private communication, 1980).

The PSCRL and JHCMRT physicians soon had an opportunity to compare experiences and discuss plans for the future. Benenson, Gordon and Greenough had visited the Calcutta unit and urged them to return the visit so that their activities could be coordinated as much as possible. Colin MacLeod also had visited the JHCMRT and had suggested they should go to Dacca, so in the second week of January 1963 Carpenter and Sack paid a visit to the PSCRL. By this time, the PSCRL physicians had handled two cases of pulmonary oedema in their own ward, and had instituted, as we have seen, a regimen of treatment that was to prove effective in avoiding this complication of the disease except in three more cases that were too far advanced by the time they came under their care. The JHCMRT physicians had seen pulmonary oedema in patients under the traditional Indian regimen and were making their plans to compare this regimen with one of their own.

The comparison of the traditional Indian rehydration regimen with the modern one developed by NAMRU-3 and -2 was made by JHCMRT after discussion with the Indian physicians who were not willing to change from the traditional regimen until they had seen it compared with the new regimen. During the period from 10 April to 14 May 1963, in the spring cholera epidemic, the first two adult males who arrived each morning at the Calcutta Infectious Disease Hospital in a state of shock and with a history of acute diarrhoea were admitted to a "metabolic" ward[4] for study [58]. After various initial studies, comparative studies were made of patients receiving hypertonic saline, the traditional regimen and a 2:1 isotonic saline lactate regimen (see below). For the comparison of the traditional and isotonic regimens, patients who were strictly comparable in regard to age, duration of illness and various other conditions were studied. The first hypotensive adult male cholera patient arriving each morning at the Infectious Disease Hospital was admitted to the special study ward and received the 2:1 saline-lactate regimen administered by Carpenter's group. The second hypotensive adult male was admitted to the main cholera ward and for four hours received the traditional regimen administered by the ward staff; thereafter he too received the isotonic saline-lactate regimen. There were 20 patients in each group [58].

---

4. In another paper, this is referred to as "a two-bed metabolic ward" [46]. Since one patient was admitted each morning and observed for three days, this seems to have been a matter of fitting a quart into a pint pot.

The 2:1 saline-lactate regimen was a modified version of the NAMRU-2 regimen. Sodium lactate was used to correct acidosis rather than sodium bicarbonate because it is as effective as bicarbonate [58], but easier to sterilize because it does not give off carbon dioxide on heating. Carpenter does not comment on the change from the NAMRU-2 3:1 (previously 8:1) ratio of saline to alkali to a 2:1 ratio; evidently, the PSCRL used a 2:1 ratio, too, until changing to the 5:4:1 solution for initial treatment as well as maintenance (see below). In fact, Carpenter used a 1 to 0.5 ratio, which meant that his patients were receiving alkali much sooner than the NAMRU-2 patients, i.e., after 1 litre rather than 3 litres of saline, because their regimen consisted of a rapid infusion (within an hour) of 1080 ml of isotonic saline to restore blood volume followed by 540 ml of isotonic (167 mEq/l) sodium lactate to counteract acidosis, followed by slower infusions of saline and lactate according to the rate of fluid loss.

The traditional regimen was applied for the first four hours only, and after that these "control" patients also received the saline-lactate regimen. All the patients had low blood pressure and were suffering from acidosis on arrival, as evidenced by the low blood pH, and all of them eventually survived, but as we have already seen, there was a marked contrast in the first four hours between the discomfort and agitation of the patients receiving the traditional treatment and the comfort and calm of those receiving the isotonic saline-lactate treatment. The difference was so dramatic as immediately to persuade the Indian physicians, Chaudhuri and Mondal, to abandon the traditional therapy.

But there was another and more important difference between the two groups of patients in the first four hours. On admittance, the blood pH of all the patients was low, pH 7.2; in those receiving lactate, it rose to the normal value of 7.4, whereas in those under the traditional regimen it remained at the dangerous level of 7.25. The latter patients were continuing to suffer from a condition that physicians doubly misname as metabolic acidosis. It has nothing to do with the metabolism (break-down or synthesis) of any substance in the body, but is due, as we know, to the abnormally high transport of alkaline sodium bicarbonate from the blood into the lumen of the gut; the blood is not "full of" acid as the suffix "-osis" implies, but merely less alkaline, with the pH reduced from about 7.4 to about 7.2 or a little below that, and very rarely below the neutral point of 7. The word "analkalaemia" could have been made up for this condition. The preceding adjective, "metabolic", is equally objectionable, and not really necessary; if an adjective much be used, "diarrhoeal" would be appropriate, and "diarrhoeic" with its decent Greek ending even better. Diarrhoeic analkalaemia is the condition we are concerned with, but, alas, custom obliges us to continue to use the expression "acidosis"; at least we will abandon "metabolic". Patients in this acidotic condition show Kussmaul's respiration, or air hunger, a deep, rapid, gasping respiration. This is not so much due to a lack of oxygen, as to a need, mediated by the central nervous system, to blow off through the lungs some of the carbon dioxide normally present in the blood in the form of carbonic acid ($H_2CO_3 = CO_2 + H_2O$). According to the famous Henderson-Hasselbach equation, the pH of blood is governed by ratio of alkaline bicarbonate to acidic carbonic acid; if the bicarbonate diminishes, the carbon dioxide must diminish, too, in an attempt to keep the blood at its proper pH. It is important to restore the alkalinity of the blood as soon as possible, and if a patient is rehydrated with saline not containing alkali, or not enough of it, the acidosis will be aggravated because the fluid that continues to pour into the gut (whether or not he is receiving alkali) will continue to take sodium bicarbonate with it. Rehydration with saline containing no alkali, or too little, may save a patient from death due to shock resulting from reduced blood pressure resulting from reduced blood volume (hypotensive, or hypovolaemic, shock), or from uraemia (urea in the blood as a result of damage to the kidney tubules, as noted by Sellards), but it will not correct the acidosis and therefore it may cause the physician to kill him by precipitating pulmonary oedema. Pulmonary oedema occurs when fluid from the capillaries of the lung spills out into the alveoli of the lung, generally as a result of failure of the left heart. This can happen with a cholera patient receiving too rapid and too copious an infusion of intravenous fluid.

Carpenter did not see pulmonary oedema in any of his own patients, who in the end all received alkali. Summing up his experiences, he stated: "Probably two factors accounted for Rogers's lack of adequate volume replacement in severely ill patients: the fear of precipitating pulmonary edema and the high incidence of pyrogen reactions caused by intravenous fluids. Fear of precipitating pulmonary edema was clearly a factor mitigating against adequate intravenous fluid administration". Carpenter then drew an important conclusion:

The fact that pulmonary edema remained a fairly common occurrence with traditional treatment on the cholera wards in Bengal in recent years, whereas it has now failed to occur in over 140 consecutive adult male cholera patients who received vigorous fluid replacement therapy with the 2:1 saline:lactate regimen, suggests that the susceptibility to pulmonary edema is decreased by 2:1 saline:lactate regimen. Since acidosis in the cholera patient is promptly corrected by the 2:1 saline:lactate regimen, but persists and often worsens during treatment with the traditional regimen, *it is suggested that the frequent occurrence of pulmonary edema with the latter regimen was due to impaired myocardial* [heart muscle] *function secondary to severe metabolic acidosis* [emphasis added] [58].

This tracing of the cause of the risk of iatric[5] pulmonary oedema to acidosis was the answer to the problem facing physicians of the Indian subcontinent who were well acquainted with pulmonary oedema and cautious about the dangers of overhydration. Chakravarti and Chaudhuri, for example, were faced by the dilemma of how to deal with a patient in a state of severe hypovolaemic shock. To treat the shock it was necessary to give him a large infusion of saline in a short time, but then instead of dying of shock he would die of pulmonary oedema [65]. They might have been better off with the old Rogers regimen (line 12, Table 1.2) or the new NAMRU-2 regimen (line 15), both of which have much more sodium bicarbonate than the traditional regimen (line 17). Chakravarti and Chaudhuri noted that pulmonary oedema and uraemia went hand in hand, but must have forgotten that Sellards (who made no mention of pulmonary oedema) had recommended alkali (incorrectly) for the prevention of uraemia [393].[6] If they had attempted to prevent uraemia in this way, they might have prevented pulmonary oedema.

The question of how uncorrected acidosis is responsible for pulmonary oedema was taken up at the PSCRL at the beginning of 1965. On clinical grounds, Greenough, who, as we have seen, had encountered five cases of pulmonary oedema in 1962 and 1963, was inclined to believe that it was due in some way to acidosis. This suggestion was later confirmed when Benenson invited Rejane M. Harvey of the Cardiopulmonary Laboratories of the Bellevue Hospital in New York to come to Dacca to study the problem. She had been studying acidosis in diabetic and nephritic patients, and in experimental animals in which acidosis had been induced, and had formed the hypothesis that when the pH of the blood was reduced the peripheral blood pressure would be reduced and the bulk of the blood would accumulate in the central circulation. With no peripheral pulse, the patient would be in shock by the usual criteria, and with all the blood pulled into the central circulation, the heart would be overloaded and would fail. Harvey and her colleagues came to Dacca and studied 23 acute patients in the PSCRL ward during the epidemic of January to March 1965 [190].

By inserting a right-heart catheter into the anticubital vein and passing

---

5. Rather than the commonly used "iatrogenic", which should mean "generating doctors" rather than "generated by doctors".

6. In fact, uraemia is not due to acidosis specifically but to extreme dehydration and hypovolaemic shock, which is generally accompanied by acidosis.

it by way of the right auricle to the right ventricle, and out to the pulmonary artery and into the farthest end of the pulmonary tree, they could measure the pressure in the capillaries of the wedge of pulmonary tissue whose arterial supply was temporarily blocked, and so determine the degree of failure of the left heart. When alkaline bicarbonate was infused, the failure of the left heart was corrected. The blood pressure studies were confirmed by studies on the pH of the blood: when plain saline was infused in an acidotic patient the blood pH went down, and when bicarbonate was infused it went up. But if the blood pH was not too low, i.e., above pH 7.2, and plain saline was infused, the kidneys were able to discriminate and correct the acidosis, and excess fluid was discharged into the bladder.

Thus, the acidotic patient's heart is overloaded with blood because the peripheral circulation is cut off due to constriction of the peripheral blood vessels. If the peripheral venoconstriction is reversed by restoring the alkalinity of the blood, the patient can safely be transfused with saline; if the acidosis is allowed to continue and the patient is not infused with saline, he may not get pulmonary oedema but he will die of hypovolaemic shock; if he is infused with saline, not even enough to restore his blood volume, it will concentrate in the central circulation and overload the left heart. Furthermore, infusion of saline alone is doubly dangerous because, as we have already seen, it aggravates the acidosis by promoting more loss of alkali, and so increases the danger of overloading the heart.

NAMRU-3 and NAMRU-2 were well aware of the phenomenon of acidosis, but in none of their papers is there any mention of pulmonary oedema. The only mention of it is in a 1979 private communication from Watten, who states that when they were feeling their way in Bangkok, not sure how fast to rehydrate, one of their older patients "went into mild pulmonary oedema during the early phase of treatment. That frightened us a bit, so we gave the fluids a little more slowly". To them, the virtue of correcting acidosis seemed to lie in their observation that it eliminated nausea and vomiting, and they state, "During the Bangkok epidemic, Watten and Phillips had no difficulties in overhydration. This was also our experience in Manila" [447]. They were not in a hurry to correct acidosis and in more of a hurry to correct hypovolaemia. This, presumably, combined with the fact that separate bottles of sterile isotonic saline and sterile sodium bicarbonate solution were available from normal naval medical stores, is why saline and alkali were administered seriatim rather than simultaneously. In Egypt, the patients had to receive 8 litres of saline before they received alkali, and in Bangkok, 3 litres of saline. Yet there was no pulmonary oedema, and one must conclude with the Pakistani and Indian physicians and with Benenson that the cholera Phillips encountered was less severe than that in Dacca and Calcutta, and, with hindsight provided by Harvey, that the pH of Phillips's patients never went lower than 7.2.

2. Tetracycline

The reader must be wondering why there has been no mention of the use of antibiotics in the treatment of cholera so far. Obviously, antibiotics were considered, and the cholera vibrio was found to be sensitive to them in laboratory tests, but in the clinical treatment of the disease they had been found wanting. The disappointment was due to their being expected to be a complete cure for cholera. Thus, Pollitzer (pp. 773–787) states, in connection with a suggestion that treatment with the antibiotic chlortetracycline might be worthwhile in conjunction with saline infusion (as we shall see, a very sensible suggestion):

> However, even if one agrees with this contention, one must stress that the aim of a specific cholera therapy is not to augment the value of the infusion treatment but to render the latter superfluous by suppressing the morbid process before dehydration and collapse have developed. Thus far no convincing evidence has been obtained that any of the methods of treatment discussed above falls into the category of a *therapia sterilisans magna*. . . . Thus, whatever the future may hold, it is difficult to visualise a time when the infusion treatment will not occupy a prominent place in the therapy of cholera [360].

At the inaugural SEATO conference in Dacca in 1960, Woodward urged that the idea of using antibiotics in the treatment of cholera should not be scrapped, but Phillips (who had used chloramphenicol and tetracycline in Bangkok [456]) would have none of it. He contended that once the epithelial cells had been affected, the harm to them could not be undone with antibiotics. It would take a week before the affected cells would be shed and replaced by fresh undamaged ones; it would also take a week before the vibrios would be cleared from the gut in the natural course of events. In the meantime, the only treatment that would help the patient was intravenous replacement of lost fluids. NAMRU-2's definitive directive for replacement therapy ends with the statement: "We do not recommend the use of sulfonamides or antibiotics although many of these drugs are bactericidal for the vibrio. There is no evidence that their use affects the pathogenesis or prognosis of the disease" [456]. Phillips's lack of enthusiasm for antibiotics must also be seen in another perspective. At the time he was treating cholera patients by fluid replacement, most physicians in Thailand and the

Philippines were, to use Watten's words (private communication, 1979) "looking for the magic bullet, one pill that would cure the whole thing, and were putting a lot of stress on the use of antibiotics". Phillips wanted to distract them from this idea and persuade them to use replacement therapy.

Shortly after Carpenter and Sack arrived in Calcutta to take up their appointments in the JHCMRT, they resolved to test the value of antibiotics again. Their senior Indian colleagues, Chaudhuri and Mondal, had studied the effect of the antibiotic chloromycetin 10 years previously in patients receiving the traditional regimen of rehydration with hypertonic saline. The death rate in patients receiving the antibiotic was no lower than in those not receiving it, i.e., about 30 percent, but the cholera vibrio was rapidly eliminated from the stools of those receiving the antibiotic, and the stools reverted to normal hardness much sooner [70].

Carpenter and Sack did not expect antibiotics to affect death rate, but they did conclude that their Indian colleagues' work showed that the duration of the disease could be reduced, and so the time of hospitalization and the volume of rehydration fluid could be reduced. They therefore resolved to test the effect of antibiotics on patients receiving the isotonic regimen. In this resolve, they were encouraged by Wallace, who came from Manila to visit them shortly after their arrival, and who did not share Phillips's views on antibiotics. They were also encouraged to test antibiotics by MacLeod when he came to visit them in November 1962. But before experimenting with antibiotics, it was necessary for them to try out the isotonic and alkaline regimen on their selected patients in the Infectious Disease Hospital.

As we have seen, before they began the trials of the regimen in the spring of 1963, they paid a visit to the PSCRL in the second week of January 1963. When they arrived in Dacca they found that Gordon, Greenough and Benenson had already been using an antibiotic, tetracycline, since New Year's Eve. On that night, a female patient—in fact, the first female patient—in the PSCRL cholera ward who had been rehydrated for hypovolaemic shock, and had repeatedly gone into shock again over several days, was in a desperate condition and so it was decided to treat her intravenously with tetracycline in the hope of eliminating the vibrio and so shortening the course of the disease. This hope was fulfilled, and on the 2nd, 3rd, 5th and 7th of January 1963 (i.e., before the arrival of Carpenter and Sack), four more severely ill cholera patients received tetracycline together with isotonic rehydration, and all made good recoveries. But now the matter becomes complicated, because all these patients were also receiving vitamins—the anti-scurvy vitamin C (ascorbic acid) and the anti–beriberi vitamin B1 (thiamine chloride) and other members of the B complex, i.e., vitamin B6, riboflavin, niacinamide, and pantothenol. The reason for the inclusion of vitamin C seems to be comparatively simple—it was present as a stabiliser in the tetracycline preparation that was formulated for intravenous use. The reason for the other vitamins is more complicated. Benenson, as we have already seen, was, and still is, interested in why Bengali patients were different from Thai, Vietnamese and Filipino patients and believed that differences in their diet, and especially their vitamin intake, might be responsible. For this reason, he had, before the arrival of Gordon and Greenough, invited Irwin H. Rosenberg to come to the PSCRL from the NIH to collaborate with Kamaluddin Ahmad of the Department of Biochemistry of Dacca University on nutritional studies in relation to cholera. Rosenberg worked in East Pakistan from October 1961 to July 1962, and returned again in January 1963 at Gordon's request. In their initial studies of convalescent cholera patients, Gordon and Greenough believed they had observed instances of deficiency of thiamine, riboflavin and folic acid. Because of this, they administered vitamins to their patients as well as the antibiotic. It might seem strange now that they tested several untried variables, an antibiotic and several vitamins, at the same time, but then they were having their first serious encounter with cholera, and they had, to use Greenough's words (private communication, 1979), "inherited all the disasters from inappropriate care [of patients] brought in from elsewhere with the hypertonic Rogers solution and inadequate replacement therapy which results in severe acidosis and renal failure". It is likely that they were more interested for the time being in dealing with the crisis they were meeting, and in curing their patients by all the means they had available, rather than in carrying out research on them.

The PSCRL had a particular interest in vitamin B1, thiamine chloride. They had determined electrocardiograms on their patients and found that they had flattened T-waves, an indication among others of potassium deficiency, but when they gave them 15 mEq of potassium the T-waves were unchanged. Later, they were to find that this was simply because they had not given enough potassium, and that the patients were indeed suffering from potassium deficiency; when this was corrected, the T-waves were no longer flattened. But for the time being, potassium deficiency was ruled out, and their thoughts turned to other causes of flattened T-waves. This led them off on a wild goose chase. Gordon remembered that beriberi, due to deficiency of vitamin B1, caused flat T-waves, thirst, nausea, vomiting and cardiac congestion such as are seen in cholera. Since beriberi occurred among rice eaters, and the patients were rice eaters, could it be that they were suffering from beriberi manifesting itself as cholera? Should they not be given vitamin

B1? And since nutritional status might be concerned, why not other vitamins?

By the time of the visit of Carpenter and Sack in the second week of January 1963, the PSCRL group had had only a few days' experience of tetracycline plus vitamins in the treatment of cholera patients. Privately communicated accounts of that meeting differ. This is not surprising. The JHCMRT physicians had planned a careful trial of antibiotics which they intended to carry out after they had made a careful comparison of the hypertonic and isotonic rehydration regimens. They were bound to feel some disappointment on hearing that the PSCRL physicians had already tried an antibiotic only a few days before their arrival. It had been a ragged trial, carried out on only five patients with no careful advance planning and with no controls. Moreover, the PSCRL physicians perhaps had their minds more on the wild goose they were chasing than on the antibiotic that had been forced on them more by circumstance than design. They had hardly any quantitative data to offer on the value of the antibiotic, except that their patients seemed rapidly to have recovered.

The PSCRL group are quite clear that they used tetracycline in order to shorten the course of the disease, but this did not stop them at the time from considering that the complications of cholera that led to heart failure and pulmonary oedema could be due to vitamin B1 deficiency. Benenson states that "we urged him [Carpenter] to evaluate the effectiveness of tetracycline without thiamine chloride [vitamin B1] to provide independent evaluation of our successful therapeutic results and to determine whether the vitamin was necessary. We were running low on cases". Sack states:

> the PSCRL physicians had no data on the effectiveness of tetracycline at the time of the visit. We knew they were using an i.v. vitamin preparation which contained tetracycline; they could get no other preparation of the vitamin to use, and felt that tetracycline was inert. We probably discussed the question of tetracycline activity at the time, but they certainly had no data on the effects of tetracycline on the duration of diarrhea and i.v. fluid requirements.

As to the "i.v. vitamin preparation which contained tetracycline", what Sack should have said is that it was rather an i.v. tetracycline preparation containing vitamin C, which had apparently been added by the manufacturers to stabilize the antibiotic [178]. Moreover, all the patients had also received vitamin C–free tetracycline by mouth. In any case, the wild goose PSCRL was chasing was not vitamin C, but vitamin B1, which they had administered to their patients both parenterally and by mouth, as is evident from an unpublished paper (to which we will return) on "Treatment of Cholera With Antibiotics and Vitamins" by Gordon, Greenough and Benenson (ca. 1964). As to lack of data on the effect of tetracycline on the duration of diarrhoea and i.v. fluid requirements, Sack is probably correct. By the time of the visit, the PSCRL had treated only five patients with tetracycline, and although their unpublished paper records good recovery of the patients, there are no precise comparative data as to the duration of diarrhoea, or on volume of intravenous fluid requirements, in patients receiving the antibiotics. These were to be acquired after the visit.

Carpenter states that "everyone at the Dacca lab was still convinced, on the basis of Phillips's work, that antimicrobials were of no value. Although Bucky Greenough felt that a definitive controlled trial might be worthwhile, neither he nor any of the other Dacca physicians in January 1963 felt that antimicrobial would be of any value in cholera".

It is likely that in early January the PSCRL group, and perhaps especially Benenson, was still enthusiastically chasing the vitamin B1 wild goose, but such a chase would not be inconsistent with a concurrent belief in the value of tetracycline. The wild goose was soon to be slain, doubly slain.

After their initial success with five acute patients, the PSCRL physicians carried out further investigations which were reported in the unpublished paper mentioned above. Twenty patients received intravenous fluid alone; 14 received fluid and vitamin B; and 18 received fluid, vitamins B and C and tetracycline. There was no difference in duration of diarrhoea or of excretion of vibrios as between those receiving fluids alone and those receiving fluids and vitamin B, whereas those receiving fluids, vitamins B and C and tetracycline suffered diarrhoea for only half the time that those in the other two groups suffered it, and excreted vibrios for only one day, compared with four to five days. These data do not support the idea that vitamin B has any value in the treatment of that cholera, and thus the wild goose received its first blow. The patients who had received tetracycline had also received vitamin C willy-nilly along with the intravenous preparations of the antibiotic, and the fact that the PSCRL group was still at some time in 1963 vitamin-minded is shown in the discussion of the unpublished paper. Tetracycline is not firmly accepted as the only cause of well-being in the group of patients receiving it, and the therapeutic value of vitamin B1 and C (another wild goose now lurking about?) is not firmly rejected. Rosenberg (at this time in the PSCRL) finally slew the vitamin B wild goose when he determined that cholera patients were in fact not deficient in that vitamin [378].

The upshot of the meeting between the PSCRL and JHCMRT physicians appears to have been an agreement that the Dacca group would continue their trials of tetracycline plus thiamine and the Calcutta groups would test tetracycline alone. The tetracycline was to be administered orally and intravenously, because if it were effective it would be far more convenient to give it by mouth. All these trials were, of course, to be done on patients receiving intravenous fluid replacement therapy. At the PSCRL, a "triple blind" trial of tetracycline was inadvertently carried out on two groups of patients—those receiving tetracycline orally and a placebo intravenously, and those receiving the placebo orally and tetracycline intravenously. Not only did the physician not know what he was administering and the patient not know what he was receiving, but later analysis showed that a mix-up in labelling had occurred so that the drug manufacturer did not know what he was supplying. In any event, all the patients did equally well in their first trials, apparently because tetracycline is so effective that a fraction of the planned dose was sufficient to destroy the vibrios in everybody. This resulted in the publication of the PSCRL paper on the subject in the *Lancet* being delayed somewhat, and it was a rather cobbled-up account of a retrospective analysis of their experiences; as the authors stated, "The present study was not planned in advance as a controlled trial, and no placebo medication was available" [178]. This study showed that tetracycline rapidly eliminated the vibrios and that its effect was manifest after the first 24 hours, after which time the output of stools was reduced, on the average from about 110 ml per kg body weight to about 8 ml; the intravenous fluid requirement per kg body weight was reduced from about 80 ml to about 2 ml; and the duration of diarrhoea was reduced from 5½ to 2½ days.

Prospective controlled trials were carried out at the JHCMRT during the Calcutta cholera epidemics in the spring of 1963 and 1964, showing the same effectiveness of tetracycline. A very brief preliminary account [57] of these trials was published seven months before the PSCRL report, and a rather more detailed account [60] appeared one month before it. Later studies were to show that it was not only cheaper and easier to administer the tetracycline by mouth rather than by vein but also more effective [50] (which is not surprising, since the former route delivers the drug immediately and without loss to where the vibrios are, in the gut). With hindsight, it is now easy to see why antibiotics (especially tetracycline, which is highly effective against the vibrio, non-toxic, easily available and comparatively cheap)[7] were not successful

---

7. Benenson (private communication, 1980) states that it has the further advantage that it "is excreted in the bile which so frequently is infected with cholera vibrios. This may be more important than being in the gut".

Introduction

In 1987 and 1988 we organized two conferences, one at the University of California (Davis) and one at the University of Chicago, to study the problem of interpersonal comparisons of well-being.[1] We enlisted philosophers, economists, political scientists, and psychologists in the hope that an interdisciplinary approach would help to make some progress on a notoriously intractable issue. The chapters in this book do not yield a complete solution to the problem. We believe, however, that they make us understand better what would count as a solution. Also, they illustrate a number of approaches to the practical task of comparing the well-being – welfare, utility, standard of living – of different people.[2]

We may distinguish among four main problems that arise in this context. First, what do we mean by well-being? Second, is a comparison of the well-being of different people at all meaningful? Third, can such comparisons actually be carried out, precisely or at least approximately, routinely or at least under ideal conditions? Last, how does the purpose for which the comparison is carried out affect the answer to the first three questions? The topic of the chapters in this book is, "How to construct a notion of well-being that is (1) interpersonally comparable, and (2) adequate for purposes of distributive justice." Whenever the contributors object to a particular concept of well-being, it is rarely on the grounds that comparisons of well-being in this sense are devoid of meaning, but rather that the concept itself is inappropriate or that it is inappropriately operationalized, given the

[1] The proceedings of an earlier conference on related topics, Foundations of Social Choice Theory, were published in the same series in 1986. In that book, Allan Gibbard and Donald Davidson discuss the problem of interpersonal comparisons of utility in papers that are widely cited in this book.
[2] Here and later, we use "well-being" as the generic term for the comparandum. As will become abundantly clear later, the specific meaning given to the term can differ widely.

normative purposes it is to serve. Consequently, we do not focus here on the issue of meaningfulness of comparison.[3]

This introduction begins in Section I by considering briefly some other purposes that might motivate the attempt to compare the well-being of different individuals. In Section II we offer a survey of interpretations of well-being. In Section III, we discuss various methods that have been proposed for actually carrying out the comparison of the well-being of different people.

I. Interpersonal comparisons for other purposes

There are at least two purposes other than to implement distributive justice for which interpersonal comparisons of well-being are necessary. First, contrary to a widespread opinion, positive or explanatory theory sometimes has to rely on such comparisons. Second, they might be needed for evaluative purposes that are unrelated to the concerns of distributive justice.

Positive theory never requires the observer or theorist to make interpersonal comparisons of well-being. To explain behavior he may, however, have to take account of the fact that the agents themselves constantly make such comparisons. An obvious example is the importance of invidious comparison in much of human life.[4] A person sufficiently concerned with relative well-being may be willing to cut off his nose to spite his face – a behavior that is hard to explain using conventional assumptions about motivation. As argued by Kahneman and Varey in their chapter, well-being itself may be determined in part through such comparisons. We then have to ask whether this concept of well-being is relevant for purposes of distributive justice – that is, whether loss of well-being due to invidious comparison is a ground for redistribution. John Rawls, in particular, argues that "excusable envy" is relevant for normative purposes.[5]

The remarks in the last paragraph illustrate the elusiveness of the concept of well-being or, rather, one of the many ways in which it is elusive. Assume that A is stagnating and B is flourishing, but that A is unaware of B's existence. Given a specific definition of well-being

---

[3] For some remarks on that issue, see Gibbard (1986), p. 183–4.
[4] For a brief survey, see Elster (forthcoming).
[5] Rawls (1971), p. 534.

and a way of measuring it, we might conclude that A's level of well-being is 4 and that of B is 7. Assume now that A becomes painfully aware of B's existence and his higher level of well-being. According to one conception, A's level of well-being remains the same, although he now suffers pangs of envy that he was previously spared. According to another conception, the awareness of B's prosperity has reduced A's well-being from 4 to, say, 3. But then A must be expected to carry out another comparison – between B's level and the level to which he, A, is reduced after the first comparison. Presumably, the process will converge to some well-defined level of well-being for A. One might wonder whether this logically impeccable construction is phenomenologically plausible. Sometimes, it probably is. The envious man can feel even more miserable when he notices his envy. More often, perhaps, it makes better descriptive sense to say that the level of well-being is unaffected, because the pangs of envy do not really belong to the same category. This approach is related to a suggestion made in Scanlon's chapter to the effect that experiential states may be a (multidimensional) vector of heterogeneous components rather than a (one-dimensional) scalar.[6]

Interpersonal comparisons also have explanatory relevance in bargaining theory. Within the framework of Nash bargaining theory, outcomes are predicted given the set of feasible utility pairs and the particular utility pair corresponding to the disagreement outcome.[7] One of the Nash axioms (linear invariance) can be interpreted as precluding the interpersonal comparison of utilities. Therefore a solution like "split the utility difference" cannot even be defined within the framework, as the difference of utilities between persons is not well-defined in Nash's model. Nevertheless, it is clear that interpersonal comparisons are made by bargainers, and that they do affect the outcome. Consider, for example, the following bargaining situation. 1 and 2 are bargaining over 100 chips. The number of chips a person has determines his probability of winning a lottery: Assuming that they agree on an efficient division $(x, 100 - x)$, 1 has a chance of $x\%$ of winning a bicycle in a lottery L_1 and 2 has $(100 - x)\%$ chance of winning a bicycle in another lottery L_2. For specificity, let us assume

[6] Cf. also Sen (1980–81).
[7] A simple exposition, sufficient for the present purposes, is Luce and Raiffa (1957), Ch. 6. See, however, Roemer (1990) for a criticism of this approach.

that they agree that each should have 50 chips. Now assume that 2's lottery is changed to L_2', with the prize now a Rolls-Royce. According to Nash's linear invariance axiom, the outcome of bargaining in terms of the distribution of chips should be the same as before, a fifty-fifty division. In actual bargaining this would never happen. Because 1 perceives that a Rolls-Royce is worth much more to 2 than a bicycle is to him (1), 1 can credibly threaten to break off the negotiations unless he gets, say, 95 of the chips. We may quote Ehud Kalai on this topic:

> The argument just presented suggests that in bargaining situations, interpersonal comparisons of utility may take place. For example, this can be detected in the statement "Player 2 stands to gain more than player 1". Many game theorists like to disregard theories involving these types of interpersonal comparisons on the grounds that they cannot be done using von Neumann–Morgenstern utilities with their arbitrary scales. However, if one believes that interpersonal comparisons do take place in bargaining situations, then it would be a mistake to ignore them because they inconvenience us when put together with individual utility theory.[8]

To repeat, the theorist need not himself carry out the task of comparing the utilities. His concern is to model the comparison made by the parties. These comparisons might well be inaccurate, based, for instance, on the kind of distortions discussed by Kahneman and Varey in their chapter.

Interpersonal comparisons may also be made for evaluative purposes that are unrelated to distributive justice. It is sometimes said, for example, that evil persons are never happy. Someone might want to verify this proposition for, let us assume, religious purposes. If it could be proved, it might make converts out of skeptics by providing evidence of divine justice. For the purpose of this comparison, the relevant notion of well-being includes the pleasures that evil persons might get from torturing others. The potential convert will not be impressed if told that evil persons are unhappy if we subtract the

---

[8]   Kalai (1985), p. 89, slightly modified to fit our example. But see Roemer (1990) for a resolution of the Rolls-Royce 'paradox' without abandoning von Neuman – Morgenstern utilities.

pleasures they derive from satisfying their evil desires. For purposes of distributive justice, however, we do not want to count satisfaction or nonsatisfaction of evil desires as grounds for redistribution (see section II).

II. The comparandum

The chapters in this book discuss a number of concepts of well-being that may lend themselves to interpersonal comparisons. Along one dimension, they may be divided into subjective mental states (hedonic satisfaction), degree of objective satisfaction of subjective desires, and objective states. Along another dimension, they may be differentiated through the principles by which states of pleasure or desire-satisfaction are admitted or discarded as components of well-being. We shall offer a selective survey of some of these concepts.

Within subjective mental states, several subdivisions can be made. First, there is Scitovsky's distinction between pleasure and comfort, explained and discussed by Kahneman and Varey. This is an old distinction. Leibniz, replying to Locke, insisted that rather than pain ("uneasiness") being the opposite of pleasure, discomfort and small pains are a core component of pleasure:

> "Je trouve que l'inquiétude est essentielle à la félicité des créatures, laquelle ne consiste jamais dans une parfaite possession qui les rendrait insensibles et comme stupides, mais dans un progrès continuel et non interrompu vers de plus grands biens".[9]

Pleasure is produced by the continual overcoming of the pain and discomfort attached to unsatisfied desires. For purposes of distributive justice, comfort is more important than pleasure. It is more important to transfer resources to people who experience constant discomfort than to help those who, because of the lack of occasional discomfort, are unable to get much pleasure out of life. The latter are just planning their lives badly, and have no claim on our assistance.

Second, we may distinguish between personal and other-directed components of subjective well-being. The latter include the sadistic

---

[9] Leibniz (1875–90), vol. 5, p. 175; see also p. 152.

and spiteful pleasures we derive from the pain of others,[10] as well as the altruistic pleasures we derive from their happiness. There is general agreement that if the purpose of interpersonal comparison is to prepare the ground for transfers of resources, the former should not count. If I am miserable because I am not allowed to indulge in my favorite activity of torturing others, I have no claim to compensation. Conversely, people should not lose claims on compensation if they happen to get a lot of pleasure from the pleasure of others. Amartya Sen's distinction between (what he calls) well-being and standard of living is relevant here.[11] The former includes, as the latter does not, other-directed pleasures.

There are strong reasons for not using subjective satisfaction, even if shorn of other-regarding pleasures, as the standard of well-being. The most important, perhaps, stems from the "happy slave" or "sour grapes" problem. The fact that people adapt to their current state, and the fact that some adapt more easily than others, make it difficult to build a theory of distributive justice on a purely subjective criterion of well-being, as emphasized by Scanlon and Kahneman–Varey in their chapters. The issues are complex. Tocqueville, for instance, asks:

> Should I call it a blessing of God, or a last malediction of his anger, this disposition of the soul that makes men insensible to extreme misery and often gives them a sort of depraved taste for the cause of their afflictions? Plunged in this abyss of wretchedness, the Negro hardly notices his ill fortune; he was reduced to slavery by violence, and the habit of servitude has given him the thoughts and ambitions of a slave; he admires his tyrants even more than he hates them and finds his joy and pride in a servile imitation of his oppressors.[12]

From one point of view, a slave is better off if he adjusts to his circumstances – the adjustment is a "blessing of God." This cannot,

---

[10]   The distinction between sadism and spite is that in the former case I derive pleasure from the pain I impose on others, whereas in the latter case, pain of any kind satisfies me equally. Acting out of spite, I may cause another to feel pain, but my pleasure derived from this pain is not larger than the pleasure derived from any equal-size pain caused by other factors. For this distinction, see also Hirschleifer (1987).
[11]   Sen (1987), p. 27ff.; also Feinberg (1984), p. 74.
[12]   Tocqueville (1969), p. 317.

of course, be relevant for evaluating justice. From another point of view, the adjustment makes him even worse off – It is "a last malediction of his anger." Marxists, especially of the Frankfurt School, argue that alienation is even more severe when (and because) it is not subjectively experienced.[13] The underlying idea is that having autonomously formed preferences is itself a component of well-being, regardless both of the actual content of those preferences and the extent to which they are satisfied. If autonomous preferences are those we would not mind having even if we knew how they had been formed,[14] an infinite regress is lurking. The trade-off between autonomy and (subjective or objective) preference satisfaction can itself be determined only by an appeal to preferences, the autonomy of which might then be questioned.

Another standard objection to the purely subjective concept of well-being is that it fails to take account of the fact that we are inclined to say that peoples' lives go well for them when their strongest desires are satisfied, even if they are not aware of the fact. Allan Gibbard writes:

> It seems clear enough . . . that people want things other than feelings of well-being: sometimes they want revenge, sometimes posthumous fame, sometimes the fidelity of friends or spouse, sometimes the well-being of others. A jealous husband may even prefer a 'fool's hell' in which his suspicions rage but his wife is in fact faithful, to a 'fool's paradise' in which his suspicions are allayed but in fact he is unknowingly cuckolded.[15]

In this book, Scanlon makes roughly the same point. There is, however, a difficulty in this view. Consider the following states:

> *A*. Jack's wife is faithful to him. He wants her to be. He believes she is not.

> *B*. Jack's wife is not faithful to him. He wants her to be. He believes she is.

---

[13] See, notably, Geuss (1979).
[14] This is roughly the concept of autonomy proposed in Elster (1983), Ch. I.
[15] Gibbard (1986), p. 169.

Now, in state A, Jack's desire is satisfied; in B it is not. In state A, Jack is unhappy; in B he is happy. Now, assuming that both preference-satisfaction and happiness are valued goods, there might be choices and trade-offs between them. Following Gibbard, we may ask Jack whether he would prefer A or B to be the true state. Assume he would prefer B, but that A is the state that actually obtains. His preference for B over A is not satisfied. Then we have to weigh that fact against the other aspects of A. Perhaps, were Jack asked to choose between the state in which he prefers B but A obtains and the state in which he prefers A and A obtains, he would prefer the latter. But then, suppose that B is the state that actually obtains, and that Jack has the preference just stated. We can go on forever; the argument seems incompletable. We should not say (and Gibbard and Scanlon are careful not to say) that A is better just because Jack's preferences are satisfied in that state, whereas in B they are not. That would be to give too much weight to objective satisfaction, and too little to hedonic well-being. But if the weights assigned to preference-satisfaction and well-being are themselves a matter of preference, we again run into an infinite regress.

An objection that can be made both to the hedonic and the desire-satisfaction conception of well-being is that they give too much weight to aspiration levels. Egalitarian concerns might lead us to transfer resources to individuals at low levels of "personal success," to use Ronald Dworkin's phrase for degree of preference-satisfaction, even if the level is low only if measured against their excessively high ambitions.[16] In his chapter, Scanlon makes a similar point when he remarks that preference-satisfaction has no moral force unless backed by an argument about what there is reason to prefer. This is in a way the converse of the "happy slave" problem. Just as we do not want to punish those who adjust to circumstances by excessively low aspiration levels, we do not want to reward those who for some reason form unrealistically high aspirations. As Dworkin remarks, the notion of ambitions being "excessively" high already presupposes a theory of just distribution, and hence cannot without circularity or regress be used as a premise of this theory.

Instead of looking to the person as the final arbiter of what is good for him, we might appeal to more impersonal standards. In this book,

16   Dworkin (1981), pp. 204ff.

both Griffin and Scanlon move in that direction. Griffin argues that we cannot assess a person's well-being as the satisfaction of private, possibly idiosyncratic desires. Instead, we must assess the desires and hence his well-being from the point of view of a world of shared values. Scanlon, moving even further away from the subjective conceptions of well-being, argues for a conception related to Rawls's notion of primary goods – goods that any person would need in order to carry out his life plan. A difficulty with Rawls's conception, from the point of view of interpersonal comparisons, is that it is a vector rather than a scalar. If one bundle of primary goods is better than another on some dimensions and worse on others, there is no way of telling which is larger and better. The best we can achieve is a partial ordering of bundles.

Amartya Sen has argued against the primary-goods conception of well-being on the grounds that it embodies a "fetishist handicap."[17] One should be concerned not with goods as such, but with what goods do for human beings and what human beings do with them. Sen advocates a different nonsubjectivist conception of the good, based on the individual's freedom and capability to act.[18] The proposal might, however, have some unacceptable consequences. Often, what matters to the handicapped is not to reach the same end-states as the nonhandicapped: It may also matter to reach them in the same way. They may prefer to go to work by train like everyone else rather than being reimbursed for taxi expenses, even if the special modifications needed for the former solution cost more than taxi subsidies and the nonhandicapped would much rather go by taxi than by train. They may prefer to work for an income rather than receiving an outright pension, even if the extra equipment needed to enable them to work costs more than the value of what they produce and the work is inherently boring and monotonous. These preferences would appear to be condoned by Sen's proposal to focus on "basic capabilities" as the target of allocation. They might, however, be thought to be somewhat irrational.[19] For purposes of resource transfers, end-state comparisons may be more relevant.

[17]   Sen (1979); see also Cohen (1989) for illuminating discussions of the issue.
[18]   Sen (1985, 1987).
[19]   Elster (1988) argues that work created solely for the purpose of promoting self-respect cannot be rationally counted on to achieve even that end.

We must distinguish between objective conceptions of well-being and objective proxies for subjective well-being. Even if one adopts a wholly subjective notion of well-being as pleasurable mental states, any attempt to measure and compare well-being thus defined would have to rely on observable features of the individuals involved. On the basis of introspection and reports from others, one might decide that the correlation between a suitable bundle of observable traits and possessions is high enough to use the bundle as a proxy for well-being. To be sure, such correlations are never perfect. A striking instance in which the subjective value of a life could not be predicted from external circumstances is found in a play planned by Jean-Paul Sartre:

> Colette Audri, with whom Sartre once discussed this play, tells us that the play was to be called *The Wager* (after Pascal's wager), and would concern a child who is not wanted by his father. The mother, however, does not let herself be pressed into abortion, although a horrible life has been prophesied for the child: severe trials and reverses, poverty, and finally death at the stake. The child is born, grows up, and everything takes place as prophesied. 'In fact he changes nothing material in his existence,' Sartre says, 'and his life ends, as foretold, at the stake. But thanks to his personal contribution, his choice and his understanding of freedom, he transforms this horrible life into a magnificent life.'[20]

For practical purposes of redistribution, it would be impossible to take account of such deviations. (On the grounds that nobody should be punished for a great fortitude of character we might not even want to do so. But that is another argument.) We now discuss matters of implementation more systematically.

III. The comparison

Let us assume that there is a *fact of the matter* in an interpersonal comparison of well-being, considered as hedonic enjoyment or satisfaction of desires. It does not follow that we could ever discover it.

[20]   Føllesdal (1981), p. 403–4.

Statements about the past pose similar problems. We tend to assume that there is a fact of the matter by virtue of which statements about the past are true if true, false if false. We may never be able to *establish* what the fact of the matter is – for example, whether it was raining when Caesar crossed the Rubicon. But that does not affect the *existence* of a fact of the matter. In one sense, other minds are just as inaccessible to us as the past. We need not entertain doubts about their existence and their essential similarity to our own, but we may despair at ever getting the details right.

To assess what it *is* like to be another person we may try to imagine what it *would be* like to be him. At the very least, we can try to imagine what it would be like to be in his circumstances. We can also draw on personal experience, psychological findings, and world literature to imagine how these circumstances would affect our personal traits and, through them, our well-being. In imagining, we may even transcend biological limitations. Flaubert said, "Madame Bovary, c'est moi." His understanding of feminine psychology might also enable him to understand what it would be like to be some actual woman. The life of a manic-depressive may seem hard to assess from the outside. Are the manic episodes "highs" that compensate for the "lows" of depression? Or are manic and depressive episodes equally unpleasant, each in their own manner? Yet even in such cases there is enough resemblance to our own experience to give us a handle on what it is like to be manic. We can come to understand that hypo-mania is an intensely enjoyable state of round-the-clock euphoria, and very different from the incoherent and tortured restlessness of the full-blown manic. The inner life of mentally retarded persons is more recalcitrant to imaginative empathy. There is no reason to reject the hypothesis that some of them enjoy life as fully as any – nor to accept it.

There are other, more general obstacles to empathy as a method of interpersonal comparison. As pointed out by Kahneman and Varey in their chapter, intuitions about end-states are often contaminated by intuitions about changes.[21] When we think of what it would be like to

21   In intrapersonal comparisons of utility, one may have the converse problem – that intuitions about changes are contaminated by intuitions about end-states. Lloyd Shapley (as reported in Shubik 1982, p. 421ff.) has constructed a cardinal measure of utility that, unlike the von Neumann–Morgenstern concept, is unaffected by attitudes toward risk. The construction rests on shaky foundations, however, because it requires

be handicapped, we are almost unavoidably affected by the thought of what it would be like to become handicapped. Also, empathy is too information-intensive to be useful for practical purposes of large-scale redistribution. It may work in the family or among friends, but hardly in larger groups.

Allan Gibbard has suggested a different approach, which relies on overlap between segments of lives rather than on empathy with whole lives. Each of us will, through our experiences, form "hypotheses about how the intrinsic reward of a course of a life depends on a range of combination of features of the person and the life he leads. Call these *personal hypotheses*."[22] If there are at least two points of overlap between the personal hypotheses of two individuals, they can be used to calibrate the degrees of intrinsic reward on a common scale. Now, for a randomly chosen pair of individuals such overlap seems implausible. In their chapter, Ortuño-Ortin and Roemer use an approach designed to overcome this difficulty. They argue that each person, through empathy or experience, can compare his well-being in a given state with that of persons sufficiently similar to himself in similar states. From such local comparisons one can then, under certain conditions, piece together a unique global ordering, which compares the well-being of any person–state pair with the well-being of any other such pair. As a consequence, one can compare two person–state pairs in which both the persons and the states are very different.

We would like interpersonal comparisons to be objective, corresponding to "the fact of the matter." Because this goal is hard to achieve, might intersubjectivity be an approximation to, or substitute for, objectivity? This is the question explored by Hylland in his chapter. As in Ortuño-Ortin and Roemer, the basic concept is that of a pair (x, s) of an individual x in state s. Hylland assumes that for all pairs $[(x, s), (y, t)]$ of such pairs, each individual in society is able to compare the well-being of x in s with that of y in t. The question then is whether we can "piece together" (in a sense of that phrase that is entirely different from that in which it applies to Ortuño-Ortin and

---

people to be able to tell whether they would rather move from state a to state b or from c to d. Responses to this question would be contaminated by the respondents' attitudes toward b and d.

²² Gibbard (1986), p. 185.

Roemer) a social comparison of well-being from the individual comparisons. Hylland shows that the answer is essentially negative, for reasons similar to those underlying Arrow's impossibility theorem for aggregation of preferences.

The approaches to interpersonal comparison mentioned so far would work, if at all, only under idealized conditions. For the time being, at least, it is hard to see how they could be used for practical redistributive purposes. Peter Hammond, in Section 5 of his chapter, surveys a number of more policy-oriented proposals. Generally speaking, he finds them wanting, in that they do not capture all ethically relevant aspects of individuals and states. Hammond's own conclusion is that the traditional approach to the matter is misleading. In that approach, one first decides on the ethically relevant concept of well-being. Next, one proceeds to measure the well-being of individuals. Finally, comparisons of well-being are used to make distributive and allocative choices. Hammond argues against the need for the first step. One should first make ethical interpersonal comparisons by asking, for example, about the utilities of persons to society, and then compare these utilities for policy-making purposes.

Two chapters in the book consider some practical approaches to interpersonal comparisons. Blackorby and Donaldson study some ways to transform an economy where the basic units are households into an economy where the basic units are identical single adults. The goal of the construction of "adult equivalence scales" is to be able to perform social evaluations by using information about the well-being of each person. Elster looks at the way in which interpersonal comparisons are made in practice, to select students for college admissions, patients for transplantation, or workers for layoffs. He finds that in some allocative arenas there is a systematic tension between giving scarce resource to those who need them most and giving them to those who can benefit most from them.

The chapters by Weymark, d'Aspremont and Gérard-Varet, and Broome attack from different angles the plausibility of utilitarianism, the view that the social good should be defined as the sum of the welfares or degrees of well-being of individuals, assuming that the latter are indeed interpersonally comparable. The most convincing axiomatic arguments in support of utilitarianism have been formulated by John Harsanyi, and Weymark provides an exposition and analysis of Harsanyi's theorems. He ramifies a rejoinder to Harsanyi first made by Amartya Sen, that Harsanyi's 'aggregation theorem' is not, in fact, a theorem about utilitarianism but rather a representation theorem for a social welfare function defined on a set of prospects and assumed to satisfy the von Neumann–Morgenstern axioms of rational choice under uncertainty. Harsanyi's theorem states that such a social welfare function U, under certain conditions, can be represented as a sum,

$$U(A) = \Sigma U_i(A) \qquad (*)$$

where U_i is a von Neumann–Morgenstern utility function for person i, and the summation is taken over the relevant population. Weymark points out that even if we assume that utility is interpersonally comparable, the functions U_i will not in general be the ones that embody the correct interpersonal calibrations. And so the view that $U(A)$ measures 'total utility' in the sense that utilitarianism supposes is wrong. Just because a social welfare function U possesses the representation (*) does not imply that the sum of the individual *welfares* is being maximized.

   In the allocation of scarce resources, incentive problems arise frequently. To increase his chances of getting a scarce good, a person may report his needs or capacities falsely. This problem is at the center of the chapter by d'Aspremont and Gérard-Varet. They assume that a social planner announces that he will maximize a weighted sum of the von Neumann–Morgenstern utility functions of the agents. To do so, he has to acquire information from them about their preferences over lotteries. The question is whether he can assign weights that will induce the agents to report their preferences truthfully. D'Aspremont and Gérard-Varet prove that the planner can indeed find such weights. There is, however, no reason to think that the utility weights that induce truthful reporting correctly convert utilities into interpersonally comparable utility. That is to say, the goals of designing a system of weights (1) that will induce people to reveal truthfully their types to the planner, and (2) that will correctly calibrate interpersonal utility, and thereby add up utilities to give the utilitarian social welfare function, are incompatible. Their result is a new variation on a previously played refrain in social choice theory –

that in the presence of asymmetric information, it is impossible to implement a social choice rule that makes interpersonal comparisons of utility.[23]

John Broome's argument against utilitarianism is somewhat more roundabout. He views the social choice problem as one of choosing from among a set of prospects, each one of which entails a certain amount of 'good' for each person at each of various times in his life. (Thus, a prospect is thought of as an event that determines the state of all persons in society during each of many years, let us say.) He relies upon Harsanyi's theorem to argue that the 'social good' can be represented as the sum of the 'good' that each person enjoys during each year, *if* two postulates hold: the Principle of Personal Good and the Principle of Temporal Good.[24] Whereas the former of these principles is defensible, the latter seems indefensible, as Broome shows by an example. Hence, Broome maintains that if we disaggregate the social good of a prospect not only over its affects on different people but over its affects at various times on each person, then utilitarianism fails as a plausible social welfare function – at least, the argument via Harsanyi does not establish its plausibility. He concludes by noting that if one subscribed to a 'disuniting metaphysics,' the Parfitian view that a human being at different times in his life should be viewed as a sequence of different persons, then the Principle of Temporal Good becomes defensible. This establishes a formal link between the Parfitian postulate and utilitarianism, modulo the Harsanyi theorem.

Jon Elster and John Roemer

[23] We refer to the Maskin (1985) result that a social choice rule is Nash-implementable only if it is monotonic. Monotonicity implies that interpersonal comparisons are not made by the social choice rule.

[24] These are the analogs of Harsanyi's Pareto principle in Broome's setup.

References

G.A. Cohen, "On the currency of egalitarian justice," *Ethics* 99 (1989), 906–44.

R. Dworkin, "What is equality? Part 1: Equality of welfare," *Philosophy and Public Affairs* 10 (1981), 185–246.

J. Elster, *Sour Grapes,* Cambridge University Press 1983.

J. Elster, "Is there (or should there be) a right to work?," in A. Guttman (ed.), *Democracy and the Welfare State,* Princeton University Press 1988, pp. 53–78.

J. Elster, "Envy in social life," forthcoming in a *Festschrift* for Thomas Schelling, edited by Mancur Olson and Richard Zeckhauser.

J. Feinberg, *Harm to Others,* Oxford University Press 1984.

D. Føllesdal, "Sartre on freedom," in P.A. Schilpp (ed.), *The Philosophy of Jean-Paul Sartre,* La Salle, IL: Open Court 1981, pp. 392–407.

R. Geuss, *The Idea of a Critical Theory,* Cambridge University Press 1979.

A. Gibbard, "Interpersonal comparisons: preference, good, and the intrinsic reward of a life," in J. Elster and A. Hylland (eds.), *Foundations of Social Choice Theory,* Cambridge University Press 1986, pp. 165–94.

J. Hirschleifer, "On the emotions as guarantors of threats and promises," in J. Dupré (ed.), *The Latest on the Best,* Cambridge, MA: M.I.T. Press 1987, pp. 307–26.

E. Kalai, "Solutions to the bargaining problem," in L. Hurwicz, D. Schmeidler, and H. Sonnenschein (eds.), *Social Goals and Social Organization,* Cambridge University Press 1985, pp. 77–106.

G.W. Leibniz, *Philosophische Schriften,* ed. Gerhardt, Leipizig 1875–90.

R. D. Luce and H. Raiffa, *Games and Decisions,* New York: Wiley 1957.

E. Maskin, "The theory of implementation in Nash equilibrium: A survey," in L. Hurwicz et al. (eds.), *Social Goals and Social Organizations,* Cambridge University Press 1985, pp. 173–204.

J. Rawls, *A Theory of Justice,* Cambridge, MA: Harvard University Press 1971.

J. Roemer, "Welfarism and axiomatic bargaining theory," *Recherches Economiques de Louvain,* 56 (1990), pp. 287–301.

A. Sen, "What is equality?," Tanner Lecture, 1979. (Reprinted as Ch. 16 of A. Sen, *Choice, Welfare and Measurement,* Oxford: Blackwell 1982.)

A. Sen, "Plural utility," *Proceedings of the Aristotelian Society* (n.s.) 81 (1980–81), 193–215.

A. Sen, *Capabilities and Commodities,* Amsterdam: North-Holland 1985.

A. Sen, *The Standard of Living,* Cambridge University Press 1987.

M. Shubik, *Game Theory in the Social Sciences,* Cambridge, MA: M.I.T. Press 1982.

A. de Tocqueville, *Democracy in America,* New York: Anchor Books 1987.

1. The moral basis of interpersonal comparisons

1. Interpersonal comparisons of welfare have been thought to raise two sorts of difficulties. First, such comparisons have been thought to involve value judgments of a kind that are not only out of place in positive economic science but also inappropriate as a basis for decisions of social policy. In addition, doubts have been raised about whether it is possible to make such comparisons at all, at least in a scientific manner, if what is to be compared are psychological states that are not open to observation. These two difficulties are related. Particular views about how to make the relevant kind of value judgments, and about how to avoid them, have led to the conclusion that what is to be compared are mental states of some kind: degrees of pleasure or happiness on the one hand, degrees of intensity or strength of preference on the other. Doubts then arise about whether comparisons of the relevant sort can in fact be made.

My own view is that, extreme forms of philosophical skepticism aside, there is no problem in general about the possibility of making interpersonal comparisons of happiness or of relative well-being. Within contemporary political philosophy and welfare economics, however, interpersonal comparisons present a problem insofar as it is assumed that the judgments of relative well-being on which social policy decisions, or claims of justice, are based should not reflect value judgments. I will argue in Sections 4 and 5 that this idea, which gives rise to the widely held view that a person's well-being should be measured by the degree to which his or her preferences are satisfied, also undermines the moral significance and even the intelligibility of the interpersonal comparisons that the proponents of that view suggest we should make.

[1] I am grateful to many people for helpful comments on earlier drafts, particularly to John Broome, James Griffin, Amartya Sen, and John Rawls.

Once this idea is given up, however, and the unavoidability of some value judgments acknowledged, the possibility of making morally significant interpersonal comparisons of well-being no longer presents a problem, although the merits of particular standards of comparison may remain controversial. This is the conclusion I will argue for in Section 6.

The aim of avoiding value judgments is, in my view, the main source of the problem of interpersonal comparisons. I will therefore begin in Section 2 by distinguishing the various kinds of value judgment that morally significant comparisons of well-being can involve. In Section 3 I will lay out the structure of the hedonistic, or, more broadly, experientialist conceptions of well-being that are the predecessors of, and in important respects the models for, the now-dominant preference-satisfaction view. In order to understand the problems raised by this view, and by the interpersonal comparisons it requires us to make, it is important to bear in mind the ways in which it differs from its hedonistic predecessors

2. The claim that one person is better off than another in the sense relevant to a certain moral question – for example, a question of justice – can involve value judgments of at least three sorts. First, it involves the moral judgment that the form of well-being in question is the one relevant to moral questions of the sort at hand – that by taking account of how a person's well-being, understood in this sense, is affected we will be giving that person the kind of consideration to which he or she is entitled.

Not all judgments of relative well-being are made with morality in mind, however. We can ask, quite apart from any question of right or justice, how well a person's life is going and whether that person is better off than another, or better off than he or she was a year ago. Answers to this question – the question of what makes a good life for the person who lives it – are value judgments of the second kind that I wish to distinguish. Although questions of this kind can be asked and answered quite apart from morality, they are also questions that have particular importance *for* morality, because one of the things that is of particular importance in moral argument is the way in which individual lives are made better or worse. In order to show, for example, that a certain standard of comparison is relevant for questions of justice, we would need to argue that that standard measured at least some of the important ways in which a person's life can be made better or worse.

It is therefore difficult to see how value judgments of either of these two kinds could be avoided when we are defending the claim that a given conception of well-being is the one that is relevant for the purpose of answering certain moral questions. But it may be that once such a conception of well-being has been selected as the relevant one, no further judgment of value is involved in making a judgment that one person is better off than another in this sense. Suppose we were to decide, for example, that a person's level of well-being, in the sense relevant to certain questions of justice, is measured simply by the amount of gold in his or her possession. The choice of this criterion would represent a moral judgment, and this might rest in turn on the value judgment (a very implausible one, perhaps) that gold is an adequate measure of a person's access to the most important means to a good life. Once these judgments had been made, however, no further judgments of value would be involved in deciding which of two people is better off in the sense indicated. Making this judgment would simply be a process of empirical investigation, weighing, and so on – literally a matter of *comparison*.

We might, however, reject this standard and decide that the only conception of well-being appropriate to questions of justice is just the general conception of "having the ingredients necessary for a good life." It would follow from this moral judgment that the process of making morally relevant judgments of relative well-being would involve, in each instance, value judgments about what a good life requires. Suppose, for example, that one person has many opportunities for achievement but little leisure and few opportunities for friendship, while another has a very easy and comfortable life, with many friends, but no challenges and few opportunities for accomplishment. In order to decide which of these people is better off we would need to determine the relative importance of achievement, comfort, and friendship as ingredients in a good life. This would not be a matter of mere comparison but would also involve a value judgment of the third sort I wish to distinguish. Like value judgments of the second kind, these are judgments about what makes a life better for the person who lives it. They differ from those judgments, however, in being made as part of the process of making particular judgments of relative well-being rather than merely as part of the process of defending a general criterion of well-being.

The three kinds of value judgments that I am distinguishing are, then, first, moral judgments about the kind of consideration we owe to one another; second, judgments about what makes a life better for the person who lives it that figure in the process of defending a general criterion of well-being; and, third, judgments about what makes a life better for the person who lives it that figure in the process of arriving at particular judgments of relative well-being. As I have said, it is difficult to see how value judgments of the first two kinds can be avoided when we are making and defending morally significant judgments of relative well-being. But it is much more plausible to think that value judgments of the third sort can be avoided. The standard mentioned earlier – the amount of gold in a person's possession – is clearly not an adequate measure of well-being, but more plausible criteria have been suggested that, like this one, would make value judgments of the third sort unnecessary and make interpersonal judgments of relative well-being literally a matter of comparison. Chief among these are hedonism and other experiential conceptions of the good. Because these views have done so much to shape the problem of interpersonal comparisons – even giving the problem its name – let me take the time to describe the structure that that problem will have if an experiential conception of the good is assumed. We can then consider what happens to the problem when such views of the good are abandoned.

3. By an experiential conception of the good I mean a view according to which a life is a good life for the person who lives it insofar as it contains certain desirable psychological states (and, perhaps, insofar as it does not contain certain undesirable ones). Hedonism, the view that what makes a life good is just pleasure and the absence of pain, is obviously one experiential view, but other such views can admit a wider variety of forms of desirable consciousness.

I have described experientialism as a class of views about what makes a life good for the person who lives it. A claim that some view of this kind is correct would thus be a value judgment of the second kind distinguished earlier. Such a claim is not yet a moral judgment. Nor is it a general account of what a person has reason to aim at, since people have reason to aim at things other than the quality of their own lives. It is only a claim about what people have reason to aim at insofar as they are concerned simply with their own lives. But such a claim leads to moral conclusions when it is conjoined with the general thesis that in moral argument we must take account of how individuals' lives are made better or worse. If some form of experientialism is correct, then it follows from this thesis that we should be concerned in moral argument with the degree to which people are caused to have various desirable or undesirable states of consciousness.

If experientialism is correct, we can easily assess the quality of our own lives at a given moment, because the presence or absence of the relevant states of consciousness is directly accessible to us. We can assess the quality of our lives in the past by remembering what our states of consciousness were like, though memory will generally need the assistance of external evidence indicating what our beliefs, desires, and external circumstances were at the time, from which we can infer "what it must have been like" to be in that situation. As far as our lives in the future, or in various hypothetical circumstances, are concerned, this process of inference is all we have to go on. We estimate the character of our experience in predicted or imagined circumstances by relying on empirical generalizations about how the felt quality of experience varies as a function of beliefs, desires, and "external" conditions (and how belief and desire in turn are shaped by these conditions). If experientialism is correct, then these estimates give us, at the same time, assessments of how good or bad our lives in those circumstances would be.

Our estimates of the character of other people's experience (and hence, if experientialism is correct, of the quality of their lives) are based on generalizations of this same kind. To deny that these generalizations are ever valid would entail a deep skepticism about the possibility of any knowledge of other people's mental states or even of our own mental states in future circumstances.

If some form of experientialism were correct as an account of what makes a life good for the person who lives it, would it follow that there was no need for value judgments of the third kind mentioned earlier? This depends on the particular form of experientialism that is taken to be correct. If one particular state of consciousness – a form of pleasure, say, or happiness understood as a particular psychological state –

is the single source of value in a life, then the process of deciding which of two lives is the better is indeed simply a matter of comparison – of deciding which life contains the greater quantity of this state. But the matter is less clear if a variety of heterogeneous forms of consciousness are held to be independently valuable. Judging whether one life is better than another will then involve deciding which of two heterogeneous collections of experiences is to be preferred. Unless the experiential account of the good provides us with some rule for making such choices, we will be required to make a value judgment in each case, just as we were in the non-experientialist example described in Section 2 involving friendship, leisure, and accomplishment.

The general structure of an experientialist view can be summarized as follows.

i.   A life is made good for the person who lives it solely by the presence in it of certain desirable states of consciousness.
ii. The presence of these states at a given time is revealed by introspection, and their occurrence over time can be summed up to yield an assessment of the value of a life as a whole.
iii. The claim that these states determine the value of a life for the person who lives it is not a moral judgment but, rather, a value judgment of the second kind described earlier. But if these states do determine how good a person's life is, then they have moral significance as well because the quality of individuals' lives is one of the things that must be taken account of in moral argument.
iv. The claim that certain states of consciousness are what makes a life desirable is itself a value judgment, but if the quality of a life is determined simply by the *quantity* of these states, then making particular judgments of relative well-being is simply a matter of comparing these quantities.

4. Hedonism is now widely rejected as an account of what makes a life good for the person who lives it, and the reasons for its rejection are reasons for rejecting other forms of experientialism as well. It is obvious that most people's concerns, even their nonaltruistic concerns, are not limited to the quality of their own mental states. I want, for example, to have loyal and devoted friends, not just to have the pleasure of believing that I do. Similarly, the value to me of having found a proof of Fermat's Last Theorem would be immeasurably greater than that of believing falsely that I had done so, even if this belief were to last for the rest of my life. If such concerns are not all mistaken (and I cannot believe that they are), then it is difficult to deny that the degree to which they are satisfied can make a difference to the quality of a person's life – for example, that my life will have been a better life from my point of view if my friends are genuine friends, my accomplishments real rather than illusory, and so on. It follows that experientialism must be rejected as an account of what makes a life a good life for the person who lives it.

This does not mean the character of a person's conscious states is of no importance in determining how good a life that person has, but rather that the character of these states is not the *only* thing of importance. In order to arrive at judgments of relative well-being, then, we will have to have some way of assessing the contribution that friendship, accomplishment, agreeable states of consciousness, and other diverse goods make to the value of a life. One conclusion to draw would be that the set of value judgments on which interpersonal comparisons of well-being depend is much more complex than some experientialist accounts have suggested. There is no single type of value to which the value of everything else can be reduced and in terms of which the value of these other things can be compared.[2]

Most contemporary discussion of interpersonal comparisons of well-being has, however, followed a different route. Within welfare economics, and to a large extent within political philosophy as well, the prevailing view has been that, at least for purposes of social justice, judgments of individual well-being should be based not on some set of "objective" value judgments taken as authoritative, or on

---

[2]   The appeal of the idea that there must be such an experiential ground of value is extremely strong. Gibbard, for example, holds that not only utilitarian ethics but also the idea of rational prudence requires that we be able to make "veridical introspective judgments" of "the intrinsic reward of a life." If he means only that we must be able to make judgments about how good a life is, then this seems unexceptionable. But the reference to introspection suggests that he thinks such judgments must be based on some quality of experience that, as he says, "could sum up the weight of good reasons" and "provide grounds for preference." See "Interpersonal Comparisons: Preference, Good and the Intrinsic Reward of a Life," in J. Elster and A. Hylland, eds., *Foundations of Social Choice Theory* (Cambridge University Press, 1986) pages 165–193. The quoted passages occur on pages 190 and 191.

the values of the person who is making the judgment, but rather on the preferences of the person whose welfare is being evaluated. Different individuals hold differing views about, for example, the relative importance of friendship, accomplishment, and pleasure in making a life good, and each person's level of well-being is determined by the degree to which that person's life accords with his or her preferences. This is the basis for Preference Utilitarianism, as it has been formulated by Harsanyi and others, and its guiding rationale is clearly stated by Harsanyi in his principle of Preference Autonomy: "The principle that, in deciding what is good and what is bad for a given individual, the ultimate criterion can only be his own wants and his own preferences."[3]

Superficially, preference satisfaction views appear to be closely related to their hedonistic or experiential predecessors, because each makes the value of various ingredients in a person's life depend on that person's subjective nature: in one case, on the degree to which those ingredients satisfy the person's preferences, and in the other, on the degree to which they bring the person pleasure (or other valued states of consciousness). But this appearance is deceiving. The two types of view are fundamentally different in character, the preference satisfaction view being at base a moral doctrine, whereas experientialism is an account of the nature of value.

Recall that an experientialist view is at base a thesis about what makes a life better for the person who lives it. Such an account, if correct, would be one that individuals should be guided by when they are assessing their own lives or when they are evaluating the lives of others, even with no specifically moral question – no question of obligation or duty, for example – in mind. As a general thesis about what makes a life better, however, the experientialist thesis becomes morally significant by virtue of the fact that the quality of people's lives is one of the things that moral argument must take into account.

Things are quite different with a preference-satisfaction view. Whereas the idea that pleasure, or happiness, is the thing that gives all other self-interested aims their value has at least some plausibility,

3   John C. Harsanyi, "Morality and the Theory of Rational Behavior," in A.K. Sen and B. Williams, eds., *Utilitarianism and Beyond* (Cambridge University Press, 1982), pages 39–62. The quoted passage is on page 55.

it is not plausible to claim that all of an agent's specific ends derived their value from the fact that they would satisfy preferences. Individuals do not, on the whole, take the fact that they have a certain preference to be a ground-level reason for doing or choosing one thing or another. More commonly, people prefer one outcome or course of action for a reason, and this reason, which is the ground of preference, is also the ground of choice. For example, a person may prefer eating fish to eating calf's liver because he finds the taste of liver disgusting. Someone else may prefer not to eat meat at all because she believes that the practice of killing animals for food is morally indefensible. A third person may prefer one painting to another because of its subtle and intriguing use of figure–ground relationships. These examples illustrate what I take to be the standard case: Preferences are typically supported by reasons, reasons that may refer to pleasant or unpleasant states of the observer but may also refer only to features of external objects or states of affairs that are taken to be valuable.

It might be argued that if we pursued the matter further we would find that these preference-grounding reasons are themselves grounded in further, more basic preferences, such as a preference not to experience nausea, a preference to do what is morally right, or a preference for paintings with novel compositional features. Even if these preferences can be correctly attributed to the agents in question, however, the fact that they have these preferences is not something that the agents themselves are likely to cite in their own processes of deliberation. In some cases, such as that of the moral vegetarian, the fact of personal preference would seem simply irrelevant. Although an observer might explain her action by saying, "She prefers to do what she thinks is right," she herself, if she takes morality seriously, could not take this to be her most basic reason for avoiding meat. In other cases, referring to the fact of preference is merely unhelpful. To ask, "Do I prefer X or Y?," is too close to asking, "What shall I decide?" for the answer to be of much guidance in reaching a decision. The more helpful question is, "Why should I prefer X? In what way would it be better?"

From an individual point of view, then, things are normally not valued because they are preferred but, rather, preferred because they are judged desirable for some other reason.[4] This point applies as well to the idea of what makes a life better from the point of view of the person who lives it: What *makes* a life[5] better from an individual point of view is not that it satisfies that individual's preferences but rather that it contains those things that the individual takes there to be reason to want. These reasons, rather than the fact of preference itself, provide the ground of value from the individual's point of view.

Now consider Harsanyi's claim that "in deciding what is good and what is bad for a given individual, the ultimate criterion can only be his own wants and his own preferences." If Harsanyi were claiming that it is a person's wants and preferences that *make* things good or bad for that person, then he would be saying something that appears on reflection to be false. There is, however, a more plausible reading of his principle of Preference Autonomy, which takes it to be making the moral claim that when we must decide what is good or bad for others, for the purposes, for example, of making decisions about the use of public resources, we should take those people's wants and preferences as our ultimate standard even though these are not what makes things good and perhaps – I will return to this in a moment – even though these wants and preferences may sometimes be mistaken. This moral

---

[4]   The idea that this way of thinking is not only common but rational is entirely compatible with the thesis that a rational individual should act so as to maximize his or her expected utility. This thesis does not assert that people should in general decide what to do by estimating the utility of the available alternatives, or that they should take utility maximization to be their most basic reason for choosing one course of action over another. It asserts only that the preferences of a rational person will satisfy certain axioms, and that when this is the case there will be a mathematical measure of expected preference satisfaction such that the individual will always prefer the alternative to which this measure assigns the greater number. In short, a rational individual will choose as if seeking to maximize this quantity, but nothing is said about the actual reasons for these choices.

[5]   Another way in which the preference-satisfaction view differs from experientialism is relevant here. States of consciousness occur at specific times and change over time, but it is at least coherent to suppose that we might determine the quality of a life by summing up the amount of desirable consciousness that it contained. Preferences also occur at a time and change over time, but as Richard Brandt has argued, the fact that the preferences a person has at different times often conflict with one another means that a simple process of summing up the degrees to which all of these preferences are satisfied fails to produce a plausible conception of how well that person's life has gone. See *A Theory of the Good and the Right* (Oxford University Press, 1979) Chapter 13. This problem, which I cannot discuss here in detail, is further evidence for the moral character of the preference-satisfaction view: The impulse behind that view is the idea that we should give a person a say about what should be done; experientialism, on the other hand, provides a way of figuring out what would be good for that person.

reading is supported by the reference to autonomy in the name of the principle, which suggests that it is intended as a rejection of paternalism – that is, as an affirmation of the idea that policy makers should not second-guess the wants and preferences of their constituents.

Almost as soon as he has formulated the principle of Preference Autonomy, Harsanyi proceeds to qualify it by specifying more precisely the class of preferences that are to be considered in defining a social welfare function, and these qualifications further illustrate the moral ideas that shape his overall theory. To begin with, the individual utility functions that are relevant for purposes of social justice are based on individuals' "personal preferences," as opposed to their "moral preferences," which include their views not only about their own well-being but also about social justice and the rights and welfare of others.[6] The preference utilitarianism that Harsanyi is expounding is itself a view about social justice. It therefore does not propose to give every competing view equal standing. What is to be given equal respect, on this view, is each individual's way of estimating his or her own welfare, considered apart from that individual's moral beliefs.[7]

Also excluded from the determination of the individual utility functions relevant for purposes of social justice according to Harsanyi are "antisocial preferences such as sadism, envy, resentment and malice." These utility functions are supposed to define the kind of goodwill toward members of society that utilitarianism requires us to have. "But no amount of goodwill to individual X can impose the moral obligation on me to help him in hurting a third person, individual Y, out of sheer sadism, ill-will or malice." These feelings are in conflict with the idea of moral community on which utilitarianism is based and consequently have "no claim for a hearing when it comes to defining our concept of social utility."[8]

6   Harsanyi, page 47.
7   This reason for excluding the degree of fulfillment of individuals' moral views from estimates of their well-being is not peculiar to Utilitarianism or to Harsanyi's theory. On the contrary, it is widely shared. Rawls, for example, would not include opportunities to put one's own theory of justice into practice as part of his list of "primary goods." For both Harsanyi and Rawls this is a way of avoiding a possible commitment to an unrealistic conception of neutrality.
8   Harsanyi, page 56. Here again, the move is not peculiar to utilitarianism. Rawls also holds that conceptions of the good that are in conflict with justice have no claim on us. (See *A Theory of Justice*, pages 31, 450.) My purpose here is not to criticize Harsanyi's view but rather to make clear the way in which ethical concerns shape the conceptions of individual well-being that are employed in theories of social justice.

Let me refer to these two qualifications taken together as Harsayni's response to the question of "Scope" – that is, to the question, "Of the many goals and aims that individuals have, which are the ones whose degree of fulfillment should be taken into account for purposes of arriving at judgments of well-being within a theory of social justice?" It is worth noticing that in one important respect these qualifications do not run contrary to the basic moral idea of preference autonomy as Harsanyi stated it. His statement of that idea ran: "*In deciding what is good and what is bad for an individual,* the ultimate criterion can only be his own wants and his own preferences."[9] The reasons I have offered for excluding "moral" and "antisocial" preferences from the determination of individual utility functions are not strictly inconsistent with this principle, because they do not assert that the fulfillment of these preferences is not good for the individuals in question. All that is asserted is that these preferences "have no claim on us" – that is, on society – for their fulfillment. Denying that they have such a claim need not involve "telling people what is good for them" – it represents a moral judgment, not a judgment of value that is in conflict with theirs.

Harsanyi's final qualification is in more direct conflict with the principle of Preference Autonomy, however. Within the sphere of those personal (as opposed to "moral") preferences that are not "antisocial," what we are supposed to take into account, according to Harsanyi, is not a person's "manifest" preferences – that is, those manifested in observed behavior – but rather his or her "true" preferences – that is, "the preferences he *would* have if he had all the relevant factual information, always reasoned with the great possible care, and were in a state of mind most conducive to rational choice."[10] Because taking these "true" as opposed to "manifest" preferences as the basis for social decision-making can involve second guessing a person's own opinion about what is good or bad for him or her, this qualification involves a clear departure from "preference autonomy." Why, then, does Harsanyi make it? He does not say very much on this point, but it seems reasonable to suppose that he introduces the notion of "true" preferences as a response to the following problem, which I will call the problem of Malleability.

[9]   Harsanyi, page 55, emphasis added.
[10]   Harsanyi, page 55.

Individual preferences are notoriously sensitive to the background of information and experience within which they are formed. We can imagine a situation where governmental policies are entirely in accord with what the people living under them currently prefer, and where this is the case because those policies, pursued over time, tend to produce exactly these preferences. Saying this need not amount to a condemnation of that situation: For all I have said, it might be positively ideal. The problem is that not enough has been said to justify this conclusion: It is also true that for all that I have said, things might be perfectly horrible even though the unfortunate citizens are prevented from realizing that this is so. In order to know which of these is the case, we need to know more about the situation. One thing that we might know is more about how the preferences in question were formed. Were the citizens deprived of relevant information? Were they subjected to "brainwashing" or other forms of manipulation? Unless we can answer these questions in the negative, the fact that the government's policies satisfy prevailing preferences does little to make them seem justified. Harsanyi's claim that it is true rather than merely manifest preferences that form the basis for the appraisal of social policy can be seen as one way of responding to this problem.

The conflict between the principle of Preference Autonomy and the move to "true" preferences reflects a fundamental moral tension, not just an inconsistency in Harsanyi's theory. On the one hand, there are good moral reasons for taking seriously other people's assessment of their own good, and these reasons apply with particular force to public officials. The principle of Preference Autonomy is meant to give these reasons their due. On the other hand, the moral justification of a policy must be concerned with the good of the people affected by it, and the problem of Malleability arises from the uncertainty of the relation between "manifest" preferences and a person's good. Moving to "true" preferences would remedy this insofar as "true" preferences can be expected to reflect a person's good even if they do not determine it.[11] But this move would involve considerable sacrifice of the values that the principle of Preference Autonomy was

[11]   I discuss this point in more detail in my paper, "Value, Desire and Quality of Life" (presented at the WIDER Conference on Quality of Life in Helsinki in July, 1988, and to be published in a volume edited by A.K. Sen and Martha Nussbaum).

supposed to protect. I will argue later that there is a better way to deal with this problem.

This, then, is the framework of Harsanyi's argument as I would reformulate it. The aim is to find a way of characterizing and comparing the levels of well-being of different individuals for the purpose of making judgments of social justice and in general for assessing social policies. Harsanyi wants to find a solution to this problem that satisfies the following moral constraints. The first is a requirement of Neutrality: We must respect the differences in individuals' conceptions of what makes their lives go better. Second, we need to give a morally defensible answer to the problem of Scope. Third, we need a way of dealing with the problem of Malleability.

Stated in this general form, these constraints are not distinctively utilitarian. Rather, they represent a moral position that many liberals would share, though they might differ over how these constraints are best interpreted. Harsanyi's claim is that if we are looking for a conception of individual well-being for use in an account of social justice that best satisfies these liberal aims – that is, that realizes most fully the aim of Neutrality while dealing satisfactorily with the problems of Scope and Malleability – then we should identify a person's well-being with the degree to which his or her true, personal, non-antisocial preferences are satisfied. This then leads Harsanyi to a particular conception of the relevant process of interpersonal comparison of well-being.

The particular details of Harsanyi's theory make it unique among preference-satisfaction views, but it nonetheless serves to illustrate the general fact, common to views of this type, that the choice of preference satisfaction as a standard of well-being, and the definition of a particular version of this standard, are decisions shaped largely by moral considerations, not merely by ideas about individual good. Bearing this in mind, I will now return to consider the form that the problem of interpersonal comparisons takes when a preference-satisfaction view of individual well-being is adopted.

5. Suppose that we have, for each individual, a complete ranking of alternative social states. In order to correlate these rankings (or the von Neumann–Morgenstern utility functions derived from them) in a way that would confer interpersonal significance we would need to establish, for each pair of individuals i and j, equivalences of the following type:

(IC) It is just as good (no better and no worse) to be an individual with i's preferences in circumstances A as to be an individual with j's preferences in circumstances B.[12]

The problem is how judgments of this type are supposed to be understood. Harsanyi's idea of Preference Autonomy seems to require that in making such a statement we are not supposed to rely on our own personal preferences but only on the specified preferences of the affected parties. Arrow, in his brief remarks[13] about "extended sympathy," suggests that this is possible because by bringing the individual's preferencess into the states that are to be evaluated we have factored out the basis of any possible disagreement, and that the resulting judgments must therefore be ones on which all individuals would agree. But even supposing that there is no difficulty involved in evaluating circumstances A on the basis of individual i's preferences and evaluating circumstances B on the basis of individual j's, how are we to understand the *inter*personal judgment that (IC) asks us to make? I can see three possible interpretations of these judgments.

The first takes these judgments literally as judgments of *value:* It is no better, no worse, but an *equally good* thing to be an individual with i's preferences in circumstances A as to be an individual with j's preferences in circumstances B. This interpretation makes perfectly good sense – there is no doubt about the possibility of making such judgments – but it is clearly incompatible with Harsanyi's principle of Preference Autonomy and with Arrow's account of "extended sympathy."

On the second interpretation, what we are to do in making judgments of the kind required by (IC) is to imagine "what it would be like" to be in the relevant circumstances while having the preferences

---

[12]   Each such judgment obviously determines an equivalence of levels, and two of these equivalences, properly chosen, determine equivalent intervals. I will therefore concentrate on judgments of type (IC). I assume that the judgments involved in establishing interval equivalences directly would involve problems of interpretation like those I am going to discuss.

[13]   See Section V of "Extended Sympathy and the Possibility of Social Choice," *American Economic Review* (1977), pages 219–225 (or Section 7 of the version of that paper published in *Philosophia* Vol. 7 (1978), pages 223–237.

in question, the idea being that once we know what this would be like we will immediately know whether one of these situations is better than, worse than, or just as good as the other (and that this is a judgment on which all will agree). This interpretation is strongly suggested by Harsanyi's discussion of interpersonal comparisons, in particularly by his suggestion that in making such comparisons we rely on psychological laws, assumed to be the same for all humans, that enable us to infer a person's psychological state from that person's objective circumstances, together with a general knowledge of his or her beliefs and preferences.[14]

As I have said, I believe that comparisons of this kind are clearly possible. The problem with this interpretation is that it represents a covert return to experientialism, because only if experientialism is correct will knowing what it would be like to be in a situation provide a basis for judging how good or bad a thing it would be to be so situated. This raises two problems. The first is that the adoption of a form of experientialism as the correct account of what makes a life good for the person who lives it is a value judgment that is incompatible with the aims of the preference-satisfaction view. The second is that the move to preference-satisfaction was supposed to provide a way of avoiding the problems of experientialism – in particular, a way of avoiding the difficulty created by the fact that there is no particular experiential state (or set of states) on which all individuals must place the same value and that can thus serve as the basis for the evaluation of all other goods. But the proposed interpretation of (IC) falls back into this very difficulty.

The third interpretation is like the second in asking us to imagine what it would be like to be a person with the specified preferences in the circumstances described. Unlike that interpretation, however, it does not ask us to draw a conclusion about how good or bad those predicaments are, but only a conclusion about how strongly the individuals in question would like or dislike their situations. (These two conclusions are different, because a person's degree of contentment with a life is clearly only one of the elements that makes that life good or bad.) This is the kind of comparison called for by the moral idea

[14]   See, especially, his discussion in Section V of "Cardinal Welfare, Individualistic Ethics, and Interpersonal Comparisons of Utility," *Journal of Political Economy* 63 (1955).

behind Preference Autonomy, according to which what we owe to individuals is not concern for the quality of their lives *simpliciter* but rather concern for the quality of their lives *as judged by their lights*.

Now it seems at first that such comparisons are clearly possible. If, for example, circumstances of type A are at the top of individual i's preference ranking, and circumstances of type B are near the bottom of j's ranking, then we would be inclined to say that i (in circumstances A and aware of this fact) would be more satisfied with her lot than j would be if he were in circumstances B (and knew that he was). But difficulties emerge when we consider in more detail what such comparisons require. The nature of the problem is clearly stated by Gibbard:

> . . . a person's level of preference for a single alternative is not fixed by the strength of his pairwise preferences between alternatives. If level of preference is to make sense at all, so that one person's level of preference for an alternative can be compared to another person's, or a person's level of preference for an alternative at one time can be compared with his level of preference for it at another time, we need to make sense of something more than a person's strength of preference at a time for one alternative over another.[15]

What might this "something else" be? It might be some information about what the individual would be willing to give up in order to change or to maintain the current position. But in order to do the job this would have to include information about how important this other thing was to that person, and hence how big a sacrifice it would be to give it up. Such information is not provided by simply knowing the place of this potential sacrifice in the agent's preference ranking. Suppose, we know, for example, that individual i would sacrifice x in order to remain in circumstances of type A, but that individual j would not give up x in order to remain in circumstances of type B. Does this mean that i cares more about A than j does about B, or only that i cares less about x than j does? On the basis of the information given there is no telling.

[15]   Gibbard, page 177.

A second possibility would be to rely on what Harsanyi[16] refers to as "verbal and nonverbal expressions of satisfaction or dissatisfaction." If *i* appears quite contented with *A*, frequently says how much she likes it, and shows no interest in looking for alternatives, and *j*, who is in circumstances *B*, frets constantly, complains loudly, and looks miserable, then it is reasonable to infer that *i* is more satisfied with *A* than *j* is with *B*. There seems to me no doubt that we do rely on evidence of this kind, but in order to see what is involved in such inferences we need to consider them in more detail. Suppose for the moment that individuals *i* and *j* are in the same external circumstances, and that whereas *i* seems quite content and certainly never complains, *j* on the other hand complains constantly and looks quite miserable. We might conclude that *i* is less dissatisfied with these circumstances than *j* is. It might be objected, however, that we have not ruled out the possibility that they are in fact equally discontent and that *j* is simply more demonstrative and more inclined to express his or her dislike of the way things are. Of course we have not ruled out this possibility, though it seems gratuitous to assume it to be the case in the absence of some information that *i* and *j* do have this general difference in psychological makeup. The objection therefore does not seem serious.

But now consider the slightly different possibility that whereas *i* and *j* have the same propensity to *express* their satisfaction or dissatisfaction with a situation, *j* is simply much harder to please than *i* and hence much more likely to *be* dissatisfied. Here again there is no special epistemological problem: Evidence from other situations can be brought to bear to support the claim that *j* does differ from *i* in this way, and in the absence of any such evidence the assumption seems gratuitous. The problem, rather, is a moral one. If *j*'s level of dissatisfaction did systematically differ from *i*'s in this way – if, for example, *j* felt greater dissatisfaction even with the states of affairs near the top of his preference ranking than *i* felt even with states that were quite far down in hers – would this, by itself, be reason to give *j*'s preferences corresponding greater weight in deciding what ought to be done? It seems to me clearly that it would not.[17] If all we have been

---

[16]   Harsanyi (1955), page 317.

[17]   I am leaving aside here (and not denying) the fact that *j*'s dissatisfaction with a state of affairs may mean that he will be unhappy if that state obtains, and therefore

given is i's and j's rankings of the alternatives (these being listed simply as A, B, and so on) together with information about how satisfied or dissatisfied they feel with certain of these alternatives, then we have as yet no way of knowing whether j's preferences have particular moral force or whether he is excessively demanding.

But what is excessive? This can be judged only by appealing to some standard other than the preference of i and j themselves – presumably to the values of the person who is making the judgment, and the defender of the preference-satisfaction view may object that this is improper. I will consider two replies to this objection.

I have interpreted Harsanyi as claiming that we can assign degrees of satisfaction and dissatisfaction to individuals simply on the basis of their preference rankings of alternatives and their behavioral manifestations of pleasure and displeasure. In particular, I have taken him to be claiming that in making these assignments we do not need to appeal to our own evaluations of the alternatives. I have so far not questioned this claim, but it is in fact quite questionable. Donald Davidson,[18] for example, has argued that we have no way of attributing preferences to others without appealing to our own notions of how good or bad certain alternatives are. As he puts it (summarizing a longer argument) ". . . the propositions I must use to interpret the attitudes of another are defined by the roles they play in my thought and feelings and behaviour; therefore in interpretation they must play appropriately similar roles. It is a consequence of this fact that correct interpretation makes interpreter and interpreted share many strategically important beliefs."[19]

This certainly seems to be correct as a claim about how we normally arrive at such understanding. In the example I presented in the previous paragraph, it was difficult to decide what to think about i's and j's preferences because the alternatives were presented in a purely abstract fashion. When we replace A, B, and so on with terms referring to familiar alternatives, however, assessment immediately

---

worse off in that respect. Under the interpretation of (IC) we are presently considering, however, j's satisfaction or dissatisfaction is being viewed not as a determinant of the quality of his life but rather as reflecting his evaluation of that life.

[18]   See his "Judging Interpersonal Interests" in J. Elster and A. Hylland, eds., *Foundations of Social Choice Theory* (Cambridge University Press, 1986), pages 195–211. Susan Hurley develops a similar argument in Chapters 4–6 of *Natural Reasons: Personality and Polity* (Oxford University Press, 1989).

[19]   Davidson, page 209.

becomes easier. This is because we can then bring to bear some common sense assumptions about how important some of these alternatives are. As Gibbard has observed,[20] for example, people understood what Patrick Henry meant when he said, "Give me liberty or give me death," because the idea of the evil of death provided them with a point of reference. They understood that he thought tyranny to be a very bad thing because they assumed that for him, as for them, the difference between a long comfortable life and a short one ending in violent death was a very great difference.

Davidson's thesis is that the use of such reference points is not simply a method that we normally use to attribute to people mental states (such as "degrees of felt dissatisfaction") that can be understood independent of these points of agreement. Rather, such areas of agreement are essential determinants of the content of the beliefs, desires, and preferences that we attribute to each other. If Davidson is correct, then there is no such thing as understanding the strength of other people's preferences without supposing that they assign the same values as we do to many alternatives. He concludes that this provides a basis for interpersonal comparison: If I cannot attribute preferences to individual i without supposing that at least many of these preferences agree with my own, and the same is true for individual j, then insofar as I understand what their preferences are I have a basis for comparing them: "The basis of interpersonal comparisons is then provided for each of us by his own central values."

My present point, however (and this is the second reply to the preference-satisfaction theorist), is that even if Davidson's thesis is mistaken and there is an intelligible notion of "degree of satisfaction" that is in principle attributable to others without appeal to our own valuations, this notion taken by itself lacks moral force. This was the point of the example considered earlier in which j was assumed to be more dissatisfied even in states near the top of his preference ranking than i was in states near the bottom of hers. This information by itself carries no moral weight: We don't yet know whether j's preferences should be given special weight or whether he is simply more demanding. If Davidson is correct, then whenever we can attribute preferences to people at all, we will always have more information about

---

[20]   In "Preference Strength and Two Kinds of Ordinalism," *Philosophia* Vol. 7 (1978), page 256.

their contents and more agreement with them about the value of these contents than this example supposes.[21] This makes it easier to assign these preferences moral weight, but this weight depends on the contents of the preferences and our assessment of them rather than on our sense of the bare strength of the person's degree of satisfaction or dissatisfaction.

This thesis about the moral force of preference satisfaction can be stated in a weaker or in a stronger form. In the weaker form it is a thesis about what is required in order to establish morally significant correlations between the preference rankings of different individuals. Such correlations cannot be established simply by equating degrees of felt satisfaction or dissatisfaction; we must rely as well on an assessment of the individuals' reasons for liking or disliking the things in question. But once these correlations have been established, this thesis permits the ranking of other alternatives in relation to these fixed points, and hence the moral importance of helping individuals to attain or avoid these alternatives, to be established entirely by the structure of each individual's preferences. The stronger thesis, on the other hand, maintains that the moral force of each preference depends on an assessment of *its* content, not merely on an assessment of the content of some other preferences in the individual's overall system.

An examination of the role of appeals to preference in ordinary interpersonal justification suggests that the stronger thesis is a better description of our normal practice. In justifying our actions and our requests to one another we normally make our case by explaining why it is that we want a certain thing rather than merely by citing the fact that we do prefer it and indicating the strength of that preference. In a situation in which there is real disagreement over what is to be done, to be willing to say only "I prefer . . ." amounts to deliberate incommunicativeness or even imperiousness. (Unless, of course, these words mean "I *just* prefer it" – that is to say, "I don't care very much or have any good reason for doing so.") Urging a serious claim in this way seems imperious[22] because it amounts to a refusal to lay

---

21   One consequence of Davidson's view is that it would be very difficult to justify the attribution of preferences like those that *j* is assumed to have in this example.

22   A good example of such "imperiousness" is the behavior of the central character in Herman Melville's story, *Bartleby the Scrivener*. All that Bartleby will say in response to the requests of his employer and co-workers is "I prefer not to." There is abundant evidence of the *strength* of his preferences: He literally prefers to die rather

out the reasons for one's preference so that others can understand them and can judge whether these are reasons that they are prepared to recognize generally as having a claim on them.

To summarize: We seemed to have found, in the third interpretation of the schema (IC), an interpretation of interpersonal comparisons that was both coherent and in accord with the aims of the preference-satisfaction view. If Davidson is correct, however, judgments of this kind cannot be made in a way that is independent of the values of the person making them – not because the *comparisons* are inherently evaluative but because the attribution of the preferences themselves depends on the attributer's evaluations. Even if Davidson is not correct, however, the bare notion of degree of satisfaction or dissatisfaction, considered apart from any assessment of the reasons behind it, appears to lack moral significance. (Just as, as I argued earlier, facts about preferences are not ultimate sources of reasons for an individual.)

This lack of significance results from the fact that the idea of the strength of a person's preferences, insofar as this is taken to be independent of value judgments about what there is reason to prefer, lacks sufficient connection with the idea of what is good for a person – what makes his or her life better.[23] This is the second problem created for the preference-satisfaction view by the weak connection between preference and good, the first being the problem that led Harsanyi to move from "manifest" to "true" preferences. Both problems result from attempting to satisfy the principle of Preference Autonomy – that is to say, they are the results of one way of responding to the moral idea of Neutrality. It is worth asking, therefore, whether there are other ways of responding to this idea. In particular, it is worth asking whether the judgments of relative well-being required by a theory of social justice can be made in a way that remains closer to the judgments of well-being that we odinarily make, thereby avoiding the difficulties just discussed, while at the same time providing an adequate solution to the problems of Neutrality, Scope and Malleability.

than comply with their requests, even when these are, by ordinary lights, quite modest, and there is no sign that he is any happier about dying than the rest of us would be. Nonetheless, the story remains a tale of dramatic failure of moral communication.

[23]   The importance of this connection (and of the lack of it) was urged on me by John Broome.

6. I believe that there is such an alternative, and this is to construct a more concrete conception of welfare in terms of particular goods and conditions that are recognized as important to a good life even by people with divergent values. The best known attempt to carry out such a strategy is Rawls's argument in *A Theory of Justice,* leading up to the selection of his list of Primary Social Goods as a standard of well-being. This standard has been the object of a number of criticisms that might be thought to apply more generally against the strategy I am recommending. First, it has been argued that such a list of exchange-able goods and institutional rights and prerogatives is too narrow and too insensitive to variation in individual needs to serve as an adequate measure of welfare. Second, such a list may seem ad hoc: Any particular selection of goods and conditions needs to be justified somehow, and it may seem that the search for justification must ultimately lead back to preference-satisfaction as the ultimate standard.

I believe that these objections rest on misinterpretations of Rawls's position. Leaving that issue aside, however, it is at least clear that they need not be fatal to the general strategy in question. To see why not, it is important to recognize that a conception of well-being that is adequate for a theory of justice will not be a simple notion but, rather, a fairly complex piece of moral theory. One thing that such a conception will include is a list of important ways in which a person's life can be better or worse. Some of the ingredients on such a list may be quite specific, such as health, freedom from physical pain, and security against attack. Others may be given by broader categories, such as having opportunities to develop one's capacities, being able to live the kind of life one wants with family and friends, and having a life that is not in conflict with one's moral and religious beliefs.

Such a shared conception of the important goods and bads in life responds to the requirement of Neutrality in two ways. The first is by the use of broad categories such as "religion," "family life," "career," and "development of capacities," which abstract from important differences in values. We may be able to agree that these are important elements in life even though we disagree sharply about which religion should be followed, which careers are worth pursuing, how family life should be lived, and so on. The second response to Neutrality is incompleteness: All that is claimed is that these are important ways in which people's lives can be better or worse, and that taken together, they are reasonably complete. Individuals may differ over the relative importance of the elements on this list, however, and where no consensus on such questions can be presumed, a conception of well-being of the kind I am describing takes no stand.

I have been concerned so far only with the question of what we could agree on as the most important elements in personal well-being. What I referred to earlier as the problem of Scope arises when we move to a slightly different question: What are the central elements of well-being that we could reasonably be asked to recognize as giving rise to moral claims against others or against our social institutions? Here the dependence of the notion of well-being on the larger moral theory of which it is a part (a dependence already present at the previous stage) becomes stronger.

Suppose that living in accord with one's deepest values has already been recognized as, in general, an important aspect of life. Absent some specification of the possible content of these values, however, there is no limit to costs that "living in accord with them" might impose on others. It is therefore not unreasonable to refuse to recognize the fulfillment of other people's moral values (no matter what these values may be) as something that always has an important claim on one. Acceptable principles must keep these potential demands within manageable proportions. One strategy for doing this, suggested by Harsanyi, would be to exclude the fulfillment of "moral preferences" altogether from the conception of well-being that is relevant to questions of justice. Another would be to distinguish between living in accord with one's values in one's private life (something of central importance) and putting these values into effect in ways that impose serious costs on others.

This seems to me the better strategy, but it must be admitted that deciding how best to carry it out involves answering a substantive moral question. Straightforward moral argument is required to construct and defend the relevant distinction between "public" and "private." Not only are there many ways of drawing such a distinction, but also, I suspect, there is no way of drawing it clearly and conclusively. Even among those who agree on the moral strategy I have just suggested, the idea of this distinction remains vague and is frequently in need of elucidation and open to argument.

Supposing, however, that we have formulated a conception of individual well-being appropriate for the purposes of moral and political argument, delimiting those personal interests that give rise to important claims on us and on our shared institutions, there remains the further question of how institutional responses to these interests are to be measured and how individual distributive shares are to be compared. This is the question to which Rawls's list of Primary Social Goods is one answer. I will refer to such an answer (whether Rawls's or some other) as an index. An index need not, like Rawls's, consist simply of exchangeable goods and institutional prerogatives. It might refer as well to levels of development of personal capacities, as Sen[24] has suggested, or even to states of consciousness. The avoidance of chronic physical pain, for example, might be one component in an index of well-being.

When an index is viewed within the context of a larger conception of well-being of the kind discussed here, it should not be seen as ad hoc. Indices can be criticized and defended in two different ways that I will refer to as the Test of Adequacy and the Test of Practicality. An index is adequate if it accurately reflects an individual's level of access to the main means for satisfying the interests that the conception of well-being recognizes as important to human life and as relevant to a person's claims on others. An index would be inadequate if, for example, it measured only a person's holdings of one good, such as gold, that was capable of satisfying (or convertible into means of satisfying) only a limited range of interests.

The question of practicality takes account of the fact that an index of well-being is something that will be used by individuals, including legislators and other officials, in assessing institutional contributions to individual welfare. The question, then, is what kind of concern we can ask others, individually or collectively, to have for our well-being, and what kind of concern would we want them to take? Both of these questions press us, I believe, toward an index defined more in terms of objective goods, rights, and prerogatives, and less in terms of the satisfaction of variable individual preferences (provided, of course, that the test of adequacy can be met). From the point of view of potential providers, a more "objective" index has the advantage of

---

[24]   See A.K. Sen, "Equality of What?" in his *Choice, Welfare and Measurement* (Cambridge, MA: MIT Press, 1982), pages 353–372.

making the level of required contribution reasonably clear and foreseeable. Such an index also has advantages from the beneficiaries' point of view, as we can see by considering the problem of Malleability.

That problem, as it arose in our discussion of Harsanyi's view, took the following form: Satisfaction of people's "manifest" preferences is not an adequate index of well-being because there are conceivable circumstances in which these preferences might be satisfied even though the individuals' true interests were far from being served. The approach I am now describing avoids this problem, because it specifies an index of well-being not in terms of preference satisfaction but rather in terms of the availability of goods and conditions deemed important for a good life. Although this approach is grounded in a particular conception (at least a partial and abstract conception) of what makes a life better, individual autonomy is protected by the fact that the index of well-being is specified in terms of particular goods, conditions, and opportunities: Governments are required to make these things available to people; what they do with them is their own business. At this point, a version of the problem of Malleability can arise again, because the degree to which having these goods and opportunities will promote a person's good will depends on the degree to which that person has the wisdom to use these things well. This problem can be addressed by requiring the index to include the presence of background conditions such as education, access to information, and so on, which provide favorable conditions for developing values and preferences and for putting them into effect in shaping one's life.

This response to the problem of Malleability strikes me as preferable to the alternative, suggested by Harsanyi, of saying that social institutions and policies are to be measured against people's "true" preferences – that is, against what they would prefer if fully informed, reasoning correctly, and so on. Accepting this as the standard of justice invites, indeed requires, governments to attempt to estimate what citizens would want if their preferences were fully informed and ideally rational. This is an invitation that I would be hesitant to issue to even the best-intentioned officials. It is much safer to require instead that citizens be provided with what are generally recognized to be favorable (or at least not obviously unfavorable) conditions for deciding what to believe and to prefer, and that they have specific kinds of opportunities to put the preferences they actually develop into practice. Decisions about what to prefer and how to pursue the satisfaction of these preferences is then left to each individual.

I do not mean to suggest that Harsanyi is complacent about the possibility of officials or others second-guessing our preferences. On the contrary, his principle of Preference Autonomy is motivated specifically by a concern to avoid this danger. What I am suggesting is that the strategy he follows is not the most promising way to do this. Because he remains committed to preferences (of some kind) as the ultimate measure of well-being, he can deal with the problem of Malleability only by moving to "true" preferences. In my view, the aims of the principle of Preference Automony are better served by moving away from preferences as the standard by which institutions and policies are measured.

It may be questioned, however, whether the conception of well-being that I have been describing actually makes this move in a fundamental way. After all, this conception begins with facts about what people prefer. Why is it not then, at base, just another version (perhaps a vaguer version) of the preference-satisfaction theory? Moreover, it may be argued that the informational needs of this account of welfare are no weaker, and perhaps even stronger, than those of the approach advocated by Harsanyi and Arrow. All that approach requires is that we be able to make, for each pair of individuals, two judgments of the type described in (IC). If an account of the kind I am advocating is workable at all, it would surely support at least this many comparative judgments. Once these judgments are made, however, we would have the basis for a more precise and complete notion of interpersonally comparable utility.

My response is that there is a difference between admitting that facts about what people prefer are relevant to an account of welfare and taking the satisfaction of some specified range of preferences to be the sole standard. Any defensible theory will do the former, but only a very special class of theories will be committed to the latter. Similarly, there is an important difference between, on the one hand, saying that individual i in circumstances A is just as well off, in the sense relevant to questions of justice, as individual j in circumstances B and, on the other, saying that this is so *by virtue of the fact that these individuals enjoy the same level of preference satisfaction*. Only the latter, stronger judgment supports a generalization from the equivalence of a pair of points on two utility scales to a comparison of other points on these scales. A judgment of the former kind need involve no commitment to preference satisfaction as the standard of relative well-being.

7. To conclude: We make "interpersonal comparisons" of at least two sorts. Some of these are comparisons of the experiential states of different people – comparisons, for example, of their degrees of happiness. Others are openly evaluative judgments about how good or bad a thing it is to be in situations of one kind or another. In each case there are philosophical problems about how we make such judgments, but little real doubt that we can in fact do so. Problems arise, however, when certain moral constraints are imposed. In order for a form of interpersonal comparisons to be morally significant, what is compared must be related to the good of the individuals in question. But a familiar moral idea of Neutrality seems to demand that the interpersonal comparisons we make in ethics not be based on our own judgments about what makes a life better for the person who lives it, all such judgments being deferred instead to the preferences of the individuals whose lives are being compared. The clash between these two moral ideas leads to an impasse. Examination of the judgments of relative well-being that figure in ordinary moral argument, and of the role of preferences in such argument, suggests that it is the latter idea that must be abandoned.

Giving up the idea that value judgments can be avoided altogether allows us to make, within moral argument, the kinds of interpersonal comparisons mentioned earlier. We can still pursue the aim of Neutrality by basing our moral arguments on a conception of the elements that are important in making a life good that is at least widely shared. The judgments supported by such a shared conception cannot be expected to yield a complete ordering of alternative social states, and the exact scope and content of the index of well-being appropriate to particular moral questions is bound to remain a subject of controversy. But the possibility of making ethically significant judgments of relative well-being – indeed the impossibility of doing without such judgments – should not be in doubt.

2. Against the taste model

JAMES GRIFFIN

1. The taste model

There are two influential models of how desire and value are related. The Perception Model gives priority to value: desired *because* valuable. That is, we judge or recognize something to be valuable and therefore form a desire for it. The Taste Model reverses the priority: valuable *because* desired. That is, given the sort of biological and psychological creatures we are, our desires come to fix on certain objects, which thereby acquire value.

Both models employ the commonplace separation of a rational side of human nature (judgment, understanding, perception) from an attitudinal side (feeling, sentiment, desire, will). One can see these attitudes either as part of a universally distributed human nature or as varying a lot between people. No doubt there is some truth in both of these views, and it is a matter of emphasis. But it is common (and, many would say, empirically plausible) to give the Taste Model the second emphasis, and I shall do that.

As these two models show, we ought to be alert to two quite different sorts of preference. Clearly, we form preferences between objects. On the Perception Model, though, I form a (derivative) preference between two options only after having independently decided on their value. No doubt some preference is like that. But on the Taste Model, desire is the basis of value. On that model I form (basic) preferences for one option over another, not derived from any independent ranking of them, just because I want the first more than the second.

The Taste Model is widespread in philosophy and, even more, in the social sciences.[1] I also think that it distorts our understanding, and

---

[1] I say something about its status in philosophy in Section 2. The following two passages represent what I take to be common (typical?) views in economics. 'Our basic theory assumes first that, for all the alternative consumption bundles he could conceiv-

I want to argue against it. But in order to be against the Taste Model, one does not have to be in favor of the Perception Model. For instance, one might instead think that there is no priority between value and desire. And one might think that the Humean distinction between reason and desire is too sharp.

2. Some of its history

Hume explains all value – aesthetic, moral, prudential – on the Taste Model.[2] He sees reason as inert, able merely to inform us of how things stand; motivation and action come only from our conative response to those things.

Kant follows Hume on prudence but emphatically refuses to do so on morality. Many think – I am one of them – that there are good reasons to reject the Taste Model for moral values. Kant's reasons are these. We all want to be happy. But what would make us happy depends upon our particular desires, interests, inclinations, and dispositions. But they are the result of such contingencies as our biological make-up, the era into which we happen to have been born, the influence of our parents, and so on. They all operate on the phenomenal level; they grow and get shaped entirely within the causal nexus. And we, so long as we are seen just on the level of desires, aims, and inclinations, are purely phenomenal selves, determined by things external to us – in Kant's term, heteronomous. What happens to us on that level is brute fact. It therefore offers no place for anything with the standing of a moral agent. We rise to the level of morality only when we manage to be autonomous, only when our actions are governed, not by contingencies, but by self-given law. To be autonomous,

---

ably face, the individual has a preference ordering. This reflects his tastes . . . from the opportunities available to him he does the best he can, best being defined according to his tastes' (P.R.G. Layard and A.A. Walters, *Micro-Economic Theory*, New York: McGraw-Hill, 1978, p. 124). 'The utility theory of choice states that the choice in any given situation depends on the interaction of the externally given obstacles [i.e., income and prices] with the *tastes* of the individual . . . The utility theory asserts, more precisely, that the tastes can be represented by an ordering according to preference of all conceivable alternatives' (K.J. Arrow, 'Utility and Expectation in Economic Behavior,' in *Collected Papers of Kenneth J. Arrow*, vol. 3, Oxford: Blackwell, 1984, section entitled 'Choice Under Static Conditions,' his italics).

  [2]   David Hume, *A Treatise of Human Nature*, bk. III pt. I.

Kant says, is 'to be independent of determination by causes in the the sensible world.'[3]

What I want to single out in this brief exegesis is that Kant is quite clearly employing the Taste Model for many prudential values (for happiness), but uses something like the Perception Model for moral values.[4] He stresses how varied persons' conceptions of happiness are indeed so varied that it is hard to see how to introduce some principled harmony between them,[5] and indeed to see how to avoid another person's compelling me to be happy on his conception of welfare.[6]

Confining the Taste Model to prudential values is widespread in contemporary philosophy. Rawls is strikingly like Kant in this respect.[7] Rawls treats our goals and aims as a matter of our psychology – in the end, the desires we come to have. When he talks about how a rational person chooses ends, this is the language he uses: A person's 'rational life plan' is the one that he would be satisfied, if he reflected properly, 'would best realize his more fundamental desires.'[8] Rawls' concern, it is true, is with a person's rational, not actual, desires, and there are important questions, to which I shall soon return, about how strong a requirement 'rational' has to be and about when it becomes too strong to be kept within the confines of the Taste Model. But Rawls seems not to leave those confines; he speaks of 'deliberative rationality' in terms of a person's learning 'the general features of his wants and ends both present and future' and 'what he really wants,' and of forms of 'criticiz-

---

[3]   *Groundwork of the Metaphysics of Morals,* transl. H.J. Paton, published with commentary as *The Moral Law,* London: Hutchinson, 1961, p. 120.

[4]   I am perhaps stretching the Perception Model in including Kant. 'Perception' suggests detection or recognition of the presence of (moral) properties, and Kant is not a moral realist. Morality, for him, is a rational requirement, and so objective in that sense, but not in the sense that there are moral 'objects' existing independently of human thought and reaction. Still, 'perception' can be taken without strain to include Kant: One perceives or recognizes a rational requirement.

[5]   'On the common saying: "This may be true in theory, but it does not apply in practice",' repr. in *Kant's Political Writings,* H. Reiss (ed.), Cambridge: Cambridge University Press, 1970, pp. 73–74.

[6]   Ibid.

[7]   For a much fuller exploration of the parallels between Kant and Rawls on these matters, see Michael Sandel, *Liberalism and the Limits of Justice,* Cambridge: Cambridge University Press, 1982, esp. Intro., but passim. Rawls himself spells out the parallels in *A Theory of Justice,* Oxford: Clarendon Press, 1972, sect. 40; he also offers corrections of Sandel's interpretation in 'Justice as Fairness: Political not Metaphysical,' *Philosophy and Public Affairs* 14 (1985), note 21.

[8]   *A Theory of Justice,* p. 417.

ing our ends which may often help us to estimate the relative intensity of our desires.'[9] In sum, our prudential values express our contingent appetitive nature; our moral values, on the other hand, express our nature as autonomous persons.

Rawls' views seem to me typical of current thought: reject the Taste Model for moral values but retain it for prudential values. The Humean tradition is still vigorous. But I doubt that the Taste Model explains prudential values either.

3. Its explanatory inadequacy: (i) In general

'Utility' is a technical term and so needs stipulation (but seldom gets much). It is also used in many different kinds of theories, and though the same term crops up in those varied contexts it is not clear that it is the same concept cropping up in them all. The conception of 'utility' needed in empirical theories (for instance, in theories of action, in the more empirical parts of decision theory and of economics) may be different from the one needed in normative theories (for instance, in moral and political theory, in welfare economics, in the more normative parts of decision theory). The conception needed in prudential theory may be different from the one needed in moral theory. The one appropriate to small-scale moral decisions may be different from the one appropriate to large-scale social decisions about distribution. I shall come back to this possible fragmentation of the notion of 'utility' at the close of the chapter.

Now the notion of 'utility' that appears in interpersonal comparisons is a fairly normative one. What we are after is comparisons of how well off people are: of their welfare, well-being, interests, quality of life. But though the Taste Model might be relevant to certain empirical theories (say, theories of motivation or action), it is not clear that it is relevant to the normative theories we are now concerned with. What relevance have peoples' *actual* desires to what is in their *interest?* One of the discouraging facts of life is that one can get what one actually wants only to find that one is not better off, and perhaps worse off. Economists are interested in *actual* desires and preferences, I think, for two reasons. First, actual desires are appro-

---

[9]   Op. cit., pp. 418–9. This, at any rate, seems to me to be the tenor of sect. 40 in particular and of the book in general.

priate to some empirical theories of behavior, but we are now interested in the more normative matter of the quality of life. Second, satisfying actual desires avoids the taint of paternalism; it grants 'consumer sovereignty.' But we must not confuse respect for autonomy with concern for quality of life. In the face of the irrelevance of *actual* desires, the common move is to shift to *rational* desires. But it is not at all clear how strong the notion of 'rational' has to become in order to give an adequate account of the quality of life. The mere fact that the term 'rational desire' still retains the word 'desire' does not show that much, or any, of the Taste Model is surviving. The very idea of a 'rational' desire is one formed by a proper appreciation of the nature of its object. But then the mere existence of a desire assumes much less importance, and recognition of the nature of the object much more. Why think that desire is left playing any more role in this revised Taste Model than it plays in the Perception Model?

Suppose, to avoid this danger, we keep the demands made by 'rational' fairly weak. We say, as Richard Brandt does,[10] that a desire is 'rational' if it survives criticism by facts and logic. That is, if we ensure that a person makes no logical errors and acknowledges all relevant facts, then, by our present definition, the desires he has are 'rational.' Brandt means 'rational' to be entirely free of value judgments, even of rich epistemological norms. To be rational, one has only to register a fact; one does not have, in some full sense, to appreciate it. So if one of my desires survives criticism by facts and logic for no better reason than that it is a stubborn one planted deep in my early childhood, or that I am not altogether in my right mind, then it is 'rational' and its fulfilment is in my 'interest.'

But is that plausible? Suppose I want always to be the center of attention. I have been told how much others resent it, how much conflict it sets up – none of which do I deny. Indeed, I spend fifteen years in psychoanalysis contemplating such facts. I am making no logical mistakes. Still, despite it all, the desire persists. It is hard to accept that its fulfillment, though perhaps avoiding some frustration for me, necessarily enhances my welfare. Is this standard for 'rational' then strong enough?

Or take John Rawls' example of the person with some crazy aim in

[10]   R.B. Brandt, *A Theory of the Good and the Right,* Oxford: Clarendon Press, 1979, p. 10, but see chs. II–VII passim.

life – say, counting the blades of grass in various lawns.[11] He accepts that no one is interested in the results, that the information is of no use, and so on. He makes no logical error. He admits that what he is doing is deadly boring, and that he could spend his time more enjoyably. In sum, we cannot begin to understand him. That, indeed, is just another way of saying that he is crazy. But it is very unlikely that we can see the fulfillment of this obsessive desire as enhancing his life – apart, that is, from preventing anxieties or tensions that might be set up by frustrating the desire. But anxiety and tension are not the point; we all recognize them as undesirable. What is hard is to see the fulfillment of the crazy desire as, in itself, improving the quality of his life. But, again, this makes it doubtful that our standard of 'rational' has become tough enough yet.

To make it tougher, though, we should have further to demote the importance of the mere fact of desire's fixing on an object. And we should have to raise the standards for *proper* appreciation of the nature of the object of the desire. The question is not whether this takes us all the way to the Perception Model, but whether it puts us at some remove from the Taste Model.

There is a stronger doubt. Does it even make sense to think that something can be valuable simply as a result of someone's desiring it? Perhaps it is too much to claim that the Taste Model covers *all* prudential values. Perhaps some things will be acknowledged to be valuable by anyone who properly takes in what they are. Still, it is a common (even common-sensical) view that other things are valuable only because seen from a personal point of view, only because somebody takes them up as a goal – call them 'personal values.'[12] Pleasure and relief of pain look valuable from any properly chosen point of view. But rock climbing or playing the piano will look valuable only from some particular points of view – though they can then look very valuable indeed. But it is doubtful that there are any such things as 'personal values.' For me to see something as of value, from any

---

[11]   *A Theory of Justice*, pp. 432–3.

[12]   Thomas Nagel makes these claims about 'personal' values. (Although his contrast between 'personal' and 'impersonal' values is not the same as my contrast between values seen on the Taste Model and those seen on the Perception Model, his 'personal' values are a subclass of values seen on the Taste Model.) See his 'The Limits of Objectivity,' in S. M. McMurrin (ed.), *The Tanner Lectures on Human Values, 1980*, Salt Lake City: University of Utah Press, 1980; and *The View from Nowhere*, New York: Oxford University Press, 1986, esp. chs. VIII–IX.

angle at all, requires my being able to see it against a backdrop of general human aims; my own personal aims are not enough. I might want to walk home tonight without once stepping on a crack in the pavement. But that is not enough for my doing it to be valuable. It might be fun for me to do it; it might stave off boredom; it might be mildly annoying for me if I fail. But fun, staving off boredom, and avoiding annoyance are values as seen from any properly chosen point of view. To see anything as valuable we have got to see it as an instance of something generally intelligible as valuable and, furthermore, as valuable for any (normal) human.

Why should this be so? It runs counter to widespread belief. One reason that we resist the conclusion is that it seems to deny plain facts about the very different things that people get out of life. But so far as I can see, it is, on the contrary, consistent with all such facts. Another reason is that we tend to overlook how central certain prudential values are to our concept of a human person or of his agency. I cannot see you as a fellow human being without seeing you as having certain aims, likes, aversions – in short, without seeing you as sharing certain basic prudential values with me. Wittgenstein and Davidson make substantially this point about language. A word has meaning only by virtue of there being rules for its use, rules that settle whether the word is correctly or incorrectly used. Wittgenstein argues that rules cannot, in the end, be satisfactorily understood except as part of shared social practices – practices that are possible only because of the human aims, interests, dispositions, sense of importance, and so on that go to make up what he calls a 'form of life.'[13] Our form of life provides the setting in which our language develops and only within which its intelligibility is possible. And a form of life seems to consist in part in a certain shared set of values. We cannot, Davidson thinks, interpret the language that others are using without assuming that we have certain basic values in common with them – that many of our aims, interests, desires, and concerns are the same.[14] Values are embodied in the language we use, which sets for us the bounds of intelligibility.

So far these arguments show at most that a certain set of values –

[13]   L. Wittgenstein, *Philosophical Investigations,* Oxford: Blackwell, 1953, sects. 19, 23, 241.
[14]   See, for example, Donald Davidson, 'Psychology as Philosophy,' p. 237, and 'Mental Events,' p. 222, both in his *Essays on Actions and Events,* Oxford: Clarendon Press, 1980.

most likely, especially basic prudential values – must be shared for there to be language, for us to be able to understand one another, for us to be able to see one another as human persons. But this is not to say that intelligibility requires our sharing all prudential values. Some important prudential values, I think, do not even have any settled term for them – in a moment I want to take up the case of what I call 'accomplishment,' which seems to me of this sort. Clearly, many persons manage to live their lives without using 'accomplishment' or any rough synonym as a value concept; many might even reject it as a value when it is put to them. None of this threatens the intelligibilities I have been talking about. But what seems to me true is not only that a basic set of prudential values is involved in the intelligibility of human persons, but also that the notion of a prudential value is: To see anything as prudentially valuable is to see it as enhancing life in a generally intelligible way, in a way that pertains to *human* life.

4. Its explanatory inadequacy: (ii) Interpersonal comparisons in particular

Just how big a problem interpersonal comparisons of utility present varies with the conception of utility in use. With some conceptions the problem is slight; with others it is great. On the Taste Model, for instance, we seem to be up against the daunting task of learning each individual's desires, calculating their intensity, and finding an interpersonal translation of the measures.

I have said that there is widespread acceptance of the Taste Model. There is also a broad consensus, within the framework of the Model, about how the comparisons work. They work, the consensus goes, by reducing interpersonal comparisons to less problematic intrapersonal ones, by appeal to a judge's own preference as to possible states of himself.[15] That is, I – supposing that I am the judge – represent two

15   John Harsanyi, Kenneth Arrow, Amartya Sen, R.M. Hare, and Donald Davidson, although they develop this root idea in different ways, all start with it. See Harsanyi, *Essays on Ethics, Social Behavior, and Scientific Explanation*, Dordrecht: Reidel, 1976, ch. 2; *Rational Behavior and Bargaining Equilibrium in Games and Social Situations*, Cambridge: Cambridge University Press, 1977, ch. 4. Arrow, 'Extended Sympathy and the Possibility of Social Choice,' *Amer. Econ. Rev. Papers and Proc.* 67 (1977); 'Extended Sympathy and the Possibility of Social Choice,' *Philosophia* 7 (1978). Sen, *On Economic Inequality*, Oxford: Clarendon Press, 1973, pp. 14–15. Hare, *Moral Thinking*, Oxford: Clarendon Press, 1981, chs. 5 and 7. Davidson, 'Judg-

personal states to myself: Say, in my shoes with my outlook on things (I should have no trouble with that) and in your shoes with your outlook (to represent that accurately I should have to know something about another person's state of mind, but let us suppose that is possible, so that we can concentrate on the comparability problem). If I can then rank these two states, I can take my indifference between them as showing them to be equal, and my preference for one of them as showing it to be higher. The judge's preference, extended beyond its normal range of operation, thus bridges the gap between persons.

But there is a problem.[16] Preference – at least on the conception of it that emerges from the Taste Model – will not do it. The conception that emerges is what earlier I called 'basic' preference – a preference formed not on the basis of some prior, independent judgment about how valuable the options are ('desired because valuable'), but one formed simply as a result of the underivative phenomenon of wanting one thing more than another ('valuable because desired'). But such basic preferences do not just happen to us as a phenomenon isolated from the rest of our psychic life; we do not observe their occurrence as we do an affliction (and as we might, for instance, certain members of that sub-class of desires, cravings). On the contrary, they are manifestations of our tastes, feelings, and attitudes.

But then how could a basic preference serve as a bridge between persons? I, as a judge, prefer the Socratic life of struggling to understand and often failing, of deep but painful personal relations, and so on, to the Fool's life of day-to-day pleasures. But *I* can form that (basic) preference because my own tastes and attitudes are there to come into play. But they must be purged; they simply distort comparison. A judge of Socratic tastes will prefer the Socratic life; a judge of Foolish tastes will prefer the Fool's life. That gets us nowhere. If we are to make headway toward an interpersonal comparison of quality of life, the relevant preference must be purged of the judge's own personal tastes, attitudes, feelings, moral views, and so on. The problem is, then, how, after that sort of purging, I can form any sort of

ing Interpersonal Interests,' in J. Elster and A. Hylland (eds.), *Foundations of Social Choice Theory,* Cambridge: Cambridge University Press, 1986.

[16]   I discuss the problem much more fully in *Well-Being,* Oxford: Clarendon Press, 1986, ch. VII sect. 2.

(basic) preference at all. What motivates the preference? After that extreme purging, all that I have left at my disposal is general knowledge of human nature and particular knowledge about individual psyches – or, more broadly, empirical knowledge generally. If one wanted to adandon the Taste Model for the Perception Model, one could also claim to have knowledge of how valuable various states are, and then preference would again be intelligible as *derived* preference. However, for the moment we are working with only the Taste Model. That is why we face a problem: If this proposal for comparability uses (basic) preference purged of any particular point of view, it looks like using preference purged of what is needed to make sense of preference.

Let us look quickly at one well-known attempt to meet the problem. John Harsanyi[17] thinks that the judge's preference is still providing the bridge, although, granted, it is preference in a rather special sense – namely, the preference the judge has when he looks at things in a certain detached way. One person's preferences, Harsanyi says, are formed by the same general causal variables that affect everyone else's. Thus, differences in preferences can be predicted, in principle, from differences in these variables. Two persons with the same biological inheritance and life history, being subject to the same general psychological laws governing the formation of desires, will end up with the same preferences. Because the utility that a judge assigns to the Socrates-state (that is, in Socrates' shoes with his outlook on things) is based on general causal knowledge of what anyone with Socrates' biological inheritance and life history prefers, the utility that all fully informed judges assign will be identical. The same holds of the Fool-state. If we call the utility that a judge would assign to his entering the one state or the other his 'extended' utility, then everyone has the same extended utility function. Therefore, although two persons' ordinary utility functions are likely to be different, their extended utility function will not be. This again gives us the favorable situation in which interpersonal comparisons are reducible to intrapersonal ones.

---

[17]   I discuss Harsanyi's solution more fully in *Well-Being,* ch. VII sect. 3. Hare has a somewhat different solution of great interest, which I discuss in 'Well-Being and Its Interpersonal Comparability,' in D. Seanor and N. Fotion (eds.), *Hare and Critics,* Oxford: Clarendon Press, 1988.

Suppose we accept that everyone's preferences are indeed determined by the same general causal variables. I might say, somewhat loosely, that if I were like you in biological make-up and life history, then I should have the preferences you have. What I should be relying upon, however, is a perfectly general causal regularity: Anyone with a certain biological make-up and life history will have certain preferences. Granting that, then with enough information about Socrates and the Fool I can come to understand the desires of each. But how do I compare their desires? There is still the gap. Harsanyi says that I, the judge, supply the bridge in my own extended preference. But Harsanyi is clinging to old talk about 'basic' preferences when he has abandoned what makes it appropriate. All that the claim that there is an extended utility function in this case means is that preferences and desires are subject to general causal regularity and that, therefore, everyone is constrained to make the same judgments about the outcome. The extended utility function is not *my* utility function. It is not, strictly speaking, a *utility function* at all. It is, rather, a psychological judgment about the strength of desires. In ranking the utilities of the Socrates-state and the Fool-state, I do not rank imagined states of me. What seems the best interpretation of the existence of a common extended utility function gives no adequate motivation for reintroducing preference. Harsanyi does not supply the solution we are looking for: an explanation of how purged (basic) preference is possible after all. Rather, it effectively abandons (basic) preference. Preference is really playing no role.

Does it matter? It might be thought that Harsanyi has still come up with a solution to the comparability problem, only not quite the one he describes, and the solution still employs (basic) preference. The solution is this. We can know how strong Socrates' desires are. We can know how strong the Fool's desires are. Now, we cannot bridge the gap by appeal to the judge's preference. But we do not need to. The mistake is to think that there is a gap to be bridged. There is not, because the judgments we can make about how strong those desires are, given general causal knowledge and facts about the particular persons, use a notion of strength from a single scale. We judge not only how strong one of Socrates' desires is compared with another, but also how strong it is absolutely – that is, on the scale of *human* desire. On the Taste Model, utility is the fulfillment of desire. If one desire is stronger than another, one utility is greater than the other. I think that if Harsanyi has a solution to the comparison problem, that is it.

But I doubt that it solves it. We come up against the problems of the last section. Even if I can determine how much someone with biological make-up *a* and life history *b* wants *c*, why should I think that that information tells me anything about the person's utility in the relevant sense – namely, interests, quality of life, welfare, well-being? We have no reason to. We should have to switch from concern with the strength of his *actual* desires to the strength of his *rational* desires. But then we do not know where that switch leaves us – in particular, whether it does not leave us well outside the Taste Model.

Also there is no solution unless we can speak coherently of relative 'strength' of desire. But 'strength' in what sense? That is always a good question to press against solutions that talk in these terms. Unless it has an answer, it is no solution. It cannot be 'strength' in the sense of felt intensity, because just how strongly we feel our desires is largely a matter of upbringing and seems to have no secure correlation with how well off we end up. You, let us say, want the last piece of cake passionately, and I, who was raised with a stiff upper lip, say merely that I would quite like it. Each of these descriptions of what we say and how we behave captures the introspectible feelings associated with our desires. But those feelings are no guide to how well off each of us would be. Nor can it be 'strength' in the sense of motivational force. Again, there is no secure correlation between a desire's actually winning through to produce action and its fulfillment's making one better off than that of any competing desire. Can the Taste Model come up with a sense of 'strength' that gives a plausible account of quality of life? Can any desire account come up with one, short of equating 'strength' with 'place in a rational preference order'? And if it makes that equation, then, to repeat, we do not know quite where we are left. We may be left outside the Taste Model and needing a very different approach to comparability.

5. One step toward adequacy

An implication of the Taste Model is that in making interpersonal comparisons, we start with one person's desires with their (possibly idiosyncratic) intensities. How do we get from this private data to public, interpersonal data? It may be, however, that some of the judgments we make about individual utility are operating with concepts, sometimes quantitative, already on an interpersonal scale. The answer to, 'How do we get to public, interpersonal data?,' may be, That's where we start. That answer already emerges from the amended version of Harsanyi's solution. It can be found in Wittgenstein's and Davidson's views of language. And in a recent paper, Davidson has developed that line of thought specifically for interpersonal comparisons of utility.[18]

Davidson argues that correct interpretation of another's speech makes interpreter and interpreted share many strategically important beliefs and values. For instance, I make your preferences and desires intelligible to myself only by fitting them, to some degree, into my own scheme of values. Because this is so, we need not, first, identify what people's desires are, and then, second, find a way of comparing them. That picture of what we have to do makes it so difficult to find any basis for their comparison that we are driven to think that we need a third step – say, some pretty strong value assumptions about justice or fairness – to get the comparison going. But the first two steps – identifying the desires and comparing them – are not separate; identifying the desires (because of the set of shared values it necessarily involves) already includes comparing them. It is true that the basis of the comparison that Davidson offers is a set of shared *values*. But these shared values are a necessary condition of intelligibility. They are not the sort of strong value-assumption that economists and decision theorists have often thought had to be resorted to in order to bring off interpersonal comparisons.

Davidson rejects one implication of the Taste Model – namely, that we need a bridge from personal to interpersonal facts. But I suspect that he accepts too much of the rest of it. He accepts, for instance, that what we compare are people's (actual) "preferences, desires or evaluations."[19] He recognizes procedures for correcting desires, but it is not clear how improved he thinks they must be in order to explain

---

[18]   Donald Davidson, 'Judging Interpersonal Interests.' For a different argument to the same conclusion – that we start with concepts that have interpersonal standing – see my *Well-Being,* ch. VII, esp. sect. 4.

[19]   Op. cit., pp. 196–7.

values. So questions arise for him to which he has, I think, no satisfactory answers.

Is the set of shared values needed for intelligibility rich enough to be the 'basis' for all interpersonal comparisons? It hardly seems so. It is likely to be limited to particularly basic values. But a lot of comparisons take us beyond those bounds. For a judge to decide whether Socrates is better off than the Fool he will have to make up his mind what accomplishing something with one's life, or achieving some understanding of one's place in the universe, add to the quality of life. The set of shared values that Davidson provides seems too meager. Can we get the rest from information about people's (actual) preferences? And how would we get from such personal data to data with interpersonal import? The old problem would crop up again, but Davidson's earlier answer would no longer apply.

Then there is the old question, 'Can one get any satisfactory account of human interests (which Davidson rightly regards as the relevant subject of comparison) out of *actual* preferences and desires?' If not, if they must be improved desires, how improved? And has Davidson any satisfactory answer to the question, 'Strength of desire in what sense?' He says that a judge must assess the interests of the two parties, "considering their own evaluations"[20] – that is, their personal

---

[20]   Op. cit., p. 197. It is clear that Davidson's topic is the interpersonal comparison of 'interests' in a different sense of the word from mine. My point is that his conception of 'interest' is not the important one for comparability. (I also find it unclear.) Davidson thinks that the choice of a conception of 'interest' is a matter that 'up to a point' may be settled by 'fiat' (p. 196). His concern, he explains, is with what persons 'are interested in, or what they value or prefer,' in contrast to 'their "true" interests, what would in some way be best for them' (p. 196). There is, I think, no single context-independent answer to the question, What is the right conception of 'interest'?, for the reasons that earlier I said that there was no one answer about the right conception of 'utility.' Davidson sometimes writes as if he has in mind a person's *actual* desires and preferences: What as a matter of fact a person is interested in. But, to repeat, there is the discouraging fact that one can get what one actually wants and be worse off. So, is Davidson talking about 'interests' in the sense that we are concerned with when we want to compare people's 'utility' or 'well-being'? And when Davidson says that he wants to discuss judgments about how well off a person is, considering that person's own evaluations (p. 197), what are we to do when, as often happens, the two elements of the judgment (well-being and actual preference) come apart? Davidson's chief example is one in which *B* and *C* both want to buy *A*'s house, and *A* decides which of them, considering their own evaluations, will end up better off getting the house (pp. 197–8). *B* and *C* both want the house to some degree, so for a comparison *A* needs to decide on the relative strength of their desires. But 'strength' in what sense? And if, to answer these questions satisfactorily, we shift from *actual* to *rational* desires, then 'rational' in what sense?

preferences, desires, attitudes, and so on. But that phrase provides no real answer to the question, 'Strength in what sense?' Davidson will have to move a long way in the direction of *rational* desires. But then he faces the question,' Once one starts, where does one stop?'

6. Further steps

Where does one stop? The answer turns largely on what standards are available to us in prudential deliberation.

There are cases that the Taste Model fits not too badly. For instance, I like both apples and pears but prefer pears. How do we explain my attaching more value to eating a pear? Well, obviously, pears taste better to me. And it is not plausible that what is going on is my perceiving that pears possess a certain feature – *tasting better* – to a greater degree than apples. What is plausible is that my liking pears more is very close to my wanting them more. And two different persons can disagree in their tastes without either's lacking perception or understanding. My preference for pears is not open to criticism (though, granted, others of my tastes might be – for lack of discrimination, experience, attention). So the direction of explanation in this case does indeed run largely from *desire* to *value*.

But other cases are very different from this one. Sometimes taste is quite peripheral, and understanding central. This seems to me true of the prudential value that one might call 'accomplishment.' Imagine what it is for someone who has frittered his life away to come to value accomplishing something with it. Accomplishment, in this rather special sense (giving one's life weight, not just frittering it away), is valuable for anyone. It is not that absolutely everyone ought to aim at accomplishment. There might be a few unusual persons who are made too anxious by any ambition for it to be worth their trying. But that would be a case of conflict of value in which accomplishment would still be a value. Nonetheless, though not everyone need aim at it, anyone failing to see accomplishment as valuable fails in understanding. Does the priority now run the other way? Here it is tempting simply to invoke the Perception Model: passively registering certain properties, seeing them as valuable, independent of human interest or aim, and the explanation now running from *value* to *desire*. But I doubt that it is as simple as that. This is not a case of perceiving facts neutrally and only then desire's coming into play to fix on an object. The perception involved seems not at all neutral: We call the value 'accomplishment,' and stipulate its sense using such terms as 'giving life weight or point.' The perception is reported in language that already picks out what we see as important, and to see something as important seems already to engage desire.

Hume was wrong to see desire and understanding (appetite and cognition, sentiment and reason) as distinct existences. It is also wrong to explain seeing something as prudentially good solely in terms of understanding. Some understanding – for instance, isolating certain features and seeing them as important – also involves elements of motivation. There is no adequate explanation of their being desirability features without some volitional element. So even though the case of accomplishment is a long way from the case of simple tastes, it does not support any sharp separation of understanding and desire. To see something as 'accomplishment,' as 'avoiding frittering one's life away,' leaves no place for desire to follow later in a subordinate place. The direction of explanation may in this case run largely in the reverse direction, from *value* to *desire*, but not exclusively.

There are many more cases to consider in which the mix between desire and understanding is different still – say, where neither dominates. But these two cases begin to show something about what is available to us for prudential deliberation. We usually start prudential deliberation by being attracted to some end that we want to understand better. You may be happy-go-lucky and not even consider doing anything special with your life, but then come upon someone whose accomplishment makes his life seem to you fulfilled in a way that yours is not. You think that you would like to start living in a way that would give your life some point and substance. But it is hard to see what sort of accomplishment would have this potent status. It cannot be bare achievement. A compulsive achiever may reach the goals he sets himself, without reaching the sort of accomplishment that we are after. The achiever may simply enjoy success in the struggle, but that, though valuable as pleasure, is not accomplishment either. In any case, bare achievements, though difficult, often lack point or substance – swallowing more goldfish than anyone else is a remarkable deed of the Guinness Book of Records sort, but itself lacks the worth that is part of accomplishment. This shows too that the development and exercise of skills, though usually satisfying, is not accomplishment either. And so on. A lot more such work would have to be done, but I shall break off there. Prudential deliberation seems to me to fall into two parts: a process of definition of the sort that I have just broken off (separation, contrast, focus) plus a judgment that the presence of *that* (what has just been defined) makes life better, though these two parts are not, in the end, separable stages.

I have whizzed through complicated subjects,[21] but I think that nonetheless we can draw a limited conclusion. Where does this leave us? My own inclination is to say that it leaves us somewhere between the Taste Model and the Perception Model. But I want to propose a weaker conclusion – at least it leaves us beyond the Taste Model.

Still, that may be doubted. What is clear is that tastes and sentiments, as such, have none of the authority that we attach to values. That is, the mere fact that my feelings prompt me to approval or disapproval would, in fact, cut no ice, even with *me*, unless I could sort my feelings into better and worse, sound and unsound. To carry the weight of values, my sentiments would have to be in some way informed, and informed in a way that makes them more than just my individual sentiments, by fitting them inside a framework of things valuable for humans generally. But, then, tastes and attitudes can improve: We accept some as more refined, sensitive, subtle than others. Perhaps there is such a thing as 'a best possible set' of them – namely, the limiting set for tastes and attitudes having gone through all improvement.

Simon Blackburn imagines a case, borrowed from Hume's essay "Of the Standard of Taste," of two persons whose evaluations diverge: a young man who prefers the tender, amorous images of Ovid, and an old man who prefers the wisdom of Tacitus.[22] Blackburn proposes that their sensibilities become better if each person recognizes and gives weight to the sensibility of the other. In this case, he thinks, the better sensibility is one that incorporates both and regards Ovid and Tacitus as of equal merit. Divergence in evaluation is prima facie

---

[21]   There is a fuller discussion in my *Well-Being*, pt. I *passim* but esp. ch. II sects. 3–4 and ch. IV.

[22]   Simon Blackburn, *Spreading the Word*, Oxford: Clarendon Press, 1984, pp. 199–202. The definition of 'a best possible set,' just above, is his; see p. 198.

reason to believe that it is wrong to maintain either of the conflicting attitudes on its own; it gives us occasion to turn two partial perspectives into a more complete one. It may, for example, find them of equal merit (as with Ovid and Tacitus), or one better than the other, or of such different merits that ranking is impossible, and so on. Widening our sensibility, Blackburn says, might end up in any of several quite different places.

Now it is true that any of these various resolutions is possible. But what determines that we accept one rather than another? The whole process of assessment, the whole mode of deliberation that is supposed to be available to us here, is left completely undescribed. So the important questions about the criticism of tastes and attitudes are not answered but ignored. When we face an attitude that diverges from our own and, following Blackburn's advice, open our eyes to this alien sensibilty, do our attitudes then just change, as a matter of brute psychological fact, and therefore become better? But what if they do not change? Or change differently for different persons? And why should this be not just change, but improvement? It is hard to find any answers in Blackburn's proposal, and we certainly need them.[23]

Take a prudential case, the one sort of example of which we have some acquaintance. Suppose the attitude of a successful sybarite clashes with that of a Socratic sort who wants to live a life of accomplishment. The sybarite is all for the pleasures of the senses; the Socratic type wants to understand something about the existence of God, the immortality of the soul, and the freedom of the will. Why think (what seems to me plausible) that the best attitude combines both? In any case, in what proportions? And why think that a certain sort of enjoyment is better, or worse, than a certain sort of accomplishment? Why think that conflicting attitudes can be reconciled, or gone beyond, at all? We have resources, I think, to answer these

---

[23]   See, e.g., his article 'Rule Following and Moral Realism' in S. Holtzman and C. Leich (eds.), *Wittgenstein: To Follow a Rule,* London: Routledge, 1981, p. 186: 'Morally I think that we profit from the sentimentalist tradition by realising that a training of the feelings rather than a cultivation of a mysterious fittingness of things is the foundation of knowing how to live.' This seems to me the dubious contrast between understanding and desire once again, helped along perhaps by an unsympathetic description of the realist position. Still, Blackburn says nothing in this paper about how one trains one's feelings. To explain this is to explain what prudential, moral, and aesthetic deliberation is like. And the explanation has the potential (realized, I think) to undercut the sentimentalist tradition.

questions; I sketched them earlier in talking about prudential deliberation. There the central notion is that of desires or attitudes shaped by appreciation of the nature of their object. The notion of 'improvement' enters through the notion of greater responsiveness to the true nature of the object. Admittedly, there is talk here of a 'true nature' and of a 'response' to it, and this may suggest that the core of the Taste Model is still intact – namely, recognition of a fact and a reaction to it. But that misses the important issue: Can the 'true nature' be described simply in natural terms?

One of the values in question is accomplishment. But as we saw earlier, it does not seem possible to give a purely natural delineation of what has this status. The prudential value that I am calling 'accomplishment' is not just an achievement; it is an achievement of the kind of thing that gives life weight or substance. To talk in terms of giving life *weight* and *substance* seems both to be necessary to fix the object to which we are now to react and, at the same time, already to embody certain favorable reactions to it. Accomplishment is of value, but not because *it* is desired, because *it* cannot be grasped as a concept without values' already coming to our assistance. The Taste Model gives clear priority to desire over value: Things are valuable because desired. But when one looks at the details of prudential deliberation, it is hard to find priority to either. This leaves the relation of understanding and desire in need of a lot of explanation. But whatever the final explanation, it seems doubtful to me that it could be anything as simple as the Taste Model would have it.

Prudential deliberation leads, I think, to some such list of prudential values as this: (1) accomplishment, (2) the components of a characteristically human existence (that is, the components of agency: autonomy, minimum material provision, liberty), (3) understanding (at least on certain basic personal and metaphysical matters), (4) enjoyment, and (5) deep personal relations.[24] It does not matter if you disagree with my list. I have not meant to go very far into substan-

[24] This list of values does not assign *enjoyment,* or any other single item, special fundamental standing: the value to which all other values can be reduced. I doubt that any substantive value has this role. But that does not mean that commensuration or maximization is an impossibility. It is just a mistake to think that commensurability of prudential values requires that there be a super substantive prudential value. All that it requires is that prudential value itself be a quantitative notion (i.e., admit of judgments as to 'more,' 'less,' 'same'), which it is. For further discussion, see *Well-Being,* ch. V.

tive prudential deliberation. I have wanted, rather, to give reasons for thinking that we should end up with some such general profile of prudential values, a chart to the various high points that human life can rise to. We all, with experience, build up such a profile of the components of a valuable life, including their relative importance. These values, if our profile is complete, cover the whole domain of prudential value.

One can acknowledge the general profile of prudential values without underrating individual differences. The values on the profile are valuable in any life; individual differences matter, not to the content of the profile, but to how, or how much, or whether a particular person can realize one or other particular value. But then they matter a great deal. We also learn how individuals deviate from the norm. For instance, one person may find accomplishment anxiety-making, and so he faces, as we do not, an unlucky clash of values. Or, being ebullient, you may enjoy things more than most persons, whereas I am depressed and enjoy nothing very much. Also the form that a value takes in different lives is bound to vary: What you can accomplish, or enjoy, in your life may well be different from what I can in mine. But all this reasoning about individual differences takes place within the framework of a set of values that apply to everyone.

This holds even of the sorts of values that the Taste Model fits most comfortably. One prudential value is enjoyment, and different persons enjoy different things, or the same things to different degrees. So we get no understanding of how well off a person is in this respect by appealing to the general profile. We have to move on to other grounds: general causal knowledge and information about particular persons. Do you enjoy wine more than I do? I need to know your powers of discrimination and your capacity for enjoyment. If I learn that your powers of enjoyment are undulled, that you have a discriminating palate (whereas I do not), and that this wine rewards discrimination, then I have my answer. Still, even with my tastes of the most literal sort, my reasoning often does not focus on me as an individual. I might make my palate as trained as yours. Should I bother? Well, most people with trained palates do not enjoy plonk less, but do enjoy most wines more. For this sort of reasoning I do not need to know what it is like in my particular skin; I need to know what makes life enjoyable and how I am placed to exploit its possibilities.

So three kinds of elements – a general profile of prudential values, general causal knowledge of human nature, and the relevant information about particular persons – make up the basis of interpersonal comparisons. The language we use in assembling our evidence already has interpersonal standing. We make judgments of the form "*A*, informed as he is, wants the thing very much. *B*, or virtually anyone, if informed, would want it the same amount; it is roughly that desirable. *C*, on the other hand, wants it less' (he, let us say, is depressed and so wants nothing very much). The quantitative phrases 'very much,' 'same amount,' and 'less' appearing in these judgments come from the same scale. These quantitative terms are not relative to other things that each of them, in his own case, wants, but relative to each other. There is no gap, so there is no need to search for the bridge. The way to remedy one deficiency in Davidson's account (that the set of shared prudential values necessary for intelligibility is not a broad enough base for interpersonal comparison) is to remedy the other (that no plausible account of *interests* can be got out of the Taste Model).

Let me return to our example one last time. What the judge needs to know is nothing about the intensity or force of Socrates' or the Fool's desires, nor anything about his own personal desires. He needs to know how desirable each of the two lives is – knowledge that can, if one wishes, be put in the language of desire: How much persons generally, when rational or informed, would want. He should have to know what various sorts of humans are capable of and the heights that human life in general can reach. Then he should have to decide how close Socrates and the Fool come to some height. What he should not particularly need to consult is their personal tastes and attitudes, nor his preferences about his landing in the one pair of shoes or the other.

It was plausible for Mill, it is true, to take as the authoritative judgment about Socrates and the Fool the *preference* of persons who have experience of both (that is, rational or informed desire). But these are not *basic* preferences, of the sort at work in the Taste Model. They are in this clear sense derivative: They are formed in the light of deliberation about the prudential values at stake. They give expression to parts of the general profile.

This may seem to make interpersonal comparisons look too easy, but that is because the Taste Model makes them look, in one respect, too hard. The Taste Model leads one to wonder: How can any judge able to think himself fully enough into Socrates' shoes to understand how well off he is also be able to think himself equally fully into the Fool's shoes; the lives are so very unlike one another that they virtually defeat finely textured comprehension by one mind. But the example of Socrates and the Fool is not meant as a comparison of, literally, their whole lives. It compares certain aspects. And those aspects can themselves be factored into elements. Let me take certain central ones. We are comparing, among other things, a life of major accomplishment with a life of short-term pleasures. It does not take great feats of imagination or especially finely textured comprehension to know what short-term pleasures are nor what it is to carry off something major in one's life. Nor does the comparison much turn on phenomenological 'feels' or fine textures. We have to do a different kind of exercise – namely, by trying to understand the values at stake (in effect, prudential deliberation), to decide what makes a life better. There are considerable epistemological problems involved, but they are not of the imagination-defeating kind presented by fine textures.

Many social scientists will resist this sort of prominence for the general profile – for ample though not, I think, sufficient reason. Some may dislike abandoning any attempt to treat interpersonal comparisons as an empirical issue. The bounds of the 'empirical' are notoriously difficult to fix, but there is a widespread use on which anything evaluative must fall outside the empirical. On this influential narrow sense (which, of course, begs all the questions about the relation of fact and value), my account clearly fails to make comparisons empirical. In contrast, if what we compare is some sort of psychological intensities of desire, then as difficult as it undoubtedly is to get reliable data about them, as puzzling as the conceptual problem has proved to be of finding an interpersonal scale between them, we at least have hope of staying within the relatively untroublesome domain of empirical truth and falsehood, narrowly conceived. It is a hope not to be given up lightly. Still, there is no getting away from the fact that what we need to compare is human *interests* or *welfare* or *well-being*. No account of interpersonal comparisons of utility is satisfactory unless it uses the relevant sense of 'utility.' Becoming irrelevant is too high a price to pay for staying (narrowly) 'empirical.'

Perhaps other social scientists are less concerned with keeping the subject empirical than with keeping it on some sort of neutral basis. Once prudential values enter, people are bound to disagree. It is hard enough to get agreement on fact; it is vastly harder on values. So there will be no agreed or accepted social basis for comparisons. But a common reason for thinking this about values is that the Taste Model still has one in its grip. If values come from personal tastes and attitudes, they are not only bound to vary but are also beyond the reach of principled convergence. Whether they are beyond that reach depends upon what critical standards are available to us in prudential deliberation. Let us suppose – in order to see how much it would settle – that there are strong critical standards: that Wittgenstein and Davidson are right that some basic prudential values are part of the ground of intelligibility, and that in general whether something is prudentially valuable is a matter of truth and falsehood in a primary, unextended sense of those terms containing some elements of correspondence with belief-independent reality.

However, even if that were so, in an important sense there still would be no agreed or accepted social basis for comparisons. There could in theory be principled convergence on prudential values. But we all know that, in practice, people's views about what makes life good are going to vary. In a liberal society, at least, disagreement is inevitable. Interpersonal comparisons of utility are a practical need. Society has to make them, we all have to be reconciled to them. Would you accept social allocation based on my very different conception of the good life?

This brings us back to a question raised at the start of the chapter. Why think that *one* notion of 'utility' will do in all theoretical contexts? I suspect that the notion we need in prudence is different from the one we need in most moral contexts, that the notion needed for moral decisions in one's personal life is different from the one needed in decisions about social allocation, and that other rather different notions are appropriate to different social allocative decisions. There are contractualist reasons for distinguishing, as Rawls does, thick conceptions of the good life from the thin conception of 'primary goods' – namely, all-purpose means to a good life on which we shall all agree – to which the state should limit itself. But there are non-contractualist reasons for much the same conclusion. There is the question of scale. I know a lot about my children. I do not, nor does anyone, nor can anyone without deplorable intrusiveness, have even roughly comparable knowledge about all the citizens of a state. I can fine-tune distributions between my children (I might know that one of them would joylessly squander any money I gave him), but I just do not know enough to do much fine-tuning of social distributions. There are the limits of prudential value theory. It does not end up with, as Aristotle thought it did, a single ideal for the human species. Lives can be lived in very different ways and still be equally good. Although I can sometimes know what would make my children's lives better, I cannot hope to know this of all citizens. So there are reasons for neutrality on the social scale between at least all respectable conceptions of the good life that do not apply on the individual scale. There is the fact that autonomy is one prudential value on the list. Even if one thought that only one conception of the good life were correct or right or true, one's respect for autonomy would require one to endorse a fair measure of social neutrality on the subject. There is the question of function. To give you a present I should find out your tastes; goverments are not in the business of giving presents but, in the main, of enhancing the possibility of solutions to cooperation problems. Doing that involves creating, defending, and improving social institutions. For the most part, a government's concern is the general framework of its citizens' lives. And there is the question of political good sense. Governments meet the need for social stability by generally steering clear of contentious issues.[25]

So there are various reasons for thinking that a narrow notion of utility is appropriate on the social scale. I doubt that they make up a case for total neutrality: So long as governments do not become too contentious, they can – and rightly do, I think – go beyond all-purpose means. But governments will generally compare different citizens' utility by appealing to things that it is assumed they all value.

The worry about there being no agreed or accepted basis for comparison is a worry about how to meet a social need, not an objection to any proposals about the nature of interpersonal comparisons. If there is to be a solution to the comparison problem, it has to work on

---

[25]   I discuss grounds for neutrality, and my reasons for preferring the noncontractualist ones, in *Well-Being*, ch. III sects. 5 and 7, ch. IV sect. 5, ch. VII sect. 6, ch. IX sect. 3.

all levels: smallest-scale personal, largest-scale social, and the levels in between. Contractualists have a plausible solution on the large social scale: They have an agreed basis for comparison in primary goods, and they have no need to find an interpersonal bridge because primary goods are already in the interpersonal sphere. But because this solution is not transferable to other levels, it lacks the generality that a solution to the comparison problem needs. We have to make comparisons on all levels; we want to understand what goes on in each of them.

3. Utilitarian metaphysics?

JOHN BROOME

Section 1

I am going to make some comparisons between interpersonal comparisons of good and intrapersonal intertemporal comparisons of good. I shall set them in the context of formal theorems that connect together these different dimensions of comparison. I hope to shed some light on the foundations of utilitarianism. Not all of utilitarianism, though; only this one part:

The Utilitarian Principle of Distribution. One alternative is at least as good as another if and only if it has at least as great a total of people's good.

Briefly: Good is the total of people's good. Utilitarians value only the total of good, regardless of whom it comes to. They do not value equality in the distribution of good. In one sense, then, they are anti-egalitarian.

It has often been suggested[1] that utilitarianism is associated with a

The argument of this chapter was first developed in an unpublished paper I wrote while I was a Visiting Fellow at All Souls College, Oxford, financed by a grant from the Economic and Social Research Council. I thank the College for its hospitality, and the ESRC for its support.

  [1] The most thorough argument to this effect is Parfit's (1984, 329–357). An article by Mirrlees (1982) makes the same suggestion, implicitly and perhaps not deliberately. Mirrlees's argument provided the stimulus for mine. On the other hand, Rawls (1974) has argued in general that moral theory is independent of metaphysical arguments about personhood. He agrees that utilitarianism may be implied by a disuniting theory of personhood. But he claims that one's theory about personhood will be determined by one's moral theory and not by independent nonmoral considerations. I think, though, that a disuniting metaphysics might be defended on nonmoral grounds, as indeed it has been by Lewis (1983c, 76–77) and Parfit (1984, Part III). So if the disuniting metaphysics can really be shown to support the Utilitarian Principle of Distribution, that will provide a metaphysical defense of the principle.

particular metaphysical theory of personhood: a "disuniting" theory that denies the full unity of a person over time. But I do not think the connection between utilitarianism and a disuniting metaphysics has yet been properly made out.[2] I hope, with the help of the formal theorems, to show how one might derive the Utilitarian Principle of Distribution from a disuniting metaphysics. I shall sketch out a line of argument, though it is far from complete. I am not committed to either the Utilitarian Principle or to a disuniting metaphysics. Deriving one from the other can serve either to support the one or to weaken the other.

Throughout this chapter, I shall speak of *good* rather than well-being or preference-satisfaction or something else. This is chiefly for the sake of generality. I want to be neutral between competing theories of what a person's good consists in. I want to talk about how goods coming at different times or to different people are compared, irrespective of what these goods might actually be. Among the competing theories of good is the theory that a person's good consists in the satisfaction of her preferences. In speaking of good rather than preference-satisfaction, I am not denying this theory, but only allowing for other possibilities as well. In speaking of good rather than *well-being,* I am allowing for the possibility of goods that cannot plausibly be counted as part of well being.[3]

I shall be concerned with how goods coming at different times or to different people go together to make up overall good. This is a matter of assessing, not just the relative magnitudes of the goods, but also their relative values or how much they count in the overall judgment. These may or may not be different things, and I do not want to preempt that issue at the beginning. *Comparing* goods suggests to me only the first task of assessing relative magnitudes. I want to include the second task too. So from now on I shall use the more general metaphor of *weighing* goods.

Sections 2 and 3 of this chapter describe the theorems and consider what conclusion can be drawn from them. Section 2 is largely a summary of a previous article of mine, "Utilitarianism and expected util-

[2] Section 6 explains why I find Parfit's argument inadequate. Schultz (1986) offers a critique of a different sort.

[3] For instance, it is plausibly good for a person to achieve literary immortality (especially if that is what she wants), but not plausibly a part of her well-being. She will be dead when it happens.

ity",[4] which deals with the interpersonal weighing of goods. Section 3 extends the argument to include intertemporal weighing too. The crucial issue turns out to be the truth of something I call "the Principle of Temporal Good." If true, this principle will give strong support, through the theorems, to the Utilitarian Principle of Distribution. Section 4 suggests that the Principle of Temporal Good is prima facie doubtful. But Section 5 argues that, nevertheless, it may be possible to defend it on the basis of a disuniting metaphysical theory. This is how I think a disuniting theory can support utilitarianism. Section 6 compares this argument with Derek Parfit's argument for the same conclusion. It argues that his is unsuccessful.

Section 2

Suppose there are h people. Suppose we are interested in prospects drawn from some set of uncertain prospects – the same set for everybody. Take the j'th person and consider her "betterness relation":

— is at least as good as — for j

where each blank is to be filled in with a prospect from the given set.

This relation will have many of the same properties as a rational preference relation. In fact, I argued in "Utilitarianism and expected utility" that j's betterness relation will satisfy the axioms of expected utility theory (when it is inserted into the theory in the place of a preference relation). I expressed doubts about one of the axioms: completeness. But I argued that the major consistency axioms of the theory, including the controversial Sure-Thing Principle, apply to this relation. I call a relation "coherent" if it satisfies the axioms of expected utility theory. So my conclusion, setting aside the reservation about completeness, is that *each person's betterness relation is coherent.*

Because it is coherent, j's betterness relation can be represented by a utility function in the manner of expected utility theory. Write this function U_j. $U_j(A)$ is at least as great as $U_j(B)$ if and only if A is at least as good for j as B. The function is unique up to positive linear transfor-

---

4   Broome (1987).

mations. And U_j is "expectational," by which I mean that the utility of an uncertain prospect is the expectation of the utilities of its possible outcomes.

Consider next the general betterness relation

__ is at least as good as __

defined on the same set of prospects. "Utilitarianism and expected utility" argued that this relation too will satisfy the axioms of expected utility theory, if we set aside doubts about completeness that arise in this context too.

These doubts are actually particularly serious for the general betterness relation. It used to be commonly claimed that interpersonal comparisons of good cannot be made. I take this to mean that one person's good cannot be weighed against another's: If, that is, A is better than B for one person, and B better than A for another, it is undetermined whether, on balance, A is better or worse than B. If this is so, then the general betterness relation is incomplete. Nevertheless, I am simply going to assume it is complete, and set aside this worry about interpersonal comparability. This is a gap in the argument. It needs to be pointed out, because it has sometimes been suggested that the theorem discussed in this section (Theorem 1) actually *overcomes* the worry: It demonstrates that interpersonal comparisons can be made.[5] Comparability, however, is an assumption of the theorem, not a conclusion.

Given that, then, *the general betterness relation is coherent.* So it can be represented by an expectational utility function U, unique up to positive linear transformations. $U(A)$ is at least as great as $U(B)$ if and only if A is at least as good as B.

In "Utilitarianism and expected utility" I also argued for this:

Principle of Personal Good. If two prospects are equally good for everybody, they are equally good. And if one prospect is at least as good as another for everybody and definitely better for somebody, it is better.

[5] Harsanyi seems to suggest this (1977b).

The following theorem can then be proved[6]:

Theorem 1. Suppose the general betterness relation is coherent, and so is each person's. And suppose the Principle of Personal Good is true. Then the general betterness relation can be represented by a utility function U that is the sum of utility functions $U_1 \ldots U_h$ representing the people's betterness relations:

$$U(A) = U_1(A) + \ldots + U_h(A) \quad \text{for all prospects } A$$

Remember that there are many utility functions representing a person's betterness relation, each a positive linear transform of the others. Theorem 1 says you can pick one function for each person, out of all her functions, in such a way that the total of all the functions you pick represents the general betterness relation.

Because the assumptions of this theorem can be supported by argument, its conclusion deserves some credence. And at first sight it looks like the Utilitarian Principle of Distribution. It seems to say that good is the total of people's good.[7] But actually we are not – or not yet – entitled to draw this inference from the theorem. The theorem says that general utility is the total of individual utilities. And an individual's utility is defined to represent her betterness relation. But it is defined only to represent the *order* of betterness for her: Of two prospects, the one with the greater utility is better for her. Utility does not necessarily represent the *quantity* of her good. But unless it does, Theorem 1 says nothing about the total of people's good.

However, it can be argued that utilities do indeed represent quantities of good. If this can be established, then Theorem 1 will genuinely support the Utilitarian Principle. So let us pursue this argument. Theorem 1 itself can contribute to it. But first let us see what can be said independently of Theorem 1.

If a utility function represents a person's betterness relation, then so does any positive linear transform of it. So the most that can be expected of a person's utility function in general is that it should be a

---

6 The first proof was Harsanyi's (1955). There is a rigorous version of Harsanyi's proof in Fishburn (1984). Proofs within different versions of decision theory include Broome (1990) and Hammond (1983).

7 Harsanyi (1977a) claims that the theorem directly supports utilitarianism.

positive linear transform of her good. The characteristic of a positive linear transformation is that it preserves the ratio of differences. Take any four prospects A, B, C, and D, which give person j these quantities of good: $G_j(A)$, $G_j(B)$, $G_j(C)$, and $G_j(D)$. Then the most that can be expected in general from j's utility function U_j is that the utility difference $\{U_j(A) - U_j(B)\}$ should bear the same ratio to $\{U_j(C) - U_j(D)\}$ as the difference in good $\{G_j(A) - G_j(B)\}$ bears to $\{G_j(C) - G_j(D)\}$.

Do utilities represent quantities of good to this extent? Take an example (Table 3.1). Suppose the person is faced with a choice between two uncertain prospects. One gives her equal chances of getting ten units of wealth or fourteen units; the other, equal chances of five or twenty units. In the table, the alternatives are:

Table 3.1

States of nature (equally likely)		States of nature (equally likely)	
H	T	H	T
10	14	5	20
Prospect A		Prospect B	

Suppose, say, that the utility difference $\{U_j(10) - U_j(5)\}$ happens to be the same as $\{U_j(20) - U_j(14)\}$. Does it follow that $\{G_j(10) - G_j(5)\}$ is the same as $\{G_j(20) - G_j(14)\}$?

The utilities are defined to represent the order of goodness. So they tell us which of A or B is the better prospect for the person. The expected utility of A, $\{U_j(10) + U_j(14)\}$, is equal to the expected utility of B, $\{U_j(5) + U_j(20)\}$. Therefore, A and B are equally good for the person. The judgment between the two can be looked at this way. It is a matter of weighing against each other the possible loss from ten units to five units in state H against the possible gain from fourteen units to twenty units in state T. Because $\{U_j(10) - U_j(5)\}$ is equal to $\{U_j(20) - U_j(14)\}$, the loss counts exactly as much as the gain.

So A and B are equally good for the person. The question is, again, does it follow that $\{G_j(10) - G_j(5)\}$ is equal to $\{G_j(20) - G_j(14)\}$?

It *would* follow if it were necessarily good for a person to maximize the expectation of her good. Then A, being equally as good for the person as B, would necessarily have the same expectation of good. That is, $\{G_j(10) + G_j(14)\}$ would necessarily be equal to $\{G_j(5) + G_j(20)\}$. Hence, $\{G_j(10) - G_j(5)\}$ would necessarily be equal to $\{G_j(20) - G_j(14)\}$. But it is quite plausible that it is not necessarily good for a person to maximize the expectation of her good. For one thing, good may not even be an arithmetic quantity, so there may not even be such a thing as the expectation (in probability theory's sense) of the person's good. And second, even if good is an arithmetic quantity, it may be good for a person to be risk-averse about her good. A is less risky than B, and this may make it as good as B even if its *expectation* of good is less. It is perfectly possible, that is, even though A is as good as B, for its expectation of good $\{G_j(10) + G_j(14)\}$ to be less than B's expectation of good $\{G_j(5) + G_j(20)\}$. If so, then $\{G_j(10) - G_j(5)\}$ will be less than $\{G_j(20) - G_j(14)\}$. Utility will not then be a positive linear transform of good.

But there is a plausible retort to this argument. It might be said that it is precisely in comparisons of the sort we are making that the notion of quantities of good gets its meaning. In assessing alternatives in the face of uncertainty, possible gains and losses are weighed against each other. In the example, the possible loss in wealth from ten units to five is weighed against the possible gain from fourteen to twenty. We know the former counts the same as the latter in determining which of the alternatives is better. This would be naturally expressed by saying that the difference between ten units of wealth and five amounts to the same as quantity of good as the difference between twenty and fourteen. In the previous paragraph I said that the difference in good between ten units of wealth and five might actually be less than the difference in good between twenty and fourteen. But what can this mean, if it is not that it counts less in determining which alternative is better? I would have to say that the difference in good *is* less, but it *counts* the same in determining the relative goodness of the alternatives. But it looks like an empty gesture to maintain a distinction between quantities of good and how much these quantities count.

I think this is a good retort. It is hard to see what use we can have for the notion of quantities of good except when weighing up differences in good in assessing alternatives.[8] So it is in weighing up differences that we can expect the notion to get its meaning. Uncertainty, however, is not the only context in which differences in good are weighed against each other. Perhaps the notion gets its meaning elsewhere. Another context is the distribution of good between people. Let us consider that.

Suppose we have to compare these two distributions of wealth for two people (Table 3.2):

Table 3.2

People		People	
1	2	1	2
10	14	5	20
Distribution *A*		Distribution *B*	

In favor of *A* is that it gives the first person ten units of wealth instead of five. In favor of *B* is that it gives the second person twenty units instead of fourteen. How should these conflicting considerations be weighed against each other? That is what Theorem 1 is about. It says that we can find the right weights from the people's utility functions. To do so, we have to make sure that for each person we have picked the appropriate utility function. Each person has many functions representing the order of her good, each an increasing linear transformation of the others, and the theorem gives no guidance about which is the right one. But it does say there is a right one. (Remember, it is an assumption of the theorem that the people's good can be compared in the first place.) And once we have it, differences in utility determine the weights that should be given to opposing considerations. In the example, once we have

---

[8] I am not appealing to a verificationist theory of meaning. Verificationism has been influential in economics. "Utility" has often been said to be meaningless except insofar as it represents *choices*, because only choices make it empirically verifiable (for example, Arrow 1973, 104). That is not what I am saying. I am not saying: Weighing differences in good gives the notion of quantities of good its meaning because it makes the notion empirically verifiable. It does not do that anyway. The result of weighing differences in good is a judgment that one or the other alternative is better, which is not empirically verifiable. I am simply appealing to a general and obvious connection between meaning and use.

functions U_1 and U_2 for the people, we compare $\{U_1(10) - U_1(5)\}$ with $\{U_2(20) - U_2(14)\}$. If the former is greater, distribution A is better; if the latter, B. This is a context where differences of good are being weighed. So according to what I said earlier, it gives us grounds for saying that these differences of utility represent differences in quantities of good. Suppose $\{U_1(10) - U_1(5)\}$ is greater than $\{U_2(20) - U_2(14)\}$, so A is better. Then we have grounds for saying that person 1 gains more in good from having ten units of wealth instead of five than person 2 gains from having twenty units instead of fourteen. Because the same utility functions supply the right weights in any distributional comparison, we have grounds for saying that these functions represent quantities of good.

But these grounds are unlikely to convince a nonutilitarian. They beg the question. They insist that when comparing the goodness of alternatives by weighing differences in good, the greater difference must always be the one that wins. The greater difference always counts more in the comparison. But this simply assumes that the better alternative is always the one with the greater total of good. And that is what has to be proved.

The strength of the utilitarian case, however, is this. The functions U_1 and U_2, which supply the weights when comparing the goodness of alternative distributions of wealth, are utility functions for the people. By their definition, therefore, they represent the order of goodness for the people of uncertain prospects. So they *also* supply the weights when comparing the goodness of alternative prospects in the face of uncertainty. These functions, then, serve the same purpose in two contexts. This very much strengthens the claim that they represent quantities of good. This is the effect of Theorem 1. This theorem provides a strong case for saying that utilities represent quantities of good. And having done so, it also says that the better of two alternatives is always the one with the greater total of good.

The answer to the nonutilitarian's objection is this. The objection relies on a distinction between quantities of good and how these quantities count in determining the goodness of alternatives: Utility tells us how good counts, but it may be distinct from good itself. We have, though, been shown no way of assigning meaning to quantities of good apart from how they count. And without that, the distinction now seems emptier than ever.

But that is not the end of the argument. All the nonutilitarian needs to do is supply a way of assigning meaning to quantities of good. What she needs is a *another* context in which differences of good are weighed against each other. The one to turn to, I think, is the weighing up of goods that come at different times in a person's life. The good in a life may be distributed across time in different ways. It may be spread evenly or unevenly, or it may come early or late. In comparing the goodness of different possible lives, good at one time has to be weighed against good at another. Perhaps this is where quantities of good get their meaning. So now I turn to these intertemporal weighings.

Section 3

Suppose there are a number of "times," say T altogether.[9] For some person j and time t consider the relation

___ is at least as good as ___ for j at t

where each blank is to be filled in with a prospect from the same set as before. It is natural to be dubious about the existence of dated bet terness relations like this. But we do often speak of how good things are for a person at one time or another. For instance, we might say that a vaccination is bad for you at the time it is done because it makes you sick for a while, but it is good for you in the long run. To be sure, we might be a little reluctant to say it is bad for you at the time. If we think it is actually good for *you,* that may make us reluctant to say it is bad for you at any time. But I think this reluctance is easily overcome. There is really no difficulty in recognizing that the vaccination may be bad for you at one time, even though the badness may be outweighed by a greater benefit later. So I think there is no real difficulty in recognizing the existence of dated betterness relations.

Furthermore, the arguments that show the coherence of the individual and general betterness relations apply to dated betterness rela-

---

[9]   The number of times has to be finite if the existing proofs of Theorem 2 are to work. I do not assume that everyone is alive at all times. It may be that all prospects are equally good for a person at all times when she is not alive, but I do not assume that either.

tions too.[10] There is, once again, a reservation to be made about completeness. But apart from that, *each dated betterness relation is coherent.*

The real worry over dated betterness relations is not, I think, whether they exist, but whether they capture all that is good or bad for a person. The claim that they do is expressed in this:

> *Principle of Temporal Good.* If two prospects are equally good for a person at every time, they are equally good for her. And if one prospect is at least as good as another for the person at every time and definitely better for her at some time, it is better for her.

This principle is the main subject of this chapter. I shall consider arguments for and against it. But first I want to explain its importance.

A simple reinterpretation of Theorem 1 gives us:

> *Theorem 2.* Suppose a person's betterness relation is coherent, and so is each of her dated betterness relations. And suppose the Principle of Temporal Good is true. Then the person's betterness relation can be represented by a utility function U_j that is the sum of utility functions $U_{jL} \ldots U_{jT}$ representing her dated betterness relations:

$$U(A) = U_{jL}(A) + \ldots + U_{jT}(A) \qquad \text{for all prospects } A$$

Putting Theorems 1 and 2 together gives us:

> *Theorem 3.* Suppose the general betterness relation is coherent, and so is each person's dated betterness relation, and so are all of each person's dated betterness relations. And suppose that both the Principle of Personal Good and the Principle of Temporal Good are true. Then the general betterness relation can be represented by a utility function U that is the sum of utility functions U_j representing each person's betterness relation. And each of these in turn

---

10   This needs better justification than I can give it here. My argument in favor of coherence appears elsewhere (Broome 1991b). It is conducted in terms of reasons, and the reasons could be confined to reasons directed toward the good of a person at a time. The argument would still work, and would then show the coherence of the person's dated betterness relation.

is the sum of utility functions U_{jt} representing the person's dated betterness relations:

$$U(A) = U_L(A) + \ldots + U_h(A)$$
$$= U_{11}(A) + \ldots + U_{1T}(A) + \ldots + U_{h1}(A) + \ldots + U_{hT}(A)$$

for all prospects A.

The various betterness relations are, I claimed, coherent, setting aside doubt about their completeness. And I claimed that the Principle of Personal Good is true. So the truth of the conclusions of these theorems turns on the Principle of Temporal Good.

Suppose the conclusions *are* true; what would that tell us? It would tell us that the same utility functions determine how differences in good weigh against each other in *three* different contexts: across time within a life, across people, and across states of nature when there is uncertainty. That would follow from a simple extension of the arguments in Section 2. And it would make it very hard to resist the conclusion that these functions represent quantities of good. I can think of no other context where the notion of quantities of good could get its meaning. Whenever there is weighing up to be done, according to the theorems, the total of utility always determines what is best. The same utilities always determine how much good counts in every context. In these circumstances, it would be impossible to maintain the distinction between good and how much it counts. Utility would represent quantities of good. And, given that, the best alternative would always be the one with the greatest total of good. This Utilitarian Principle of Distribution would be irresistible.

So if the Principle of Temporal Good is true, that will give very strong support to the Utilitarian Principle. That is the significance of the Principle of Temporal Good. Sections 4 and 5 consider whether it is true.

This conclusion, notice, is derived from considerations of *meaning* only. The Utilitarian Principle looks like a substantive and important principle that is, in one way, opposed to egalitarianism. But the effect of this argument in its defense is to make it much less important. The argument concludes, in effect, that the notion of a quantity of good acquires its meaning in such a way that it turns out to be best to maximize the total of people's good. I think there is a lesson to be learned from this. The substantive and important questions about equality will be to do with equality in *income* or resources or other things that come with a natural metric. Questions about equality in the distribution of *good* seem at first to be more fundamental. But in the end they boil down to questions of meaning. They only seem substantive if one assumes in advance a natural metric for good. I very much doubt if there is such a metric apart from the ones, derived from comparisons in various contexts, that I have considered.

Section 4

The prima facie evidence is against the Principle of Temporal Good.[11] Consider this example (Table 3.3). Imagine for simplicity that there are only two times, and compare this pair of prospects for a person:

Table 3.3

		States of nature (equally likely)				States of nature (equally likely)	
		H	*T*			*H*	*T*
Times	1	*x*	*y*	Times	1	*x*	*y*
	2	*x*	*y*		2	*y*	*x*
		Prospect *A*				Prospect *B*	

---

[11]   It is easy to think of things that seem good for a person without being good for her at any particular time. One example is success. Suppose someone works to achieve some aim, and succeeds. Her success seems, prima facie, to be good for her. But it is often hard to know at what date it can be good for her. Derek Parfit's example (1984, 151) is a person who works for much of her life to save Venice from the sea. If Venice really is saved, this will make her work worthwhile, whereas if Venice is eventually swamped, her work will have been pointless. That her work is worthwhile seems good for her, but it is hard to know when she receives this good. Whether or not Venice is saved may not even be determined until after her death.

Examples like this are inconclusive. Someone who believes in the Principle of Temporal Good can deal with it in two ways. She can deny that there really are goods of this sort; for instance, she might deny that success (as opposed to feeling successful or believing you are successful) is really a good. Or she can assign some date to the good. For instance, she might date the good of success to all the dates when a person is working for it.

The example in the text is a different sort because it links time and uncertainty.

In this table, x and y refer to the quantities of good that come to the person at the times.[12] Assume x and y are different. Prospects A and B are equally good for the person at both times, because at both times they each give her an equal chance of x and y units of good. The Principle of Temporal Good, then, implies that prospects A and B are equally good for her. But it is plausible that actually B is better for her. This is because B gives the person, for sure, $x + y$ units of good altogether, whereas A gives her either $2x$ or $2y$. A is risky, then. So if there is any value in avoiding risk to the person's good, B is better. Its superior value appears from the standpoint of the person as a whole, and does not show up in either of the times taken separately.

Compare this formally similar example that has two people instead of two times (Table 3.4):

Table 3.4

		States of nature (equally likely)				States of nature (equally likely)	
		H	T			H	T
People	1	x	y	People	1	x	y
	2	x	y		2	y	x
		Prospect A				Prospect B	

Prospects A and B are equally good for each person. So the Principle of Personal Good implies they are equally good. And in this case there is no analogous reason for doubting this conclusion. There is no standpoint analogous to the standpoint of the person as a whole. There is no plausible reason why it should be good to avoid risk to the total good of the two people taken together. The Principle of Personal Good is not threatened by the example in the same way as the Principle of Temporal Good.

On the face of it, however, there seems to be an opposite threat. Although there is nothing in the interpersonal example to recommend B over A, there may seem to be something to recommend A over B: A leads inevitably to an equal distribution of good, and B to

[12]   For simplicity, think of them as quantities (numbers). But actually they might be elements in some partially ordered scale. It is not necessary for this example that good should be measurable on a numerical scale.

an unequal one. If this really makes A better than B, then that contradicts the Principle of Personal Good.

But what, if anything, is good about equality and bad about inequality? It can only be that equality is fair and inequality unfair. Inequality is unfair to the people at the bottom. This is a harm done them as individuals. Equality is good because it avoids this individual harm.[13] In Table 3.4 the figures stand for the people's total good. Any harm of unfairness that may be caused by inequality has already been taken into account. Once this has been done, the value of equality can then provide no further reason for favoring prospect A over B. So this value turns out to be no threat to the Principle of Personal Good.

This pair of examples, then, shows a disanalogy between the Principle of Personal Good and the Principle of Temporal Good. The latter is on more shaky ground because prospects can be judged from a standpoint that links different times together: the standpoint of a person as a whole. There is no analogous standpoint that links different people together.

Section 5

The example of Table 3.3 constitutes a prima facie case against the Principle of Temporal Good. Now I shall consider how, nevertheless, this principle might be defended. I shall consider, in particular, whether any metaphysical argument might be made for it.[14]

Some metaphysical theories about personhood deny the full unity of a person over time, and instead assimilate the relationships between different times in a person's life to the relationships between

---

[13]   This individualist account of the value of equality is spelt out in Broome (1989 and 1991a, Chapter 9.)

[14]   A different argument might rely on some particular theory of what a person's good consists in. Take, for instance, the theory that it consists in good experiences such as pleasure. Good experiences must all occur at some time or other. So it may look as though the Principle of Temporal Good would follow from this theory. But actually that is not so. This experience theory of good says only what the goodness of an *outcome* consists in; it says nothing about the goodness or badness of *risk*. Look again at the example of Table 3.3. The symbols x and y stand for quantities of good, which according to the experience theory are quantities of good experiences. A subscriber to the experience theory might reasonably think that prospect B is better than A, because from the standpoint of the person as a whole it is less risky. The experience theory of good is consistent with recognizing the standpoint of the person as a whole. So this theory, at least, cannot support the Principle of Temporal Good. It may be that some other theory of good might do so, though.

different people. "We regard the rough subdivisions within lives as, in certain ways, like the divisions between lives," says Derek Parfit.[15] I shall call this vaguely defined class of theories "disuniting." It seems plausible that a disuniting theory might be able to give support to the Principle of Temporal Good. It might assimilate the Principle of Temporal Good to the Principle of Personal Good. Because the latter is plausible, this might support the former. Specifically, a disuniting metaphysics might deny the standpoint of the person as a whole.

On the face of it, the two principles are metaphysically not closely analogous. The Principle of Personal Good is about putting together the good of different things – people. The Principle of Temporal Good is about putting together the good of a single thing – a person – that comes to her at different times. At all times in her life, a person is the same person, one thing. This is what makes available the standpoint of the person as a whole. It is the source of reasonable doubts about the Principle of Temporal Good. Across people, there is nothing analogous to this fact that a person is the same person at all times. There is nothing that is the same for all people.

But a disuniting metaphysical theory makes an analogy where, on the face of it, there is not one. It supposes a person is in some way made up of temporal segments. Each segment is a thing on its own. That a person is the same person at different times is more accurately expressed by saying that person-segments existing at different times make up a single person. This fact, then, is analogous to the fact that different people make up a single society. And this theory supposes that the good of a person at a time is the good of the person-segment that exists at that time. The Principle of Temporal Good, therefore, is about putting together the good of different things, just like the Principle of Personal Good. With this analogy in place, the reasons that support the latter principle may be able to support the former.

This, then, is roughly how a metaphysical argument might go. The rest of this section lays out an argument along these lines. But it leaves some gaps. The beginning of the task will be to establish that people are made up of temporal segments in the first place. In this chapter, though, I am not concerned with the merits of the disuniting theory itself, only with its implications. So I shall take this much for granted.

---

[15]   Parfit (1984, 333–334).

The notion "made up of" is vague. Societies are made up of people and water is made up of molecules, but the relation between a society and its people is not very similar to the relation between water and its constituent molecules. Different disuniting theories are possible, each with its own account of the relation between a person's segments and the person. One view is that this relation is membership: a relation formalized in set theory. Another is that it is the relation of part to whole: a relation formalized in mereology.[16] All the theories, though, must share this implication: The properties of a person must supervene on the properties of her segments.[17] If a person might have been different in some way without any of her segments being different, then she could not be said to be made up of her segments.

The Principle of Temporal Good says that the good of a person supervenes on her dated goods: Her good could not have been different without one of her dated goods being different. (It also says the direction of supervenience is positive: More good for the person implies more good for her at some time. But in this chapter I shall leave aside this question of direction. This is one gap in the argument.) The disuniting metaphysics treats the person's good at a time as the good of one of her segments. So, granted the metaphysics, the Principle of Temporal Good says that the good of a person supervenes on the good of her segments.

The disuniting metaphysics implies, as I say, that the good of a person (being one of her properties) supervenes on the properties of her segments. But that it supervenes on the *good* of her segments is a big further step. Compare a different example. I am made up of my

[16]   This is a popular view, but it weakens the analogy between a person and a society. It is not plausible that a person is a part of a society, at least as mereology conceives a part. In mereology, a part of a part is a part. But it is not very plausible that a part of a person, such as her finger, is a part of society. For an account of mereology, see Simons (1987).

[17]   In a trivial sense, this must be so. Suppose the person has the property F. If, instead, she had not had this property, then all of her segments would have been different in at least this respect: They would have had the property of being segments of a person who does not have property F. But I am speaking of supervenience in a nontrivial sense. To define it adequately I would need to rule out in some way such trivial properties of segments. Lewis's way (1983a, 359) would be to define supervenience in terms of the *intrinsic* or nonrelational properties of the segments. But this will not do, at least for my purposes. Whether or not a person has the property of leading a worthwhile life may depend on whether or not she is in love at some time, and we would want this to be consistent with supervenience. But being in love is not an intrinsic property, at least as Lewis understands "intrinsic" (see also Lewis 1983b).

spatial parts. My properties supervene on the properties of my parts. But my good does not supervene on the good of my parts. It is even true that my parts have their own goods: Exercise is good for my muscles and fish is said to be good for my brain. But things can be good for me without being good for any of my parts.

The theory that a person is made up of temporal segments, then, is not enough. Something needs to be added to it.

Another example shows the sort of thing it needs to be. A society is made up of people. And it is natural to think that the good of the society *does* supervene on the good of its members; nothing can be good for the society without being good for one of its members. This, at any rate, is an implication of the Principle of Personal Good. So what is the difference between the example of me and my parts and the example of a society and its members? It must be something to do with the *way* in which the parts and the members go to make up me and the society. And this must be something to do with the relations among them. It must be that my parts are related together in such a way that they make up an aggregate – me – whose good does not supervene on the good of the parts. On the other hand, this must not be true of the members of a society.

So we need to examine the relations between a person's temporal segments. Are they such that the segments form an aggregate – the person – whose good does not supervene on the good of the segments? (I shall call such a good "autonomous"). Could one argue that they do not?

Here is a way. Suppose we add to the disuniting metaphysics this further premise: that the relations between a person's segments, in virtue of which the segments make up a person (I shall call these "the unifying relations"), are not significant in respect of good ("axiologically significant," I shall say). I shall discuss later whether this premise is defensible. But first I shall show it is enough to give us the argument we are looking for. An outline of the argument is this. If these relations between segments are not significant in respect of good, then it makes no difference to good whether or not a collection of segments makes up a person. And this implies that when a collection does happen to make up a person, this person cannot have an autonomous good of her own. What follows fills out this outline.

I need first to define more precisely the notion of axiological significance. Our premise is that the unifying relations are not axiologically
significant. What does this mean? Clearly it should be understood
counterfactually. A first approach is: If the unifying relations between
a person's segments did not hold, then the good and bad in the world
would be just as it actually is. This formula, however, picks up causal
factors that I do not mean to be picked up. If these relations did not
hold, that is likely, for causal reasons, to make a difference to the
good of individual segments. Suppose, for instance (as Parfit believes) that among the unifying relations are relations of memory. If
some wizened person-segment remembers the achievements of some
youthful person-segment, that is part of what makes these two segments components of the same person; it is one of the unifying relations. Now, if *this* relation did not hold, so the wizened segment did
not have this memory, the wizened segment would probably be less
content than it actually is. There would therefore be less good in the
world than there actually is. One could say, then, that this relation of
memory is axiologically significant in a causal way. But when I say
that the unifying relations are not axiologically significant, I do not
mean to deny their causal significance. I mean they have no axiological significance *apart* from a causal one.

What I mean by the premise is this: If the unifying relations between a person's segments did not hold, but the good and bad of each
segment was just as it actually is, then the good and bad in the world
would be just as it actually is. Granted this, we can argue as follows
that a person can have no autonomous good.

Take a person, and imagine what it would be like if the unifying
relations between her segments did not hold, but the good and bad of
each segment remained the same. Imagine, say, that halfway through
her life the person was magically swept out of existence and in her
place appeared a new person similar in all respects, who then lived
out the rest of her life. The details of the magic required for this trick
will depend on what the unifying relations are, and there are different
theories about that. There might have to be an infinitesimal gap in
spatio-temporal continuity, say. Or the new person might have to be
made out of new matter. Or something else. But, whatever it is,
imagine the magic done in such a way that it leaves unaltered the
good and bad of every segment. For one thing, all the segments'

experiences, including memory-experiences, will have to be the same as the experiences of the actual person.

Now, suppose that the person had an autonomous good independent of the good of her segments. According to our premise, if the magic I described was done, the good or bad in the world would be just as it actually is. So the person's good would still exist. But there would be no one it could belong to. There would be no one taking the place of this person. Instead there would be a conflation of two people. A conflation is not a person, and it is not the sort of thing that could possibly have an autonomous good. So the person could not have had an autonomous good after all. QED.

This argument leaves something to worry about. The magic it requires may seem to be impossible. It may seem that magic could not possibly sever the unifying relations without altering the good or bad of segments. To put it another way: The premise from which I am arguing is a counterfactual conditional that may seem to have an impossible antecedent. We already know the antecedent is *causally* impossible because severing the unifying relations will cause the good or bad of segments to alter. But it may also seem *metaphysically* impossible. Whether or not one takes this view will depend on one's theory of what the good or bad of segments consists in. But here is a plausible example. It might plausibly be claimed that it is bad for a segment to be deceived about its past by its memory-experiences. And the magic will surely cause bads of this sort. After the magic has happened, later segments will have memory-experiences of actions that will lead them to believe these actions were done by earlier segments of the same person. But actually they were not. Because the magic has severed the unifying relations, the person who performed these actions was someone different. So the later segments are deceived by their memory-experiences.

I think, however, that this worry can be overcome. The antecedent of the conditional is not impossible, though it may be a more remote possibility than I have described so far. If necessary, we can envision the possibility as follows.[18] Take a possible world in which there are *two* perfect duplicates of our person, living duplicate lives on duplicate planets. Call them P and Q. And in this possible world, let the

[18] In this paragraph I am adopting the terminology and modal semantics of Lewis (1986).

counterparts of segments from the first half of the actual person's life be the corresponding segments of *P*'s life, and let the counterparts of segments from the second half of the actual person's life be the corresponding segments of *Q*'s life. In these circumstances I cannot see how the good and bad of each segment could fail to be just the same as the good and bad of its counterpart. Certainly, no segment in the possible world is deceived by its memory-experiences; each segment will have genuine memories of the actions of earlier segments of the same person. But this collection of counterpart segments in the possible world is not linked by the unifying relations. So the counterparts of the actual segments have just the same good and bad as the actual segments, but the unifying relation does not hold between them. That is what was wanted.[19]

I conclude, then, that the argument is successful. The premise that the unifying relations are not axiologically significant, taken together with a disuniting metaphysics, implies that a person does not have an autonomous good. Her good supervenes on the good of her segments. This is (apart from the matter of direction I mentioned) the Principle of Temporal Good. So it only remains to ask whether the premise can be defended.

Derek Parfit's work[20] provides one model for a defense. It contains extensive arguments about what "matters" (as Parfit puts it) in the relations between person-segments. Parfit argues for a disuniting metaphysics, and he argues that the unifying relations between a person's segments, in virtue of which they make up a person, are psychological connections. He includes connections of memory, intention, and so on: One segment of a person remembers what another did, one carries out intentions formed by another, and so on. Normally (excluding some fictional cases of fission and suchlike), a chain of segments will make up a person if and only if each segment is connected psychologically in the appropriate way to another.

On Parfit's account, then, our premise amounts to the claim that these psychological connections are not axiologically significant. Parfit

---

[19]   Taking the counterfactual in this more elaborate way also makes the final step of my argument particularly clear. If the person had an autonomous good, then so would the collection of counterpart segments in the possible world. But it is particularly clear that this collection is not the sort of thing that can have a good of its own. It is a collection of segments living on different planets.

[20]   Parfit (1984, Part III).

calls such a view "extreme," but says it is defensible on the basis of his arguments.[21] So here is one way the premise might be defended.

Parfit's work also offers another way. Parfit believes that, speaking roughly, a person's life may be divided into periods that are not very closely connected psychologically. An old person is not very closely connected with the young person she once was. These are the "rough subdivisions within lives" mentioned in the quotation at the beginning of this section. Suppose we treat each of these periods as a segment.[22] They are connected psychologically, and they therefore make up a person. But the connections may be weak enough to be axiologically insignificant, or at least unimportant. Parfit does not consider this an extreme view; indeed, it appears to be his own. It is a defense of our premise, if an imprecise one.

So Parfit's arguments may offer a basis for the premise that the unifying relations are not axiologically significant. Is it a metaphysical basis? There are two steps to the argument: first, that the unifying relations are psychological connections, and second, that psychological connections are not axiologically significant. Parfit's defense of the first is purely metaphysical; it is about the nature of a person. But he does not really defend the second. It may turn out to require a less purely metaphysical argument.[23]

Section 6

Section 5 does not contain a complete argument. But suppose a complete argument *was* made out deducing the Principle of Temporal Good from a disuniting metaphysics. Section 3 shows that the Principle of Temporal Good, if true, lends very strong support to the Utilitarian Principle of Distribution. So what would have been

---

[21] Parfit (1984, 343).

[22] Theorems 2 and 3 do not require there to be many "times." Two is enough.

[23] Susan Wolf (1986) has argued, in response to Parfit, that what matters ethically is not a metaphysical question. She says there is a reason why we should care about people rather than, say, person-segments: If we cared about person-segments and not people, the world would be less good than it actually is. This reason is independent of metaphysics; it will still exist even if a disuniting metaphysics is true. I am sure Wolf is right. But it does not affect what I am saying. I am concerned with whether the unifying relations are ethically significant as I defined ethical significance. This is not a question about what we should care about. (I believe, too, that what Parfit means by "mattering" is much closer to what I mean by "axiologically significant" than it is to Wolf's meaning.)

achieved is an argument from the disuniting metaphysics to the Utilitarian Principle.

This link between a disuniting metaphysics and the Utilitarian Principle has been argued for before. But I believe, first, that my argument, if completed, could provide a new and much tighter link. The Principle of Temporal Good is a precise objective for the metaphysical argument to aim for. If it can reach it, then the theorems and their associated formal arguments will bring the Utilitarian Principle in train.

And I believe, second, that the previous arguments have not actually succeeded in making the link properly. I am going to review the most thorough attempt – Derek Parfit's[24] – in order to explain where I think it fails.

Parfit's argument starts from his disuniting metaphysics, which implies that "the rough subdivisions within lives [are], in certain ways, like the divisions between lives."[25] He takes this to imply that the distribution of good across time should be regarded, to an extent, in the same way as distribution across people. If, for instance, it is unfair to impose a burden on one person for the sake of benefiting someone else to a greater extent, then it may be unfair to impose a burden on a child for the sake of benefiting her to a greater extent in later life. Or if some value should be attached to equality in the distribution of good between people, then some value should be attached to evenness in the distribution of good through a life. To put it another way: Principles of distribution,[26] whatever they are, should be applied, not to people, but to smaller units: person-segments.

Parfit takes this to be a consequence of his disuniting metaphysics. Because the subdivisions within lives are, in certain ways, like the divisions between lives, then to some extent the same principles of distribution should apply. This is not obvious. It is not obvious that the ways in which the divisions are alike are ways that make it right to regard distribution similarly. But Parfit supposes that the ways in which they are alike include all the ways that matter ethically. So the conclusion follows. Let us take that for granted.

[24]   Parfit (1984, 329–347).
[25]   Parfit (1984, 333–334) quoted earlier.
[26]   Parfit himself confines the term "distributive principles" to principles other than the utilitarian one. My usage differs from his.

The disuniting metaphysics, then, implies that distribution between lives and within lives should be regarded similarly to some extent. But it does not obviously have any implications about whether it is the Utilitarian Principle or some other that should be applied both between and within lives. It is this step that is negotiated by the theorems and the argument of Section 3. That is what I think this formal argument contributes.

Parfit, however, believes he can get from the metaphysics to the Utilitarian Principle without the help of the formal argument. At least, he believes that without its help, he can use the metaphysics to make the Utilitarian Principle plausible.[27] Here is part of his argument[28]:

> Consider the relief of suffering. Suppose that we can help only one of two people. We shall achieve more if we help the first; but it is the second who, in the past, suffered more. Those who believe in equality may decide to help the second person. This will be less effective; so the amount of suffering in the two people's lives will, in sum, be greater; but the amounts in each life will be made more equal. If we accept the Reductionist View [Parfit's disuniting metaphysics], we may decide otherwise. We may decide to do the most we can to relieve suffering. To suggest why, we can vary the example. Suppose that we can help only one of two nations. The one that we can help the most is the one whose history was, in earlier centuries, more fortunate. Most of us would not believe that it could be right to allow mankind to suffer more, so that the suffering is more equally divided between the histories of different nations. In trying to relieve suffering, we do not regard nations as the morally significant unit. On the Reductionist View, we compare the lives of people to the histories of nations. We may therefore think the same about them. We may believe that, when we are trying to relieve suffering, neither persons nor lives are the morally significant unit. We may again decide to aim for the least possible suffering, whatever its distribution.

I do not think, however, that this has moved us forward. We have already granted, given the disuniting metaphysics, that we should take

[27] Parfit (1984, 342).
[28] Parfit (1984, 341).

the same attitude to distribution within a life as we take to distribution across lives. This is because the boundaries within lives are like the boundaries between lives. So we do not regard people as the morally significant units. This only means that if we are concerned with distribution at all, we shall be concerned with distribution between what *are* the morally significant units – namely, person-segments or whatever these divisions of a person are. So certainly the fact that a person has suffered more in the *past* will not make us give extra weight to relieving her suffering now. But if she is suffering more *now,* we may give extra weight to it. We may be concerned to equalize the distribution of good between person-segments. So all this argument does is remind us that we have changed the units of distribution. It does not suggest that we should be less interested in distribution between them.[29]

Parfit also says[30]: On the Reductionist View "it becomes more plausible to focus less upon the person, the subject of experiences, and instead to focus more upon the experiences themselves. It becomes more plausible to claim that . . . we are right to ignore whether experiences come within the same or different lives." Once again I can make the same answer. Focusing on experiences is not the same thing as aiming to maximize the total goodness of experiences. Suppose an experience is "the morally significant unit," so the unit has shrunk to something even smaller than the person-segment. We still might be interested in equality between units. We might be interested in equalizing the goodness of experiences.

But Parfit argues that if the morally relevant unit is shrunk so small as to be just an experience, then distributive principles become less plausible.[31] His argument seems to be this. If we apply distributive principles with experiences as the units, we shall give the greatest importance to reducing the badness of the worst experiences, to reducing the greatest suffering. Is this plausible? What is so bad about great suffering that it should require such particular attention? Well, suffering strikes us intuitively as *really* bad when it is the same person who is constantly suffering. But once we have shrunk our morally relevant unit, the fact that it is the same person constantly suffering

29   Nagel (1979, 124–125 note) makes this point too, in response to an earlier argument of Parfit's. Parfit (1984, 343–344) replies to Nagel, but I do not think his reply adds much to the earlier argument.
30   Parfit (1984, 341).
31   Parfit (1984, 345).

cannot actually count. So we have removed the reason for giving special importance to reducing the badness of the worst experiences.

I think this argument is inadequate. The question is: Should we apply distributive principles across experiences? If we can reduce the badness of an experience by some particular amount, is that a better thing to do if the experience is originally a very bad one than if it is originally less bad? This is a subtle quantitative question, and you cannot answer it without having some metric of badness for experiences. Parfit's argument does not have the necessary quantitative precision. My argument, on the other hand, examined the metric of goodness and badness in detail, and that was crucial to the argument.

I conclude, therefore, that Parfit's argument does not get where it wants to go. Even if we grant, on the basis of the disuniting metaphysics, that the units of distribution are person-segments or something smaller, that does not establish the Utilitarian Principle of Distribution.

Section 7

My own argument is not complete. But I hope it could be more successful in the end. Its linchpin is the Principle of Temporal Good. The disuniting metaphysics may be able to support this principle, and it in turn supports the Utilitarian Principle of Distribution. This second step is achieved using the formal theorems of Sections 2 and 3. These theorems are needed, and Parfit's argument fails because he does not use them.

References

Arrow, Kenneth J (1973) "Some ordinalist-utilitarian notes on Rawls's theory of justice" *Journal of Philosophy* 70 245–263. Reprinted in his *Collected Papers Volume 1: Social Choice and Justice* Blackwell 1984. (Page reference to the reprinted version.)

Broome, John (1987) "Utilitarianism and expected utility" *Journal of Philosophy* 84 405–422.

Broome, John (1989) "What's the good of equality?" in Hey (1989).

Broome, John (1990) "Bolker–Jeffrey decision theory and axiomatic utilitarianism" *Review of Economic Studies* 57 477–502.

Broome, John (1991a) *Weighing Goods* Blackwell.

Broome, John (1991b) "Rationality and the sure-thing principle" in Meeks (1991).

Elster, Jon (ed) (1986) *The Multiple Self* Cambridge University Press.

Fishburn, Peter C (1984) "On Harsanyi's utilitarian cardinal welfare theorem" *Theory and Decision* 17 21–28.

Hammond, Peter J (1983) "Ex-post optimality as a dynamically consistent objective for collective choice under uncertainty" in Pattanaik and Salles (1983) 175–205.

Harsanyi, John C (1955) "Cardinal welfare, individualistic ethics, and interpersonal comparisons of utility" *Journal of Political Economy* 63 309–321.

Harsanyi, John C (1977a) "Morality and the theory of rational behavior" *Social Research* 44, reprinted in Sen and Williams (1982) 39–62.

Harsanyi, John C (1977b) *Rational Behavior and Bargaining Equilibrium in Games and Social Situations* Cambridge University Press.

Hey, John (ed) (1989) *Current Issues in Microeconomics* Macmillan.

Jeffrey, Richard (1971) "On interpersonal utility theory" *Journal of Philosophy* 68 647–656.

Lewis, David (1983a) "New work for a theory of universals" *Australasian Journal of Philosophy* 61 343–377.

Lewis, David (1983b) "Extrinsic properties" *Philosophical Studies* 44 197–200.

Lewis, David (1983c) *Philosophical Papers, Volume 1* Oxford University Press.

Lewis, David (1986) *On the Plurality of Worlds* Blackwell.

Meeks, Gay (ed) (1991) *Thoughtful Economic Man* Cambridge University Press.

Mirrlees, J A (1982) "The economic uses of utilitarianism" in Sen and Williams (1982) 219–238.

Nagel, Thomas (1979) *Mortal Questions* Cambridge University Press.

Parfit, Derek (1984) *Reasons and Persons* Oxford University Press.

Pattanaik, P K and Salles, M (eds) (1983) *Social Choice and Welfare* North-Holland 175–205.

Rawls, John (1974) "The independence of moral theory" *Proceedings of the American Philosophical Association* 48 5–22.

Schultz, Bart (1986) "Persons, selves and utilitarianism" *Ethics* 96 721–745.

Sen, Amartya, and Williams, Bernard (eds) (1982) *Utilitarianism and Beyond* Cambridge University Press.

Simons, Peter (1987) *Parts: A Study in Ontology* Oxford University Press.

Wolf, Susan (1986) "Self-interest and interest in selves" *Ethics* 96 704–720.

4. Local justice and interpersonal comparisons

JON ELSTER

I. Introduction

The problem of interpersonal comparisons of utility or welfare can be studied from several perspectives. First, there is a conceptual issue: Are such comparisons at all meaningful? Second, there is a question of operationalization. Assuming that the notion of comparing the utility or welfare of different people is meaningful, can it be reliably and validly implemented in practice? Here, "in practice" can mean anything from procedures that would work only under ideal conditions to methods that could be routinely used under a wide variety of circumstances. Third, we can start from the fact that people carry out these comparisons all the time, and ask how they do it. This question, or rather a subvariety of it, is the main topic of this chapter.

This issue – how people actually make interpersonal comparisons – can be studied in many ways. Coming from experimental psychology, one may search for heuristics, biases, and inconsistencies. Experimental techniques also allow us to test perceptions of relative need, and to bring out the features of an allocative situation and of potential recipients that shape this perception.[1] The focus of this chapter is on the allocative behavior of institutions. In allocating the scarce goods at their disposal – organs for transplantation, exemption from military service, or admission to higher education – institutions often (but not invariably) make comparisons between potential recipients. These

The research reported here has been supported by a grant from the Russell Sage Foundation. I am grateful to Steven Laymon, Stuart Romm, and, especially, Michael Dennis for skillful research assistance; and to G.A. Cohen, Fredrik Engelstad, Aanund Hylland, and Menachem Yaari for comments on an earlier draft.
[1] M. Yaari and M. Bar-Hillel, "On dividing justly," *Social Choice and Welfare* 1 (1985), 1–14; M. Bar-Hillel and M. Yaari, "Judgments of justice" (unpublished manuscript 1987).

comparisons are sometimes made in terms of utility or welfare, more frequently in terms of proxies for well-being.

Hence the structure of the chapter is as follows. In Section II I sketch the notion of "local justice" that is at the core of my analysis. In addition to the market and the global redistributive system of taxes and transfers, determinants of life chances include the local, decentralized, in-kind allocation of scarce goods by hospitals, draft boards, universities, and similar institutions, using a variety of distributive mechanisms and criteria. In Section III I focus on the subset of these criteria that involve comparisons among individuals, based on their merit, worth, effort, ability, contribution, or need. In Section IV the focus is further narrowed to the smaller subset of criteria that in some sense involve interpersonal comparisons of welfare or utility. I consider at some length the special case of selecting recipients for organ transplantations. Section V offers a few conclusions on the use of proxies for welfare in local justice contexts.

II. The concept of local justice

Conceptions of justice that are held by individuals or implemented by institutions can be global or local, end-state, or procedural. Global theories of justice have as their main object the overall design of society, with special emphasis on political freedom and schemes for redistributive taxation. End-state global theories include utilitarianism,[2] egalitarianism,[3] and John Rawls' theory of justice.[4] The best known procedural global theory is that associated with Robert Nozick.[5]

End-state global theories can be distinguished from each other along two dimensions, by the nature of the good to be allocated through the redistributive system and by the chosen principle of redistribution. The good may be utility (as in utilitarianism and welfare-

[2] See for instance the essays collected in B. Williams and A. Sen (eds.), *Utilitarianism and Beyond*, Cambridge University Press 1982.

[3] See R. Dworkin, "What is equality? Part 1: Equality of welfare," *Philosophy and Public Affairs* 10(1981), 185–246, and "What is equality? Part 2: Equality of resources," ibid., 283–345; J. Roemer, "Equality of talent," *Economics and Philosophy* 1(1985), 151–88, and "Equality of resources implies equality of welfare," *Quarterly Journal of Economics* 101(1986), 751–84.

[4] J. Rawls, *A Theory of Justice*, Cambridge, MA: Harvard University Press 1971.

[5] R. Nozick, *Anarchy, State and Utopia*, New York: Basic Books 1974.

egalitarianism), a bundle of primary goods (as in Rawls) or of basic capabilities (as in Sen),[6] or opportunities for self-realization (as in Marxism).[7] The principle may be that of equal distribution of the good, a distribution that maximizes the amount of the good that accrues to those who get least, or one that maximizes the total production of the good. What all global theories have in common, however, is that they single out *one* good (or one type of goods) and *one* principle of distribution.[8]

Local justice, by contrast, concerns a variety of different goods (including exemptions from burdens), allocated by a number of different principles. Illustrations are the distribution of scarce human organs for transplantation, the decision about whom to induct into military service, and the choice by a firm of which workers to lay off in a recession. Often, global theories have no clear implications for who should get what or do what in these situations.[9] Indeed, they are often not intended to have implications for small-scale problems.[10] This fact is reflected in actual practices. These nonfungible goods are not part of a global redistributive system, but allocated in an uncoordinated, decentralized fashion. Although the institutions allocating them are to some extent bound by national regulations or guidelines, they usually have considerable discretionary power. Some of these decisions are crucial for the life chances of the citizen. Others are of small or medium-sized importance. For any individual citizen, their sum-total is certain to be overwhelmingly important. Their interaction and correlation with market decisions and global redistributive schemes is complex and variable. Institutions that allocate on the

[6] A. Sen, "Equality of what?," in his *Choice, Measurement and Welfare*, pp. 353–69, Oxford: Blackwell, 1979.

[7] For a survey, see G.A. Cohen, "The currency of egalitarian justice," *Ethics* 99(1989), 906–44.

[8] M. Walzer's *Spheres of Justice*, New York: Basic Books 1983, is an exception. He proposes, in fact, a theory that is partly global and partly local, as the terms are used here.

[9] The application of global theories often requires more information than is available. For instance, it may not be in the interest of the social agents to reveal their preferences and productive capacities. See the chapter by d'Aspremont and Gerard-Varet in this volume.

[10] John Rawls makes it clear, for instance, that his two principles of justice are intended only for the design of the basic institutions in society, not for the solution of specific allocative problems.

basis of merit or worth tend to reinforce the biases of the market, whereas allocations on the basis of need tend to go along with the transfer system in offsetting these biases.

To illustrate the working of local justice, I shall first give some examples of (procedural) *mechanisms* and (individualized) *criteria* used in allocating scarce goods, and then some prominent examples of the goods themselves. A fuller discussion of individualized criteria is given in Section III. In the following, the term *principle* is used to denote both mechanisms and criteria, as well as any combination thereof.

Absolute equality

When the good can be infinitely divided without (too much) loss of value, it is often divided equally among all applicants or potential beneficiaries. When it would lose all value by division, the principle of absolute equality dictates that it should not be given to anyone. The latter prescription is often found in Jewish ethics.[11] The recent Oregon moratorium on non-renal transplantations provides an example of such all-or-none reasoning,[12] as does (albeit more controversially) Massachusetts policy on liver transplants.[13]

Lotteries

Goods that cannot be divided without loss of value are often allocated by a lottery that gives equal chances to all applicants of getting them.[14]

---

[11]   E. Cahn, *The Moral Decision,* Bloomington: Indiana University Press 1955, p. 61 ff; I. Jakobovits, *Jewish Medical Ethics,* New York: Bloch 1975, p. 98; F. Rosner, *Modern Medicine and Jewish Ethics,* New York: Yeshiva University Press 1986.

[12]   "Pointing to federal Medicaid statutes requiring equal treatment for similarly situated patients, the [Oregon Division of Adult and Family Services] stressed that there was no way the state could limit its funding to a prescribed number of transplant patients." (H. Gilbert and E.B. Larson, "Dealing with limited resources: The Oregon decision to curtail funding for organ transplantation," *The New England Journal of Medicine,* July 21 1988, pp. 171–73, at p. 171.)

[13]   C.M. Havighurst and N.M. King, "Liver transplantation in Massachusetts: Public policy making as a morality play," *Indiana Law Review* 19(1986), 955–87.

[14]   For a survey, see J. Elster, "Taming chance: Randomization in individual and social decisions," Ch. II of *Solomonic Judgements,* Cambridge University Press 1989.

Queuing and seniority[15]

Often, the good is distributed on a first-come first-served basis. Some queues require that one actually wastes time standing in them, whereas others only involve mailing or depositing a claim. A closely related principle is that of seniority, which also gives major importance to the sheer passage of time.

Status

In many premodern societies, goods were allocated according to ascribed status. Slaves have been treated differently from the free, nobles differently from non-nobles, blacks from whites, men from women, and children from adults. The non-induction of women into military service and the refusal of certain rights to minors are contemporary examples.

Individual welfare

Very often the scarce resource is allocated on the basis of individual welfare. One version of this criterion is in marginal terms, so that the good should be given where it produces the greatest *increment* of utility or welfare. Another version, emphasizing need rather than efficiency, tells us to channel the good to people at low welfare *levels*. I return to these criteria in Section IV.

Productivity

Often the allocation follows the principle of efficiency or productivity. Thus X may derive greater personal benefits from a good than Y, yet Y may use it more productively, in the sense of making a larger contribution to the goals of the allocating institution or more generally, of society.

---

[15]   For case studies and some general observations, see B. Schwartz, *Queuing and Waiting: Studies in the Social Organization of Access and Delay,* University of Chicago Press 1976.

Contribution

Sometimes goods are allocated according to earlier contributions. They serve, then, as a reward for good behavior. This criterion has a backward-looking element, unlike need and productivity, which are forward-looking. Using goods as rewards may, nevertheless, have good effects on productivity.

Social worth

When used in the allocation of scarce medical resources, this criterion has been interpreted both in the backward-looking sense of contribution to society and in the forward-looking sense of productivity.

Effective demand

This is the principle used by the market. When the creation of a market requires an explicit institutional decision, use of this principle can also be seen as a form of local justice. The proposal to create a market in procreation rights illustrates this idea.

Mixed principles

In addition to these "pure" mechanisms and criteria, various combinations have been used. Occasionally, lotteries with uneven chances are employed, with the weights being determined by individualized criteria. Examples include the Georgian land lottery of 1832, which gave two chances to orphans, Revolutionary War veterans, and heads of families, or the Dutch system for admission to medical school, which admits candidates with a probability that depends on their grades. To allocate a given scarce good, one can first use criteria of need or productivity to form a pool of those who are eligible, and then use queuing or lotteries as secondary criteria to choose within the pool. Or one may use a point system, so that individuals are ranked by an aggregate index that takes account of productivity, need, contribution, seniority, and experience. A point system used to allocate kidneys for transplantation is described in detail later.

Here is a fuller list of some local allocative problems.

Allocation of scarce medical resources

Naturally or artificially scarce medical resources include: organs for transplantation, expensive medication, admission to intensive-care units, and the labor power of doctors or nurses. Allocation has been made according to such criteria as medical efficiency, medical need, queuing, lotteries, social worth or effective demand.[16]

Allocation of places in nursery schools and old-age homes

Often, people seek institutional care for their children or their old parents. When places in these institutions are scarce, criteria of allocation are needed. Queuing, need, and effective demand are frequently used criteria.

Allocation of military service

Often there is no military purpose in having universal, compulsory military service. Criteria for choosing a subset of the relevant age group have included opportunity costs (production foregone), mental and physical fitness, lotteries, ability to buy a substitute, or some combination of these.[17] A related problem concerns demobilization: Who should be allowed to leave the army first? In the U.S. Army in the Second World War this was solved by an elaborate point system that took account of contribution as well as of need.[18]

Admission to college and professional schools

There is great variety in the admission principles that have been used by different kinds of schools in different countries: effective demand, negative or positive discrimination on grounds of sex or race, athletic

[16]   Good general discussions are G. Winslow, *Triage and Justice,* Berkeley: University of California Press 1982, and D. Note, "Scarce medical resources," *Columbia Law Review* 69 (1969), 620–92.

[17]   Useful discussions are F. Choisel, "Du tirage au sort au service universel," *Revue Historique des Armees* 37(1981); A. Blum, "Soldier or worker: A revaluation of the selective service system," *The Midwest Quarterly* 13 (1972), 147–67; N. de Bohigas, "Some opinions on exemption from military service in nineteenth-century Europe," *Comparative Studies in Society and History* 10 (1968), 261–88.

[18]   S. Stouffer et al., *The American Soldier,* Princeton University Press 1949, vol. II, Ch. 11.

ability, scholastic ability, documented experience, or one or more of these combined with a procedural principle such as queuing or lottery. Point systems are extensively used.

Allocation of water, energy, and similar resources

When water, electricity, or gasoline (for consumption or production) have been scarce, several mechanisms have been used to allocate them: queuing, rationing according to need, rationing according to productivity, and auctioning.[19]

Allocation of public housing[20]

Municipalities allocate public housing by need, as defined by income and present housing conditions, often combined with queuing and lotteries.

Allocation of jobs

Most firms and public agencies have policies for preferential hiring and (especially) firing. Criteria such as sex, race, age, seniority, need (for example, family dependents) and productivity are often used.[21]

Allocation of children

In divorce cases and in child placement cases, courts and welfare agencies use various criteria (the interest of the child, the needs and rights of parents, the needs of society) to determine whether children should be with the mother or the father, or with the biological parents or in a foster home.[22]

[19] See A. Olmstead and P. Rhode, "Rationing without government: The West Coast gas famine of 1920," *American Economic Review* 75(1985), 1044–55, and E.J. Zajac, "Perceived economic justice: The example of public utility regulation," in H.P. Young (ed.), *Cost Allocation,* Amsterdam: Elsevier 1985, 119–53.

[20] See J.R. Prescott, *Economic Aspects of Public Housing,* Beverly Hills: Sage 1974, and J.S. Fuerst (ed.), *Public Housing in Europe and America,* New York: Wiley 1974.

[21] See, for instance, E. Yemin (ed.), *Workforce Reductions in Undertakings,* Geneva: International Labour Office 1982.

[22] For a survey, see J. Elster, "Solomonic judgments," *University of Chicago Law Review* 54 (1987), 1–45.

Allocation of procreation rights

Some societies have found it necessary to limit the number of children a family can have, by the use of negative and positive incentives. In China, only individuals without siblings who marry each other receive the right to have two children.

Allocation of tasks within the household

Adult members of a household must allocate tasks among themselves. In doing so, they can use the criterion of equality of time spent on household tasks. They can also take account of the differences between more and less pleasant tasks, of differential efficiency in carrying them out, and of work load outside the household.

Other examples include allocation of broadcasting licenses, allocation of land to settlers, allocation of extra educational resources to the least gifted or to the most gifted children, allocation of help in disaster situations ("women, children, and doctors first"), allocation of sites for nuclear waste, allocation of space (for example, parking space or office space), allocation of time (for example, longer holidays for older workers or shorter working days for parents of young children), allocation of food stamps, allocation of means of transportation (bus or rail service), and selective abortions on the basis of sex among multiple fetuses.[23]

III. Interpersonal comparisons

When an institution has to choose a mechanism or criterion to allocate the scarce good at its disposal, it usually reaches a compromise between ideal and practical considerations.

On the one hand, decision-makers can usually formulate a principle of *local justice* that they deem to be inherently fit, appropriate, efficient or fair, given the nature of the good and the goal of the institution. To select soldiers for military service, physical fitness would seem appropriate. In admitting students to the university, scholastic ability stands out as the natural criterion. In allocating medical goods,

[23]   On the last issue, see *New York Times* January 25 1988: "Multiple fetuses raise new issues tied to abortion."

medical need is paramount. (Some would say, though, that medical efficiency is more appropriate. The issue is further discussed in Section IV.) In selecting workers for layoffs, managers would ideally want to retain the most productive. The choice of a custodial parent should follow the best interest of the child.

On the other hand, the institution's choice of allocative principle is shaped by a number of practical considerations that necessitate compromise.

1. Sometimes, the central government forces administrators to deviate from these local criteria by imposing *global considerations*. Thus, people in the work force are sometimes given priority in the health queues, as are soldiers whose wounds are so slight that they can be made fit for combat duty. Positive discrimination on grounds of sex or race offers another example.

2. Often, institutions take account of the *incentive effects* of criteria.[24] (a) They may want to avoid criteria that create negative incentives. Examples include the incentive for self-mutilation created by selection for military service by physical fitness, or the incentive for wasteful occupation created by systems that take account of work experience in admitting students to medical school. (b) Institutions may want to use criteria that create positive incentives. Examples include layoffs by seniority in firms (see point 6) and admission to university by grades. Interestingly, positive incentive schemes are little used in the health sector. For instance, nonsmokers are not given priority in heart operations, nor are wearers of safety belts in rehabilitation after car accidents. The fact that in many countries people are supposed to bear the full costs of their dental care may, however, be part of an incentive scheme.

3. Sometimes, institutions take account of the *costs of decision-making,* preferring the least costly methods over the more costly ones even when the latter more closely approximates the locally just criterion. Fine-tuned, discretionary criteria are often time-consuming and costly; hence, mechanical criteria like queuing, lotteries, or seniority

---

[24]   I discuss this issue in my "Incentives and local justice," Working Paper #7 from the Local Justice Project, Department of Political Science, University of Chicago.

(within a pool that satisfies some minimal substantive criterion) may be preferred. On the other hand, the use of mechanical criteria may be more costly if more individuals become eligible.

4. Sometimes, institutions are influenced by the *fear of complaints* and, especially in the United States, of *litigation*. This points in the same direction as the previous consideration – away from discretionary criteria and toward mechanical, automatic principles.

5. Sometimes, the institution takes account of possible *"Catch-22" effects* that deter the most eligible individuals from receiving the scarce goods. Needs-based criteria often require the most needy – usually the least advantaged individuals – to orient themselves in a jungle of regulations and forms. As a consequence, those who deserve the good most sometimes don't get it. The alternative – using simple, mechanical criteria of allocation – harbors the opposite problem, that some who don't deserve the good nevertheless get it.

6. Sometimes, institutions choose the criteria through *bargaining* with the potential recipients of the scarce goods. The use of seniority in layoffs is the outcome of bargaining between trade unions and firms. Patient associations may well come to play a similar role in the allocation of medical goods.

7. Sometimes, the choice of criterion may be influenced by a desire to *channel more resources* toward the institution. Thus it has been argued that in choosing principles for allocating organs for transplantation, one should take account of their impact on the willingness to donate organs. If, for instance, foreign nationals or resident aliens are treated on a par with citizens, the willingness to donate organs might fall off.[25] If in the name of medical efficiency local transplantation centers are forced to share their organs with other institutions, their incentive to procure organs might be reduced.[26]

[25]   J.F. Childress, "Some moral connections between organ procurement and organ distribution," *Journal of Contemporary Health Law and Policy* 3(1987), 85–110.
[26]   P.S. Russell, "Organ allocation: how can we assure equitable distribution?," *Transplantation Proceedings* 20(1988), 1022–24; G. Opelz, "Allocation of cadaver kidneys for transplantation," *Transplantation Proceedings* 20 (1988), 1028–32.

8. Sometimes, institutions are constrained or influenced by *public opinion*. Thus the use of weighted lotteries in admitting students to medical school in Holland is said to be a compromise between the institution's meritocratic preferences and the very egalitarian public opinion. According to Tocqueville, this constraint also explains the institution of compulsory military service in democratic societies.

A distinction can be made between the criteria that look mainly to the past (up to and including the present), those that look mainly to the future, and those that do both. Backward-looking criteria tend to be easier to apply than forward-looking ones, which usually require an element of discretionary judgment. Against this, substantive considerations of fairness or efficiency may favor the forward-looking principles.

Backward-looking comparisons were central in the demobilization scheme for the American Army in World War II.[27] Both the scheme and the method by which it was defined are of considerable interest. A proposal to retain the combat fighting teams and to discharge the service troops and the untrained soldiers was discarded in favor of an individualized, backward-looking system. To implement this idea, the Army considered and then discarded a "first in, first out" system, preferring a scheme that took account of several factors. It finally chose a point system that accorded 1 point per month in the army, 1 point per month in overseas service, 5 points per campaign star or combat decoration, and 12 points per child under 18, up to three. Except for the last, these are all backward-looking variables.[28]

To determine the variables and their weights, the army conducted large-scale surveys among enlisted men. In one survey the criteria were held up against each other in pairwise comparisons. In another, the respondents were asked to name the category of soldiers to be released first and the category to be released last. In a third survey they were given thumbnail descriptions of three soldiers, and asked who should be released first. The individual rankings showed a high

---

[27] The following draws on Stouffer et al., loc. cit.

[28] In this context, the number of children was a proxy for the forward-looking principle of social value. In other contexts, one might want to reward people for having many children, as in France under the "familles nombreuses" system. This is a mixed system, both forward and backward-looking.

degree of consistency, but also a clear self-serving bias.[29] They also showed some collective inconsistency,[30] but not so much as to render them useless for the purposes of constructing a point system that reflected fairly well the preferences of the respondents.[31] The system was widely accepted as fair, and met with few complaints.

Forward-looking comparisons can be defined in terms either of individual or social welfare. On the one hand, we can ask whether person X or person Y will benefit more personally from the scarce good. On the other hand, we can ask whether society as a whole will benefit more if X or Y is given the scarce good. I shall say more about individual welfare in the next section, but let me say something here about social productivity.

Consider, first, medical decisions. Some writers have explicitly argued that (forward-looking) social value should be one of several criteria[32] or even the main criterion[33] in allocating scarce life-saving resources. The principle has also been used in practice, either as a rule of exclusion[34] or as a rule of final selection.[35] If it sounds unacceptably elitist by suggesting that a brilliant pianist should take precedence over an unskilled worker, we should note that it also favors recipients with many dependents over those who have none. When

[29]   For instance, the percentage saying that married men with children should be let out first was 60 among married men with children, 37 for married men without children, and 24 for single men. For a discussion of self-serving biases in such contexts, see D.M. Messick and K. Sentis, "Fairness, preference, and fairness biases," in D.M. Messick and K. Cook (eds.), *Equity Theory*, pp. 61–94, New York: Praeger 1983.

[30]   Thus, 55% thought that a single man with two campaigns of combat should be released before a married man with two children who had not been in combat; 52% rated 18 months overseas as more important than two children; and 60% rated two campaigns as worth more than 18 months overseas. Apropos this finding, Stouffer et al. write (*The American Soldier,* p. 528) that "a high degree of internal consistency on such intricate hypothetical choices was hardly to be expected," thus suggesting that the problem was one of individual inconsistency. Had they written after the publication of Arrow's impossibility theorem a few years later, they might have preferred the interpretation in terms of collective inconsistency. As Aanund Hylland has pointed out to me, a sure sign of individual inconsistency would have been if the majorities had added up to more than 200%. In the present case, they add up only to 167%.

[31]   For the problems inherent in any attempt to construct interpersonal comparisons on the basis of individual rankings, see Aanund Hylland's contribution to this volume.

[32]   N. Rescher, "The allocation of exotic lifesaving therapy," *Ethics* 79 (1969), 173–86.

[33]   L. Shatin, "Medical care and the social worth of a man," *American Journal of Orthopsychiatry* 36 (1966), 96–101.

[34]   "Scarce medical resources," p. 655.

[35]   Ibid., p. 657 ff.

restricted to the latter interpretation, the principle need no longer rest on a utilitarian basis. We might be absolutely confident that the death of a childless genius would cause a greater social loss than the death of an unskilled worker with many small children, and yet give precedence to the latter. One may want avoidance of a few large losses to count for more than the avoidance of many small losses, even if the sum-total – assuming it can be measured – is larger in the latter case.

Consider, next, selection for military service. Here, the notion of productivity is ambiguous. It can be taken to mean usefulness for military duty or social usefulness more generally. In the former sense, the criterion cannot be justified on a utilitarian basis. In the latter, utilitarian sense the productivity criterion was widely used in the nineteenth century to justify exemptions or the possibility of buying a substitute for privileged groups, on the grounds that their value to society was so high that they should not waste their time in the army.[36] Even if we assume that they make better soldiers than others, their comparative advantage is elsewhere. Once again, exemption because of family dependents provides a more acceptable version of this argument.

Finally, there is a mixed category of comparisons that embody both backward- and forward-looking considerations.[37] At any given point in time, resources are allocated according to behavior in the past. The creation of this backward-looking system is justified, however, by a forward-looking argument from incentives. Schematically – at time t_1 it is made known that at time t_3 rewards shall be allocated according to behavior at time t_2. The demobilization scheme was a pure backward-looking system, because it was not even envisaged at the time at which it might, if known, have had good incentive effects. Soldiers might have fought harder if they had known that combat experience would get them sooner out of the army, but they didn't know. The advantage of the scheme was fairness, not efficiency.

Pure backward-looking systems easily become mixed, however, if

---

[36]   De Bohigas, "Some opinions on exemption from military service."
[37]   Systems can also be mixed in a different sense. The demobilization scheme was mixed, in that it accorded points both for backward-looking considerations (time spent in the army, battle citations) and for forward-looking ones (numbers of dependents). As used in the text, however, by a mixed system I mean a backward-looking system that has been created for forward-looking reasons.

they persist over time. Religious doctrines that promise salvation in return for good works usually go on to add that the reward will not be forthcoming if the works are undertaken for the sake of salvation.[38] In practice, the warning is rarely heeded.[39] Conversely, mixed systems may come to be perceived as pure backward-looking ones, based on *entitlements* rather than *incentives*. The rule of "finders keepers," which makes good sense on the mixed interpretation, is often and more obscurely presented as a rights-based principle. The principle of lay-offs by seniority (discussed later) is similarly ambiguous.

Access to institutions of higher education is regulated by a mixed system. By and large, students are not admitted on the basis of their future potential, nor on the basis of meritorious behavior (special treatment of veterans is an exception). Instead, they are admitted on the basis of grades and test scores. Because it is publicly known that institutions admit students by these criteria, an incentive is created to work hard in high school and when cramming for test scores. The effect is socially valuable, because it induces people to acquire more socially useful knowledge than they would otherwise have done.[40]

This, at least, is the standard account, and there is probably a lot to it. A study of Harvard admission policies, by a former admissions chairman at the Kennedy School of Government, suggests that things are somewhat more complicated.[41] In addition to studying the Kennedy School, he studied admission policies in Harvard College, in the graduate school of arts and sciences, and in the professional schools. Some of the more salient findings follow.

The Kennedy School tried to select future leaders for the public sector. They based their choices partly on character and personality, whereas "some very smart students were rejected because their essays or recommendations made them sound poorly motivated, egocentric, or immature." In Harvard College we also find deviations

[38]   Salvation, in other words, is essentially a byproduct, as that notion is defined in Ch. II of my *Sour Grapes*, Cambridge University Press 1983.

[39]   A similar degeneration of reward according to ideological merit is described in A. Walder, *Communist Neo-Traditionalism*, Berkeley: University of California Press 1986.

[40]   I am assuming that education is productive, and does not simply function as a signaling device (for the latter idea, see M. Spence, *Market Signaling*, Cambridge, MA: Harvard University Press 1974).

[41]   R. Klitgaard, *Choosing Elites*, New York: Basic Books 1985. The following citations are taken from Ch. 2 of this book.

from scholastic merit, justified by various (and curious) arguments. One is that "the top high school student is often, frankly, a pretty dull and bloodless or peculiar fellow." In a similar (albeit opposite) vein, a dean of admission is on record as asking what would happen if "the precious, the brittle and the neurotic take over." Another argument is that "the most academically able students might not want to join a college that selected on purely academic criteria." Still another argument stems from "the search for the happy bottom quarter," summarized as follows. "Inevitably . . . 25 percent of the entering students would end up in the bottom quarter of the class. If they were former academic stars, they would be unhappy – perhaps they would even be broken by the experience. So, intentionally admitting less academically able students as 'the bottom quarter,' who were strong in sports or social life or the arts and would therefore not care so much about their academic standing, would make everyone's educational experience happier." Some of these arguments were probably rationalizations to justify the admission of children of alumni.

A backward-looking criterion that also has forward-looking effects is *seniority,* which is used to select workers for promotion or layoffs as well as to allocate numerous other work-related benefits. Seniority tends to reduce turnover, and lower turnover makes for higher productivity.[42] On the other hand, seniority is usually enforced by unions,[43] and unionism tends to reduce profits.[44] Managers of non-unionized firms might want to use seniority because of the good incentive effects, but without a union with which to make an agreement they may be unable to make credible promises to this effect. Managers of unionized firms might prefer to have no union, but given that one exists they may prefer seniority rules over a system that gives them discretionary power. All in all, therefore, whenever seniority can be enforced, it is in the interest of both workers and management to have it. Although the principle is often perceived by workers as springing from an entitlement, created by time and custom,[45] manage-

[42]   R. Freeman and J. Medoff, *What do Unions do?,* New York: Basic Books 1984 pp. 107, 174.
[43]   "In the nonunion sector, management often takes account of seniority but can ignore it when it chooses" (Ibid., p. 123).
[44]   Ibid., Ch. 11.
[45]   See Zajac, "Perceived economic justice," for a discussion of the process whereby an accidentally created status quo is transformed into a property right.

ment might have fought harder against it had it not also good effects on productivity.

The principle of seniority might appear to be utterly simple and mechanical. A brief look at collective bargaining agreements that specify how seniority is to be interpreted and implemented dispels this impression.[46] The need and scope for secondary criteria to break ties increase when date of hiring is given by a month rather than by day. The unit – company, plant, or department – within which seniority is to be counted must be specified. Seniority may or may not accumulate during probation period or during layoffs. Unlike age, seniority can be lost – for example, when a worker refuses to accept promotion. Sometimes, seniority determines the order in which workers are laid off, but not the order in which they are recalled to work. As was also the case in the demobilization scheme, the principle does not apply to "indispensable" workers.

These examples show how local justice works in practice. The main impression is that it is a messy business. Usually, the institution acknowledges that more than one feature of the individual is relevant for the allocation decision. Sometimes, as in the demobilization scheme, explicit weights are assigned to the various features. More frequently, this weighting is left to the discretionary decision of the administrators. Often, there is some discrepancy between the official principles and actual practice. Sometimes, tortuous explanations are given to reconcile practice and principle, as in the Harvard admissions system. More frequently, the principles are just violated in secret. Reaching agreement on a principle is often achieved at the cost of some vagueness about interpretation and implementation.

IV. Interpersonal comparisons of welfare

The *welfare* of the potential recipients often plays a major role in the allocation process, either to define a pool of eligibles or to define the criteria of final selection. The allocating institution may then be forced to make unit-comparisons or level-comparisons of the welfare of different individuals.[47] Suppose that there are two individuals, X and Y, who

[46] See "Layoff, recall and worksharing procedures" and "Administration of seniority," Bulletins 1425–13 and 1425–14 of the U.S. Department of Labor 1972.
[47] For this distinction, see Hammond's contribution in this volume.

would both benefit from one unit of a scarce good. We may (1) give the unit to X if X's initial *level* of welfare is lower than that of Y, or (2) give the unit to X if the *increment* in welfare it will produce in X is higher than the increment it will produce in Y. Both correspond to well-known ideas of justice: We should compensate the worst-off or allocate resources to those who would benefit most from them.

Input level and input-output increment must be sharply distinguished from output level as a criterion – that is, giving a unit of the scarce good to X if it would bring him to a higher level of welfare than what would be achieved by Y if he were given the good. One survey article of scarce medical resources writes that "It is an almost universally accepted standard for selection that the patient whose chances of survival will be most greatly increased by a resource will be preferred over others." In a footnote, the authors document this effect, drawing on interviews with doctors which show that "The shift from the 'most critical' to the 'most salvageable' standard in the allocation of intensive care ward space can have a dramatic effect. Under the former standard the Los Angeles County-University of Southern California Hospital Intensive Care Unit had a mortality rate of 80%. By shifting to the latter standard the rate has been reduced to 20%. . . . The corresponding figures to the Jackson Memorial Hospital Surgical Intensive Care Unit are 25–30% with critical admissions and 4–5% with salvageable admissions."[48] These figures, however, refer to output, not to increments. Clearly, mortality rates can always be reduced by concentrating on less severe cases, but it would defeat the purpose of medical treatment to use this as a criterion of admission.[49]

For many purposes, it does not matter whether we choose the level criterion or the increment criterion. When X and Y are reasonably similar individuals, and consumption of the scarce good has diminish-

[48]   "Scarce medical resources," p. 655, n. 188.
[49]   For-profit hospitals sometimes concentrate on the easy cases, leaving the hard ones for the public sector. There is also some evidence that there is "substantial waste in the provision of mental health services – that large numbers of highly trained provider groups are being well paid mostly to talk about personal matters to people with mild emotional problems" (D.J. Knesper, D.J. Pagnucco, and J.R.C. Wheeler, "Similarities and differences across mental health services providers and practice settings in the United States," *American Psychologist* 40(1985), 1352–69, at p. 1367. A more legitimate reason for preferring the easy cases arises in warfare, where the overriding consideration is to get soldiers combat ready and not to cure them (Winslow, *Triage and Justice*, Ch. 1).

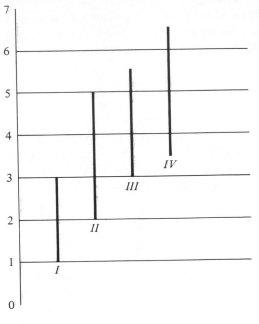

Figure 4.1

ing marginal utility, then a person at a lower level will always derive a larger increment than a person at a higher level. This corresponds to the relation between individuals II and III in Figure 4.1. Here, each vertical line represents a person. The line begins at the welfare level of the person before allocation of the scarce good, and ends at the level that he would reach if allocated one unit of the good.

The criteria diverge in two cases. First, the good may produce *increasing* marginal utility over some range. A person who already has four units might benefit more from an additional one than a person who has three, even assuming that the two have the same skills and preferences. This corresponds to the relation between III and IV in Figure 4.1. This argument was made by Leibniz, initially with respect to all sorts of goods.[50] Later he limited it to "useful" goods, as distinct from "necessary" goods.[51] With respect to some

[50]   Leibniz, *Philosophische Schriften,* ed. Gerhardt, vol. I, p. 74.
[51]   G. Mollat, *Mittheilungen aus Leibnizens ungedruckten Schriften,* Leipzig 1893, p. 85.

goods, the argument is not palpably absurd. If X and Y are identical except that X is at a higher level of education and hence of welfare than Y, X may benefit more from an additional unit of education because he possesses more prior information with which the new information can be combined. A little learning may not be a dangerous thing, but it can be somewhat pointless. By and large, however, the assumption of decreasing marginal utility is more plausible, and in most cases overwhelmingly more plausible.[52]

The other case in which the two criteria point in different directions is more interesting. Some people might be inherently less efficient in converting goods into welfare. This corresponds to the relation between I and II in Figure 4.1. We may suppose that I suffers a handicap that causes him both to be at a lower level of welfare – for instance because he earns less – and to derive less welfare from an additional unit of the good. In such cases, those who make allocative decisions face a dilemma. Should schools, for instance, allocate extra resources – smaller classes or additional equipment – to the least gifted or to the most gifted children? Should agencies for the mentally retarded give priority to those who are so severely retarded that they are unlikely to enjoy life much under any circumstances, or to those who can benefit substantially from supportive measures? Should agencies for rehabilitation of prisoners give priority to recalcitrant high-risk or to more promising low-risk cases? If a judge is allowed to take account of the circumstances of persons to be sentenced, should he emphasize their current level of welfare or the drop in welfare they would experience if severely sentenced? Should he reason that "This person has already suffered enough," or "This person would suffer excessively if imprisoned"?

In many cases of this kind we are not comparing people's welfare directly. Rather, we are comparing observable proxies for welfare. The principal of a school looks at levels and increments of knowledge, not of welfare. The prison visitor considers risks of recidivism with or without assistance, not welfare. To be sure, we usually assume that welfare is correlated with knowledge and with recidivism. And presumably this correlation is a major reason for caring about such

---

[52]   For an argument that *necessary* goods have increasing marginal utility, see C. Karellis, "Distributive justice and the public good," *Economics and Philosophy* 2(1986), 101–26.

things as knowledge and recidivism. It is not the only reason, however. When someone acquires more knowledge or keeps away from crime more of the time, other people tend to benefit in various ways, and they can do so even if the person concerned actually suffers a loss in welfare.[53] I shall, however, neglect this complication because my main example will be one in which it does not matter very much. This is the allocation of scarce life-saving medical resources, such as access to dialysis or organ transplantation. The outcome of treatment is evaluated solely by its impact on the person in question, not also by the effect on other people.

With respect to these life-saving resources, the distinction between level and increment takes two main forms. On the one hand, the proxy for welfare may be number of life years.[54] The level criterion then takes the simple form of age, suggesting that younger patients should be given priority over older patients. The increment criterion takes the form of additional life expectancy, suggesting that the scarce good should be directed where it would produce more extra life years. On the other hand, the proxy for welfare may be the probability of eliminating the specific medical problem that calls for intervention, regardless of life chances in general. The level criterion then tells us to give more to the person whose chances of spontaneous remission are the smallest – that is, the person in the most critical condition. The increment criterion tells us to give the resources to the person for whom the chance of eliminating the relevant condition would be most increased by the intervention.

I shall mainly consider the second interpretation, in which the tension between the level and increment criteria appears most clearly.

[53]   Some scholars become more unhappy as they grow more accomplished. As they learn more about the subject matter, they also learn more about the extent of their ignorance, and hence tend to think of themselves as unworthy frauds. (When the circle of light expands, so does the surrounding area of darkness.) But other people can still benefit from their work.

[54]   I shall not discuss the notion of "quality-adjusted" life years, except for the following remarks. What must be meant by quality in this context is *not* subjective level of well-being. Assume, namely, that we had constructed the perfect hedonometer so that people's cardinal levels of welfare could be measured and compared with precision. Nobody, I am sure, would propose that in allocating organs for transplantation one should prefer people with a sunny disposition over people with a morose temperament. The only relevant quality-of-life aspects are those that stem directly from the medical condition itself, such as pain and the ability to function. Moreover, I do not think one can construct valid trade-offs between quantity and quality thus defined, or, within quality, between pain and functioning.

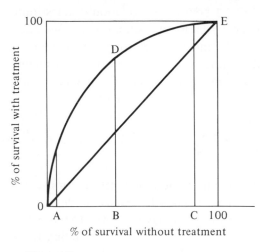

Figure 4.2

Giving an organ to a young person will usually produce more additional life years than giving it to an older person, so that the two criteria point in the same direction. There may be exceptions, which may make for hard choices, but there is no systematic tendency for the two criteria to diverge. I believe, however, that there is a systematic tendency for the level and increment criteria to diverge under the second interpretation.[55] From the inception of medical triage, it has been recognized that patients fall into three categories.[56] At one extreme, some patients are too ill to benefit from treatment: They will die in any case. At the other extreme, some patients do not need treatment: They will recover by themselves without it. In between are the patients who can benefit substantially from treatment and to whom, therefore, it should preferentially be given. The relation between severity of illness and efficacy of treatment can thus be summarized as follows (Figure 4.2):

The increment criterion tells us to concentrate on patients around *B*. The level criterion would have us prefer patients around *A*. The output-maximizing criterion, to which reference was made earlier,

[55] The statement that "sometimes there is tension between urgency of need and probability of success" (J.F. Childress, "Some moral connections between organ procurement and organ distribution," p. 99) is therefore too weak.
[56] Winslow, *Triage and Justice*, p. 1.

focuses on patients around C.[57] I believe this relation obtains quite frequently, not just for medical treatment. Among the cases cited earlier, education, support to the mentally retarded, and rehabilitation of prisoners are probably subject to similar constraints. Roughly speaking, efficiency dictates concentration on intermediate cases, compassion on the hard ones, and laziness on the easy ones.

Heart transplantations offer a direct illustration of the level-increment distinction. I shall quote at some length a passage that makes the point with exemplary clarity:

> A major conflict with the efficient or "best" use criteria for use of a heart arises once patients have been selected as candidates for transplant. The current selection system gives priority to those candidates on the list whose cases are most urgent, including those who have rejected a transplant and those who have received a temporary artificial heart as a bridge to transplant. A strict concern with efficacious use of donated hearts might argue against such an allocation, for the most urgent cases are less likely to do as well as healthier candidates. Yet is it not clear that decisions in favor of these candidates are ethically unacceptable. While efficiency is important, a strong equity consideration is to avoid abandonment of critically ill patients. Once on a candidate list one could argue that there is a special need not to abandon those in greatest need. . . . Retransplantation after rejection of a heart also appears to conflict with efficiency by allocating a second heart to a patient who does not have as good a chance of surviving as a healthier candidate. Yet aggressive efforts on behalf of a recipient in acute rejection are viewed by some physicians as essential to demonstrate commitment and to avoid abandonment. Such a choice is not unreasonable, and could justify a second transplant even if some patients receive two hearts and still die and others receive none.[58]

[57]   I am assuming here that treatment never makes things worse. Sometimes, this assumption is false. For instance, "selection of patients who are not sick enough [for a heart transplantation] may result in the premature death of a 'successful' recipient" (J.G. Copeland et al., "Selection of patients for cardiac transplantation," *Circulation* 75(1987), 1–9, at p. 1).

[58]   J.A. Robertson, "Supply and distribution of hearts for transplantation: Legal, ethical, and policy issues," *Circulation* 75(1987), 77–87, at p. 82. See also F.M. Kamm, "The Report of the U.S. Task Force on Organ Transplantation: Criticisms and Alternatives," *The Mount Sinai Journal of Medicine* 56 (1989), 207–220, esp. pp. 214 ff.

By emphasizing that urgent cases are *less likely* to do as well as healthier candidates, the passage supports the view that there is a systematic tension between level and increment criteria, or between compassion and efficiency. By emphasizing the value of commitment, it also brings an additional factor to our attention. This is the norm of *thoroughness* in treatment that is inculcated in doctors. Doctors would much rather treat a few patients intensively than more patients less intensively. Once a person has been granted patient status, medical ethics tells the doctor to do everything in his power to treat him. "As individual physicians, we must do the very best we can for our patients. The patient rightly expects his physician to act single-mindedly in his best interests. If very expensive care is indicated, then the physician should do his utmost to obtain it for his patients. . . . [The] physician cannot serve two masters – his patient and society's coffers."[59]

Taken in isolation, the medical norms of giving maximal attention to each patient and of treating the most serious cases first conflict with the principle of efficiency.[60] Outcome-oriented efficiency suggests that doctors spread their attention more thinly over a larger number of patients, and that they focus on cases of intermediate severity. It is not clear, however, that the norms of compassion and thoroughness can be isolated from the medical training in which they are embedded. Without them, it might indeed be difficult to induce in doctors the commitment and attention to detail that we do value on outcome-oriented grounds. A remote analogy might be the desirable side effects of the apparently pointless perfectionism of the postal services in some countries, especially in the past. By imposing the principle of next-day delivery for all letters, no matter how remote the destination, costs were incurred that would also appear excessive if taken in isolation. Yet the unbreakable principle, together with the heroic tales spun around its strict implementation, may have contributed to an occupational pride and motivation that led to better service than any efficiency-oriented system could ever realize at the same cost.

Kidney transplantations, too, require moral choices, but not the

---

[59]   M. Angell, "Cost containment and the physician," *Journal of American Medical Association,* 254 (1985), 1203–1207, at p. 1206.
[60]   For a more general discussion of social norms and their relation to rational, outcome-oriented behavior, see Ch. 3 of my *The Cement of Society,* Cambridge University Press 1989.

same ones. These operations differ from heart transplantations in that medical urgency or need is less important, because most patients can be kept alive on dialysis while they wait for a transplantation. Nevertheless there is a conflict between efficiency and equity, as the following account will show.

The allocation of kidneys – that is, the matching of an available kidney with a recipient – is made under a number of medical constraints. First, the donor and the recipient must be of the same blood type. Second, the recipient must not have cytotoxic antibody formation against the donor kidney. This constraint can be severe, as some candidates for transplants have antibody formation against most kidneys in the population at large. These patients are referred to as "sensitized." Third, the recipient should be well matched to the donor, in the sense of having as many as possible of six antigens in common. Unlike the first two constraints, this is not an absolute one, but is an important determinant of the probability of success.[61] Last, donor and recipient should not be too far from the transplantation center, as organs deteriorate rapidly with time.

Currently, the allocation of kidneys is regulated by the United Network for Organ Sharing (UNOS). I shall describe the regulations later, but first say a few words about the earlier, unregulated and decentralized practice, drawing on a study of a Renal Network in the American Midwest.[62] Assume that a kidney becomes available to a transplantation center.[63] First, blood type and antibody formation are used to exclude a certain number of potential recipients on the center's waiting list.[64] Next, the final recipient is chosen on the basis of antigen match and other medical considerations. In this network, kidneys were usually given only to patients who had a two or more antigen match with the donor. Some sensitized patients were offered kidneys even if the match was less good.

[61]   Although the medical literature is divided, this statement appears to remain true even after the introduction of cyclosporin. See, notably, Opelz, "Allocation of cadaver kidneys for transplantation."

[62]   M. Kjellstrand, "Age, sex, and race inequality in renal transplantation," *Archives of Internal Medicine* 148(1988), 1305–1309.

[63]   Actually, kidneys often are made available in pairs. The transplantation center then keeps one for itself, offering the other on a rotating basis to one of the other centers in the network.

[64]   Here and in the following I neglect problems relative to the formation of the waiting list. Kjellstrand argues that much of the bias in transplantation is due to unequal access to the waiting list, not or not only to unfair selection from the list.

The other medical considerations are partly related to the origin of the renal disease. Renal disease caused by diabetes has more complications than that caused by hypertension, yet patients with diabetic renal disease had higher transplant rates. The author of the study suggests that "this may be due to the thought that these patients' conditions do particularly badly while receiving dialysis."[65] If correct, this fact might have one of two explanations. Either the compassion of doctors leads them to prefer patients who are suffering more. Or efficiency considerations lead them to prefer patients whose conditions can be improved more: Although the outcome is less good in absolute terms than it would have been for other patients, the improvement in relative terms is bigger because they start out being worse off.

Following a pathbreaking article of Thomas Starzl and his coworkers at the University of Pittsburgh,[66] a new centralized system of kidney allocation has been created, based on a scheme for allocating points to potential recipients of a donated kidney and then selecting the person with the largest number of points. As in the scheme used for demobilizing American soldiers after World War II, it gives points both on backward-looking and on forward-looking grounds.[67] I shall describe only the parts of the scheme that are relevant for my concerns here.[68]

First, patients receive points – from 0 to 10 – for their time on the waiting list. Peyton Young has shown that the particular way in which waiting time generates points violates a condition similar to the social-choice condition of independence of irrelevant alternatives.[69] The relative ranking of two persons on the list can be reversed if a third person drops out. Young also shows that the paradox can be overcome by allocating points by (cardinal) length of waiting time,

[65]   Kjellstrand, op. cit., p. 1308.

[66]   T. Starzl et al., "A multifactorial system for equitable selection of cadaver kidney recipients," *Journal of American Medical Association* 257(1987), 3073–75.

[67]   The scheme is not, however, a mixed scheme in the technical sense defined earlier, because it does not rely on incentive effects of any kind.

[68]   Actually, I describe the system that was in force up to April 1989, at which time extensive changes were made. For a description of the earlier system and the reasons adduced for changing it, see the Memorandum of April 7 1989 from the United Network for Organ Sharing. The underlying arguments from efficiency and equity are, however, the same under the new system.

[69]   H.P. Young, "On the use of priority formulas for determining organ transplant recipients," *Journal of the American Medical Association* 261 (1989), p. 2957.

perhaps discounted by some factor, rather than by (ordinal) place in the queue.

Second, the patients receive points – from 0 to 12 – for the number of matched antigens. This part of the scheme embodies efficiency considerations.

Third, patients receive points – from 0 to 10 – for "panel reactive antibody formation." As explained earlier, many patients have pre-formed antibodies that make them strictly unsuitable as recipients for particular kidneys. Suppose that a person has antibodies against 60% of a panel of kidneys drawn at random from the population. For this he receives 6 points in the scheme. Antibody formation thus plays a double role in the scheme. By medical necessity, it retains its exclusionary function in matching individual recipients with individual kidneys. In addition, however, the point allocation just described ensures that a low chance of ever finding a suitable kidney can offset low antigen matching when a suitable kidney is finally found. As we saw, this practice also occurred under the earlier, unregulated regime. The UNOS regulations have incorporated this requirement in a formal manner. By giving extra weight to the patients who have the bad luck to be incompatible with most donated kidneys, it embodies consider-ations of equity or compassion. The same patients also tend to accumu-late more points from being on the waiting list. As they usually get some points from antigen matching as well,[70] their selection is virtually ensured *if* a suitable kidney becomes available. (Note, however, that the more points they get from antibody formation, the bigger the if.)

The system provides insurance against two forms of bad luck, or "medical and biological fate."[71] One, just mentioned, is that of hav-ing a high panel antibody formation. The other is that of having an unusual antigen pattern that makes it unlikely that one will ever achieve a good antigen match.[72] If efficiency – that is, number of antigen matches, were all that counted, patients with such patterns would stand a low chance. Adding points for time on the waiting list

---

[70]   Antibody formation and antigen matching do not vary independently of each other. "Widely reacting cytotoxic antibodies often have specificity against the class I antigens of the A and B histocompatibility loci; because of this, the demonstration of a negative cytotoxic cross match for a highly sensitized patient should predict a good antigen match. Thus, the antibody and antigen credits tend to be reinforcing." (Starzl et al, op. cit, p. 3075.)

[71]   This phrase is used in the UNOS document cited in note 68.

[72]   Ibid.

partially offsets that handicap. The first handicap – high antibody formation – is offset both by the waiting list and by explicitly according points for the antibodies.

This contrast between efficiency and compensation for bad luck has at most a family resemblance to the distinction between increment and level criteria for allocating medical goods. People with high antibody panel formation or unusual antigen patterns are not badly off *in terms of their disease,* as are critically ill heart patients who receive a new heart in spite of the fact that their condition makes them less likely to benefit from it. They are just unlucky with respect to the availability of efficient treatment.

V. Concluding remarks

In allocating scarce goods, one would often want to compare some aspect of welfare of the potential recipients: How well off they are without the good, how much difference would it make to their welfare if they get it, how well off they will be with the good. For practical purposes, we must measure welfare by an operational proxy. Claims based on supernormal or subnormal efficiency in converting goods into welfare are ruled out unless they are based on observable features that standardly go together with these abilities or inabilities. Similarly, people who claim to have expensive tastes, but do not differ from others in observable ways, cannot expect a favorable hearing. Observable criteria for allocating scarce goods are never perfectly correlated with the underlying unobservable feature – such as levels or increments of welfare – that we would really want to implement if we could observe it. This fact provided Marx with what he believed was a knockdown argument against the very possibility of a theory of justice. Any such theory, he argued, would sometimes treat different people – for example, people who are alike in all observable respects but different in others – equally and hence potentially unjustly.[73] For some reason, he did not notice that in appealing to the injustice of such procedures he was implicitly denying the claim that talk about justice is meaningless. More importantly, he confused first-best notions of justice with second-best implementations.

[73]   Marx, *Critique of the Gotha Program.*

Some reasons why welfare itself cannot be used directly in the comparison are mentioned in the Introduction to this book. Some are due to limitations in empathy and amounts of shared experience. Others are due to incentive problems: People may overreport or underreport the strength of their needs in order to get more of scarce goods or pay less for them. Still others are squarely normative. We might stop short of more individualized measures, even assuming that there were no information and incentive problems to prevent us from carrying them out. Some handicapped people might, because of a naturally sunny disposition, be at high levels of welfare. Or, because of their greater flexibility, they might have adapted successfully to their handicap. Some of the nonhandicapped might, because of a naturally morose disposition, be at a lower utility level than most handicapped people. Or, as in an example of Ronald Dworkin's, they might be unhappy because their religion makes them afraid they might be damned to eternal pain. In all these cases, we might feel disinclined to use this individualized information, even assuming it could be costlessly obtained. Most of us have strong intuitions that for purposes of compensation, such things as natural tempers, the ability to adapt to difficult circumstances, and religious beliefs neither offset handicaps nor constitute the analogue of handicaps.

In contexts of local justice, additional constraints arise. Fear of litigation promotes mechanical procedures at the expense of more individualized criteria. More importantly, doctors and other specialist allocators do not see their role as that of redressing social injustice. They are specialized providers of specific services, not promoters of overall welfare. They may be willing to compensate for bad luck that falls within their specific domain, but not for bad luck overall. A person in need of a kidney may be compensated for kidney-related bad luck, but usually not for other kinds of medical bad luck, and definitely not for nonmedical bad luck. If the specialists are aware that there is a bigger picture, they leave it to others. Often, however, nobody feels responsible for the big picture. The many local-justice decisions that are made by different institutions with respect to the same individual can add up to a global injustice.

5. Notes on the psychology of utility

DANIEL KAHNEMAN AND CAROL VAREY

The aim of this chapter is to introduce some psychological considerations that are relevant to the conception of utility and to the task of
comparing utilities. The standard approach to utility in decision science is an objectivist view, which focuses on tangible goods as the
carriers of utility, and on observable preferences as the proper measure of it. In contrast, a psychological view tends to focus on interpreted objects and events as the carriers of utility, and on experiences
of pleasure or satisfaction as the proper measure of it. Drawing on the
psychology of perception, we discuss the problem of predicting future
tastes and provide illustrative examples of two central facts of experience that are likely to be ignored in an objectivist analysis of utility:
adaptation and loss aversion. We show that lay intuitions about loss
aversion are at the root of everyday judgments of fairness in interpersonal dealings, and we consider some implications of these notions
for problems of allocation and reallocation.

Two concepts of utility

In the essay that initiated the modern analysis of decision making,
Daniel Bernoulli (1738) proposed that people evaluate financial options by weighting the utilities of possible outcomes by their probabilities. His argument and his references to earlier writings by Gabriel
Cramer identify utility as satisfaction – a subjective state or experience. Jeremy Bentham and John Stuart Mill also used the term utility
to refer to the hedonic quality of experience. Bentham spoke of the
two sovereign masters that govern mankind – pleasure and pain –

This work was supported in part by a grant from the Alfred P. Sloan Foundation.
We thank Amos Tversky, Richard Thaler, and Jon Elster for their helpful comments
and discussions.

and developed the notion of a 'hedonic calculus.' Indeed, the basic tenet of utilitarianism is variously referred to as 'the principle of utility' and as 'the greatest happiness principle.'[1] Sen (1986) finds a similar interpretation of utility in more recent writings by many economists, notably Pigou. However, the modern view of utility has abandoned any explicit reference to hedonic experience or happiness. The positivistic movement that swept the social sciences between the two world wars gave us behaviorism, strict operational definitions, and a suspicious attitude to mentalist notions. In this spirit it was natural to seek a definition of utility in terms of observable choices – revealed preferences. The definition of utility in terms of choices still rules the sciences of decision, although operationalism and behaviorism have largely lost their hold on psychology.

It should be clear that the original and the modern notions of utility are different concepts, and that the use of the same term for both is likely to produce confusion. In referring to Bentham's concept we shall speak of *experience utility:* the hedonic quality of experience, broadly construed to include satisfaction as well as pleasure. The value associated with a particular consequence in a decision context is its *preference utility.* The distinction between experience and preference utility suggests another notion, *predicted utility:* the individual's reflective assessment of future experience utility (Kahneman and Snell, 1990).

The three notions of utility are separable in measurement as well as in principle, and how they relate to each other is an empirical issue. As will be shown, there is reason to believe that the correspondence between the measures is not always close. The empirical dissociation of experience and decision utility has significant implications: Unless it can be shown that experience utility and preference utility correspond very closely, any utilitarian ethics, and indeed any attempt to perform interpersonal comparisons of utility or intrapersonal comparisons of utility across time, must be explicit about the notion of utility that is involved. The task of interpersonal comparison of utility is best stated as a comparison of strengths of preference only if people know what will be good for them and if this knowledge is appropriately reflected in their preferences. However, if people do not know their

---

[1]   A collection of readings illustrating the historical development of the concept of utility can be found in Page (1968).

future experience utilities, or if their preferences of the moment do not accurately reflect what they do know, a case can be made for using experience utility rather than preference as the unit of account in utilitarian calculations. The task of evaluating and comparing subjective experiences of utility will be central to such an approach. The task is not an easy one, but perhaps not as hopelessly impossible as the positivist dogma holds it to be. In this chapter we borrow some methods and results from the psychological study of perception to argue that many relevant facts about experience utility can be established–and that quite a few are already known. Our aim will be to present informative examples, rather than claim to be exhaustive.

Objectivist versus psychological approaches

There are characteristic differences between the approaches of various disciplines to the measurement and interpretation of utility. From the perspective of psychology, the methodological and conceptual presuppositions of the analysis of utility and choice in economics and in the formal sciences of decision share an *objectivist* core. In this section we sketch – or perhaps caricature – the objectivist position on utility and contrast it to the presuppositions that guide a psychological analysis of that topic.

We have already mentioned that the objectivist position favors a notion of utility based on publicly (objectively) observable choices. Several arguments bolster the implicit rejection of subjective experience as the criterion of welfare analysis. The methodological argument is the standard behaviorist one – that subjective experience is irrelevant to scientific analysis because it is not publicly observable. Sen (1986, p. 18) notes that "The popularity of this view in economics may be due to a mixture of an obsessive concern with observability and a peculiar belief that choice (in particular, market choice) is the only human aspect that can be observed." The substantive argument for measuring utility from choices is that people know what is good for them – or at least that they know it better than any observer, certainly better than any agency of society. Thus, the objectivist stance requires faith in the consistency and stability of preferences, and implicitly invokes the standard assumption of rationality. There is also an ideological and moral attitude to the act of choice: whether or not they choose wisely, individuals are responsible for their decisions and for the consequences of these decisions.

The psychological stance on these matters is different: Psychologists may be more tolerant of measures of subjective experience and more inclined to doubt the rationality of agents – and the wisdom of their choices. Thus, the objectivist and the psychological analyses favor different responses as measures of utility and different objects as carriers of utility. In an objectivist analysis, utility is assigned mainly (or only) to tangible and objectively identifiable aspects of the decision maker's situation at a given time. Not all economic analyses are objectivist in this sense: Treatments that incorporate regret (Loomes and Sugden, 1982) or positional considerations (Frank, 1985) focus on determinants of utility that are less than perfectly tangible, and Sen (1982, 1986) has offered a view of the mainsprings of action and of the evaluation of their consequences that is too broad to fit under the label of utility. In spite of such notable exceptions, there is a distinct tendency in economics and decision theory to view material assets as the main carriers of utility.

The psychological stance on the carriers of utility puts more weight on intangibles as factors of utility. The utilities of outcomes depend on how they are framed – in violation of the principle of invariance or extensionality that is often invoked in economic analyses (Arrow, 1982; Tversky and Kahneman, 1986). In particular, utilities depend on a neutrally evaluated reference level, and the main carriers of utility are said to be changes or differences (gains or losses) relative to that reference level. Psychological analyses are also likely to put considerable weight on emotions such as hope, fear, disappointment, regret, pride, and guilt, which do not fit easily into an objectivist treatment.

There is much to be said for an objectivist stance on utility, especially with regard to tractability. Revealed preferences are more satisfactory than measures of experience utility, and problems of distribution are more comfortably treated in terms of tangible assets than when the objects of distribution are subjective states. However, the facts of the matter are relevant. The case for using preferences as the measure of utility in welfare calculations is weakened if these preferences do not maximize experience utility, and the statement of distribution problems in terms of tangible assets may yield unjust solutions if intangible factors account for much of the variance in the utility of experience.

Maximizing redness

In this section we develop the argument for a conceptual separation of preference utility and experience utility. We begin by raising the problem of maximization of an attribute of experience in an unusual context, and we follow this with a review of some preliminary data on the issue of the accuracy with which people can predict changes in their tastes.

A basic observation of sensory psychology is that the quality and intensity of the experience associated with a particular stimulus depends on an *adaptation level* (AL), which is determined by the recent history of exposure to relevant stimuli (Helson, 1964). A special feature of sensory adaptation to some dimensions is that the neutral adaptation level defines two regions in which stimulation elicits different *qualities* of experiences. Temperature provides a salient example. The adaptation level varies with the prevailing temperature within a fairly broad range, and the same temperature can be experienced as warm or cold. Furthermore, the experiences associated with stimuli on the two sides of the adaptation level differ in quality: To be cold is not the same as to be hot only a little. Complementary colors, such as red and bluish-green, provide another example. When spotlights in such complementary colors are mixed on the theater stage, the resulting impression is of desaturated red or green-blue, depending on the relative intensity of the two sources. One particular mixture will yield an impression of white or gray. However, the mixture of complementary wavelengths that produces the 'colorless' experience of white or gray is not fixed. A mixture that appears distinctly red to an observer previously adapted to green light will appear distinctly green to an observer preadapted to red light. As in the case of temperature, the same physical stimulus can produce experiences that differ not only in degree but in quality.

The analogy to hedonic experience should be obvious. Pleasure and displeasure are another pair of qualitatively distinct dimensions, separated by a neutral value that can shift with adaptation. Exposure to a maintained state or to repeated occurrences of a hedonically relevant event can cause the neutral level to shift. The sugar concentration that produces the preferred level of sweetness varies with dietary habits. The same level of noise can be experienced as pleasantly low or unpleasantly high, depending on recent experience; an animal can respond to a particular quantity of food reward with evidence of frustration or satisfaction; and of course a given income can be perceived as opulence or as misery.

Let us now pursue the analogy between utility and other perceptual experiences, to see what it might teach us about maximization. Imagine an individual who seeks to maximize over a period of time her total subjective experience of redness – the characteristic experience associated with long wavelengths for that individual. What advice can be given to such a redness maximizer? The question is difficult, but technical considerations can take us at least part of the way to a reasonable answer, and will block several simple moves. In particular, it will do little good to follow a simple 'objective' strategy and filter out all short wavelengths by red goggles, or provide only 'red' illumination, because continuous homogeneous stimulation will soon produce complete adaptation – and a null response. Adaptation is the enemy to be vanquished, and contrast – both simultaneous and successive – is the essential weapon. A considerable amount of green stimulation will undoubtedly be required to maximize redness, with strong differences in the amount of 'red' stimulation between different areas at any one time, and frequent changes in the illumination of any area over time. How much green, how many different areas at any one time, how to use abrupt and gradual changes – these are technical questions.

The technical nature of the redness maximization problem is the point of this fable. We would not be tempted to believe that an individual who wishes to solve the redness maximization problem would know how to go about it. The consumer sovereignty argument – that people know what is red for them – has no appeal in this case. The analogy raises the question of whether people are much better in judging what will be good for them. Do individuals know much more about their adaptation to hedonically relevant stimuli than they do about their adaptation to lights of varying wavelength? Of course, most of us exert more effort in the pursuit of happiness than of redness, and the experience may bring about some skill, but a high level of expertise should not be taken for granted.

Predicting future tastes

Rational decisions about delayed outcomes require accurate predictions of future tastes, and the prediction of adaptation is an important part of the task. Thus, the decisions about whether to quarrel with one's spouse over wallpaper that now seems hideous, or to organize the community against the building of a noisy highway, cannot be made reasonably without considering the possibility of tastes and sensibilities being modified by continued exposure.[2] The significance of unpredictable tastes was noted in a well-known essay by March (1978), but there has been little systematic study of this important obstacle to rational choice.

Early results suggest that people's ability to predict their future tastes is sometimes quite poor (Kahneman and Snell, 1990). Participants in several experiments were repeatedly exposed to a mundane experience – for example, consuming a helping of their favorite ice-cream flavor while listening to the same piece of rock music, on eight visits to a laboratory on consecutive working days. They predicted their future ratings of the experiences after the first day. The daily repetitions of the experience produced rather substantial changes in the rated liking for the ice cream and the music. Most of the changes were negative, but about 20% were in the direction of a more favorable response. Overall, the correlation between actual and predicted *changes* in liking was close to zero. Similarly negative results were obtained consistently in several other studies of the same general kind.

These preliminary observations are of course insufficient to support a general claim that people cannot predict future tastes. However, they suffice to indicate the possibility of failures in such tasks. The issue is pertinent in assessing the feasibility of rational action and the justification of commitment (Elster, 1979; Schelling, 1981, 1983). In the situations for which Ulysses at the mast provides a model, the decision maker accurately predicts values and tastes in two future states: the moment of temptation and the end of the episode, when

[2]   In one study (Weinstein, 1982), residents close to a newly opened highway were optimistic that they would adapt to the noise. After one year there was little adaptation, and the residents were actually lobbying to have the road closed. In the years leading to the opening of the highway there had been no organized opposition to it – a clear failure to predict the impact of the new road on the residents.

current preferences will be restored. This assumption is reasonable in many cases. Difficult issues arise, however, when there is substantial uncertainty about future tastes. And an important class of irrational actions emerges: actions that are based on a wrong assignment of utilities to consequences. The next section describes a particular instance of this general problem.

The utility of escalating bads

Consider experiences of extended outcomes, such as carrying a suitcase over several street blocks on a hot day, performing push-ups as a form of military punishment, or suffering several days of continuous headaches. Most people readily agree that these experiences escalate, becoming progressively worse over time – in contrast to other unpleasant experiences where adaptation predominates. We have recently begun a study of beliefs and preferences about such escalating experiences (Varey and Kahneman, in preparation).

Beliefs about the changing experience of repeated or sustained exposure to stimuli must be relevant to the utility of an aggregate, such as six consecutive days of headache or fifty push-ups. A normative issue arises in considering the weighting of constituent experiences in the evaluation of the aggregate. In the absence of uncertainty, the most obvious contender is a form of within-person utilitarianism in which the constituent experiences are weighted equally.[3] Because the aversiveness of the experiences is assumed to escalate, equal weighting implies an accelerating or risk-averse utility function. This implication is interesting because of the rather consistent finding of risk-seeking preferences in choices that involve only negative outcomes (Kahneman and Tversky, 1979; Tversky and Kahneman, 1986). A risk-seeking utility function is easily justified for experiences that habituate with time or repetition, but not for escalating experiences.

Our initial results indicate significant dissociation of decisions from beliefs about the dynamics of the experience. Choices about escalat-

---

[3]   Jon Elster (personal communication) has suggested to us that in cases of uncertainty people may allocate intrapersonal goods or experiences over time according to a maximin principle, or by a compromise between the two strategies: maximizing subject to a floor constraint. This is an extension to the within-person domain of a strategy observed for between-person allocation choices under conditions of uncertainty (Frohlich, Oppenheimer, and Eavey, 1987).

ing aversive outcomes do not reflect the level of risk aversion that appears to be entailed by such beliefs. For example, the choices imply that the utility difference between fifty push-ups and sixty push-ups is no bigger than the utility difference between ten and twenty push-ups, although a large majority of respondents believe that the experience of successive push-ups is increasingly painful. Such choices do not maximize expected experience utility.

A thought experiment may help explain the apparent discrepancy between choices and beliefs in such situations: Imagine the experience of being told that you will have to perform a large number of push-ups. We propose that the intensity of the response to the *news* will turn out to be a sub-additive function of the number of push-ups – in accord with many studies of the psychophysics of number. This could well be true although the *experience* of the push-ups is increasingly aversive. For many years, Tversky and Kahneman have wondered about the possibility of distinguishing between the hedonic significance of a repeated event or maintained state and the hedonic significance of the news that one will be exposed to these events or this state. Our speculaton was that the weight assigned to outcomes in evaluating prospects (what we have here called preference utility) corresponds to their 'hedonic news value' more closely than to their 'actual' hedonic value, whenever the two diverge.

The hypothesis that news value and actual value can differ raises the question of which of the two provides a better guide to rational choice. Amos Tversky has suggested that the discrepancy may be mitigated if outcomes are consumed not only as actual events but also as memories, because the psychophysics of news might also apply to memories. In fact, experience utility broadly conceived should probably incorporate three separate factors: the experience as it happens, the experience of remembering it, and the experience of anticipating it (savoring the pleasure or dreading the pain).[4] These correspond to Jevons' (1905) enumeration of three distinct ways in which pleasurable or painful feelings are caused (cited in Loewenstein, 1987).

However, we should not undervalue the effect of the experience itself. A case can be made that acting according to news value alone is simply a mistake, when the experience of the relevant outcome will

---

[4]   Loewenstein (1987, 1988) has studied the value that individuals place on waiting periods in which to enjoy or suffer anticipation of future hedonic events.

be spread over time. The mistake is most serious where it is avoidable, as is the case if the individual would reach different conclusions by focusing on the experience rather than on the psychophysics of quantity. The value function of prospect theory (Kahneman and Tversky, 1979) may not be a good guide to action in such cases, although it may be appropriate if the outcome will be experienced as a single undesirable event, or if the response to repeated exposure produces habituation rather than sensitization. The indications of systematic conflicts between preference utility and the relevant beliefs about experience provide a new argument in the debate about the standard assumption of rationality, and raise a new question about the status of choice as the sole measure of utility.

Adaptation and comparison

In the next sections we consider two important determinants of experience utility: processes of adaptation and processes of comparative judgment.

Sensory adaptation

The phenomenon of adaptation (or habituation) to maintained states is a fundamental biological regularity, which is observed at all levels of functioning, from the single cell to the whole organism. At all these levels, the maintenance of a state and the frequent repetition of a stimulus event are associated with a decreasing response to that state or that event (Thompson and Spencer, 1966). Adaptation has obvious functional advantages for an organism limited in its information carrying capacity: There is no need for the system to deal with redundant messages, and it may deploy its discriminative abilities to best effect by focusing on deviations from the prevalent or expected state of affairs. Light adaptation, for instance, is essential in permitting the visual system to function effectively over a million-fold range of variation in luminance.

Adaptation has two general consequences for subjective experience. The first is that exposure to repeated stimulation tends to produce a neutral subjective experience, or null state, in response to that stimulation. In many cases, as we saw earlier, stimuli on the two sides of the neutral reference point are associated with different experiential qualities, such as red versus green, cold versus warm, pleasant versus unpleasant. The second consequence of adaptation is that contrast is the primary determinant of the intensity of experience.

Two broad categories of contrasting events are changes and differences. Special mechanisms are in place to enhance the response to changes and differences, while suppressing the response to steady states or to homogeneous stimuli. Abrupt changes and sharp discontinuities are most effective in producing a contrast effect. In the case of vision, for example, spatial discontinuities in the distribution of luminance create contours, and a mechanism of lateral inhibition sharpens apparent contrast at these contours. Abruptness is important: Gradual changes that fail to produce contours may not be noticed at all. Perceptual mechanisms such as visual opponent processes tend to segregate the experienced world into regions, exaggerating the differences between regions and smoothing variations within them. The notion of inhibition between opponent processes has been extended to hedonic stimuli by Solomon (1980). His hypotheses go beyond the range covered here, but are as yet supported by little evidence.

Before discussing the implications of adaptation, we should mention two important restrictions on the phenomenon. First, although there is substantial evidence for adaptation to stimuli as varied as noise, pollution, population density, temperature, and electric shocks (Glass and Singer, 1972), people do not adapt to everything. In general, the speed of adaptation depends on the intensity of the stimulus, and there may be little adaptation to stimuli that are extremely painful or intense (Epstein, 1973). This serves as a reminder that there is a *range of tolerance* within which adaptation effects can operate. Second, adaptation to stressors can be affected by coping strategies and by cognitive appraisal (Baum, Singer, and Baum, 1982; Lazarus, 1968, 1981).

The phenomenon of sensory adaptation has suggestive implications for the task of making interpersonal comparisons of subjective experiences. It is plausible to assert that adapted null states can be matched for a given individual: A woman could be said to have the same response to the weight of her hair – whether short or long – after she completely adapts to the current weight, whatever it may be. Similarly, experiences at the threshold of sensitivity, which are also affected by adaptation, may be subjectively equivalent. Imagine walking into a room that appears totally dark. After a while your eyes adjust and you see a door, which you walk through into total darkness. You progress in this manner through a sequence of rooms, where the level of illumination may decrease by several orders of magnitude, but the initial experience in each room is the same. Thus, the subjective experience of total darkness may be matched at different levels of night adaptation.

The argument that would allow matching states of an individual at different times appears almost equally compelling for interpersonal comparisons. Two individuals who are fully adapted to different levels of stimulation on a particular attribute can be said to be matched in their *absence* of response to their states, and their responses to stimuli that differ in the same direction from their respective adaptation levels can be matched in sign, if not in magnitude. The implications of this argument for interpersonal comparisons of utility are obvious and potentially significant, but a note of caution is surely in order. In the cases of complete sensory adaptation that we have mentioned, experiences that are subjectively very similar or even undistinguishable can be produced by different combinations of adapting states and stimulus intensities.

Comparative coding

There is a large class of perceptual phenomena that bear a family resemblance to sensory adaptation, but are certainly mediated by different mechanisms. The characteristic of these cases is that the evaluation of an experience is relative to a norm – also called a frame of reference, a reference level, and sometimes an adaptation level. A tall man may appear slight in the company of professional basketball players. A stern rebuke may appear compassionate or even friendly, if a diatribe were expected. A poor man may feel wealthy after a raise, and a rich man may feel poor after a loss in the market. In the classic studies of adaptation level, an observer may come to consider a weight of 50 grams 'heavy' in one context, and a weight of 300 grams 'light' in another (Helson, 1964). In another illustrative study (Wohlwill and Kohn, 1973), migrants to a medium-sized city coming from a rural environment or from a large metropolitan area were found to have different impressions of the size, pollution level, noise level, and pace of life in their new environment. Unlike the case of sensory adaptation, the observer in such situations usually retains some ability to discriminate absolute as well as relative values on the judgment dimension.

Context effects should not be dismissed as a mere adjustment of the response scale. An experiment by Russell and Fehr (1987) illustrates the power of the effect. Subjects were asked to describe the facial expression of a woman seen on a photograph. When seen on its own, the woman's face appears almost enigmatically unemotional. In the experiment, however, the target face was judged immediately after another photograph that expressed a strong emotion. In that context, the target face was judged to express a moderately intense contrasting emotion. From personal observation we can report that this simple situation induces a remarkable subjective experience: The neutral face actually appears to smile next to a scowling neighbor and to express sadness after judging an exuberant expression, to the extent that even a sophisticated observer finds it difficult to believe that the same picture of the face was shown on both occasions. Results of other experiments (Higgins and Lurie, 1983) imply that an observer would make systematic errors in attempting to recognize the 'neutral' face originally seen in one emotional context, if the test of memory were conducted in a different context.

Several experiments have demonstrated context effects on affect and mood. Strack, Schwarz, and Gschneidinger (1985) found contrast effects on judgments of happiness and life satisfaction when subjects were instructed to remember emotional events occurring in the past, except when the memories affected present mood – in which case assimilation effects on happiness ratings were observed.[5] Even vicarious stimuli can provide a context. Dermer, Cohen, Jacobsen, and Anderson (1979) found contrast effects on life satisfaction when subjects were shown films depicting either 'the good old days' or the 'bad old days.'

Other studies have suggested that counterfactual alternatives can

---

[5] In a later section, in which we discuss Parducci's (1984) theory of happiness, we return to the roles of two component effects of an experience – the experience itself, and its effect on the standard of comparison. Tversky and Griffin (in press) refer to these respectively as the endowment and contrast effects.

define the norms to which reality is compared (Kahneman and Tversky, 1982; Kahneman and Miller, 1986). Consider an individual who arrives late at the airport, expecting to have missed his flight by half an hour, and is now told that his plane was delayed and actually left only three minutes ago. Why does this information make things worse? Easily imagined scenarios in which he would have caught the plane evidently provide the context of comparison. A similar explanation applies to the special poignancy of 'unnecessary' accidental deaths – such as that of the traveler who made a special effort to get onto a flight that crashed. Miller and McFarland (1986) found that people recommended larger compensation for victims of crimes and accidents with readily available alternative scenarios, probably as a result of heightened sympathy.

The rules that govern the availability of imagined alternatives to reality were discussed by Kahneman and Miller (1986). Some events evoke alternatives more strongly than others. The cognitive rules of availability may explain, for example, why greater regret is commonly associated with acts of commission than with acts of omission, or why there is more regret about harm that was caused by deviating from standard operating procedures than by following them. In general, such considerations point to the high cost of choice – in an intriguing tension with the emphasis that Sen (1982, 1987) has placed on the value of freedom.

Comparisons with others are an important source of context effects in the evaluation of one's outcomes. There has been considerable psychological research on the factors that control social comparisons and there is also a history of mild interest in these factors among economists (Duesenberry, 1952; Frank, 1985). In general, comparisons are most salient if individuals perceive the reference person or group as in some way similar to themselves. This makes the fate of the reference group appear to be feasible, thereby setting up a reference level against which to evaluate one's own circumstances. Brickman and Bulman (1977) point out that people may try to avoid the unpleasant consequences of some comparisons, either by looking for ways in which they differ from those who are beset by misfortune, or by refraining from comparison altogether if an unwelcome contrast is anticipated.

The comparison processes that have been discussed in this section illustrate a fundamental aspect of what we have called the psychological stance, in opposition to an objectivist stance. A basic tenet of psychological analysis is that the contents of subjective experience are coded and interpreted representations of objects and events. An objective description of stimuli is not adequate to predict experience because coding and interpretation can cause identical physical stimuli to be treated as different and different ones to be treated as identical – or at least similar in important respects. The contrastive coding and interpretation that is routinely assigned to stimuli is not an extraneous addition to perceptual experience – it is a central aspect of the immediate experience, and perhaps an even more important aspect of its representation in memory.

Determinants of satisfaction

The thrust of the present argument is that utility should be viewed as a dimension of experience and, as such, it is expected to obey the usual laws of perception and memory. The preceding sections have identified two sets of factors that are likely to affect the experience utility that an individual will associate with a particular event or state: the history of prior experiences and the context to which the relevant object, state, or event will be compared.

Much information about people's evaluations of different aspects of their lives has been obtained from surveys of well-being and satisfaction (for a review of this literature, see Argyle, 1987). A useful generalization is that the correlation between objective circumstances of different *populations* and the average reported well-being of these populations is very low (Campbell, 1981; Diener, 1984; Easterlin, 1974). A representative observation is that satisfaction with standard of living did not increase among Detroit area wives between 1955 and 1971, although real income increased by 40% during that period (Duncan, 1975). These results are just what would be expected from the idea that adaptation to improving circumstances causes people to move on a hedonic treadmill (Brickman and Campbell, 1971), with little real gain in actual welfare.

The argument for the existence of a hedonic treadmill was brought to an almost absurd extreme in a study by Brickman, Coates, and Janoff-Bulman (1978) in which recent lottery winners were found to be no happier than a control group. Paraplegics were less happy, but still above the midpoint on the scale. However, the paraplegics described their pre-injury past as much happier than the other groups did. These results are indeed difficult to accept, perhaps because we are certain that *becoming* a paraplegic is a tragic event, that recovering from paralysis is cause for joy, and that the hedonic responses to sudden large changes in wealth are almost equally unequivocal. However, the thought experiment of imagining the utility of a change from one state to another does not necessarily provide a useful assessment of the utility of being permanently in that state. It would therefore be rash to dismiss the results of this and other surveys of well-being because they do not agree with our intuitions.

If individual adaptation to circumstances were complete, we might expect most people to rate themselves at the neutral point on scales of satisfaction or well-being. This is not the case, of course. There is large variation in such ratings within any one population. Furthermore, most surveys indicate a positive correlation between economic standing and relevant measures of satisfaction within each population, accounting for up to 10–15% of the variance. The joint finding of no cross-population effects and of a moderately strong within-population effect suggests that a tendency to adapt to one's particular circumstances is counteracted by comparisons with other people or with one's past.

Sociological studies of soldiers' morale in World War II identified relative deprivation as a more important factor than objective circumstances: Morale in a unit tended to be low if its circumstances were significantly worse than those of a comparable unit (Stouffer et al., 1949). More recent work on relative deprivation has focused on women – some writers have expressed frustration with women whose morale is high although they are paid much less than men for the same work (Crosby, 1982). Morale and satisfaction tend to be high so long as women compare themselves to other women rather than to men.

Some of the best information about the determinants of individuals' satisfaction with their income was obtained in Dutch and Belgian surveys, in which respondents were asked to give a range of income they would judge as satisfactory, insufficient, excellent, and so on (van Praag, 1971). The extensive results of these surveys have been used to evaluate the role of different comparisons, such as to one's past circumstances and to those of comparable others, in determining the 'welfare income function.' The analysis suggests that the income of others is not the most important factor that controls the subjective definition of adequate income, although it does have some influence. Modeling income satisfaction as a function of a perceived distribution of incomes, the authors concluded that one's own past and present income is allocated twice as much weight as others'. The weight accorded to each preceding year gets smaller and smaller, but the total contribution of previous years is about four times that of the present year (van de Stadt, Kapteyn, and van de Geer, 1985).

The relativity of subjective hedonic experience and implications for planning 'the good society' were explored in a thoughtful essay by Brickman and Campbell (1971). Drawing on adaptation-level theory (Helson 1964) and on surveys of well-being, they raised the possibility that any beneficial effects of improved circumstances may be canceled by adaptation. The notion of such a hedonic treadmill is consistent with a generally pessimistic view of human prospects, with an indifferent attitude toward attempts to reduce social inequities – or perhaps with a combination of these unattractive positions. If people can adapt to anything, there may be little point in attempting to improve their circumstances (Ittleson et al., 1974). In a more positive spirit, adaptation effects can be viewed as a challenge, to be overcome by a just distribution of resources (Brickman and Campbell, 1971) and by rational planning of income and consumption patterns (Scitovsky, 1976).

The pitfalls of intuitions about utility

We have tried to argue that any treatment of interpersonal utility comparison must assign a central role to two factors that an objectivist approach is likely to neglect: adaptation and the relative coding of experiences. Taken to the extreme, the notion of adaptation might suggest that tolerable sustained states have no utility at all and that stable differences in the endowments of individuals can be ignored. This claim is too strong, but we advance it as a useful corrective to a set of powerful intuitions that tend to exaggerate utility differences between states.

We have proposed that two people who are fully adapted to their current state could have equal states of subjective well-being – null states – at very different objective levels of a desirable attribute such as health, youth, or income. However, the two individuals would not view themselves as equal: One would be reluctant to trade because the change would be in a negative direction; the other would desire a change. Are such attitudes to changes of state relevant to assessing the utility of these states? Our intuitions about the emotional significance of a sustained state are often based on images of the transition into that state. As we mentioned earlier, it is tempting to evaluate the utility of being a paraplegic by imagining the horror of becoming one, or the joy of a cure – but the temptation should be resisted.[6] In the presence of major adaptation effects, the utility of a transition provides little information about the adapted experience. Many a blissful ocean swim begins in shivering agony. After repeated experiences with this sequence, people will learn to look forward to the swim (although perhaps with less enthusiasm than if the two stages of the experience occurred in reverse order). In dealing with unfamiliar states, however, most people probably have a more accurate view of the utility of the transition than of the steady state. As a consequence, adaptation will tend to be neglected or underestimated and differences between states correspondingly exaggerated.

The issue raised here applies to many forms of introspective thought experiments, those conducted by philosophers as well as by respondents in surveys of well-being. By their nature, such exercises take place in the head of one individual. They are, perforce, a within-subject design, even when the intention is to perform an interpersonal comparison. Thus, powerful intuitions are likely to lead us astray when we compare the utilities of different individuals, or alternative states for a given individual. As we have shown, methods requiring evaluation of a single stimulus and methods using a comparative design may yield quite different intuitions. In addition, as will be shown in the next section, comparative designs with different reference levels can yield conflicting results because of loss aversion. Thus the thought experiment may not only be a poor source for

[6]   A paraplegic commented on a television interview: "You probably think I am unhappy but you are wrong. And I used to think that I knew what suffering was, but I was wrong."

comparisons of experience utility, it may also be an invalid indicator of preference utility. The reluctance to accept the surprising results of surveys of well-being may reflect this difficulty.

Prescriptive implications

Considerations of adaptation have rather obvious implications for the individual pursuit of happiness and for welfare policy.[7] Applying only a standard utilitarian calculus – without any suggestion of exclusivity for these considerations – priority must be assigned to events and states that resist adaptation: The aversive ones should be eliminated, and the positive ones should be provided, within the constraints of feasibility. A much lower priority should be accorded to improving those circumstances that are likely to yield rapid adaptation, when the starting point is within the acceptable range. In this section we review some proposals that have been advanced in this prescriptive spirit.

Scitovsky (1976) drew an important distinction between comforts and pleasures, on the basis of psychological evidence relating pleasure to novelty and arousal value (Berlyne, 1960). The distinctive mark of comforts is that their presence gives no pleasure, and indeed no affective experience at all. Comfort is a state in which one is at or close to optimal arousal, whereas pleasures are derived from a change in state toward optimal arousal. Thus one achieves comforts at the expense of the possibility of pleasure. In the terms of the present analysis, comforts are sources of initially pleasant stimuli to which adaptation is essentially complete. The main experience of a comfort is the displeasure that accompanies its withdrawal. In contrast, pleasures are stimuli that are treated as exceptions to some routine, and therefore attract attention and increase arousal. Some examples of pleasures that Scitovsky discusses are vacations, flowers, feasts, and skilled consumptions. Scitovsky shows little respect for the idea that people can be trusted to maximize the benefits of the resources at their disposal. Indeed, he argues that some cultures are distinctly

[7] Ethical problems can arise when policy makers consider imposing a bad in the belief that people will get used to it. For an exchange on how this differs from choices for oneself operating on one's own belief that one will adapt, see Elster (1979, pp 81–82; 1983, pp 112–113), and Sen (1981, pp 203–204).

worse than others in using economic resources to produce enjoyment. In a related vein, Brickman and Campbell (1971) claim that it may be worth fasting in order to obtain pleasure from feasting. This was once widely customary, and still is in some religious communities.

Parducci (1968, 1984), a psychophysicist with an interest in the study of happiness, has offered an analysis that contrasts in intriguing ways with Scitovsky's. The starting point for Parducci's analysis is that the relative coding of an experience depends on its location in the *range* of experiences to which it is compared, as well as on its position in the frequency distribution of these experiences. The neutral point on the subjective scale is located between the median and the midrange of the relevant set. This hypothesis suggests that a positively skewed distribution is detrimental to the average quality of experience, because the isolated pleasures exert a strong pull on the norm, causing most experiences to appear unsatisfactory. Parducci suggests the peak experiences are not worth their costs, and views a negatively skewed distribution as the key to happiness. Amos Tversky has also been concerned for some time with the dual effects of hedonic experiences. Pleasurable experiences have the direct effect of increasing one's endowment, but the memory of them also induces a contrast effect that can reduce other pleasures in the future. The overall benefit depends on the relative weights of these two contributions (Tversky and Griffin, in press).

Parducci's analysis is intuitively compelling for some cases. Consider a family that has a tradition of celebrating birthdays by a restaurant meal. It does appear unwise for such a family to pick out one arbitrary birthday for a much more expensive feast than they plan for future occasions – subsequent birthday feasts could well lose some of their charm. However, an analysis of the effects of similarity and categorization on the adaptation level suggests that an extravagant outing on a different occasion, such as a wedding anniversary, would have relatively little effect on the norm for birthday celebrations (Kahneman and Miller, 1986). To have the benefits of the unusual pleasure without paying the cost in the form of a raised adaptation level, the special occasion must be cognitively isolated from other experiences that might be compared to it. Scitovsky's recommendations for the investment of greater resources in pleasures is especially appealing when the contrast effect of these experiences can be minimized. A similar conclusion is implied by Tversky and Griffin's analysis of endowments and contrasts.

The analysis of the effects of skewed distribution is usefully extended to another domain: the schedule of distribution of a remuneration package (Kahneman and Thaler, 1987). The immediate question is the allocation of the package to regularly scheduled payments and to occasional bonuses – with a secondary question of the extent to which the size and timing of these bonuses should be predictable. Practices vary widely among countries: The proportion of bonuses in the total remuneration package of line workers is much higher in Japan than in the United States, and many firms in Europe pay a 'thirteenth month salary' in December, and perhaps a fourteenth one in June as well. These are positively skewed distributions. Our analysis suggests that such arrangements should have hedonic advantages over a uniform schedule of payments if the bonuses are cognitively segregated from regular income. Systematic experimental studies are lacking, but a recent review concluded that workers are generally enthusiastic about bonus plans (Lawler, 1986). A survey conducted with Cornell undergraduates also indicated that a positively skewed distribution of monthly incomes was preferred to a rectangular distribution of the same total. A negatively skewed distribution (for example, distributing yearly income over nine months) was almost unanimously rejected, perhaps because of the problems of self-control that such a distribution raises (Kahneman and Thaler, 1987).

Conventional economic wisdom would suggest that the schedules of payment should be irrelevant, because employees would be expected to save and borrow so as to even out their consumption. However, a Japanese study indicates that the pattern of spending for bonus income differs substantially from normal spending (Shefrin and Thaler, 1988). Workers save more from bonuses, whether or not these bonuses are expected. We suspect that workers also spend more bonus money on extravagances – as Scitovsky would surely recommend.

Loss aversion

Preceding sections documented the claim that people are relatively insensitive to steady states, but highly sensitive to *changes* from the neutral adaptation level that separates positive from aversive experiences, gains from losses, advantages from disadvantages. These are the considerations that justify the proposal made in prospect theory (Kahneman and Tversky, 1979) that the main carriers of value are gains and losses rather than overall wealth. We now turn to a fundamental property of the value function, which has been called *loss aversion* (Kahneman and Tversky, 1984): Losses loom larger than gains, both as they are anticipated in the context of decision and as they are ultimately experienced.

Loss aversion is a particular manifestation of an asymmetry in the evaluation of avoidance and approach tendencies – a biological rule of obvious adaptive value, which is manifest in the priority accorded to signals of pain and danger in neural processing. In this section we briefly describe some recent demonstrations of loss aversion in risky and riskless choice, and we raise the question of the normative status of the value function. We also assess the expressions of loss aversion in intuitive notions of fairness.

Loss aversion and the avoidance of risk

It is generally accepted that people's preferences for uncertain prospects are predominantly risk averse, and that fact is commonly given a unitary explanation by invoking a concave utility function for wealth. The analysis of risky choice in prospect theory abandoned this unitary treatment, by distinguishing three factors that contribute to risk-averse preferences: (1) The overweighting of sure outcomes favors risk-averse preferences for gains that are offered with certainty over gains that are merely probable; (2) the concavity of the value function in the positive domain favors risk-averse preferences for positive prospects, as in standard treatments; (3) loss aversion, the differential steepness of the value function in the positive and negative domains, favors risk aversion in the evaluation of mixed prospects.[8]

There are important quantitative differences in the extent of risk aversion that is produced by these contributing factors, and loss aversion is by far the strongest effect. The relative magnitude of risk aversion in strictly positive and in mixed prospects was compared in a

---

[8]   In choices between purely negative prospects, risk-seeking is often observed because of the combined effect of the decision weights and the convexity of the value function.

recent experiment, which used auction techniques to establish equivalences between pairs of prospects (Kahneman and Tversky, in preparation). Participants in that experiment were indifferent between the following prospects: (1) equal chances to win $15 or to win $40, with a .5 chance to win nothing; (2) equal chances to win $5 or to win $52, with a .5 chance to win nothing. The value-difference between gains of $40 and $52 is matched to the difference between gains of $5 and $15, a ratio of 1.2. Quite different results were obtained for mixed prospects, where the following two options were equally attractive: (3) equal chances to win $20 or lose $5, with a .5 chance to win and lose nothing; (4) equal chances to win $60 or lose $15, with a .5 chance to win and lose nothing. Here, a chance to win $60 rather than $20 was needed to compensate for the risk of losing $15 rather than $5 – a ratio of 4:1 between matched differences of losses and of gains. Other experiments of the same type (all conducted with low stakes) yield similar estimates (between 2 and 4) for the ratio by which gains must exceed equally probable losses to make a risky prospect acceptable.

The abrupt changes in the level of risk aversion observed in these experiments cannot be explained by any reasonable utility function for overall wealth. The extremely risk-averse choices of our subjects appear almost absurd – if evaluated in terms of monetary outcomes. Furthermore, they appear unreasonable when considered as a *policy* regarding the acceptability of small gambles, because of the risk-reducing effects of statistical aggregation. Indeed, risk aversion is considerably reduced when people are required to make a decision about a set of plays on the same gamble (Keren and Wagenaar, 1987). When left to their own devices, however, decision makers focus myopically on problems taken one at a time, and their choices appear to be dominated by the anticipated emotional consequences of individual losses. Can such myopic and extremely risk-averse decisions be viewed as mistakes? Should we wish to influence people to modify the value function that they apply, or their ways of framing the problems?

The issue raised here is another form of a question raised earlier: What is the utility that should be considered in welfare calculations? Unlike the problems of escalating bads, there is no obvious conflict between experience utility and preference utility in these cases of extreme risk aversion. The decisions of subjects indicate that they are very reluctant to accept a risk of loss, and we have no reason to believe that they act on a mistaken assessment of the immediate hedonic consequences of winning or losing their bets. However, a problem arises because extreme risk aversion in risky choices for small stakes is very costly in the long run – the conflict is between the subjects' preferences and an objective assessment of their best interest. The susceptibility of the decisions to aggregate framing is another reason for doubt. It is difficult to accord much respect to foolish or labile preferences.

The endowment effect

In the context of decisions about riskless multi-attribute options, loss aversion appears to be implicated in the following two observations, among others. First, the *same* difference between attribute levels of two options will have greater impact on the preference between them if it is coded as a difference between disadvantages than if it is coded as a difference between advantages. Thaler (1980) has given the example of the attitudes to a price difference that is labeled as a discount or as a surcharge; it appears easier to forego a discount than to accept a surcharge. Second, loss aversion may induce a reluctance to trade one bundle for another, if the goods that are given up are evaluated as losses whereas the goods that are obtained are evaluated as gains. This effect of ownership on value has been called the *endowment effect* (Thaler, 1980).

A recent series of experiments (Kahneman, Knetsch, and Thaler, 1990) illustrate the power of the endowment effect and the ease with which it can be induced. The experiments are conducted in a class setting. One third of the participants, arbitrarily selected by the seats they occupy, are given an object – such as a decorated mug worth about $5 at the university bookstore. These participants (called sellers) are asked to indicate in writing the lowest price at which they are willing to sell their mug, with instructions that are intended to discourage strategic bids. Another group (the buyers) are asked to state the highest price that they are willing to pay to acquire a mug. Finally, a third group (the choosers) are given a choice between receiving a mug and receiving a sum of money, and are asked to indicate the smallest amount of cash that they would prefer to the mug. In one of several experiments conducted in this design, the median responses of sellers, buyers, and choosers were $7.12, $2.87, and $3.12, respectively. The highly significant difference between the value assigned to the mug by sellers and by choosers is worthy of note because the choices faced by the two groups are objectively equivalent. The attitude to a mug appears to be greatly altered by taking possession of it, illustrating the instantaneous induction of an endowment effect.[9]

The endowment effect represents an embarrassment for the theory of value, and for the more general assumption that tastes are stable. The doubling of the monetary value associated with an object when it becomes part of one's endowment is not easily reconciled with the stability assumption. Because the sellers and the choosers face extensionally equivalent options, their discrepant preferences can be viewed as a framing effect (Tversky and Kahneman, 1981, 1986), a violation of the principle that preferences should be invariant over changes of the problem representation that the decision maker, upon reflection, would consider irrelevant. The discrepant evaluations of the mug made by sellers and by choosers who objectively face the same choice illustrate the difficulty: If a chooser who is prepared to set a value of $3.12 on the mug were to learn that acquiring the mug would raise its value (to him or her) above $7, what should that chooser do?

Although the existence of a large endowment effect may be a threat to standard value theory, it is surely a blessing that goods that people acquire thereby become more valuable: This property of evaluation tends to stabilize choices by causing the disadvantages of the alternatives relative to the status quo to be weighted more heavily than their advantages (Kahneman and Tversky, 1984). Consider an individual who would have some difficulty choosing between a mug and a large chocolate bar, if given the choice between the two. Now imagine that the individual is arbitrarily assigned the mug, takes possession of it, and is then offered the opportunity to exchange it for a chocolate bar. Loss aversion implies that the initial indifference between the two prizes has now been replaced by a definite preference for the mug. Of course, another individual whose tastes were originally similar but

[9] The effect seems to be restricted to goods that are intended for personal use. There is no reluctance to trade in money tokens (Knetsch, Thaler, and Kahneman, 1987), and presumably no loss aversion for goods that are acquired to be traded, or for money that is used to pay for a purchase. Thus, most routine economic transactions do not involve loss aversion.

who has been given the chocolate bar will be equally reluctant to accept the mug in its place. Just such an experiment was reported by Knetsch, Thaler, and Kahneman (1987); fewer than 15% of participants were willing to exchange the prize they had been given. If the same phenomenon applies on a grander scale, loss aversion may have a great deal to do with the (relative) stability of long-term choices of spouses, jobs, and homes.

Another beneficial consequence of loss aversion is that it tends to combat the effects of time discounting in determining preferences for future streams of rewards. Loss aversion favors social arrangements that provide a steady improvement of rewards or benefits over time, in preference to schedules in which the same total benefit is handed out in equal or diminishing quantities. Many of us, including all academics, live under explicit or implicit contracts that almost guarantee nondecreasing or slowly increasing income – and that clearly violate the theoretical expectation that workers are paid the value of their marginal product. The present analysis of the effects of adaptation and of loss aversion confirms that such contracts are likely to offer a good hedonic return per dollar of pay received.

The fairness of transactions

A study of lay opinions about the fairness of various economic transactions produced much evidence of asymmetric treatment of gains and losses (Kahneman, Knetsch, and Thaler, 1986a,b). Respondents in telephone surveys were asked to evaluate the fairness of actions in which a firm (merchant, landlord, or employer) sets a price, rent, or wage that affects one or more transactors (customer, tenant, or employee). As illustrated by the following example, each brief scenario specified a potentially relevant precedent, an occasion for the firm to reconsider a price or a wage it had set, and an actual decision that was to be evaluated.

> A hardware store has been selling snow shovels for $15. The morning after a large snowstorm, the store raises its price to $20. Please rate this action as
>
> *Completely fair   Acceptable   Unfair   Very unfair*

Although the merchant's response to increasing demand appears reasonable in the light of the standard logic of price setting, 82% of respondents considered it distinctly unfair.

The same general procedure was used to investigate a variety of common pricing decisions. Can a landlord put up rent in a housing shortage? Is it fair for a retailer to retain the entire benefit of a decrease of wholesale price? Is it fair for a firm to lower the wage of an employee to the level at which it could hire a replacement? When an employee quits, is it fair for the firm to pay his replacement at the lower prevailing wage?

A concept of *reference transaction* provided a satisfactory account of the results. The reference transaction is a relevant precedent that defines a reference price or wage for the transactor and a reference profit for the firm. Outcomes are coded in relation to the reference transaction: In the snow shovel example the outcome is a loss to consumers and a gain to the firm. The main conclusion of the research is that judgments of fairness are governed by a principle of *dual entitlement:* Transactors have an entitlement to the reference terms and the firm has an entitlement to its reference profit. A firm that imposes a loss on a transactor to achieve an increased profit violates the transactor's entitlement. On the other hand, a firm is allowed to impose a loss on its transactors in order to prevent a loss of profit – for example, by cutting wages when business is poor. The asymmetric treatment of gains and losses that is built into any concept of entitlement (or right) is evident in the following result: Lay rules of fairness permit increases in costs to be passed on to customers, but they do *not* obligate the firm to share the benefits of decreasing costs (Kahneman, Knetsch, and Thaler, 1986b). This observation is incompatible with the common notion that cost-plus is the rule of fair pricing (Okun, 1981).

Lay judgments of fairness draw a sharp distinction between new and continuing transactions. An employee's current wage and a tenant's current rent have the moral force of entitlements in further transactions with the same employer or landlord. However, the employee and the tenant do not carry this entitlement with them in transactions with new firms, and a firm is allowed to set the terms of transactions with new workers or tenants according to prevailing market prices.

The psychological rules that govern lay judgments of fairness have much in common with the rules that govern the evaluation of outcomes of individual decisions. In both cases, precedents and expectations define a reference outcome, with sharply asymmetric reactions to positive and negative deviations from the reference level. The moral counterpart of loss aversion is a strong condemnation of actions in which the actor achieves a gain by imposing a loss on another person. There is no correspondingly strong injunction to share one's gains with others. Furthermore, losses need not be shared: A firm that is threatened by a loss in a transaction may fairly pass the total loss to its transactors. Judgments of fairness assign a central role to a distinction that is considered fallacious in standard economic analysis, between 'real' losses and the opportunity costs associated with foregone gains. Failing to maximize profit has the force of a loss in the calculation of 'rational fools,' but not in lay intuitions.

Distribution and redistribution

Problems of just allocation can often be framed in two distinct ways that are analogous to two modes of framing consequences of individual decisions with monetary outcomes: as states of wealth, or as changes in wealth (Kahneman and Tversky, 1979). (1) In the *distribution* frame, the object of moral evaluation is a pattern of final individual endowments, into which the allocation is incorporated. (2) In the *redistribution* frame, the outcomes to affected individuals are described in terms of gains and losses relative to an existing endowment, and the pattern of these changes is the object of evaluation.

The two framings of the problem of just allocation appear to be associated with distinct moral intuitions. In particular, considerations of loss aversion, which are suppressed in the distribution frame, tend to play a dominant role when the allocation problem is framed in terms of redistribution. The powerful intuitive appeal of the conflicting theories of justice offered by Rawls (1971) and by Nozick (1974) arises in large part from the different frames that they establish. Incompatible intuitions are brought to bear when allocations are judged from a position of null endowment behind a veil of ignorance, or in relation to existing endowments and entitlements.

The outcome of any individual in a distribution problem is naturally evaluated with respect to a norm defined by the outcome of other individuals. Individuals who are below the norm are seen as losers; individuals whose outcomes exceed the norm are gainers. In conjunction with a utilitarian criterion, a shared-value function that attaches greater weight to losses than to gains will tend to favor an egalitarian distribution. A strong preference for egalitarian distribution is typically observed when lay subjects solve distribution problems on a fixed bundle of goods (Yaari and Bar-Hillel, 1984). When the bundle is not fixed, however, some trade-offs in equality may be tolerated to increase the absolute amount being distributed (Frohlich, Oppenheimer, and Eavey, 1987). There are quite strong individual differences in the extent to which egalitarian and utilitarian values are weighted in trade-off situations (Rohrbaugh, McClelland, and Quinn, 1980).

The redistribution frame states the allocation problem in relation to a prior set of endowments. The gains and losses of individuals are then coded in relation to their respective prior states, rather than in comparison to the endowments of others. In this frame, the psychophysics of loss aversion tend to reduce the appeal of redistribution: A utilitarian calculation will only support the transfer of a good from Peter to Paul if the disutility of Peter's loss is less than the utility of Paul's gain.

We recently compared intuitions about distribution and redistribution in a small study, patterned after Yaari and Bar-Hillel's landmark research. Several versions of an allocation problem were constructed. An example of a distribution question follows:

A doctor has two patients, A and B, who both suffer from a rare and debilitating disease. Medication can provide total relief from the symptoms of the disease. Unfortunately, the drug is in very short supply – the doctor's supply is exactly forty-eight pills per day. She must decide how to allocate the forty-eight pills to her patients. The following information is known to the doctor and to her two patients:

Patient A's metabolism is such that it takes three pills to give him one hour of relief.

Patient B's metabolism is such that it takes one pill to give him one hour of relief.

If you were the doctor, how would you divide the forty-eight pills between A and B? (No trades can be made after the division takes place.)

In accord with the findings reported by Yaari and Bar-Hillel, most of our respondents opted to equalize hours of pain, and rejected an equal split of pills or a compromise solution; 77% of respondents endorsed an equal-pain allocation in this question. There were also redistribution questions, which explicitly specified an initial equal allocation for two patients whose metabolism was equal. The occasion to reconsider the allocation was an improvement or deterioration in the metabolism of one of the patients. Each redistribution problem corresponded to one of the distribution problems presented to other respondents. The following is an example of a redistribution problem:

Previously, A and B's metabolism was such that taking one pill gave one hour of relief.

For several months, A and B have each received twenty-four pills daily, and hence have been suffering no pain.

Today, however, it is discovered that B's metabolism has suddenly deteriorated and now it takes three pills to give him one hour of relief.

Patient A's metabolism has remained the same, so that it takes one pill to give him one hour of relief.

Should the doctor reconsider the distribution of the forty-eight pills? If you were the doctor, how would you divide the forty-eight pills between A and B? (No trades can be made after the division takes place.)

Here, only 50% of respondents endorse an equal-pain rule. Some respondents evidently feel that individuals have the right not to be forced to share others' misfortune. When a redistribution problem arose because of an improvement in the condition of one of the patients, however, almost the same percentage as before (70%) opted for redistributing the gain in order to equalize pain.

Utilitarian psychophysics for Robin Hood

We end this discussion with a question and a speculation. The problems of distribution and redistribution that were discussed in the preceding section were concerned with the proper response to an exogenous change that turns an initially equal allocation into one that is unequal in terms of utility. A different redistribution issue arises from an initially unequal distribution. We call it the Robin Hood problem. An interesting special case of this problem arises when the rich and the poor are assumed fully adapted to their current state of wealth, but differentially sensitive to changes in their wealth. A utilitarian Robin Hood with such a view of value would consider a proposed redistribution of wealth in terms of the balance of disutility to the rich, who will lose, and of utility to the poor, who will benefit – not in terms of their utilities for the final states of wealth. What value function should Robin Hood apply?

A relevant observation, first articulated by Daniel Bernoulli, is that the rich are less sensitive than the poor to equal changes in their wealth – the assumption of proportional sensitivity applies the familiar Weber law to this case. Other qualitative observations that constrain the choice of a value function are loss aversion and the (approximate) proportional risk aversion that is commonly observed in choices between sure gains and positive prospects (Kahneman and Tversky, 1979; Swalm, 1966). These notions are applied in a sample value function, which relates value to an initial wealth w and to a change of wealth x:

$$V(x,w) = bx^a/w \qquad \text{for } x > 0, \text{where } a < 1 \text{ and } b > 0$$
$$V(0,w) = 0$$
$$V(x,w) = -Kb(-x)^a/w \quad \text{for } x < 0, \text{where } K > 1$$

The results of studies of loss aversion summarized earlier suggest that an estimate $2 < K < 4$ could be reasonable. A utilitarian Robin Hood who believes that Peter and Paul have the same value function with $K = 3$, will take from Peter and give to Paul only so long as Paul's wealth is less than one third of Peter's. Are there cases in which moral intuitions conform to such a threshold model?

Concluding remarks

Before we can compare the utilities of different persons we must reach some agreement on the proper objects of comparisons. A central theme of this chapter has been that the standard position that utilities are to be derived from preferences is questionable. We pointed out the pitfalls of an extreme objectivist position, with its emphasis on observable measures of utility and on tangible carriers of utility. We proposed that anyone attempting to compare utilities should take into consideration the complex psychology of hedonic experience. Our initial argument was that the proper currency for welfare calculation is experience utility, that people do not always know enough about themselves to predict their future experiences, and that they sometimes make decisions that are inconsistent with their own beliefs about these experiences.

The consideration of adaptation raised a dilemma: The data suggests that there is fairly complete adaptation to different states within a region of tolerance. By some criteria, individuals at different levels of wealth can be equally adapted to their circumstances, much as individuals can feel equally warm at different temperatures. However, an exchange of endowments will cause pleasure to one of these individuals and even greater displeasure to the other, because of loss aversion. Thus, different measures of satisfaction may lead to different conclusions about the existence and extent of welfare differences. Another implication is that the simple thought experiment of imagining oneself in another's situation is fraught with problems. In particular, evaluations of the welfare of others are likely to be contaminated by inevitable comparisons to one's own circumstances.

A characteristic of perception in general, and of hedonic response in particular, is that people are more sensitive to changes than to steady states. Preferences reflect this characteristic of experience utility: There is ample evidence that outcomes are evaluated as gains and losses rather than as states. The normative issues that arise here are particularly difficult. Decision theorists teach that the proper way to evaluate options is in terms of final states, and that the proper way to view decisions is in terms of global policies. This is reasonable but unrealistic. Gains and losses do loom large in subjective experiences, and the response to steady states is muted by adaptation. It is not obvious that one can maximize experience utility without considering these psychological facts.

References

Arrow, K.J. Risk perception in psychology and economics, *Economic Inquiry*, 1982, *20*:1, 1–9.

Argyle, M. *The Psychology of Happiness*. London: Methuen, 1987.

Baum, A., Singer, J.E., and Baum, C.S. Stress and the environment. In G.W. Evans (Ed.), *Environmental Stress*. Cambridge, England: Cambridge University Press, 1982.

Berlyne, D.E. *Conflict, Arousal and Curiosity*. New York: McGraw-Hill, 1960.

Bernoulli, D. Exposition of a new theory on the measurement of risk. *Econometrica*, 1954, *22*, 23–36. Translated by Louise Sommer from "Specimen Theoriae Novae de Mensura Sortis," *Commentarii Academiae Scientiarum Imperialis Petropolitanae*, Tomus V, 1738.

Brickman, P., and Bulman, R.J. Pleasure and pain in social comparison. In J.M. Suls and R.L. Miller (Eds.), *Social Comparison Processes: theoretical and empirical perspectives*. New York: Wiley/Halsted, 1977.

Brickman, P., and Campbell, D.T. Hedonic relativism and planning the good society. In M.H. Appley (Ed.), *Adaptation-Level Theory: a symposium*. New York: Academic Press, 1971.

Brickman, P., Coates, D., and Janoff-Bulman, R. Lottery winners and accident victims: is happiness relative? *Journal of Personality and Social Psychology*, 1978, *36*:8, 917–927.

Campbell, A. *The Sense of Well-being in America: recent patterns and trends*. New York: McGraw-Hill, 1981.

Crosby, F. *Relative Deprivation and Working Women*. New York: Oxford University Press, 1982.

Dermer, M., Cohen, S.J., Jacobsen, E., and Anderson, E.A. Evaluative judgments of aspects of life as a function of vicarious exposure to hedonic extremes. *Journal of Personality and Social Psychology*, 1979, *37*:2, 247–260.

Diener, E. Subjective well-being. *Psychological Bulletin*, 1984, *95*:3, 542–575.

Duesenberry, J.S. *Income, Saving and the Theory of Consumer Behavior*. Cambridge, Massachusetts: Harvard University Press, 1952.

Duncan, O. Does money buy satisfaction? *Social Indicators Research*, 1975, *2*, 267–274.

Easterlin, R.A. Does economic growth improve the human lot? Some empirical evidence. In P.A. David and M.W. Reder (Eds.), *Nations and Households in Economic Growth*, New York: Academic Press, 1974.

Elster, J. *Sour Grapes: studies in the subversion of rationality*. Cambridge, England: Cambridge University Press, 1983.

Elster, J. *Ulysses and the Sirens: studies in rationality and irrationality*. Cambridge, England: Cambridge University Press, first edition, 1979; second edition, 1984.

Elster, J. Sadder but wiser? Rationality and the emotions. *Social Science Information*, 1985, *24:*2, 375–406.

Epstein, S. Expectancy and magnitude of reaction to a noxious UCS. *Psychophysiology*, 1973, *10:*1, 100–107.

Frank, R.H. *Choosing the Right Pond: human behavior and the quest for status*, Oxford, England: Oxford University Press, 1985.

Frohlich, N., Oppenheimer, J., and Eavey, C. Laboratory results on Rawls's distributive justice. *British Journal of Political Science*, 1987, *17*, 1–21.

Glass, D.C., and Singer, J.E. *Urban Stress: experiments in noise and social stressors*, New York: Academic Press, 1972.

Helson, H. *Adaptation Level Theory*, New York: Harper and Row, 1964.

Higgins, E.T., and Lurie, L. Context, categorization, and recall: the "change-of standard" effect. *Cognitive Psychology*, 1983, *15*, 525–547.

Ittleson, W.H., Proshansky, H.M., Rivlin, L.G., and Winkel, G.H. *An Introduction to Environmental Psychology*. New York: Holt, Rinehart and Winston, 1974.

Jevons, W.S. *Essays on Economics*. London: Macmillan, 1905.

Kahneman, D., Knetsch, J.L., and Thaler, R.H. Fairness and the assumptions of economics. *Journal of Business*, 1986, *59:*4, s285–s300.

Kahneman, D., Knetsch, J.L., and Thaler, R.H. Fairness as a constraint on profit seeking: entitlements in the market. *The American Economic Review*, 1986, *76:*4, 728–741.

Kahneman, D., Knetsch, J.L., and Thaler, R.H. Experimental tests of the endowment effect and the Coase theorem, *Journal of Political Economy*, 1990, 98, 1325–1348.

Kahneman, D. and Miller, D. Norm theory: comparing reality to its alternatives, *Psychological Review*, 1986, *93*, 136–153.

Kahneman, D., and Snell, J. Predicting utility. In R. Hogarth (Ed.), *Insights in Decision Making*. Chicago: University of Chicago Press, 1990.

Kahneman, D., and Thaler, R. How much rationality does economics need? Paper presented at American Economics Association, Chicago, Dec. 1987.

Kahneman, D., and Tversky, A. Prospect theory: an analysis of decision under risk. *Econometrica*, 1979, *47:*2, 263–291.

Kahneman, D., and Tversky, A. The simulation heuristic. In D. Kahneman, P. Slovic, and A. Tversky (Eds.), *Judgment Under Uncertainty: heuristics and biases*. Cambridge, England: Cambridge University Press, 1982.

Kahneman, D., and Tversky, A. Choices, values and frames. *American Psychologist*, 1984, *39:*4, 341–350.

Keren, G., and Wagenaar, W.A. Violation of utility theory in unique and repeated gambles. *Journal of Experimental Psychology: Learning, Memory and Cognition*, 1987, *13:*3, 387–391.

Lawler, E.E. III. *High Involvement Management*, San Francisco: Jossey-Bass, 1986.

Lazarus, R.S. Emotions and adaptation: conceptual and empirical relations.

In W.J. Arnold (Ed.), *Nebraska Symposium on Motivation*. Lincoln, Nebraska: University of Nebraska Press, 1968.

Lazarus, R.S. The stress and coping paradigm. In C. Eisdorfer, D. Cohen, A. Kleinman, and P. Maxim (Eds.), *Models for Clinical Psychopathology*. New York: Spectrum, 1981.

Loewenstein, G. Anticipation and the valuation of delayed consumption. *Economic Journal*, 1987, *97*, 666–684.

Loewenstein, G. Frames of mind in intertemporal choice. *Management Science*, 1988, *34*, 200–214.

Loomes, G., and Sugden, R. Regret theory: an alternative theory of rational choice under uncertainty. *Economic Journal*, 1982, *92*, 805–824.

March, J. G. 1978. Bounded rationality, ambiguity, and the engineering of choice, *Bell Journal of Economics*, 1978, *9:2*, 587–608.

Miller, D.T., and McFarland, C. Counterfactual thinking and victim compensation: a test of norm theory. *Personality and Social Psychology Bulletin*, 1986, *12:4*, 513–519.

Nozick, R. *Anarchy, State and Utopia*. New York: Basic Books, 1974.

Okun, A. *Prices and Quantities: a macro economic analysis*, Washington: The Brookings Institution, 1981.

Page, A.N. *Utility Theory: a book of readings*. New York: Wiley, 1968.

Parducci, A. The relativism of absolute judgments. *Scientific American*, 1968, *219*, 84–90.

Parducci, A. Value judgments: toward a relational theory of happiness. In J.R. Eiser (Ed.), *Attitudinal Judgment*. New York: Springer-Verlag, 1984.

Rawls, J. *A Theory of Justice*. Cambridge, Massachusetts: Belknap, 1971.

Rohrbaugh, J., McClelland, G., and Quinn, R. Measuring the relative importance of utilitarian and egalitarian values: a study of individual differences about fair distribution. *Journal of Applied Psychology*, 1980, *65*, 34–49.

Russell, J.A., and Fehr, B. Relativity in the perception of emotion in facial expressions. *Journal of Experimental Psychology: General*, 1987, *116:3*, 223–237.

Schelling, T.C. Economic reasoning and the ethics of policy. *The Public Interest*, 1981, *63*, 37–61.

Schelling, T.C. The mind as a consuming organ. In D.E. Bell, H. Raiffa, and A. Tversky (Eds.), *Decision making: Descriptive, normative, and prescriptive interactions*. Cambridge, England: Cambridge University Press, 1988.

Scitovsky, T. *The Joyless Economy*, Oxford, England: Oxford University Press, 1976.

Sen, A. Plural utility. *Proceedings of the Aristotelian Society*, 1981, *81*, 193–215.

Sen, A. *Choice, Welfare and Measurement*, Oxford, England: Basil Blackwell, 1982.

Sen, A. The standard of living. In S. McMurrin, *Tanner Lectures on Human Values, vol. VII*. Cambridge, England: Cambridge University Press, 1986.

Sen, A. *On Ethics and Economics*. Oxford, England: Basil Blackwell, 1987.

Shefrin, H.M., and Thaler, R.H. The behavioral life-cycle hypothesis. *Economic Inquiry*, 1988, *26*, 609–643.

Solomon, R.L. The opponent-process theory of acquired motivation: the costs of pleasure and the benefits of pain. *American Psychologist*, 1980, 691–712.

Stouffer, S.A., (Ed.) *The American Soldier: adjustment during wartime life*, Vol. I., 1949, Princeton, New Jersey: Princeton University Press.

Strack, F., Schwarz, N., and Gschneidinger, E. Happiness and reminiscing: the role of time perspective, affect, and mode of thinking. *Journal of Personality and Social Psychology*, 1985, *49:6*, 1460–1469.

Swalm, R.O. Utility theory: insights into risk taking, *Harvard Business Review*, 1966, *44*, 123–136.

Thaler, R. Toward a positive theory of consumer choice, *Journal of Economic Behavior and Organization*, 1980, *1*, 39–60.

Thompson, R.F., and Spencer, W.A. Habituation: a model phenomenon for the study of neuronal substrates of behavior. *Psychological Review*, 1966, *73:1*, 16–43.

Tversky, A., and Griffin, D. On the dynamics of hedonic experience: endowment and contrast in judgments of well-being. In F. Strack, M. Argyle, and N. Schwarz, *Subjective Well-being* (in press).

Tversky, A., and Kahneman, D. The framing of decisions and the psychology of choice. *Science*, 1981, *211*, 453–458.

Tversky, A , and Kahneman, D. Rational choice and the framing of decisions. *Journal of Business*, 1986, *59:* 4, s251–s278.

van de Stadt, H., Kapteyn, A., and van de Geer, S. The relativity of utility: evidence from panel data. *The Review of Economics and Statistics*, 1985, *67:2*, 179–187.

van Praag, B.M.S. The individual welfare function of income in Belgium: an empirical investigation. *European Economic Review*, 1971, *2*, 337–369.

van Praag, B.M.S. *Individual Welfare Functions and Consumer Behavior*, Amsterdam, Netherlands: North-Holland Publishing Company, 1968.

Varey, C.A., and Kahneman, D. Experiences extended across time: Evaluation of moments and episodes. (Manuscript in preparation).

Weinstein, N.D. Community noise problems: evidence against adaptation. *Journal of Environmental Psychology*, 1982, *2*, 87–97.

Wohlwill, J.F., and Kohn, I. The environment as experienced by the migrant: an adaptation-level view. *Representative research in social psychology*, 1973, *4:1*, 135–164.

Yaari, M.E., and Bar-Hillel, M. On dividing justly. *Social choice and welfare*, 1984, *1*, 1–24.

6. Adult-equivalence scales, interpersonal comparisons of well-being, and applied welfare economics

CHARLES BLACKORBY AND DAVID DONALDSON

1. Introduction

Social evaluations in economic environments are often performed with consumer's-surplus tests. For example, one such test employs each household's "willingness to pay" net of costs (Hicksian consumer's surplus) for an economic change, and declares the change worthwhile if and only if the simple sum of these numbers is positive.

If household demand behavior is consistent with a standard indifference map, then a positive willingness to pay indicates an improvement for the household in question, according to household preferences. No account is taken of household members as individuals, however, and, at the aggregate level, no attention is paid to income distribution. Further, these tests do not order social alternatives consistently unless a strong (and implausible) restriction on household preferences is satisfied (Blackorby and Donaldson [1985, 1990]).

In this chapter we investigate adult-equivalence scales and their potential for applied welfare economics. These scales permit comparisons of levels of well-being between people who are members of different households, and the social-evaluation procedure described uses these comparisons to perform consistent social evaluations that:

1. Deal with the general equilibrium problem (price change).
2. Explicitly model the fact that economic behavior rests on household decisions while individual household members experience well-being or utility.
3. Take account of economies of scale in household consumption.

We are indebted to Kenneth Arrow, Martin Browning, Dale Jorgenson, Joseph Ostroy, Shelley Phipps, Daniel Slesnick, Terry Wales, John Weymark, and the participants in the ICU conference for comments and criticisms. Earlier versions were presented at Dalhousie, McGill, and UBC, whom we also thank.

4. Base social evaluations on individual (rather than "household")
   well-being.
5. Take account of inequality of well-being and therefore of
   incomes.

Two general approaches to adult-equivalence scales are discussed.
Commodity-independent scales assign a single number to each household. If a household of four people has an equivalence number of
three, then the household is equivalent, in terms of well-being, to
four (reference) single adults, each with one third of the household's
income. Commodity-specific scales assign a different equivalence
number to each good or service.

These scales permit the conversion of an actual economy into an
"as if" economy of identical single adults. Each of these has the same
utility function. Individual utilities may be aggregated with a symmetric social-evaluation function that gives equal weight to each person
and pays attention to inequality of well-being.

Our discussion focuses on two particular models of equivalence
scales. The first is Equivalence-Scale Exactness (ESE) (Blackorby
and Donaldson [1988], Browning [1988], Lewbel [1988, 1989]),
which structures (a priori) both household preferences and interhousehold comparisons of well-being in a way that permits estimation of commodity-independent equivalence scales from demand behavior alone (Blackorby and Donaldson [1988]). The second is
Barten's [1964] model of commodity-specific scales. We compare
these two models theoretically with respect to their usefulness in
applied welfare economics. At the same time we suggest that empirical tests are needed to discover the strengths and weaknesses of
each.

In Section 2 we outline our model of household behavior. In Section 3 we show that the ability to make comparisons of *levels* of utility
between households is always sufficient to implement any (welfarist)
social-evaluation function, given the appropriate measurability condition on household preferences. This means that the level comparisons
provided by adult-equivalence scales are always sufficient − no direct
comparisons of utility gains and losses, for example, are needed.
Section 4 introduces equivalence scales, and Sections 5 and 6 discuss
ESE and its two special cases. In Section 7 we investigate the ways

that ESE and the Barten scales structure interhousehold comparisons. Section 8 contains a comparison of the two models with the main alternatives from the point of view of welfare-economic applications, and a further demonstration that the Barten model with independent scales and ESE overlap very little – equivalence requires all household preferences to be homothetic. Section 9 concludes the chapter.

2. The model

In this section we construct a model of household behavior for use in social evaluation. We consider a simple model of utilities and preferences of household members in an economic environment with n people and m private goods.[1] Society is grouped into H households, where $2 < H \leq n$. Households are indexed by superscripts and are described by vectors of characteristics. n^h is the number of people in household h. Hence,

$$\sum_{h=1}^{H} n^h = n. \tag{2.1}$$

A is the set of all possible vectors of household characteristics ($|A| \geq 2$), and $\alpha^h \in A$ describes household h. α^h may contain the names of household members, their ages, sexes, locations, states of health, and so on.

The relationship between consumption vectors of individual household members and household consumption (or demand) is complicated by the fact that some goods and services that are private in the economy are public or semipublic in the household. Household consumption is given by an m-vector x^h. We assume that the intrahousehold distributions of commodities and the levels of the public and semipublic goods are such that every member of the household has the same utility. This can be rationalized by a household maximin social-evaluation function.[2]

---

[1]   These are private goods to the economy; within the household they may be public or semipublic.

[2]   More realistic intrahousehold structures can be dealt with in this context, but their complexity tends to cloud the interpersonal comparison issue on which we focus.

Because our focus is on economic well-being only, we assume that the well-being or utility of each person in household h is given by a function (U) of household consumption and household characteristics α^h,

$$u^h = U(x^h, \alpha^h). \tag{2.2}$$

The function U is continuous, nondecreasing, and locally nonsatiated in x^h. U does not need the superscript h because α^h is sufficient to describe all the relevant characteristics of the household. This means, of course, that households with the same characteristics have the same utility functions.

Comparisons of utility levels between members of different households are assumed to be meaningful (the definitions of equivalence scales require these comparisons). This means that inequalities such as

$$U(\hat{x}^k, \alpha^k) \geq U(\bar{x}^h, \alpha^h) \tag{2.3}$$

together with strict inequality and equality, are allowed. We assume, further, that for any $\bar{\alpha}, \hat{\alpha} \in A$ and any $\bar{x} \in E_+^m$, there exists $\hat{x} \in E_+^m$ such that

$$U(\bar{x}, \bar{\alpha}) = U(\hat{x}, \hat{\alpha}). \tag{2.4}$$

This means that changes in consumption can bring members of different households to equality of well-being, no matter what their characteristics.

We use a social-evaluation function for society that depends upon the well-being of each person by assigning the household utility value to each household member. Hence the social-evaluation function depends on n arguments, and the utility of household h appears n^h times in the function.

A social change that moves society from an allocation $\bar{x}:\ = (\bar{x}^1, \ldots, \bar{x}^H)$ to allocation $\hat{x}:\ = (\hat{x}^1, \ldots, \hat{x}^H)$ may be ranked by a social-evaluation function $W: E^n \to E$ that depends on *all* n individuals utilities. $\hat{x}$ is ranked as no worse than $\bar{x}$ if and only if

$$W \underbrace{(U(\hat{x}^1, \alpha^1), \ldots, U(\hat{x}^1, \alpha^1)}_{n^1}, \ldots, \underbrace{U(\hat{x}^H, \alpha^H), \ldots, U(\hat{x}^H, \alpha^H)}_{n^H})$$

$$\geq W (\underbrace{U(\overline{x}^1, \alpha^1), \ldots, U(\overline{x}^1, \alpha^1)}_{n^1}, \ldots, \underbrace{U(\overline{x}^H, \alpha^H), \ldots, U(\overline{x}^H, \alpha^H)}_{n^H}). \tag{2.5}$$

A social preference requires a strict inequality in (2.5).

Several comments on the model are in order.

1. We assume that each household's market behavior results from maximization of the utility function $U(x, \alpha)$ subject to its budget constraint. Thus, household demands are rationalizable by simple utility maximization. This is an extreme assumption. Competing models, such as Nash bargaining by parents, may be more realistic but are too complex given our current knowledge (see Sen [1987] for a discussion).

2. We assume that each household member enjoys the same level of well-being. Although some ethically significant intrahousehold inequality is missed, this procedure is dictated by practical considerations because consumption data typically describes household rather than individual behavior.

3. The model allows *every* member of a household, including children, to count in social evaluations.[3] Other interpretations of the household utility function are possible. For example, Browning [1988], Grunau [1988], and Deaton and Muellbauer [1986] interpret U as measuring parental utility or well-being, and Pollak and Wales [1979,1981] assume that the household allocation problem has been solved somehow. Nelson [1986, 1987, 1988] assumes the existence of a household social-welfare function but does not use her results for social evaluation. Jorgenson and Slesnick [1983, 1984a, 1984b, 1987] assume that the "kth consuming unit" has a utility function whose image is used in social evaluation. Because the utility of every member of society ought to appear in the social-evaluation function – in principle at least – these approaches are not as useful for applications of welfare economics.

---

[3]   Children's well-being is assumed to be promoted by parental decisions.

4. Social evaluations can be made with functions that exhibit any degree of inequality aversion, ranging from the utilitarian social-evaluation function (with no aversion to inequality of utilities) to maximin utilities (with maximum inequality aversion).

5. The model assumes that households with identical characteristics have the same preferences. Because α may contain the names of household members, no harm is done in that case, and the model generalizes the usual consumer model. In practical applications, α will not name household members, and this assumption is a real restriction. Fisher [1987] has criticized the Barten model for linking preferences to interhousehold comparisons in an unreasonable way, a priori. In the non-homothetic case, our ESE (discussed later) links preferences to interhousehold comparisons in a way that we believe is, a priori, plausible. Fisher's criticisms are discussed in Sections 7.2 and 8.

6. The model allows changes in preferences caused by changes in α to be incorporated into social evaluations in a consistent way. If, for example, a project results in a family member receiving a service that changes his or her health status, the project may be evaluated by changing α in the before – and after – project description. Because household utility measures the (equal) economic well-being of all household members, preferences of parents for children are not part of the model.

3. Interpersonal comparisons and social evaluation

"Welfarist" social evaluation (Sen [1977]) is based on individual well-being (utility), and no additional information – about individual liberty, for example – is needed. Social values, such as liberty, are treated as instrumental values; they count because of the contributions they make to well-being.

Almost all welfarist social-evaluation functions require some interhousehold comparisons of utility (that is, between people in different households). For example, maximin utility requires interhousehold comparisons of *levels* of utility. In addition, different functions require different standards of measurability of utilities. Utilitarianism requires household utilities to be cardinally measurable and units of measurement to be comparable so that utility gains and losses can be compared.

However, cardinal measurability and level comparability alone are sufficient to implement utilitarianism (see Theorem 1).

A natural way to think about this is to partition the set of all possible utility functions satifying our assumptions into "information-equivalence classes." Usable information for a particular utility function consists of the information that is shared by all other members of the equivalence class. For example, suppose that the equivalence class for a particular utility function $\overline{U}$ consists of all the utility functions that are household – specific increasing transforms of $\overline{U}$. Formally, the equivalence class $E(\overline{U})$ for $\overline{U}$ is the Ordinal Noncomparability (ONC) set for $\overline{U} - E^{ONC}(\overline{U})$ – where

$$E(\overline{U}) = E^{ONC}(\overline{U}): = \{U \in U \,|\, \exists \, \phi \ni U(x, \alpha) = \phi(\overline{U}(x, \alpha), \alpha)\}. \qquad (3.1)$$

U is the set of all utility functions satisfying our assumptions, and ϕ is increasing in its first argument. The only common information in $E(\overline{U})$ is preference information for individual households; different members of $E(\overline{U})$ make interhousehold comparisons differently. If all the information-equivalence classes have the same structure as $E(\overline{U})$, then the information environment is called Ordinal Noncomparability (ONC). Similarly, if household utilities are cardinally measurable and

$$\begin{aligned} E(\overline{U}) = E^{CNC}(\overline{U}): & = \{U \in U \,|\, \exists \, a(\alpha) > 0, b(\alpha) \in E \ni U(x, \alpha) \\ & = a(\alpha)\overline{U}(x, \alpha) + b(\alpha)\} \end{aligned} \qquad (3.2)$$

for each $\overline{U} \in U$, then the information environment is called Cardinal Noncomparability (CNC). The numbers $a(\alpha)$ and $b(\alpha)$ can be different for each α.

It is also possible to describe information environments in which utilities are fully comparable and either ordinally or cardinally measurable. If utilities are ordinally measurable, then the equivalence classes for Ordinal Full Comparability (OFC) are given by

$$E^{OFC}(\overline{U}): = \{U \in U \,|\, \exists \, \Psi \ni U(x, \alpha) = \Psi(\overline{U}(x, \alpha))\}. \qquad (3.3)$$

In this case, each U in the information-equivalence class is the *same* increasing transform of $\overline{U}$.[4] The equivalence classes for OFC are therefore smaller than the equivalence classes for ONC, and they

    [4] See d'Aspremont and Gevers [1977], Blackorby, Donaldson and Weymark [1984], Bossert and Stehling [1989], and Sen [1977] for general discussions.

contain more usable information – namely interhousehold comparisons of utility *levels,* such as the ones in (2.3) and (2.4).

The information-equivalence classes for Cardinal Full Comparability (CFC) are defined by

$$E^{CFC}(\overline{U}): = \{U \in U \mid \exists \, a > 0, \, b \in E \ni U(x, \alpha)$$
$$= a\overline{U}(x, \alpha) + b\}. \tag{3.4}$$

In this case, the allowable transforms are affine, and the same for all α. This information structure permits utility levels to be compared *and* allows gains and losses to be compared as well.

Information environments corresponding to other measurability assumptions such as "ratio-scale" ($b = 0$ in (3.5)) are discussed in Blackorby and Donaldson [1982] and Blackorby, Donaldson, and Weymark [1984].[5]

It is useful to think of information environments that contain all the information corresponding to one of the environments described, and, perhaps, additional information as well. We say that a given information environment with information-equivalence classes $\{E$ $(U)\}$ *supports* Ordinal Full Comparisons of utility (OFC+) if and only if

$$E(U) \subseteq E^{OFC}(U) \tag{3.5}$$

for all $U \in U$. The partition of U may be finer than the OFC partition, but because (3.5) holds, all the utility functions in $E(U)$ are the *same* (α-independent) increasing transform of U. Hence, interhousehold comparisons like (2.4) are usable. CFC+ is defined in a similar fashion. We say that the information environment supports Cardinal Full (interhousehold) Comparisons (CFC+) if and only if, for all $U \in U$,

$$E(U) \subseteq E^{CFC}(U). \tag{3.6}$$

This information environment contains at least as much information as CFC does.

It is tempting to say that social-evaluation functions such as the utilitarian one require more or different comparisons than simple comparisons of *levels* of well-being. This is *not* the case, however.

---

[5] In addition, see d'Aspremont and Gevers [1977] and Sen [1977].

Suppose that in an information environment, utilities are individually cardinally measurable. Then, for all $U \in U$,

$$E(U) \subseteq E^{CNC}(U) \tag{3.7}$$

and we say that CNC+ is satisfied. At the same time, suppose that levels of utility are comparable (OFC+). This means that for any U,

$$E(U) \subseteq E^{OFC}(U). \tag{3.8}$$

But (3.7) and (3.8) together imply CFC+. (3.7) implies that for any $\bar{U}$ in E (U), there exist $a(\alpha)$ and $b(\alpha)$ such that

$$\bar{U}(x, \alpha) = a(\alpha)U(x, \alpha) + b(\alpha). \tag{3.9}$$

However, (3.8) implies that for each $\bar{U}$ in $E(U)$ there exists an increasing function Ψ such that

$$\bar{U}(x, \alpha) = \Psi(U(x, \alpha)). \tag{3.10}$$

The two together imply that $a(\alpha)$ and $b(\alpha)$ are independent of α for all $\bar{U}$ in E (U). Hence,

$$E(U) \subseteq E^{CFC}(U). \tag{3.11}$$

and $CFC+$ is satisfied. This result is summarized in Theorem 1.

Theorem 1. If, in an information environment, utilities are Cardinally Measurable (CNC+) and levels of utility are comparable (OFC+), then the environment supports Cardinal Full Comparisons (CFC+).

This result can easily be extended to other measurability assumptions, such as ratio-scale. The conclusion is the same – namely, that interhousehold comparisons of levels of utility are sufficient to extend individual ratio-scale measurement to Ratio-Scale Full Comparability (or more).[6]

A simple example may develop the intuition behind this result.

6   Bossert and Stehling [1989] show that Theorem 1 is not true if the ranges of utility functions are not restricted. Our assumption that consumption can always produce utility equality (2.4) is needed in Theorem 1. It means that all utility functions have the same range.

Suppose that the members of household 1 gain from a change and the members of household 2 lose. Level comparability lets us find commodity bundles for household 1 that yield the same utilities for it that household 2 experiences before and after the change. If household 1's utility is cardinally measurable, then the utility gain that household 1 actually gets may be compared with the loss it would get if it consumed the commodity bundles that give it household 2's utility levels. Thus, household 1's gain can be compared with household 2's loss. This information is sufficient for application of the utilitarian social-evaluation function (or any other function for which CFC+ is sufficient information).

Adult-equivalence scales provide interhousehold comparisons of levels of utility. Given Theorem 1, these comparisons are sufficient for the implementation of *any* welfarist social-evaluation function, assuming the appropriate measurability condition at the household level. We therefore assume, in the rest of this discussion, that interhousehold comparisons of *levels* of utility are meaningful – that is, that the information environment satisfies OFC+.

4. Interpersonal comparisons and adult-equivalence scales

The simplest and probably the most common form of interhousehold comparison is made through the use of adult-equivalence scales.[7] These scales deal with two phenomena. The first concerns the fact that different households contain different numbers and types of people (adults, children, disabled people, and so on), and therefore have different preferences and needs. The second concerns the fact that there are economies of scale in household consumption (due to public and semipublic consumption within the household). As an example, consider a case where the number of adult equivalents is not commodity-specific.[8] Suppose that a house-

---

[7]   Adult equivalence scales are discussed by Barten [1964], Blackorby and Donaldson [1987,1989], Beach, Card, and Flatters [1981], Browning [1988], Canadian Senate [1971], Deaton [1980], Deaton and Muellbauer [1980, 1986], Gorman [1976], Jorgenson and Slesnick [1983, 1984a, 1984b, 1987], King [1983], Kwong [1985], Lewbel [1988, 1989], Muellbauer [1974, 1977], Nelson [1986, 1987, 1988], and Pollak and Wales [1979, 1981].

[8]   Commodity-specific scales will be considered later.

hold consists of two adults with an income of $30,000. If we say that the number of adult equivalents in the household is 1.5, then we mean that the household is equivalent, for utility purposes, to two *single reference* adults with incomes of $20,000 each ($30,000 divided by 1.5). The farther the number of adult equivalents is below 2, the greater is the economy of scale. If, on the other hand, a single disabled person has an adult-equivalence number of 3, this disabled adult with an income of $60,000 is equivalent for utility purposes to an able-bodied (reference) single adult with an income of $20,000.[9] These effects are combined in equivalence scales for families with different numbers of adults and children, but the arithmetic is the same. If a family of two adults and two children contains three adult equivalents, then a family income of $60,000 is equivalent for utility purposes to four (reference) single adults with $20,000 each.

Commodity-specific equivalence scales, such as Barten's [1964], are similar except they attach a (potentially) different number of adult-equivalents to each commodity. This permits economies of scale in housing, for example, but not in food.

In this section we construct two general classes of adult-equivalence scales, both of which structure the function U. One of them is commodity-specific and the other is not. To do this, we use two dual representations of the utility function U. The indirect utility function V is given by

$$u = V(p, y, \alpha) = \max_x \{U(x, \alpha) \mid p \cdot x \le y\}, \tag{4.1}$$

where p is a vector of positive prices and y is household income (consumption expenditure). $V(p, y, \alpha)$ is the maximum utility that each member of a household with characteristics α can obtain when facing prices p with income y. The expenditure or cost function corresponding to U is C, where

$$C(u, p, \alpha) = \min_x \{p \cdot x \mid U(x, \alpha) \ge u\}. \tag{4.2}$$

---

[9] Equivalence scales of the welfarist type discussed here may not be the best way to deal with people who have special needs. An alternative, based on capabilities rather than well-being, is discussed by Sen [1985], and scales based on needs are discussed by Atkinson and Bourguignon [1987].

$C(u, p, \alpha)$ is the minimum amount that a household with characteristics α must spend in order to achieve a utility level u for each member of the household while facing prices p. For each α, V is continuous and homogeneous of degree zero in p and y, increasing in y, and quasi-convex, nonincreasing and locally nonsated in p. C, on the other hand, is continuous in (u, p), increasing in u, and homogeneous of degree one, concave, and nondecreasing in p.[10] If U is concave in x, then V is concave in y and C is convex in u.[11] In addition, C and V are related by the identity

$$C(u, p, \alpha) = y \leftrightarrow u = V(p, y, \alpha). \tag{4.3}$$

4.1. Commodity-independent equivalence scales

Let d be the number of adult equivalents in a household with characteristics α and income y facing prices p; d is defined implicitly by

$$u = V(p, y, \alpha) = V\left(p, \frac{y}{d}, \alpha^r\right). \tag{4.4}$$

α^r is the characteristics vector of a *reference household* consisting of one single adult. Given our assumptions (see equation 2.4)), a solution for d in (4.4) exists. The solution is unique because V is increasing in y.

It is important to notice that the definition of d in (4.4) is not meaningful unless the information structure supports level comparisons of utilities (OFC+). If V is replaced by $\tilde{V}$, where (as in (3.1))

$$\tilde{V}(p, y, \alpha) = \phi(V(p, y, \alpha), \alpha), \tag{4.5}$$

then the number of adult equivalents can change. However, if V is replaced by $\tilde{V}$, where (as in (3.3))

$$\tilde{V}(p, y, \alpha) = \Psi(V(p, y, \alpha)), \tag{4.6}$$

[10]   Blackorby, Primont, and Russell [1978] contains a discussion of these assertions in Chapter 2 and proves them in an appendix.
[11]   This is proved in Diewert [1978].

then the number of adult equivalents (defined by (4.4)) remains unchanged. Hence, *level* comparability of utilities is required.

(4.4) implicitly defines a function $d = D(u, p, \alpha)$. If the reference adult has an income $y/D(u, p, \alpha)$ and faces prices p, then he or she enjoys a utility level exactly equal to the utility of each member of a household with characteristics α and income y, facing prices p. Using (4.3), d is given by[12]

$$d = D(u, p, \alpha) = \frac{C(u, p, \alpha)}{C(u, p, \alpha^r)}. \tag{4.7}$$

The function D depends on the utility level of the members of the household, a number that is normally unobservable. (4.7) implies that $D(u, p, \alpha^r) = 1$ for all u and p.

4.2. Commodity-specific equivalence scales

Commodity-specific equivalence scales were introduced by Barten [1964]; letting U^r be the utility function of the reference household, $U(\cdot, \alpha^r)$, the Barten scales are described by

$$U(x, \alpha) = U^r \left(\frac{x_1}{\Delta_1(\alpha)}, \ldots, \frac{x_m}{\Delta_m(\alpha)} \right) \tag{4.8}$$

with $\Delta_j(\alpha^r) = 1$ for all j. The scales deflate each commodity to an amount that brings a reference adult to the same level of utility as a household with characteristics α. $\Delta_j(\alpha^h)$ may be interpreted as an index of the "degree of publicness" of commodity j to household h. If $\Delta_j(\alpha^h) = 1$, then commodity j is a pure public good for household h, and if $\Delta_j(\alpha^h) = n^h$, then j is pure private good. If $1 < \Delta_j(\alpha^h) < n^h$, j is a semipublic good. Given this interpretation, (4.8) implies that *each* member of *each* household has the *same* preferences. Again, (4.8) makes no sense unless interhousehold comparisons of levels of utility are possible (OFC+).

---

[12]   This general formula is the same as the one defined on page 205 of Deaton and Muellbauer [1980]. They do not mention the need for interhousehold comparability.

(4.8) is equivalent to the requirement that the cost function C can be written as

$$C(u, p, \alpha) = C^r(u, \Delta_1(\alpha)p_1, \ldots, \Delta_m(\alpha)p_m) \tag{4.9}$$

where C^r is defined by

$$C^r(u, p) := C(u, p, \alpha^r).^{13} \tag{4.10}$$

(4.9) implies that the effective price of good j to a person in a household with characteristics α is $\Delta_j(\alpha)p_j$. (4.3) can be used to find the indirect utility function corresponding to (4.9). It is given by

$$V(p, y, \alpha) = V^r(\Delta_1(\alpha)p_1, \ldots, \Delta_m(\alpha)p_m, y), \tag{4.11}$$

where V^r, the indirect utility function of the reference household, is defined by

$$V^r(p, y) = V(p, y, \alpha^r). \tag{4.12}$$

(4.9) has been generalized by Gorman [1976] (see Pollak and Wales [1981]) and Browning [1988]). The commodity-specific scale for good j is allowed to depend on α *and* on p_j, so that (4.9) becomes

$$\begin{aligned} C(u, p, \alpha) &= \tilde{C}(u, \tilde{\Delta}_1(p_1, \alpha)p_1, \ldots, \tilde{\Delta}_m(p_m, \alpha)p_m) \\ &\quad + \hat{C}(p, \alpha). \end{aligned} \tag{4.13}$$

This generalization is analogous to ESE (see Section 5) in the commodity-independent case, because the equivalence scales are independent of u.[14] Unfortunately, it is possible to demonstrate that the functions $\{\tilde{\Delta}_j\}$ must be *independent* of their first arguments.

Theorem 2. The generalized Barten scales $\{\tilde{\Delta}_j\}$ (4.13) are independent of their first arguments, and (4.13) can be rewritten as

$$C(u, p, \alpha) = \tilde{C}(u, \Delta_1(\alpha)p_1, \ldots, \Delta_m(\alpha)p_m) + \hat{C}(p, \alpha). \tag{4.14}$$

---

[13]   See Barten [1964], Gorman [1976], Muellbauer [1974, 1977], and Nelson [1986, 1987a, 1987b] for additional discussion.

[14]   Muellbauer has also generalized the Barten scales by including utility instead of prices in the equivalence scales. We discuss this briefly in section 8.

Proof. See the appendix.

Thus, the addition of the function $\hat{C}$ in equation (4.13) is the only generalization of Barten's model that this model provides.

5. Equivalence-scale exactness (ESE) and commodity-independent scales

The commodity-independent equivalence scale $D(u, p, \alpha)$ contains an unobservable – the utility of each member of the household. An adult-equivalent *index* can be constructed to approximate D by setting u equal to a particular reference level of utility (such as poverty utility). We define an index, $\bar{d}$, by

$$\bar{d} = \bar{D}(p, \alpha): = D(u^r, p, \alpha) = \frac{C(u^r, p, \alpha)}{C(u^r, p, \alpha^r)} . \tag{5.1}$$

If u^r is the poverty utility level, then $\bar{d}$ is the ratio of the poverty line for the household in question to the poverty line for the reference household (at the same prices).

$\bar{D}$ uses much less information than D. All that is necessary is that a single indifference surface (corresponding to u^r) be identified for each α. This means that interhousehold comparisons need only be made for a *single level* of utility. Nevertheless, even here, some comparability is required in order to define the equivalence scale. A method for doing this is to find reference consumption bundles $X(\alpha)$, $\alpha \in A$, such that

$$U(X(\alpha), \alpha) = u^r. \tag{5.2}$$

If u^r is the poverty utility level, then $X(\alpha)$ is a poverty consumption bundle for a household with characteristics α. To make the interhousehold comparisons needed for D, reference consumption bundles for each α *and* each utility level are needed.

Social evaluations can be made with the index $\bar{D}$. The utility of each member of a household with characteristics α is

$$u = V(p, y, \alpha) = V^r\left(p, \frac{y}{D(u, p, \alpha)}\right) \tag{5.3}$$

and it can be approximated as

$$\bar{u} = V^r \left(p, \frac{y}{\overline{D}(p, \alpha)} \right).$$ (5.4)

This approximation can be used in a social-evaluation function (such as the utilitarian one) for each member of the household.

The social evaluation that results will be approximate unless $\overline{D}$ is *exact*–that is, unless

$$\overline{D}(p, \alpha) = D(u, p, \alpha).$$ (5.5)

Exactness requires that D be independent of u. The necessary and sufficient condition for exactness is

$$C(u, p, \alpha) = \overline{C}(u, p)\hat{C}(p, \alpha)$$ (5.6)

for all (u, p, α).

When (5.6) or (5.5) holds, we say that utilities satisfy Equivalence Scale Exactness (ESE).[15] (5.6) is a restriction on U, V, and C; more specifically, it restricts them both *interpersonally* and *intrapersonally*. The exact equivalence scale Δ is given by

$$\Delta(p, \alpha): = D(u, p, \alpha) = \frac{C(u, p, \alpha)}{C(u, p, \alpha')} = \frac{\hat{C}(p, \alpha)}{\hat{C}(p, \alpha')}$$ (5.7)

and, in this case, (5.5) holds. It is homogeneous of degree zero in p because C is homogeneous of degree one in p. Given (5.6) and (5.7), we can rewrite the cost function as

$$C(u, p, \alpha) = C(u, p, \alpha') \frac{C(u, p, \alpha)}{C(u, p, \alpha')} = C^r(u, p)\Delta(p, \alpha).$$ (5.8)

Equation 5.8 suggests that one household's preferences may be chosen arbitrarily (corresponding to $C^r(u, p)$). The equivalence scales

---

[15]   See Blackorby and Donaldson [1989], Theorem 4.1. This condition has also been noticed by Browning [1988] and Lewbel [1988, 1989]. The results that follow are from Blackorby and Donaldson [1989].

are allowed to depend on p, a reasonable condition because econo-mies of scale in consumption are likely to be different for different goods and services. Choice of an equivalence scale for each house-hold ($\Delta(p, \alpha)$) completely determines household preferences for all α, making a significant restriction on preferences, *given C'*.

Given (5.8), (4.3) can be used to find the indirect utility function given ESE. It is

$$V(p, y, \alpha) = V^r\left(p, \frac{y}{\Delta(p, \alpha)}\right) \tag{5.9}$$

and (5.9) is equivalent to (5.8) and (5.6). In fact, (5.9) can be sepa-rated into two conditions: ESE requires *preferences* to satisfy

$$u = V(p, y, \alpha) = \phi\left(V^r\left(p, \frac{y}{\Delta(p, \alpha)}\right), \alpha\right) \tag{5.10}$$

where ϕ is increasing in its first argument *and* ESE requires ϕ to be independent of α, a condition on interpersonal comparisons. The condition that ϕ be independent of α can be thought of as a conse-quence of OFC+, the necessary information requirement for equiva-lence scales. OFC+ implies that information-equivalence classes are smaller than they would be with ONC; if ϕ were to depend on α, then (5.10) would move V out of its information class.

ESE ((5.8) or (5.9)) admits two important special cases. In the simpler case, the function $\hat{C}$ is independent of p, and therefore the equivalence scale Δ is independent of p. We call this case Engel Equivalence Exactness. In the second case, $\overline{C}$ is independent of p, and each household's preferences are homothetic. We call this case *Full Homotheticity*.

6. Special cases of equivalence-exactness: Engel equivalence and full homotheticity

Engel Equivalence Exactness requires that

$$\Delta(p, \alpha) = \mathring{\Delta}(\alpha). \tag{6.1}$$

In this case, the cost function is

$$C(u, p, \alpha) = C^r(u, p)\mathring{\Delta}(\alpha). \tag{6.2}$$

The indirect utility function is

$$V(p, y, \alpha) = V^r\left(p, \frac{y}{\mathring{\Delta}(\alpha)}\right) \tag{6.3}$$

and the direct utility function is

$$U(x, \alpha) = U^r\left(\frac{x}{\mathring{\Delta}(\alpha)}\right). \tag{6.4}$$

These characterizations imply that the reference indifference map is very similar to the indifference map for an arbitrary household. A given indifference surface is scaled along rays – toward the origin if $\mathring{\Delta}(\alpha) > 1$ and away from it if $\mathring{\Delta}(\alpha) < 1$. (6.4) makes it clear that Engel-Equivalence Exactness is the same as Barten equivalence (4.8) with identical commodity-specific scales.

The second special case is called Full Homotheticity; it requires preferences to be homothetic (if one household's preferences are homothetic, ESE implies that all are homothetic). Homotheticity requires that C be multiplicatively separable, with

$$C(u, p, \alpha) = \Gamma(u)\Pi(p, \alpha) \tag{6.5}$$

where Π is homogeneous of degree one in prices. ESE prevents Γ from depending on α. Π can be a different function for each α, and so each household type may have different homothetic preferences. The equivalence scale is

$$\Delta(p, \alpha) = \frac{\Pi(p, \alpha)}{\Pi(p, \alpha^r)} \tag{6.6}$$

and it is homogeneous of degree zero in p (and, of course, $\Delta(p, \alpha^r) = 1$).

Full Homotheticity provides a method for constructing the equivalence scale in the general case of ESE. To do it, simply select arbitrary homothetic preferences for each household type satisfying (6.5); then construct Δ using (6.6).

In the Cobb–Douglas case, for example.

$$\Delta(p, \alpha) = \frac{A(\alpha)p_1^{\gamma_1(\alpha)}p_2^{\gamma_2(\alpha)}\cdots p_m^{\gamma_m(\alpha)}}{A(\alpha^r)p_1^{\gamma_1(\alpha^r)}p_2^{\gamma_2(\alpha^r)}\cdots p_m^{\gamma_m(\alpha^r)}} \tag{6.7}$$

where $\gamma_j(\alpha) > 0$ and

$$\sum_{j=1}^{m} \gamma_j(\alpha) = 1 \tag{6.8}$$

for all α. (6.7) may be rewritten as

$$\Delta(p, \alpha) = S(\alpha)p_1^{\sigma_1(\alpha)}p_2^{\sigma_2(\alpha)}\cdots p_m^{\sigma_m(\alpha)} \tag{6.9}$$

where $S(\alpha)$ is a "scaling factor" corresponding to $\mathring{A}(\alpha)$ in the Engel case, $\sigma_j(\alpha) := \gamma_j(\alpha) - \gamma_j(\alpha^r)$, and

$$\sum_{j=1}^{m} \sigma_j(\alpha) = 0 \tag{6.10}$$

for each α (this follows from (6.8)). Then Δ may be used in combination with V^r or C^r to find the general utility or cost function.

This example illustrates the fact that ESE is more general than Engel equivalence (the condition implicitly used by poverty researchers). Engel equivalence implies in the Cobb–Douglas case that $\sigma_j(\alpha) = 0$ for all α, or that commodity j is just as important to each household as it is to the reference household. On the other hand, ESE (in the Cobb–Douglas case) permits different goods to be more or less important to a household with characteristics α than to a reference household. If $\sigma_j(\alpha) > 0$, commodity j is more important; if $\sigma_j(\alpha) < 0$, it is less important.

Barten commodity-specific equivalence scales may be built into Δ, but not into the prices that appear in V^r, when ESE is satisfied. Remembering that the Barten scale for commodity j is $\Delta_j(\alpha)$, and that $\Delta_j(\alpha') = 1$ for all j, the equivalence scale (6.6) becomes

$$\Delta(p, \alpha) = \frac{\Pi(\Delta_1(\alpha)p_1, \ldots, \Delta_m(\alpha)p_m, \alpha)}{\Pi(p, \alpha')}. \qquad (6.11)$$

In the Cobb–Douglas example, the $\Delta_j(\alpha)$'s simply affect $A(\alpha)$, and no generalization of (6.9) occurs. But in the general case, (6.11) is different from (6.6) (an example is the homothetic translog).

7. Equivalence scales and interpersonal comparisons

In this section we investigate the interhousehold comparisons that characterize ESE and Barten equivalence scales (including generalized Barten scales).

7.1 Equivalence scale exactness and income-ratio comparability

ESE is completely described by

$$V(p, y, \alpha) = V^r\left(p, \frac{y}{\Delta(p, \alpha)}\right). \qquad [(5.9)]$$

Suppose that two household types, $\hat{\alpha}$ and $\tilde{\alpha}$, face the same prices and have income $\hat{y}$ and $\tilde{y}$ such that their utilities are the same. This means that

$$V^r\left(p, \frac{\hat{y}}{\Delta(p, \hat{\alpha})}\right) = V^r\left(p, \frac{\tilde{y}}{\Delta(p, \tilde{\alpha})}\right) \qquad (7.1)$$

which is true if and only if

$$\frac{\hat{y}}{\Delta(p, \hat{\alpha})} = \frac{\tilde{y}}{\Delta(p, \tilde{\alpha})}$$

$$\leftrightarrow \frac{\lambda \hat{y}}{\Delta(p, \hat{\alpha})} = \frac{\lambda \bar{y}}{\Delta(p, \bar{\alpha})}$$

$$\leftrightarrow V^r \left(p, \frac{\lambda \hat{y}}{\Delta(p, \hat{\alpha})} \right) = V^r \left(p, \frac{\lambda \bar{y}}{\Delta(p, \bar{\alpha})} \right) \tag{7.2}$$

for any nonnegative number λ. (7.2) says that if the households have the same utility at $\hat{y}$ and $\bar{y}$, then any common scaling of their incomes (by λ) preserves equality of their utilities. We call this condition Income-Ratio Comparability (IRC), and (7.2) shows that it is a consequence of ESE. In Blackorby and Donaldson [1989, theorem 5.1] we show that IRC completely characterizes ESE (that is, it is both necessary and sufficient for ESE).

We believe that IRC is a plausible condition on interhousehold comparisons. It is important, however, that prices for the two household types in (7.2) be the same. If income-scaling preserves utility equality when prices for the households are different, then Full Homotheticity results [1988b, theorem 6.5].

In order to illustrate the implications of IRC, consider Figure 6.1 where the indifference maps of two households, g and h, whose preferences satisfy IRC are represented. Depicted are three levels of utility (which can be chosen to be the same for both households by virtue of level comparability)[16] and the income-consumption curves associated with two different price vectors, ICC (1) and ICC (2). At points $[a]$, g and h spend y_g^1 and y_h^1, respectively, to obtain one unit of utility each while facing prices p^1. Raising g's income to $\bar{\lambda} y_g^1$ brings g up to utility level β at point $[b]$ for some $\bar{\lambda} > 0$. IRC guarantees that $\bar{\lambda} y_h^1$ will bring household h up to level β (at point $[b]$) as well. We now choose another price vector; pick p^2 so that y_g^1 just suffices to bring g to the unit level of utility at these prices (point $[c]$); this is always possible because demands are homogeneous of degree zero in prices and income. Suppose that $\bar{\lambda} y_g^1$ brings g up to utility level α at point $[d]$ (we have arbitrarily chosen $\alpha \leq \beta$). At prices p^2 it takes y_h^2 to bring h up to the unit level (note that y_g^1 is not in general equal to y_h^2); then, IRC guarantees that $\bar{\lambda} y_h^2$ will bring h up to level α as well.

---

[16]   Note, however, that they do not have to be the same locus of points in the two maps. The unit indifference curve could be a rectangular hyperbola for household g and a straight line for household h.

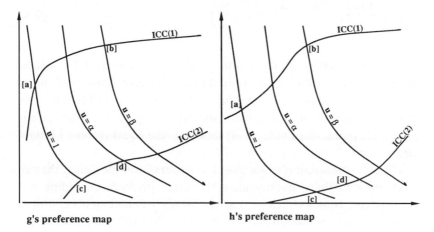

g's preference map   h's preference map

Figure 6.1

7.2 Barten interhousehold comparisons

Barten equivalence scales $\{\Delta_j(\alpha)\}$ can be chosen arbitrarily for all $\alpha \neq \alpha'$ because $\Delta_j(\alpha') = 1$ for all j. When, in addition, the indirect utility function of the reference adult is specified, preferences are determined for every household type, and

$$V(p, y, \alpha) = V^r(\Delta_1(\alpha)p_1, \ldots, \Delta_m(\alpha)p_m, y). \qquad [(4.8)]$$

The most appealing interpretation (to us at least) of (4.8) is that everyone has the *same preferences* and that $\Delta_j(\alpha)$ is an index of the degree of publicness of commodity j in a household of type α. If this interpretation is accepted, then $\Delta_j(\alpha^h)$ should depend on n^h, the number of people in the household. This can be formalized by writing

$$\Delta_j(\alpha^h) = \bar{\Delta}_j(n^h). \qquad (7.3)$$

For a private good, $\bar{\Delta}_j(n^h) = n^h$, and for a pure public good, $\bar{\Delta}_j(n^h) = 1$. Because V is homogeneous of degree zero in (p, y),

$$V(p, y, \alpha) = V^r(\Delta_1(\alpha)p_1, \ldots, \Delta_m(\alpha)p_m, y)$$

$$= V^r \left(\frac{\Delta_1(\alpha)}{n} p_1, \ldots, \frac{\Delta_m(\alpha)}{n} p_m, \frac{y}{n} \right). \tag{7.4}$$

(7.4) implies that for a pure public good, the price to each household member is p_j/n^h, which is the Lindahl price for each household member given that the household members have the same utility functions and household income is equally shared among them. When goods are purely public or private, (7.4) describes the equal-income Lindahl equilibrium.

This interpretation is attractive, but suffers from the defect that all *individuals* in the economy have the same preferences, ruling out type-specific commodities such as children's toys and men's clothing.

Another interpretation is that the scales allow different households to have different preferences. Fisher [1987] criticizes this interpretation on the grounds that (4.8) implies that any two households with the *same preferences* have the *same utilities* when their incomes are the same and they face the same prices. He suggests that a priori realism requires that (4.8) ought to be amended so that V is allowed to be an α-specific transform of the right side of (4.8). Unfortunately, such a move is not likely to be empirically tractable because behavior is independent of such transforms. The issue is, really, not whether preferences are linked to interpersonal comparisons or not, but rather whether the link, if it exists, is reasonable a priori, and whether the interhousehold comparisons discovered by using the model are consistent with other comparisons, such as the ones implicit in the poverty lines.

The Gorman–Browning generalization of the Barten model (4.13) cannot be given the semipublic-goods interpretation, and must be seen as conditioning the way preferences vary across household types. It may be able to fit the data better than the simple Barten model, but is open to the same objection that Fisher makes to the Barten model itself.

8. ESE Versus Barten: Strengths and weaknesses

It is possible to generalize any of the equivalence scales presented here by allowing utility to appear in the equivalence scale. We think that such generalizations are likely to be of little importance empirically. The presence of u in the scales adds an unobservable variable, and it is a variable that must be compared across households. This creates a serious problem both for estimation and for welfare-economic applications.

Browning [1988] has shown that *all* the equivalence scale models can be interpreted as imposing structure on the cost function C. For example, the "Engel method" (Muellbauer [1977]), a generalization of our Engel equivalence, requires

$$C(u, p, \alpha) = f(u, p)\, g\,(u, \alpha) \tag{8.1}$$

which does not satisfies ESE. The commodity-independent equivalence scale is

$$D\,(u, p, \alpha) = \frac{g(u, \alpha)}{g(u, \alpha')} \tag{8.2}$$

a generalization of Engel equivalence, because it does not depend on prices. The presence of u in D suggests that an index number approach might be used in practice, in which case Engel equivalence is implicitly satisfied.

The Generalized Cost Scaling (GCS) model of Ray [1986] requires

$$C(u, p, \alpha) = f^1(u, p)f^2(u, \alpha)f^3(p, \alpha)\,[17] \tag{8.3}$$

with

$$D(u, p, \alpha) = \frac{f^2(u, \alpha)f^3(p, \alpha)}{f^2(u, \alpha')f^3(p, \alpha')}. \tag{8.4}$$

D is the product of a utility-independent function

$$\frac{f^3(p, \alpha)}{f^3(p, \alpha')} \tag{8.5}$$

---

[17]   Browning writes this as $f^1(u, p)f^2(u, \alpha)f^3(\alpha)f^4(p, \alpha)$ and, without loss of generality, we have absorbed f^3 into f^4.

(which resembles our $\Delta(p, \alpha)$) multiplied by a term

$$\frac{f^2(u, \alpha)}{f^2(u, \alpha')} \tag{8.6}$$

(which resembles generalized Engel equivalence (8.2)).[18]

An alternative to the Gorman generalization of the Barten model would be an equivalence scale $\hat{\Delta}_j(u, p_j, \alpha)$ that depends on u as well as p_j and α. The scale must be independent of p_j (Theorem 2), and this is analogous to Muellbauer's generalized Engel equivalence. As long as the scales actually depend on u, the model is difficult to implement, both normatively and positively.

This discussion suggests that we may want to focus on ESE in the commodity-independent case and on the Barten model in the commodity-specific case. Fisher's objection to the Barten model is that preferences and interpersonal comparisons are not linked in a reasonable way, a priori. The semipublic goods interpretation of Barten is plausible, but suffers from the serious defect that preferences must be the same for *all* individuals. If the model is interpreted as a simple conditioning of preferences across households for demand-system estimation, then there is no reason to require

$$u = V^r(\Delta_i(\alpha)p_l, \ldots, \Delta_m(\alpha)p_m, y) \tag{8.7}$$

rather than

$$u = \phi(V^r(\Delta_1(\alpha)p_1, \ldots, \Delta_m(\alpha)p_m, y), \alpha). \tag{8.8}$$

Both (8.7) and (8.8) exhibit the same preferences and therefore the same demand functions. What is needed for welfare economics is a reason supporting the interhousehold comparisons in (8.7) as opposed to those in (8.8) (for some specific function ϕ). For example, suppose, as a specific example of (8.8), that

$$u = S(\alpha)V^r(\Delta_1(\alpha)p_1, \ldots, \Delta_m(\alpha)p_m, y). \tag{8.9}$$

---

[18]   Browning also discusses the Modified Cost Function of Lewbel [1985], which does not restrict C at all.

(8.7) and (8.9) have the same preferences, but $S(\alpha)$ scales utilities up or down to produce different interhousehold comparisons. If V^r and the scales $(\Delta_1, \ldots, \Delta_m)$ are estimated from behavior, then S could be found from a set of external interhousehold judgments, such as the ones implicit in the poverty lines. We see no reason to believe, a priori, that $S(\alpha)$ must be set equal to one for all α.

On the other hand, ESE structures interhousehold comparisons in a way that may be more acceptable. ESE is equivalent to IRC. It requires that if any two households facing the same prices have incomes such that their utilities are the same, then any common scaling of their incomes preserves utility equality. Thus, if a disabled adult has an adult equivalence number of 3 at a particular price vector, then an income for the disabled adult of *three times* the income of a reference adult results in utility equality. The ratio three is sufficient for equality without reference to income levels. It seems to us that this is an appealing structuring of interhousehold comparisons a priori, at least if we focus on comparisons of *economic* well-being only.

In the special case of Full Homotheticity, the equivalence scale (6.6) may be scaled arbitrarily without changing preferences. In that case,

$$V^r(p, y) = \Psi\left(\frac{y}{\Pi(p, \alpha^r)}\right) \tag{8.10}$$

where Π is homogeneous of degree one in p (this follows from (6.5) and (4.3)). The utility function for a household with characteristics α is

$$V^r(p, y, \alpha) = \Psi\left(\frac{y}{\Pi(p, \alpha)}\right) \tag{8.11}$$

$$= \Psi\left(\frac{y}{\Pi(p, \alpha^r)} \Big/ \frac{\Pi(p, \alpha)}{\Pi(p, \alpha^r)}\right)$$

$$= \Psi\left(\frac{y}{\Pi(p, \alpha^r)} \Big/ \Delta(p, \alpha)\right).$$

If $\Delta(p, \alpha)$ in (8.11) is replaced by

$$\tilde{\Delta}(p, \alpha) = S(\alpha)\Delta(p, \alpha) \tag{8.12}$$

then the utility function becomes

$$\tilde{V}(p, y, \alpha) = \Psi \left(\frac{y}{\Pi(p, \alpha')} \bigg/ \tilde{\Delta}(p, \alpha) \right) \tag{8.13}$$

$$= \Psi \left(\frac{y}{\Pi(p, \alpha')} / S(\alpha)\Delta(p, \alpha) \right)$$

$$= \tilde{\Psi} \left(\left[\frac{y}{\Pi(p, \alpha')} / \Delta(p, \alpha) \right], \alpha \right)$$

where $\tilde{\Psi}$ is defined by

$$\tilde{\Psi}(t, \alpha) = \Psi(t/S(\alpha)). \tag{8.14}$$

(8.13) means that $\tilde{V}(\cdot, \cdot, \alpha)$ and $V(\cdot, \cdot, \alpha)$ are ordinally equivalent for each α. Scaling the equivalence scale (8.12) changes utility levels but *not* preferences or (utility-maximizing) household behavior. Consequently, in the case of Full Homotheticity, the equivalence scale Δ cannot be determined uniquely by behavior alone. Some external comparisons, such as the ones implicit in the poverty lines, must be supplied.[19]

Given ESE, either *all* households have homothetic preferences, resulting in FH (homothetic Engel Equivalence is a special case), or none does. If preferences are *not* homoethetic, then the equivalence scale Δ is *uniquely* determined by household preferences. The proof (Blackorby and Donaldson [1989, theorems 6.1 and 6.2]) requires that the cost function be regular (increasing in u for all p, nondecreasing in p, etc.). Unfortunately, some specifications of C^r take the form

$$C^r(u, p) = A(p)[f(u)]^{B(p)} \tag{8.15}$$

or equivalently,

$$\ln C^r(u, p) = \ln A(p) + B(p) \ln [f(u)] \tag{8.16}$$

[19]   See Blackorby and Donaldson [1987] for a more detailed discussion.

where $f(u)$ is any increasing function of u. However, $f(u)$ can take on *any* nonnegative value, and so C' will not be regular in p unless $B(p)$ is a constant (homotheticity).[20] However, if (8.15) holds, then Δ cannot be determined uniquely because it implies that

$$C(u, p, \alpha) = A(p)[f(u)]^{B(p)}\Delta(p, \alpha) . \tag{8.17}$$

If $\Delta(p, \alpha)$ is replaced by

$$\tilde{\Delta}(p, \alpha) = S(\alpha)^{B(p)}\Delta(p, \alpha), \tag{8.18}$$

C becomes

$$\tilde{C}(u, p, \alpha) = A(p)[f(u)S(\alpha)]^{B(p)}\Delta(p, \alpha) \tag{8.19}$$

which has the same demand functions as C. Consequently, when (8.12) is satisfied, Δ cannot be determined uniquely from behavior.

On the other hand, suppose that a functional form for Δ is constructed from a cost function satisfying Full Homotheticly, as illustrated in Section 6, possibly incorporating commodity-specific features to account for household semipublic goods, and a C' that represents regular nonhomothetic preferences or a C' that does not satisfy (8.15) is chosen. Then C' and Δ may be uniquely estimated. Of course, IRC is a maintained hypothesis. One way to check is to test it against the "poverty relatives" – ratios of poverty lines to the reference poverty line. There is no completely compelling reason to believe that the equivalence scale estimated in this way will be reasonable. However, previous work (see Jorgenson and Slesnick [1983, 1984a, 1984b, 1987] and Kwong [1985]) in this area that has used a combination of (non-independent) Barten commodity-specific scales and ESE has found equivalence scales that are not unreasonable. Kwong performed the poverty-related test and found close agreement between them and his estimated scales. Using ESE alone as a maintained hypothesis, Phipps [1989] has estimated price-dependent commodity-independent equivalence scales for Canada. Her estimates are reasonable – they lie in the right ranges and are sensitive to prices in the expected way. They

---

[20]   If C' is not regular, there is no direct utility function from which it could have been derived.

exhibit smaller economies of scale in household formation, however, than some poverty relatives indicate.

A natural question that emerges from this discussion is whether or not Barten scales and ESE are compatible. That is, when can it be true that

$$V^r\left(p, \frac{y}{\Delta(p, \alpha)}\right) = V^r(\Delta_1(\alpha)p_1, \ldots, \Delta_m(\alpha)p_m, y)? \tag{8.20}$$

An untransformed V^r can be used on both sides of (8.20) because $\Delta(p, \alpha') = \Delta_j(\alpha') = 1$ for all j.

If the $\Delta_j(\alpha)$'s are not functionally independent, then it is possible for (8.20) to be satisfied by a nonhomothetic V^r. However, suppose that α is, in part, a continuous variable (age may be a continuous component, for example), and that $(\Delta_1(\alpha), \ldots, \Delta_m(\alpha))$ may be moved through a set

$$T: = \{x \in E_+^m | \underline{x}_j \leq x_j \leq \overline{x}_j, j = 1, \ldots, m\} \tag{8.21}$$

where $\underline{x}_j < \overline{x}_j$ for each j. This means that the $\Delta_j(\alpha)$'s can be moved *independently* by suitable choices of α. In this case, (8.20) may be satisfied if and only if V^r represents homothetic preferences, and therefore, Full Homotheticity holds.

Theorem 3. The Barten model with *independent* commodity-specific equivalence scales satisfies ESE if and only if Full Homotheticity is satisfied.[21]

Proof. See the appendix.

To see sufficiency, suppose preferences are homothetic, with

$$V^r(p, y) = \Psi\left(\frac{y}{\tilde{\Pi}(p)}\right) \tag{8.22}$$

where $\tilde{\Pi}$ is homogeneous of degree one in p. Then, using the Barten method,

---

[21]   This has been discovered and proved independently by Lewbel [1988] in Corollary 2. His main theorem is more general than ours and concerns the case where the scales are not completely independent.

$$V(p, y, \alpha) = \Psi \left(\frac{y}{\tilde{\Pi}(\Delta_1(\alpha)p_1, \ldots, \Delta_m(\alpha)p_m)} \right), \qquad (8.23)$$

$$C(u, p, \alpha) = \Psi^{-1}(u)\tilde{\Pi}(\Delta_1(\alpha)p_1, \ldots, \Delta_m(\alpha)p_m), \qquad (8.24)$$

and

$$\Delta(p, \alpha) = \frac{\tilde{\Pi}(\Delta_1(\alpha)p_1, \ldots, \Delta_m(\alpha)p_m)}{\tilde{\Pi}(p)} \qquad (8.25)$$

which satisfies ESE.

This result suggests that in the general case, the Barten and Gorman models of commodity-specific scales are very different from commodity-independent scales that satisfy ESE. They have different consequences, both for behavior and for interpersonal comparisons. Although we prefer the ESE commodity-independent scales for welfare applications, the ultimate test is the reasonableness of estimated scales and their compatibility with the data.

9. Conclusion

Both the Barten commodity-specific equivalence scales and the ESE commodity-independent scales are independent of the utility level of the household, and this makes them empirically tractable. This feature is not shared by their main competitors.

At the same time, the two approaches structure household preferences quite differently, allowing ESE and independent Barten scales to overlap only when Full Homotheticity is satisfied. Because homotheticity fits household demand behavior poorly, the models are empirically distinct.

The main strength of the Barten model is its capacity for the explicit inclusion of household public and semipublic goods, and its main weaknesses are that (i), in the public-good interpretation, everyone, including children, must be assumed to have the same preferences, and (ii), in interpretations that see the scales as allowing for preference differences across households, the implied interhousehold comparisons of well-being are arbitrary and unconvincing.

ESE's main strength is the independence of the scale from household utility, and this property makes it possible to estimate the scale from behavior when preferences are not homothetic. Its main weakness is that household public goods can be explicitly incorporated into the equivalence scale, but not into the reference utility function (section 6). At the same time, ESE structures interhousehold comparisons in a way that is reasonable, a priori. It is equivalent to the condition that the scaling – up or down – of the incomes of two households (facing the same prices) preserves utility equality (this is Income-Ratio Comparability (IRC)).

Both models provide interhousehold comparisons of levels of utility and, given the appropriate measurability of individual household utilities, welfarist social evaluations can be performed.

It is true, of course, that comparisons of fit with data and with external norms such as poverty lines provide the ultimate tests of these models. At the same time, ESE is clearly better suited to some applications, such as poverty-line estimation because the "poverty relatives" (the ratios of poverty lines to the reference line) are simply the values of the equivalence scale. ESE allows these numbers to depend on prices, a significant generalization of the common price-independent poverty relatives.

Appendix

1. Generalized Barten equivalence

Browning [1988] generalizes Gorman's generalization of Barten's model by writing

$$C(u, p, \alpha) = \tilde{C}(u, h_1(p_1, \alpha), \ldots, h_m(p_m, \alpha)) + \hat{C}(p, \alpha). \qquad \text{(a.1)}$$

Without loss of generality, $h_j(p_j, \alpha^r)$ may be set equal to p_j by a suitable normalization of $\tilde{C}$. Thus,

$$C^r(u, p,) = \tilde{C}(u, p) + \overline{C}(p) \qquad \text{(a.2)}$$

where $\overline{C}(p) := \hat{C}(p, \alpha^r)$. Homogeneity of C^r requires $\tilde{C}$ and $\overline{C}$ to be homogeneous of degree one in p.

Define the functions $\{\tilde{\Delta}_j\}$ by

$$\tilde{\Delta}_j(p_j, \alpha) := \frac{h_j(p_j, \alpha)}{p_j} . \qquad \text{(a.3)}$$

Then,

$$C(u, p, \alpha) = \tilde{C}(u, \tilde{\Delta}_1(p_1, \alpha)p_1, \ldots, \tilde{\Delta}_m(p_m, \alpha)p_m) + \hat{C}(p, \alpha). \quad \text{(a.4)}$$

C must be homogeneous of degree one in p, and this implies that the compound function $\tilde{C}(u, \tilde{\Delta}_1(p_1, \alpha)p_1, \ldots, \tilde{\Delta}_m(p_m, \alpha)p_m)$ is homogeneous of degree one in p. Hence

$$\tilde{C}(u, \tilde{\Delta}_i(\lambda p_1, \alpha) \lambda p_1, \ldots, \tilde{\Delta}_m(\lambda p_m, \alpha)\lambda p_m) \qquad \text{(a.5)}$$

$$= \lambda \tilde{C}(u, \tilde{\Delta}_1(\lambda p_1, \alpha) p_1, \ldots, \tilde{\Delta}_m(\lambda p_m, \alpha)p_m)$$

$$= \lambda \tilde{C}(u, \tilde{\Delta}_1(p_1, \alpha)p_1, \ldots, \tilde{\Delta}_m(p_m, \alpha)p_m).$$

The second line of (a.5) follows from the homogeneity of $\tilde{C}$ and the third from the homogeneity of the compound function. Because p_k, $k \neq j$, can be made as close to zero as one likes, (a.5) implies that for each j, $\tilde{\Delta}_j$ is homogeneous of degree zero in p_j, and this means (because p_j is a singleton) that $\tilde{\Delta}_j$ is independent of p_j. This result is summarized in Theorem 2.

Theorem 2. The generalized Barten scales $\{\tilde{\Delta}_j\}$ (4.13) are independent of their first arguments, and (4.13) can be rewritten as

$$C(u, p, \alpha) = \tilde{C}(u, \Delta_1(\alpha)p_1, \ldots, \Delta_m(\alpha)p_m) + \hat{C}(p, \alpha) \qquad \text{(a.6)}$$

2. Independent Barten scales and ESE

Theorem 3. The Barten model with *independent* commodity-specific equivalence scales (see the text and (8.21)) satisfies ESE if and only if Full Homotheticity is satisfied.

Proof. Sufficiency is demonstrated in the text. Suppose, therefore, that (8.20) is satisfied, and define

$$\delta_j: = \Delta_j(\alpha) \tag{a.7}$$

for each j. If the Barten scales satisfy ESE, then

$$C(u, p, \alpha) = C^r(u, \{\delta_j p_j\}) = C^r(u, p)\Delta(p, \alpha). \tag{a.8}$$

Defining

$$q: = (\delta_1 p_1, \ldots, \delta_m p_m), \tag{a.9}$$

$\Delta(p, \alpha)$ may be written as

$$\mathring{D}(p, q) = \Delta(p, \alpha) \tag{a.10}$$

so that (a.8) becomes

$$C(u, p, \alpha) = C^r(u, q) = C^r(u, p)\mathring{D}(p, q). \tag{a.11}$$

For fixed p, α may be used to move $\{\delta_j\}$ through T, and so q may be moved independently of p. Hence, q must be separable from u in C^r (because of separability on the right side of (a.11)). But this means that C^r corresponds to a homothetic $U^r: = U(\cdot, \alpha^r)$ with

$$C(u, p, \alpha) = C^r(u, q) = \Gamma(u)\tilde{\Pi}(q) \tag{a.12}$$

$$= \Gamma(u)\tilde{\Pi}(\{\Delta_j(\alpha)p_j\})$$

$$= \Gamma(u)\Pi(p, \alpha)$$

which is Full Homotheticity.

References

Atkinson, A., and F. Bourguignon, "Income Distribution and Differences in Needs," in *Arrow and the Foundations of the Theory of Economic Policy,* edited by G. Feiwel, London, Macmillan, 1987, 350–370.

Barten, A.P., "Family Composition, Prices and Expenditure Patterns," in *Econometric Analysis for National Economic Planning,* edited by P. Hart, G. Mills, and J. K. Whittaker, 16th Symposium of the Calston Society, London, Butterworth, 1964, 277–292.

Beach, C.M., D.E. Card, and F. Flatters, *The Distribution of Income and Wealth in Ontario: Theory and Evidence.* Toronto: University of Toronto Press, 1981.

Blackorby, C., and D. Donaldson, "Ratio-Scale and Translation-Scale Full Comparability Without Domain Restrictions: Admissible Social-Evaluation Functions," *International Economic Review,* 23, 1982, 249–268.

Blackorby, C., and D. Donaldson, "Consumers' Surpluses and Consistent Cost-Benefit Tests," *Social Choice and Welfare,* 1, 1985, 251–262.

Blackorby, C., and D. Donaldson, "Welfare Ratios and Distributionally Sensitive Cost-Benefit Analysis," *Journal of Public Economics,* 34, December, 1987, 265–290.

Blackorby, C., and D. Donaldson, "The Case Against the Use of the Sum of Compensating Variations in Cost-Benefit Analysis," *Canadian Journal of Economics,* 23, 1990, 471–494.

Blackorby, C., and D. Donaldson, "Adult-Equivalence Scales and the Economic Implementation of Interpersonal Comparisons of Well-Being," University of British Columbia Disscussion Paper 88-27, 1988, revised 1989.

Blackorby, C., D. Donaldson, and J.A. Weymark, "Social Choice with Interpersonal Utility Comparisons: A Diagrammatic Introduction," *International Economic Review,* 25, 1984, 327–356.

Blackorby, C., D. Primont, and R.R. Russell, *Duality, Separability and Functional Structure: Theory and Economic Applications.* New York: Elsevier North-Holland, 1978.

Bossert, W., and F. Stehling, "Admissible Transformations for Interpersonally Comparable Utilities: A Rigourous Derivation," mimeo, Universität Karlsruhe, 1989.

Browning, M. "The Effects of Household Characteristics on Behavior and Welfare," mimeo, Department of Economics, McMaster University, 1988.

Canadian Senate, *Poverty in Canada,* Information Canada, Ottawa, 1971.

D'Aspremont, C., and L. Gevers, "Equity and the Informational Basis of Collective Choice," *Review of Economic Studies,* 44, 1977, 199–209.

Deaton, A., "The Measurement of Welfare: Theory and Practical Guidelines," Living Standards Measurement Study Working Paper No. 7, World Bank, 1980.

Deaton, A., and J. Muellbauer, *Economics and Consumer Behavior.* Cambridge: Cambridge University Press, 1980.

Deaton, A., and J. Muellbauer, "On Measuring Child Costs: With Applications to Poor Countries," *Journal of Political Economy,* 94, 1986, 720–744.

Diewert, W.E., "Hicks' Aggregation Theorem and the Existence of a Real Value-Added Function," in *Production Economics: A Dual Approach to Theory and Applications,* edited by M. Fuss and D. McFadden, Amsterdam: North Holland, 1978.

Fisher, F.M., "Household Equivalence Scales and Interpersonal Comparisons," *Review of Economic Studies,* 54, 1987, 519–524.

Gorman, W.M., "Tricks With Utility Functions," in *Essays in Economic Analysis,* edited by M. Artis and R. Nobay, Cambridge: Cambridge University Press, 1976.

Grunau, R., "Consumption Technology and the Intrafamily Distribution of Resources: Adult Equivalence Scales Reexamined," *Journal of Political Economy,* 96, 1988, 1183–1205.

Jorgenson, D., and D. Slesnick, "Individual and Social Cost-of-Living Indexes," in *Price Level Measurement,* edited by W. Diewert and C. Montmarquette, Ottawa, Statistics Canada, 1983, 241–336.

Jorgenson, D., and D. Slesnick, "Inequality in the Distribution of Individual Welfare," in *Advances in Econometrics,* 3, edited by R. Basmann and G. Rhodes, Greenwich, Conn. JAI Press, 1984a, 67–130.

Jorgenson, D., and D. Slesnick, "Aggregate Consumer Behavior and the Measurement of Inequality," *Review of Economic Studies,* 51, 1984b, 369–392.

Jorgenson, D., and D. Slesnick, "Aggregate Consumer Behavior and Household Equivalence Scales," *Journal of Business and Economic Statistics,* 5, 1987, 219–232.

King, M.A., "Welfare Analysis of Tax Reforms Using Household Data," *Journal of Public Economics,* 21, 1983, 183–214.

Kwong, S., *Price-Sensitive Inequality Measurement,* Ph.D. Thesis, University of British Columbia, 1985.

Lewbel, A., "A Unified Approach to Incorporating Demographic or Other Effects into Demand Systems," *Review of Economic Studies,* 52, 1985, 1–18.

Lewbel, A., "Household Equivalence Scales and Welfare Comparisons," *Journal of Public Economics,* 39, 1989, 377–392.

Lewbel, A., "Cost of Characteristics Indices and Household Equivalence Scales," Brandeis Discussion Paper No. 206, 1988, forthcoming in the *European Economic Review.*

Muellbauer, J., "Household Composition, Engel Curves and Welfare Comparisions between Households: A Duality Approach," *European Economic Review,* 5, 1974, 103–122.

Muellbauer, J., "Testing the Barten Model of Household Composition Effects and the Costs of Children," *Economic Journal,* 87, 1977, 460–487.

Nelson, J., *A Model of Household Joint Utility Maximization with Public Goods,* unpublished Ph.D dissertation, University of Wisconsin, 1986.

Nelson, J., "Household Demands with Public Goods," mimeo, University of California, Davis, 1987.

Nelson, J., "Household Economics of Scale in Consumption: Theory and Evidence," *Econometrica*, 56, 1988, 1301–1314.

Phipps, S., "Price-Sensitive Adult-Equivalence Scales for Canada," mimeo, Dalhousie University, Halifax, 1989.

Pollak, R.A., and T.J. Wales, "Welfare Comparisons and Equivalence Scales," *American Economic Review*, 69, 1979, 216–221.

Pollak, R.A., and T.J. Wales, "Demographic Variables in Demand Analysis," *Econometrica*, 49, 1981, 1533–1551.

Ray, R., "Demographic Variables and Equivalence Scales in a Flexible Demand System: The Case of AIDS," *Applied Economics*, 18, 1986, 265–278.

Sen, A.K., "On Weights and Measures: Informational Constraints in Social Welfare Analysis", *Econometrica*, 45, 1977, 1539–1572.

Sen, A.K., *Commodities and Capabilities*, North-Holland, Amsterdam, 1985.

Sen, A.K., "Gender and Cooperative Conflicts," Discussion Paper No. 1342, Harvard Institute of Economic Research, Discussion Paper 1342, 1987.

Weymark, J., "Optimality Conditions for Public and Private Goods," *Public Finance Quarterly*, 7, 1979, 338–351.

7. Interpersonal comparisons of utility: Why and how they are and should be made

PETER J. HAMMOND

. . . I still believe that it is helpful to speak as if inter-personal comparisons of utility rest upon scientific foundations – that is, upon observation or introspection. . . . I still think, when I make interpersonal comparisons . . . that my judgments are more like judgments of value than judgments of verifiable fact. Nevertheless, to those of my friends who think differently, I would urge that, in practice, our difference is not very important. They think that propositions based upon the assumption of equality are essentially part of economic science. I think that the assumption of equality comes from outside, and that its justification is more ethical than scientific. But we all agree that it is fitting that such assumptions should be made and their implications explored with the aid of the economist's technique.

Robbins (1938, pp. 640–641)

1. Introduction

1.1. Background

Personal ethics should be about living a good life (cf. Williams, 1985), ethics in public policy about making good public decisions, and ethics

This chapter is an extensive revision of a paper presented at the Sloan Conference on "Interpersonal Comparability of Welfare" at the University of California at Davis, April 17–18, 1987. That paper was was based on a much earlier paper prepared in connection with the workshop on "Interpersonal Comparisons of Utility" (organized jointly with Menaham Yaari) at the Institute for Mathematical Studies in the Social Sciences, Stanford University, on August 20, 1981. Research support from the National Science Foundation under Grant No. SES 79-24831 for preparing that workshop, and later from the Guggenheim Foundation, is gratefully acknowledged. I am particularly indebted to Kenneth Arrow, Frank Hahn, James Mirrlees, Amartya Sen, and Menaham Yaari for fruitful discussion in connection with the earlier paper, and to Charles Blackorby, Daniel Hausman, Christian Seidl, and John Weymark for helpful comments on various revisions.

in economics about choosing economic policies that improve the allocation of resources. This brings ethics very close to normative decision theory. Indeed, ethics may even become, at one and the same time, both an application and an ideal form of that theory.

Many approaches to ethical decision making have received the attention of moral philosophers and practical people. In my view, none is as satisfactory as an idealized form of utilitarianism based upon an ethical concept of utility. Indeed, if one takes an individualistic view of ethics, then utilitarianism can be made virtually tautologous by defining an individual's utility function as that whose expected value ought to be maximized in all the personal matters affecting that individual alone. What is more, utilitarianism itself can be derived from the even more primitive normative principle called "consequentialism." This last principle (Hammond, 1986, 1988a, 1988b) requires that a prescribed norm of behavior should be explicable solely by its consequences. That is, a "consequentialist" behavior norm must reveal a "consequence choice function" according to which the consequences of behavior are chosen from the feasible set of consequences in any decision tree. When the space of consequences is defined broadly enough to accommodate everything of ethical relevance, consequentialism also becomes a tautology (cf. Sen, 1987a, p. 40, note 13). Under the conditions spelled out in Hammond (1987a, 1988c) it also implies an idealized form of Harsanyi utilitarianism, based on a single and fully interpersonal comparable "fundamental" utility function for all possible types of individual.

This leaves us with the difficulty of constructing the interpersonally comparable fundamental utility function. Indeed, for many years this has usually been seen as the main problem with Harsanyi utilitarianism in particular. The same is true of Rawlsian maximin, of course, and more generally with the construction of any suitable Bergson social welfare function for use in welfare economics.

Many problems have been created in social choice theory and in welfare economics by the extreme reluctance to make any kind of interpersonal comparison of utility (ICU). The main exception has been the almost certainly unethical comparisons that result from weighing all individuals' dollars equally. Such comparisons emerge implicitly when the "Kaldor–Hicks" compensation principle (actually due to Pareto (1894, 1895) and Barone (1908), as explained by Chipman and Moore (1978) and Chipman (1987)) is applied without any actual compensation occurring. They are quite explicit in the aggregate wealth criterion advocated by Strotz (1958, 1961), Harberger (1971), and Posner (1981), and criticized by Fisher and Rothenberg (1961) and Hammond (1982a). Goldstick (1971) suggested valuing the dollars of those with equal wealth equally, but did not suggest how to compare the dollars of those whose wealth differs.

So great was the reluctance to consider other interpersonal comparisons that it took almost twenty years after the publication of the first editions of Arrow's *Social Choice and Individual Values* before Sen (1970a,b) and others started a systematic study of the implications of relaxing Arrow's most restrictive assumption – namely, the total avoidance of all ICUs in his definition of a "social welfare function." It is true that "independence of irrelevant alternatives" is formulated in a way that excludes interpersonal comparisons (Hildreth, 1953). Nevertheless, it is really the definition of a social welfare function that makes this exclusion almost inevitable and so leads inexorably to a dictatorship (cf. Hammond, 1991).

1.2. Coverage

This chapter presents an incomplete yet still quite long survey of that part of the literature on ICUs which seems most relevant to social choice theory and welfare economics. One example of an entirely different approach that I shall not discuss is Wittman (1974) and Nozick's (1985, pp. 166–167) suggestion for using ICUs in criminology in order to compare offenders' punishments with their victims losses, so that sufficient retribution can be exacted.

Nor shall I say much about Shapley's (1969) ingenious proposal, lucidly explained as well as extended by Yaari (1981), and also expounded by Brock (1978b, 1979a, 1980). Shapley suggested constructing a cooperative game of transferable λ-weighted utility, and determining a weight λ_i for each individual i so that the utility distribution emerging from this artificial cooperative game is a feasible distribution in the original game. Yaari's theory only applies when there is a convex set of possible social states. And in applications such as Aumann and Kurz (1977), the theory also presumes the kind of lump-sum redistribution that, as I have argued in Hammond (1979a, 1987b), is generally "incentive incompatible," so not truly feasible. Nevertheless, d'Aspremont (1991) has begun work on extending the idea to Bayesian incentive-compatible procedures. See also Keeney and Kirkwood (1975) for related work, and particularly Roth (1980, 1986), Shafer (1980), Scafuri and Yannelis (1984), and Aumann (1985, 1986, 1987) for an intense debate on the significance of the fact that such "NTU value allocations" are often asymmetric.

Another common use of ICUs has been in bargaining theory. Works such as Kalai (1977), Myerson (1977), Neilsen (1983), Kalai and Samet (1985), and Bovens (1987) can be consulted in this connection. In effect, bargaining problems represent a very special kind of social decision tree in which a great deal of redistribution is possible. In this and other work, I have chosen to concentrate on social decision procedures that in principle can be applied to a much broader domain of social decision trees.

Finally, yet another important problem neglected here is that of reconciling conflicting interpersonal comparisons without either imposition or dictatorship. Arrow mentioned this in his oral discussion of Phelps (1977), and there is some published discussion in Kelly (1978) and Pazner (1979). It has remained a comparatively neglected area. This is in contrast to the very extensive work on "social welfare functionals" (SWFLs) embodying utility information that reflects interpersonal comparisons. I shall have very little to say about SWFLs for two reasons. First is that d'Aspremont (1985) and Sen (1986) have both conducted extensive surveys quite recently. Second is that this literature has never explained precisely where this additional utility information comes from, which will be my main concern here.

1.3. Outline

After this introduction, Section 2 briefly discusses some of the history behind the general reluctance of economists to make ICUs, as well as the impasse that this creates in both welfare economics and social choice theory. Section 3 considers what different forms ICUs may take and distinguishes between interpersonal comparisons of utility levels (ICULs) and interpersonal comparisons of utility differences (ICUDs). Sections 4 and 5 consider what alternative methods for making such

ICUs have been suggested. Section 4 considers the "impersonal" preferences that emerge when individuals are in the hypothetical original position of either Harsanyi or Rawls. Section 5 examines suggestions for inferring interpersonal comparisons from different aspects of individuals' actual behavior. It seems, however, that such "behaviorist" empirical methods are fundamentally unsatisfactory. I believe this is because ethically relevant ICUs are tantamount to normative statements and so cannot be derived just from empirical observation. So, finally, in Section 6, a number of explicitly ethical methods of making interpersonal comparisons are considered. In particular, a procedure is put forward for deriving "decision-theoretic" ICUs from a general framework for ethical decision-making, and for integrating such comparisons within that framework by considering the implicit or "revealed" preferences for types of people. Section 7 concludes.

2. Social choice without interpersonal comparisons of utility

2.1. Logical positivism

In the 1930s, the philosophical doctrine of logical positivism was imported to England from Vienna. Primarily responsible for this, perhaps, was Sir Alfred Ayer, whose *Language, Truth and Logic* was published in 1936. There he wrote:

> We can now see why it is impossible to find a criterion for determining the validity of ethical judgements. It is not because they have an 'absolute' validity which is mysteriously independent of ordinary sense-experience, but because they have no objective validity whatsoever . . . They are pure expressions of feeling and as such do not come under the category of truth and falsehood. They are unverifiable for the same reason as a cry of pain or a word of command is unverifiable [as a statement] – because they do not express genuine propositions.
>
> *Ayer (1936, 1971), p. 144.*

As he remarks in Magee (1971), Ayer himself regarded logical positivism as "a blending of the extreme empiricism of Hume with the modern logical techniques developed by people like Bertrand Russell." Even before this, however, in 1932 when Ayer was still only twenty-two, Robbins – perhaps influenced by the Vienna Circle, perhaps not – had published his *Essays on the Nature and Significance of Economic Science*. The logical positivists saw all ethical statements as "unverifiable" (see Ayer's conversation in Magee, 1971, p. 49) – in fact, as just so much noise or exhaust. Actually, Ayer eventually withdrew somewhat from his extreme position – even in the introduction to the second edition of *Language, Truth and Logic* in 1946 – but we shall return to this later in Section 4. Meanwhile, Robbins pointed out that ICUs – at least those of the kind used to argue for equality – were also ethical statements of a particular kind without scientific foundation. Indeed, Jevons had made a similar claim earlier:

> The reader will find again, that there is never, in any single instance, an attempt to compare the amount of feeling in one mind with that in another. I see no means by which such comparison can be accomplished. The susceptibility of one mind may, for what we know, be a thousand times greater than that of another. But provided that the susceptibility was different in a like ratio in all directions, we should never be able to discover the difference. Every mind is thus inscrutable to every other mind, and no common denominator of feeling seems to be possible . . . the motive in one mind is weighed only against other motives in the same mind, never against the motives in other minds.
>
> *Jevons (1871, 1970)* (Introduction, Measurement of Feelings and Motives)

Cooter and Rappoport (1984) discuss how Fisher (1892) saw that price theory relies only on ordinal utility that is not interpersonally comparable. And Chipman and Moore (1978, p. 548, fn. 2) and Chipman (1987) discuss briefly how Pantaleoni and Barone had persuaded Pareto (1894, p. 58) to use the monetary interpersonal comparisons implicit in the compensation principles, before he turned to a general differential form of Bergson social welfare function in Pareto (1913) – see also Bergson (1983).

2.2. The new welfare economics

Following Robbins, it became fashionable for economists to eschew ICUs, apparently in an attempt to be "scientific." Positive economics, of course, could easily do without them, but even normative economists were swept up by the "new welfare economics" and insisted on limiting themselves to identifying Pareto efficient outcomes, or at least actual or potential Pareto improvements to the existing economic allocation. Without ICUs they could do nothing else. Choosing one Pareto efficient social state over another requires trading off the gains of some individuals against the losses of others. Policy measures that alleviate extreme poverty may be highly desirable, but will not be Pareto improvements if they involve sacrifices by the rich. As Dobb (1969, p. 81) points out, this drastic weakness of welfare economics without ICUs had been noted by Harrod (1938) just before the appearance of Robbins' (1938) influential article. Yet the habit has persisted for many years. For instance, Archibald (1959, 1965) forcefully advocated the view that welfare economists need not proceed beyond identifying changes everybody desires. And where interpersonal comparisons really have to be made, because the gainers from a change were not going to compensate the losers, the monetary comparisons that result from valuing all individuals' dollars equally still seem to be the most popular among economists, who then wonder why their policy advice does not receive wider acceptance.

On social choice theory without ICUs there is also an enormous literature – see, for example, Sen's (1986) survey. It is virtually impossible, however, to get any acceptable stronger choice rule than the Pareto criterion of the new welfare economics (Sen, 1970a). Indeed, after Arrow's original contribution, not much of this literature seems all that useful in retrospect. The reason is that most of it has tried to circumvent one or other of the conditions of Arrow's impossibility theorem. Elsewhere (Hammond, 1986) I have offered what may seem to be a stronger "consequentialist" defense of these conditions than Arrow and various successors have offered. This suggests that the most important condition of the impossibility theorem is one not stated as a formal assumption, though it was clearly expressed as follows:

The viewpoint will be taken here that interpersonal comparison of utilities has no meaning and, in fact, there is no meaning relevant to welfare comparisons in the measurability of individual utility.

Arrow (1951, 1963, p. 9)

Indeed, Arrow's theorem really is an "impossibility" rather than a "dictatorship" theorem because ultimately even the choice of the dictator requires interpersonal comparisons. And, of course, majority rule attempts to value all individuals' preferences equally, which is another kind of interpersonal comparison.

3. The forms of interpersonal comparisons

3.1 Interpersonal comparisons of utility levels

Suppose there is a society of individuals i in the finite set N, each of whom has a utility function $U^i(\cdot)$ that represents i's personal welfare ordering R^i on the domain X of social states. A comparison of utility levels between two individuals $i, j \in N$ is then simply a statement such as $u^i \geq u^j$, where u^i and u^j are two particular levels of the utility functions U^i, U^j for persons i and j.

Thus, ICULs are simply ordinary comparisons of real numbers. So far, we have not given them any significance, either empirical or ethical. Economists usually give individual utilities empirical significance by considering preferences. Thus the statement

$$U^i(x) \geq U^i(y) \Leftrightarrow x \, R^i y \tag{1}$$

gives meaning to the ordering of the two utility levels $U^i(x)$ and $U^i(y)$ for person i. But what are we to make of the inequality $U^i(x) \geq U^j(y)$ when $i \neq j$? Person i cannot choose to be person j and person j cannot choose to be person i. But person i can want to change places with person j, and vice-versa, so we might interpret $U^i(x) > U^j(y)$ to mean that if x is the social consequence, person i would rather not become person j if y were then the resulting social consequence. Or we can interpret it to mean that if y has occurred, person j would rather be person i if x were to result. Alternatively, it might mean that a third person k would rather become person i in state x than person j in state y.

Whatever their interpretation, it follows that such ICULs correspond to an interpersonal preference ordering $\bar{R}$ on the space $X \times N$, so that $U^i(x) \geq U^j(y)$ if and only if $(x, i)\ \bar{R}\ (y, j)$. Notice that, as in Suppes (1966), different individuals k in N will usually have their own interpersonal ordering $\bar{R}^k$ on $X \times N$; there is no guarantee that they will have the same estimate of what it means in welfare terms to be another person. Indeed, different individuals k can even have their own personal opinions of what constitutes the utilities of individuals i and j, so that we really need to write

$$U^{ik}(x) \geq U^{jk}(y) \Leftrightarrow (x, i)\ \bar{R}^k\ (y, j) \tag{2}$$

where $U^{ik}(\cdot)$, $U^{jk}(\cdot)$ denote k's assessments of the utility functions of i and j respectively.

However, as both Harsanyi (1955) and Sen (1970a) discuss at some length, it is usual to assume that the different individuals k in N can at least agree on what constitutes the welfare orderings of person i and person j. It is not at all clear to me that this is a very good assumption, but it may be all right if we suppose that each individual i is closely consulted on what makes up his utility, and each other individual k uses this information. This is the axiom of identity. Then the interpersonal ordering of each individual $k \in N$ must respect the welfare orderings of other individuals, so that, for all i, k, x, y, one has

$$(x, i)\ \bar{R}^k\ (y, i) \Leftrightarrow x\ R^i y \Leftrightarrow U^{ik}(x) \geq U^{ik}(y) \tag{3}$$

It follows that each $U^{ik}(x) \equiv \phi^{ik}[U^i(x)]$, where ϕ^{ik} is an increasing transformation of i's personal utility function. The ICULs become comparisons of different individuals' indifference curves. Nevertheless, in future the possible dependence of ICULs on k will be ignored throughout.

The question of what it means to want to be another person has still not really been faced, however, as it must be if this approach to ICULs is to have proper empirical significance. I shall return to this later in Sections 4, 5, and 6. For the moment, assuming that ICULs do have ethical significance, we ask what kind of ethical significance are they likely to have.

If $U^i(x) > U^j(x)$, the presumption has generally been that an egalitarian, who will tend to favor equalizing utility levels if possible, will want to try to alter social state x somewhat in order to increase person j's utility, perhaps by a transfer of income from i to j, even if this may mean lowering person i's utility (cf. Sen, 1973). How much the egalitarian is prepared to sacrifice i's utility in order to increase j's remains unclear, however. Indeed, if it is possible to increase i's utility a lot by moving away from state x, even though this means decreasing j's utility, a mild egalitarian may even be prepared to accept this inegalitarian change. Of course, these considerations really only make sense if intensities or differences in utility can be compared interpersonally, as well as levels.

An extreme egalitarian would presumably see $U^i(x) > U^j(x)$ as justifying any change that promoted j's welfare, even at the expense of i, provided it did not go so far as to make i even worse off than j was in state x. In other words, if $U^i(x)$, $U^i(y)$, and $U^j(y)$ all exceed $U^j(x)$, and if all other individuals are indifferent between x and y, then y should be socially preferred to x. This is exactly the equity axiom and the two-person leximin rule discussed in Hammond (1976a, 1979b) and Sen (1977). Under the conditions of unrestricted domain and independence of irrelevant alternatives, as well as Pareto indifference, it becomes equivalent to the leximin criterion of Sen (1970a). This form of extreme egalitarianism is also related to Strasnick's (1976a, 1976b, 1977, 1979) idea of "preference priority." Under this idea, for each pair of individuals $i, j \in N$ and each pair of alternatives $x, y \in X$, we say that i's preference for x over y *takes priority* over j's preference for y over x if $x P y$ when $x P^i y$, $y P^j x$, and all other individuals are indifferent between x and y.

Such extreme egalitarianism is ethically unappealing because, when $U^i(x)$ is much bigger than $U^j(x)$, it may prescribe very large sacrifices in i's welfare even when the gains to person j are extremely small. Such arguments evidently rest on being able to compare i's losses with j's gains, and this is a different kind of interpersonal comparison that I shall come to consider in a moment. It should be noted, however, that the ethical significance of ICULs on their own remains somewhat unclear in this framework, unless we do accept extreme egalitarianism and so Rawls' difference principle. Of course, ICULs do allow egalitarian allocations to be identified in economic models with a sufficiently rich feasible set from which to choose, as in Dworkin (1981), Roemer (1985), Cohen (1989), and other related bargaining models. They do not, however, tell us how to compare different inegalitarian allocations, or even how to compare egalitarian allocations with inegalitarian ones.

3.2. Interpersonal comparisons of utility units or differences

Interpersonal comparisons of utility differences (ICUDs) amount to comparisons of the form $u_1^i - u_2^i > u_1^j - u_2^j$, where u_1^i, u_2^i are two levels of person i's utility function, and u_1^j, u_2^j are two levels of person j's utility function. What then is the empirical significance of a statement such as

$$U^i(x) - U^i(y) > U^j(w) - U^j(z) \tag{4}$$

Insofar as $U^i(x) - U^i(y)$ measures the "preference intensity" of person i for x over y, and $U^j(w) - U^j(z)$ the "preference intensity" of person j for w over z, this seems to be just a straightforward comparison of preference intensities. But what empirical significance do we attach to person's "preference intensity," and on what empirical basis do we "compare" the preference intensities of different people? Some suggestions for answers to both these questions are discussed in Section 5, but none is very satisfactory.

At its face value, (4) means something like preferring moving from state y to state x if one is person i to moving from state z to state w if one is person j. This is hardly an operational preference, however. But suppose $w = y$ and $z = x$, so that (4) becomes

$$U^i(x) - U^i(y) > U^j(y) - U^j(x) \tag{5}$$

This means that moving i from y to x is preferable to the reverse move of j from x to y. It suggests that if we are only considering what happens to persons i and j, then we should prefer x to y because i's gain outweighs j's loss. As an empirical statement, this means very little indeed, but as an ethical statement, its immediate implications seem rather clear at first sight.

Even as an ethical statement, however, we may not always want to infer from (5) that x should be preferred to y if we take account only of persons i and j. Consider the following possibility, of the kind discussed by Sen (1973). Although $U^i(x) - U^i(y)$ may be greater than $U^j(y) - U^j(x)$, it may also be true that $U^i(x) > U^i(y) > U^j(y) > U^j(x)$ and that actually $U^j(y)$ may be very much greater than $U^i(y)$. Of course, this amounts to an ICUL. It suggests, however, that we should try to increase j's welfare on egalitarian grounds, even if this has to be done at the expense of i. Moving from x to y, as suggested on the basis of ICUDs, is therefore inegalitarian when one judges on the basis of ICULs.

With both types of comparison, one has "dual" comparisons of the kind considered in Hammond (1977), and there will usually be tensions between the ethical prescriptions suggested by the two different types of comparison. Such tensions seem hard to avoid in general social choice problems, although, as shown in that paper, the two types of comparison could be reconciled sometimes when the problem is to choose a first-best optimal income distribution (in the absence of any incentive constraints). Basically, when both $U^i(x) - U^j(y) > U^j(y) - U^j(x)$ and $U^i(x) > U^i(y) > U^j(y) > U^j(x)$, there has to be a judgment of whether the excess of i's gain over j's loss is more than enough to outweigh the inegalitarian results of the move from y to x. These are the kind of questions that are difficult to resolve without a single coherent decision framework in which ICUs can both be made and used in ethical decisions. For this reason I regret that the discussion of Hammond (1977, 1980) now seems largely irrelevant.

Having discussed the form of ICUs, it is now time to consider their meaning.

4. Impersonality and fundamental preferences

In the first edition of *Language, Truth and Logic* I had maintained that propositions about oneself, one's own feelings, were to be taken at their face value, so that when I was talking about my own thoughts I was talking about thoughts, feelings and so on, but that propositions about the mental states of other people were propositions about their behaviour. This was a fairly natural deduction from the principle of verifiability, but I came to see that it was wrong and in fact even inconsistent, that it could be shown to lead to a contradiction, and these two classes of propositions had to be taken symmetrically. And once you take the view that they have to be symmetrical, then either you can treat yourself behaviouristically, which means, as Ogden and Richards once put it, feigning anaesthesia, or you can ascribe thoughts and feelings to others in the literal way in which one ascribes them to oneself.

Ayer, in Magee (1971) pp. 54–5.

"Impersonality" is the term used by Harsanyi (1953b, 1955) to describe the idea that, in order to free oneself from an unduly selfish perspective in weighing moral issues, an ethical observer should pretend to be completely uncertain which individual he will become after the issue is decided. In this formulation of utilitarianism, therefore, individuals are meant to choose as though behind a "veil of ignorance" – to borrow Rawls's (1971) felicitous term – uncertain what positions they will eventually occupy in the society being affected by the decisions under consideration. This Kantian idea is similar to Hare's (1951, 1963) principle of "universalizability," under which any person should only prescribe what he would still be willing to prescribe even if he were somebody else completely. And it is perhaps even close in spirit to what Rawls describes as "the original position" – see Rawls (1959, 1971).

Harsanyi and Rawls both use this concept of impersonality or the original position in order to arrive at alternative specific forms of social ordering. Harsanyi assumes that a person who acts as though he does not yet know who he is will be "Bayesian rational" and maximize the expected utility of a von Neumann–Morgenstern utility function, giving equal probability to becoming each possible individual in the society. Rawls, on the other hand, hypothesizes a much less orthodox view of behavior under uncertainty in the original position, which focuses upon the person who one would least like to be. This leads to his "difference principle." If one restricts oneself to a utilitarian framework (which Rawls does not), this would suggest maximizing the minimum utility level – that is, maximin. This could conceivably be an acceptable ethical criterion if one lived in a world where the only risk is in the original position. When individual consequences are risky, however, rules like maximin violate the independence axiom, as Harsanyi (1975a,b, 1977b, 1978) pointed out. In fact, as Lyons (1972), Arrow (1973), Gordon (1973), and, in particular, Barry (1973) have discussed with some care, Rawls's defense of the difference principle is not at all convincing. Harsanyi's defenses of his version of the original position are possibly rather better argued, but much controversy still surrounds them. For this reason, one of my aims in Hammond (1987a) was precisely to avoid any arguments based upon an original position or a veil of ignorance. The main idea will now be recapitulated.

Indeed, to go beyond ICULs we can follow Harsanyi's idea of considering lotteries to get ICUDs as well. Thus, let Θ denote the set of all possible individual characteristics. Let $\Delta(X \times \Theta)$ denote the set of all simple probability measures or lotteries (with finite support) on $X \times \Theta$. Each measure μ in $\Delta(X \times \Theta)$ is a finite collection of possible threesomes (x_k, θ_k, p_k) consisting of a social state x_k and a personal characteristic θ_k, together with the nonnegative probability p_k that (x_k, θ_k) will occur. Of course, $\Sigma_k \, p_k = 1$. Suppose that the ethical observer imagines himself facing decision trees with random consequences in the space $\Delta(X \times \Theta)$ of such lotteries. Such decision trees include but are not restricted to those in which decisions must be taken behind a veil of ignorance. Provided that the observer recommends behavior that is (with probability one) both dynamically consistent in each possible decision tree, and also depends only on the consequences of his choices, then he must maximize some preference ordering over this space of lotteries that satisfies the independence axiom. If one also imposes a rather weak continuity condition on behavior, it can also be shown that all three axioms of Herstein and Milnor (1953) are satisfied (see Hammond, 1983, 1987a and 1988a,b). Therefore the observer must maximize the expected value of some von Neumann-Morgenstern utility function (NMUF) which I shall write as $u(x, \theta)$.

Note that the resulting "fundamental" utility function contains within it interpersonal comparisons of *both* utility levels *and* utility differences. For the ICUL $u(x, \theta_i) > u(y, \theta_j)$ can be taken to mean that the ethical observer prefers to be a θ_i-person in state x rather than a θ_j-person in state y. And the ICUD $u(z, \theta_i) - u(y, \theta_i) > u(z, \theta_j) - u(w, \theta_j)$ can be taken to mean that the ethical observer prefers a 50-50 lottery with (x, θ_i) and (w, θ_j) as possible outcomes to one with (y, θ_i) and (z, θ_j) as possible outcomes.

Two special cases deserve to be mentioned. Rawlsian ICULs alone emerge when one excludes lotteries altogether and simply chooses between sure pairs in $X \times \Theta$. Harsanyi's ICUDs alone emerge when one restricts attention to lotteries in which the probabilities of different social states x are independent of the probability distribution over θ, and when the latter corresponds to the actual distribution of personal characteristics in the population under consideration, as in Harsanyi's version of the original position.

Such impersonal preferences may have a superficial appeal in seeming to fit what we perhaps think of when we make ICUs. The empirical basis of the resulting ICUs, however, is not very strong, unless we find a lot of people who are used to thinking in this precise impersonal way, and ask them their views. Nor are their ethical implications all that clear, because we still have to construct a social ordering based on such ICUs, and there are many possibilities, as Roberts (1980a,b), Blackorby, Donaldson, and Weymark (1984), d'Aspremont (1985), and Sen (1986), for instance, have all discussed. This problem is by no means limited to "impersonal" ICUs, however, though we may be able to circumvent it by considering ethical ICUs directly, as in Section 6.

5. Behaviorist approaches

5.1. Introduction

It would seem empirically ideal if we were able to base ICUs on personal behavior. Not surprisingly, therefore, there have been many attempts to do so. Yet one can see immediately that this is unlikely to succeed completely, inasmuch as different ethical observers are likely to find different behaviorist criteria more appealing.

Let me nevertheless consider some of the behaviorist approaches that have been proposed. To do so, it will be convenient to consider two rather different aspects of these behaviorist approaches separately. The first concerns the construction of a cardinal utility function to represent each individual's preferences, which is clearly necessary if one is to make ICUDs. The second aspect is the comparison of different individual's utility functions as such, once they have been cardinalized.

5.2. Preference intensities

The most common suggestion for cardinalizing individual utility functions before comparing their differences interpersonally is to use NMUFs. These are assumed to describe each individual's personal attitudes towards risk. Relative differences of utility are taken as measures of preference intensity for a single individual. I have already discussed this procedure at some length in Hammond (1982b, 1983, 1987a). I find it more compelling than many other approaches, but not all that compelling. Initially, its chief advocates, apart from Harsanyi (whose arguments are rather different anyway), were Vickrey (1945, 1960) and Jeffrey (1971). Its many critics have included Friedman and Savage (1948, 1952), Arrow (1951), Diamond (1967), Sen (1970a, 1973) and, of course, Rawls (1971). A general discussion of this and other kinds of intensity approach can also be found in Weirich (1983, 1984).

One apparent source of confusion should be cleared up at once. It has been argued by some, and is hinted at by Arrow (1951), that using NMUFs to cardinalize is unacceptable when there is no risk, but quite acceptable when there is risk. Yet this leads to a discontinuity. If the NMUF cardinalization is right for risky prospects, then it is right, presumably, for a sequence of risky prospects that converges to a sure prospect. Why then is this same cardinalization not right in the limit, when we converge to a sure prospect? Instead, I prefer to regard the usual NMUF cardinalization as being inappropriate for ICUs in all situations, be they risky or sure.

Of course, even if one accepts the NMUF cardinalization of individual utilities, that does not yet make them interpersonally comparable. To do so, Isbell (1959) had an ingenious suggestion. To avoid St. Petersburg-like paradoxes, one can argue that each individual i must have an NMUF u_i that is bounded both above and below. Otherwise, as Menger (1934) and Arrow (1972) showed, there are discontinuities in preferences for some sequence of probability distributions that converges in the limit to a distribution attaching positive probability to each of an infinite sequence of consequences. Then Isbell suggested normalizing each individual's utility function by an affine transformation that puts equal upper and lower bounds on all individuals' utilities – for example, a lower bound of 0 and an upper bound of 1. Summing normalized utilities then gives a well-defined social ordering. So does a similar normalization procedure suggested by Schick (1971) and criticized by Jeffrey (1974). The ethical appeal of equating different person's upper and lower bounds remains unconvincing, however, at least to me. Consider some undemanding person who achieves his upper bound at a low level of consumption. Do we normalize that person's utility scale so that it has the same upper and lower bounds as that of a greedy person? If so, and if we distribute goods to each individual so that each achieves, say, 90% of maximum utility (which is now a well-defined utility level), then the greedy person is likely to be given much more than one feels he deserves.

Most other cardinalizations also rest more or less on some way of trying to infer the intensities of an individual's preferences from personal behavior. One prominent method is the use of "just noticeable differences". This derives from Edgeworth (1881). It is assumed that each individual has a preference semi-ordering of the kind formalized by Luce (1956), in which a transitive indifference relation is replaced by an intransitive incomparability relation. Then, under certain additional assumptions such as those presented by Suppes and Winet (1955) and Kaneko (1984), there exists a utility function $U^i(\cdot)$ for each individual i and a positive number δ^i such that

$$x \; P^i \; y \Leftrightarrow U^i(x) - U^i(y) > \delta^i \tag{6}$$

Evidently, such inequalities enable *intra*personal comparisons of utility differences and so a cardinalization. Normalizing each individual's utility function U^i by multiplying the function by the constant $1/\delta^i$, it can even be arranged that all the δ^i's are equal to one, which Goodman and Markovitz (1952) and more recently Ng (1975, 1984b, 1985b) have used to make ICUDs. Svensson (1985) and others have raised obvious objections to adding individuals' utilities that have been cardinalized in this way. But such ICUDs themselves are ethically unattractive, as Arrow (1963, pp. 115–8) for one has argued. This is because they tend to favor the sensitive or those who are most able to complete their indifference map. If we think about income distribution impersonally, for instance, do we believe that we would value income more if our personal characteristics became those of a person who noticed more differences in his utility ranking? And even if we confine ourselves to intrapersonal comparisons, does it really make sense to value an income change half as much just because it moves a person through half as many just noticeable differences? The fundamental problem in that the relationship of just noticeable differences to idealized ethical decisions is tenuous at best. As Arrow also points out, the same is true of Dahl's (1956) suggestion of using willingness to incur enough trouble to vote for x over y as an indication that intensity of preference is sufficient to make voting worthwhile.

A somewhat related proposal is to cardinalize utility by looking at the probability that the person chooses x over y. It is assumed, of course, that this probability may not be unity even when x is better than y. Instead, we have probabilistic choice models of the kind considered by psychologists such as Luce (1959) and reviewed in Becker, DeGroot, and Marschak (1963) (see Edwards and Tversky, 1967) using such probabilities of choice, but over the whole domain of options. Intriligator (1973) equated "utilities" with probabilities of choice, in effect. A related proposal is due to Waldner (1972), who suggests that if possible one should construct a utility function for each individual so that the probability of choosing x over y is an increasing function of $U^i(x) - U^i(y)$ (for example, as in a probit econometric equation – see Amemiya, 1981). Alternatively, the "latency" of choice – the time it takes for the person to decide for x over y – could be assumed to be some function of $U^i(x) - U^i(y)$. And, in a later paper, Waldner (1974a) combines the ideas of probabilistic choice with just noticeable differences by looking for "bare preferences," defined so that "x is barely preferred to y" means that x is chosen over y with probability 0.75 (see also Becker 1974 and Waldner 1974b).

Now, it may be that we can get a good measure of an individual's utility by the looking at the right-hand side exogenous variables of some probit (or logit) econometric equation, which is what this kind of procedure would seem to lead to eventually. Yet I remain unconvinced. For, bearing in mind that an individual's "utility" should surely be based on idealized choices, I have to ask why such superficial irrationalities as imperfect discrimination and the failure to choose the best with probability one should have any ethical relevance at all.

5.3. Social indicators

Two entirely different suggestions for cardinalizing individual utilities, as well as for comparing the cardinalized utilities interpersonally, are contained in the article by Simon (1974) – with comments by Toharia (1978) and a reply by Simon (1978) – and also in the "Leyden" approach of van Praag and his associates – see van Praag (1968, 1971), van Praag and Kapteyn (1973), Kapteyn and van Praag (1976), Kapteyn (1977), van Herwaarden, Kapteyn and van Praag (1977), Tinbergen (1980, 1985, 1987a,b), Hagenaars (1986), van Praag and van der Saar (1988), and especially Seidl's (1987) careful review of Hagenaars' monograph.

Simon lists a number of aspects of individual behavior that are correlated with personal income and so, Simon claims, might be used to construct a measure of welfare. They include the propensity to commit suicide on the one hand or murder on the other (both negatively correlated with income), statements about how happy a person feels, and also different aspects of personal health – how well the person thinks he is, worries, psychological anxiety, severe mental illness, and so on. Some economic variables that he also considers include a function defining the utility of consumption for each time period, which would be a cardinal utility function if preferences over consumption streams were additively separable, which almost certainly they are not.

A second economic variable Simon considers is labor supply, based on the observation by Kindleberger (1965) that hours worked per week in manufacturing industry are higher in countries with lower incomes per head. Even as some measure of "national" utility, however, this measure seems extremely suspect; as a measure of individual utility, it is clearly useless, because it would suggest that the unemployed are the best off of all! As for Simon's other measures, do we really want to say that extra money means most to an individual whose propensity to commit suicide or to fall ill is thereby most reduced? Or even to say that it means most to an identifiable group of individuals whose collective propensity to commit suicide or to fall ill is thereby most reduced? And even if we do, what is the appropriate *cardinalization* of utility based on such propensities?

The Leyden approach of van Praag and his associates uses a different technique. This involves constructing a "social indicator" of well-being – as discussed by sociologists such as Levy and Guttman (1975) or McKennell (1978) – supplemented, however, by explicit interpersonal comparisons of such social indicators. The construction is based on the intervals of net family income levels that each individual in a sample reports as being necessary to achieve an income that is "excellent," or "good," or "barely sufficient," or "bad" – in fact, they use up to nine different quality descriptions. They rank the eight different boundaries between quality intervals on a scale from 0 to 1, and then fit a lognormal cumulative probability distribution function to these reports. The result is taken as the "individual welfare function of income." Different types of individuals are characterized by the mean and the standard deviation of the distribution of the logarithm of income that best fits their reports. They find that the mean is positively related to income and to family size, whereas the standard deviation increases for people whose incomes have fluctuated in the past, or whose "social reference group" consists of people with widely differing income levels. Thus, the utility of income function for a particular group of people is a smoothing of the function obtained by looking at the proportions of people who regard any particular income level as "good," "sufficient," "bad," and so on. The smoothing occurs, as explained earlier, by fitting a cumulative lognormal distribution. Reasons for choosing this distribution are especially unclear, as Seidl (1987) also points out.

This is an ingenious device very similar to that suggested by Rescher (1967, 1969) for more general decisions than the choice of income distribution. But it faces a number of questions concerning the significance of the findings – particularly their ethical significance. If one only thinks how one would oneself go about completing the questionnaire that these researchers used, one begins to realize that the survey results must be based on extremely tenuous foundations. The questionnaire actually seems harder to fill in, moreover, when one realizes that the results will be used to construct a cardinalized utility function in order to decide what is an appropriate income distribution. Unless, that is, one has some confidence already in what is the right cardinalization. The approach also faces considerable problems when one tries – as van Praag (1968) and also Kapteyn (1977) indeed did – to go beyond a purely one good framework and allow different consumers to have different tastes for many consumption goods. If there were public goods as well, the method would be very stretched indeed.

It therefore seems to me that there has not yet emerged any thoroughly satisfactory behaviorist approach to cardinalizing individual utility functions. The fact that so many different approaches have been tried, all of which have some merits but also some serious faults, suggests that even at this level we cannot overcome "Hume's law," which claims that one cannot derive an "ought" from an "is." Indeed, in Hume's own words:

> In every system of morality, which I have hitherto met with, I have always remark'd, that the author proceeds for some time in the ordinary way of reasoning, and establishes the being of a God, or makes observations concerning human affairs; when of a sudden I am surpriz'd to find, that instead of the usual copulations of propositions, *is,* and *is not,* I meet with no proposition that is not connected with an *ought,* or an *ought not.* This change is imperceptible; but is, however, of the last consequence. For as this *ought,* or *ought not,* expresses some new relation or affirmation, 'tis necessary that it shou'd be observ'd and explain'd; and at the same time that a reason should be given, for what seems altogether inconceivable, how this new relation can be a deduction from others, which are entirely different from it. But as authors do not commonly use this precaution, I shall presume to recommend it to the readers; and am persuaded, that this small attention wou'd subvert all the vulgar systems of morality, and let us see, that the distinction of vice and virtue is not founded merely on the relations of objects, nor is perceiv'd by reason.

> *Hume (1739–40; 1969, p. 521)*

As Hume foresaw, there is just no way we can use empirical observations on their own to produce an ethically satisfactory cardinalization, let alone an ethically satisfactory social welfare ordering. As Samuelson (1937, p. 161) put it more than fifty years ago:

> In conclusion, any connection between utility as discussed here and any welfare concept is disavowed. The idea that the results of such a statistical investigation could have any influence upon ethical judgment of policy is one which deserves the impatience of modern economists.

5.4. Fundamental preferences and isomorphy

All men are born equal: it's their habits that make them different.

Attributed to Confucius

The idea that deep down we are really all alike is rather an old one in moral philosophy. And it would be helpful, particularly in making interpersonal comparisons of utility *levels,* if there were a universally accepted preference ordering on the space that everybody shares. Then the comparison $(x, \theta_1)\ \bar{R}(y, \theta_2)$ would mean that *everybody* weakly prefers being in state x with characteristics θ_1 to being in state y with characteristics θ_2. Among economists, an ordering of this kind has been postulated by Tinbergen (1957) and Kolm (1972). Under standard assumptions, it gives rise to a utility function $u(x, \theta)$ that enables ICULs to be made. The utility still needs cardinalization, however, if we are to compare utility differences as well. This is what Harsanyi (1955) tried to provide.

Such "fundamental preferences," as Kolm calls them, make especial sense when we recognize that individuals do not have fixed characteristics, and so find themselves choosing what characteristics to have as well as making the usual economic and other decisions. This is the topic of Section 5.5. Unfortunately, it is by no means clear why a universally accepted interpersonal preference ordering should emerge, as Mac-Kay (1986), for one, discusses.

An alternative, rather less general, approach is that of "iso-morphy," to use Mirrlees' (1982) term. A general formulation of this principle is found in Arrow (1977); it is related to the Gorman (1956, 1980) and Lancaster (1966) "characteristics" approach to consumer demand theory. A similar approach is also used by Stigler and Becker (1977) to construct what is in effect a fundamental utility function shared by all, though they do not care to use the function to make interpersonal comparisons. There is a space Z of "characteristics" such that, for each consequence y in Y and each individual i in N, there is a characteristic vector $G_i(y)$ in Z that describes the effect of y on i. Each z in Z is supposed to include not only Gorman–Lancaster characteristics but, in some cases, tastes too (Arrow, 1977). Then there is a utility function u on Z that is the same for each individual. A similar but simpler version is discussed by Mirrlees (1982), who assumes that individuals differ only in their skill level n, and that each individual has the same utility function $u(x, y/n)$, where x is consumption and y is output in efficiency units from the labor that the individual supplies.

Yet another kind of "isomorphy" arises in connection with family equivalence scales. These were introduced by Barten (1964), then used by Muellbauer (1974a,b,c, 1975, 1977) especially in order to make interfamily comparisons of utility levels. Such comparisons have been criticized by Pollak and Wales (1979) – see also Muellbauer (1987) and Blackorby and Donaldson (1991). For these family equivalence scales it is assumed that each household has a utility function for consumption vectors of the form $u(x_1/m_1, x_2/m_2, \ldots, x_n/m_n)$, where x_g denotes family consumption of good g, and m_g is a scaling factor for good g that depends on family composition. These scaling factors can be derived from demand data, because household's demand for good g at given prices and incomes can be expressed as $m_g h_g^*(p_1 m_1, p_2 m_2, \ldots, p_n m_n; I)$, where I denotes income. This is a very special functional form, however, and although some generalizations are possible, they only permit inferences about the form of u for different households to be made in exceptional cases.

Yet the main objection to these approaches is rather different. It is simply that if we measure utility interpersonally by $u(x, y/n)$ in the Mirrlees model, we neglect the possibility that being more skilled actually confers extra utility in its own right. Any class of utility functions of the form

$$\bar{u}(n, x, y/n) \equiv \phi(n, u(x, y/n)) \tag{7}$$

with $\phi(n, \cdot)$ increasing in u for each fixed n, produces identical utility maximizing demand and supply behavior, but usually very different interpersonal comparisons. Similarly, in the model with household composition effects, if we measure utility interfamilially by $u(x_1/m_1, x_2/m_2, \ldots, x_n/m_n)$. Then, as Pollak and Wales (1979), Deaton and Muellbauer (1986), and Fisher (1987) have all pointed out, we neglect the possibility that a household with more children may be better off just because it has more children, even if it consumes an equivalent bundle of goods. Indeed, any class of utility functions of the form

$$\bar{u}(m_1, m_2, \ldots, m_n; x_1, x_2, \ldots, x_n) \tag{8}$$

$$\equiv \psi\left(m_1, m_2, \ldots, m_n; u\left(\frac{x_1}{m_1}, \frac{x_2}{m_2}, \ldots, \frac{x_n}{m_n}\right)\right)$$

where $\psi(m_1, m_2, \ldots, m_n, \cdot)$ is increasing in u for each fixed m_1, $m_2, \ldots, m_n$, generates identical utility maximizing demands for commodities, but usually very different interfamily comparisons. The postulate of isomorphy in this simple form forces us to neglect such possibilities altogether. In the more general Arrow (1977) approach, however, we can include things like skill and children as characteristics that are desirable in themselves.

It has been suggested that simple isomorphy may be recoverable if we consider the choice of family size and of household composition within a utility maximizing framework, or the choice of skill level when this results from decisions concerning education. But even if one believes in utility maximization as strongly as does Becker (1981) when it comes to "human capital" or family composition decisions, it is far from clear that the appropriate utility function is being maximized. Family composition is chosen for reasons that are not purely self-interested – or at least one hopes this is usually the case. And the choice of how skilled one wants to be is a difficult one to make according to usual expected utility maximizing criteria, because it is virtually impossible to appreciate all the possible consequences of acquiring skills without actually acquiring them.

It seems that to make isomorphy a basis for ICULs requires doing as Arrow (1977) suggests and including lots of extraneous variables. Then, however, we have gone beyond a purely behaviorist model because many of the extraneous variables will be inherited or exogenous rather than consequences of the individual's own behavior. We have virtually reverted to "fundamental preferences." And, as I remarked before, such preferences are unlikely to be observable. Little is gained, it seems, by considering preferences under isomorphy instead of fundamental preferences, which they closely resemble.

5.5. Intrapersonal comparisons

Gibbard (1986, 1987) has pursued an idea that had earlier been developed by Harsanyi (1955, and 1977a, p. 59) and Jeffrey (1971). This suggests basing the notional ICUs ethical theory seems to require upon the *intra*personal comparisons of utility that many of us find ourselves implicitly making throughout our lives. Similar ideas are also considered by Griffin (1991), Broome (1991), and many others. After all, the argument goes, we are confronted many times with opportunities to make decisions that affect our personal characteristics, including our tastes, habits, predilections, and so on. Implicitly, at least, any such decision involves comparing different potential personal characteristics. It happens that these are different characteristics for the same person, but why should that make any difference? Thus, this approach supplies us with the beginnings of a theory based on actual preferences. Two serious problems remain, however, both of which Gibbard for one readily admits. In fact, Gibbard even uses these problems as arguments for why one should be skeptical about the possibility of basing an *individual* welfare function on *intra*personal comparisons, let alone the possibility of basing a *social* welfare function on *inter*personal comparisons.

The first difficulty, which is more obvious, is that any given individual – particularly a mature adult to whose preferences we might want to give much more weight than to those of a child – is only likely to face choices between a rather limited range of different possible personal characteristics. Somebody who does not learn in youth a particular kind of skill like mathematics, foreign languages, ability with a particular musical instrument, or gymnastics or ball games will find it much harder to achieve real mastery of the skill later on in life. Some personal characteristics are virtually impossible to change, such as one's genetic inheritance. Indeed, how does one completely forget one's upbringing? So the range of interpersonal comparisons of utility that can be inferred from such practical intrapersonal comparisons of utility is unfortunately rather limited. Ortuño-Ortin and Roemer (1991) have an interesting suggestion for piecing together local intrapersonal comparisons into a global intrapersonal welfare function, but it depends on assumptions that may limit its applicability too severely.

The second difficulty with this theory relates to the general issue of whether it is right to infer how to make ethical decisions from individual's actual preferences. In economics, the "consumer sovereignty" value judgment states that the goods and services an individual wants to buy enhance that individual's welfare and so are ethically desirable. As Lerner (1972) put it:

> As a social critic, I may try to change some desires to others of which I approve more, but as an economist I must be concerned with the mechanisms for getting people what they want, no matter how these wants are acquired.

Lerner (1972, p. 258)

Many economists accept this value judgment so unquestioningly that they even forget that it is a value judgment. Yet, when it comes to individuals who reveal a preference for becoming addicted to certain drugs, most people – even most economists – generally reject consumer sovereignty. Such self-destructive behavior is clearly just one extreme instance of the general possibility noticed by Harsanyi (1953a) and Pollak (1976), for instance, that people do not always make ethically appropriate intrapersonal comparisons of utility, because they wind up acquiring inappropriate personal characteristics. So it is doubtful whether individual behavior can be relied on to reveal fundamental preferences, partly because the relevant characteristics include tastes that themselves have to be inferred from behavior, and partly because individuals will usually be too myopic to maximize consistently any such fundamental preferences.

Of course, Harsanyi also claimed to be using intrapersonal comparisons. His approach rests on "the postulate that the preferences and utility functions of all human individuals are governed by the same basic psychological laws" (Harsanyi, 1975b, p. 600). But, unlike the theory just enunciated, Harsanyi allows comparisons to extend to all "hypothetical conditions" in which a person has a different characteristic. Some such "hypothetical conditions" could never be met in practice; an individual cannot become a younger person, for instance, or have different natural parents. For this reason, I prefer to regard Harsanyi as postulating a fundamental utility function.

6. Interpersonal comparisons and ethical decisions

6.1. The direct approach to social welfare measurement

The attempt to base ethically relevant ICUs upon empirical observations, particularly observations of behavior, has not surprisingly run into Hume's law, which claims that normative statements cannot rest upon purely empirical foundations. The only alternative is to recognize from the start that ethically relevant ICUs are bound to depend upon ethical value judgements, at least in part, and so will almost certainly also have to be subjective. Indeed, even intrapersonal comparisons, and the construction of an ethically relevant individual welfare function, are bound to contain similar subjective ethical value judgments. There is no system of ethical standards that is not largely subjective, at least when we try to come up with as precise a system as that implied by a social welfare ordering.

Once we recognize that such ICUs are bound to be subjective, and so that any derived social welfare ordering is bound to be subjective, there is much to be said for looking directly at the ordering itself. This is particularly true in economic contexts, where the issue of how to trade off total real income against inequality of real income may even suffice to determine a social welfare function – cf. Atkinson (1970), and Sen's (1978) criticism of ethical inequality measures. This is the direct approach to social welfare measurement. It is, of course, the one that Bergson (1938) and many others have adopted, at least implicitly. Such an approach typically relies on ICUs because otherwise we would have a dictatorship (see Roberts, 1980c, and the papers cited therein, as well as Kemp and Ng, 1987). But if it is easier to think what is a good social welfare ordering, rather than how to make ICUs, why should we not start with the ordering and have it reveal the ICUs, instead of starting with ICUs and trying to derive a social ordering? Especially if it is not at all clear anyway how to incorporate ICUs into a social ordering even if we believe we have made securely founded and ethically relevant interpersonal comparisons of both utility levels and utility differences. This direct approach is well exemplified by the experiments of Yaari and Bar-Hillel (1984) and Schokkaert and Overlaet (1989). It is also advocated in the conclusion of Kaneko (1984).

6.2. Can interpersonal comparisons have ethical significance?

The direct approach to distributional judgments, however, essentially only masks the key question: What ethical significance can we attach to the implicit ICUs, if any (cf. Sen, 1979)? To summarize, as pointed out by Rothenburg (1961, pp. 268–9), most existing treatments of ICUs consider only hypothetical decisions requiring that individuals imagine themselves becoming other individuals. The same is true of Arrow's (1963) discussion of "extended sympathy." As Adam Smith put it:

> How selfish soever man may be supposed, there are evidently some principles in his nature, which interest him in the fortune of others, and render their happiness necessary to him, though he derives nothing from it except the pleasure of seeing it. Of this kind is pity or compassion, which we feel for the misery of others, when we either see it, or are made to conceive it in a very lively matter . . .
>
> That this is the source of our fellow feeling of the misery of others, that it is by changing places in fancy with the sufferer, that we come either to conceive or to be affected by what he feels, may be demonstrated by many observations, if it should not be thought sufficiently evident of itself.

> *Smith (1759), pp. 1–3*

Harsanyi (1977a, fn. 4, p. 293) seeks to rebut Rothenburg's argument that ICUs depend on "changing places" in this way. Indeed, the transition from being nobody in particular in an original position, to a particular person later on, really is different. But there is a sense in which person *A* becomes *B* as the result of two transitions: first, back from being *A* to the original position; second, forward from the original position to being *B*. In any case, the ethical relevance of such original position arguments remains controversial.

Indeed, the reason for not allowing ICUs that Arrow offered in *Social Choice and Individual Values*, as quoted at the end of Section 2, was recently repeated somewhat more forcefully:

> Interpersonal comparisons of utility cannot be given decision-theoretic significance. That is, there is no decision-theoretic meaning for a statement such as, 'a movie gives me more utility than an opera gives you,' because neither of us could ever be forced to choose between being me at a movie and you at an opera.
>
> *Myerson (1985, pp. 238–9)*

The real trouble with most existing approaches to ICUs is precisely the failure to integrate them properly within a comprehensive framework based on ethically relevant decisions. People cannot change places, or be put into an original position. Information regarding utility comparisons cannot just be postulated, without explaining what decisions it explains or relates to.

Sen (1970a,b) and many succeeding articles published during the 1970s incorporate ICUs in formal social choice theory in a different way. But that work mostly treated ICUs as additional information that merely places restrictions on the invariance class of transformations to individuals' utility functions required to leave the social decision norm unchanged. No practical procedures for making such ICUs were suggested. In Sen's approach, ICUs were not directly related to any ethical decisions that could possibly arise in practice.

The time has come to see what is possible when interpersonal comparisons are explicitly related to choices of people.

6.3. Interpersonal comparisons revealed by choice of people

There are certainly many real life decisions that do involve genuine interpersonal comparisons, if not always interpersonal comparisons of utility. We choose people as spouses, friends, colleagues, employees, employers, landlords, tenants, doctors, lawyers, investment advisers, members of our sports teams or social clubs. Doctors choose people as candidates for organ transplants. Immigration officers choose people, or reject them, as do governments with the power to withhold exit visas. To a certain extent, even conference organizers and participants choose each other, as do writers and their readers. The opening two sentences of Harsanyi (1987b) recognize this:

> Suppose I am left with a ticket to a Mozart concert I am unable to attend and decide to give it to one of my closest friends. Which friend should I actually give it to?

Indeed, consider the choice between person i at a film and person j at an opera, which Myerson claimed could not be given decision-theoretic meaning. Myerson was right that it may be hard for a film enthusiast like i to imagine becoming an opera-lover like j, or for person j to imagine becoming somebody like i who prefers the cinema to the opera. And he was right that this is *exactly* the kind of comparison that virtually all existing work on ICUs would have us contemplate. Yet other much more meaningful comparisons by third parties are certainly possible, even between film- and opera-goers. A municipal authority, for example, may be contemplating whether to use a certain piece of land or an existing building for either a cinema or an opera house – it is then involved in rather direct interpersonal comparisons between having more people in the city who see more films, or more people who see more opera. A private profit-maximizing entertainment company, making a similar decision, will value cinema- and opera-goers by the profits they are expected to generate, which is even a quantitative interpersonal comparison.

At first it might seem that such choices of people have no bearing on our problem of making interpersonal comparisons of *utility*. One chooses friends mostly for the value of their friendship, not because of their individual utility. Yet, in a sense, friends are being chosen precisely for their *utility as friends* to the person choosing to befriend them. Interpersonal comparisons of this utility as friends are being revealed by the choice of one's friends, according to this view. The entertainment company, or any other profit-maximizing company, attaches a measure of "utility" to each customer equal to the profit that customer is expected to generate. Of course, these are personal preferences and personal measures of utility, which need not necessarily have any ethical significance.

6.4. The utilities of persons to society

The ethical interpersonal comparisons of utility that are hidden in the idealized version of Harsanyi's utilitarianism are actually rather similar to those just discussed. They represent, in a sense, preferences for the kinds of people it is desirable to have in the society. An ethical interpersonally comparable utility function measures an ethical observer's view of the *utility of a person* to the society as a whole. Moreover, the utility of a person can change along with that person's circumstances, such as income or social status. Indeed, it could happen that this measure of the utility of a person increases if and only if the person moves to situations that he himself prefers, although this is by no means necessary.

To understand this approach properly requires examining carefully the precise form that idealized or "fundamental" utilitarianism takes. As explained in Hammond (1987a, 1988c), it requires choosing among the feasible probability distributions over possible values of (x, θ^M, M) in order to maximize the expected value of the welfare sum

$$W(x, \theta^M, M) \equiv \sum_{i \in M} v(x, \theta_i) \tag{9}$$

Here, M denotes the variable set of individuals in the society, x denotes the usual social state (or economic allocation), θ^M denotes the profile $(\theta_i)_{i \in}M$, where θ_i denotes individual i's personal characteristics, which determine tastes, values, and so on, and v denotes the common fundamental NMUF. This is just (the expected value of) the total utility objective of classical utilitarianism, but with a very different concept of an individual's "utility."

As Yaari (1981) points out, Edgeworth (1881, p. 117) dismissed what Hutcheson called "the greatest happiness for the greatest numbers" as meaningless, like "greatest illumination with the greatest number of lamps." But Yaari's argument (p. 17) that maximization of (9) is "meaningless" is at best incomplete. Because the special form of distribution problem he considers places no natural limit on numbers of individuals, the maximand can indeed become arbitrarily large. An analogy is that the consumer's utility function in neoclassical demand theory may also be made arbitrarily large, unless it happens to be bounded above. Realistically, however, the set of feasible intertemporal population streams is bounded, for any finite time horizon. This also disposes of G. Dworkin's (1982) (apparently deliberately frivolous) rejection of utilitarianism, which is very similar to Yaari's. Anyway, one is usually choosing among a small number of different feasible policies affecting both population and resource allocation. Yaari's ingenious reformulation of classical utilitarianism therefore strikes me as being neither necessary nor convincing. Other objections to this population objective are discussed, for instance, in Dasgupta (1988), Hammond (1988c), the work cited in those papers, and in Schwartz (1979). None seems to me very persuasive when the welfare objective (9) is properly understood.

Implicit in (9) are at least three different types of ICUs, all of which have received considerable attention in the past. Now, in addition, they will be related to hypothetical ethical choices of potential persons, as befits ethical ICUs.

First, one has level comparisons of utility of the form

$$v(x_1, \theta_i) > v(x_2, \theta_j) \tag{10}$$

This typical comparison has the obvious meaning that if it were possible to replace an individual i in situation (x_1, θ_i) with the same or another individual j in situation (x_2, θ_j), then that would be a desirable change, *ceteris paribus*.

Second, one has difference comparisons of utility of the typical form

$$v(x_1, \theta_i) - v(x_2, \theta_j) > v(x_3, \theta_k) - v(x_4, \theta_l) \tag{11}$$

This can be interpreted as follows. If it were possible to have an increase in the probability of replacing an individual i in situation (x_1, θ_i) with another individual j in situation (x_2, θ_j) that is exactly equal to the decrease in the probability of replacing an individual k in situation (x_3, θ_k) with another individual l in situation (x_4, θ_l), then that would be a desirable change, *ceteris paribus*.

The third kind of comparison is of an individual's utility level with zero, and it takes one of the two alternative forms

$$v(x, \, \theta_i) > 0 \tag{12}$$

or

$$v(x', \, \theta_j) < 0 \tag{13}$$

The typical comparison (12) has the obvious meaning that if it were possible to replace a society in which individual i will never exist with another society in which individual i will exist and be in situation (x, θ_i), then that would be a desirable change, *ceteris paribus*. On the other hand, the reverse typical comparison (13) has the obvious meaning that if it were possible to replace a society in which individual j will exist and be in situation $(x', \, \theta_j)$ with another society in which j will never exist, then that would also be a desirable change, *ceteris paribus*.

These interpretations of the three kinds of comparison that have received most attention in the past are rather obvious, given that one accepts the desirability of the utilitarian welfare objective (9) for all kinds of policy decision, including those that affect the future numbers of individuals in the society, as well as the distribution of personal characteristics within it.

6.5. Utility Ratios as Marginal Rates of Substitution

In fact, once we allow the possibility of grouping individuals into one of several categories of "ethically identical" individuals, the fundamental utility function can be given another interpretation that should be familiar to economists. For if $N(x, \theta)$ denotes the number of individuals who have personal characteristic θ when the social state is x, then (9) can be written as

$$W(x, \, \theta^M, \, M) \equiv \Sigma_\theta \, N(x, \, \theta) \, v(x, \, \theta) \equiv V(\mathbf{N}(x, \, \cdot)) \tag{14}$$

Here, $V(\mathbf{N}(x, \, \cdot))$ is a linear function of the vector $\mathbf{N}$ with components $N(x, \, \theta)$ (all $\theta \in \Theta$). Then (14) says that the social ordering should have linear indifference curves in the space of possible vectors $\mathbf{N}$, with constant marginal rates of substitution $v(x, \theta)/v(x, \theta')$ between the numbers of individuals with any pair θ, θ' of personal characteristics. Such constant marginal rates of substitution determine, for each fixed x, an interpersonally comparable utility function $v(x, \cdot)$ on the domain of possible values of θ. This function is unique up to cardinal ratio scale transformations of the form

$$\tilde{v}(x, \theta) \equiv \alpha(x)\, v(x, \theta) \tag{15}$$

for any $\alpha(x) > 0$ that is independent of θ. This implies that the entire fundamental utility function $v(x, \theta)$ can be constructed by combining:

(i) any one type of individual's von Neumann–Morgenstern utility function $v(\cdot, \bar{\theta})$ defined on all social states x, whose expected value represents the utility to society of a $\bar{\theta}$-person for any given lottery over such social states;

(ii) the unique marginal rates of substitution $v(x, \theta)/v(x, \bar{\theta})$ between θ-persons and $\bar{\theta}$-persons in each social state x.

The result is a function $v(x, \theta)$ that is unique up to ratio-scale transformations of the form

$$\tilde{v}(x, \theta) \equiv \alpha\, v(x, \theta) \tag{16}$$

where now $\alpha > 0$ is also independent of x.

Take the specific case where $x = y(\cdot)$, an income distribution function $y(\theta)$ defined for all types of individual θ, and where each individual's welfare becomes just $w(y(\theta))$, a function of just own income. Then equation (14) becomes

$$V(n(\cdot)) = \sum_y n(y)\, w(y) \tag{17}$$

where $n(y)$ is the number of individuals who share income level y. Then the interpersonally comparable utility of income function $w(y)$ is simply determined from marginal rates of substitution between numbers of people with different incomes. Notice that $w(y)$ could be negative for some values of y. Nor is there any presumption yet that w is increasing in y, though that is probably a restriction that one's ethics would imply – the utility to a society of richer people exceeds that of poorer.

Finally, it is tempting to explore the implications of assuming that a function like (17) represents a nation's preferences not only over income distributions but also over immigration policies. For then the ratios $w(y)/w(y')$ represent marginal rates of substitution between immigrants (and existing residents too, indiscriminately) of different earning capacities. If immigration policy is then insensitive to earning capacity beyond a certain threshold $\bar{y}$, that would imply that the marginal utility of income drops to zero, for $y > \bar{y}$! On the other hand, if immigrants with income y below some lower limit $\underline{y}$ are regarded as undesirable – that is, $w(y) < 0$ for all $y < \underline{y}$ – that tends to suggest that there may be exceptional benefit from raising the incomes of existing poor residents to at least $\underline{y}$. It also suggests, of course, that society would be better off if it could prevent the birth of individuals with incomes below $\underline{y}$. No doubt function (17) is far too simplistic for discussing immigration or population policy, even assuming that objectives are limited to national rather than world welfare, that only the distribution of income is ethically relevant, and that immigrants are treated on the same basis as nationals. Yet it does illustrate some of the possibilities that begin to emerge from integrating the choice of people into our welfare objectives.

Despite the promise of such an approach, there has been a remarkable reluctance, apparently, to try to relate the ICUs that utilitarian ethical theory needs to explicit decisions of this kind. That may well be because we feel uncomfortable when confronted with such decisions, because they tend to remind us of the evils of Hitler's *Mein Kampf,* which were put into practice, or those of Aldous Huxley's *Brave New World,* which have not been as yet. But then any all-encompassing ethical theory of this kind is bound to embrace many different possible values, some of which may be extremely unethical. It seems to me high time that the ethical issues regarding the choice of persons should be confronted more openly and honestly.

Summary of where we stand

Needless to say I do not at all deny that, in the course of evolution of economics as we know it, there has been a good deal of intermixture of political and ethical discussion with the scientific discussion of fact and possibility. I shall shortly be discussing this matter further in the light of certain specific instances; and it will not appear that, *provided the logical difference between the two kinds of propositions is clearly kept in mind,* I am in the least hostile to the combination. In that youthful book of mine which evoked such fervid denunciation, I expressly denied that my position involved the view that 'economists should not discuss ethical or political questions any more than the position that botany is not aesthetics means that botanists should not have views on the layout of gardens.' On the contrary I went on to argue, 'it is greatly to be desired that economists should have speculated long and widely on these matters.' As you will see later on, my position today only involves a slight purely semantic modification of this pronouncement. I still hold that the distinction of the different kinds of propositions is inescapable and that we run the dangers of intellectual confusion on our own part and justifiable criticism from outside if we do not explicitly recognize it.

Robbins (1981, p. 4)

Interpersonal comparisons of utility (ICUs) have to be made if there is to be any satisfactory escape from Arrow's impossibility theorem, with its implication that individualistic social choice has to be dictatorial (or at least oligarchic), or else that it has to restrict itself to recommending Pareto improvements. Even dictatorship, in fact, embodies interpersonal comparisons in the choice of the dictator, as do oligarchies in their choices of the oligarchs.

ICUs can be comparisons of utility levels or of utility differences, but even after they have been made, traditional theory does not really tell us how they should be incorporated into a social welfare functional (cf. Roberts, 1980a,b; Blackorby, Donaldson, and Weymark, 1984; and d'Aspremont, 1985). Nor have existing attempts to derive ICUs from imaginary decisions behind a veil of ignorance, or from preferences about the type of person one might wish to become, or from individual behavior, yet yielded anything sufficiently definite and specific to apply to a broad class of ethical decision problems. It is true that for some purposes one could circumvent the problem just by specifying what seems an ethically attractive Bergson social welfare function, based on a fundamental form of Harsanyi's utilitarianism, and letting ICUs emerge from the analysis. Yet this would seem to be unnecessarily evasive.

These considerations then suggest the need to consider the relationship between ICUs and explicit ethical choices regarding numbers of different types of people in the population. The result is an enriched social choice theory, capable of handling a broader range of ethical decision problems, in which the ICUs are explicit and play a clear role in the analysis. Utility becomes determined up to a cardinal ratio scale, with zero signifying the level at which society is indifferent between creating that type of person as a new member and not. Utility ratios are marginal rates of substitution between numbers of differents types of people.

The primary content of all such ICUs, however, is entirely ethical. Indeed, even the primary content of the utility or individual welfare functions that are being compared interpersonally must be entirely ethical, because such functions represent the relative ethical desirability of different decisions that affect only one individual. Empirical evidence can be of great relevance, but judgments of what sort of empirical evidence bears on the question of how to construct a fully comparable fundamental utility function, as required by the kind of extension of Harsanyi's theory that I am contemplating, are inevitably ethical value judgments. Hume's law refuses to release its iron grip. The empirical content of the fundamental interpersonally comparable utility function is precisely the empirical content of the utilitarian ethical theory based on maximizing the expected sum of this utility function over all individuals and all potential individuals – no more, and no less.

In a sense, we have gone back to the "fundamental preferences" considered in Section 4. The difference is that these preferences need not be derived from individuals' "impersonal preferences" in some kind of original position, behind a veil of ignorance. Instead, they are based on the values of the ethical observer, as influenced by that observer's understanding of the individual's psychology and the observer's view of how society benefits from creating that individual or changing the individual's situation. As Scanlon (1991) suggests, we need to construct a more concrete conception of welfare in terms of particular goods and conditions generally recognized as important to a good life even by people with divergent values.

Similar ideas received extensive discussion in Sen (1980, 1984, 1985, 1987b), Griffin (1986, 1991), and so on.

To repeat, ethical ICUs really do require that an individual's utility be the ethical utility or worth of that individual to the society.

Bibliography

In addition to all the items referred to in this chapter, several other works discussing interpersonal comparisons have been added, but the resulting list is almost certainly incomplete – possibly seriously so. Articles in collected volumes or reprinted therein may not be listed individually unless they are referred to in the chapter. D'Aspremont (1985) and Sen (1986) also contain extensive references.

For bibliographic research assistance, especially in using the DIA-LOG and *Philosopher's Index* databases, my thanks to Jeffrey Coles, who was my research assistant in 1981, and to Peter Kennealy and Milica Uvalic of the European University Institute Library.

P.W. Abelson (1987), "Fairness in the Real World: Rules, Choices, Expectations, and Policies," *Australian Economic Papers,* **26:** 1–19.

T. Amemiya (1981), "Qualitative Response Models: A Survey," *Journal of Economic Literature,* **19:** 1483–1536.

G.C. Archibald (1959, 1965), "Welfare Economics, Ethics and Essentialism," and "A Reply," *Economica,* **26:** 316–27, and **32:** 226–7.

W.E. Armstrong (1951), "Utility and the Theory of Welfare," *Oxford Economic Papers,* **3:** 259–271.

K.J. Arrow (1951, 1963), *Social Choice and Individual Values (2nd edn.).* New Haven: Yale University Press.

K.J. Arrow (1972), "Exposition of the Theory of Choice under Uncertainty," in *Decision and Organization* edited by C.B. McGuire and R. Radner (Amsterdam: North-Holland), ch. 2, pp. 19–55; reprinted in Arrow (1984).

K.J. Arrow (1973), "Some Ordinalist-Utilitarian Notes on Rawls' Theory of Justice," *Journal of Philosophy,* **70:** 245–263; reprinted in Arrow (1983).

K.J. Arrow (1977), "Extended Sympathy and the Possibility of Social Choice," *American Economic Review (Papers and Proceedings),* **67:** 219–25; reprinted in Arrow (1983).

K.J. Arrow (1983), *Collected Papers of Kenneth J. Arrow, Vol. 1: Social Choice and Justice.* Cambridge, Mass.: Harvard University Press.

K.J. Arrow (1984), *Collected Papers of Kenneth J. Arrow, Vol. 3: Individual Choice under Certainty and Uncertainty.* Cambridge, Mass.: Harvard University Press.

K.J. Arrow (1987), "Reflections on the Essays," in Feiwel (1987), ch. 35. pp. 727–734.

C. d'Aspremont (1985), "Axioms for Social Welfare Orderings," in Hurwicz, Schmeidler, and Sonnenschein, ch. 2, pp. 19–76.

C. d'Aspremont (1988), "Utility Comparisons and Bayesian Revelation Mechanisms," presented to the Sloan conference on "Interpersonal Comparability of Welfare," University of Chicago.

C. d'Aspremont and L. Gevers (1977), "Equity and the Informational Basis of Collective Choice," *Review of Economic Studies,* **44:** 199–209.

A.B. Atkinson (1970), "On the Measurement of Inequality," *Journal of Economic Theory,* **2:** 244–63.

R.J. Aumann (1985), "Value, Symmetry, and Equal Treatment: A Comment on the Roth-Shafer Examples," *Econometrica,* **53:** 667–677.

R.J. Aumann (1986), "Rejoinder," *Econometrica,* **54:** 985–989.

R.J. Aumann (1987), "On the Non-transferable Utility Value: A Comment on Scafuri and Yannelis," *Econometrica,* **55:** 1461–1464.

R.J. Aumann and M. Kurz (1977), "Power and Taxes," *Econometrica,* **45:** 1137–1161.

A.J. Ayer (1936, 1971), *Language, Truth and Logic.* Harmondsworth: Penguin Books.

E. Barone (1908), "Il ministero della produzione nello stato colletivista," *Giornale degli Economisti,* **37:** 267–293, 391–414; translated as "The Ministry of Production in the Collectivist State," in F. A. Hayek (ed.) (1935), *Collectivist Economic Planning* (London: Routledge & Paul), pp. 310–334, and reprinted in P. Newman (ed.), *Readings in Mathematical Economics, Vol. I: Value Theory* (Baltimore: The Johns Hopkins Press).

B. Barry (1973), *The Liberal Theory of Justice.* Oxford: Clarendon Press.

A.P. Barten (1964), "Family Composition, Price, and Expenditure Patterns," in *Econometric Analysis for National Economic Planning (16th Symposium of the Colston Society)* edited by P. Hart, G. Mills, and J. K. Whitaker (London: Butterworth), pp. 277–292.

G. Becker (1974), "Difficulties with Bare Preferences," *Theory and Decision,* **5:** 329–331.

G.M. Becker, M.H. DeGroot, and J. Marschak (1963), "Stochastic Models of Choice Behavior," *Behavioral Science,* **8:** 41–55.

G.S. Becker (1981), *A Treatise on the Family.* Cambridge, Mass.: Harvard University Press.

A. Bergson (1938), "A Reformulation of Certain Aspects of Welfare Economics," *Quarterly Journal of Economics,* **52:** 310–334.

A. Bergson (1983), "Pareto on Social Welfare," *Journal of Economic Literature,* **21:** 40–46.

L. Bergstrom (1982), "Interpersonal Utility Comparisons," *Grazer Philosophical Studies,* **16/17:** 283–312.

T. Bezembinder and P. van Acker (1987), "Factual versus Representational Utilities and Their Interdimensional Comparisons," *Social Choice and Welfare,* **4:** 79–104.

C. Blackorby and D. Donaldson (1982), "Ratio-scale and Translation-scale Full Interpersonal Comparability without Domain Restrictions: Admissible Social Evaluation Functions," *International Economic Review,* **23:** 249–268.

C. Blackorby and D. Donaldson (1987), "Adult-Equivalence Scales and the Economic Implementation of Interpersonal Comparisons of Well-Being," presented to the Sloan Conference on "Interpersonal Comparability of Welfare" at the University of California, Davis (in this volume).

C. Blackorby, D. Donaldson, and J. Weymark (1984), "Social Choice with Interpersonal Utility Comparisons: A Diagrammatic Introduction," *International Economic Review,* **25:** 327–356.

R.W. Boadway and N. Bruce (1984), *Welfare Economics.* Oxford: Basil Blackwell.

P.J.M. van der Bogard and J. Versluis (1960), "The Design of Socially Optimal Decisions," in *Proceedings of the Second International Conference on Operations Research* (New York: John Wiley).

L. Bovens (1987), "On Arguments from Self-Interest for the Nash Solution and the Kalai Egalitarian Solution to the Bargaining Problem," *Theory and Decision,* **23:** 231–260.

R.B. Brandt (1979), *A Theory of the Good and the Right.* Oxford: Clarendon Press.

D. Braybrooke (1982), "The Maximum Claims of Gauthier's Bargainers: Are the Fixed Social Inequalities Acceptable?" *Dialogue (Canada),* **21:** 411–429.

K. Breault (1981), "Modern Psychophysical Measurement of Marginal Utility: A Return to Introspective Cardinality?" *Social Science Quarterly,* **62:** 672–684.

D.W. Brock (1973), "Recent Work in Utilitarianism," *American Philosophical Quarterly,* **10:** 241–276.

H.W. Brock (1978a), "A Critical Discussion of the Work of John C. Harsanyi," *Theory and Decision,* **9:** 349–367.

H.W. Brock (1978b), "A New Theory of Social Justice Based on the Mathematical Theory of Games," in *Game Theory and Political Science* edited by P.C. Ordeshook (New York: New York University Press), pp. 563–627.

H.W. Brock (1979a), "A Game Theoretic Account of Social Justice," *Theory and Decision,* **11:** 239–265; reprinted in Brock (1979b).

H.W. Brock (ed.) (1979b), *Game Theory, Social Choice and Ethics.* Dordrecht: D. Reidel.

H.W. Brock (1980), "The Problem of 'Utility Weights' in Group Preference Aggregation," *Operations Research,* **28:** 176–187.

J. Broome (1988), "Utilitarian Metaphysics?" presented to the Sloan Conference on "Interpersonal Comparability of Welfare" at the University of Chicago.

S.T. Buccola (1988), "Social Welfare and Interpersonal Utility Comparisons in Applied Policy Research," *American Journal of Agricultural Economics,* **70:** 454–58.

A. Camacho (1986), "Individual Cardinal Utility, Interpersonal Comparisons, and Social Choice," in *Recent Developments in the Foundations of Utility and Risk Theory* edited by L. Daboni, A. Montesano, and M. Lines (Dordrecht: D. Reidel), pp. 185–200.

A. Camacho and J. Sonstelie (1974), "Cardinal Welfare, Individualistic Ethics, and Interpersonal Comparisons of Utility: A Note," *Journal of Political Economy*, **82:** 607–611.

J.S. Chipman (1987), "Compensation Principle," in Eatwell, Milgate and Newman.

J.S. Chipman and J.C. Moore (1978), "The New Welfare Economics, 1939–1974," *International Economic Review*, **19:** 547–584.

G.A. Cohen (1989), "On the Currency of Egalitarian Justice," *Ethics*, **99:** 906–944.

R.D. Cooter and P. Rappoport (1984), "Were the Ordinalists Wrong about Welfare Economics?" *Journal of Economic Literature*, **22:** 507–530.

R.D. Cooter and P. Rappoport (1985), "Reply to I.M.D. Little's Comment," *Journal of Economic Literature*, **23:** 1189–1191.

R.A. Dahl (1956), *A Preface to Democratic Theory*. Chicago: University of Chicago Press.

P.S. Dasgupta (1974), "On Some Problems Arising from Professor Rawls' Conception of Distributive Justice," *Theory and Decision*, **4:** 325–344.

P.S. Dasgupta (1988), "Lives and Well-Being," *Social Choice and Welfare*, **5:** 103–126; reprinted in Gaertner and Pattanaik.

D. Davidson (1986), "Judging Interpersonal Interests," in Elster and Hylland, ch. 7. pp. 195–211.

A.S. Deaton and J. Muellbauer (1986), "On Measuring Child Costs: With Applications to Poor Countries," *Journal of Political Economy*, **94:** 720–744.

R. Deschamps and L. Gevers (1977), "Separability, Risk-Bearing and Social Welfare Judgements," *European Economic Review*, **10:** 77–94.

R. Deschamps and L. Gevers (1978), "Leximin and Utilitarian Rules: A Joint Characterization," *Journal of Economic Theory*, **17:** 143–163.

P.A. Diamond (1967), "Cardinal Welfare, Individualistic Ethics, and Interpersonal Comparisons of Utility: Comment," *Journal of Political Economy*, **75:** 765–766.

M. Dobb (1969), *Welfare Economics and the Economics of Socialism: Towards a Commonsense Critique*. Cambridge: Cambridge University Press.

G. Dworkin (1982), "A Journal of Mathematical Ethics: A Proposal," *Philosophical Forum*, **13:** 413–415.

R. Dworkin (1981), "What is Equality, I: Equality of Welfare," and "What is Equality, II: Equality of Resources," *Philosophy and Public Affairs*, **10:** 185–246 and 283–345.

J. Eatwell, M. Milgate, and P. Newman (Eds.) (1987), *The New Palgrave Dictionary of Economics*. London: Macmillan.

F.Y. Edgeworth (1881), *Mathematical Psychics*. London: Kegan Paul.

W. Edwards and A. Tversky (Eds.) (1967), *Decision Making*. Harmondsworth: Penguin Books.

J. Elster (1986), "The Market and the Forum: Three Varieties of Political Theory," in Elster and Hylland, ch. 4. pp. 103–132.

J. Elster and A. Hylland (Eds.) (1986), *Foundations of Social Choice Theory*. Cambridge: Cambridge University Press, and Oslo: Universitetsforlaget.

G.R. Feiwel (Ed.) (1985), *Issues in Contemporary Microeconomics and Welfare*. London: Macmillan.

G.R. Feiwel (Ed.) (1987), *Arrow and the Foundations of the Theory of Economic Policy*. London: Macmillan.

B. Fine (1975), "A Note on 'Interpersonal Aggregation and Partial Comparability'," *Econometrica*, **43:** 169–172.

B. Fine (1985), "A Note on the Measurement of Inequality and Interpersonal Comparability," *Social Choice and Welfare*, **1:** 273–277.

F.M. Fisher (1956), "Income Distribution, Value Judgements and Welfare," *Quarterly Journal of Economics*, **70:** 380–424.

F.M. Fisher (1987), "Household Equivalence Scales and Interpersonal Comparisons," *Review of Economic Studies*, **54:** 519–24.

F.M. Fisher and J. Rothenberg (1961), "How Income Ought to Be Distributed: Paradox Lost," *Journal of Political Economy, 69:* 162–180.

I. Fisher (1892, 1925), *Mathematical Investigations in the Theory of Value and Prices*, in the Transactions of the Connecticut Academy of Sciences: reprinted. New Haven: Yale University Press.

M. Fleming (1957), "Cardinal Welfare and Individualistic Ethics: A Comment," *Journal of Political Economy*, **65:** 355–357.

M. Friedman and L.J. Savage (1948), "The Utility Analysis of Choices Involving Risk," *Journal of Political Economy*, **56:** 279–304.

M. Friedman and L.J. Savage (1952), "The Expected Utility Hypothesis and Measurement of Utility," *Journal of Political Economy*, **60:** 463–474.

W. Gaertner and P.K. Pattanaik (Eds.) (1988), *Distributive Justice and Inequality*. Berlin: Springer Verlag.

P. Gärdenfors (1978), "Fairness without Interpersonal Comparisons," *Theoria*, **44:** 57–74.

L. Gevers (1979), "On Interpersonal Comparability and Social Welfare Orderings," *Econometrica*, **47:** 75–90.

A.F. Gibbard (1978), "Preference Strength and Two Kinds of Ordinalism," *Philosophia (Israel)*, **7:** 255–264.

A. Gibbard (1986), "Interpersonal Comparisons: Preference, Good, and the Intrinsic Reward of a Life," in Elster and Hylland, ch. 6, pp. 165–193.

A. Gibbard (1987), "Ordinal Utilitarianism," in Feiwel (1987), ch. 2, pp. 135–153.

D. Goldstick (1971), "Assessing Utilities," *Mind*, **80:** 531–541.

R.E. Goodin (1975), "How to Determine Who Should Get What," *Ethics*, **85:** 310–321.

L.A. Goodman and H. Markovitz (1952), "Social Welfare Functions Based on Individual Rankings," *American Journal of Sociology*, **58:** 257–62.

S. Gordon (1973), "John Rawls' Difference Principle, Utilitarianism, and the Optimum Degree of Inequality," *Journal of Philosophy*, **70:** 275–280.

W.M. Gorman (1956, 1980), "A Possible Procedure for Analysing Quality Differentials in the Egg Market," *Review of Economic Studies*, **47:** 843–56.

J. Griffin (1981), "Interpersonal Comparisons of Utility (in Polish)," *Etyka*, **19:** 45–68.

J. Griffin (1986), *Well-Being: Its Meaning, Measurement, and Moral Importance*. Oxford: Clarendon Press.

J. Griffin (1987), "Well-Being and its Interpersonal Comparability," presented to the Sloan Conference on "Interpersonal Comparability of Welfare" at the University of California, Davis (in this volume).

A.J.M. Hagenaars (1986), *The Perception of Poverty*. Amsterdam: North-Holland.

F.H. Hahn and M. Hollis (Eds.) (1979), *Philosophy and Economic Theory*. Oxford: Oxford University Press.

A. Hallam (1988), "Measuring Economic Welfare: Is Theory a Cookbook for Empirical Analysis," *American Journal of Agricultural Economics*, **70:** 443–447.

P.J. Hammond (1976a), "Equity, Arrow's Conditions, and Rawls' Difference Principle," *Econometrica*, **44:** 793–804; partly reprinted in Hahn and Hollis (1979).

P.J. Hammond (1976b), "Why Ethical Measures of Inequality Need Interpersonal Comparisons," *Theory and Decision*, **7:** 263–274.

P.J. Hammond (1977, 1980), "Dual Interpersonal Comparisons of Utility and the Welfare Economics of Income Distribution"; and "——: A Corrigendum," *Journal of Public Economics*, **7:** 51–71 and **14:** 105–106.

P.J. Hammond (1979a), "Straightforward Individual Incentive Compatibility in Large Economies," *Review of Economic Studies*, **46:** 263–282.

P.J. Hammond (1979b), "Equity in Two Person Situations: Some Consequences," *Econometrica*, **47:** 1127–35.

P.J. Hammond (1982a), "The Economics of Justice and the Criterion of Wealth Maximization," *Yale Law Journal*, **91:** 1493–1507.

P.J. Hammond (1982b), "Utilitarianism, Uncertainty and Information," in Sen and Williams, ch. 4, pp. 85–102.

P.J. Hammond (1983), "Ex-Post Optimality as a Dynamically Consistent Objective for Collective Choice under Uncertainty," in *Social Choice and Welfare* edited by P. K. Pattanaik and M. Salles (Amsterdam: North Holland), ch. 10, pp. 175–205.

P.J. Hammond (1985), "Welfare Economics," in Feiwel (1985), ch. 13, pp. 405–434.

P.J. Hammond (1986), "Consequentialist Social Norms for Public Decisions," in *Social Choice and Public Decision Making: Essays in Honor of Kenneth*

J. Arrow, Vol. 1 edited by W.P. Heller, R.M. Starr, and D.A. Starrett (Cambridge: Cambridge University Press), ch. 1, pp. 3–27.

P.J. Hammond (1987a), "On Reconciling Arrow's Theory of Social Choice with Harsanyi's Fundamental Utilitarianism," in Feiwel (1987), ch. 4, pp. 179–222.

P.J. Hammond (1987b), "Markets as Constraints: Multilateral Incentive Compatibility in Continuum Economies," *Review of Economic Studies*, **54:** 399–412.

P.J. Hammond (1987c), "Social Choice: The Science of the Impossible?" in Feiwel (1987), ch. 1B, pp. 116–131.

P.J. Hammond (1988a), "Consequentialism and the Independence Axiom," in *Risk, Decision and Rationality* edited by B.R. Munier (Dordrecht: D. Reidel), pp. 503–516.

P.J. Hammond (1988b), "Consequentialist Foundations for Expected Utility," *Theory and Decision*, **25:** 25–78.

P.J. Hammond (1988c), "Consequentialist Demographic Norms and Parenting Rights," *Social Choice and Welfare*, **5:** 127–145; reprinted in Gaertner and Pattanaik.

P.J. Hammond (1991), "Independence of Irrelevant Interpersonal Comparisons," *Social Choice and Welfare*, **8:** (in press).

A.C. Harberger (1971), "Three Basic Postulates for Applied Welfare Analysis," *Journal of Economic Literature*, **9:** 785–797.

R.M. Hare (1951), *The Language of Morals*. Oxford: Clarendon Press.

R.M. Hare (1963), *Freedom and Reason*. Oxford: Clarendon Press.

R.M. Hare (1981), *Moral Thinking: Its Levels, Method and Point*. Oxford: Clarendon Press.

R.F. Harrod (1938), "Scope and Method of Economics," *Economic Journal*, **48:** 383–412.

J.C. Harsanyi (1953a), "Welfare Economics of Variable Tastes," *Review of Economic Studies*, **21:** 204–13.

J.C. Harsanyi (1953b), "Cardinal Utility in Welfare Economics and in the Theory of Risk-Taking," *Journal of Political Economy*, **61:** 434–5; reprinted in Harsanyi (1976).

J.C. Harsanyi (1955), "Cardinal Welfare, Individualistic Ethics, and Interpersonal Comparisons of Utility," *Journal of Political Economy*, **63:** 309–321; reprinted in Phelps (1973) and Harsanyi (1976).

J.C. Harsanyi (1975a), "Nonlinear Social Welfare Functions: Do Welfare Economists Have a Special Exemption from Bayesian Rationality?" *Theory and Decision*, **6:** 311–32; reprinted in Harsanyi (1976).

J.C. Harsanyi (1975b), "Can the Maximin Principle Serve as a Basis for Morality? A Critique of John Rawls's Theory," *American Political Science Review*, **69:** 594–606; reprinted in Harsanyi (1976).

J.C. Harsanyi (1976), *Essays on Ethics, Social Behavior, and Scientific Explanation*. Dordrecht: D. Reidel.

J.C. Harsanyi (1977a), *Rational Behavior and Bargaining Equilibrium in Games and Social Situations*. Cambridge: Cambridge University Press.

J.C. Harsanyi (1977b), "Morality and the Theory of Rational Behavior," *Social Research*, **44**: 623–56.

J.C. Harsanyi (1978), "Bayesian Decision Theory and Utilitarian Ethics," *American Economic Review (Papers and Proceedings)*, **68**: 223–8.

J.C. Harsanyi (1979), "Bayesian Decision Theory, Rule Utilitarianism, and Arrow's Impossibility Theorem," *Theory and Decision*, **11**: 289–317; reprinted in Brock (1979b).

J.C. Harsanyi (1987a), "Von Neumann-Morgenstern Utilities, Risk Taking, and Welfare," in *Arrow and the Ascent of Modern Economic Theory* edited by G.R. Feiwel (London: Macmillan; and New York: New York University Press), ch. 17, pp. 545–558.

J.C. Harsanyi (1987b), "Interpersonal Utility Comparison," in Eatwell, Milgate, and Newman.

D.M. Hausman (Ed.) (1984), *The Philosophy of Economics: An Anthology.* Cambridge: Cambridge University Press:

P. Hennipman (1987), "A Tale of Two Schools: Comments on a New View of the Ordinalist Revolution," *De Economist*, **135**: 141–162.

P. Hennipman (1988), "A New Look at the Ordinalist Revolution: Comments on Cooter and Rappoport," *Journal of Economic Literature*, **26**: 80–91.

I.N. Herstein and J. Milnor (1953), "An Axiomatic Approach to Measurable Utility," *Econometrica*, **21**: 291–297.

F. van Herwaarden, A. Kapteyn, and B.M.S. van Praag (1977), "Twelve Thousand Individual Welfare Functions," *European Economic Review*, **9**: 283–300.

C. Hildreth (1953), "Alternative Conditions for Social Orderings," *Econometrica*, **21**: 81–94.

A. Hirayama (1983), "Interpersonal Comparison and Criteria of Justice," *Economic Studies Quarterly*, **34**: 156–70.

D. Hume (1739–40, 1969), *A Treatise of Human Nature*. Harmondsworth: Penguin Books.

L. Hurwicz, D. Schmeidler, and H. Sonnenschein (Eds.) (1985), *Social Goals and Social Organization*. Cambridge: Cambridge University Press.

M. Intriligator (1973), "A Probabilistic Model of Social Choice," *Review of Economic Studies*, **40**: 553–60.

J.R. Isbell (1959), "Absolute Games," in *Contributions to the Theory of Games, Vol. IV* edited by A.W. Tucker and R.D. Luce (Princeton: Princeton University Press), pp. 357–396.

J.Y. Jaffray (1985), "Interpersonal Level Comparability Does Not Imply Comparability of Utility Differences – A Comment on Ng," *Theory and Decision*, **19**: 201–203.

R.C. Jeffrey (1971), "On Interpersonal Utility Theory," *Journal of Philosophy*, **68**: 647–56.

R.C. Jeffrey (1974), "Remarks on Interpersonal Utility Theory," in *Logical Theory and Semantic Analysis* edited by S. Stenlund (Dordrecht: D. Reidel), pp. 35–44.

W.S. Jevons (1871, 1970), *The Theory of Political Economy*. London: Macmillan; Harmondsworth: Penguin Books.

R.E. Just (1988), "Making Economic Welfare Analysis Useful in the Policy Process: Implications of the Public Choice Literature," *American Journal of Agricultural Economics*, **70:** 448–453.

E. Kalai (1977), "Proportional Solutions to Bargaining Situations: Interpersonal Utility Problems," *Econometrica*, **45:** 1623–1630.

E. Kalai and D. Samet (1985), "Monotonic Solutions to General Cooperative Games," *Econometrica*, **53:** 307–27.

M. Kaneko (1984), "On Interpersonal Utility Comparisons," *Social Choice and Welfare*, **1:** 165–175.

P. Kantor and R.J. Nelson (1979), "Social Decision Making in the Presence of Complex Goals, Ethics and the Environment," *Theory and Decision*, 10: 181–200.

A. Kapteyn (1977), *A Theory of Preference Formation*. 's-Gravenhage: Drukkerij J.H. Pasmans.

A. Kapteyn and B.M.S. van Praag (1976), "A New Approach to the Construction of Family Equivalence Scales," *European Economic Review*, **7:** 313–35.

R.L. Keeney and C.W. Kirkwood (1975), "Group Decision Making Using Cardinal Social Welfare Functions," *Management Science*, **22:** 430–437.

R.L. Keeney and H. Raiffa (1976), *Decisions with Multiple Objectives: Preferences and Value Trade-Offs*. New York: John Wiley.

J.S. Kelly (1978), *Arrow Impossibility Theorems*. New York: Academic Press.

M.C. Kemp and Y.-K. Ng (1987), "Arrow's Independence Condition and the Bergson-Samuelson Tradition," in Feiwel (1987), ch. 5, pp. 223–241.

L. Kern (1980), "Zur Axiomatischen Charakterisierung alternativer Vertragsprinzipen [On the axiomatic characterization of alternative contract principles]," *Erkenntnis*, **15:** 1–31.

C.P. Kindleberger (1965), *Economic Development (2nd edn)*. New York: McGraw-Hill.

K. Klappholz (1964), "Value Judgements and Economics," *British Journal for the Philosophy of Science*, **15:** 97–114; reprinted in Hausman (1984).

S.-C. Kolm (1972), *Justice et Equité*. Paris: Editions du Centre National de la Recherche Scientifique.

S.-C. Kolm (1974), "Sur les conséquences économiques de principes de justice et de justice pratique," *Revue d'Economie Politique*, **84:** 80–107.

K.J. Lancaster (1966), "A New Approach to Consumer Theory," *Journal of Political Economy*, **74:** 132–57.

A.P. Lerner (1944), *The Economics of Control*. London: Macmillan.

A.P. Lerner (1972), "The Economics and Politics of Consumer Sovereignty," *American Economic Review (Papers and Proceedings)*, **62:** 258–263.

S. Levy and L. Guttman (1975), "On the Multivariate Structure of Well-Being," *Social Indicators Research*, **2:** 361–388.

I.M.D. Little (1957), *A Critique of Welfare Economics (2nd edn.)*. Oxford: Oxford University Press.

I.M.D. Little (1985), "Robert Cooter and Peter Rappoport, 'Were the Ordinalists Wrong about Welfare Economics?': A Comment," *Journal of Economics Literature*, **23:** 1186–1188.

R.D. Luce (1956), "Semi-Orders and a Theory of Utility Discrimination," *Econometrica*, **24:** 178–91.

R.D. Luce (1959), *Individual Choice Behavior*. New York: John Wiley.

R.D. Luce and H. Raiffa (1957), *Games and Decisions: Introduction and Critical Survey*. New York: John Wiley.

D. Lyons (1972), "Rawls versus Utilitarianism," *Journal of Philosophy*, **69:** 535–545.

A.F. MacKay (1975), "Interpersonal Comparisons," *Journal of Philosophy*, **72:** 535–549.

A.F. MacKay (1980), *Arrow's Theorem: The Paradox of Social Choice*. New Haven: Yale University Press.

A.F. MacKay (1986), "Extended Sympathy and Interpersonal Utility Comparisons," *Journal of Philosophy*, **83:** 305–322.

B. Magee (1971), *Modern British Philosophy*. London: Secker and Warburg.

E. Maskin (1978), "A Theorem on Utilitarianism," *Review of Economic Studies*, **45:** 93–96.

E. Maskin (1979), "Decision-making under Ignorance with Implications for Social Choice," *Theory and Decision*, **11:** 319–337; reprinted in Brock (1979b).

A.C. McKennell (1978), "Cognition and Affect in Perceptions of Well-Being," *Social Indicators Research*, **5:** 389–426.

G. McKenzie (1988), "Applied Welfare Economics and Frisch's Conjecture," in *Welfare and Efficiency in Public Economics* edited by D. Bös, M. Rose and C. Seidl (Berlin: Springer-Verlag), pp. 1–20.

K. Menger (1934), "Das Unsicherheitsmoment in der Wertlehre, Betrachtungen im Anschluss an das sogenannte Petersburger Spiel [Expectation in value theory; considerations in connection with the so-called St. Petersburg paradox]," *Zeitschrift für Nationalökonomie*, **5:** 459–485.

J.A. Mirrlees (1982), "On the Economic Uses of Utilitarianism," in Sen and Williams, ch. 3, pp. 63–84.

R. Möller (1983), *Interpersonelle Nutzenvergleiche: Wissenschaftliche Möglichkeit und politische Bedeutung* [Interpersonal comparisons of utility: scientific possibility and political meaning]. Göttingen: Vandenhoeck and Ruprecht.

J. Muellbauer (1974a), "Prices and Inequality: The United Kingdom Experience," *Economic Journal,* **84:** 32–55.

J. Muellbauer (1974b), "Household Composition, Engel Curves and Welfare Comparison between Households: A Duality Approach," *European Economic Review,* **5:** 103–22.

J. Muellbauer (1974c), "Inequality Measures, Prices and Household Composition," *Review of Economic Studies,* **41:** 493–504.

J. Muellbauer (1975), "Identification and Consumer Unit Scales," *Econometrica,* **43:** 807–809.

J. Muellbauer (1977), "Testing the Barten Model of Household Composition Effects and the Cost of Children," *Economic Journal,* **87:** 460–87.

J. Muellbauer (1987), "Professor Sen on the Standard of Living," in Sen (1987b), pp. 39–58.

D.C. Mueller, R.D. Tollison, and T.D. Willett (1974), "The Utilitarian Contract: A Generalization of Rawls' Theory of Justice," *Theory and Decision,* **4:** 345–367.

R.B. Myerson (1977), "Two-Person Bargaining Problems and Comparable Utility," *Econometrica,* **45:** 1623–1630.

R.B. Myerson (1981), "Utilitarianism, Egalitarianism, and the Timing Effect in Social Choice Problems," *Econometrica,* **49:** 883–897.

R.B. Myerson (1985), "Bayesian Equilibrium and Incentive Compatibility: An Introduction," in Hurwicz, Schmeidler, and Sonnenschein, ch. 8, pp. 229–259.

L. Narens and R.D. Luce (1983), "How We May Have Been Misled into Believing Interpersonal Comparisons of Utility," *Theory and Decision,* **15:** 247–260.

L.T. Neilsen (1983), "Ordinal Interpersonal Comparisons in Bargaining," *Econometrica,* **51:** 219–21.

Y.-K. Ng (1972), "Value Judgements and Economists' Role in Policy Recommendation," *Economic Journal,* **82:** 1014–1018.

Y.-K. Ng (1975), "Bentham or Bergson? Finite Sensibility, Utility Functions and Social Welfare Functions," *Review of Economic Studies,* **42:** 545–69.

Y.-K. Ng (1982), "Beyond Pareto Optimality: The Necessity of Interpersonal Cardinal Utilities in Distributional Judgements and Social Choice," *Zeitschrift für Nationalökonomie,* **42:** 207–233.

Y.-K. Ng (1984a), "Interpersonal Level Comparability Implies Comparability of Utility Differences," *Theory and Decision,* **17:** 141–147.

Y.-K. Ng (1984b), "Expected Subjective Utility: Is the Neumann-Morgenstern Utility the Same as the Neoclassical's?" *Social Choice and Welfare,* **1:** 177–186.

Y.-K. Ng (1985a), "Some Fundamental Issues in Social Welfare," in Feiwel (1985), ch. 14, pp. 435–469.

Y.-K. Ng (1985b), "The Utilitarian Criterion, Finite Sensibility, and the Weak Majority Reference Principle: A Response," *Social Choice and Welfare,* **2:** 37–38.

Y.-K. Ng (1989), "Interpersonal Level Comparability Implies Comparability of Utility Differences: A Reply," *Theory and Decision,* **26:** 91–93.

R. Nozick (1985), "Interpersonal Utility Theory," *Social Choice and Welfare,* **2:** 161–179.

I. Ortuño-Ortin and J.E. Roemer (1991), "Deducing Interpersonal Comparability from Local Expertise," in this volume.

V. Pareto (1894), "Il massimo di utilità dato dalla libera concorrenza [The utility maximum given by free competition]," *Giornale degli Economisti,* **9:** 48–66.

V. Pareto (1895), "Teoria matematica del commercio internazionale" [Mathematical theory of international trade]," *Giornale degli Economisti,* **10:** 476–498.

V. Pareto (1913), "Il massimo di utilità per una colletività in Sociologia" [The utility maximum for a collective in sociology]," *Giornale degli Economisti,* **46:** 337–341.

P.K. Pattanaik (1968), "Risk Impersonality, and the Social Welfare Function," *Journal of Political Economy,* **76:** 1152–1169; reprinted in Phelps (1973).

E.A. Pazner (1979), "Equity, Nonfeasible Alternatives and Social Choice: A Reconsideration of the Concept of Social Welfare," in *Aggregation and Revelation of References* edited by J.-J. Laffont (Amsterdam: North-Holland), pp. 161–173.

E.S. Phelps (Ed.) (1973), *Economic Justice.* Harmondsworth: Penguin Books.

E.S. Phelps (1977), "Recent Developments in Welfare Economics: Justice et Equite in *Frontiers of Quantitative Economics* edited by M.D. Intriligator (Amsterdam: North-Holland), ch. 16, pp. 703–730.

R.A. Pollak (1976), "Habit Formation and Long-Run Utility Functions," *Journal of Economic Theory,* **13:** 272–97.

R.A. Pollak and T.J. Wales (1979), "Welfare Comparisons and Equivalence Scales," *American Economic Review (Papers and Proceedings),* **69:** 216–21.

R.A. Posner (1981), *The Economics of Justice.* Cambridge, Mass.: Harvard University Press.

B.M.S. van Praag (1968), *Individual Welfare Functions and Consumer Behavior.* Amsterdam: North Holland.

B.M.S. van Praag (1971), "The Welfare Function of Income in Belgium: An Empirical Investigation," *European Economic Review,* **2:** 337–69.

B.M.S. van Praag and A. Kapteyn (1973), "Further Evidence on the Individual Welfare Function of Income: An Empirical Investigation in the Netherlands," *European Economic Review,* **4:** 33–62.

B.M.S. van Praag and N.L. van der Sar (1988), "Household Cost Functions and Equivalence Scales," *Journal of Human Resources,* **23:** 193–210.

D. Rae et al. (1981), *Equalities.* Cambridge, Mass.: Harvard University Press.

P. Rappoport (1988), "Reply to Professor Hennipman," *Journal of Economic Literature,* **26:** 86–91.

J. Rawls (1959), "Justice as Fairness," *Philosophical Review,* **67:** 164–94.

J. Rawls (1971), *A Theory of Justice.* Cambridge, Mass: Harvard University Press.

N. Rescher (1967), "Notes on Preference, Utility and Cost," *Synthese,* **19:** 332–43.

N. Rescher (1969), *Introduction to Value Theory.* Englewood Cliffs: Prentice Hall.

L. Robbins (1932), *An Essay on the Nature and Significance of Economic Science.* London: Macmillan; partly reprinted in Hausman (1984).

L. Robbins (1938), "Interpersonal Comparisons of Utility: A Comment," *Economic Journal,* **48:** 635–41.

L. Robbins (1981), "Economics and Political Economy," *American Economic Review (Papers and Proceedings),* **71:** 1–10.

K.W.S. Roberts (1980a), "Possibility Theorems with Interpersonally Comparable Welfare Levels," *Review of Economic Studies,* **47:** 409–420.

K.W.S. Roberts (1980b), "Interpersonal Comparability and Social Choice Theory," *Review of Economic Stuides,* **47:** 421–439.

K.W.S. Roberts (1980c), "Social Choice Theory: The Single-Profile and Multi-Profile Approaches," *Review of Economic Studies,* **47:** 441–50.

J. Roemer (1985), "Equality of Resources Implies Equality of Welfare," *Quarterly Journal of Economics,* **101:** 751–784.

G. Ross (1974), "Utilities for Distributive Justice: The Meshing Problem and a Solution to It," *Theory and Decision,* **4:** 239–258.

A.E. Roth (1980), "Values for Games without Side Payments: Some Difficulties with Current Concepts," *Econometrica,* **48:** 457–465.

A.E. Roth (1986), "On the Non-transferable Utility Value: A Reply to Aumann," *Econometrica,* **54:** 981–984.

J. Rothenburg (1961), *The Measurement of Social Welfare.* Englewood Cliffs: Prentice-Hall.

L.R. Rovig (1976), "On the Measurement of Extent of Preference, Interpersonal Comparisons, and Rates of Substitution," *Intermountain Economic Review,* **71:** 83–84.

S. Roy (1984), "Considerations on Utility, Benevolence and Taxation," *History of Political Economy,* **16:** 349–362.

L. Sacconi (ed.) (1986), *La Decisione: Razionalità collettiva e strategica nell'amministrazione e nelle organizzazioni.* Milano: Franco Angeli.

P.A. Samuelson (1937), "A Note on Measurement of Utility," *Review of Economic Studies,* **4:** 155–61.

P.A. Samuelson (1947), *Foundations of Economic Analysis.* Cambridge, Mass.: Harvard University Press.

P.A. Samuelson (1987), "Sparks from Arrow's Anvil," in Feiwel (1987), ch. 3, pp. 154–178.

A.J. Scafuri and N.C. Yannelis (1984), "Non-symmetric Cardinal Value Allocations," *Econometrica,* **52:** 1365–68.

T.M. Scanlon (1987), "The Moral Basis of Interpersonal Comparisons," presented to the Sloan Conference on "Interpersonal Comparability of Welfare" at the University of California, Davis (in this volume).

A. Schäfer and R.W. Trapp (1989), "Distributional Equality in Non-classical Utilitarianism – A Proof of Lerner's Theorem for 'Utilitarianism Incorporating Justice'," *Theory and Decision*, **26:** 157–173.

F. Schick (1971), "Beyond Utilitarianism," *Journal of Philosophy,* **68:** 657–666.

E. Schokkaert and B. Overlaet (1989), "Moral Intuitions and Economic Models of Distributive Justice," *Social Choice and Welfare,* **6:** 19–31.

T. Schwartz (1970), "On the Possibility of Rational Policy Evaluation," *Theory and Decision,* **1:** 89–106.

T. Schwartz (1975), "On the Utility of MacKay's Comparisons," *Journal of Philosophy,* **72:** 549–551.

T. Schwartz (1979), "Welfare Judgments and Future Generations," *Theory and Decision,* **11:** 181–194; reprinted in Brock (1979b).

T. Seidenfeld, J.B. Kadane, and M.J. Schervish (1989), "On the Shared Preferences of Two Bayesian Decision Makers," *Journal of Philosophy,* **86:** 225–244.

C. Seidl (1987), Review of Hagenaars (1986), *Zeitschrift für National-ökonomie,* **47:** 92–98.

A.K. Sen (1969), "Planner's Preferences: Optimality, Distribution and Social Welfare," in *Public Economics* edited by J. Margolis and H. Guitton (London: Macmillan), ch. 8, pp. 201–221.

A.K. Sen (1970a), *Collective Choice and Social Welfare.* San Francisco: Holden-Day.

A.K. Sen (1970b, 1972), "Interpersonal Aggregation and Partial Comparability," and "A Correction," *Econometrica,* **38:** 393–409 and **40:** 959–960; reprinted in Sen (1982).

A.K. Sen (1973), *On Economic Inequality.* Oxford: Clarendon Press.

A.K. Sen (1974), "Rawls versus Bentham: An Axiomatic Examination of the Pure Distribution Problem," *Theory and Decision,* **4:** 301–309; reprinted in N. Daniels (ed.) (1975) *Reading Rawls: Critical Studies of "A Theory of Justice"* (New York: Basic Books).

A.K. Sen (1977), "On Weights and Measures: Informational Constraints in Social Welfare Analysis," *Econometrica,* **45:** 1539–72; reprinted in Sen (1982).

A.K. Sen (1978), "Ethical Measurement of Inequalities: Some Difficulties," in *Personal Income Distribution* edited by W. Krelle and A. Shorrocks (Amsterdam: North Holland; reprinted in Sen, 1982).

A.K. Sen (1979), "Interpersonal Comparisons of Welfare," in *Economics and Human Welfare: Essays in Honor of Tibor Scitovsky* edited by M.J. Boskin (New York: Academic Press), pp. 183–201; reprinted in Sen (1982).

A.K. Sen (1980), "Equality of What?" in *The Tanner Lectures on Human*

Values, Vol. I edited by S. McCurrin (Cambridge: Cambridge University Press; reprinted in Sen, 1982).

A.K. Sen (1982), *Choice, Welfare and Measurement.* Oxford: Basil Blackwell, and Cambridge, Mass.: MIT Press.

A.K. Sen (1984), "The Living Standard," *Oxford Economic Papers,* **36** (*Supplement*): 74–90.

A.K. Sen (1985), *Commodities and Capabilities.* Amsterdam: North-Holland.

A.K. Sen (1986), "Social Choice Theory," in *Handbook of Mathematical Economics, Vol. III* edited by K.J. Arrow and M.D. Intriligator (Amsterdam: North-Holland), ch. 22. pp. 1073–1181.

A.K. Sen (1987a), *On Ethics and Economics.* Oxford: Basil Blackwell.

A.K. Sen et al. (1987b), *The Standard of Living.* Cambridge: Cambridge University Press.

A.K. Sen and B. Williams (Eds.) (1982), *Utilitarianism and Beyond.* Cambridge: Cambridge University Press.

W.J. Shafer (1980), "On the Existence and Interpretation of Value Allocation," *Econometrica,* **48:** 467–474.

L.S. Shapley (1969), "Utility Comparison and the Theory of Games," in *La Décision: Agrégation et dynamique des ordres de préférence* edited by G.Th. Guilbaud (Paris: Centre National pour la Recherche Scientifique).

C.L. Sheng (1987), "A Note on Interpersonal Comparisons of Utility," *Theory and Decision,* **22:** 1–12.

C.L. Sheng (1989), "Some Quantitative Concepts of Value and Utility from a Utilitarian Point of View," *Theory and Decision,* **26:** 175–195.

J.L. Simon (1974), "Interpersonal Welfare Comparisons Can be Made – and Used for Redistribution Decisions," *Kyklos,* **27:** 63–98.

J.L. Simon (1978), "Interpersonal Welfare Comparisons: A Reply," *Kyklos,* **31:** 315–317.

A. Smith (1759, revised 1790, reprinted 1975), *The Theory of Moral Sentiments.* Oxford: Clarendon Press.

R.A. Sorensen (1986), "Did the Intensity of My Preferences Double Last Night?" *Philosophy of Science,* **53:** 282–285.

R.J. Stefanik (1981), "Harsanyi's Critical Rule Utilitarianism," *Theory and Decision,* **13:** 71–80.

G.J. Stigler and G.S. Becker (1977), "De Gustibus Non Est Disputandum," *American Economic Review,* **67:** 76–90.

S.S. Stevens (1966), "A Metric for the Social Consensus," *Science,* **151:** 530–541.

S. Strasnick (1976a), "Social Choice and the Derivation of Rawls's Difference Principle," *Journal of Philosophy,* **73:** 85–99.

S. Strasnick (1976b), "The Problem of Social Choice: Arrow to Rawls," *Philosophy and Public Affairs,* **5:** 241–273.

S. Strasnick (1977), "Ordinality and the Spirit of the Justified Dictator," *Social Research,* **44:** 668–690.

S. Strasnick (1979), "Extended Sympathy Comparisons and the Basis of Social Choice," *Theory and Decision,* **10:** 311–328.

R.H. Strotz (1958), "How Income Ought to Be Distributed: A Paradox in Distributive Ethics," *Journal of Political Economy,* **66:** 189–205.

R.H. Strotz (1961), "How Income Ought to Be Distributed: Paradox Regained," *Journal of Political Economy,* **69:** 271–278.

P. Suppes (1966), "Some Formal Models of Grading Principles," *Synthese,* **6:** 284–306.

P. Suppes and M. Winet (1955), "An Axiomatization of Utility Based on the Notion of Utility Differences," *Management Science,* **1:** 259–270.

L.-G. Svensson (1985), "The Utilitarian Criterion, Finite Sensibility, and the Weak Majority Preference Principle: A Further Analysis," *Social Choice and Welfare,* **2:** 23–35.

J. Tinbergen (1957), "Welfare Economics and Income Distribution," *American Economic Review (Papers and Proceedings),* **47:** 490–503.

J. Tinbergen (1980), "Two Approaches to Quantify the Concept of Equitable Income Distribution," *Kyklos,* **33:** 3–15.

J. Tinbergen (1985), *Production, Income and Welfare: The Search for an Optimal Social Order.* Lincoln, Neb.: University of Nebraska Press.

J. Tinbergen (1987a), "The Optimum Order Revisited," in Feiwel (1987), ch. 9, pp. 281–327.

J. Tinbergen (1987b), "The Tension Theory of Welfare," in Feiwel (1987), ch. 15, pp. 410–417.

L. Toharia (1978), "Interpersonal Welfare Comparisons and Welfare Economics: A Comment," *Kyklos,* **31:** 311–314.

W.S. Vickrey (1945), "Measuring Marginal Utility by Reactions to Risk," *Econometrica,* **13:** 319–33.

W.S. Vickrey (1960), "Utility, Strategy and Social Decision Rules," *Quarterly Journal of Economics,* **74:** 507–35.

W.S. Vickrey (1961), "Risk, Utility and Social Policy," *Social Research,* **28:** 205–217; reprinted in Phelps (1973).

I. Waldner (1972), "The Empirical Meaningfulness of Interpersonal Utility Comparisons," *Journal of Philosophy,* **69:** 87–103.

I. Waldner (1974a), "Bare Preference and Interpersonal Utility Comparisons," *Theory and Decision,* **5:** 313–328.

I. Waldner (1974b), "Value Neutrality," *Theory and Decision,* **5:** 333–334.

V.C. Walsh (1964), "Discussion: The Status of Welfare Comparisons," *Philosophy of Science,* **31:** 149–155.

P. Weirich (1983), "Utility Tempered with Equality," *Noûs,* **17:** 423–439.

P. Weirich (1984), "Interpersonal Utility in Principles of Social Choice," *Erkenntnis,* **21:** 295–317.

B. Williams (1985), *Ethics and the Limits of Philosophy,* London: Fontana Press/Collins.

D. Wittman (1974), "Punishment as Retribution," *Theory and Decision,* **4:** 209–237.

D. Wittman (1979), "A Diagrammatic Exposition of Justice," *Theory and Decision,* **11:** 207–237; reprinted in Brock (1979b).

M.E. Yaari (1981), "Rawls, Edgeworth, Shapley, Nash: Theories of Distributive Justice Re-examined," *Journal of Economic Theory,* **24:** 1–39.

M.E. Yaari and M. Bar-Hillel (1984), "On Dividing Justly," *Social Choice and Welfare,* **1:** 1–24.

8. A reconsideration of the Harsanyi–Sen debate on utilitarianism

JOHN A. WEYMARK

1. Introduction

John Harsanyi, in a classic series of writings – most notably in Harsanyi (1955, 1977a) – uses expected utility theory to develop two axiomatizations of "weighted utilitarian" rules. I refer to these results as Harsanyi's Aggregation Theorem and Harsanyi's Impartial Observer Theorem. Both propositions are single-profile social choice results – that is, they assume that there is a single profile of individual preference orderings and a single social preference ordering of a set of social alternatives. The set of alternatives considered by Harsanyi consists of all the lotteries generated from a finite set of certain alternatives.

In Harsanyi's Aggregation Theorem, Harsanyi assumes that individual and social preferences satisfy the expected utility axioms and that these preferences are represented by von Neumann–Morgenstern utility functions. With the addition of a Pareto condition, Harsanyi demonstrates that the social utility function is an affine combination of the individual utility functions – that is, social utility is a weighted sum of individual utilities once the origin of the social utility function is suitably normalized.

In Harsanyi's Impartial Observer Theorem, Harsanyi introduces a hypothetical observer who determines a social ordering of the alternatives based on a sympathetic but impartial concern for the interests of all members of society. The observer is sympathetic because he imagines how he would evaluate an alternative if he were placed in, say, person i's position, with i's tastes and objective circumstances. Harsanyi supposes the impartial observer has preferences over these hypothetical alternatives that satisfy the expected utility

The ideas expressed in this chapter have been greatly influenced by my joint work with Charles Blackorby and David Donaldson. I am also indebted to Aanund Hylland for his comments and to Diana Weymark for preparing the diagrams.

axioms, and that these preferences are represented by a von Neumann–Morgenstern utility function. He also supposes that the observer respects the individuals' orderings of the social alternatives. The observer's utility from an alternative is the utility associated with the hypothetical lottery in which the alternative is received for certain but there is an equal chance of being any member of society. This results in alternatives being ranked by their average (over members of society) utility.

Harsanyi's contributions have spawned a considerable literature, much of which takes issue with Harsanyi's analysis. In part, this controversy has arisen because Harsanyi often states his assumptions and theorems imprecisely and because he frequently makes use of unstated assumptions in his proofs. Consequently, there is a great deal of confusion in the literature about the correct statement of Harsanyi's theorems.

There has also been considerable controversy about the ethical significance of Harsanyi's work and its relationship to utilitarianism. These issues have been the subject of a lively exchange between Harsanyi and Amartya Sen that appears in Harsanyi (1975, 1977b) and Sen (1976, 1977, 1986).[1] Although a number of issues are addressed in this debate, here I am concerned with Sen's claim that Harsanyi's theorems are not about utilitarianism. Sen argues that in Harsanyi's theorems, utility is only used to represent preferences and has no other independent basis.[2] As a consequence, Sen regards Harsanyi's results as theorems about the representability of social preferences and not about utilitarianism, as the latter requires a concept of utility that is not based exclusively on preference.[3] Further, Sen argues that when such a concept of utility is used, utility functions

[1]   Sen also considers Harsanyi's theorems in Sen (1969, 1970).
[2]   In the terminology of Bezembinder and van Acker (1987), Sen is arguing that Harsanyi's utilities are "representational" and not "factual."
[3]   Harsanyi (1955, 1977a) presents a third theorem, due to Fleming (1952), in support of using sums of utilities to rank alternatives. This theorem does not appeal to the expected utility hypothesis, as the alternatives considered have no random elements. Fleming's theorem makes use of an axiom that requires that the social ranking of a pair of alternatives should depend only on the rankings of these alternatives by concerned individuals. As Fleming's introductory comments make clear, the utility (welfare) functions in his theorem are representational in nature and need not be based on an independent concept of well-being (such as happiness). Thus, Sen's critique of Harsanyi's Aggregation and Impartial Observer Theorems is also relevant to Harsanyi's version of Fleming's theorem.

may not be von Neumann–Morgenstern functions, even if the expected utility axioms are satisfied. If this is the case, Harsanyi's theorems imply that the social welfare function is nonlinear in these welfare-relevant utilities, and hence obviously nonutilitarian.

Sen does not develop his argument in much detail, nor does he spell out the formal model underlying his largely verbal discussion. As a result, Sen's argument may be misunderstood, as seems to be the case in Harsanyi's (1977b) rejoinder to Sen's critique. Furthermore, there is some textual evidence to suggest that at least, on occasion, Harsanyi does view utility in terms of satisfaction, and not just preference, and this is overlooked by Sen.

This chapter has two major goals. First, I want to clarify exactly what Harsanyi has established in his theorems. Second, I want to review and evaluate the Harsanyi–Sen debate. In order to make the discussion accessible to a wide audience, intuitive arguments and illustrative examples are used in place of proofs wherever a proof is long and available elsewhere.

The plan of this chapter is as follows. In Section 2 I review the relevant features of expected utility theory. In Section 3 I present a number of variants of Harsanyi's Aggregation Theorem. In Section 4 I consider the implications for Harsanyi's Aggregation Theorem of relaxing the requirement that preferences be represented by von Neumann–Morgenstern utility functions. In Section 5 I discuss Harsanyi's Impartial Observer Theorem. In Section 6 I review the Harsanyi–Sen debate and consider the implications for that debate of regarding utility as measuring something other than just preference. In Section 7 I provide some brief concluding remarks.

2. Expected utility theory[4]

Following Harsanyi (1955), the set of alternatives under consideration consists of all lotteries with prizes drawn from a finite set of certain alternatives. Let $X = \{x_1, \ldots, x_M\}$, with $M \geq 2$, denote the set of *certain alternatives*. A *lottery* $p = (p_1, \ldots, p_M)$ offers the outcome x_m as a prize with probability p_m. The *set of all lotteries* is

---

[4] Nontechnical introductions to expected utility theory may be found in Luce and Raiffa (1957), Sugden (1986), and Machina (1987).

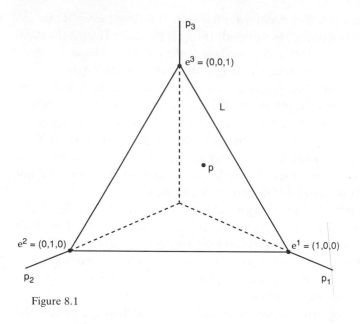

Figure 8.1

$$L = \{p \in \mathbb{R}^M \mid p_m \geq 0 \text{ for all } m \text{ and } \sum_{m=1}^{M} p_m = 1\}$$

Lotteries are sometimes referred to as *prospects* and alternatives in X are sometimes referred to as *pure* (or sure) *prospects*. There is no need to treat sure prospects separately from lotteries as the certain alternative x_m is equivalent to the lottery $e^m = (e_1^m, \ldots, e_M^m)$ where $e_i^m = 1$ if $i = m$ and $e_i^m = 0$ otherwise. In other words, X is equivalent to the set of lotteries $\{e^1, \ldots, e^M\}$ where e^m offers x_m as the prize for certain.

When $M = 3$ – that is, when there are three pure alternatives – the set of lotteries L has the simple geometric representation shown in Figure 8.1. The set L is a simplex (that is, a triangle including the interior) with vertices given by the sure prospects $\{e^1, e^2, e^3\}$. As L is two-dimensional when $M = 3$, henceforth I shall depict L as lying flat in the page. This is what L would look like to an observer looking down at L from a position directly over the lottery (1/3, 1/3, 1/3).

The lotteries in L are *simple lotteries* because the prizes are pure alternatives. One could also consider *compound lotteries,* which have lotteries as prizes. However, in expected utility theory it is assumed that only the ultimate consequences of a lottery matter.[5] An implication of this assumption is that for any compound lottery there is an equivalent simple lottery. For example, suppose p = (1/4, 1/2, 1/4), q = (1/2, 1/4, 1/4), and that the compound lottery r offers the lottery p as a prize with probability 1/4 and the lottery q as a prize with probability 3/4. The compound lottery r is equivalent in its consequences to the simple lottery

$$s = \frac{1}{4}p + \frac{3}{4}q = (7/16, 5/16, 1/4)$$

In some axiomatizations of expected utility theory, the set of alternatives is expanded to include all lotteries, both simple and compound, generated from the set of pure prospects. In this approach, r and s are distinct alternatives. However, an axiom is then introduced that requires r to be ranked as indifferent to s. Alternatively, the set of alternatives can be taken to be L. In this second approach, r and s are regarded as being two alternative descriptions of the same lottery. The latter approach is adopted here.

A ranking of the lotteries in L is given by a *weak preference relation R*. From R, a *strict preference relation P* and an *indifference relation I* are defined in the usual fashion.[6] Expected utility theory is concerned with the implications of requiring the weak preference relation R to satisfy ordering, continuity, and independence axioms. Although different axiomatizations of expected utility theory use alternative ver-

---

[5] By adopting this form of consequentialism, it is implicitly being assumed that preferences do not exhibit any intrinsic attitude towards gambling – that is, toward the activity of gambling in and of itself. See Harsanyi (1987) for an extended discussion of this point. Harsanyi argues that the attitudes toward gambling found in expected utility theory are instrumental in nature; they express the willingness to take on or avoid risks in order to obtain particular outcomes.

[6] Formally, for all p, $q \in L$, (a) pPq iff pRq and not (qRp), and (b) pIq iff pRq and qRp.

sions of these axioms, all axiomatizations of expected utility theory have this basic structure.[7]

The ordering axiom is standard.

Ordering

R is an ordering – that is, R is a reflexive, complete, and transitive binary relation.

Continuity

For any $p \in L$, the set of weakly preferred lotteries $R^+(p)=\{q \in L | qRp\}$ and the set of weakly worse lotteries $R^-(p)=\{q \in L | pRq\}$ are both closed sets.

This axiom is simply a reinterpretation of the continuity axiom used in the theory of choice over certain alternatives. The continuity axiom implies that if p is strictly preferred to q, then for any lottery r close to p, r is also strictly preferred to q.

Independence

For any $p, q, r \in L$, if pRq, then $[\lambda p+(1-\lambda)r]R[\lambda q+(1-\lambda)r]$ for any $\lambda \in (0, 1)$.

In words, if p is weakly preferred to q, then any mixture (convex combination) of p and r is weakly preferred to the same mixture of q and r, independent of the weight λ used to form the mixture.[8]

Together these three axioms, which I refer to as the *expected utility axioms,* have strong implications for the structure of the preference relation R.

Theorem 1. A preference relation R on the set of lotteries satisfies the expected utility axioms if and only if either (a) all lotteries are indifferent to each other, or (b) all indifference curves are parallel hyperplanes with a uniform direction of increasing preference.[9]

---

[7]   My axiomatization is essentially the same as the one in Laffont (1989). Different axiomatizations appear in von Neumann and Morgenstern (1947), Marschak (1950), and Herstein and Milnor (1953). See Samuelson (1952) and Malinvaud (1952) for further discussion of the independence axiom.

[8]   In Savage's (1954) discussion of expected utility theory, his independence condition is the sure-thing principle.

[9]   A hyperplane is a linear surface. In one dimension a hyperplane is a line, and in two dimensions a hyperplane is a plane.

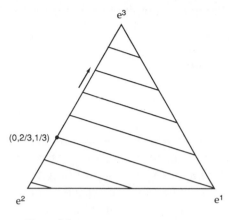

Figure 8.2

In the nondegenerate case, the continuity and ordering axioms by themselves imply that there are well-defined indifference curves that vary continuously over L. Adding the independence condition forces the indifference curves to be parallel and linear with a uniform direction of preference. Clearly, any preference relation with indifference curves satisfying (a) or (b) satisfies the expected utility axioms.

Case (b) is illustrated in Figure 8.2, where the arrow indicates the direction of preference. In this example, e^3Pe^1, e^1Pe^2, and $e^1I(0, 2/3, 1/3)$ – that is, x_3 is preferred to x_1, x_1 is preferred to x_2, and x_1 is indifferent to a lottery that yields x_2 with probability 2/3 and x_3 with probability 1/3.[10]

A *utility function* U defined on L *represents* the preference relation R if for all $p, q \in L$,

$$U(p) \geq U(q) \text{ iff } pRq \tag{2.1}$$

Whether the function U represents R or not depends solely on the ordinal properties of U. Consequently, if U is a utility function representing R, then any monotone increasing transform of U is also a utility function representing R. It is well known that if R is a continu-

---

[10] It is inconsistent with the expected utility axioms for the indifference curves to be as depicted in Figure 8.2 but with, for example, the curve through e^1 containing the most preferred alternatives in L.

ous ordering, then there exists a continuous utility function U representing R.[11]

A *von Neumann–Morgenstern* (1947) *utility function* is a function V defined on L with the property that for any $p \in L$,

$$V(p) = \sum_{m=1}^{M} p_m V(e^m) \tag{2.2}$$

In (2.2), $V(e^m)$ is the utility number assigned to receiving x_m for certain. Consequently, with a von Neumann–Morgenstern utility function, the utility assigned to a lottery is the lottery's expected utility. The function V is linear in the probabilities p, which implies that the contours of V must be of the form described in Theorem 1.

Suppose the von Neumann–Morgenstern utility function V represents R – that is, for all p, $q \in L$,

$$V(p) \geq V(q) \quad \text{iff} \quad pRq \tag{2.3}$$

Now let

$$V'(p) = \alpha + \beta V(p) \tag{2.4}$$

for all $p \in L$ where $\beta > 0$; V' is a positive affine transformation of V. Because V' is an increasing monotone transformation of V and because V represents R, V' is also a utility function representing R. Multiplying both sides of (2.2) by β and adding α to both sides of the resulting equation, we obtain

$$\alpha + \beta V(p) = \sum_{m=1}^{M} p_m [\alpha + \beta V(e^m)]$$

Substituting from (2.4) yields

$$V'(p) = \sum_{m=1}^{M} p_m V'(e^m)$$

---

[11]   For example, see Debreu (1959).

Thus V' is also a von Neumann–Morgenstern utility function. In fact, if V is a von Neumann–Morgenstern utility function representing R, then V' is also a von Neumann–Morgenstern utility function representing R if and only if V' is a positive affine transform of V.

Theorem 2 is the *Expected Utility Theorem*.

Theorem 2. If a preference relation R on the set of lotteries L satisfies the expected utility axioms, then there exists a von Neumann–Morgenstern utility function V representing R. Furthermore, V' is also a von Neumann–Morgenstern utility function representing R if and only if V' is a positive affine transform of V.

Faced with the problem of choosing from a subset $\overline{L}$ of L, it is supposed that an individual makes this choice by choosing the most preferred alternative(s) in $\overline{L}$ according to R. If V is a von Neumann–Morgenstern representation of R, the Expected Utility Theorem implies that this individual is behaving *as if* he or she is maximizing expected utility on $\overline{L}$ using the utility function V.

For the preference relation R illustrated in Figure 8.2, the function is defined by setting

$$V(p) = 35p_1 + 30p_2 + 45p_3 \tag{2.5}$$

for all $p \in L$ is a von Neumann–Morgenstern utility function representing R. Here we have $V(e^1) = 35$, $V(e^2) = 30$, and $V(e^3) = 45$. These numbers cannot be chosen independently. For example, fix the values assigned to e^2 and e^3 as before. Because $e^1 I(0, 2/3, 1/3)$, we must have

$$V(e^1) = V(0, 2/3, 1/3)$$

or, using (2.2),

$$V(e^1) = \frac{2}{3} V(e^2) + \frac{1}{3} V(e^3) = 35$$

All other von Neumann–Morgenstern utility representations of R are obtained using (2.4). For example, setting $\alpha = -10$ and $\beta = 2$, it follows from (2.4) and (2.5) that

$$V'(p) = 60p_1 + 50p_2 + 80p_3$$

is also a von Neumann–Morgenstern utility representation of R.

It is of fundamental importance to note that the Expected Utility Theorem does *not* say that if R satisfies the expected utility axioms, then *all* utility representations of R must be von Neumann–Morgenstern utility functions. For example, the function defined by setting

$$U(p) = \log(35p_1 + 30p_2 + 45p_3) \tag{2.6}$$

is a utility function for the preference relation shown in Figure 8.2 because U is an increasing transform of (2.5). However, U is not linear in the probabilities, so it cannot be a von Neumann–Morgenstern utility function. Theorem 1 completely characterizes the structure imposed on R by the expected utility axioms. These axioms are only concerned with the properties of R – that is, the *ranking* of alternative lotteries. The expected utility axioms do not, and cannot, single out von Neumann–Morgenstern utility representations for special treatment. An individual's choice behavior is rationalized by *any* utility function representing R, not just von Neumann–Morgenstern representations.[12]

3. Harsanyi's aggregation theorem

Harsanyi (1955) supposes that there is a group of individuals each of whom has a preference relation on the lotteries in L. Based on these individual preferences, a collective or social preference relation on L is determined. Thus, Harsanyi is concerned with a problem in what is now known as single-profile social choice theory. That is, there is only one profile (list) of individual preferences and, correspondingly, one social preference.

Formally, there is a finite set of individuals indexed by $i = 1, \ldots, I$. A *profile* is a list of preference relations on the set of

[12]   This point is particularly clear in Arrow (1951, p. 10). Arrow remarks that what distinguishes von Neumann–Morgenstern representations from other equally acceptable utility representations is the simple way that the former summarize preferences (or, in Arrow's words, "the laws of rational behavior").

lotteries L, one for each person. The profile under consideration is denoted by $(R_1, \ldots, R_I)$ where R_i is *person i's preference relation*. The *social preference relation* is denoted by R.

Harsanyi assumes that the individual preference relation R_i and the social preference relation R satisfy the expected utility axioms. He also supposes that the individual and social preferences are related by a Pareto principle. I consider three alternative Pareto conditions:

Pareto Indifference

For all $p, q \in L$, if pI_iq for all i, then pIq.

Semistrong Pareto[13]

For all $p, q \in L$, if pR_iq for all i, then pRq.

Strong Pareto

For all $p, q \in L$, if pR_iq for all i, then pRq and if, furthermore, there exists an i such that pP_iq, then pPq.

Pareto Indifference says that if everyone is indifferent between a pair of lotteries, then so is society. Similarly, Semistrong Pareto says that if everyone weakly prefers one lottery to a second, then so does society. Strong Pareto says that (a) if everyone weakly prefers one lottery to a second, then so does society, and (b) if in addition at least one individual's preference is strict, then society's preference over these lotteries is strict as well. Note that Strong Pareto implies Semistrong Pareto, which in turn implies Pareto Indifference. Each of the Pareto principles is a formalization of the idea that unanimity should be respected. In the various versions of Harsanyi's Aggregation Theorem, Pareto conditions provide the only link between individual and social preferences.

With both the individual and social preferences satisfying the expected utility axioms, it is possible to represent each individual's

---

[13] There appears to be no standard name for this principle in the literature. Weak Pareto refers to the axiom obtained by using strict instead of weak preferences in the definition of Semistrong Pareto. Note that Semistrong Pareto does not imply Weak Pareto.

preference relation R_i by a von Neumann–Morgenstern utility function V_i, and it is possible to represent the social preference relation R by a von Neumann–Morgenstern utility function V. *Harsanyi's Aggregation Theorem* states that the social utility function V must be an affine combination of the individual utility functions V_i if Pareto Indifference is satisfied.

Theorem 3.[14] Suppose R_i, $i = 1, \ldots, I$, and R satisfy the expected utility axioms and also suppose that Pareto Indifference is satisfied. Let V_i be a von Neumann–Morgenstern utility representation of R_i, $i = 1, \ldots, I$, and let V be a von Neumann–Morgenstern utility representation of R. Then there exist numbers a_i, $i = 1, \ldots, I$, and b such that for all $p \in L$,

$$V(p) = \sum_{i=1}^{I} a_i V_i(p) + b \tag{3.1}$$

This is a rather remarkable result. The functions V_i and V are arbitrary von Neumann–Morgenstern utility representations for the underlying preference orderings. Given Pareto Indifference, (3.1) must hold: The social utility function must be a weighted combination of the individual utility functions with the origin translated by b units. Note that the theorem does *not* say that the weights a_i must be positive or even nonnegative. Nor does it say that only one vector of coefficients $(a_1, \ldots, a_I, b)$ satisfies (3.1).

It is instructive to consider some examples. In each of these examples, there are two individuals and three pure prospects.

In the first example, the von Neumann–Morgenstern utility functions are given by

$$V_1(p) = 15p_1 + 10p_2 + 20p_3 \tag{3.2}$$

$$V_2(p) = 5p_1 + 15p_2 + 25p_3 \tag{3.3}$$

[14] Theorem 3 is Fishburn's (1984) restatement of Harsanyi's Aggregation Theorem. Theorem 3 is proved by Border (1981). Border's proof is reproduced in Selinger (1986) and in Weymark (1990). Theorem 3 is a special case of related theorems established by Domotor (1979), Fishburn (1984), Border (1985), and Coulhon and Mongin (1989). Harsanyi's original proof is unsatisfactory as it makes use of an implicit assumption not included in the theorem statement. This additional assumption and its implications are discussed later in this section.

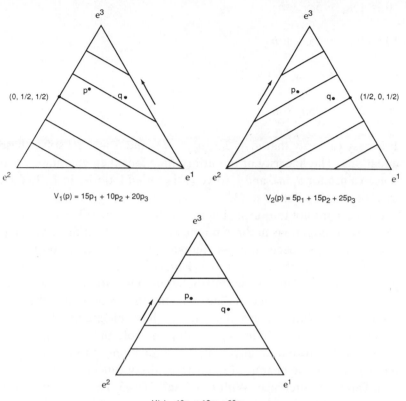

Figure 8.3

and

$$V(p) = 10p_1 + 10p_2 + 20p_3 \tag{3.4}$$

for all $p \in L$. These functions are illustrated in Figure 8.3. Harsanyi's Aggregation Theorem establishes that (3.1) holds for any $p \in L$. In particular it holds for the lotteries $\{e^1, \ldots, e^M\}$, each of which offers a certain alternative with probability one. Considering eaco of the three pure prospects e^1, e^2, and e^3 in turn, substituting from (3.2), (3.3), and (3.4) into (3.1) yields

$$10 = 15a_1 + 5a_2 + b$$

$$10 = 10a_1 + 15a_2 + b$$

and

$$20 = 20a_1 + 25a_2 + b$$

It is easy to verify that $a_1 = 2/3$, $a_2 = 1/3$, and $b = -5/3$ solve these equations. The linearity of the utility functions then guarantees that these values for a_1, a_2, and b solve (3.1) for *all* lotteries in L. In fact, this is the only solution to (3.1).

It is perhaps not too surprising to find that we can solve a system of three linear equations in three unknowns. However, if there are, say, twenty pure prospects and two individuals, there would be twenty equations in only three unknowns. Harsanyi's Aggregation Theorem guarantees that in this situation the equations also have a solution.

The example illustrated in Figure 8.3 has the property that there do not exist two distinct alternatives that both people are indifferent between. Thus, Pareto Indifference plays no role in this example. In other words, given the individual utility functions in (3.2) and (3.3), *any* social von Neumann–Morgenstern utility function is consistent with Pareto Indifference. With $I = 2$ and $M = 3$, Pareto Indifference only restricts the functional form of V (given V_1 and V_2), if (a) at least one person is indifferent between all alternatives, (b) both people have the same preferences, or (c) the individuals have diametrically opposed preferences (that is, the same indifference curves, but with opposite directions of preference). With four or more pure prospects, there is more scope for Pareto Indifference to play a role in the analysis.

To see why Pareto Indifference is important for Harsanyi's Aggregation Theorem, consider setting

$$V_1(p) = 2p_1 + p_2 + p_3 \tag{3.5}$$

$$V_2(p) = p_1 + 2p_2 + 2p_3 \tag{3.6}$$

and

$$V(p) = p_1 + p_2 + 2p_3 \tag{3.7}$$

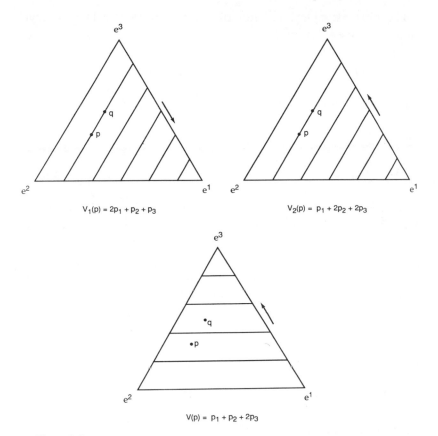

$$V_1(p) = 2p_1 + p_2 + p_3$$

$$V_2(p) = p_1 + 2p_2 + 2p_3$$

$$V(p) = p_1 + p_2 + 2p_3$$

Figure 8.4

for all $p \in L$. These functions are illustrated in Figure 8.4. Here the two individuals have the same indifference curves but opposite directions of preference. To satisfy the expected utility axioms and to also be consistent with Pareto Indifference, the social preference relation must either (a) coincide with person one's preference ordering, (b) coincide with person two's preference ordering, or (c) exhibit universal indifference. As the social preferences do not satisfy any of these alternatives, Pareto Indifference is violated. In this example, it is not possible to find values for a_1, a_2, and b that satisfy (3.1) for all lotteries in L. To see this, consider the lotteries p and q shown in Figure 8.4. Because pI_1q and pI_2q, the right-hand side of (3.1) has the same value for both p and q. However, the values on the left-hand side of (3.1) differ for p and q because qPp.

The next example illustrates the possibility that (3.1) may have more than one solution. Let

$$V_1(p) = 10p_1 + p_2 + p_3 \tag{3.8}$$

$$V_2(p) = p_1 + 10p_2 + 10p_3 \tag{3.9}$$

and

$$V(p) = 99p_1 \tag{3.10}$$

for all $p \in L$. These functions are illustrated in Figure 8.5. Individual one and society have the same preference ordering, with person two having diametrically opposed preferences. It is clear from the diagram that Pareto Indifference is satisfied, so Theorem 3 applies. To solve for (a_1, a_2, b), I, proceed as above by considering the three pure prospects. They yield the pair of equations

$$99 = 10a_1 + a_2 + b$$

and

$$0 = a_1 + 10a_2 + b \,[15]$$

The general solution to these two equations is

$$a_2 = a_1 - 11$$

and

$$b = -a_1 - 10a_2$$

There are an infinite number of values for (a_1, a_2, b) that solve these equations. For example, letting $a_1 = 12$, $a_2 = 1$, and $b = -22$, Harsanyi's Aggregation Theorem implies that

---

[15]   The prospects e^2 and e^3 both result in the second equation.

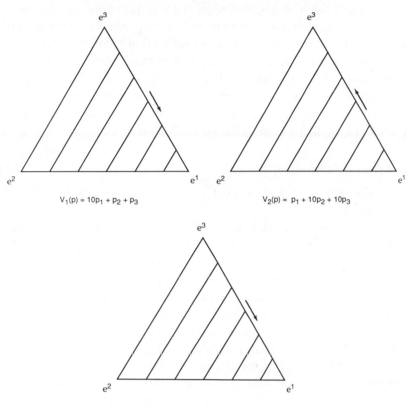

$V_1(p) = 10p_1 + p_2 + p_3$ $V_2(p) = p_1 + 10p_2 + 10p_3$

$V_1(p) = 99p_1$

Figure 8.5

$$V(p) = 12V_1(p) + V_2(p) - 22 \tag{3.11}$$

for all $p \in L$, as can be readily checked by direct calculation.[16] Setting $a_1 = 10$, $a_2 = -1$, and $b = 0$, it is also true that

$$V(p) = 10V_1(p) - V_2(p) \tag{3.12}$$

for all $p \in L$. As the function V is the same in both (3.11) and (3.12), we find that V can be thought of as an affine combination of the V_i with each person receiving positive weights, or as an affine combina-

[16] In performing these calculations, recall that $p_2 + p_3 = 1 - p_1$.

tion of the V_i with one person receiving a negative weight. Furthermore, if a_1 is chosen to be less than zero, both people receive negative weights. This indeterminacy creates problems in the interpretation of Theorem 3 as a theorem about weighted utilitarianism.

Harsanyi's (1955) proof of Theorem 3 makes use of an unstated assumption. Although this means that Harsanyi did not prove his theorem, as noted earlier, others have subsequently done so. I call Harsanyi's implicit axiom *Independent Prospects*.

Independent Prospects

For each $i = 1, \ldots, I$, there exist $p^i, q^i \in L$ such that $p^i I_j q^i$ for all $j \neq i$ and $p^i P_i q^i$.[17]

This condition says that for each person we can find a pair of prospects for which that person is not indifferent and for which everyone else is indifferent. This axiom is satisfied for the profile illustrated in Figure 8.3 but is violated for the profiles illustrated in Figures 8.4 and 8.5. Clearly, this assumption rules out the possibility of any individual expressing universal indifference. If each person's preferences satisfy the expected utility axioms, this assumption cannot be satisfied if the number of individuals is at least as large as the number of pure prospects. For example, for the profile depicted in Figure 8.3 it is impossible to add one more person and have the new profile satisfy Independent Prospects, as there are no distinct prospects that both person one and person two are indifferent between.

Independent Prospects implies that the coefficients that appear in Harsanyi's Theorem are unique.

Theorem 4.[18] Suppose the assumptions in Theorem 3 are satisfied. Then the coefficients $(a_1, \ldots, a_I, b)$ in (3.1) are unique *if and only if* Independent Prospects is satisfied.

This result clarifies why there is a unique solution to (3.1) for the

---

[17]   Assuming that each person's preferences satisfy the expected utility axioms, Independent Prospects is equivalent to assuming that $\{V_1, \ldots, V_I\}$ are affinely independent, where V_i is any von Neumann–Morgenstern utility function representing R_i. The functions $\{V_1, \ldots, V_I\}$ are affinely independent if the only solution to $\sum_{i=1}^{I} \lambda_i V_i(p) + \mu = 0$ for all $p \in L$ is $\lambda_1 = \ldots = \lambda_I = \mu = 0$. See Coulhon and Mongin (1989) and Weymark (1990).

[18]   Theorem 4 appears explicitly in Coulhon and Mongin (1989) and is implicit in Fishburn (1984). See also Weymark (1990).

example depicted in Figure 8.3, whereas there is not a unique solution to (3.1) for the example depicted in Figure 8.5. In the former example, Independent Prospects is satisfied, whereas in the latter example it is not.

In the first example, the unique solution to (3.1) is (a_1, a_2, b) = $(2/3, -1/3, -5/3)$. Here the weights on the individual utility functions are positive. If V_2 is replaced by

$$V_2(p) = -5p_1 - 15p_2 - 25p_3 \qquad (3.13)$$

there is again a unique solution to (3.1). It is given by (a_1, a_2, b) = $(2/3, -1/3, -5/3)$. This follows from the fact that (3.13) is just the negative of (3.3). As a consequence, in this new example there is no solution to (3.1) that gives a nonnegative weight to each person's utility function. The essential difference between this example and the original example is that the former satisfies Semistrong Pareto and the latter does not. For the p and q shown in Figure 8.3, in the new example qP_1p and qP_2p, but pPq, violating Semistrong Pareto.

The conclusion in (3.1) can be strengthened if Pareto Indifference is replaced by Semistrong Pareto.

Theorem 5.[19] Suppose R_i, $i = 1, \ldots ,I$, and R satisfy the expected utility axioms, and also suppose that Semistrong Pareto is satisfied. Let V_i be a von Neumann–Morgenstern utility representation of R_i, $i = 1, \ldots ,I$, and let V be a von Neumann–Morgenstern utility representation of R. Then there exist numbers $a_i \geq 0$, $i = 1, \ldots ,I$, and b such that (3.1) is satisfied for all $p \in L$. Furthermore, the coefficients in (3.1) are unique if and only if Independent Prospects is satisfied.

When there are multiple solutions to (3.1) – that is, when Independent Prospects is violated – Theorem 3 only guarantees that *a* solution to (3.1) exists with nonnegative weights on the individual utility functions; it does not say that *all* solutions to (3.1) weight individuals nonnegatively. The example depicted in Figure 8.5 illustrates this point. We have already seen that Pareto Indifference is satisfied for this example. Semistrong Pareto is satisfied as well, as there are no lotteries p and q for which one person strictly prefers p to q and the

[19]   The first part of Theorem 5 is a special case of theorems in Domotor (1979) and Fishburn (1984). The uniqueness result follows immediately from Theorem 4. Theorem 5 is also proved in Weymark (1990).

other person weakly prefers p to q. To satisfy (3.1), we can choose any (a_1, a_2) satisfying $a_2 = a_1 - 11$, so both weights are nonnegative if and only if $a_1 \geq 11$.

A third version of Harsanyi's Aggregation Theorem is obtained using Strong Pareto.

Theorem 6.[20] Suppose R_i, $i = 1, \ldots ,I$, and R satisfy the expected utility axioms and also suppose that Strong Pareto is satisfied. Let V_i be a von Neumann–Morgenstern utility representation of R_i, $i = 1, \ldots ,I$, and let V be a von Neumann–Morgenstern utility representation of R. Then there exist numbers $a_i > 0$, $i = 1, \ldots ,I$, and b such that (3.1) is satisfied for all $p \in L$. Furthermore, the coefficients in (3.1) are unique if and only if Independent Prospects is satisfied.

Analogous to Theorem 5, in the absence of the Independent Prospects assumption, Theorem 6 does not say that *all* solutions to (3.1) weight individuals positively.[21]

To illustrate the difference between Theorems 5 and 6, consider setting

$$V(p) = V_1(p) = p_1 \tag{3.14}$$

and

$$V_2(p) = p_2 \tag{3.15}$$

for all $p \in L$. These preferences are illustrated in Figure 8.6. Independent Prospects is satisfied, so the coefficients that solve (3.1) are unique; they are given by $(a_1, a_2, b) = (1, 0, 0)$. Thus, it is not possible to satisfy (3.1) with a positive weight for person two. This example satisfies Semistrong Pareto, but not Strong Pareto. The violation of

---

[20]   The first part of Theorem 6 is a special case of a theorem in Domotor (1979). The uniqueness result was originally established in Fishburn (1984). See also Weymark (1990) for an alternative proof of Theorem 6.

[21]   Harsanyi's (1977a, 1979) statements of the version of his theorem that uses Strong Pareto includes the claim that the a_i that satisfy (3.1) *must* be positive. The example illustrated in Figure 8.5 shows that this claim is false. Resnick (1983) appears to be the first person to construct a counterexample to Harsanyi's claim. Note, however, that Harsanyi's claim is true with the addition of the Independent Prospects assumption, an assumption that Harsanyi implicitly uses in his proof.

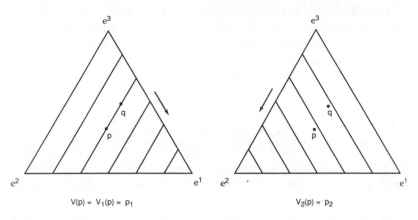

$V(p) = V_1(p) = p_1$ $V_2(p) = p_2$

Figure 8.6

Strong Pareto can be seen from considering the prospects p and q shown in Figure 8.6.

For the moment, let me drop the requirement that preferences satisfy all of the expected utility axioms and consider a profile $(R_1, \ldots ,R_I)$ and an associated social preference relation R on the set of lotteries L for which each preference relation is a continuous ordering. Suppose that U_i is a continuous individual utility function representing R_i, $i = 1, \ldots ,I$, and U is a continuous *social utility function* representing R. For each $p \in L$, there is a corresponding vector of utility numbers $u := (u_1, \ldots ,u_I)=(U_1(p), \ldots ,U_I(p))$. Let $\mathcal{U}$ be the set of all such vectors of utility numbers as p varies over L. The set $\mathcal{U}$ is a subset of $\mathbb{R}^I$; it is the set of *attainable utility vectors*.

If Pareto Indifference is satisfied, it is possible to express the social ordering R in terms of a *social welfare ordering* R^* of $\mathcal{U}$. More precisely, there exists an ordering R^* of $\mathcal{U}$ such that for all $p, q \in L$,

$$pRq \quad \text{iff} \quad (U_1(p), \ldots ,U_I(p))R^*(U_1(q), \ldots ,U_I(q)) \qquad (3.16)$$

In fact, (3.16) can be used to construct the ordering R^* from R. If Pareto Indifference is violated, this would not be possible, as we could then find lotteries p and q such that $(U_1(p), \ldots , U_I(p)) = (U_1(q), \ldots , U_I(q))$ but for which pPq, in which case (3.16) cannot be satisfied.

The relation R^* is obviously reflexive and complete on $\mathcal{U}$. To show that it is transitive, consider any $u, \overline{u}, \overline{\overline{u}} \in \mathcal{U}$ with $uR^*\overline{u}$ and $\overline{u}R^*\overline{\overline{u}}$. Because each of these utility vectors is in $\mathcal{U}$, we can find lotteries $p, q,$ $r \in L$ such that $u = (U_1(p), \ldots, U_I(p)), \overline{u} = (U_1(q), \ldots, U_I(q)),$ and $\overline{\overline{u}} = (U_1(r), \ldots, U_I(r))$. By (3.16), pRq iff $uR^*\overline{u}$ and qRr iff $\overline{u}R^*\overline{\overline{u}}$. Because R is transitive, we must have pRr, which by (3.16) implies that $uR^*\overline{\overline{u}}$. This establishes that R^* is transitive.

The continuity of the individual utility functions and the continuity of the social preference relation imply that R^* is continuous and can be represented by a continuous *social welfare function* W.[22] Formally, there exists a continuous function $W: \mathcal{U} \to \mathbb{R}$ such that for all $p, q \in L$,

$$pRq \quad \text{iff} \quad W(U_1(p), \ldots, U_I(p)) \geq W(U_1(q), \ldots, U_I(q)) \qquad (3.17)$$

One way to construct such a social welfare function is to set

$$W(u) = U(p) \qquad (3.18)$$

whenever $u = (U_1(p), \ldots, U_I(p))$. In (3.18), the social utility function U on L is used to number the contours of the social welfare ordering R^* on $\mathcal{U}$. This construction is possible because all utility vectors on an indifference curve of R^* must correspond to prospects that are socially indifferent. However, because W is merely a representation of R^*, there is no need to choose this particular representation; any increasing monotonic transform of the W defined in (3.18) would do just as well.

The implications for R^* and W of strengthening the Pareto condition are easy to discern. If Semistrong Pareto is satisfied, the social welfare ordering R^* is weakly monotonic and the social welfare function W is weakly increasing in all of its arguments. If Strong Pareto is satisfied, R^* is strictly monotonic and W is strictly increasing in all of its arguments.

The main points of the previous discussion are summarized in Theorem 7.

---

[22] Such functions are commonly referred to as Bergson (1938)–Samuelson (1947) social welfare functions because W is defined on vectors of utility numbers and the utility vectors are generated from a single profile of individual preference orderings. In contrast, an Arrow (1951) social welfare function assigns a social preference ordering to each profile of individual preference orderings in some domain of profiles.

Theorem 7.[23] Suppose R_i, $i = 1, \ldots, I$, and R are continuous order-ings of L. Let U_i be a continuous utility function representing R_i, $i = 1, \ldots, I$.[24] (a) If Pareto Indifference is satisfied, there exists a con-tinuous social welfare ordering R^* of $\mathcal{U}$ satisfying (3.16) and R^* can be represented by a continuous social welfare function W satisfying (3.17). (b) If Semistrong Pareto is satisfied, R^* is weakly monotonic and W is weakly increasing. (c) If Strong Pareto is satisfied, R^* is strictly monotonic and W is strictly increasing.

Theorem 7 applies whenever the individual and social preferences are continuous orderings. Now suppose that these preference rela-tions satisfy the expected utility axioms and that the individual prefer-ence relations are represented by von Neumann−Morgenstern utility functions V_i, $i = 1, \ldots, I$. In this case, the set $\mathcal{U}$ is convex because the set of lotteries L is convex and the utility functions are linear in the probabilities. Combining the previous theorems in this section yields Theorem 8.

Theorem 8.[25] Suppose R_i, $i = 1, \ldots, I$, and R satisfy the expected utility axioms. Let V_i be a von Neumann−Morgenstern utility repre-sentation of R_i, $i = 1, \ldots, I$. (a) If Pareto Indifference is satisfied, then there exist $a_i \in \mathbb{R}$, $i = 1, \ldots, I$, such that (3.17) is satisfied with the social welfare function

$$W(u) = \sum_{i=1}^{I} a_i u_i \qquad (3.19)$$

for all $u \in \mathcal{U}$. (b) If Semistrong Pareto is satisfied, then the weights in (3.19) may all be chosen to be nonnegative. (c) If Strong Pareto is satisfied, then the weights in (3.19) may all be chosen to be positive. (d) If in (a), (b), or (c), Independent Prospects is also satisfied, then the weights in (3.19) are unique up to a positive factor of proportionality.

The social preference relation R is an ordering of the lotteries in L.

---

[23]   Part of Theorem 7, in the special case of von Neumann−Morgenstern utility functions, appears in Harsanyi (1955) in a slightly different form.
[24]   A representation of the social preference relation R is not used in this theorem.
[25]   Part (a) of this theorem corresponds to Harsanyi's (1955) original statement of his Aggregation Theorem. Harsanyi chooses a representation of R^* in which (3.18) is satisfied.

Theorem 7 can be interpreted as saying that with Pareto Indifference, society is behaving *as if* it is using a social welfare function W to generate the social ranking R – that is, society is behaving as if the social ordering R is being determined from W using (3.17). Theorem 8 can be similarly interpreted; society is behaving *as if* the social ordering R is being determined using a linear social welfare function whenever individual and social preferences satisfy the expected utility axioms and von Neumann–Morgenstern utility representations are used. However, it should be stressed that the social preference relation R is the primitive and the social welfare function W is a derivative construct.

It is easy to see why Theorem 8 follows from the earlier theorems. We know from Theorem 1 that for all $p, q \in L$,

$$pRq \quad \text{iff} \quad \sum_{i=1}^{I} a_i V_i(p) + b \geq \sum_{i=1}^{I} a_i V_i(q) + b \qquad (3.20)$$

Cancelling the b's yields (3.17) for the social welfare function (3.19). Theorem 4 demonstrates that the coefficients in (3.1) are unique if Independent Prospects is satisfied. Uniqueness of the coefficients in (3.1) corresponds to uniqueness up to a factor of proportionality of the weights in (3.20), as multiplying all the weights in (3.20) by a positive constant preserves the inequality.

Figure 8.7 shows some contours of the social welfare function W in (3.19) for the case in which both Strong Pareto and Independent Prospects are satisfied. Strong Pareto implies that the indifference curves of W are negatively sloped. Independent Prospects implies that we can find lotteries $p, q, r \in L$, for which, for example, (a) person one prefers q to p while person two is indifferent between p and q, and (b) person two prefers r to p while person one is indifferent between p and r. The corresponding utility vectors are $u, \bar{u}, \bar{\bar{u}}$, respectively, as shown in Figure 8.7.

For the example illustrated in Figure 8.5, Independent Prospects is violated as

$$V_2(p) = 11 - V_1(p)$$

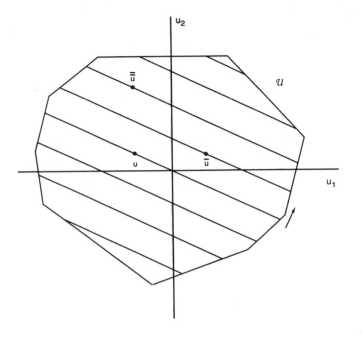

$$W(u) = a_1u_1 + a_2u_2$$

Figure 8.7

for all $p \in L$. The set $\mathcal{U}$ for this example is shown in Figure 8.8. The endpoints of $\mathcal{U}$ follow from the fact that $1 \leq V_1(p) \leq 10$ for all $p \in L$. As the social preference relation coincides with person one's preference relation, the social welfare ordering R^* must be increasing as u_1 increases. Because $\mathcal{U}$ is one-dimensional, many linear welfare functions represent R^*. Two examples are shown in Figure 8.8.[26]

In the preceeding discussion, not only has the profile $(R_1, \ldots ,R_I)$ and the social ordering R been fixed, so has the von Neumann–Morgenstern utility representations V_i, $i = 1, \ldots ,I$, and V used to represent them. The coefficients in (3.1) depend on the particular representations chosen and must be adjusted if the representations are changed. In the previous section it was noted that von Neumann–

---

[26]   Strictly speaking, W need only be defined on $\mathcal{U}$. Defining W on all of $\mathbb{R}^2$ or $\mathbb{R}^2_+$ makes it easier to see that the weights a_1 and a_2 are not unique up to a factor of proportionality.

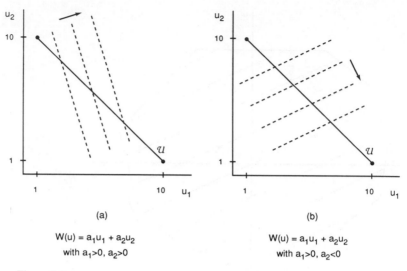

(a)

$W(u) = a_1u_1 + a_2u_2$
with $a_1 > 0$, $a_2 > 0$

(b)

$W(u) = a_1u_1 + a_2u_2$
with $a_1 > 0$, $a_2 < 0$

Figure 8.8

Morgenstern utility representations are unique up to a positive affine transformation. Consider replacing V_i with

$$\overline{V}_i = \alpha_i + \beta_i V_i \qquad i = 1, \ldots ,I \tag{3.21}$$

and replacing V with

$$\overline{V} = \alpha + \beta V \tag{3.22}$$

where $\beta_i > 0$, $i = 1, \ldots ,I$, and $\beta > 0$. Solving for V_i and V, we obtain

$$V_i = -\frac{\alpha_i}{\beta_i} + \frac{1}{\beta_i} \overline{V}_i \qquad i = 1, \ldots ,I$$

and

$$V = -\frac{\alpha}{\beta} + \frac{1}{\beta} \overline{V}$$

Substituting these expressions in (3.1) yields, after some simple algebra,

$$\overline{V} = \sum_{i=1}^{I} \bar{a}_i \overline{V}_i + \overline{b} \tag{3.23}$$

where

$$\bar{a}_i = \frac{\beta a_i}{\beta_i} \qquad i = 1, \ldots, I \tag{3.24}$$

and

$$\overline{b} = \beta b + \alpha - \beta \sum_{i=1}^{I} \left[\frac{a_i \alpha_i}{\beta_i} \right] \tag{3.25}$$

As was to be expected from Theorem 3, (3.23) has the same basic form as (3.1), but the coefficients have been altered to correspond to the new choice of utility representations.

Because the weights a_i have changed, so must the social welfare function. It is now given by

$$\overline{W}(u) = \sum_{i=1}^{I} \bar{a}_i u_i \tag{3.26}$$

for all $u \in \overline{\mathcal{U}}$, where $\overline{\mathcal{U}}$ is the set of attainable utility vectors that are feasible using the new utility functions $\overline{V}_i$, $i = 1, \ldots, I$. Even though there has been no change in the profile $(R_1, \ldots, R_I)$ or in the social preference relation R, because new individual utility representations are being employed, it is necessary to use a new social welfare function. Simply because new utility representations have been adopted, society behaves as if it has changed the way it aggregates individual utilities. This discussion suggests that great care should be taken in drawing inferences from the functional form of the social welfare function.[27]

---

[27] Social welfare orderings are also used in multiprofile social choice theory. In Arrow's (1951) problem, a social preference ordering is determined for every conceivable profile of individual orderings of a set of alternatives. If Pareto Indifference is

Suppose that for the von Neumann–Morgenstern utility functions $V_i, i = 1, \ldots, I$, and V, (3.1) is satisfied with $a_i > 0$ for all i. Using the representations given in (3.21) and (3.22) with $\alpha_i = 0$, $\beta_i = a_i$, $\alpha = -b$, and $\beta = 1$, (3.23) becomes

$$\overline{V} = \sum_{i=1}^{I} \overline{V}_i \qquad\qquad (3.27)$$

and (3.26) becomes

$$\overline{W}(u) = \sum_{i=1}^{I} u_i \qquad\qquad \cdot \quad (3.28)$$

for all $u \in \overline{\mathcal{U}}$. Thus, provided that (3.1) can be satisfied with positive weights, by carefully choosing the von Neumann–Morgenstern utility representations, the social ranking can be interpreted to be the one obtained by ranking lotteries in terms of their total utility.[28]

4. Nonlinear social welfare functions and Harsanyi's aggregation theorem

With the exception of Theorem 7, the discussion in the preceding section supposes that all preference orderings are represented by von

satisfied, then for each profile there is a social welfare ordering R^*, an ordering that depends on the utility representations being used, unless R^* is dictatorial. However, also requiring Independence of Irrelevant Alternatives (an interprofile condition) to be satisfied forces the orderings R^* to be independent of both the profile being considered and the utility representations being used. This conflict leads to Arrow's Theorem. See Sen (1979) or Blackorby, Donaldson, and Weymark (1984) for details.

[28]   The versions of Harsanyi's Aggregation Theorem presented here presuppose that the set of alternatives is the set of lotteries L. In economic applications, it is often more natural to work with state contingent alternatives in which the probability of each state occuring is fixed. Blackorby, Donaldson, and Weymark (1991) demonstrate (by means of a counterexample) that Harsanyi's Aggregation Theorem is not valid when alternatives are modeled in this way. They also show that a version of Harsanyi's Aggregation Theorem holds in their framework if an extra (rather strong) assumption is made concerning the images of the utility functions. This theorem reproduces, with a minor correction, an unpublished result circulated in Blackorby, Donaldson, and Weymark (1980). Hammond (1983, 1987) also presents versions of Harsanyi's Aggregation Theorem in which state contingent alternatives are used. Hammond does not state this extra assumption in his theorems, but it is used in his proof. Hammond notes that when applied to state contingent alternatives, Harsanyi's Aggregation Theorem requires the consistency of ex ante and ex post welfare evaluations.

Neumann–Morgenstern utility functions. As discussed in Section 2, satisfaction of the expected utility axioms merely permits the use of a von Neumann–Morgenstern utility representation; any other kind of utility representation is equally satisfactory. In this section I consider the implications for Harsanyi's Aggregation Theorem of dropping the requirement that only von Neumann–Morgenstern representations be used as utility functions.

Again, suppose that the profile $(R_1, \ldots, R_I)$ and the social preference relation R are fixed. Further suppose that all of the individual and social preference relations satisfy the expected utility axioms. Let U_i be a utility representation of R_i, $i = 1, \ldots, I$, and let U be a utility representation of R. Consider any *arbitrary* von Neumann–Morgenstern representations V_i, $i = 1, \ldots, I$, and V of the orderings R_i and R. Because U_i and V_i [resp. U and V] are ordinally equivalent, we must have

$$U_i = f_i(V_i) \qquad i = 1, \ldots, I \tag{4.1}$$

and

$$U = f(V) \tag{4.2}$$

where f_i, $i = 1, \ldots, I$, and f are increasing monotone transformations. If U_i [resp. U] is a von Neumann–Morgenstern utility function, then f_i [resp. f] is a positive affine transform. If U_i [resp. U] is not a von Neumann–Morgenstern utility function, then f_i [resp. f] is nonaffine.

Because the transforms in (4.1) and (4.2) are increasing, they may be inverted to obtain

$$V_i = f_i^{-1}(U_i) \qquad i = 1, \ldots, I$$

and

$$V = f^{-1}(U)$$

If Pareto Indifference is satisfied, then Harsanyi's Aggregation Theorem applies to the functions V_i, $i = 1, \ldots, I$, and V. Therefore, there must exist numbers a_i, $i = 1, \ldots, I$, and b such that (3.1) holds – that is, for all $p \in L$,

$$f^{-1}(U(p)) = \sum_{i=1}^{I} a_i f_i^{-1}(U_i(p)) + b$$

or, equivalently,

$$U(p) = f[\sum_{i=1}^{I} h_i(U_i(p)) + b] \tag{4.3}$$

where

$$h_i(u_i) := a_i f_i^{-1}(u_i) \qquad i = 1, \ldots, I \tag{4.4}$$

In other words, for all $p, q \in L$, we have

$$pRq \qquad \text{iff} \qquad \sum_{i=1}^{I} h_i(U_i(p)) \geq \sum_{i=1}^{I} h_i(U_i(q)) \tag{4.5}$$

Consequently, the associated social welfare ordering R^* is represented by the social welfare function given by

$$W(u) = \sum_{i=1}^{I} h_i(u_i) \tag{4.6}$$

for all $u \in \mathcal{U}$.

If every individual utility function U_i is a von Neumann–Morgenstern utility function, then this social welfare function is affine – that is, W has linear contours. This conclusion follows from (4.4) and the observation that f_i^{-1} is an affine function if U_i and V_i are both von Neumann–Morgenstern utility representations of R_i. However, if U_i is a nonaffine transform of V_i, then h_i is not an affine function. Provided

Independent Prospects is satisfied, if any h_i is nonaffine, then the contours of W are nonlinear.[29]

The social welfare function in (4.6) is additive, but it need not be increasing in its arguments. Because f_i^{-1} is increasing, the function h_i in (4.4) is (a) increasing if $a_i > 0$, (b) constant if $a_i = 0$, and (c) decreasing if $a_i < 0$. In other words, the monotonicity properties of the social welfare function do not depend on the choice of utility functions used to represent the individual preferences.

What is affected by the choice of utility representations is the curvature properties of the welfare function. With von Neumann–Morgenstern representations, the contours of the welfare function are linear. If each person's von Neumann–Morgenstern utility function is subjected to an increasing strictly convex transformation f_i, the functions h_i in (4.4) would be strictly concave, and the contours of the new welfare function would be bowed away from the origin (provided $\mathcal{U}$ is not one dimensional). On the other hand, if each person's von Neumann–Morgenstern utility function is subjected to a strictly concave transformation f_i, the functions h_i in (4.4) would be strictly convex, and the contours of the new welfare function would be bowed toward the origin (provided $\mathcal{U}$ is not one dimensional).

To make these ideas more concrete, let me reconsider the example illustrated in Figure 8.3. Initially, suppose that the von Neumann–Morgenstern utility representations in (3.2), (3.3), and (3.4) are employed. Applying Harsanyi's Aggregation Theorem, we then have

$$pRq \quad \text{iff} \quad \frac{2}{3} V_1(p) + \frac{1}{3} V_2(p) \geq \frac{2}{3} V_1(q) + \frac{1}{3} V_2(q) \quad (4.7)$$

for all $p, q \in L$. Now replace V_1 with

$$U_1 = e^{V_1} \quad (4.8)$$

---

[29]   Even if h_i is nonaffine, it is possible for the contours of W to be linear if Independent Prospects is violated. For example, with $I = 2$ suppose $U_1 = U_2$; $\mathcal{U}$ is a subset of the 45° line. With Strong Pareto, R^* is increasing along this line; each contour of W is a single point, and so is trivially linear.

and V_2 with

$$U_2 = e^{V_2^{30}} \tag{4.9}$$

From (4.4), we see that

$$h_1(u_1) = \frac{2}{3} \log u_1 \tag{4.10}$$

and

$$h_2(u_2) = \frac{1}{3} \log u_2 \tag{4.11}$$

Thus, for the utility functions U_1 and U_2, the social welfare function in (4.6) is

$$W(u) = \frac{2}{3} \log u_1 + \frac{1}{3} \log u_2 \tag{4.12}$$

whereas the social welfare function using V_1 and V_2 as the representations is

$$W(u) = \frac{2}{3} u_1 + \frac{1}{3} u_2 \tag{4.13}$$

Whereas the welfare function in (4.13) is linear, the welfare function in (4.12) is a Cobb–Douglas function, and so is nonlinear. Some contours of (4.12) are shown in Figure 8.9.[31,32]

It should be stressed that both (4.12) and (4.13) correspond to a single social ordering R of the lotteries in L. The functional forms of

---

[30]   Here e stands for the exponential function and should not be confused with the lotteries e^m considered earlier.

[31]   In Figure 8.9, $A = (e^{15}, e^5)$ is the utility vector associated with receiving x_1 for certain, $B = (e^{10}, e^{15})$ is the utility vector associated with receiving x_2 for certain, and $C = (e^{20}, e^{25})$ is the utility vector associated with receiving x_3 for certain.

[32]   If logarithms had been used in place of exponentials in (4.8) and (4.9), (4.12) would have exponentials instead of logarithms. The contours of the welfare function would then be bowed toward the origin.

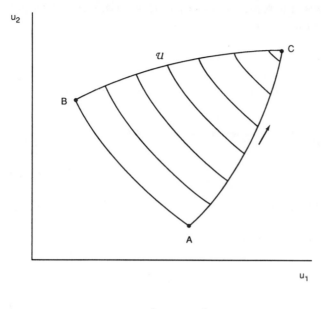

$$W(u) = \tfrac{2}{3} \log u_1 + \tfrac{1}{3} \log u_2$$

Figure 8.9

the welfare functions in (4.12) and (4.13) differ because they are based on alternative utility representations of the individual utility functions.

For a given profile $(R_1, \ldots , R_I)$ and a given social preference ordering R, we have seen that the social welfare ordering R^* depends on the choice of utility functions $(U_1, \ldots , U_I)$ used to represent the profile. In deriving the social welfare function W in (4.6), the function h_i depends on the functional relationship between U_i and some von Neumann–Morgenstern utility representation V_i of R_i. If a different von Neumann–Morgenstern representation $\overline{V}_i$ of R_i is used in place of V_i, the function h_i changes, resulting in a new welfare function. However this new welfare function must be ordinally equivalent to (4.6), and hence represent the same social welfare ordering R^*. The social welfare ordering R^* is unchanged because the social welfare function is still defined using the U_i scales.

Formally, let $\overline{V}_i$ be an affine transform of V_i, $i = 1, \ldots , I$, as in

(3.21), and suppose the representation V of R is fixed. Because U_i and $\overline{V}_i$ are ordinally equivalent,

$$U_i = \bar{f}_i(\overline{V}_i) \qquad i = 1, \ldots ,I \tag{4.14}$$

for some increasing functions $\bar{f}_i$, $i = 1, \ldots ,I$. It then follows that for all $p \in L$,

$$U_i(p) = f_i(V_i(p)) \qquad\qquad\qquad\qquad\qquad \text{[by (4.1)]}$$

$$= \bar{f}_i(\overline{V}_i(p)) \qquad\qquad\qquad\qquad\qquad \text{[by (4.4)]}$$

$$= \bar{f}_i(\alpha_i + \beta_i V_i(p)) \qquad\qquad\qquad\qquad \text{[by (3.21)]}$$

$$= \bar{f}_i(\alpha_i + \beta_i f_i^{-1}(U_i(p))) \qquad\qquad\qquad \text{[by (4.1)]}$$

for all $i = 1, \ldots ,I$. Thus, for all $p \in L$,

$$\bar{f}_i^{-1}(U_i(p)) = \alpha_i + \beta_i f_i^{-1}(U_i(p)), \qquad i = 1, \ldots ,I \tag{4.15}$$

For $i = 1, \ldots ,I$, we have

$$\overline{h}_i(u_i) := \bar{a}_i \bar{f}_i^{-1}(u_i) \qquad\qquad\qquad\qquad \text{[by (4.4)]}$$

$$= \bar{a}_i(\alpha_i + \beta_i f_i^{-1}(u_i)) \qquad\qquad\qquad \text{[by (4.15)]}$$

$$= \frac{a_i}{\beta_i}(\alpha_i + \beta_i f_i^{-1}(u_i)) \qquad\qquad\qquad \text{[by (3.24)]}$$

$$= (a_i\alpha_i/\beta_i) + h_i(u_i) \qquad\qquad\qquad\qquad \text{[by (4.4)]}$$

Thus, using the functions $\overline{V}_i$ as a basis for constructing the functions $\overline{h}_i$, the social welfare function is

$$\overline{W}(u) = \sum_{i=1}^{I} [(a_i\alpha_i/\beta_i) + h_i(U_i)]$$

$$= W(u) + \sum_{i=1}^{I} (a_i\alpha_i/\beta_i) \tag{4.16}$$

for all $u \in \mathcal{U}$. The functions W and $\overline{W}$ are ordinally equivalent; they are alternative representations of a common social welfare ordering R^*.

5. Harsanyi's impartial observer theorem

In Harsanyi (1953), Harsanyi describes a way of modeling moral value judgments in terms of an impartial observer who is sympathetic to the interests of each person in society. In Harsanyi (1955), and more completely in Harsanyi (1977a), Harsanyi uses this framework to obtain what I call Harsanyi's Impartial Observer Theorem. In this section I review the main features of this theorem.

As in the previous sections, there is a fixed profile $(R_1, \ldots ,R_I)$ of individual orderings of the lotteries in L, with each ordering satisfying the expected utility axioms. In contrast to Harsanyi's Aggregation Theorem, we do not start with a given social preference relation on L. Instead, it is supposed that the impartial observer, who plays the role of society in this discussion, has preferences on the set of lotteries that have as prizes being person i with the social alternative x_m.

Formally, an *extended alternative* is a pair $(x_m, i) \in X \times \{1, \ldots ,I\}$. When faced with this extended alternative, the observer is to imagine himself being person i with the social alternative x_m. In making this sympathetic identification with person i, not only is the observer supposed to consider himself with i's objective circumstances in x_m, he is also supposed to imagine himself with i's subjective characteristics, including i's preferences as given by the ordering R_i. There are thus MI pure extended alternatives. The set of (simple) lotteries generated by these MI alternatives is denoted by $\hat{L}$. To distinguish lotteries in $\hat{L}$ from lotteries in L, the former are called *extended lotteries*. An extended lottery is a vector such as $\pi = (\pi_{11}, \ldots ,\pi_{1I}, \ldots ,\pi_{MI})$ where π_{mi} is the probability of being person i with alternative x_m.[33]

The observer is assumed to have an *extended preference relation* $\hat{R}$ on the set of lotteries $\hat{L}$. This preference relation $\hat{R}$ is assumed to satisfy the expected utility axioms for the set of lotteries $\hat{L}$. Thus, $\hat{R}$ can be represented by a von Neumann–Morgenstern utility function $\hat{V}$ on $\hat{L}$. That is, there exists a function $\hat{V}$ such that for all $\pi, \rho \in \hat{L}$,

[33]   Obtaining the pure extended alternative (x_m, i) for certain corresponds to setting $\pi_{mi} = 1$ and $\pi_{nj} = 0$ if either $n \neq m$ or $j \neq i$.

$$\pi \hat{R} \rho \quad \text{iff} \quad \hat{V}(\pi) \geq \hat{V}(\rho) \tag{5.1}$$

and for which

$$\hat{V}(\pi) = \sum_{m=1}^{M} \sum_{i=1}^{I} \pi_{mi} \hat{V}(x_m, i) \tag{5.2}$$

for all $\pi \in \hat{L}$.[34] As before, I want to stress that $\hat{R}$ can be equally well represented by a utility function that is not a von Neumann–Morgenstern representation – that is, by a function that satisfies (5.1) but not (5.2).

Suppose that the extended lotteries π and ρ have the property that for all m, $\pi_{mj} = \rho_{mj} = 0$ for all $j \neq i$. In both of these extended lotteries, it is certain that the observer will take on person i's features. Consequently, in ranking π and ρ, the observer is essentially ranking a pair of lotteries in L from person i's perspective. The observer is supposed to be sympathetic to i's interests, and so should rank the extended lotteries π and ρ in the same way i would rank the corresponding lotteries in L. This principle is Harsanyi's (1977a) *Principle of Acceptance*.[35]

Principle of Acceptance

For all $i = 1, \ldots, I$, for all $\pi, \rho \in \hat{L}$, if for all $m = 1, \ldots, M$, $\pi_{mj} = \rho_{mj} = 0$ for all $j \neq i$, then $\pi \hat{R} \rho$ if and only if $p R_i r$ where $p = (\pi_{1i}, \ldots, \pi_{Mi})$ and $r = (\rho_{1i}, \ldots, \rho_{Mi})$.

Suppose that $\hat{R}$ satisfies both the expected utility axioms and the Principle of Acceptance. Further suppose that $\hat{R}$ is represented by the von Neumann–Morgenstern utility function $\hat{V}$. By considering lotteries in which the observer is i for certain, $\hat{V}$ can be used to *define* the functions V_i, $i = 1, \ldots, I$, on L by setting

$$V_i(p) := \hat{V}(\pi) \tag{5.3}$$

[34] Writing (5.2) in this way involves a slight abuse of notation as (x_m, i) should be replaced by its formalization as an extended lottery.
[35] Note that it would not be possible for $\hat{R}$ to satisfy both the expected utility axioms and the Principle of Acceptance if some individual's ordering R_i of L violated the expected utility axioms.

where for all m, $\pi_{mj} = 0$ if $j \neq i$ and $\pi_{mj} = p_m$ if $j = i$. The function V_i is a particular von Neumann−Morgenstern utility representation of person i's preference relation R_i on L.

For the extended lottery $\pi \in \hat{L}$, if the probability of being person i is independent of the probability of alternative x_m occurring, then there exists a lottery $p = (p_1, \ldots, p_M) \in L$ and a probability distribution $z = (z_1, \ldots, z_I)$ on the set of individuals, where z_i is the probability of being person i, such that for all $m = 1, \ldots, M$, for all $i = 1, \ldots, I$,

$$\pi_{mi} = p_m z_i \tag{5.4}$$

For such an extended lottery, by combining (5.2) and (5.3) we obtain

$$\hat{V}(\pi) = \sum_{i=1}^{I} z_i V_i(p) \tag{5.5}$$

The observer's utility from the extended lottery π can be computed by first calculating each person's expected utility in the lottery p and then taking the weighted sum of the individual expected utilities, using the probabilities of being each person as weights.

The observer is supposed to be not only sympathetic to each person's interests, but also impartial. Harsanyi models this impartiality by supposing that the observer restricts attention to lotteries that satisfy (5.4) and for which there is an equal probability of being any particular person in society. Put another way, the observer is engaging in a thought experiment in which he is imagining that he has an equal chance of being any person in society, complete with that person's objective and subjective circumstances. The observer could in fact be one of the individuals in society who has temporarily adopted an impartial perspective from which to judge the relative desirability of alternative outcomes. By adopting this impartial perspective, the resulting judgments can be thought of as moral judgments, as they give equal consideration to each person's interests.[36]

[36]   A related notion of impartiality is considered by Vickery (1945). In common with Rawls (1971), Harsanyi and Vickery develop ethical judgments by considering a rational egoist making decisions under a hypothetical "veil of ignorance." The individual operating under this veil is supposed to be provided with all morally relevant information concerning society and its alternative courses of actions and is supposed to

I call an extended lottery $\pi \in \hat{L}$ that satisfies (5.4) with $z_i = 1/I$ for all i an *impartial lottery*. Let $\hat{L}^\circ$ denote the set of impartial lotteries. By considering impartial lotteries, it is possible to derive a preference relation R for the observer over the lotteries in L. Formally, for all p, $r \in L$, R is *defined* by setting

$$pRr \quad \text{iff} \quad \pi \hat{R} \rho \tag{5.6}$$

where $\pi_{mi} = p_m/I$ and $\rho_{mi} = r_m/I$ for all m and for all i. In Harsanyi's Aggregation Theorem, the social preference relation R is a primitive in the model. Here, the impartial observer's preference relation R is a derived construct.

It is straightforward to verify that this derived relation R on L satisfies the expected utility axioms provided the extended preference relation $\hat{R}$ on $\hat{L}$ satisfies the expected utility axioms. If, in addition, $\hat{R}$ satisfies the Principle of Acceptance, then for all lotteries p, $r \in L$,

$$pRr \quad \text{iff} \quad \frac{1}{I} \sum_{i=1}^{I} V_i(p) \geq \frac{1}{I} \sum_{i=1}^{I} V_i(r)^{37} \tag{5.7}$$

Equation (5.7) follows immediately from (5.1), (5.5), and (5.6) after setting $z_i = 1/I$ in (5.5). For all $p \in L$, *define*

$$V(p) := \frac{1}{I} \sum_{i=1}^{I} V_i(p) \tag{5.8}$$

It is clear from (5.7) that V is a utility function representing R. Because all of the individual utility functions V_i are von Neumann–Morgenstern utility functions, they are linear in the probabilites. Adding linear functions preserves linearity, so V is also linear in the probabilities, and hence is a von Neumann–Morgenstern utility function for R.

---

be stripped of any information that is morally irrelevant. The differences between the conclusions of these three authors in part stems from differences in what information is permitted behind the veil of ignorance.

[37]   Of course, we could multiply both sides of the inequality by I. I follow Harsanyi (1977a) in not doing so.

These results can be reexpressed in terms of a social welfare function. Given the individual utility representations in (5.3), $\mathcal{U}$ is again used to denote the set of all vectors of utility numbers that are attainable using the lotteries in L. From (5.7) it is obvious that Strong Pareto, and hence Pareto Indifference, is satisfied. It then follows that the social welfare ordering R^* given by

$$uR^*\overline{u} \quad \text{iff} \quad \frac{1}{I}\sum_{i=1}^{I} u_i \geq \frac{1}{I}\sum_{i=1}^{I} \overline{u}_i \tag{5.9}$$

for all $u, \overline{u} \in \mathcal{U}$, corresponds to R – that is, the R^* in (5.9) satisfies (3.16). The ordering R^* can be represented by the social welfare function W given by

$$W(u) = \frac{1}{I}\sum_{i=1}^{I} u_i \tag{5.10}$$

for all $u \in \mathcal{U}$. Consequently, the social welfare function is a symmetric linear function.

This discussion has established *Harsanyi's Impartial Observer Theorem*.

Theorem 9. Suppose R_i, $i = 1, \ldots, I$, are preference relations on the set of lotteries L that satisfy the expected utility axioms. Suppose $\hat{R}$ is an extended preference relation on the set of extended lotteries $\hat{L}$ that satisfies the expected utility axioms and the Principle of Acceptance. Let $\hat{V}$ be a von Neumann–Morgenstern utility representation of $\hat{R}$. Then the impartial observer's preference relation R on the set of lotteries L defined in (5.6) satisfies the expected utility axioms. Furthermore, for the individual von Neumann–Morgenstern utility functions defined in (5.3), R satisfies (5.7) and can be represented by a von Neumann–Morgenstern utility function of the form given in (5.8). In addition, the social welfare ordering R^* in (5.9) satisfies (3.16) and the social welfare function in (5.10) represents this R^*.

For the individual utility representations used in the theorem, (5.7) and (5.9) say that the impartial observer is behaving *as if* his rankings of the lotteries in L are being obtained by calculating the average expected utility of each lottery. In Harsanyi's Aggregation Theorem, the weights need not be equal (or even be all positive).

The choice of the von Neumann–Morgenstern function $\hat{V}$ to represent the extended preference ordering $\hat{R}$ is arbitrary. Suppose instead that $\hat{R}$ is represented by the utility function $\hat{U}$ – that is, for all $\pi, \rho \in \hat{L}$,

$$\pi\hat{R}\rho \quad \text{iff} \quad \hat{U}(\pi) \geq \hat{U}(\rho) \tag{5.11}$$

As before, for all $i = 1, \ldots, I$, for all $p \in L$, define

$$U_i(p) := \hat{U}(\pi) \tag{5.12}$$

where for all m, $\pi_{mj} = 0$ if $j \neq i$ and $\pi_{mj} = p_m$ if $j = i$. The function U_i is the utility function representing individual i's preferences that is implicit in the new calibration of the observer's extended preferences. As $\hat{U}$ need not be a von Neumann–Morgenstern utility function, U_i need not be one either.

Because $\hat{U}$ and $\hat{V}$ are both utility functions for $\hat{R}$, there exists an increasing transform $\hat{f}$ such that

$$\hat{U} = \hat{f}(\hat{V}) \tag{5.13}$$

In view of how the individual utility functions are constructed, it follows that

$$U_i = \hat{f}(V_i) \tag{5.14}$$

for all $i = 1, \ldots, I$. Note that both (5.13) and (5.14) employ the same transform $\hat{f}$. Inverting (5.14) and substituting in (5.7), we find that for all $p, r \in L$,

$$pRr \quad \text{iff} \quad \frac{1}{I}\sum_{i=1}^{I}\hat{f}^{-1}[U_i(p)] \geq \frac{1}{I}\sum_{i=1}^{I}\hat{f}^{-1}[U_i(r)] \tag{5.15}$$

and that R is represented by the utility function defined by

$$U(p) := \frac{1}{I}\sum_{i=1}^{I}\hat{f}^{-1}[U_i(p)] \tag{5.16}$$

for all $p \in L$. The corresponding social welfare function is given by

$$\hat{W}(u) = \frac{1}{I} \sum_{i=1}^{I} \hat{f}^{-1}(u_i) \tag{5.17}$$

for all $u \in \hat{\mathcal{U}}$, the set of utility vectors obtainable from the lotteries in L using the new individual utility representations (5.12).

If $\hat{U}$, like $\hat{V}$, is a von Neumann–Morgenstern representation of $\hat{R}$, the transform $\hat{f}$ is affine. In this case (5.13) becomes

$$\hat{U} = \alpha + \beta \hat{V} \tag{5.18}$$

for some α and β with $\beta > 0$. Simple algebra then shows that the utility function in (5.16) is given by

$$U(p) = -\frac{\alpha}{\beta} + \frac{1}{\beta I} \sum_{i=1}^{I} V_i(p) \tag{5.19}$$

for all $p \in L$, and the social welfare function in (5.17) is given by

$$\hat{W}(u) = -\frac{\alpha}{\beta} + \frac{1}{\beta I} \sum_{i=1}^{I} u_i \tag{5.20}$$

for all $u \in \hat{\mathcal{U}}$. As in Theorem 9, we have a symmetric linear function. For the utility vectors attainable using either set of representations, – that is, for $u \in \mathcal{U} \cap \hat{\mathcal{U}}$, (5.10) and (5.20) have identical contours; they differ only in how the contours are numbered.

If $\hat{U}$ is not a von Neumann–Morgenstern representation of $\hat{R}$, the transform $\hat{f}$ and its inverse $\hat{f}^{-1}$ are nonaffine. The social welfare $\hat{W}$ in (5.17) is then symmetric but nonlinear and, provided $\hat{\mathcal{U}}$ is not degenerate, the contours of $\hat{W}$ are also symmetric and nonlinear.[38]

It should not be forgotten that the impartial observer's ordering R of the lotteries in L does not depend on the choice of representation for the observer's extended preferences $\hat{R}$. Thus, the functions in

---

[38]   For example, if $\hat{f}$ is the exponential function, $\hat{f}^{-1}$ is the logarithmic function. However, unlike the example illustrated in Figure 8.9, the contours of $\hat{W}$ are symmetric with respect to the 45° line.

both (5.8) and (5.16) are simply alternative utility representations of R. Merely by choosing different representations of $\hat{R}$, the observer's ranking of the lotteries in L can appear to be generated using a symmetric linear welfare function or to be generated using a symmetric nonlinear welfare function.

In the model discussed in Sections 3 and 4, whether or not the social welfare function has linear contours depends solely on whether all individual preference relations R_i are represented by von Neumann–Morgenstern utility functions. The representation used for the social preference relation does not affect the shape of the contours of the social welfare function. In contrast, in the model discussed in this section, whether or not the social welfare function has linear contours depends solely on whether the impartial observer's extended preference relation $\hat{R}$ is represented by a von Neumann–Morgenstern function. Whether the utility functions representing R_i and R are von Neumann–Morgenstern functions is completely determined by the choice of representation for $\hat{R}$.[39]

Although the social preference relation R that appears in Harsanyi's Aggregation Theorem need not be identified with any particular individual, Harsanyi often does so. Harsanyi prefers to interpret R as being some individual's *ethical preferences* with the individual preference relations R_i interpreted as being the *subjective preferences* of the members of society. Harsanyi (1955, p. 315) describes the distinction between these two kinds of preferences as follows:

> . . . the former must express what this individual prefers (or, rather, would prefer) on the basis of impersonal social considerations alone, and the latter must express what he actually prefers, whether on the basis of personal interests or on any other basis.

With this interpretation, the social preference relation R does not belong to some abstract entity called society, but belongs instead to some particular individual.

The notion of ethical preferences provides a way of linking Harsanyi's two theorems together. The social preference relation R derived from the extended preference relation $\hat{R}$ in the Impartial

---

[39]   The claims in this paragraph need appropriate qualification if $\mathcal{U}$ is degenerate in a way that forces all social indifference curves to be trivially linear.

Observer Theorem is based on impersonal considerations, and so could serve as the social preference relation that is used in the Aggregation Theorem. The Impartial Observer model incorporates one particular notion of impartiality. The use of a different concept of impartiality could possibly result in a different ethical preference relation, in which case the two theorems could be concerned with different social orderings.[40]

In both of Harsanyi's theorems, the profile of individual preferences $(R_1, \ldots, R_I)$ is fixed from the outset. In the Impartial Observer Theorem, the social preference relation R is derived from a previously determined extended preference relation $\hat{R}$. Once a utility representation is chosen for $\hat{R}$, the individual utility functions representing the profile are completely specified [see (5.3) or (5.12)]; the individual utility functions cannot be chosen independently. In the aggregation model, whether the individual utility representations can be chosen independently depends on the interpretation of the social preference relation R. If R is a primitive of the model and is exogenously specified, then the choice of R places no restrictions on the individual utility representations. On the other hand, with some interpretations of R as an ethical preference, the choice of R does restrict the set of permissible individual utility representations.

6. Representation theorems or utilitarianism?

Sen (1976, 1977, 1986) raises two, essentially independent, objections to Harsanyi's analysis. First, following Diamond (1967), Sen questions the appropriateness of the expected utility axioms for social decision-making. Diamond and Sen argue that the Independence (or sure-thing) axiom does not permit society (or the impartial observer) to take account of the fairness of the process by which outcomes are generated. The expected utility axioms force the social decision-maker to be outcome oriented, and Diamond and Sen find this to be

[40]   It should be stressed that Harsanyi's Aggregation Theorem does not presuppose that R is an ethical preference. For example, in Theorem 3 it is possible to have $R = R_1$, and these social preferences would hardly qualify as ethical preferences in a heterogeneous society. Of course, the axioms on R in the Aggregation Theorem are not meant to be a complete list of the properties that R should satisfy.

morally unacceptable. As this issue has received considerable attention in the literature, I do not consider it further here.[41]

My chief concern is with Sen's second objection. The main point of this objection is that Harsanyi's theorems do not provide axiomatizations of (weighted) utilitarianism. Sen (1986, p. 1123) notes that utilitarianism starts with an *"independent* concept of individual utilities of which social welfare is shown to be the sum."* In contrast, Sen argues that Harsanyi's theorems do not employ such an independent concept of utility.[42] Furthermore, Sen argues that when an independently based concept of utility is used, the social welfare function may well be nonlinear, and hence nonutilitarian. In Sen's view, Harsanyi's theorems are primarily representation theorems.[43] By this Sen means that the social utility functions given in (3.1) and (5.8) only have significance as representations of the underlying social preferences; the fact that these representations are expressed in terms of weighted sums of utilities has no necessary connection with utilitarianism. In part, Sen is objecting to the utilitarian *interpretation* Harsanyi attaches to his theorems. However, Sen is also taking issue with Harsanyi's implicit assumption, made explicit here, that only von Neumann–Morgenstern utility functions be considered when preferences satisfy the expected utility axioms.

When Sen says that Harsanyi has no independently based concept of utility, he means that utility is only being used to represent preferences over lotteries or extended lotteries. However, even if Sen is correct in claiming that this is the kind of utility used by Harsanyi, Sen's argument does not establish that Harsanyi's theorems have no relevance for utilitarianism. Harsanyi's theorems do not preclude the use of an alternative utility concept and, in fact, there is some textual evidence to suggest that Harsanyi regards utility as measuring satisfaction. Later in this section I consider whether a non-preference-based concept of utility permits one to interpret Harsanyi's theorems as propositions concerning utilitarianism.

[41] For detailed discussions of this issue, see Diamond (1967), Harsanyi (1975, 1977b, 1987), Sen (1970, 1976, 1977), Deschamps and Gevers (1977), and Broome (1987, 1989).

[42] Selinger (1986) makes the same point. See also Nunan (1981).

[43] McClennen (1981, p. 601) shares this view. He writes that Harsanyi's "sum-of-utilities theorem is really a theorem about the representability of social preferences, and not directly about the proper way to evaluate social states, although the axioms do restrict the range of acceptable evaluative approaches."

It is useful to begin by clarifying what is meant by (weighted) utilitarianism.[44] Utilitarian theories evaluate the relative desirability of social alternatives in terms of a weighted sum of the utilities obtained by each person in society from the alternatives being considered. The weights used to aggregate the individual utilities are specified *a priori*. In total (or classical) utilitarianism, the weights are all equal to one, resulting in the simple sum-of-utilities criterion. In average utilitarianism, the weights are all equal to $1/I$, so alternatives are ranked according to their average utilities. With a fixed population, average and total utilitarianism obviously yield the same social ordering.

In traditional formulations of utilitarianism, individual utility is a quantitative measure of personal well-being.[45] Different concepts of well-being result in different versions of utilitarianism. For the early utilitarians, the focus is on mental states, and well-being is equated with pleasure, happiness, or, more generally, satisfaction. Some subsequent utilitarians identify well-being with desire fulfillment. For my purpose here, it is unimportant which of these concepts of utility is adopted. There is a third interpretation of utility in which utility is viewed as measuring preference.[46] As shall become clear later, I do not believe that this concept of utility can provide an adequate basis for utilitarianism.

In the first two interpretations of utility, utility is not derived from preference, but is instead a measure of satisfaction or desire fulfillment. With these interpretations of utility, there may or may not be a causal link between utility and preference. If there is, preference has no independent meaning; it is defined in terms of utility. Starting with individual i's utility function U_i on the set of alternatives (here the set of lotteries L), the preference relation R_i is *defined* by setting

$$pR_iq \quad \text{iff} \quad U_i(p) \geq U_i(q) \tag{6.1}$$

for all $p, q \in L$. Alternatively, utility and preference could have independent bases. In this case, there may be no reason to expect that

[44]   Henceforth, I use the term "utilitarianism" to refer to any weighted utilitarian theory.

[45]   See Sen (1987) for an overview of different concepts of utility. Nunan (1981, p. 587) notes the importance for utilitarianism of having utility be a measure of "some particular dimension of human experience."

[46]   Preferences could in turn be defined in terms of observed or hypothetical choice behavior.

(6.1) holds. If (6.1) is satisfied, I say that the preference ordering R_i and the utility function U_i are *congruent*. Henceforth, when utility has a non-preference basis, I assume that either preference is defined in terms of utility or is congruent with utility. In the third interpretation of utility, utility does not have meaning independent of preference. In this case, utility is the derived concept; the utility function is merely a representation of preferences.

Given exogenously specified utility functions U_i and exogenously specified weights a_i, $i = 1, \ldots ,I$, define

$$U(p) := \sum_{i=1}^{I} a_i U_i(p) \tag{6.2}$$

for all $p \in L$. In utilitarianism, the social ordering R is *defined* by setting

$$pRq \quad \text{iff} \quad U(p) \geq U(q) \tag{6.3}$$

for all $p, q \in L$. Although it is true that the social utility function U defined in (6.2) represents the social ordering R defined in (6.3), it is inappropriate to describe utilitarianism in terms of social utility representations, because the social ordering R is derived from the social utility function U, and not the other way round.

As noted, utilitarianism regards utility as measuring some aspect of personal well-being. As with any measure, utility may not be completely determinate. In (6.2), particular utility functions are used – namely, the vector of utility functions $(U_1, \ldots ,U_I)$. However, there may well be other utility functions that are equally satisfactory measures of the well-being of each person in society. The set of permissible substitutes for the utility functions $(U_1, \ldots ,U_I)$ is $\mathcal{I}(U_1, \ldots , U_I)$, the *information set* for $(U_1, \ldots ,U_I)$. If the vector $(\overline{U}_1, \ldots ,\overline{U}_I)$ is in $\mathcal{I}(U_1, \ldots ,U_I)$, the two sets of utility functions are said to be *informationally equivalent*. Different assumptions concerning the measurability and comparability of well-being (utility) result in different information sets for $(U_1, \ldots ,U_I)$.[47]

[47]   See Blackorby, Donaldson, and Weymark (1984), d'Aspremont (1985), or Sen (1986) for introductions to the literature on the measurability and comparability of utility functions.

For example, suppose that personal well-being is an ordinal concept and that well-being is interpersonally noncomparable. In this case, utility is said to be *ordinally measurable and noncomparable*. With this information assumption, if person i's well-being is measured by the utility function U_i, then it is equally well measured by the function $\overline{U}_i$ given by

$$\overline{U}_i(p) = \phi_i[U_i(p)] \qquad i = 1, \ldots ,I \tag{6.4}$$

for all $p \in L$ where ϕ_i is *any* increasing transform. The information set generated by this class of transforms is denoted $\mathcal{I}^{ON}(U_1, \ldots ,U_I)$. Because

$$U_i(p) \geq U_i(q) \qquad \text{iff} \qquad \phi_i[U_i(p)] \geq \phi_i[U_i(q)]$$

for all $p, q \in L$, for all $i - 1, \ldots ,I$, whenever ϕ_i is increasing, the class of person-specific transforms in (6.4) preserves intrapersonal comparisons of levels of well-being. However, because the transforms ϕ_i for different people can be chosen independently, this class of transforms does not, in general, preserve comparisons of levels of well-being interpersonally.

Utility is *ordinally measurable and fully comparable* if well-being is an ordinal concept and levels of well-being are interpersonally commensurate. In this case, (6.4) is replaced by

$$\overline{U}_i(p) = \phi[U_i(p)] \qquad i = 1, \ldots ,I \tag{6.5}$$

where ϕ is any increasing transform. The corresponding information set is denoted $\mathcal{I}^{OF}(U_1, \ldots ,U_I)$. Because the transform ϕ is common to all individuals,

$$U_i(p) \geq U_j(q) \qquad \text{iff} \qquad \phi[U_i(p)] \geq \phi[U_j(q)]$$

for all $p, q \in L$, for all $i, j = 1, \ldots ,I$. For $i \neq j$, this says that interpersonal comparisons of levels of well-being are meaningful and for $i = j$, this says that intrapersonal comparisons of well-being are meaningful.

Utility is *cardinally measurable and noncomparable* if (6.4) is replaced by

$$\overline{U}_i(p) = \alpha_i + \beta_i U_i(p) \tag{6.6}$$

for any $\alpha_i \in \mathbb{R}$ and any $\beta_i > 0$. The corresponding information set is denoted by $\mathcal{I}^{CN}(U_1, \ldots, U_I)$. In (6.6), U_i is subjected to an increasing affine transform. A transform ϕ_i is *difference-preserving* if

$$U_i(p) - U_i(q) \geq U_i(r) - U_i(s) \quad \text{iff} \quad \phi_i[U_i(p)] - \phi_i[U_i(q)] \geq \phi_i[U_i(r)] - \phi_i[U_i(s)]$$

for all p, q, r, $s \in L$. Clearly, an affine transform is difference-preserving, so the class of transforms in (6.6) preserves comparisons of both levels and increments of well-being intrapersonally, but not interpersonally.[48]

Utility is *cardinally measurable and unit comparable* if (6.4) is replaced with

$$\overline{U}_i(p) = \alpha_i + \beta U_i(p) \quad i = 1, \ldots, I \tag{6.7}$$

for any $\alpha_i \in \mathbb{R}$ and any $\beta > 0$. The corresponding information set is denoted by $\mathcal{I}^{CU}(U_1, \ldots, U_I)$. Because β is common to all individuals, we have

$$U_i(p) - U_j(q) \geq U_i(r) - U_j(s) \quad \text{iff} \quad \overline{U}_i(p) - \overline{U}_j(q) \geq \overline{U}_i(r) - \overline{U}_j(s)$$

for all p, q, r, $s \in L$ and for all $i, j = 1, \ldots, I$, so that this class of transforms preserves intrapersonal and interpersonal comparisons of gains and losses in well-being. However, because the α_i can be chosen independently, this class of transforms does not preserve interpersonal comparisons of levels of well-being.

---

[48]   For the set of lotteries L, if the preference ordering R_i corresponding to U_i is continuous, then the set of increasing affine transforms is equivalent to the set of difference-preserving transforms. If R_i is not continuous or if the set of alternatives is not connected, the class of difference-preserving transforms may well be larger than the class of increasing affine transforms. For discussions of this issue and its implications for utilitarianism, see Basu (1983) or Bossert (1989).

Utility is *cardinally measurable and fully comparable* if (6.4) is replaced with

$$\overline{U}_i(p) = \alpha + \beta U_i(p) \qquad i = 1, \ldots ,I \tag{6.8}$$

for any $\alpha \in \mathbb{R}$ and any $\beta > 0$. The corresponding information set is denoted by $\mathcal{I}^{CF}(U_1, \ldots ,U_I)$. Because α and β are common to all individuals, both levels and differences in well-being can be compared both intrapersonally and interpersonally.

Utility is *cardinally measurable and level comparable* if the set of permissible transforms consists of the transforms satisfying *both* (6.5) and (6.6). Provided the images of the utility functions U_i, $i = 1, \ldots ,I$, are the same for all individuals, it follows that utility is necessarily also cardinally measurable and fully comparable. In effect, the fact that interpersonal comparisons of levels of well-being are possible permits one to infer interpersonal comparisons of increments from intrapersonal comparisons of increments of well-being.[49]

In some circumstances, it is not necessary to exactly specify how precisely well-being can be measured. For example, it may be that the information set is a subset of $\mathcal{I}^{CU}(U_1, \ldots ,U_I)$, but the exact subset is left unspecified. In this case, the utility functions are said to satisfy *cardinal unit plus comparability*. With cardinal unit plus comparability, all vectors of utility functions $(\overline{U}_1, \ldots ,\overline{U}_I) \in \mathcal{I}(U_1, \ldots ,U_I)$ satisfy (6.7) but not all vectors of functions that satisfy (6.7) need be in $\mathcal{I}(U_1, \ldots ,U_I)$.

For utilitarianism to be a meaningful doctrine, it is necessary that the same social ordering R be obtained for all vectors of utility functions in the information set corresponding to $(U_1, \ldots ,U_I)$. Utilitarianism is meaningful if utility is cardinally measurable and unit comparable because the substitution of any vector of utility functions from $\mathcal{I}^{CU}(U_1, \ldots ,U_I)$ into (6.2) and (6.3) yields the same social ordering R found using $(U_1, \ldots ,U_I)$. That is,

$$\sum_{i=1}^{I} a_i \overline{U}_i(p) \geq \sum_{i=1}^{I} a_i \overline{U}_i(q) \quad \text{iff} \quad \sum_{i=1}^{I} a_i U_i(p) \geq \sum_{i=1}^{I} a_i U_i(q) \tag{6.9}$$

[49]   See Blackorby and Donaldson (1991) for details.

for all p, $q \in L$ whenever $(\overline{U}_1, \ldots, \overline{U}_I)$ satisfies (6.7). As a consequence, utilitarianism is meaningful if utility satisfies cardinal unit plus comparability.

Utilitarianism is not meaningful if utility is *only* ordinally measurable, even if utility levels can be compared.[50] For example, if the transform ϕ in (6.5) is given by $\phi(t) = t^3$, in general (6.9) will not hold, and the social ordering in (6.3) will depend on whether the functions $(U_1, \ldots, U_I)$ or the functions $(\overline{U}_1, \ldots, \overline{U}_I)$ are used to measure individuals' well-being.

An implication of these remarks is that the third interpretation of utility discussed here does not provide an adequate foundation for utilitarianism. Recall that in this interpretation, utility is regarded as measuring preference. If the preferences being measured are the individual orderings, R_i, $i = 1, \ldots, I$, of the lotteries in L, then utility is ordinally measurable and noncomparable. If the preference being measured is an extended ordering $\hat{R}$ of the extended lotteries $\hat{L}$, then only the ordinal properties of any extended utility function $\hat{U}$ representing $\hat{R}$ have any significance. This means that $\widehat{\overline{U}}$ and $\hat{U}$ are informationally equivalent whenever there exists an increasing transform ϕ such that

$$\widehat{\overline{U}}(\pi) = \phi[\hat{U}(\pi)] \tag{6.10}$$

for all $\pi \in \hat{L}$. Provided that the Principle of Acceptance is satisfied, it then follows from (5.12) that (6.5) is satisfied – that is, utility is ordinally measurable and fully comparable.[51,52] Preference over lotteries, whether simple or extended, is an ordinal concept. In either case, the

[50] Strictly speaking, this statement depends on $\mathcal{U}$, the image of $(U_1, \ldots, U_I)$ over L, not being too degenerate.

[51] Note that for $i \neq j$, $U_i(p)$ and $U_j(p)$ are defined using different extended lotteries; the former using a lottery in which the observer is i for certain, and the latter using a lottery in which the observer is j for certain.

[52] Harsanyi (1978, p. 227) recognizes that his Aggregation Theorem "*does not depend on the possibility of interpersonal utility comparisons.*" See also Harsanyi (1979, p. 294). However, Harsanyi (1978, p. 228) mistakenly claims that his Impartial Observer Theorem "as well as the equiprobability model itself, does presuppose the possibility of interpersonal comparisons of utility differences (increments)." See also Harsanyi (1979, p. 295). This statement is clearly wrong, as the extended preference ordering makes use of interpersonal comparisons of utility levels, not differences. Harsanyi (1977a, pp. 55–57) recognizes that utilitarianism requires the use of interpersonal comparisons of utility differences but, as I argue later, his discussion of this issue is flawed by his mistaken belief that the expected utility axioms require the use of a von Neumann–Morgenstern utility function.

admissible utility representations are too indeterminate to be used to construct a utilitarian social ordering.

The implications of this discussion for Harsanyi's theorems are clear. If utility *only* has meaning as a representation of preferences on lotteries or extended lotteries, then Sen is right in arguing that Harsanyi's theorems do not provide characterizations of utilitarianism, but are instead merely social representation theorems. Furthermore, with this view of utility, it is arbitrary to only consider von Neumann—Morgenstern utility functions, as Harsanyi does. As a consequence, no significance should be attached to the shape of the contours of the social welfare function. As we have seen, whether or not these contours are linear depends solely on whether individual preferences in the Aggregation Theorem or extended preferences in the Impartial Observer Theorem are represented by von Neumann—Morgenstern utility functions.[53]

As noted earlier, preferences could be defined in terms of observed or hypothetical choice behavior. In this behaviorist approach to preference, pR_iq means that person i is willing to choose lottery p when offered a choice between lotteries p and q. It then follows that pP_iq means that person i is only willing to choose p, and pI_iq means that person i is willing to choose either p or q when choosing from the set $\{p, q\}$. Similarly, $\pi\hat{R}\rho$ means that the impartial observer is willing to choose the extended ordering π when offered the choice of π and ρ.

Harsanyi claims that if behavior is consistent with the expected utility axioms, then observing how person i makes choices over lotteries permits one to make inferences concerning utility gains and losses for this individual.[54] The argument is as follows. Suppose the compound lottery A offers the lotteries p and q with equal probability, and the compound lottery B offers the lotteries r and s with the same

---

[53]   The discussion in this paragraph also applies to Hammond's (1983, 1987) versions of Harsanyi's theorems. Hammond does not start with preferences but instead considers individual and social choice correspondences (behavior norms, in his terminology) on a class of dynamic decision trees. (Hammond points out a number of problems with respecting individual choices and so formulates the individual choice correspondences in a way that need not completely respect consumer sovereignity.) Using revealed preference arguments, Hammond shows that these choices are rationalized by individual and social preference relations on the set of consequences that satisfy the expected utility hypothesis. Hammond represents these preferences by von Neumann—Morgenstern utility functions, but offers no justification for choosing these particular representations.

[54]   This argument is developed at length in Harsanyi (1979, pp. 296–297) and more briefly in Harsanyi (1977a, p. 293).

probabilities. Further suppose that person i chooses A over B – that is, strictly prefers A to B. If i's preferences are represented by the von Neumann–Morgenstern utility function V_i, it then follows from the Expected Utility Theorem that

$$\frac{1}{2} V_i(p) + \frac{1}{2} V_i(q) > \frac{1}{2} V_i(r) + \frac{1}{2} V_i(s)$$

or, equivalently,

$$V_i(p) - V_i(s) > V_i(r) - V_i(q) \tag{6.11}$$

Equation (6.11) is interpreted as saying that the utility gain obtained by replacing lottery s with lottery p exceeds the utility gain obtained by replacing lottery q with lottery r. This statement is taken to be meaningful because the inequality in (6.11) is satisfied for any von Neumann–Morgenstern representation of i's preferences.

However, this argument presupposes that only von Neumann–Morgenstern utility functions are to be used to represent this person's preferences. This is unjustified, as *any* ordinal transform of V_i also rationalizes i's choices and, in general, the inequality in (6.11) is not invariant to arbitrary increasing transforms of V_i. The Expected Utility Theorem merely says that i's preferences *can* be represented by a von Neumann–Morgenstern utility function; it does not say that i's preferences *must* be represented by a von Neumann–Morgenstern utility function.[55],[56]

[55]   The mistaken belief that expected utility theory allows one to make comparisons of utility differences is so commonplace that Luce and Raiffa (1957, p. 32) single it out as Fallacy 3 on their list of common misinterpretations of the theory. See Fishburn (1989) for a detailed historical discussion of this issue.

[56]   Similar remarks apply to extended preference orderings. Suppose the impartial observer prefers a fifty-fifty chance of obtaining π or ρ to a fifty-fifty chance of obtaining σ or τ, where π and τ are extended lotteries in which the observer is i for certain and ρ and σ are extended lotteries in which the observer is j for certain. Using the von Neumann–Morgenstern utility function $\hat{V}$ to represent the extended preferences, it follows from (5.3) that the analogue to (6.11) is

$$V_i(p) - V_i(t) > V_j(s) - V_j(r)$$

where $p_m = \pi_{mi}$, $t_m = \tau_{mi}$, $s_m = \sigma_{mj}$, and $r_m = \rho_{mj}$, for all $m = 1, \ldots ,M$. One cannot use this inequality to make interpersonal comparisons of utility differences as the inequality is not invariant to an arbitrary increasing transform of $\hat{V}$, and such transforms are permissible if utility is only a measure of preference.

In the *formal* statement and development of Harsanyi's theorems, preferences are primitives of the model. In the aggregation model, these primitives are the individual and social preference relations on L. In the impartial observer model, these primitives are the individual preference relations on L and the extended preference relation on $\hat{L}$. In the formal development of the Aggregation Theorem and the Impartial Observer Theorem, utility functions are only used as representations of these preference orderings. As we have seen, if utility *only* has meaning as a representation of preference, then Harsanyi's theorems should not be interpreted as being theorems about utilitarianism, but should instead be regarded as theorems about the representability of social preferences.

But what if one of the other interpretations of utility is adopted? Harsanyi's theorems do not preclude an alternative interpretation of well-being, provided utility and preference are congruent. Indeed, in Harsanyi's discussion of the nature of interpersonal utility comparisons, he appears to regard well-being as involving something more than just preference.

Harsanyi (1979, p. 301) provides a nice summary of his views on the nature of interpersonal utility comparisons:

> From a logical point of view, interpersonal utility comparisons are based on what I have called the *similarity* postulate. . . . By this I mean the principle that, given the basic similarity in human nature (i.e., in the fundamental psychological laws governing human behavior and human attitudes), it is reasonable to assume that different people will show very *similar* psychological reactions to any given objective situation, and will derive much the *same* utility or disutility from it—*once proper allowances have been made for any empirically observed differences* in their biological make-ups, in their social positions, in their educational and cultural backgrounds and, more generally, in their past life histories. . . . Thus, from a philosophical point of view, interpersonal utility comparisons have the status of *empirical* hypotheses based on a *nonempirical* a priori principle, the similarity postulate.[57]

---

[57] The phrase "similarity postulate" first appears in Harsanyi (1977c), although the basic idea occurs in Harsanyi (1955, 1977a), as well as in many of Harsanyi's other articles.

After describing some everyday examples of the use of interpersonal utility comparisons, Harsanyi (1977c, p. 638) says:

> Simple reflection will show that the basic intellectual operation in such interpersonal comparisons is imaginative empathy. We imagine ourselves to be in the shoes of another person, and ask ourselves the questions, "If I were now really in *his* position, and had *his* taste, *his* education, *his* social background, *his* cultural values, and *his* psychological make-up, then what would now be *my* preferences between various alternatives, and how much satisfaction or dissatisfaction would I derive from any given alternative?"

In effect, Harsanyi is saying that all interpersonal utility comparisons can in principle be reduced to intrapersonal comparisons. He regards everyone as being fundamentally the same (his similarity postulate), so that an individual's well-being (utility) can be thought of as a function of the alternative (the lottery) obtained and the "objective causal variables" determining this person's background and makeup, with the function relating well-being to the alternative and the causal variables being the same for everyone. Thus, any individual i could, in principle, determine the well-being of any other individual j by simply imagining how well off i himself would be with j's alternative and j's causal variables.[58] As we have seen in the previous section, this kind of imaginative empathy is central to Harsanyi's impartial observer model and to his notion of ethical preferences.

The references to "psychological reactions" and "satisfaction" in these passages suggest that Harsanyi regards individual well-being as involving more than just preference. Indeed, these passages also suggest that Harsanyi has a concept of well-being that shares much in common with the early utilitarians. This raises the possibility that utility satisfies cardinal unit plus comparability, the necessary precondition for utilitarianism to be meaningful.

Implicit in Harsanyi's discussion of the Impartial Observer Theorem is what I call the *Principle of Welfare Identity*.

---

[58] See Harsanyi (1977a, pp. 57–61) for an elaboration of this point.

Principle of Welfare Identity

For any $i = 1, \ldots, I$ and any $\pi \in \hat{L}$, if for all $m = 1, \ldots, M$, $\pi_{mj} = p_m$ if $j = i$ and $\pi_{mj} = 0$ otherwise, then the well-being of the impartial observer with the extended lottery π is equivalent to the well-being of person i with the lottery p.

The Principle of Welfare Identity implies the Principle of Acceptance – that is, the impartial observer's ordering of extended lotteries in which he is i for certain agrees with i's ordering of the corresponding simple lotteries. For example, suppose that π and ρ are lotteries in which the observer is i for certain with corresponding simple lotteries p and r, respectively. Suppose person i's well-being is measured by the utility function U_i. Then by the Principle of Welfare Identity, we can set $\hat{U}(\pi) = U_i(p)$ and $\hat{U}(\rho) = U_i(r)$, where $\hat{U}$ is a utility function for the observer.[59] The Principle of Acceptance then follows from (6.1) applied to $\hat{U}$ and U_i.

Given the individual utility functions, the Principle of Acceptance completely determines the ranking of any two extended lotteries in which the observer is the same person for certain. The Principle of Welfare Identity also completely determines the ranking of any two extended lotteries in which the observer is someone for certain, with the person possibly differing between the two lotteries. For example, suppose that π is an extended lottery in which the observer is i for certain with corresponding simple lottery p and ρ is an extended lottery in which the observer is j for certain with corresponding simple lottery r. Suppose i's and j's well-beings are measured with the utility functions U_i and U_j, respectively, where the scales have been calibrated so that $U_i(q) = U_j(s)$ means that person i is as well off with lottery q as person j is with lottery s. By the Principle of Welfare Identity, we can set $\hat{U}(\pi) = U_i(p)$ and $\hat{U}(\rho) = U_j(r)$. It then follows that $\pi \hat{R} \rho$ if and only if i is as well off with p as j is with r.[60]

With the explicit adoption of the Principle of Welfare Identity, Harsanyi's Impartial Observer Theorem can be used to justify utili-

---

[59]   Note that here I am starting with the individual utility function and using it to define $\hat{U}(\pi)$ and $\hat{U}(\rho)$. This is the reverse of the procedure set out in (5.3).

[60]   This argument presupposes that levels of well-being are comparable. Note that this argument does not require that U_i and U_j be von Neumann–Morgenstern utility functions, nor even that individual preferences satisfy the expected utility axioms.

tarianism if (i) well-being is cardinally measurable and fully comparable, and (ii) each person's well-being, including that of the impartial
observer, is measured by a von Neumann–Morgenstern utility function.[61] To see this, suppose that person i's well-being is measured by
the von Neumann–Morgenstern utility function V_i, $i = 1, \ldots ,I$,
where the functions have been calibrated to incorporate the interpersonal comparisons. Let $\hat{V}$ be the impartial observer's extended utility
function calibrated so that $\hat{V}(\pi) = V_i(p)$ if π guarantees that the
observer will be person i with the lottery p. Now consider any $\pi \in \hat{L}$.
Because $\hat{V}$ is a von Neumann–Morgenstern utility function, (5.2) is
satisfied. By the Principle of Welfare Identity, it then follows that

$$\hat{V}(\pi) = \sum_{m=1}^{M} \sum_{i=1}^{I} \pi_{mi} V_i(e^m) \tag{6.12}$$

for all $\pi \in \hat{L}$. Thus, for all $\pi, \rho \in \hat{L}$,

$$\pi \hat{R} \rho \qquad \text{iff} \qquad \sum_{m=1}^{M} \sum_{i=1}^{I} \pi_{mi} V_i(e^m) \geq \sum_{m=1}^{M} \sum_{i=1}^{I} \rho_{mi} V_i(e^m) \tag{6.13}$$

In other words, the extended ordering $\hat{R}$ is completely determined by,
and can be constructed from, knowledge of how well off each person
is with each pure alternative x_m. This implies that all observers will
agree on the extended ordering $\hat{R}$ provided they have sufficient information to determine the individual utility functions and perform the
interpersonal comparisons.[62] Furthermore, the ordering in (6.13) is
unaffected if $(V_1, \ldots ,V_I)$ is replaced by any other list of utility functions in the information set corresponding to $(V_1, \ldots ,V_I)$. By restricting attention to lotteries in which there is an equal chance of
being any member of society, we obtain the ordering R over L in
(5.7). Because the utility functions $(V_1, \ldots ,V_I)$ measure the well-
being of the members of society, and because the ordering R is invariant to the choice of this profile (from the information set) to measure

[61]   The following argument also holds if utility can be determined more exactly
than is possible with cardinal measurability and full comparability.

[62]   Harsanyi (1977a, pp. 57–60) notes that $\hat{R}$ could be observer-dependent if observers possess incomplete information about the causal variables characterizing each person's background and make-up or incomplete information about the general psychological laws relating well-being to the alternatives and to the causal variables.

well-being, one can conclude from the additive form of (5.7) that R is the average utilitarian ordering.[63]

This discussion has established the following theorem.

Theorem 10. Suppose (i) that well-being is cardinally measurable and fully comparable, and (ii) that each person's well-being, including that of the impartial observer, is measured by a von Neumann–Morgenstern utility function. Let V_i be person i's utility function on L $i = 1, \ldots, I$, and $\hat{V}$ be the impartial observer's utility function on $\hat{L}$. If the Principle of Welfare Identity is satisfied, then $\hat{V}$ is uniquely determined from $(V_1, \ldots, V_I)$ by (6.12). The impartial observer's extended ordering $\hat{R}$ of $\hat{L}$ satisfies (6.13) and his preference ordering R defined in (5.6) satisfies (5.7). In addition, the social ordering R^* in (5.9) satisfies (3.16) and the social welfare function in (5.10) represents R^*. Furthermore, the same orderings $\hat{R}$, R, and R^* are obtained using any list of utility functions $(\overline{V}_1, \ldots, \overline{V}_I)$ in $\mathcal{I}^{CF}(V_1, \ldots, V_I)$.

Pattanaik (1968, pp. 1158–1160) appears to accept the assumptions of Theorem 10 but does not believe that they imply that all observers will agree on the derived social ordering R. He argues instead that R also depends on the risk attitudes of the observer. Pattanaik's argument is captured in the following example. Suppose $I = 2$ and the observer wants to rank e^1 and e^2 – that is, either x_1 or x_2 occurs for certain. Further suppose that $V_1(e^2) > V_1(e^1) = V_2(e^1) > V_2(e^2)$. The impartial observer ranks e^1 and e^2 using the corresponding impartial lotteries. In the first impartial lottery the observer obtains utility $V_1(e^1) = V_2(e^1)$ for certain. In the second impartial lottery there is a fifty-fifty chance of receiving $V_1(e^2)$ or $V_2(e^2)$. Pattanaik claims that a sufficiently risk-averse observer will prefer e^1 to e^2 but will instead prefer e^2 to e^1 if he is sufficiently risk-loving. This argument is flawed, because the observer's expected utility for the second lottery must be

$$\frac{1}{2} V_1(e^2) + \frac{1}{2} V_2(e^2)\text{[64]}$$

[63] If for all $\pi \in \hat{L}$ there exists a $p \in L$ and an $i \in \{1, \ldots, I\}$ such that $\hat{V}(\pi) = V_i(p)$, then the assumption that $\hat{V}$ is a von Neumann–Morgenstern utility function can be weakened to the requirement that $\hat{R}$ satisfies the expected utility axioms. It then follows from the assumption that each V_i is a von Neumann–Morgenstern function that $\hat{V}$ must be one as well.

[64] The risk attitudes of the members of society affect the orderings $\hat{R}$ and R through their influence on the functional forms of the utility functions V_i. There is a

For the argument used to establish Theorem 10 to be valid, it is essential that utility not be simply a measure of preference. Although comparisons of levels of well-being are sufficient to construct the extended ordering in (6.13) and from it the social ordering in (5.7), it must be possible to compare increments in well-being for the extended ordering $\hat{R}$ and hence the social ordering R to be invariant to the choice of the particular utility functions used to measure well-being from the relevant information set.

It is also important that everyone, including the impartial observer, has his well-being measured by a von Neumann–Morgenstern utility function. It is not sufficient to merely assume that each person's utility function is congruent with preferences that satisfy the expected utility axioms. For an extended lottery π in which there is some uncertainty as to which person the observer will become, the determination of $\hat{V}(\pi)$ in (6.12), from knowledge of the well-being obtained from each of the pure alternatives by each individual, makes critical use of the fact that von Neumann–Morgenstern utility functions satisfy (2.2).

Harsanyi has never provided satisfactory justifications for either of these critical assumptions. He restricts attention to von Neumann–Morgenstern utility functions because he mistakenly believes that their use is *required* by the adoption of the expected utility axioms. He compounds this error by also claiming that these axioms imply that utility is cardinally measurable. Combining this measurability condition with interpersonal comparisons of utility levels results, as we have seen, in utility being cardinally measurable and fully comparable. Thus, although both of the critical assumptions used in the preceding argument are present, at least implicitly, in Harsanyi's analysis, they are obtained using fallacious arguments.

It is perhaps not too difficult to use Harsanyi's theory of interpersonal utility comparisons to justify assuming that both utility levels and differences can be compared. However, it is more problematic to justify the assumption that each utility function is a von Neumann–Morgenstern function. In Harsanyi's theory, interpersonal comparisons are empirical statements. It is therefore an empirical matter

large literature on the role attitudes toward risk play in Harsanyi's theorems. Particularly good introductions to the issues involved may be found in Hammond (1983, 1987).

whether it is appropriate to measure utility using von Neumann–Morgenstern functions or not. Although satisfaction of the expected utility axioms is necessary for utility to be von Neumann–Morgenstern, it is not sufficient.[65]

This observation has implications both for Harsanyi's version of the Impartial Observer Theorem (Theorem 9) and my own version of the Impartial Observer Theorem (Theorem 10). If well-being is not measured by von Neumann–Morgenstern functions, but, for example, the assumptions of Theorem 9 are satisfied, then the individual utility functions U_i in (5.12) represent individual preferences but they do not measure well-being. It then follows from the discussion in the previous section that although the social welfare function is linear in terms of individual von Neumann–Morgenstern values, it is not linear in terms of individual welfare, as Sen (1976, 1977, 1986) has observed.[66]

The assumption that interpersonal comparisons are empirically based also raises new concerns about the reasonableness of supposing that the impartial observer's preferences satisfy the expected utility axioms. For example, one could well imagine that the facts of the case require person i's well-being to be measured by a von Neumann–Morgenstern utility function, whereas they require person j's well-being to be measured by a non-von Neumann–Morgenstern utility function, even if both people's preferences satisfy the expected utility axioms. But then it is impossible for the impartial observer's extended preferences to satisfy both the Principle of Welfare Identity and the expected utility axioms.[67] It thus seems that although identifying well-being with satisfaction, or some other mental state, opens up the possibility of interpreting Harsanyi's Impartial Observer Theorem as a theorem about utilitarianism, doing so raises issues that Harsanyi has not treated in a satisfactory manner.

Adopting a non-preference-based view of well-being and supposing

[65]   Sen's (1979, 1976) discussion of individual welfares not being "V-values" is making the point that when well-being (welfare) is non-preference-based, utility functions may not be von Neumann–Morgenstern functions even if the expected utility axioms are satisfied.

[66]   The examples in Arrow (1973, pp. 256–257) and Sen (1986, pp. 1123–1124) illustrate this point.

[67]   For $\hat{R}$ to satisfy the expected utility axioms it is necessary that everyone's utility functions be a von Neumann–Morgenstern function or that there is a single ordinal transform that can convert everyone's utility functions into von Neumann–Morgenstern functions.

that interpersonal comparisons of utility differences are possible has implications for Harsanyi's Aggregation Theorem as well. When such comparisons are possible, Harsanyi (1979, p. 294) proposes adding an additional axiom.[68] In his words:

> *Axiom D: Equal treatment of all individuals.* If all individuals' utility functions $U_1, \ldots, U_n$ are expressed in *equal utility units* (as judged by individual j on the basis of interpersonal utility comparisons), then the social welfare function W_j of individual j must assign the *same* weight to all these utility functions.

In this passage, Harsanyi is interpreting the social preference ordering as j's ethical preferences, and his W_j function corresponds to the social utility function V in Theorem 3. By "expressed in equal utility units" he means that utility differences are comparable.

What is particularly noteworthy about this quotation is that Harsanyi simply assumes that the individual utility weights are equal. The justification for this assumption is spelled out in Harsanyi (1975, p. 322):

> When we are assigning the same quantitative measure to utility changes affecting two individuals . . . , then we are implicitly asserting that these utility changes for both individuals involve human needs of equal urgency. But, this being so, it would be highly unfair – and, in many cases, quite inhumane – discrimination to claim that, as a matter of principle, satisfaction of one man's needs should have a lower social priority than satisfaction of the other man's needs should have.

If these quotations are to be taken at face value, it seems that Harsanyi is *constructing* the social ordering as in (6.3). But that means Harsanyi is simply assuming utilitarianism, and is not deriving it from more fundamental principles.[69] If this interpretation is correct, it lends credence to Sen's (1975, p. 251) remark that "an

---

[68]   See also Harsanyi (1978, p. 227). The same axiom appears in earlier writings, but is not as clearly expressed.

[69]   The discussion in Harsanyi (1977a, pp. 81–82) seems to support this interpretation of Harsanyi's theory.

axiomatic justification of utilitarianism would have more content to it if it started off at a place somewhat more distant from the ultimate destination."

7. Conclusion

The main points to emerge from the Harsanyi–Sen debate can be summarized quite easily.

If utility only has meaning as a representation of preference, then Sen is correct in regarding Harsanyi's theorems as social utility representation theorems. In this interpretation, Harsanyi is simply mistaken in believing that the expected utility axioms (i) require the use of von Neumann–Morgenstern utility functions, and (ii) imply that utility is cardinally measurable. No significance should be attached to the linearity or nonlinearity of the social welfare function, as the curvature of this function depends solely on whether or not von Neumann–Morgenstern representations are used, and the use of such representations is arbitrary.

If utility does not simply measure preference, Harsanyi's Impartial Observer Theorem can be interpreted as an axiomatization of utilitarianism provided (i) well-being is cardinally measurable and fully comparable, (ii) each person's well-being, including that of the impartial observer, is measured by a von Neumann–Morgenstern utility function, and (iii) the Principle of Welfare Identity is satisfied. However, such a concept of utility raises concerns about the appropriateness of assuming that utility takes on a von Neumann–Morgenstern form and about the appropriateness of assuming that the impartial observer's preferences satisfy the expected utility axioms. With this interpretation of utility, the use of Harsanyi's Axiom D appears to trivialize the Aggregation Theorem, as this axiom essentially assumes that the social welfare function is utilitarian.

To conclude on a more positive note, let me concur with Sen (1986, p. 1124) in saying:

. . . . the failure to provide a fully-fledged axiomatic derivation of utilitarianism does not render Harsanyi's results useless. Indeed, far from it. The representation theorem is of much interest in itself, and Harsanyi's framework of impersonal choice has proved to be one of the most fruitful ones in social ethics.

To which I can add that Harsanyi's discussion of the nature of interpersonal utility comparisons is an important contribution to a topic on which there is much disagreement and confusion.

References

K.J. Arrow (1951), *Social Choice and Individual Values*, New York: John Wiley.

K.J. Arrow (1973), "Some Ordinalist-Utilitarian Notes on Rawls' Theory of Justice," *Journal of Philosophy*, 70, pp. 309–321. Reprinted in Arrow (1983), pp. 96–114.

K.J. Arrow (1983), *Collected Papers of Kenneth J. Arrow, Volume 1: Social Choice and Justice*, Cambridge, Mass.: Harvard University Press.

K.J. Arrow and M.D. Intriligator, eds. (1986), *Handbook of Mathematical Economics: Volume III*, Amsterdam: North-Holland.

K. Basu (1983), "Cardinal Utility, Utilitarianism, and a Class of Invariance Axioms in Welfare Analysis," *Journal of Mathematical Economics*, 12, pp. 193–206.

A. Bergson (1938), "A Reformulation of Certain Aspects of Welfare Economics," *Quarterly Journal of Economics*, 52, pp. 310–334.

T. Bezembinder and P. van Acker (1987), "Factual Versus Representational Utilities and Their Interdimensional Comparisons," *Social Choice and Welfare*, 4, pp. 79–104.

C. Blackorby and D. Donaldson (1991), "Adult-Equivalence Scales, Interpersonal Comparisons of Well-being, and Applied Welfare Economics," this volume.

C. Blackorby, D. Donaldson, and J.A. Weymark (1980), "On John Harsanyi's Defences of Utilitarianism," Discussion Paper No. 8013, Center for Operations Research and Econometrics, Université Catholique de Louvain.

C. Blackorby, D. Donaldson, and J.A. Weymark (1984), "Social Choice with Interpersonal Utility Comparisons: A Diagrammatic Introduction," *International Economic Review*, 25, pp. 327–356.

C. Blackorby, D. Donaldson, and J.A. Weymark (1991), "Single Profile Social Choice with State Contingent Alternatives," manuscript in preparation.

K. Border (1981), "Notes on von Neumann−Morgenstern Social Welfare Functions," unpublished manuscript, California Institute of Technology.

K. Border (1985), "More on Harsanyi's Utilitarian Cardinal Welfare Function," *Social Choice and Welfare*, 1, pp. 279–281.

W. Bossert (1989), "On Intra- and Interpersonal Utility Comparisons," Discussion Paper No. 89-25, Department of Economics, University of British Columbia.

J. Broome (1987), "Utilitarianism and Expected Utility," *Journal of Philosophy*, 84, pp. 405–422.

J. Broome (1989), "Should Social Preferences be Consistent?," *Economics and Philosophy*, 5, pp. 7–17.

R. Butts and J. Hintikka, eds. (1977), *Foundational Problems in the Special Sciences*, Dordrecht: D. Reidel.

T. Coulhan and P. Mongin (1989), "Social Choice Theory in the Case of von Neumann–Morgenstern Utilities," *Social Choice and Welfare*, 6, pp. 175–187.

C. d'Aspremont (1985), "Axioms for Social Welfare Orderings," in L. Hurwicz, D. Schmeidler, and H. Sonnenschein (1985), pp. 19–76.

G. Debreu (1959), *Theory of Value*, New York: John Wiley.

P.A. Diamond (1967), "Cardinal Welfare, Individualistic Ethics, and Interpersonal Comparisons of Utility: Comment," *Journal of Political Economy*, 75, pp. 765–766.

R. Deschamps and L. Gevers (1977), "Separability, Risk-Bearing and Social Welfare Judgements," *European Economic Review*, 10, pp. 77–94. Reprinted in Laffont (1979), pp. 145–160.

Z. Domotor (1979), "Ordered Sum and Tensor Product of Linear Utility Structures," *Theory and Decision*, 11, pp. 375–399.

G.R. Feiwel, ed. (1987a), *Arrow and the Ascent of Modern Economic Theory*, London: Macmillan.

G.R. Feiwel, ed. (1987b), *Arrow and the Foundations of the Theory of Economic Policy*, London: Macmillan.

P.C. Fishburn (1984), "On Harsanyi's Utilitarian Cardinal Welfare Theorem," *Theory and Decision*, 17, pp. 21–28.

P.C. Fishburn (1989), "Retrospective on the Utility Theory of von Neumann–Morgenstern," *Journal of Risk and Uncertainty*, 2, pp. 127–158.

M. Fleming (1952), "A Cardinal Concept of Welfare," *Quarterly Journal of Economics*, 66, pp. 366–384.

P.J. Hammond (1983), "Ex-Post Optimality as a Dynamically Consistent Objective for Collective Choice Under Uncertainty," in P.K. Pattanaik and M. Salles (1983), pp. 175–205.

P.J. Hammond (1987), "On Reconciling Arrow's Theory of Social Choice with Harsanyi's Fundamental Utilitarianism," in G.R. Feiwel (1987b), pp. 179–221.

J.C. Harsanyi (1953), "Cardinal Utility in Welfare Economics and in the Theory of Risk-Taking," *Journal of Political Economy*, 61, pp. 434–435. Reprinted in Harsanyi (1976), pp. 3–5.

J.C. Harsanyi (1955), "Cardinal Welfare, Individualistic Ethics, and Interpersonal Comparisons of Utility," *Journal of Political Economy*, 63, pp. 309–321. Reprinted in Harsanyi (1976), pp. 6–23.

J.C. Harsanyi (1975), "Nonlinear Social Welfare Functions: Do Welfare Economists Have a Special Exemption from Bayesian Rationality?," *Theory and Decision*, 6, pp. 311–332. Reprinted in Harsanyi (1976), pp. 64–85.

J.C. Harsanyi (1976), *Essays on Ethics, Social Behavior, and Scientific Explanation*, Dordrecht: D. Reidel.

J.C. Harsanyi (1977a), *Rational Behavior and Bargaining Equilibrium in Games and Social Situations*, Cambridge: Cambridge University Press.

J.C. Harsanyi (1977b), "Nonlinear Social Welfare Functions: A Rejoinder to Professor Sen," in R. Butts and J. Hintikka (1977), pp. 293–296.

J.C. Harsanyi (1977c), "Morality and the Theory of Rational Behavior," *Social Research,* 44, pp. 623–656.

J.C. Harsanyi (1978), "Bayesian Decision Theory and Utilitarian Ethics," *American Economic Review, Papers and Proceedings,* 68, pp. 223–228.

J.C. Harsanyi (1979), "Bayesian Decision Theory, Rule Utilitarianism, and Arrow's Impossibility Theorem," *Theory and Decision,* 11, pp. 289–317.

J.C. Harsanyi (1987), "Von Neumann–Morgenstern Utilities, Risk Taking, and Welfare," in G.R. Feiwel (1987a), pp. 545–558.

I.N. Hernstein and J. Milnor (1953), "An Axiomatic Approach to Measurable Utility," *Econometrica,* 21, pp. 291–297.

L. Hurwicz, D. Schmeidler, and H. Sonnenschein, eds. (1985), *Social Goals and Social Organization,* Cambridge: Cambridge University Press.

J.-J. Laffont, ed. (1979), *Aggregation and Revelation of Preferences,* Amsterdam: North-Holland.

J.-J. Laffont (1989), *The Economics of Uncertainty and Information,* Cambridge, Mass.: MIT Press.

R.D. Luce and H. Raiffa (1957), *Games and Decisions,* New York: John Wiley.

M. Machina (1987), "Choice Under Uncertainty: Problems Solved and Unsolved," *Journal of Economic Perspectives,* 1, pp. 121–154.

E. Malinvaud (1952), "Note on von Neumann–Morgenstern's Strong Independence Axiom," *Econometrica,* 20, p. 679.

J. Margolis and H. Guitton, eds. (1969), *Public Economics,* London: Macmillan.

J. Marschak (1950), "Rational Behavior, Uncertain Prospects, and Measurable Utility," *Econometrica,* 18, pp. 111–141.

E.F. McClennen (1981), "Utility and Equity: Sen vs. Harsanyi," *Journal of Philosophy,* 78, pp. 600–601.

R. Nunan (1981), "Harsanyi vs. Sen: Does Social Welfare Weigh Subjective Preferences?," *Journal of Philosophy,* 78, pp. 586–600.

P.K. Pattanaik (1968), "Risk, Impersonality, and the Social Welfare Function," *Journal of Political Economy,* 76, pp. 1152–1169.

P.K. Pattanaik and M. Salles, eds. (1983), *Social Choice and Welfare,* Amsterdam: North-Holland.

J. Rawls (1971), *A Theory of Justice,* Cambridge, Mass.: Harvard University Press.

M.D. Resnick (1983), "A Restriction on a Theorem of Harsanyi," *Theory and Decision,* 15, pp. 309–320.

P.A. Samuelson (1947), *Foundations of Economic Analysis,* Cambridge, Mass.: Harvard University Press.

L.J. Savage (1954), *The Foundations of Statistics,* New York: John Wiley.

S. Selinger (1986), "Harsanyi's Aggregation Theorem without Selfish Preferences," *Theory and Decision,* 20, pp. 53–62.

A.K. Sen (1969), "Planners' Preferences: Optimality, Distribution and Social Welfare," in J. Margolis and H. Guitton (1969), pp. 201–221.

A.K. Sen (1970), *Collective Choice and Social Welfare,* San Francisco: Holden-Day.

A.K. Sen (1976), "Welfare Inequalities and Rawlsian Axiomatics," *Theory and Decision,* 7, pp. 243–262. Reprinted in R. Butts and J. Hintikka (1977), pp. 271–292.

A.K. Sen (1977), "Non-Linear Social Welfare Functions: A Reply to Professor Harsanyi," in R. Butts and J. Hintikka (1977), pp. 297–302.

A.K. Sen (1986), "Social Choice Theory," in K.J. Arrow and M.D. Intriligator (1986), pp. 1073–1181.

A.K. Sen (1987), *The Standard of Living,* Cambridge: Cambridge University Press.

R. Sugden (1986), "New Developments in the Theory of Choice Under Uncertainty," *Bulletin of Economic Research,* 38, pp. 1–24.

W. Vickery (1945), "Measuring Marginal Utility by Reactions to Risk," *Econometrica,* 13, pp. 319–333.

J. von Neumann and O. Morgenstern (1947), *Theory of Games and Economic Behavior, Second Edition,* Princeton: Princeton University Press.

J.A. Weymark (1990), "Harsanyi's Social Aggregation Theorem with Alternative Pareto Principles," Discussion Paper No. 90-28, Department of Economics, University of British Columbia.

9. Deducing interpersonal comparisons from local expertise

IGNACIO ORTUÑO-ORTIN AND JOHN E. ROEMER

1. Introduction

Economists accept the idea that a person can have a coherent ordering over the states of the world; yet it is commonplace to balk at the notion that there exists a coherent interpersonal ordering, which would give sense to statements of the form 'person i is better off in state x than person j is in state y.' The reason for such skepticism is that whereas in the first case one mind is making judgments about states of the world, there is no universal mind that can make interpersonal judgments. Nevertheless, most of us feel capable of making some interpersonal comparisons, perhaps by virtue of the limited empathy we feel, because we believe at some level all people are relevantly similar. We will argue that it may be quite reasonable to suppose the existence of an interpersonal ordering of the states of the world, based on a kind of empathy that a person can legitimately feel, because he has, during his life, indeed been a person of various different types.

Interpersonally comparable utility has had a checkered history. In the nineteenth century (see Cooter and Rappoport (1986)), the possibility of interpersonal comparisons was taken for granted by many social theorists. The ordinalist revolution dissolved this innocent presumption; its supporters claimed that interpersonal comparisons were necessarily normative, hence not within the purview of positive economics (see also Sen (1979) for a discussion).[1] There are, it seems, two different bases for the current agnosticism, or rather nihilism,

This research was partially supported by a grant from the National Science Foundation. We are also indebted to David Donaldson for his comments.

[1] Although interpersonal comparisons may be made for normative *reasons*, the comparisons themselves may be matters of fact. We wish to argue that this may be so, quite generally.

with respect to the existence of an interpersonal ordering. First, positive economics (including general equilibrium theory) does not require interpersonal comparability. Hence, parsimony suggests that such information not be assumed. Second, it is widely believed that to assume interpersonal comparability presupposes some kind of supra-person authority who makes the decisions that no individual can make. Such authoritarian decisions would have either an objective or a dictatorial quality that would cut against the grain of the twentieth-century subjective approach to preference.

But the necessity of establishing foundations for interpersonal comparability need hardly be mentioned if one is interested in social choice and distributive justice. Without interpersonal comparability, one can hardly move beyond Pareto optimality as a social criterion for evaluating alternative states, but with it social choices can be made (see, for example, Blackorby, Donaldson, and Weymark (1984)). In the late 1960s and throughout the 1970s, attempts were made to move beyond Pareto optimality without imposing an assumption of interpersonal comparability with the development of the notion of fairness (envy-free, Pareto efficient allocations) and the related notions of egalitarian equivalent allocations and fair net trades[2] (see Foley (1967), Kolm (1972), and Thomson and Varian (1986) for a survey of this literature). Fairness, so defined, however, does not reach very far in resolving questions of distributive justice. Fair allocations do not always exist; but more importantly, when the distribution of internal traits of persons becomes a topic for distributive justice – and this is central to the contemporary theories of Rawls (1971), Dworkin (1981), and Sen (1981) – then fairness becomes an almost useless concept (see Roemer (1985) for an explanation).

The tension between the necessity for positing interpersonal comparability in order to make progress on questions of social choice and distributive justice, and the agnosticism with respect to the possibility of making interpersonal judgments in an objective way is seen, for example, in the following quotation from Arrow:

In a way that I cannot articulate and am not too sure about defending, the autonomy of individuals, an element of mutual incommen-

---

[2] See, however, the introduction of Kolm (1972), in which the author writes that the concept of fairness was discussed by J. Tinbergen in 1953.

surability among people, seems denied by the possibility of interpersonal comparisons. No doubt it is some such feeling as this that has made me so reluctant to shift from pure ordinalism, despite my desire to seek a basis for a theory of justice (Arrow (1977, p. 225)).

We hope to chip away at this incommensurability; in particular, to show that a supra-personal authority is not necessary, but that people can be expected to make interpersonal comparisons themselves by combining their individual judgments, based on local expertise.

2. Local expertise

Let X denote the set of states of the world over which a person has a preference ordering. If we had to design an experiment to deduce the person's preferences, we would probably ask him to rank the alternatives in small subsets of X. In carrying out this revealed preference experiment, it is likely that inconsistent answers will be given. Most persons, when confronted with an agenda of such requests, will produce intransitivities, if X is large enough. (We assert this as a piece of conventional wisdom.) But faced with such demonstrated inconsistencies, we do not declare the incoherence of the notion of intrapersonal comparability. We are prone to say, instead, that the person has made a mistake or that he has bounded rationality; the ideal of an intrapersonal ordering remains acceptable.

We suggest that such errors are made in the revealed preference experiment because the person does not have sufficient remembered experience of all the states he has been asked to rank.[3] Some of the states are distant from his personal experience, so he does not have a good basis on which to rank them against some other states. Perhaps it would be appropriate, if this were the case, to say that he really has incomplete preferences over X.

We propose to extend the charity that we show in assuming people have coherent intrapersonal orderings, despite evidence to the contrary, to the ideal of interpersonal comparability.[4] Let T be the set of

[3]   This differs from May's (1954) proposal. If a person has n orderings of the states, each according to one of n criteria that are important to him, there will not in general exist an overall ordering that satisfactorily aggregates the n criteria-specific orderings. This is an application of Arrow's impossibility theorem.

[4]   But see Gibbard (1986) for a discussion of the difficulties in constructing a coherent intrapersonal ordering.

types of persons. The information summarizing a person's type is sufficient to determine his ordinal preferences. A type is a long vector, some components of which describe salient aspects of a person's history and, perhaps, his biochemical and genetic makeup. We will assume that a distinction can be made between the characteristics that determine type, and the attributes of the social alternatives, or states, that comprise X – an important and perhaps controversial assumption. An interpersonal ordering of X is an ordering of the set $X \times T$, interpreted as follows: $(x, t) \gtrsim (y, s)$ means a person of type t is at least as well off in state x as a person of type s is in state y.

Suppose we conduct an experiment in which we ask different people to rank subsets of $X \times T$. If everyone agreed on these rankings, we might feel confident in asserting the coherence of an interpersonal ordering. But in all likelihood there will be disagreements among people, even when they are posed the problem of comparing some pairs of states in $X \times T$. We suggest that two people, say of types i and j, disagree about the ranking of (x, s) and (y, t) for essentially the same reason that one person commits inconsistencies in his intrapersonal ordering of X. At least one of the *positions* (x, s) or (y, t) is too distant from the personal experience of i or j. This might be so either because, say, x is too far from the states in X that the type i person has experienced, or because a person of type s is too far from a person of type i. Thus, the person in question cannot be considered a competent judge of interpersonal comparisons when his experience – say (z, i) – is 'too far' from (x, s) or (y, t).

Just as each person has had experience with different states in X, it is the case that each person has had experience with different types in T. He himself has been different types. Some of the characteristics that define a type vary with personal experience – age, health, and wealth. Thus each person has traveled through some, perhaps small, subset of the set of types T. If we are willing to assume that a person has a coherent intrapersonal ordering on X, then we should be willing to assume he is capable of providing an *interpersonal* ordering on $X \times T_i$, where T_i is the subset of types in his remembered experience. Not only can the person who is currently of type i report the intrapersonal orderings (of X) for types in the set T_i; he can, as well, make intertype comparisons.

(We could say that a particular person has experienced types i, j, k and that he experienced subsets of X denoted X_i, X_j, X_k, respectively, while of those types. He would then be capable of providing an interpersonal ordering only on the set $(X_i \times \{i\} \cup (X_j \times \{j\}) \cup (X_k \times \{k\})$. But our goal is to establish the cogency of interpersonal comparability given the cogency of intrapersonal comparability. Therefore we assume that a person has a complete order of X for each type he has experienced.)

That is, a person is assumed to have accurate memory, or one mind, that can unify the perceptions he has had as his type has varied, and so he is capable not only of rendering accurate intrapersonal orderings for each type he has experienced, but of recalling the interpersonal ordering among these types: "I was happier living in that dump as a student than I am in this palace in middle age." These comparisons are not ones made from the point of view of his current type, but are of his actual experienced welfare levels at the two positions in question. In fact, we will not require people to remember how they felt many years ago; it will be sufficient if they can remember their feelings only for types very 'close' to their present type, which is to say, types they have experienced in the recent past.

The assumption suggested by this discussion is that each person is competent to make interpersonal comparisons – or, more accurately, intertype comparisons – on some neighborhood in state-type space of the point at which he is currently situated. It follows that if the neighborhoods of competence of two people intersect, then the interpersonal orderings on the intersection must agree, because they have both experienced the positions in the intersection.[5] This is so, in particular, because those comparisons are not made from the point of view of one's current position.

In the next section we present a simple model in which this condition suffices to determine a partial ordering on the space $X \times T$. We use the opinion of local experts to piece together a consistent (but perhaps incomplete) interpersonal ordering of $X \times T$.

---

[5]   What if two people, each of whom is putatively a local expert in regard to two positions (x, s) and (y, t) disagree on their ordering? Then we must say that the space of types has not been sufficiently disaggregated to distinguish properly between these two persons and between types s and t.

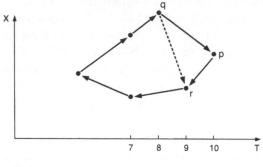

Figure 9.1

3. A simple model

In this model, it will be assumed that the set of types can be represented by a discrete one-dimensional set. We identify the types with integers. The set X is an abstract set. A position in $X \times T$ is schematically represented by a point in the plane in Figure 9.1 whose first coordinate is an integer. It is assumed that each type i has experienced one neighboring type on each side. Thus, the set $T_i = \{i - 1, i, i + 1\}$. We assume that the person of type i has an ordering on the set $X \times T_i$. Agents of types i and j agree on the interpersonal ordering on the intersection $X \times (T_i \cap T_j)$.

By linking together the judgments of individuals of neighboring types, we induce a partial binary relation on $X \times T$. The question is whether this procedure will be consistent, or whether it will generate intransitivities. Under the earlier assumptions, this procedure leads to no intransitivities.

Denote i's preference ordering on $X \times T$ by $>_i$. We only respect his ordering on his domain of competence, $X \times T_i$. Let $p, q \in X \times T_i$, and suppose $p <_i q$. If $q, r \in X \times T_j$ and $q <_j r$, then we define $p < r$, where $<$ represents the interpersonal ordering under construction. Suppose there is a cycle under this procedure, as illustrated in Figure 9.6. We draw an arrow $p \to q$ to indicate that $p <_i q$ for some i.[6]

If there is a cycle, there is one involving a smallest number of types. Consider such a minimal cycle. We derive a contradiction by showing

---

[6] $p <_i q$ means $p \leq_i q$ and p and q are not indifferent. (Indifference is the conjunction of $p \leq_i q$ and $q \leq_i p$.)

that a cycle can be constructed that does not involve the agent on the right-hand extreme, position p in Figure 9.1. There are only several possibilities for what the cycle looks like near p. One is illustrated in Figure 9.1, where the position q immediately inferior to p is a position of type 8, and the position r, which is immediately superior to p, is a position of type 9. But then $r, q \in X \times T_8$, and so it must be that $r >_8 q$, or else there would be smaller cycle created among r, p, q, which is impossible, for all three positions lie within the local ordering of 8. But if $r >_8 q$, then agent 10 can be removed from the cycle, as the dotted line indicates, which completes the argument. There are several other possible configurations for p, q, and r, but the same argument works. Hence the procedure for aggregating the opinion of local experts works.

Note, first, that this procedure does not necessarily lead to a complete order on $X \times T$. Second, this piecing-together procedure for deducing interpersonal comparability does not verify the conventional wisdom that if everyone agrees on the order of two positions, then that must be the correct interpersonal order. Although it may be the case that everybody believes that (x, i) is better than (y, j), we might deduce that $(x, i) \lesssim (y, j)$. No one person may be competent to make judgments comparing these two positions, and when the opinions of local experts are linked together, the opposite conclusion may hold. Thus, we do not concur with the conventional wisdom that universal agreement about the ordering of two positions is sufficient grounds for concluding that that is the correct interpersonal ordering. We trust only the opinions of people who are competent to judge.

We proceed to show how a complete interpersonal ordering can be deduced from the opinions of local experts when the set of types is a discrete, n-dimensional set.

4. Interpersonal comparability on a lattice

We suppose now that the set of types T can be represented as the points in an n-dimensional rectangular lattice. Each dimension is interpreted as one of a set of traits, which together characterize a type. The set X, as before, is any abstract set.

We work with a two-dimensional lattice T, although the definitions and theorems are general for a lattice of any finite dimension. A *type* in T is denoted (i, j), after its integer coordinates. We postulate that a person located at any type has experienced, as well, the four closest types in the lattice.[7] Thus, his neighborhood of competence, in type space, is:

$$T_{i,j} = \{(i, j), (i - 1, j), (i + 1, j), (i, j - 1), (i, j + 1)\}$$

It is postulated that (i, j) has an ordering on $X \times T_{i,j}$, which will be denoted $\succeq_{i,j}$. Furthermore, it is postulated that:

Axiom of Coincidence The orderings $\succeq_{i,j}$ and $\succeq_{k,l}$ agree on $X \times (T_{i,j} \cap T_{k,l})$.

We furthermore postulate:

Axiom of Continuity. If $(x; k, l) \in X \times T_{i,j}$, then there exists $(y; i, j) \in X \times \{(i, j)\}$ such that $(x; k, l) \sim_{i,j} (y; i, j)$.

We call this an axiom of continuity because it is plausible if the types that are neighbors in the lattice are 'close' to each other, in a psychological sense, and if the set X is sufficiently dense that this kind of indifference curve can be drawn as the types vary. The Axiom of Continuity is perhaps only plausible if X is a continuum, such as the set of all possible allocations of some continuously divisible set of commodities, although the theory does not require X be such a set.

Theorem 1. Let T be an n-dimensional square lattice and let $t = (i_1, i_2, \ldots, i_n)$ represent an arbitrary type in the lattice. Let the neighborhood of t, denoted T_t, consist of the $2n$ points of unit distance from t, plus t itself. Let X be any set, and let $\succeq_t$ be a complete order of $X \times T_t$, for every t. Suppose the axioms of coincidence and continuity hold. Then the local orderings $\succeq_t$ can be extended to a complete ordering of $X \times T$ in a unique way.

Proof: Section 6.

One might object that it is unreasonable to suppose that there is an order $\succeq_t$ associated with every point in the lattice. Perhaps there are persons associated only with some proper subset of types on the

---

[7]   This condition may seem too strong. Our age, for example, is now the maximum we have ever had, so we should not postulate that we have experienced ages older than we are. This difficulty is easily resolved: The type where a person is located in the lattice does not need to be his present type, only a type he has experienced in the recent past.

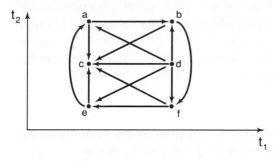

Figure 9.2

lattice. In this case, it is still possible to recover a partial ordering of $X \times T$.

Without the axiom of continuity it is not difficult to find examples of intransitivities. Let a, b, c, d, e, f be six different types in a two-dimensional lattice $T_{i, j}$ (see Figure 9.2). Suppose that the set of states of the world contains just one element: $X = \{x\}$. Call $A = (x, a) \in X \times T$, $B = (x, b) \in X \times T$, and so on. We now write $A \gtrsim_k B$ for $(x, a) \gtrsim_k (x, b)$ for $k \in T$. Let the orderings for the six types in each of their neighborhoods of competence be as follows:

$$C >_a B >_a A$$
$$B >_b A >_b D$$
$$C >_c A >_c E >_c D$$
$$C >_d F >_d B >_d D$$
$$C >_e E >_e F$$
$$E >_f F >_f D$$

It is easy to check that the axiom of coincidence holds, but we can form the intransitivity $A <_b B <_d F <_f E <_c A$. This is illustrated in Figure 9.2, where an arrow from a to b means $B >_a A$, and so on.

As a corollary to Theorem 1, a similar result follows if $T = R^n$.

The theorem remains true for a continuum of types. For this we need:

Generalized Axiom of Continuity. Let T and X be sets, and for each $p \in T$, let $T_p \subset T$, and let $\gtrsim_p$ be an order on $X \times T_p$. $\gtrsim_p$ satisfies the axiom of continuity if, for all $q \in T_p$, $x \in X$ *there exists* $y \in X$ *such that* $(x, p) \sim_p (y, q)$.

Theorem 2. Let $T = R^n$, X be any set, and ε be a positive number. Let T_p be an arc-connected neighborhood of p containing a ball of radius at least ε about p. For all $p \in T$, let $\gtrsim_p$ be an order on $X \times T_p$. Suppose the axioms of coincidence and continuity hold. Then the local orders extend uniquely to a complete order of $X \times T$.

Proof: Available from authors.

Remark. An alternative model for our problem does not distinguish between the states X and the types T but postulates a set Y – say, a rectangular lattice of many dimensions – whose members are identified with positions (in some state-type space). Each point in Y specifies everything about a person, where his type is not distinguished from the state. Associated with each $y \in Y$ is an ordering $>_y$ of a small neighborhood of y. The axiom of coincidence is postulated. The axiom of continuity, however, no longer makes sense because type and state cannot be distinguished. What other conditions on the local orders are sufficient to guarantee that the induced binary relation on Y is an order? The problem is trivial if $n = 1$; there is a strong condition that suffices for $n = 2$; but the problem becomes very difficult at $n = 3$. The advantage of the approach we have taken – of distinguishing states from types – is that the problem becomes tractable because dimension no longer plays a critical role. Hence the assumption that type can be distinguished from state is perhaps the most important, and contentious, assumption of the model.

5. Conclusion

Our theorems provide a basis for legitimating a belief in interpersonal comparability, if the idea of local expertise is accepted. If each person is competent to make interpersonal judgments locally, among positions occupied by types close to his own, then a unique complete order on state-type space exists, which is the transitive extension of the local orders. We interpret this global ordering as *the* interpersonal ordering. More accurately, we can say that *if* an interpersonal ordering exists, this must be it, for it is the unique order that coincides with all the orderings of local experts. It may still be objected that no interpersonal ordering exists, and so the order whose existence we have proved has no significance – other than being the transitive extension of local

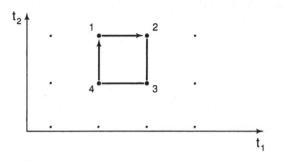

Figure 9.3

orders. But we find this nihilism unconvincing. It would be more convincing to argue that we have merely reduced the problem of interpersonal comparability to one of communicating one's type. As Arrow[8] has said, that may be the insurmountable problem.

6. Proofs

Proof of Theorem 1:

We prove the theorem for the two-dimensional lattice $T = N \times N$, where N is the non-negative integers. T_{ij} is the five-point neighborhood of (i, j). Let $I(y^1)$ be an intransitivity $y^1 \gtrsim y^2 \gtrsim \ldots \gtrsim y^n$, $I(y^1) \subset X \times T$ and for all $m \in \{1, 2, \ldots, n\}$, y^m and y^{m+1} belong to $X \times T_{ij}$ for some $(i, j) \in N \times N$. We write the mth term in $I(y^1)$ as y^m or $(x^m; i^m, j^m)$.

The proofs of this theorem and Theorem 2 are easier if we work with the projection of $I(y^1)$ on T: We associate each point in $X \times T$ with its coordinate in T and we relate these points in T in such a way that $(i, j) \gtrsim (i', j')$ if there exists a pair $(y^p, y^{p+1}) \subset I(y^1)$ such that $y^p = (x, i, j) \gtrsim (x', i', j') = y^{p+1}$. This projection of $I(y^1)$ on T produces an intransitivity on T.

Lemma 1 There cannot be an intransitivity $I(y^1)$ such that its projection on T, $I_T(y^1)$, is a square of area equal to one.

Proof. See Figure 9.3, where an arrow (or undirected segment) from a to b means $a < b$ (or $a \sim b$). Note that $\{4, 2\} \in T_1$; therefore type 1

Figure 9.1

Figure 9.2

Figure 9.3

says that $2 > 4$ – that is, that the states y^2, y^4 in $X \times T$ associated with 2 and 4, respectively, are such that $y^2 > y^4$. But $\{4, 2\} \in T_3$ and type 3 says that $4 \sim 2$. This contradicts the postulated agreement of agents of types 1 and 3 about types 2 and 4 that lie in $T_1 \cap T_3$.

Now we assign a utility function over the set X to each type in T. Choose the type $(0, 0)$ and assign a utility function u_{00} to his ordering over the set X – that is, a function $u_{00}: X \to R$ such that $u_{00}(x) \geq u_{00}(y)$ $\Leftrightarrow (x; 0, 0) \geq (y; 0, 0)$. To simplify the notation, let $(0, 0) = a$, $(1, 0) = b$, $(0, 1) = c$, and $(1, 1) = d$. Type a has experienced types b and c, so given u_a he can construct utility functions for type b and c, as follows: Define the function $u_b: X \to R$ by $u_b(x) = u_a(y)$, where y is such that $(x; b) \sim_a (y; a)$. This is well defined by the axiom of continuity. We define u_c in a similar way. These utility functions can then be used to define utility functions for types to the right and above, and so on. The utility functions so defined will provide us with a complete ordering over the set $X \times T$. We first have to show that the utility function that type d receives from type b coincides with the one that type c gives to type d.

Lemma 2 Let u_{dc} (u_{db}) be the utility function assigned to type d by type c (type b). Then $u_{dc}(x) = u_{db}(x) \qquad \forall\, x \in X$.

Proof. Suppose not – that is, $\ni x \in X$ such that $u_{dc}(x) \neq u_{db}(x)$. Then by the axiom of continuity and the definition of u_{dc}, u_c, and u_a there exists x', $x'' \in X$ such that $u_{dc}(x) = u_c(x') = u_a(x'')$, and this is equivalent to

$$(x; d) \sim_c (x'; c) \sim_a (x''; a) \tag{i}$$

For the same reason there exists y, $y' \in X$ such that $u_{db}(x) = u_b(y) = u_a(y')$, which is equivalent to

$$(x; d) \sim_b (y; b) \sim_a (y'; a) \tag{ii}$$

Clearly $u_a(x'') \neq u_a(y')$. Assume that $u_a(x'') > u_a(y')$, then (i) and (ii) imply the intransitivity

$$(x''; a) \sim_a (x'; c) \sim_c (x; d) \sim_b (y; b) \sim_a (y'; a) < (x''; a)$$

which clearly contradicts Lemma 1.

Now we will show that if we repeat the same process – that is, where each type receiving a utility function endows utility functions to the types immediately to the right and above him, we can construct a complete ordering on $X \times T$. After that we will prove that the ordering is the unique one that respects all of the local orderings given by the local experts.

Let $c = \langle l^0, l^1, l^2, \ldots , l^k \rangle$ be a finite chain of elements of T. Let C be the set of all chains such that $\forall c \in C$, $c = \langle l^0, l^1, \ldots , l^k \rangle$, $l^0 = (0, 0)$, and $l^s \in T_{l^{s-1}}$, $(s = 1 \text{ to } k)$.

Definition: A finite chain $c = \langle l^0, l^1, l^2, \ldots , l^k \rangle$ has the northeast (NE) property if

$$(i_s, j_s) \in \{(i_{s-1} + 1, j_{s-1}), (i_{s-1}, j_{s-1} + 1)\} \qquad s = 1, \ldots , k$$

Let C^{NE} be the family of all chains with the NE property such that $l^0 = (0, 0)$. Clearly $\forall c \in C^{NE}$ and $l^s \in c$, $l^s \in T_{l^{s-1}}$. Therefore we can assign utility functions to all types in c in the way described here – that is, given the chain $c \in C^{NE}$, $c = <l^0, l^1, \ldots , l^k>$, we assign a utility function over the set $X \times l^0$ to the first type in the chain, denoted by u^{c_0}; then type l^0 endows a utility function u^{c_1} over the set $X \times l^1$ to type l^1, and so on.

For each $(m, n) \in T$ we can find a chain $c \in C^{NE}$, $c = <l^0, l^1, \ldots , l^l>$ such that $l^l = (m, n)$. Therefore we can assign utility functions to all elements of T. We have to show that the utility function assigned to any type in T does not depend on the chain $c \in C^{NE}$ we choose to connect that point with the origin.

Lemma 3 For all $c, c' \in C^{NE}$, $c = <l^0, l^1, \ldots , l^k>$, $c' = <l^0, l^1, \ldots , l^l$ such that $l^k = l^l$ we have $u^{c_k} = u^{c'}_l$.

Proof. Let $C_n \in C^{NE}$ be the set of all C^{NE} chains such that $\forall c \in C_n$, $\forall l^s \in c$, $l^s \in \{(i_s, 0), (i_s, 1), (i_s, 2), \ldots , (i_s, n)\}$.

(a) It is evident that the lemma is true for all members of C_0.

(b) Now we consider elements that can be reached by C_1 chains. If $c \in C_1$ has endpoint $l^k = (i_k, 0)$ we are in case (a). The lemma holds trivially for the type $(0, 1)$ in T because there exists only one $c \in C^{NE}$ with end point $(0, 1)$. Now take the type $(1, 1)$. There are two chains $c, c' \in C_1$ with endpoint $(1, 1)$. By Lemma 2 we know that $u^{c}_{(1, 1)} = u^{c'}_{(1, 1)}$. There are three chains $c_1, c_2, c_3 \in C_1$ with endpoints equal to $(2, 1)$:

$$c_1 = \ <(0, 0), (0, 1), (1, 1), (2, 1)>, c_2 = \ <(0, 0), (1, 0), (1, 1), (2, 1)>$$

and

$$c_3 = \ <(0, 0), (1, 0), (2, 0), (2, 11)>.$$

As shown, $u^{c1}_{(1, 1)} = u^{c2}_{(1, 1)}$, and therefore $u^{c1}_{(2, 1)} = u^{c2}_{(2, 1)}$, so it remains to be proved that $u^{c2}_{(2, 1)} = u^{c3}_{(2, 1)}$: Clearly this is true because we can apply Lemma 2 by rewriting types in this way: $(1, 0) = a$, $(1, 1) = b$, $(2, 0) = c$, and $(2, 1) = d$. In the same way we can show that the four chains with endpoint $(3, 1)$ will assign the same utility function to type $(3, 1)$. We do the same for the rest of the types that can be reached by chains in C_1. This proves that the utility function assigned to any element that belongs to a C_1 chain is well-defined – that is, it does not depend on the chain we choose.

(c) For types that belong to C_2 chains, we can prove the lemma by the argument we used in (a) and (b) because the utility functions assigned to types with the second coordinate equal to 1 are unique; therefore we can view a chain $c \in C_2$ with endpoint $(i_k, 2)$ as a C_1 chain after taking type $(0, 1)$ as the origin (instead of type $(0, 0)$). If we do the same for all chains C_n, $n \in N$, we prove the lemma.

Lemma 3 provides us with a complete ordering on the set $X \times T$ that respects the local orderings of all local experts. The next step is to prove that it is unique.

Denote by u^t the utility function that type t receives when we allow only C^{NE} chains. Let u^{ct} be the utility function assigned to type $t \in T$ using the chain $c \in C$. There are two cases to consider:

(a) Let C^a be the set of chains of C such that

$$\forall c \in C^a, c = \ <l^0, l^1, \ldots, l^k >, l^s \in \{(i_{s-1} + 1, j_{s-1}), (i_{s-1}, j_{s-1} + 1),$$
$$(i_{s-1}-1, j_{s-1}), (j_{s-1}, j_{s-1}-1)\}, s = 1 \ldots k.$$

Suppose that t is the last type in a chain $c \in C^a$. We want to show that $u^t = u^{ct}$. If $c \in C^{NE}$, there is nothing to prove; otherwise, assume $u^t \neq u^{ct}$.

Let $l^P = t'$ be the first term in c such that $u^{t'} \neq u^{ct'}$; without loss of generality assume that $l^P = (i_p, j_p) = (i_{p-1}-1, j_{p-1})$. Now rename types in the following way: $t' = b$, $(i_{p-1}, j_{p-1}) = d$, $(i_{p-1}, j_{p-1}-1) = c$, $(i_{p-1}-1, j_{p-1}-1) = a$. The assumption says that $u^b \neq u^{cb}$. Using the axiom of continuity in the same way we did for Lemma 2, we can show that there exists an intransitivity in the square a, c, d, b, which is impossible by Lemma 1. Therefore $u^{t'} = u^{ct'}$. We have proved that for any type, the utility function assigned to it using chains in C^a coincides with the one assigned using chains in C^{NE}.

(b) There is a different way to assign utility functions to types in T. Given the utility function for type (i, j), we allow for the possibility that type $(i + 1, j)$ assigns a utility function to type $(i + 2, j)$ (and the same for j) – that is, we can have "jumps". Evidently this is not a problem because type (i, j) can assign a utility function to type $(i + 1, j)$, and given this utility function, type $(i + 1, j)$ assigns one to type $(i + 2, j)$, which must coincide with the one he assigned first, for otherwise we would have an intransitivity within $T_{(i+1, j)}$.

All chains of c are studied in cases (a) and (b). It therefore follows that the complete ordering is unique.

The proof for the n-dimensional case — that is, when $T = N x \ldots$ xN, parallels the proof earlier. First, we prove the equivalent of Lemma 1 for the n-cube with sides of area equal to one. Next, we assign a utility function over the set X to the type $(0, 0, \ldots, 0)$. In turn this type will assign utility functions to the n types having just one coordinate equal to one and the rest zeros, and we continue in the same way as before, with the natural modifications for the definitions of the different types of chains.

Theorem 2 is a corollary of Theorem 1. Its proof is available from the authors.

References

Arrow, Kenneth. 1977. "Extended Sympathy and the Possibility of Social Choice," *American Economic Review* 67, 219–225.

Blackorby, C., Donaldson, D., and Weymark, J. 1984. "Social Choice with Interpersonal Utility Comparisons: A Diagrammatic Introduction," *International Economic Review* 25, 327–356.

Cooter, Robert, and Peter Rappoport. 1986. "Were the Ordinalists Wrong About Welfare Economics?" *Journal of Economic Literature* 22, 507–530.

Dworkin, Ronald. 1981. "What is Equality? Part 1: Equality of Welfare," *Philosophy and Public Affairs* 10, 185–246.

Foley, Duncan. 1967. "Resource Allocation and the Public Sector," *Yale Economic Essays* 7, 45–98.

Gibbard, Allan, 1986. "Interpersonal comparisons: Preference, good, and the intrinsic reward of a life," in Elster, J., and A. Hylland, *Foundations of Social Choice Theory,* Cambridge: Cambridge University Press.

Kolm, Serge-Christophe. 1972. *Justice et Equité,* Paris: Editions du Centre National de la Recherche Scientifique.

May, Kenneth. 1954. "Intransitivity, Utility, and the Aggregation of Preference Patterns," *Econometrica* 22, 1–13.

Rawls, John. 1971 *A Theory of Justice.* Cambridge, Mass.: Harvard University Press.

Roemer, John. 1985. "A Note on Interpersonal Comparability and the Theory of Fairness," Dept. of Economics, University of California, Davis: Working Paper No. 261.

Sen, Amartya. 1979. "Interpersonal Comparisons of Welfare," in M. Boskin (ed.), *Economics and Human Welfare: Essays in Honor of Tibor Scitovsky,* New York: Academic Press.

Sen, Amartya. 1980. "Equality of What?" In *The Tanner Lectures on Human Values,* Volume I. Salt Lake City and New York: University of Utah Press and Cambridge University Press.

Thomson, William, and Hal Varian. 1986. "Theories of Justice Based on Symmetry," in Leonid Hurwicz et al. (eds.), *Social Goals and Social Organization: Essays in Memory of Elisha Pazner,* New York: Cambridge University Press.

10. Subjective interpersonal comparison

AANUND HYLLAND[1]

1. Introduction

Social choice theory has traditionally been dominated by negative results. Starting with Arrow's famous impossibility theorem, authors have formulated seemingly reasonable conditions that a preference aggregation procedure ought to satisfy, and then proved that the conditions are logically inconsistent.

As has been observed by several authors,[2] one reason for this state of affairs is the extremely weak informational basis on which a social choice function is supposed to work: The input to the function consists of ordinal and noncomparable preferences.

In this chapter, I shall investigate the consequences of introducing a certain type of preference comparability, which I shall call *subjective comparability*. I explain and motivate the concept in this Introduction; details come later. Throughout the chapter, I stick to the standard assumption that preferences are purely ordinal.[3]

Previous authors have incorporated interpersonally comparable preferences into the social choice framework in the following way[4]: The input to the social choice function is an ordering of the pairs (x, i), where x is a social state and i is an individual. This ordering includes information about each individual's ranking of the states,

[1] The author is a professor of economics and decision theory at the University of Oslo and the Norwegian School of Management. A preliminary version of the chapter was presented in April, 1987, at the conference on "Interpersonal Comparison of Welfare," Davis, California, USA. I thank the participants at the conference, and John Broome in particular, for useful comments.

[2] See, for example, the thorough discussion in Sen (1977).

[3] It is well known that introducing cardinal preferences, without any form of interpersonal comparison or normalization, does not change matters much; this, however, is not the subject of the chapter.

[4] See, for example, Hammond (1976), d'Aspremont and Gevers (1977), Gevers (1979), Roberts (1980), and Blackorby et al. (1984).

but it also contains answers to questions of the type: "Is it better to be individual i in state x than individual j in state y?" If one now introduces conditions analogous to the standard conditions of social choice theory, many of the negative results – including Arrow's impossibility theorem – do not reemerge. In particular, the maximin rule is a well-defined procedure in this setting, and it has many desirable properties.[5]

In the model just mentioned, it is essential that the input to the social choice function be *one* ordering of the pairs (x, i). Thus the interpersonal comparisons of preferences must themselves not be the subject of disagreement. Either the persons involved unanimously agree on how one should compare the condition of being individual i in state x to that of being j in y, or there is an objective standard accepted by everybody, or everybody yields to the judgment of an ethical observer, or the like. In any case, the interpersonal comparisons must in some sense be *objective*.[6]

There are conceptual problems concerning interpersonal comparison of preferences, and even if these were solved, there would be obvious difficulties involved in operationalizing the comparisons. Still, there are strong intuitive grounds for not dismissing the concept completely. In everyday life and in ordinary political debate, interpersonal comparisons of a kind are made all the time. We talk about groups or individuals being better or worse off than others, and at least sometimes we have in mind not simply income or other directly measurable indices of well-being, but something like the individual's (or group's) subjective feeling of welfare. Political proposals are often justified on the grounds that they will be particularly beneficial to "the worst-off group," and behind this there must lie some conception of comparison of preferences.[7]

One can discuss how much genuine comparison of preference there is in such everyday statements, but it is not the purpose of this chapter to pursue that debate. I take it for granted that informal interpersonal comparison has a strong intuitive appeal. These informal compari-

---

[5]   The maximin rule is defined and discussed in Section 5.

[6]   Perhaps the word "objective" does not cover all the cases mentioned here, but I use it for lack of a better phrase.

[7]   Such arguments are probably more common in societies where equality is an almost universally acclaimed ideal, such as in Norway, and less common where inequality is more accepted, such as in the United States.

sons are not, however, of the objective type described earlier. The statement that one individual or group is better off than another is always the *subjective* point of view of the person who makes the statement. Different people may agree to a greater or lesser extent when expressing this kind of judgment, but there is neither any theoretical nor any practical reason to expect complete unanimity.

If we take seriously the intuitive arguments for accepting interpersonal comparisons, the model where the input to the social choice function is *one* ordering of the pairs (x, i) is inadequate. The input should be a *vector* of orderings of these pairs, one ordering for each individual. This ordering represents the subjective interpersonal comparisons of the individual.

Each individual enters the picture in two different ways. Suppose that (x, i) is ranked above (y, j) in the subjective interpersonal comparisons of individual k. Then something is said about the *interests* of individuals i and j, according to the *judgment* of k. Hence an individual both has interests and expresses judgments, and we shall distinguish between these two aspects of the person. It is even possible that those individuals whose interests count in the social choice function, are not the same as those to whose judgments the function pays attention. This is discussed further in Section 3.

In this chapter, I study axiomatically the possibility of constructing "acceptable" social choice functions in the model where interpersonal comparison of preferences is subjective.[8] For reasons of comparison, I stay as close as possible to Arrow's impossibility theorem (the 1963 version). Analogous versions of Arrow's conditions Pareto Optimality, Independence of Irrelevant Alternatives, and Unrestricted Domain are imposed as axioms, and the consequences of the resulting axiom system are investigated.

The condition Unrestricted Domain (UD) is perhaps too strong. It implies that a person $k \neq i$ is allowed to express the judgment that (x, i) is better than (y, i), even if i, who is the only person whose interests are involved in this comparison, prefers (y, i) to (x, i). Alternatively, one can modify UD by ruling out such "paternalistic" judgments; this

---

[8]   The model introduced here is not unknown in the literature. See Sen (1970), Chapter 9*; the concluding remarks in Hammond (1976); and Roberts (1980), Section 5. Roberts' approach is similar to mine; I comment on his work in connection with Theorems 1 and 2 in Sections 5 and 6.

amounts to weakening the condition. The issue is discussed further in Section 4.

The most interesting question is the following:

Does Arrow's theorem reemerge in the framework of subjective interpersonal comparison, so that any social choice function that satisfies the imposed conditions is dictatorial, or do there exist nondictatorial functions that satisfy the conditions?

The answer is positive: When UD is modified as described, there exist nondictatorial functions satisfying the conditions. However, the class of acceptable functions is still quite small; in an intuitive sense, every member of the class is close to being dictatorial. This is explained further in Section 7.

The chapter is organized as follows: In order to formulate conditions and results precisely, it is convenient to introduce some formal notation. This is done in Section 2. Section 3 contains comments on the two different roles an individual plays in the model, as one who has interests and one who expresses judgments. In Section 4 I formulate and comment on the conditions that are to be used in the main theorems.

The results are found in Sections 5–7. In the first of these sections I consider the case where interpersonal comparisons are objective. The subjective case is treated in Sections 6 and 7. First, a direct analogy of Arrow's condition Unrestricted Domain is imposed, and a completely negative result is obtained. Finally, in Section 7, the domain condition is weakened so that paternalistic judgments are ruled out; this leads to a somewhat more positive result, as already indicated.[9]

In the Appendix I give a short outline of the most important proofs. Complete proofs are not included in this chapter, but are available separately.[10]

2. Notation

In this section, concepts are introduced, and to some extent explained and discussed. In a couple of cases, however, only the bare definition is given; its significance is made clear in later sections.

[9]   The original contribution of the chapter is Theorem 3 of Section 7.
[10]   Hylland (1991). The paper can be obtained from the author.

The basic framework is that of social choice theory. We consider a given society with a fixed set of members. There is also a given and fixed set of social states.[11] Input to the social choice process consists of some kind of individual preferences, and the output is a ranking of the social states. The connection between input and output is represented by a function, referred to as the aggregation process, the social choice function, or the like. Conditions are imposed on this function, and it is asked which functions, if any, satisfy the conditions.

Many interesting and important questions are not discussed at all. Some of these are:

- How is it determined who shall be considered members of the society?

- How are the social states found (or determined); how is the set of possible states delineated?

- How are individual preferences determined?

- How can (those who administer) the process get reliable information about individual preferences?

The set of social states is denoted A. Typical members of A are x, y, z. The set A is assumed to be finite and have at least three members.[12]

Throughout the chapter, I shall assume that all orderings that occur as input to a social choice function are strict. This is a great technical simplification. In my opinion, it leads to no loss in insight or understanding.[13] The orderings that occur as values of a social choice func-

[11]   What is here referred to as the set of social states could instead, for example, be thought of as the set of possible outcomes of a collective decision process. In general, the basic concepts of social choice theory can be given different interpretations. In this chapter, I do not want to commit myself to any one of these, and my choice of terminology is to some extent arbitrary. I discuss the consequences of there being several possible interpretations in Hylland (1986).

[12]   See, however, remarks at the end of Sections 6 and 7, where the possibility that A contains only two elements is considered.

[13]   Most authors in social choice theory discuss non-strict as well as strict individual preferences. In particular, this is true for Arrow (1963). Hence the simplification runs counter to my expressed wish to stay as close as possible to Arrow's impossibility theorem. In spite of this, I have found that the benefits of simplifying outweigh the costs. The case of non-strict preferences is considered in Hylland (1991).

tion are not a priori assumed to be strict; it will, however, follow from other conditions that they are strict.

Let m and n be positive integers. Define $M = \{1, 2, \ldots m\}$ and $N = \{1, 2, \ldots n\}$. Typical members of M are denoted i and j, while k and k' are the typical members of N. Both M and N can be thought of as sets of individuals. As described in the Introduction and in Section 3, individuals play two different roles in the model; therefore, it is convenient to distinguish the sets M and N. An individual $i \, \varepsilon \, M$ is one who has interests, whereas $k \, \varepsilon \, N$ denotes an individual who expresses judgments. In a specific interpretation, the sets M and N may or may not be equal.

Let $\underline{P}$ be the set of strict orderings on A, $\underline{R}$ the set of weak orderings on A, and $\underline{Q}$ the set of strict orderings on the Cartesian product of A and M. Typical members are denoted P, R, and Q, respectively.

If $Q \, \varepsilon \, \underline{Q}$, then Q is an ordering on the set of pairs (x, i), and the expression $(x, i) \, Q \, (y, j)$ is interpreted as "being individual i in state x is better than being individual j in state y (according to Q)."

A *social choice function for subjective interpersonal comparison,* abbreviated SIC-function, is a function defined on $\underline{Q}^n$ or a subset thereof, with values in $\underline{R}$. Hence if F is an SIC-function, a typical expression is

$$F(Q_1, Q_2, \ldots Q_n) = R$$

If $n = 1$, the input to the social choice function consists of only one ordering of the pairs (x, i). In the Introduction I referred to this as the case of objective interpersonal comparison. Hence the following definition is appropriate: A *social choice function for objective interpersonal comparison,* abbreviated OIC-function, is a function defined on $\underline{Q}$ or a subset thereof, with values in $\underline{R}$. When F is such a function, the typical expression is

$$F(Q) = R$$

Note that the latter concept is a special case of the former; any OIC-function is also an SIC-function.

Let Σ be the set of strict orderings on M. Typical elements of Σ will be denoted π and σ. For given $x \, \varepsilon \, A$ and $Q \, \varepsilon \, \underline{Q}$, we define $\sigma \, \varepsilon \, \Sigma$ by

$i \, \sigma \, j$ if and only if $(x, i) \, Q \, (x, j)$

This σ is called the *characteristic* of x with respect to Q.

We shall need the concept *pre-filter*. It can be defined generally for any set, but because we shall only deal with pre-filters on M and N, we might as well keep the definition specific. It is given here for M; for N, definition, discussion, and examples are completely analogous.

A *pre-filter* on M is a set Φ of subsets of M, satisfying the following conditions:

   (1). The set M is an element of Φ.
   (2). The empty set is not an element of Φ.
   (3). If M_1 and M_2 are subsets of M, M_1 is a subset of M_2, and $M_1 \varepsilon \Phi$, then $M_2 \varepsilon \Phi$.

Intuitively, we can think of the elements of Φ as the "big" or "powerful" subsets of M. The three conditions say that the whole of M is powerful, the empty set is not, and if a subset of a given set is powerful, then that given set is also powerful. It is not, however, just a question of size; in example (a) next, there exist subsets M_1 and M_2 of M such that M_1 is an element of Φ_1, M_2 is not, but M_1 has fewer elements than M_2.

Examples of pre-filters on M:

   (a). Let $i \varepsilon M$ be given, and let Φ_i consist of exactly those subsets of M that contain i.
   (b). Let I be a non-empty subset of M, and let Φ_I consist of exactly those subsets of M that have a non-empty intersection with I.
   (c). Let an integer q be given, satisfying $1 \le q \le m$. Let Φ_q^* consist of all subsets of M that have q or more elements.
   (d). Assign to each element of M a nonnegative weight, at least one of the weights being strictly positive. Let a be the sum of the weights, and fix a number b satisfying $0 < b \le a$. A subset M' of M belongs to Φ_W if and only if the sum of the weights of the elements of M' is at least b.

Example (a) is a special case of (b), with $I = \{i\}$. Moreover, (b) for $I = M$ coincides with (c) for $q = 1$. All of (a), (b), and (c) are special cases of (d).[14] When $m \geq 4$, the examples do not exhaust the whole class of pre-filters on M.

For a given pre-filter Φ on M we define Φ^d, the *dual* of Φ, as follows: A subset of M' of M belongs to Φ^d if and only if its complement $M\backslash M'$ does not belong to Φ. It is not difficult to prove that Φ^d is itself a pre-filter on M. Examples: (a) The pre-filter Φ_i is its own dual. (b) When I is a non-empty subset of M, the dual of Φ_I consists of all subsets of M that contain I. (c) For $1 \leq q \leq m$, the dual of Φ_q^* is Φ_{m+1-q}^*.

Let a pre-filter Φ on M be given. We shall define the *corresponding function* of Φ. This is a function f from Σ to M, and the definition is the following: For $\sigma \, \varepsilon \, \Sigma$, find $i \, \varepsilon \, M$ such that

$$\{j \, \varepsilon \, M \mid j \, \sigma \, i\} \notin \Phi,$$

and

$$\{j \, \varepsilon \, M \mid j \, \sigma \, i \text{ or } j = i\} \, \varepsilon \, \Phi$$

It follows from conditions (1)–(3) that this i exists and is unique. We let $f(\sigma) = i$. Because $\sigma \, \varepsilon \, \Sigma$ was arbitrary, the function f is thereby defined.

Intuitively, we can think of the process for computing $f(\sigma)$ this way: We start from the top of the ordering σ, collecting the elements of M one by one as they occur in the ranking given by σ. At some point, the subset of M that we have collected becomes an element of Φ. The value $f(\sigma)$ is the element of M that made the collected subset a member of Φ. In other words, $f(\sigma)$ is the individual who turned the subset into a powerful one.

Examples:

  (a). The function f_i corresponding to the pre-filter Φ_i is a constant function, with $f_i(\sigma) = i$ for all $\sigma \, \varepsilon \, \Sigma$.
  (b). The function f_I corresponding to the pre-filter Φ_I is defined as follows: For each $\sigma \, \varepsilon \, \Sigma$, $f_I(\sigma)$ is the first element of I according to the ordering σ.

---

[14]   In (a), we give i weight 1, every other element of M weight 0, and choose $b = 1$. In (b), every element of I has weight 1, the other elements of M have weight 0, and $b = 1$. In (c), every element of M has weight 1, and $b = q$.

(c). The function f_q^* corresponding to the pre-filter Φ_q^* is defined as follows: For each $\sigma \, \epsilon \, \Sigma$, $f_q^*(\sigma)$ is the qth element in the ranking given by σ.

To every pre-filter on M there corresponds a function from Σ to M, but not vice-versa. (An example of an f that is not the corresponding function of any pre-filter is given in Section 5.) We want to formulate a condition that characterizes the corresponding functions of pre-filters.

For $\sigma \, \epsilon \, \Sigma$ and $i, j \, \epsilon \, M$, $i \, \sigma! \, j$ shall mean that i is immediately ahead of j in the ordering given by σ. In that case, we denote by σ^{ji} the element of Σ that is obtained by interchanging i and j in σ, leaving the rest of the ordering unchanged.

We shall look at the possible effect on the f-value of interchanging the two adjacent elements i and j in σ. The following condition requires that either there be a change from i to j, or a change from j to i, or no change at all. In the last case, $f(\sigma) = f(\sigma^{ji})$ can be equal to i or j or any other element of M.

Condition A. A function f from Σ to M satisfies Condition A if the following holds, for all $i, j \, c \, M$ and all $\sigma \, \epsilon \, \Sigma$ with $i \, \sigma! \, j$: If $f(\sigma)$ and $f(\sigma^{ji})$ are not equal, *then* $f(\sigma), f(\sigma^{ji}) \, \epsilon \, \{i, j\}$.

It can be proved that a function from Σ to M satisfies Condition A if and only if it is the corresponding function of a pre-filter on M. There is a one-to-one correspondence between pre-filters and functions satisfying the condition; to every pre-filter there corresponds exactly one such function, and vice-versa.

3. Judgments and interests

The expression

$$(x, i) \, Q_k \, (y, j)$$

is interpreted as follows: According to the ordering $Q_k \, \epsilon \, \underline{Q}$, which is supposed to represent the subjective views of individual k, it is better being individual i in state x than being individual j in state y. Expressions of this type make up the input to an SIC-function.

As previously pointed out, the role played by individual k in the expression is different, in an important way, from the role played by i and j. For i and j, their *interests* are at stake; the question is who of the two is better off, according to a certain evaluation and given specific social states. On the other hand, it is the *judgment* of k, or a part of it, that is being represented by the expression and thus enters the aggregation process.

If all members of a society are considered fundamentally equal, it seems reasonable that they all shall have both their interests and their judgments count in the social choice process. In the notation of Section 2, we will then have $M = N$. The sets M and N contain the same individuals, and we might as well assume that they are numbered in the same way, so that $i \in M$ and $i \in N$ refer to the same person. We can think of this as the "standard" case, and most of the motivating remarks in the Introduction were written with that case in mind.

It is possible, however, that a society contains members whose interest one wants to take account of, but whose judgments are not found worthy of consideration. These individuals will be members of the set M, but not of N. Examples could be small children, drug addicts, and the mentally retarded.

Conversely, there may exist persons who are not really members of the society in question and who have no personal interest in the social choice (or no interest that should legitimately count), but whose good judgment is appreciated. Hence their judgment, in the technical sense of the word, might be considered relevant and taken into account in the social choice process. These persons will belong to N but not M.

The members of N need not even be persons. A $k \in N$ could represent a "consideration," or a "point of view," or a "criterion," or the like, which is considered relevant for the social choice.

It is quite possible that there exists no person whose interests and judgments are both counted. Issues that are important for one group of people, are sometimes decided by – or on the basis of judgments made by – one or more outside referees. The referees do not have, or are at least supposed not to have, any personal or direct interest in the issues. It is not difficult to find institutions functioning in this manner in actual societies.

I shall not pursue this discussion further, because it is not the main topic of the chapter. I just emphasize the distinction between on the one hand the *standard* case, where M and N are equal and contain the same individuals, similarly numbered, and on the other hand all other cases. (Even outside the standard case it may happen that M and N have the same number of members and thus are formally equal, but that is irrelevant for the distinction made here.)

An SIC-function gets as its input information about interests and judgments, and aggregates this into a ranking of the social states. The aggregation is, or may at least be, simultaneous; nothing in the formalism allows us to distinguish aggregation of judgments from aggregation of interests.

Because judgments and interests are quite different phenomena, one might question the wisdom of formulating a model in which the two forms of aggregation are completely intermingled.[15] An alternative formalism could be the following:

The input to the process is a vector $(Q_1, Q_2, \ldots Q_n)$ ε $\underline{Q}^n$ of individual judgments. First, these are aggregated into a social or collective judgment Q ε $\underline{Q}$. Formally, this part of the process can be represented by a function G from $\underline{Q}^n$ to $\underline{Q}$. Then the social judgment forms the basis for interest aggregation, resulting in a ranking R of the social states. The formal representation of this stage is a function H from $\underline{Q}$ to $\underline{R}$ – that is, an OIC-function.

The whole process is represented by the composite function $H \cdot G$, and a typical expression of the result will be:

$$H(G(Q_1, Q_2, \ldots Q_n)) = R$$

The composition $H \cdot G$ is an SIC-function, but not all SIC-functions can be expressed in this form. Requiring separate aggregation of judgments and interests reduces the set of potentially acceptable aggregation procedures.

One can impose on G and H conditions similar to, or with motivation similar to, the conditions of Section 4. At the end of Sections 6 and 7 I comment on the consequences of doing this.

---

[15] This point was raised by John Broome at the conference mentioned in note 1.

4. Conditions

As pointed out in the Introduction, the strategy of the chapter is to impose on SIC-functions the conditions of Arrow's impossibility theorem, except the nondictatorship condition.

The definition of an SIC-function requires that a value of the function be an element in $\underline{R}$ – that is, an *ordering* on the set A. Thus all values of the function are transitive and complete relations. This is implicit in the definition, and transitivity and completeness need not be explicitly imposed as conditions.

Because SIC-functions and social choice functions in Arrow's sense are defined on different domains, the original conditions cannot be applied directly; they must be reformulated to fit the present model. My reformulation of the conditions Pareto Optimality (PO), Independence of Irrelevant Alternatives (IIA), and Unrestricted Domain (UD) reads as follows:

Pareto Optimality. The SIC-function F satisfies PO if the following holds for all $(Q_1, Q_2, \ldots Q_n)$ on which F is defined, and for all $x, y \in A$: *If* $(x, i) Q_k (y, i)$ for all $i \in M$ and all $k \in N$, *then* x is ranked ahead of y in the ordering $F(Q_1, Q_2, \ldots Q_n)$.

Independence of Irrelevant Alternatives. The SIC-function F satisfies IIA if the following holds for all $(Q_1, Q_2, \ldots Q_n)$ and $(Q_1', Q_2', \ldots Q_n')$ on which F is defined, and for all $x, y \in A$: *If*, for all k, Q_k and Q_k' are equal when restricted to the Cartesian product of $\{x, y\}$ and M, *then* $F(Q_1, Q_2, \ldots Q_n)$ and $F(Q_1', Q_2', \ldots Q_n')$ are equal when restricted to $\{x, y\}$.

Unrestricted Domain. The SIC-function F satisfies UD if it is defined on all $(Q_1, Q_2, \ldots Q_n) \in \underline{Q}^n$.

The question of whether Arrow's conditions PO, IIA, and UD are reasonable in his model, is discussed at length in the literature.[16] Most of the arguments for and against are also relevant in the present model. I make no attempt to repeat or summarize them.

---

[16]   Reviews of the discussion can, for example, be found in Sen (1970), Kelly (1978), and several of the articles in Elster and Hylland (1986).

Another question is whether my conditions are correct analogies of those of Arrow, or whether I have somehow changed the significance of one or more of the conditions when translating them into my own formalism.

Concerning IIA, it seems obvious to me that my translation is correct; I can see no alternative version.[17]

As for PO, we note that the usual distinction between weak and strong Pareto Optimality has disappeared, because the orderings Q_k are assumed to be strict. However, I can think of two alternative formulations of the condition, one weaker and one stronger than the version given earlier.

First, an alternative to the final clause in the definition could be the following:

If (x, i) Q_k (y, j) for all $i, j \varepsilon M$ and all $k \varepsilon N$, *then x is ranked ahead of y in the ordering* $F(Q_1, Q_2, \ldots Q_n)$.

This gives a weaker condition, placing fewer restrictions on $F(Q_1, Q_2, \ldots Q_n)$. To make the difference clear, let a vector $(Q_1, Q_2, \ldots Q_n) \varepsilon \underline{Q}^n$ of individual judgments be given. Suppose that (x, i) Q_k (y, i) for all $i \varepsilon M$ and all $k \varepsilon N$ – that is, each person is, in everybody's judgment, better off under x than under y. At the same time, we have (y, i) Q_k (x, j) for some i and j and some k; for example, i is definitely better off than j (in k's opinion). Hence it is not the case that all outcomes that have to do with x are considered superior to all outcomes related to y. The original PO requires that the ordering $F(Q_1, Q_2, \ldots Q_n)$ rank x ahead of y; the alternative places no restrictions on $F(Q_1, Q_2, \ldots Q_n)$ in relation to x and y. In my view, there is in this case genuine unanimity that x is better than y, so the idea behind Pareto Optimality implies that x should be socially ranked above y. Therefore, the alternative considered here is not reasonable and is not discussed further.

The second alternative is a strengthening of PO, to the following condition PO^+. It only makes sense in the standard case, where $M = N$.

---

[17] Other authors use the same condition. For example, Condition I** in Roberts (1980), Section 5, is equivalent to IIA.

Pareto Optimality$^+$. The SIC-function F satisfies PO$^+$ if the following holds for all $(Q_1, Q_2, \ldots Q_n)$ on which F is defined, and for all $x, y \in A$: If $(x, i) Q_i (y, i)$ for all $i \in M = N$, *then x is ranked ahead of y in the ordering $F(Q_1, Q_2, \ldots Q_n)$*.

This condition becomes operative as soon as every $i \in M$ considers (x, i) to be superior to (y, i); it ignores a possible judgment by some $k \neq i$ that $(y, i) Q_k (x, i)$. Hence PO$^+$ puts more restrictions on $F(Q_1, Q_2, \ldots Q_n)$ than PO does.[18]

The condition UD requires some further comments. There can be no doubt that my version of the condition is a correct translation of that of Arrow. There are, however, some arguments against the condition that do not apply in Arrow's model.

We consider the standard case described in Section 3; that is, M and N contain the same individuals, numbered in the same way. For $k \neq i$, the following statements could both be true:

$$(x, i) \; Q_i \; (y, i)$$

$$(y, i) \; Q_k \; (x, i)$$

Hence i is better off in x than in y, according to i's own judgment. In spite of this, k expresses the judgment that i is better off in y than in x. In other words, k's judgment is paternalistic.

If one does not like paternalism, it seems reasonable to rule out this kind of judgment, and only require that an SIC-function be defined when paternalism does not occur. This motivates the following weakened version of UD:

Unrestricted Domain Subject to Weak Anti-Paternalism (UD-WAP). The SIC-function F satisfies UD-WAP if it is defined on all $(Q_1, Q_2, \ldots Q_n) \in \underline{Q}^n$ that satisfy the following: For all $x, y \in A$ and all $i, k \in M = N$, $(x, i) Q_k (y, i)$ if and only if $(x, i) Q_i (y, i)$.

When weak anti-paternalism is assumed, the conditions PO and PO$^+$ coincide.

[18]   Roberts (1980) refers to PO$^+$ as the (weak) Pareto criterion; PO is equivalent to his condition "universal unanimity." In a sense, PO$^+$ implies that one refuses to take account of paternalistic judgments, and hence it is related in spirit to anti-paternalism.

It is possible to formulate a stronger concept of anti-paternalism than the one given. Let i, j, and k be three different individuals. Suppose the following relations hold:

$$(x, i) \ Q_i \ (y, j)$$

$$(x, i) \ Q_j \ (y, j)$$

$$(y, j) \ Q_k \ (x, i)$$

In this case, k also expresses a paternalistic judgment. The choice between (x, i) and (y, j) concerns only the interests of i and j. Because i and j happen to agree that (x, i) is better than (y, j), a person who rejects paternalism may say that the matter is thereby decided; everybody must respect the joint judgment of the two persons involved. (If i and j do not agree on which is the better of (x, i) and (y, j), k is allowed to make an independent judgment; neither $(x, i) \ Q_k \ (y, j)$ nor $(y, j) \ Q_k \ (x, i)$ can be called paternalistic.)

The condition reads as follows:

Unrestricted Domain Subject to Strong Anti-Paternalism (UD-SAP). The SIC-function F satisfies UD-SAP if it is defined on all $(Q_1, Q_2, \ldots Q_n) \ \varepsilon \ \underline{Q}^n$ that satisfy the following: For all $x, y \ \varepsilon \ A$ and all i, j, $k \ \varepsilon \ M = N$, if $(x, i) \ Q_i \ (y, j)$ and $(x, i) \ Q_j \ (y, j)$, *then* $(x, i) \ Q_k \ (y, j)$.

If we let $i = j$ in the strong condition, it reduces to the weak one. (The cases $k = i$ and $k = j$ are vacuous.) Strong anti-paternalism is really stronger than weak anti-paternalism, and the domain condition UD-SAP is weaker than UD-WAP. They are both weaker than UD.

Should anti-paternalism be imposed? I do not want to express any definite view on this; it could also depend on factors that are not specified in the abstract framework of social choice theory.

On the one hand, one could argue that i has a right, based on individual freedom and autonomy, to decide the choice between (x, i) and (y, i); this supports (weak) anti-paternalism. On the other hand, there could be individuals whose judgments are not considered reliable, for example, small children. In Section 3 I discussed the possibility that such persons could be included in the set M but not in N; then their interests are taken account of, but their judgments are ignored.

Less radically, one can include these individuals in both M and N and thus in principle take account of their judgments as well as their interests, but reject anti-paternalism and allow others to express independent judgments about these interests.

I do not continue this discussion. In this chapter, my task is to explore the consequences of imposing the anti-paternalism condition.

Still we might ask whether there are any reasons for imposing weak anti-paternalism and not strong. If one accepts the arguments for anti-paternalism, do not these arguments immediately lead to the strong version?

I know of one argument that supports weak anti-paternalism but not strong[19]: Suppose that we reject the view that i has a *right* to decide the choice between (x, i) and (y, i). Still, weak anti-paternalism can be defended on the grounds that nobody knows better than person i what it is like to be person i. We can reasonably regard i as an expert on the choice between (x, i) and (y, i), and hence require that i's judgment on this point be respected by everybody. If i and j are different persons, however, there is no reason to assume that i has special expertise concerning the choice between (x, i) and (y, j), and the same holds for j. If they agree on this choice, it is probably just an accident; the shared view of two uninformed persons does not make up an expert opinion. Hence strong anti-paternalism is rejected.

Weak anti-paternalism is equivalent to saying that everybody agrees on which is the better of (x, i) and (y, i). In particular, they shall all agree with i's judgment, but that is not the point here. Hence we can equivalently formulate the condition UD-WAP like this:

Unrestricted Domain Subject to Weak Anti-Paternalism (UD-WAP). The SIC-function F satisfies UD-WAP if it is defined on all $(Q_1, Q_2, \ldots Q_n) \varepsilon \underline{Q}^n$ that satisfy the following: For all $x, y \varepsilon A$, all $i \varepsilon M$ and all $k, k' \varepsilon \overline{N}$, $(x, i) Q_k (y, i)$ if and only if $(x, i) Q_{k'} (y, i)$.

The advantage of this formulation is that it also makes sense when M and N do not contain the same individuals. If a certain i belongs to both M and N, the last definition says exactly the same as the previous one. Then consider an individual i who belongs to M but not to N. For example, the reason could be that i is not trusted to make sound

---

[19]   It has been suggested by John Roemer.

judgments about interpersonal comparison. Still one might trust and respect i's choices between pairs of the type (x, i) and (y, i). This would amount to all judgments being equal on the set $\{(x, i), (y, i)\}$, exactly as the last definition requires. Another possiblity is that i is not trusted to make any judgment, but still there could be a specific ranking over pairs involving i that has a special status and should be respected by everybody. This could, for example, be the ranking determined by the parents of a child or the guardian of a retarded person. Again, the last version of UD-WAP says what we want it to say.[20]

If we are not in the standard case, the definition of strong anti-paternalism still makes sense for all i and j that belong to the intersection of M and N, and for all $k \, \varepsilon \, N$. But a general formulation of the condition does not seem possible in this case.

In Section 7, UD is weakened to UD-WAP, and an interesting result emerges. I have not, however, been able to prove any results using UD-SAP.

5. Objective interpersonal comparison

In this section, the case $n = 1$ will be discussed; in other words, we consider OIC-functions. The question is: Which functions of this type satisfy PO, IIA, and UD? Because OIC-function is a special case of SIC-function, the conditions defined in Section 4 can be applied directly.

In the Introduction I said that this model is inadequate, if one takes seriously the intuitive arguments for accepting interpersonal comparisons. I nevertheless study the model, partly as background for what comes later, partly because it has been extensively discussed in the literature.

From Arrow's theorem and other well-known results, we would expect that there exists a class of *dictatorial* OIC-functions satisfying PO, IIA, and UD. This is indeed the case, and these functions are defined as follows:

Fix an individual $i \, \varepsilon \, M$. We shall define an OIC-function F_i. For a given $Q \, \varepsilon \, \underline{Q}$, ignore all pairs of the form (x, j) for $j \neq i$, and concentrate attention on the pairs (x, i), where x varies over A. The order in

---

[20]   In these cases, the phrase "anti-paternalism" may be misplaced, but the condition is a meaningful one.

which Q ranks these pairs, defines an ordering on A – that is, an element of $\underline{R}$. This ordering is the value $F_i(Q)$. Formally, $x \, F_i(Q) \, y$ if and only if $(x, i) \, Q \, (y, i)$, for all $x, y \, \varepsilon \, A$.

These are not the only acceptable functions. An example of a nondictatorial OIC-function satisfying the conditions is the *maximin rule*.[21] For reasons that will become clear later, I call it F_m^*, and it can be described in this way:

Let $Q \, \varepsilon \, \underline{Q}$ be given; we shall compute $F_m^*(Q)$. For any $x \, \varepsilon \, A$, look at the way in which Q ranks the pairs (x, i), where i varies over M. Find the lowest ranked of these pairs, and find the corresponding individual i; this i is denoted $m(x)$. It is the individual who is worst off, which is the same as being mth best off, according to Q if x is realized. Similarly, we define $m(y)$, $m(z)$, and so on, for $y \, \varepsilon \, A$, $z \, \varepsilon \, A$, and so on. The ranking of x compared to y in $F_m^*(Q)$ shall be the same as the ranking of $(x, m(x))$ compared to $(y, m(y))$ in Q.

Intuitively, we can say that we rank x, y, z, and so on by considering only the position of the worst-off individual. It must be noted, however, that there is not *one* worst-off individual; there is one who is worst off if x is realized, possibly another who is worst off under y, and so on. In addition, everything depends on the chosen $Q \, \varepsilon \, \underline{Q}$.

More generally, instead of looking at the worst-off individual, we can choose an integer q satisfying $1 \le q \le m$ and consider the individual who is qth best off. In exact analogy with the earlier description, we can define an OIC-function F_q^*. The maximin rule corresponds to $q = m$. If $q = 1$, only the position of the best-off individual is taken into account; this can be called the *maximax rule*. Collectively, the functions F_q^* are referred to as *positional dictatorships;* each of them gives all power not to a specific individual, but to a specific position in the relevant ranking.

It is not difficult to prove that all positional dictatorships satisfy the three conditions PO, IIA, and UD. If we in addition require that the function be *anonymous,* which essentially means that it shall treat all individuals equally, the converse also holds: An OIC-function satisfies these four conditions if and only if it is a positional dictatorship.[22]

---

[21]   It is often called Rawls' maximin rule because of resemblance to philosophical ideas presented in Rawls (1971).

[22]   This was proved in Roberts (1980), Theorem 4. A similar result, but with slightly stronger conditions, can be found in Gevers (1979), Theorem 4.

Still we have not exhausted the class of OIC-functions satisfying PO, IIA, and UD. In a positional dictatorship we always use the same principle when deciding which individual shall determine the ranking of x compared to other members of A. Would it be possible to let this principle vary and depend on x and Q? Could we, for example, in some cases look at the best-off individual, in other cases the one who is second best off, and so forth?

The conditions PO, IIA, and UD together imply that the OIC-function has a property called *neutrality;* it essentially treats all elements of A equally. Therefore, the principle by which the deciding individual is chosen cannot depend on x itself. But it can depend on properties of x; in particular, it can depend on how the pairs (x, i), where i varies over M, are ranked in Q. In other words, it can depend on the characteristic of x with respect to Q; see the definition in Section 2.

Let f be a function from Σ to M. If $\sigma \; \varepsilon \; \Sigma$ is the characteristic of x with respect to Q, we choose $f(\sigma)$ as the deciding individual in the case of x and Q.

The procedure can be more formally described as follows: We shall define an OIC-function F derived from f. Choose $Q \; \varepsilon \; \underline{Q}$ and $x, y \; \varepsilon \; A$. We must determine whether $F(Q)$ ranks x ahead of y or vice versa. Let π be the characteristic of x with respect to Q, while σ is the characteristic of y with respect to Q; π and σ are elements of Σ. Consider the pairs $(x, f(\pi))$ and $(y, f(\sigma))$, and look at their relative ranking in Q. If the former is ranked higher than the latter, we rank x ahead of y in $F(Q)$; otherwise, we rank y above x. Because x and y were arbitrary elements of A, $F(Q)$ is now fully specified. Then F is completely defined, because Q was an arbitrary element of $\underline{Q}$.

The resulting F is a well-defined OIC-function, and it satisfies IIA and UD. It may, however, violate PO, as shown by the following example: Let $m = 3$ and $M = \{1, 2, 3\}$, let π and σ be the elements of Σ given by $1 \; \pi \; 2 \; \pi \; 3$ and $1 \; \sigma \; 3 \; \sigma \; 2$, and let $f(\pi) = 1, f(\sigma) = 3$. The rest of the function f need not be specified. Choose x and y in A, and find a $Q \; \varepsilon \; \underline{Q}$ that ranks the six pairs that involve x and y in the following way:

$$(y, 1) \; Q \; (x, 1) \; Q \; (y, 3) \; Q \; (y, 2) \; Q \; (x, 2) \; Q \; (x, 3)$$

We have $(y, i)\, Q\, (x, i)$ for all $i\, \varepsilon\, M$; hence PO requires that $F(Q)$ rank y above x. The characteristic of x with respect to Q is π, and that of y is σ. According to the definition of F, we shall look at the pairs $(x, f(\pi)) = (x, 1)$ and $(y, f(\sigma)) = (y, 3)$. In Q, the former is ranked above the latter, which implies $x\, F(Q)\, y$. This proves that F violates PO.

Note that f does not satisfy Condition A, formulated in Section 2. We have $2\, \pi!\, 3$ and $\sigma = \pi^{32}$, but the change from $f(\pi)$ to $f(\sigma)$ is not of the type permitted by the condition.

In order to guarantee that PO be satisfied, we must impose some restriction on the function f. It turns out that Condition A is necessary and sufficient for F to satisfy PO. This, in turn, is equivalent to the statement that there exists a pre-filter Φ on M such that f is the corresponding function of Φ.

Given a pre-filter Φ on M, we can first find the corresponding function f of Φ; this is a function from Σ to M. Then we can construct an OIC-function F from f as described earlier. We say that F is *derived* from Φ.

The function F derived from a pre-filter Φ is always a well-defined OIC-function, satisfying PO, IIA, and UD. The converse also holds, and we have the following result:

Theorem 1. An OIC-function F satisfies PO, IIA, and UD if and only if there exists a pre-filter Φ on M such that F is derived from Φ.

For given A and M, there is a one-to-one correspondence between the class of pre-filters on M and the class of OIC-functions satisfying the three conditions; one such function corresponds to exactly one pre-filter, and vice-versa.

Equivalently, we can characterize the class of OIC-functions that satisfy PO, IIA, and UD by the class of functions from Σ to M that satisfy Condition A. Again, there is a one-to-one correspondence between the two classes.[23]

Finally, I shall point out the connection between the examples considered earlier in this section and some of the examples of pre-filters given in Section 2.

Example (a) of Section 2: If we start with the pre-filter Φ_i, we will

---

[23]   Theorem 1 is essentially proved in Section 4 of Roberts (1980); see his Theorems 2 and 3. He does not, however, put the results together to formulate explicitly a result like my Theorem 1. The notation is different, but the conclusion of his Theorem 3 corresponds to my Condition A.

derive the OIC-function F_i that makes individual i an ordinary dictator.

Example (b): From the pre-filter Φ_I is derived the function that ignores all individuals not in I, and then applies the maximax rule.

Example (c): From the pre-filter Φ_q^* is derived the qth positional dictatorship F_q^*.

6. Unrestricted domain

Now we assume $n > 1$ – that is, we look at the genuine case of subjective interpersonal comparison. The following result can be proved[24]:

Theorem 2. Let F be an SIC-function satisfying PO, IIA, and UD. Then there exist (i) a $k \ \varepsilon \ N$, and (ii) an OIC-function F_0 that satisfies PO, IIA, and UD, such that

$$(*) \qquad F(Q_1, Q_2, \ldots Q_n) = F_0(Q_k) \text{ for all } (Q_1, Q_2, \ldots Q_n) \ \varepsilon \ \underline{Q}^n.$$

Conversely, if k and F_0 satisfy (i) and (ii) and F is given by $(*)$, then F is an SIC-function, and it satisfies PO, IIA, and UD.

The function F_0 must belong to the class described by Theorem 1. The two theorems give a complete characterization of the class of SIC-functions satisfying the three conditions.

For a given F satisfying the conditions, the individual k and the OIC-function F_0 are uniquely determined. Conversely, k and F_0 uniquely determine F.

Any function F covered by Theorem 2 is dictatorial, in the sense that it takes account of the *judgments* of only one individual $k \ \varepsilon \ N$. We call such a function a *judgment dictatorship*. On the other hand, F may take account of the *interests* – as viewed by k – of several, possibly all, individuals in M. For example, F_0 could be the maximin rule or some other positional dictatorship, which treats everybody equally as far as interests are concerned.

If PO is strengthened to PO$^+$ in Theorem 2, the class of acceptable

[24]   It corresponds to Roberts (1980), Theorem 5.

functions is further restricted.[25] Then F_0 must be equal to the dictatorship F_k, defined in Section 5. In that case, k is really a dictator; the only things that count, are k's interests as judged by k.

A function that satisfies the conditions of Theorem 2 will aggregate judgments and interests separately. The judgment aggregation is in a sense trivial, because there is a specific individual whose personal judgment always becomes the social judgment. No further restriction is imposed by the alternative formalism described at the end of Section 3. This holds if A has at least three elements, as is assumed earlier. Things change, however, if A has only two elements; let us say $A = \{x, y\}$. This case is empirically important, but it is usually considered trivial and not discussed in social choice theory. Then Theorems 1 and 2 do not apply; the condition IIA is vacuous, and an SIC-function can use essentially all information from $Q_1, Q_2, \ldots Q_n$ when deciding whether x is socially ranked above or below y, subject only to Pareto Optimality. If we now require separate aggregation of judgments and interests, assume $m \geq 2$, and impose on the judgment aggregation process G conditions corresponding to PO, IIA, and UD, it follows that G even in this case must be dictatorial. Thus the composite function $H \cdot G$ must be of type (*), but Theorem 1 does not apply, and the OIC-function $F_0 = H$ can use more information than is allowed according to that theorem. In any case, the conclusion is that separate aggregation of judgments and interests is a real restriction when A has two elements.

7. Weak anti-paternalism

When UD is weakened to UD-WAP, the functions covered by Theorem 2 are still acceptable.[26] The question is whether there are any others.

Before answering the question, let me make a couple of other remarks. In the comments to Theorem 2, it was pointed out that if the SIC-function F is a judgment dictatorship, the dictator $k \, \varepsilon \, N$ is uniquely determined. This need not be true in the present case.

Let $i \, \varepsilon \, M$ be given and fixed. Choose $k \, \varepsilon \, N$ arbitrarily, and let F_{ik} be

---

[25]   See Roberts (1980), Theorem 6.
[26]   To be pedantic, they are not the same functions, because they are now defined on a smaller domain.

the dictatorial function that only takes account of the interests of i, as judged by k. Hence $F_{ik}(Q_1, Q_2, \ldots Q_n)$ depends only on Q_k, and as a function of Q_k it behaves exactly as the dictatorial OIC-function F_i, defined in Section 5. Formally we have

$$F_{ik}(Q_1, Q_2, \ldots Q_n) = F_i(Q_k)$$

for all $(Q_1, Q_2, \ldots Q_n)$ that are admissible under weak anti-paternalism.

Because of weak anti-paternalism, it does not matter which k we choose in the earlier construction. That is, for all k and k' in N and all admissible $(Q_1, Q_2, \ldots Q_n)$, we have

$$F_{ik}(Q_1, Q_2, \ldots Q_n) = F_{ik'}(Q_1, Q_2, \ldots Q_n)$$

It follows that every $k \ \varepsilon \ N$ is a dictator for the function F_{ik}. There are n different SIC-functions defined on the whole domain $\underline{Q}^n$, each of them dictatorial and having a unique dictator, which coincide when restricted to the domain admitted by UD-WAP.

Saying that everybody is a dictator is unnatural use of language; a dictator ought to be unique. Therefore, we should perhaps regard a function of the type just described not as a judgment dictatorship with any k as a dictator, but as a special kind of SIC-function called *interest dictatorship*. The interest dictator i is unique, and the fact of the matter is that i's interests alone determine the social ranking of the alternatives in A. I emphasize, however, that any interest dictatorships formally is a judgment dictatorship.

Then suppose F is a "genuine" judgment dictatorship with a unique dictator k. Even in this case, an individual $i \neq k$ is not necessarily without influence on the social ranking. By weak anti-paternalism, Q_k is partially determined by the preferences of i; hence these preferences may play a role. This contrasts with the situation in Section 6, where Q_k is determined independently of the preferences of every $i \neq k$.

I now return to the question asked at the beginning of the section. The answer is in the positive; there exist nondictatorial SIC-functions that satisfy PO, IIA, and UD-WAP. I first give an example.

Suppose n is odd. Let i and j be two members of M, given and fixed throughout the discussion. The SIC-function F_{ij}^*, to be constructed, will depend on the judgments of all $k \varepsilon N$, but only on the interests of i and j.

Fix a vector $(Q_1, Q_2, \ldots Q_n)$ that satisfies weak anti-paternalism. We shall compute $F_{ij}^*(Q_1, Q_2, \ldots Q_n)$, which is an element of $\underline{R}$ – that is, an ordering on A. For simplicity, we call it R. In particular, we choose x and y in A, in order to determine which is the better of these two states according to R.

For any $k \varepsilon N$, consider the way in which Q_k ranks the four pairs (x, i), (x, j), (y, i), and (y, j). Apply the maximin rule to this reduced ranking. If this rule declares that x is better than y, we say that k votes for x; otherwise, k votes for y. We do this exercise for all $k \varepsilon N$ and count the votes for x and y. The one that gets a majority is ranked above the other one in R.

The process is repeated for all choices of $x, y \varepsilon A$, and the whole of R is determined. This is again repeated for all $(Q_1, Q_2, \ldots Q_n)$ that satisfy weak anti-paternalism, and the description of F_{ij}^* is complete.

Majority vote often leads to intransitive results. In the present setting, this would amount to the following: Let x, y, and z be three elements of A. When considering x and y, we conclude that R ranks x ahead of y; when y and z are compared, y is preferred; and when z and x are considered, z is placed above x. If this happens, $R = F_{ij}^*(Q_1, Q_2, \ldots Q_n)$ is not an ordering, and F_{ij}^* is not an SIC-function.

It can be proved that this does not happen. The proof uses weak anti-paternalism in an essential way. If we try to use the earlier description to define $F_{ij}^*(Q_1, Q_2, \ldots Q_n)$ for all $(Q_1, Q_2, \ldots Q_n) \varepsilon \underline{Q}^n$, intransitivities will occur. Moreover, it can be proved that the SIC-function F_{ij}^* satisfies PO and IIA on the domain where it is defined. It has all the required properties.

Clearly, the specific function F_{ij}^* is not the only nondictatorial function that satisfies PO, IIA, and UD-WAP. Compared with the earlier description, generalizations can be made in three ways:

For one thing, any two individuals i and j from M can be chosen as those whose interests are to count.

Moreover, instead of using the maximin rule, one can use the maximax rule. Because only two individuals from M are considered, these are the only positional dictatorships that are possible.

Finally, the "voting" described before need not be an ordinary majority vote. Let a pre-filter Θ on N be given. It is no longer assumed that n is odd. Suppose that i prefers x to y, while j ranks them the other way. Formally, this means that (x, i) Q_k (y, i) and (y, j) Q_k (x, j); the choice of k makes no difference by weak anti-paternalism. Instead of counting votes, we ask whether those $k \ \varepsilon \ N$ who vote for x make up an element of Θ. If so, x is socially preferred to y; otherwise, y is preferred to x. In the case in which both i and j prefer x to y, the condition PO requires that x socially be ranked above y.

It may appear that x and y are treated asymmetrically. This, however, is not the case. We just use the name "x" for that of the two alternatives under consideration that is preferred to the other one by i. There is, in general, asymmetric treatment of i and j, but all elements of A are treated equally. For example, if $k \geq 2$ and the chosen pre-filter is Θ_1^* – constructed in analogy with Example (c) in Section 2 – i's interests are given more weight than those of j: If at least one of the individuals in N make an interpersonal comparison on a certain issue that supports i, then i wins on that issue; j needs unanimous support to win. Conversely, if the pre-filter is O_n^*, then j has the advantage. If we interchange the roles of i and j in the earlier description, and replace Θ with its dual (see Section 2 for a definition), the resulting SIC-function is unchanged.

An SIC-function that can be constructed in one of these ways is called a *binary interest rule*. The reason for the name is that only two persons' interests are taken account of. This result can be proved:

Theorem 3. An SIC-function satisfies PO, IIA, and UD-WAP if and only if it is either a dictatorship in the sense of Theorem 2, or a binary interest rule.

If we insist on separate aggregation of judgments and interests and impose on G the appropriate versions of PO, IIA, and UD-WAP, then binary interest rules are possible for $m = 2$ but not for $m \geq 3$. That is, if there exist other individuals in M than i and j, separate aggregation is a real restriction. The remarks in Section 6 about the case $A = \{x, y\}$ still apply, provided $m \geq 3$.

8. Conclusion

When Universal Domain is modified by assuming weak anti-paternalism, there exist aggregation procedures for subjective interpersonal comparison that satisfy reasonable analogies of Arrow's conditions Pareto Optimality, Independence of Irrelevant Alternatives, and Non-dictatorship. However, the class of acceptable functions is still quite small; in an intuitive sense, every member of the class is close to being dictatorial.

It is an open question whether more functions will satisfy the conditions if strong anti-paternalism is imposed.

Appendix

The complete proofs of the theorems are rather long; they are given in detail in Hylland (1991). Here, I give an outline of the main ideas of the proofs. Most technical details are omitted.

As a mathematical preliminary, we study functions from Σ^n to M; these are called *selection functions*.

Two conditions are imposed on such functions. The first one is analogous to Condition A of Section 2 and is given the same name; it is only modified to take account of the possibility $n > 1$. If two adjacent elements are interchanged in any one of the arguments of the selection function f, then the value of f does not change at all, or it changes as permitted by the previously formulated Condition A. In symbols:

Condition A. A selection function f satisfies Condition A if the following holds for all $i, j \in M$, all $k \in N$, all $\sigma \in \Sigma$ with $i \, \sigma! \, j$, and all $\sigma_1, \ldots \sigma_{k-1}, \sigma_{k+1}, \ldots \sigma_n \in \Sigma$: Define

$$i^* = f(\sigma_1, \ldots \sigma_{k-1}, \sigma, \sigma_{k+1}, \ldots \sigma_n)$$

and

$$j^* = f(\sigma_1, \ldots \sigma_{k-1}, \sigma^{ji}, \sigma_{k+1}, \ldots \sigma_n)$$

If i^* and j^* are not equal, then $i^*, j^* \in \{i, j\}$

In order to formulate the second condition, let $i, j \in M$ and $(\sigma_1, \sigma_2, \ldots \sigma_n) \in \Sigma^n$ be given, let K be a subset of N, and suppose that for every $k \in K$, $i \, \sigma_k! \, j$. We shall keep $\sigma_{k'}$ constant for $k' \notin K$, and consider the effect of changing σ_k to σ_k^{ji} for some or all $k \; \varepsilon \; K$. To simplify the notation, suppose $K = \{1, 2, \ldots n'\}$, with $n' \leq n$. Define a function g from $\{i, j\}^K = \{i, j\}^{n'}$ to M by

$$g(i_1, i_2, \ldots i_{n'}) = f(\pi_1, \pi_2, \ldots \pi_{n'}, \sigma_{n'+1}, \ldots \sigma_n)$$

where, for each $k \; \varepsilon \; K$, if $i_k = i$ then $\pi_k = \sigma_k$, and if $i_k = j$ then $\pi_k = \sigma_k^{ji}$. If f satisfies Condition A, then either g is constant, or all its values belong to the set $\{i, j\}$. In the latter case, we want to impose a monotonicity condition on g, and hence on f. Suppose that there is a case in which a change in one of the arguments of g from i to j, changes the value from i to j. Then we require that a change in the opposite direction never occurs; that is, it never happens that a change in one of the arguments of g from i to j changes the value from j to i. Similarly, if there is a case where changing one of the arguments from i to j changes the value from j to i, then there shall be no case where changing an argument from i to j changes the value from i to j.

This may sound complicated, but the intuition is simple: Either all changes in the value go in the same direction as the change in the argument, or it is always the other way round. Formally, the following condition expresses this:

Condition B. A selection function f satisfies Condition B if the following holds for all $i, j \; \varepsilon \; M$, all subsets K of N, and all $(\sigma_1, \sigma_2, \ldots \sigma_n) \; \varepsilon \; \Sigma^n$ such that $i \; \sigma_k! \; j$ for every $k \; \varepsilon \; K$: Define g as before. Then either g is constant, or

$$g(i, i, \ldots i) \neq g(j, j, \ldots j)$$

In other words, if the "extreme values" of g are equal, the function must be constant. Note that if g is given and K' is a subset of K, the condition shall also hold if we replace K by K' and redefine g. This guarantees that the original g is really monotone, as described earlier. It should also be noted that if we have two situations that satisfy the premise of Condition B, and define g_1 and g_2 in the obvious way, it is perfectly possible that $g_1(i, i, \ldots i) = i$ and $g_1(j, j, \ldots j) = j$, while $g_2(i, i, \ldots i) = j$ and $g_2(j, j, \ldots j) = i$. Hence f need not be globally monotone in its response to interchanges of i and j in the arguments;

monotonicity is a local phenomenon in each of the situations covered by Condition B.

Two lemmas can be proved:

Lemma 1. Let $n = 1$. A selection function f satisfies Condition A if and only if there exists a pre-filter Φ on M such that f is the corresponding function of Φ.

Lemma 2. Let f be a selection function that satisfies Conditions A and B. Assume that the range of f contains at least three elements. Then there exist (i) a $k \; \varepsilon \; N$, and (ii) a function f_0 from Σ to M that satisfies Condition A, such that

$$(**)\qquad f(\sigma_1, \sigma_2, \ldots \sigma_n) = f_0(\sigma_k) \text{ for all } (\sigma_1, \sigma_2, \ldots \sigma_n) \; \varepsilon \; \Sigma^n$$

A converse result also holds: If k and f_0 satisfy (i) and (ii) and f is given by $(**)$, then f is a selection function that satisfies Conditions A and B.

We say that a function f of the form $(**)$ is *unilateral*. Lemma 2 is an interesting result only for $n > 1$; it is vacuously true when $n = 1$.

There is a connection between Lemma 2 and the famous theorem of Gibbard and Satterthwaite on manipulation of voting schemes; see Gibbard (1973) and Satterthwaite (1975). An element $\sigma \; \varepsilon \; \Sigma$ can be thought of as a strict preference ordering on the set M, and then a selection function can be viewed as a voting scheme in Gibbard's sense. (Here M is interpreted as the set of possible outcomes or social states, whereas N is the set of individuals taking part in the voting.) It is not difficult to prove that if this voting scheme is not manipulable, it must satisfy Conditions A and B, but these two conditions are together weaker than nonmanipulability. Given the premise of Condition A, nonmanipulability implies that either $i^* = j^*$, or $i^* = i$ and $j^* = j$. Condition A also admits the possibility $i^* = j$ and $j^* = i$. Under the premise of Condition B, nonmanipulability requires either that g be constant, or $g(i, i, \ldots i) = i$ and $g(j, j, \ldots j) = j$; Condition B in addition allows the two latter values to be interchanged.

The conclusion of the Gibbard–Satterthwaite theorem implies that if the range of a voting scheme contains at least three elements, then the scheme is unilateral. In Lemma 2, the same conclusion is proved from weaker assumptions. This does not mean that Lemma 2 is strictly stronger than the Gibbard–Satterthwaite theorem, because the latter has a stronger conclusion, but it shows that there is a connection.

Theorem 1, sketch of proof. It is not difficult to prove that an OIC-function derived from a pre-filter on M, satisfies PO, IIA, and UD.

Conversely, suppose that the OIC-function F satisfies the conditions. Let $\sigma \varepsilon \Sigma$ be given. We shall define a function G from $\underline{P}^m$ to $\underline{R}$ as follows: Let $(P_1, P_2, \ldots P_m) \varepsilon \underline{P}^m$ be given. Define $Q \varepsilon \underline{Q}$ by

$$(x, i) \ Q \ (y, j) \quad \text{if either } i \ \sigma \ j, \text{ or } i = j \text{ and } x \ P_i \ y$$

for all $x, y \varepsilon A$ and all $i, j \varepsilon M$. That is, we primarily rank the pairs (x, i) on the basis of the second component and according to σ, but if the second component is equal, we look at the first component and use the appropriate P_i. Then G is defined by

$$G(P_1, P_2, \ldots P_m) = F(Q)$$

This G is a social choice function in the sense of Arrow's original theory. The set of social states is A and the set of individuals is M. From the fact that F satisfies PO, IIA, and UD, as defined in Section 4 of this chapter, we can deduce that G satisfies the corresponding conditions in Arrow's original versions. Hence G is dictatorial; the dictator is an individual in M.

The construction of G depends on σ; therefore, the dictator may also depend on σ. Let f be the function from Σ to M such that for every $\sigma \varepsilon \Sigma$, $f(\sigma)$ is the dictator for G. We can prove that this function satisfies Condition A. By Lemma 1, it is the corresponding function of a pre-filter Φ on M.

The final part of the proof consists in showing that F is actually the OIC-function derived from Φ (or from f) in the way described in Section 5. That is, we must show that F has the following form: Let x, $y \varepsilon A$ and $Q \varepsilon \underline{Q}$ be given, and let π be the characteristic of x and σ the characteristic of y with respect to Q. Then

$$x \ F(Q) \ y \quad \text{if and only if} \quad (x, f(\pi)) \ Q \ (y, f(\sigma))$$

It is not really difficult to prove this, but it is technically complicated.

Theorem 2, sketch of proof. The last statement of the theorem can easily be proved.

In order to prove the first statement, let F be an SIC-function satisfying PO, IIA, and UD. The structure of the proof resembles that of Theorem 1. Let $(\sigma_1, \sigma_2, \ldots \sigma_n) \, \varepsilon \, \Sigma^n$ be given. We shall define a function G from $\underline{P}^{mn}$ to $\underline{R}$. The input to this function will be a vector of the form

$$(P_{ik}; i \, \varepsilon \, M, k \, \varepsilon \, N)$$

Given such a vector, we define $(Q_1, Q_2, \ldots Q_n) \, \varepsilon \, \underline{Q}^n$ by

$$(x, i) \, Q_k \, (y, j) \text{ if either } i \, \sigma_k \, j, \text{ or } i = j \text{ and } x \, P_{ik} \, y$$

for all $x, y \, \varepsilon \, A$, all $i, j \, \varepsilon \, M$, and all $k \, \varepsilon \, N$. The value of G at the given vector is determined by

$$G(P_{ik}; i \, \varepsilon \, M, k \, \varepsilon \, N) = F(Q_1, Q_2, \ldots Q_n)$$

As before, G is a social choice function in Arrow's sense. The set of social states is A. The set of individuals, however, is more complicated; it is the Cartesian product of M and N. The function G inherits the properties PO, IIA, and UD from F. Hence we can again conclude that G is dictatorial. The dictator is a pair (i, k), with $i \, \varepsilon \, M$ and $k \, \varepsilon \, N$.

Let two vectors $(\sigma_1, \sigma_2, \ldots \sigma_n)$, $(\sigma_1', \sigma_2', \ldots \sigma_n') \, \varepsilon \, \Sigma^n$ be given. The earlier construction leads to two functions, G and G', with possibly different dictators (i, k) and (i', k'). We can prove that k and k' are equal. Hence there is a specific $k \, \varepsilon \, N$ such that the dictator for G is always of the form (i, k), for some $i \, \varepsilon \, M$. Next, it can be proved that $F(Q_1, Q_2, \ldots Q_n)$ depends only on Q_k. Finally, we use Theorem 1 to wind up the proof of Theorem 2.

Theorem 3, sketch of proof. An SIC-function that is a dictatorship in the sense of Theorem 2 satisfies PO and IIA on the whole domain $\underline{Q}^n$, and it is easy to show that it is defined and satisfies these conditions on the smaller domain permitted by UD-WAP.

It is also easy to prove that a binary interest rule satisfies PO and IIA whenever it is defined. But is it defined for all $(Q_1, Q_2, \ldots Q_n) \, \varepsilon \, \underline{Q}^n$ that satisfy weak anti-paternalism? The only possible problem is intransitive social preferences. Let the binary interest rule F be given, let i and j be the two individuals in M whose interests count, and suppose that F is defined by the maximax rule and some pre-filter on N. (The proof is similar for binary interest rules based on the maximin rule.) Choose some $(Q_1, Q_2, \ldots Q_n) \, \varepsilon \, \underline{Q}^n$ that satisfies weak anti-paternalism, let $x, y, z \, \varepsilon \, A$, and assume that an attempt to define $F(Q_1, Q_2, \ldots Q_n)$ leads to intransitive social preferences: x is preferred to y, y to z, and z to x. First, suppose that i and j agree on the ranking of some pair from $\{x, y, z\}$ – for example, $(x, i) \, Q_i \, (y, i)$ and $(x, j) \, Q_j \, (y, j)$. Then any $k \, \varepsilon \, N$ who votes for y over z, must necessarily also vote for x over z; hence it is impossible that y beats z and z beats x. (Here we use (3) in the definition of a pre-filter.) Second, assume that i and j have strictly opposite interests concerning x, y, and z – for example,

$$(x, i) \, Q_i \, (y, i) \, Q_i \, (z, i)$$

and

$$(z, j) \, Q_j \, (y, j) \, Q_j \, (x, j)$$

Suppose $k \, \varepsilon \, N$ votes for z when x and z are compared. This means that z beats x in Q_k according to the maximax criterion, when only the pairs (x, i), (z, i), (x, j), and (z, j) are considered. The top-ranked of these pairs in Q_k must then be (z, i) or (z, j), but it cannot be the former by weak anti-paternalism. Hence (z, j) is the top-ranked pair, which implies $(z, j) \, Q_k \, (x, i)$ and, by weak anti-paternalism and transitivity of Q_k, $(z, j) \, Q_k \, (y, i)$. If we now consider the comparison of y and z, it follows that k votes for z. That is, any $k \, \varepsilon \, N$ who votes for z over x also votes for z over y. It is impossible that z beats x and y beats z. By symmetry, any intransitivity must be of one of the two types now considered. We conclude that intransitivities cannot occur, and F satisfies UD-WAP.

Conversely, suppose that the SIC-function F satisfies PO, IIA, and UD-WAP. Again, the proof is structured like the proofs of the previous theorems. Let $(\sigma_1, \sigma_2, \ldots \sigma_n) \varepsilon \Sigma^n$ be given. Here we shall define a function G from $\underline{P}^m$ to $\underline{R}$. Let $(P_1, P_2, \ldots P_m) \varepsilon \underline{P}^m$ be given. Define $(Q_1, Q_2, \ldots Q_n) \varepsilon \underline{Q}^n$ by

$(x, i) \, Q_k \, (y, j)$ if either $i \, \sigma_k \, j$, or $i = j$ and $x \, P_i \, y$

for all $x, y \, \varepsilon \, A$, all $i, j \, \varepsilon \, M$, and all $k \, \varepsilon \, N$. We note that $(Q_1, Q_2, \ldots Q_n)$ satisfies weak anti-paternalism. The value of G is given by

$$G(P_1, P_2, \ldots P_m) = F(Q_1, Q_2, \ldots Q_n)$$

Exactly as in the proof of Theorem 1, G is a social choice function, the set of social states is A and the set of individuals is M, and G satisfies PO, IIA, and UD. There is a dictator, but the identity of the dictator may depend on $(\sigma_1, \sigma_2, \ldots \sigma_n)$. Let f be the function from Σ^n to M such that for every $(\sigma_1, \sigma_2, \ldots \sigma_n) \varepsilon \Sigma^n$, $f(\sigma_1, \sigma_2, \ldots \sigma_n)$ is the dictator for G.

This f is a selection function, and we can prove that it satisfies Conditions A and B. Lemma 2 can be used. It is convenient to distinguish three cases, depending on the number of elements in the range of f.

First, suppose that the range has only *one element* – that is, f is a constant function. Let $i \, \varepsilon \, M$ be the value. Then F is an *interest dictatorship;* only the interests of i count when the social ordering is determined. As noted in Section 7, any interest dictatorship is formally a judgment dictatorship, with any $k \, \varepsilon \, N$ as a dictator.

Second, assume that the range has *at least three* elements. Then, by Lemma 2, f is unilateral; it depends only on its kth argument, for the $k \, \varepsilon \, N$ given in (i) of Lemma 2. Then we can prove that F only depends on its kth argument. That is, F is a *judgment dictatorship*.

Finally, there is the case in which the range of f contains *two* elements. Let them be i and j. We can prove that F depends only on the interests of i and j.

By Condition A, the value $f(\sigma_1, \sigma_2, \ldots \sigma_n)$ depends only on how i and j are ranked relatively to each other in $\sigma_1, \sigma_2, \ldots \sigma_n$. For $(\sigma_1, \sigma_2, \ldots \sigma_n) \varepsilon \Sigma^n$, let

$K(\sigma_1, \sigma_2, \ldots \sigma_n) = \{k \ \varepsilon \ N \mid i \ \sigma_k \ j\}$

It follows that $f(\sigma_1, \sigma_2, \ldots \sigma_n)$ depends only on $K(\sigma_1, \sigma_2, \ldots \sigma_n)$. We define:

$$\Theta = \{K(\sigma_1, \sigma_2, \ldots \sigma_n) \mid f(\sigma_1, \sigma_2, \ldots \sigma_n) = i\}$$

This Θ is a set of subsets of N. Suppose $N \ \varepsilon \ \Theta$ – that is, assume that the value of f is i if i is ranked ahead of j in all the arguments. From Condition B and the fact that j belongs to the range of F, we can prove that Θ is a pre-filter on N. Then we can prove that F is a *binary interest rule,* based on the maximax rule and the pre-filter Θ.

Then assume $N \ \not\varepsilon \ \Theta$. Let Θ' consist of the complements of the elements of Θ. It is a pre-filter on N. In this case, F is also a binary interest rule. It is based on the maximin rule and Θ'.

This completes the proof.

References

Arrow, K.J. (1963): *Social Choice and Individual Values,* second edition, New York: John Wiley and Sons (first edition published 1951).

Blackorby, C., D. Donaldson, and J. Weymark (1984): "Social choice with interpersonal utility comparisons: A diagrammatic introduction," *International Economic Review,* **25,** 327–356.

d'Aspremont, C., and L. Gevers (1977): "Equity and the informational basis of collective choice," *Review of Economic Studies,* **44,** 199–209.

Elster, J., and Aa. Hylland, eds. (1986): *Foundations of Social Choice Theory,* Cambridge: Cambridge University Press.

Gevers, L. (1979): "On interpersonal comparability and social welfare orderings," *Econometrica,* **47,** 75–89.

Gibbard, A. (1973): "Manipulation of voting schemes: A general result," *Econometrica,* **41,** 587–601.

Hammond, P.J. (1976): "Equity, Arrow's conditions and Rawls' difference principle," *Econometrica,* **44,** 793–804.

Hylland, Aa. (1986): "The purpose and significance of social choice theory: Some general remarks and an application to the 'Lady Chatterley problem'," Chapter 2 in Elster and Hylland (1986).

Hylland, Aa. (1991): "Aggregation procedures with interpersonal comparisons," working paper from the Norwegian School of Management.

Kelly, J.S. (1978): *Arrow Impossibility Theorems,* New York: Academic Press.

Rawls, J. (1971): *A Theory of Justice,* Cambridge, Massachusetts: Harvard University Press.

Roberts, K.W.S. (1980): "Possibility theorems with interpersonally comparable welfare levels," *Review of Economic Studies,* **47,** 409–420.

Satterthwaite, M.A. (1975): "Strategy-proofness and Arrow's conditions: Existence and correspondence theorems for voting procedures and social welfare functions," *Journal of Economic Theory,* **10,** 187–217.

Sen, A.K. (1970): *Collective Choice and Social Welfare,* San Francisco: Holden-Day.

Sen, A.K. (1977): "On weights and measures: Informational constraints in social welfare analysis," *Econometrica,* **45,** 1539–1572.

11. Utilitarian fundamentalism and limited information

C. D'ASPREMONT AND L.A. GÉRARD-VARET

Introduction

There is a long-standing tradition in moral philosophy to found a theory of distributive justice on some concept of "impartiality" as a prerequisite to the acceptance of its principles as being universal moral obligations. In this tradition there are two non-independent strands. One, found in most "social contract" theories, emphasizes the procedural justification to moral principles: The moral imperatives are "impartial" because the procedure by which they were determined is "impartial." The second, eminently represented by the Kantian categorical imperative, emphasizes individual autonomy as a basis for moral laws, and the impartiality of these laws results from the universality of reason.

The idea of "original position" as used in recent theories of distributive justice, in particular Rawls' and Harsanyi's, is a convenient way to integrate the two strands – although differently, because in the case of Rawls the original position is thought of as an original negotiation between rational representatives, whereas in Harsanyi the original position consists in one individual playing the role of a "sympathetic but impartial" decision maker facing the equal-chance lottery of being anyone in society. The original position is always described as a hypothetical situation in which any person, as a moral observer, is supposed to forget his own characteristics. The parties in the original position are put "behind a veil of ignorance." However, in order to choose principles of justice, essentially based on interpersonal comparisons, a given amount of common information is required. In

We thank C. Blackorby and J. Roemer for their comments. Support from "Accords Scientifiques franco-belges" and "Directions des Relations Internationales du Ministere de la Recherche et de la Technologie" (European networks) are gratefully acknowledged.

Rawls [1972] the parties are supposed to agree on a single "index of primary goods" to be applied to all individuals: "The same function holds for all citizens and interpersonal comparisons are made accordingly" (Rawls, 1982, p. 178, fn 21). Similarly in Harsanyi ([1977] p. 51) we find the two assumptions:

> "1. All individuals i have full information about the von Neumann–Morgenstern utility functions of all individuals making up the society
> 2. All individuals i agree on how to make interpersonal utility comparisons among different members j of society."

One may ask what would happen to the proposed procedures if the information required in the original position included at least some pieces that are private to some individuals, and thus relied on their truthful revelation. The problem seems to be avoided by Rawls because the vector of "all features of the person which may affect satisfaction is here replaced by a constant vector p which has entries only for the characteristics of free and equal moral persons presumed to be fully cooperating members of society over a complete life" (Rawls [1982] p. 178, fn 21). So, the parties in the original position are to agree on the characteristics that idealized moral persons should have. Still the question remains about the general objectives of these parties, representing the individuals in the original negotiation, and the knowledge they mutually have about those objectives. In the following we shall not address this question requiring a formal extension of Rawls's theory. We shall instead examine, in the context of Harsanyi's Impersonal Choice Utilitarianism, the theoretical difficulties arising when the two assumptions just quoted are abandoned, by embedding the foundation of morality and social welfare in the framework of the theory of games with incomplete information.

Without assumption 1, one has to face the problem of obtaining, from every individual, truthful information concerning his own utility function, and without assumption 2, the problem of choosing conversion ratios that are to be applied to the individual utility units, "in order to convert them to the common units which are to be aggregated in evaluating the social welfare" (Vickrey [1960]). A "pragmatic" solution will consist in choosing conversion ratios ensuring truthful revelation. But for someone who believes in meaningful inter-personal comparability, there will be no reason to think that these ratios correctly convert each utility into interpersonally comparable utility. Before looking at this problem in Section II, we shall recall in Section I Harsanyi's Impersonal Choice Utilitarianism.

I. The fundamental theory of impersonal choice utilitarianism

The starting argument of Harsanyi's foundation of utilitarianism is that the theory of individual decision making in face of risky alterna-tives could be used for utility measurement in social choice. This was already advocated by Vickrey [1945]: Considering the foundation of the utilitarian approach for the comparison of various distributions of income, Vickrey proposed a procedure involving a particular notion of fairness; to quote:

> "If utility is defined as that quantity the mathematical expectation of which is maximized by an individual making choices involving risk, then to maximize the aggregate of such utility over the popula-tion is equivalent to choosing that distribution of income which such an individual would select were he asked which of various variants of the economy he would like to become a member of, assuming that once he selects a given economy with a given distribu-tion of income, he has an equal chance of landing in the shoes of each member of it" (Vickrey [1945] p. 329).

This argument involves two ideas. First, an idea of "extended sym-pathy" by which any individual in society is capable not only of evalu-ating the social alternatives from a personal viewpoint, but can take, hypothetically, the position of any other individual and evaluate the social alternatives from this other individual's viewpoint. This evalua-tion is based on the rationality postulates of decision theory. A second idea, introduced to ensure a particular form of impartiality, is that the procedure is based on the construction of an equal-chance lottery for every social alternative. Following Harsanyi, social alternatives can

receive various interpretations (as moral rules, institutional arrangements, or patterns of redistribution), but they should determine the
condition under which the individuals will live in the society.

These two ideas are at the basis of Harsanyi's formalization. Let N
$= \{1, 2, \ldots, i, \ldots, n\}$ be the set of individuals in society. We have a
set X of social alternatives. The interpretation of these alternatives
may remain unspecified, but Harsanyi insists that they should be
viewed as alternative rules of actions (and not alternative actions).
For instance, these rules might be moral rules or institutional arrangements governing individual actions, or they might be alternative patterns of redistribution of several kinds of goods (including primary
goods in the sense of Rawls). Besides the social alternatives, which
determine the objective conditions under which an individual will live
in the society, there are other variables that are supposed to determine the personality of every individual as a member of the society.
These are the personal characteristics of an individual such as personal talents, biological inheritance, socio-economic and cultural endowments, personal conceptions and convictions, and so on. In the
fundamental preference approach of Harsanyi, this list of characteristics is assumed to allow for a complete description of the type of every
individual and thus to give a theoretical meaning to the possibility of
any one to "land in the shoes" of any other. We denote by B the finite
set of all *possible types* for any one individual: an element β of B is a
complete description of the features an individual could have. In fact,
Harsanyi considers only the subset

$$B_n = \{\beta_1, \beta_2, \ldots, \beta_n\}$$

of *actual types,* those that can be associated to the n individuals in the
given society, and introduces "imaginary" alternatives, or "extended"
alternatives, as pairs (x, β_j) representing what it is to have the type of
individual j in social alternative x.

Therefore, we have two sets of alternatives, the set of social alternatives X and the set of extended alternatives $X \times B_n$ and, correspondingly, for every individual i, two kinds of preferences. We consider
also "simple lotteries" defined on these two sets of alternatives: These
are probability measures l on X (resp. L on $X \times B_n$) such that $l(x)$
(resp. $L(\alpha, \beta_j)$) is positive for at most a finite number of outcomes x in

X (resp. (x, B_j) in $X \times B_n$), equal to zero elsewhere, and $\Sigma_x l(x) = 1$ (resp. $\Sigma(x, \beta_j) \, L(x, \beta_j) = 1$), the sum being taken over all positive values. Moral value judgments should be based on the second kind of preferences, those defined on imaginary alternatives. More specifically, the procedure that an individual i should adopt for choosing (according to his moral preferences) between two social alternatives x and y is to face the risky choice of one among two equal-chance lotteries involving imaginary alternatives: one lottery (say $\hat{L}_x$) giving each outcome $(x, \beta_1), (x, \beta_2), \ldots , (x, \beta_n)$ a probability $\frac{1}{n}$, the other (say $\hat{L}_y$) giving each outcome $(y, \beta_1), (y, \beta_2), \ldots , (y, \beta_n)$, also a probability $\frac{1}{n}$. We may call such lotteries "*original position lotteries.*" The result of Harsanyi is to show that for one individual i, to adopt a utilitarian criterion amounts to having both kinds of preferences obeying von Neumann–Morgenstern axioms for rational decision-making in the face of risk and to follow a principle of acceptance. This last principle says that he should follow the preference of any other individual, say j, whenever choosing between two imaginary alternatives both involving the type of j, say (x, β_j) and (y, β_j). To take Sen's example (1970, p. 149), if type β_j implies being a devout Muslim, if x is a social organization promoting beef consumption and y a social organization promoting pork consumption, then individual i should prefer (x, β_j) to (y, β_j), as j does, even though his type β_i implies that he is a devout Hindu who would never consider eating beef.

Formally, the fundamental utilitarianism theorem can be stated as follows.

Axiom O (von Neumann–Morgenstern preferences on X for each β_j in B_n). Each individual of type β_j has, over the set of all simple lotteries on X, a preference ordering satisfying the von Neumann–Morgenstern axioms. It is denoted by the binary relation $\geq_{\beta_j}$ and is representable by a cardinal utility function – that is, there exists U_{β_j}, a function defined on X such that for any two simple lotteries on X, say l and l',

$$\Sigma_x l(x) U_{\beta_j}(x) \geq \Sigma_x l'(x) U_{\beta_j}(x) \qquad \text{if and only if} \qquad l \geq_{\beta_j}$$

This function is unique up to an affine transformation (a change of origin and a change of unit: We could take any U'_{β_j} defined on X such that $U'_{\beta_j}(x) = \lambda_{\beta_j} U_{\beta_j}(x) + \mu_{\beta_j}$ for all x in X, any number μ_{β_j}, and any $\lambda_{\beta_j} > 0$).

Axiom 1 (von Neumann–Morgenstern preferences on $X \times B_n$ for each i in N). Each individual i has, over the set of all simple lotteries on $X \times B_n$, a preference ordering satisfying the von Neumann–Morgenstern axioms. It is denoted by the binary relation R^i and it is representable by a cardinal utility function – that is, there exists U^i, a function defined on $X \times B_n$, such that for any two simple lotteries on $X \times B_n$, say L and L',

$$\Sigma_{(x,\,\beta_j)} L(x, \beta_j) U^i(x, \beta_j) \geq \Sigma_{(x,\,\beta_j)} L'(x, \beta_j) U^i(x, \beta_j) \qquad \text{if and only if} \quad L R^i L'.$$

This function is unique up to an affine transformation (a change of origin and a change of unit).

Axiom 2 (Principle of acceptance). For every individual i, the preference ordering R^i is "congruent" to each preference ordering $\geq_{\beta_j}$ – that is, for every i and every β_j, R^i is representable by a utility function U^i and $\geq_{\beta_j}$ by a utility function U_{β_j} such that for every (x, β_j), $U^i(x, \beta_j) = U_{\beta_j}(x)$.

Theorem 1. There exists a cardinal utility function U defined on $X \times B_n$, such that for every i and for any two original position lotteries, say $\hat{L}_x$ and $\hat{L}_y$,

$$\hat{L}_x R^i \hat{L}_y \qquad \text{if and only if} \qquad \Sigma_{\beta_j} U(x, \beta_j) \geq \Sigma_{\beta_j} U(y, \beta_j)$$

The argument to prove this theorem is simple to give. Because by Axiom 0, all preference orderings $\geq \beta_j$ are representable by a cardinal utility function, and by Axiom 1 all preference orderings R^i are representable by a cardinal utility function, and because by Axiom 2 all these preference orderings are congruent (congruence is a transitive relation), we can choose all these utility functions to get, for all i, β_j and x:

$$U^i(x, \beta_j) = U_{\beta_j}(x)$$

Hence, using the von Neumann–Morgenstern expected utility theorem (see Fishburn [1969] chapt. 8), for any i and any two original position lotteries $\hat{L}_x$ and $\hat{L}_y$, $\hat{L}_x R^i \hat{L}_y$ if and only if

$$\Sigma_{\beta_j} \tfrac{1}{n} U_{\beta_j}(x) = \Sigma_{\beta_j} \tfrac{1}{n} U^i(x, \beta_j) \geq \Sigma_{\beta_j} \tfrac{1}{n} U^i(y, \beta_j) = \Sigma_{\beta_j} \tfrac{1}{n} U_{\beta_j}(y)$$

Define the function U on $X \times B_n$ by letting $U(x, \beta_j) = U_{\beta_j}(x)$ for all (x, β_j), and the result follows.

This result has been criticized on several grounds. First, to quote Sen, following Arrow [1973], "This is a theorem about utilitarianism in a rather limited sense" because: "there is no *independent* concept of individual utilities of which social welfare is shown to be the sum, and as such the result asserts a good deal less than classical utilitarianism does" (Sen [1986] p. 1122). According to this view, one can think of the function $U(x, \beta_j)$ as a monotone transformation of the individual utility (say, V_j, and let, for example, $U(x, \beta_j) = \tfrac{1}{b_j}[V_j(x)]^{b_j}$ for some parameter $b_j > 0$); hence the social welfare criterion can cover a very large class of non-utilitarian rules including (at the limit) the maximin rule. Actually this critique should not apply to the fundamental preference approach to Impersonal Choice Utilitarianism such as given by Harsanyi [1977] (see pages 58–89). Indeed, recalling the first basic informational assumption of Harsanyi, quoted in our introduction and formally included in our Axiom 0, and assuming that the description given by the type β_j of any individual exhausts all his personal features, the function $U(x, \beta_j)$ is to be identified with the von Neumann–Morgenstern utility of individual j (of type β_j) (and not to a monotone transformation of it). In particular, in the example given, the risk-aversion parameter b_j is to be thought of as a component of the type β_j of individual j, the function V_j being specified by the remaining components of β_j.

The critique can of course be considered differently and viewed as a rejection of Harsanyi's fundamental preference approach. This is the view adopted by Rawls when he argues in favor of his conception of justice as fairness:

"The notion of a shared highest order preference function is plainly incompatible with the conception of a well-ordered society in justice as fairness. For the circumstances of justice citizens' conception of the good are not only said to be opposed but to be incommensurable" (Rawls [1982], p. 179).

This is somewhat a view shared by Arrow (see Arrow [1977]). Furthermore, one may distinguish two lines of arguments against a fundamentalist approach to distributive justice. Indeed there are, broadly, two basic kinds of fundamentalism that, in a Kantian terminology, we may call an "a priori fundamentalism" and "an empirical fundamentalism." In a Kantian tradition such as Rawls', one would mainly argue against the second kind and reject the empirical positivism of Harsanyi's theory based on the presumption that "the different individuals choice behavior and preferences are at least governed by the *same basic psychological laws*" (Harsanyi [1977], p. 58). It should be noticed, though, that an a priori fundamentalist reformulation of Harsanyi's theory can be easily proposed. Just replace in the earlier formulation the set B_n of actual types by the finite set B of a priori possible types. It implies that Axiom 0 applies to individual preferences $\geq_\beta$ defined for every β in B, that Axiom 1 assumes von Neumann–Morgenstern preferences on $X \times B$, and that Axiom 2 is restated accordingly. Then, of course, an original position lottery, say $\hat{L}_x$ is evaluated by $\frac{1}{|B|}\Sigma U(x, \beta)$. But such an a priori fundamentalism is subject to the same questioning as the one addressed by Arrow to Rawls's search for a universal concept of justice:

"An actual individual must necessarily have limited information about the world, and different individuals have different information. Hence, they cannot possibly argue themselves back into an original position with common information, even if they succeed in 'forgetting' who they are" (Arrow [1973] p. 262).

However, the limited information argument has even greater force if one adopts (either a priori or a posteriori) an empirical viewpoint. The implication, for Harsanyi's theory, is to modify his two initial assumptions, complete information on individual utilities and agreement on conversion ratios. It then suggests linking the problem of finding a formal definition of distributive justice and the problems of its implementation to the recent theory of incentives. We address this issue in the following.

II. Incomplete information, incentives, and interpersonal comparisons

The purpose of this section is to show how problematic it is to define a universal concept of distributive justice, with some empirical bearing, as soon as Harsanyi's initial assumptions are weakened. To weaken the first assumption we shall use another of Harsanyi's doctrines, the one concerned with games with incomplete information. Under this doctrine, the actual types of the n individuals are selected according to some a priori probability distribution – that is, we have a joint probability distribution p on the set of all vectors of individual types $\beta = (\beta_1, \beta_2, \ldots, \beta_n)$ in the space B^N. This joint distribution is common knowledge, but actually the individuals are only informed of their own type. Thus they have incomplete information about the types of the others, and may simply compute the probability distribution of the others' types conditional on their own – that is, for every individual i of type β_i we have the conditional probability distribution

$$p(\beta_{-i}|\beta_i) = p(\beta_i, \beta_{-i}) \, / \, \Sigma_{\beta_{-i}} p(\beta_i, \beta_{-i})$$

with $\beta_{-i} = (\beta_1, \ldots, \beta_{i-1}, \beta_{i+1}, \ldots, \beta_n)$ a vector in the space $B^{N-\{i\}}$.

Likewise, for the weakening of the second initial assumption, we shall follow Harsanyi (see [1977] p. 59–60) and introduce explicitly the conversion ratios in the utilitarian criterion, which becomes for any given $(\beta_1, \beta_2, \ldots, \beta_n)$,

$$\text{Max } \Sigma_{\beta_i} \lambda(\beta_i) U(\mathrm{x}, \beta_i)$$
$$x \in X$$

with $\lambda(\beta_i) > 0$. In order to have this expression well-defined, we take X to compact in some Euclidean space and U to be continuous (more structure will result from later assumptions). Thus the individuals need to agree, as a basic ingredient, upon the distribution λ of conversion ratios, defined on the set B of all possible types. For any such λ-distribution and any vector of actual types $\beta = (\beta_1, \beta_2, \ldots, \beta_n)$, we denote by $x(\beta, \lambda)$ the outcome selected as a solution to maximization problem. We call $x(., \lambda)$ the λ-*utilitarian outcome function,* because it is parametrized by the λ-distribution. The choice of the λ-distribution is to be made "a priori" by the individuals' accepting their roles of sympathetic and impartial observers, but the realization of the outcome depends on the personal incentives of everyone, motivated by his actual preferences to give the information he holds – that is, to reveal correctly his actual type. In other words, one should introduce explicitly "(Bayesian) incentive constraints" on the chosen outcome function whereby the expected utility of individual i should be greatest when he reports his true type β_i instead of b_i:

$$\Sigma_{\beta_{-i}} U(x(\beta, \lambda), \beta_i) \, r(\beta_{-i}|\beta_i) \geq \Sigma_{\beta_{-i}} U(x(b_i, \beta_{-i}, \lambda), \beta_i) p(\beta_{-i}|\beta_i)$$

for all β_i and b_i in B and every individual i. This means that individual i, of actual type β_i, has no interest (in expected utility terms) to pretend to be of type b_i, knowing the outcome function $x(., \lambda)$ for the given conversion ratios λ. The explicit introduction of these incentive constraints makes clear the major dilemma of a "pragmatic" approach to distributive justice: Either the "true" conversion ratios are used, in which case the individuals are inclined to distort the information concerning their actual types, or distorted conversion ratios are chosen so that the "true" types are revealed. In any case, the basis for interpersonal comparison is shaken. Because "true" conversion ratios are not obtainable, the only possibility is to check whether or not the modest goal of finding conversion ratios leading to truthful revelation can be achieved.

It should be noticed, moreover, that the formal problem of finding an outcome function maximizing the weighted sum of the utilities for some distribution λ may also receive a noncardinal interpretation in relation to the literature on "mechanism design" (for references, see the survey by Myerson [1985]). Indeed, finding a distribution λ and taking the corresponding λ-utilitarian outcome function $x(., \lambda)$ amount to defining a "mechanism" that for every vector of actual type β, leads to a Pareto optimal outcome $x(\beta, \lambda)$ – that is, a social alternative such that for no other alternative y in X, $U(y, \beta_i) \geq U(x(\beta, \lambda), \beta_i)$, for all i

(with a strict inequality for at least one). As is well known, this condition is purely ordinal, and for any given β varying the λ-values is nothing but describing the set of all Pareto optimal alternatives. A function $\tilde{x}$ from B^N to X satisfying this condition may be called a *Pareto optimal outcome function*.

In this new interpretation, the goal becomes: Look for a Pareto-optimal outcome function satisfying the incentive constraints. In such a process, efficiency and incentive considerations receive priority over consideration of distributive justice. But it is possible to show that under some structural assumptions, this problem has a solution satisfying in addition minimal "symmetry" requirements that are incorporated in the utilitarian outcome function by construction. Indeed, observe that the fundamental utility construction introduces a basic symmetry in the problem: For any vector of types $\beta = (\beta_1, \beta_2, \ldots, \beta_n)$, for any permutation σ of the individuals and the corresponding permuted vector of types $\beta_\sigma = (\beta_{\sigma(1)}, \beta_{\sigma(2)}, \ldots, \beta_{\sigma(n)})$ with $\beta_i = \beta_{\sigma(i)}$, we obviously have that $U(. , \beta_i) = U(., \beta_{\sigma(i)})$ for all i. The symmetry property of the outcome function $x(., \lambda)$ is that for any permutation of individual types we get the corresponding permutation of final utility levels – that is, for any distribution λ and any permutation σ of the individuals:

$$U(x(\beta, \lambda), \beta_i) = U(x(\beta_\sigma, \lambda), \beta_{\sigma(i)})$$

We shall call *symmetric* any outcome function $\tilde{x}$ satisfying this property.

To get a symmetric Pareto optimal outcome function satisfying the incentive constraints, we need the following structural assumptions:

Assumption 0 (symmetry and independence). There is a probability distribution q over B such that every individual type is randomly and independently drawn according to this distribution – that is,

$$p(\beta_1, \ldots, \beta_i, \ldots, \beta_n) = \mathop{\times}_{i=1}^{n} q(\beta_i)$$

and the individual beliefs are for every i:

$$p(\beta_{-i} | \beta_i) = \underset{j \neq i}{\times} \quad q(\beta_j)$$

Assumption 1 (0-normalization). The final utility level $u(x(\beta, \lambda), \beta_j)$ of any individual of type β_j is null if and only if $\lambda(\beta_j) = 0$.

Assumption 2 (nonlevelness). If for some distribution λ an individual changes from a zero-weight type to a positive-weight type, the other types remaining fixed, the weighted sum of the final utilities of these others should decrease (choosing a Pareto optimal outcome is a strictly competitive problem). Moreover $x(\beta, \lambda)$ should be a continuous function of λ.

Theorem 2. There exists a Pareto optimal, symmetric outcome function satisfying the incentive constraints. It is given by the λ^*-utilitarian outcome function $x(., \lambda^*)$ for some distribution λ^*. (To avoid technical developments, the proof is sketched in the appendix.)

The first assumption of this theorem is in fact a symmetry condition on the basic probability distribution. In a fundamental utility approach, this symmetry seems natural. However, it should be better to maintain symmetry without imposing simultaneously independent random drawings of the individual types. This could be achieved by requiring the basic probability distribution p to be "exchangeable" (de Finetti [1970]) that is, invariant to permutations of individual types. Indeed independence is a strong requirement. To take an example, if we think of X as the set of possible allocations of some given bundle of resources, and if the individual's initial endowment in these resources is part of his type, for any particular individual the observation of his own endowment affects the probability that he assigns to the endowments of the others. However, extending the present result to this enlarged situation is an open problem.

Assumption 2 of Theorem 2 is a nonlevelness condition of the kind used by Aumann [1985], restricting the shape of the Pareto frontier for any given configuration. Essentially it says that when the weight of an individual is increased, ceteris paribus the utility level obtained by the others must decrease. This is illustrated in Figure 11.1, where

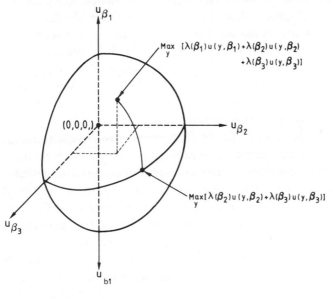

Figure 11.1

we measure final utility levels for two types, β_1, b_1, of individual 1, and one type of individuals 2 and 3, respectively β_2, β_3.

Finally, Assumption 1, the 0-normalization condition, appears to be an "individual rationality" requirement, because it implies that the final utility levels will all be positive. However, it is the weakest form of individual rationality one can think of because the condition implies that the set of individually rational utility levels coincides with the Pareto frontier for any given type configuration. Classical individual rationality is based on some given reference point, usually interpreted as a status quo point. Assumption 1 in effect eliminates the possibility of such a point. In the present approach, individual rationality is also represented by another kind of condition – namely the incentive constraints.

Conclusion

The purpose of this chapter has been to stress the difficulties in developing a universal concept of distributive justice. We have followed the particular attempt given by Harsanyi's fundamental utility theory. This kind of development should be seen as a Kantian idealistic project to found morality on reason. Harsanyi's distinction between "personal preferences" and "moral preferences" may be related to the Kantian opposition between the "assertorical imperative" of personal happiness and the "categorical imperative" of morality. Also, to have the moral principles rationally chosen by an individual according to his moral preferences may be viewed as a particular expression of the Kantian autonomy of the will. In that perspective, whereby moral laws are to be adopted freely by all rational persons, there is no need to reduce, as Harsanyi does, fundamental preference to basic "psychological laws." What we have shown is that the problem of limited information remains critical from a pragmatic point of view. Even an impartial observer can make a moral decision only on the information he gets. If the moral principles are to be implemented in concrete situations, and, in particular, are to be based on meaningful interpersonal comparisons, then some communicability of the individual experiences is necessary. The contribution of incentive theory is precisely to show the limits of this program.

Appendix

Sketch of the proof of Theorem 2. Consider the symmetric outcome function given by

$$x(\beta, \lambda) = \operatorname*{Arg\,Max}_{y \in X} \sum_{i=1}^{n} \lambda(\beta_i) U(y, \beta_i)$$

Define for every i

$$t_i(\beta, \lambda) = g(\beta_i, \lambda) - \frac{1}{n-1} \sum_{j \neq i} g(\beta_j, \lambda)$$

with

$$g(\beta_i, \lambda) = \sum_{\beta_{-i}} \lambda(\beta_j) \sum_{j \neq i} U(x(\beta_i, \beta_{-i}, \lambda), \beta_j) p(\beta_{-i})$$

Clearly $\Sigma^n_{i=1} t_i(., \lambda) = 0$, and for every individual i, every permutation σ and every vector β, $t_i(\beta, \lambda) = t_{\sigma(i)}(\beta_\sigma, \lambda)$. Select any strictly positive distribution λ; by Theorem 6 in d'Aspremont–Gérard-Varet [1979a], the pair $(x(., \lambda), t(., \lambda))$ is an outcome function that is Pareto optimal with respect to individual utilities given by $\lambda(\beta_i)u(x(\beta, \lambda), \beta_i) + t_i(\beta, \lambda)$, and satisfies the corresponding incentive constraints. Furthermore, it is by Assumption 2 a continuous function of λ. Define the continuous function f for any strictly positive λ distribution:

$$f_b(\lambda) = |B|g(b, \lambda) - \sum_{b' \in B} g(b', \lambda) \qquad b \in B$$

If there exists some λ^* at which $f(\lambda^*) = 0$, then for every $b \in B$

$$g(b, \lambda^*) = 1/|B| \sum_{b' \in B} g(b', \lambda^*)$$

implying that for every $\beta \in B^N$ and every i, $t_i(\beta, \lambda^*) = 0$

Thus, at such λ^*, the outcome function $x(., \lambda^*)$ gives the result. To prove the existence of some strictly positive λ^*-distribution such that $f(\lambda^*) = 0$, we can use degree theory and verify the boundary behavior of the function f. A theorem by Schulz [1985] gives sufficient conditions that can be checked (see d'Aspremont and Gérard-Varet [1989]).

References

d'Aspremont C., L.A. Gérard-Varet (1979) "Incentives and Incomplete Information," *Journal of Public Economics,* vol. 11, pp. 25–45.

d'Aspremont C., L.A. Gérard-Varet (1989) "Utility Comparisons and Bayesian Incentives," Document de Travail GREQE 89A03, April 1989.

Aumann R.J. (1985) "An Axiomatization of the Non-transferable Utility Value," *Econometrica,* vol. 53, pp. 599–612.

de Finetti B. (1970) *Theory of Probability,* J. Wiley and Sons, London.

Fishburn P.C. (1970) *Utility Theory for Decision Making,* J. Wiley and Sons, New York.

Harsanyi J.C. (1955) "Cardinal Welfare, Individual Ethics and Interpersonal Comparisons of Utility," *Journal of Political Economics,* vol. 63, pp. 309–321.

Harsanyi J.C. (1967–68) "Games of Incomplete Information Played by 'Bayesian' Players" Part I–III, *Management Science,* vol. 14, pp. 159–182, 320–334, 486–502.

Harsanyi J.C. (1977) *Rational Behavior and Bargaining Equilibrium in Games and Social Situations,* Cambridge University Press, Cambridge.

Myerson R.B. (1985) "Bayesian Equilibrium and Incentive-Compatibility: An Introduction," in Hurwicz, L., D. Schmeidler, and H. Sonnenschein (Eds), *Social Goals and Social Organization,* Cambridge University Press, Cambridge, pp. 229–259.

Rawls J. (1972) *A Theory of Justice,* Harvard University Press, Cambridge, Massachusetts.

Rawls J. (1982) "Social Unity and Primary Goods," in Sen A., B.W. Williams (Eds), *Utilitarianism and Beyond,* Cambridge University Press, Cambridge, pp. 159–185.

Schulz N. (1985) "Existence of Equilibria Based on Continuity and Boundary Behaviour," *Economic Letters,* vol. 19, pp. 101–103.

Sen A. (1970) *Collective Choice and Social Welfare,* Holden Day, San Francisco.

Sen A. (1986) "Social Choice Theory," in Arrow, K.J., M.D. Intriligator, *Handbook of Mathematical Economics,* vol. III, North Holland, Amsterdam, pp. 1073–1181.

Vickrey W. (1945) "Measuring Marginal Utility by Reaction to Risk," *Econometrica,* vol. 13, pp. 319–333.

Vickrey W. (1960) "Utility, Strategy and Social Decision Rules," *The Quarterly Journal of Economics,* vol. 14, pp. 507–535.

Index